Dick Wilson has observed and commented on Chinese affairs for over forty years. A journalist and lecturer, his first work to be published was a series on Japan in an Indian newspaper in 1953. As well as working for the *Financial Times*, *Far Eastern Economic Review* and the *China Quarterly*, he has contributed to *The Times*, the *Guardian*, *International Herald Tribune* and *The Times Literary Supplement*, and lectured frequently to academic and civic audiences around the world. His many acclaimed books include *A Quarter of Mankind* (1966) and *Mao, The People's Emperor* (1979). *China, The Big Tiger* is Dick Wilson's considered, and, he believes, final book on Chinese life.

Also by Dick Wilson

A Quarter of Mankind
Asia Awakes
The Long March 1935
East Meets West – Singapore
The Future Role of Singapore
The Neutralisation of Southeast Asia
Mao Tse-tung in the Scales of History (editor)
Mao, The People's Emperor
When Tigers Fight, The Sino-Japanese War 1937–45
Chou, The Story of Zhou Enlai 1898–1976
Another Bite at the Cherry, The European View of Japan
The Sun at Noon, An Anatomy of Modern Japan
A Bank for Half the World, The Story of the Asian Development Bank
Hong Kong! Hong Kong!
China's Revolutionary War
Japan In Britain – Partners and Competitors
British Windows on Japan

With Luo Zewen, J.P. Drege and H. Delahaye: *The Great Wall*
With Elliott Kulick: *Thailand's Turn*
With Matthew Grenier: *Chinese Communism*

CHINA
THE BIG TIGER
A NATION AWAKES

DICK WILSON

An *Abacus* Book

First published in Great Britain by Little, Brown and Company 1996
This edition published by Abacus 1997
Reprinted 1997

A CIP catalogue record for this book
is available from the British Library.

ISBN 0 349 10874 9

Typeset by Solidus (Bristol) Limited
Printed and bound in Great Britain by
Clays Ltd, St Ives plc

Abacus
A Division of
Little, Brown and Company (UK)
Brettenham House
Lancaster Place
London WC2E 7EN

Dedicated to Malee

CONTENTS

LIST OF MAPS

LIST OF DIAGRAMS AND TABLES

TECHNICAL NOTE

Spelling of Names

The *pinyin* system used in China to adapt Chinese characters to the Roman alphabet is used here except for a handful of names (e.g. Sun Yatsen) which became internationally well known in the spelling of the previously accepted Wade-Giles system. People in Hongkong, Taiwan and Singapore do not follow the *pinyin* system, so it seems best to give their names as they themselves choose. A further complication is that Chinese put their family name first, the given name second (the reverse of the European habit), and that is how almost all the names will appear in this book.

There are a few minor variations: Taiwan and Hongkong favour the hyphenated given name (Tang Chi-lien) whereas Singapore prefers three separate capitalised syllables (Tang Chi Lien). But a Chinese meeting foreigners usually knows now that a Westerner will instinctively misread his name Tang Chilien as 'Mr. Chilien', so he tries to avoid indignity in one of two ways. He may put on his name card 'Chilien Tang', or he may give himself a Western personal name as 'Terry Tang Chilien', or even 'Terry C.L. Tang'. A Chinese living in the West might simply call himself 'Terry Tang'. The scope for variety and misunderstanding is huge. For readers unfamiliar with these names a list of main characters with brief description follows.

TECHNICAL NOTE

Currencies

Trying to convert currencies over fifty years of variable exchange rates is not very useful. Most of the sums in this book are in *Renminbi* (the Chinese currency), or £ sterling or US dollars: the few instances of Hongkong and Singapore dollars are so described. At the time of going to press one *RMB* roughly equalled 12 American cents or 7.5 pence sterling.

THE MAIN ACTORS

Chiang Kai-shek (*pinyin*: Jiang Jieshi) (1887–1975) Commander-in-chief of Nationalist Army 1928–75, President of the Republic of China (Taiwan) 1950–75. The 'Generalissimo' succeeded Sun Yatsen as leader of the Guomingdang (Nationalist Party) after Sun died in 1925. In 1949 he lost control of the Chinese mainland to Mao Zedong's Communist Party, moving his armies, government and supporters to Taiwan where the Republic of China still survives.

Chen Yun (1905–95) A printer who became the Communist Party's economic expert in the early years of the People's Republic, originator of the 'birdcage' theory for limited free enterprise. After 1978 he became the most influential of the elderly 'Immortals', restraining Deng Xiaoping's enthusiasm for reform.

Dalai Lama (1933–) The religious and political leader of the Tibetans who fled into exile in India in 1959 after the Chinese government crushed a popular Tibetan uprising against Chinese occupation. In 1989, he won the Nobel Peace Prize.

Deng Xiaoping (1904–) Though short in stature, Deng became the most powerful leader of China after the death of Mao, opening China's doors to economic reforms, foreign investment and the market system. He retired from all public offices in 1989 but continued to be 'paramount ruler' behind the scenes. The succession struggle following his demise is the most pressing political problem faced by China today.

Fang Lizhi (1936–) Dissident astrophysicist sometimes described as China's Sakharov, outspoken on academic freedom and the freedom of speech. After Tiananmen in 1989, he sought asylum in the US embassy and sheltered there for more than a year. He lives in exile in the USA, ranking as China's most celebrated dissident critic.

Hu Jintao (1942–) The youngest of the Communist Party's seven-man Politburo Standing Committee, Hu was the Party Secretary in Tibet before being elevated. A disciple of Hu Yaobang, though less liberal.

Hu Qili (1928–) A key liberal in the early 1980s, reaching the Standing Committee of the Central Committee, but his conciliatory attitude to the students at Tiananmen in 1989 cost him his job.

Hu Yaobang (1915–89) Party General Secretary 1981–87. A leading reformer and advocate of 'Chinese'-style socialism, organiser of the Communist Party's Youth League and a protégé of Deng who regarded him as his successor in the early 1980s. Ousted by political hardliners in 1987. Widely admired by the intellectual community, his death sparked the student protests of 1989 and the subsequent Tiananmen crisis.

Jiang Zeming (1926–) Communist Party General Secretary since 1989, President of the Republic from 1993. He was mayor of Shanghai 1984–87, and a surprise choice for the top leadership. With a background in science and technology, he is the first graduate to hold the highest post. He took an early tough stance on student protest, winning the endorsement of hardliners like Chen Yun, and later of Deng. With no clear political stance, he functions as the balance between conflicting factions within the Party.

Lee Kuan Yew (1923–) Prime Minister of Singapore 1959–91, Senior Minister from 1991. Lee's long tenure as prime minister began when his People's Action Party was voted into power in 1959. Educated at Cambridge in law, his paternalistic and strict rule of the city-state has produced a clean, efficient but somewhat regimented society with a high standard of living and strong economy. He is hailed by some as the model of neo-Confucianism. He has spoken publicly against Western presumptions about democracy, for the Asian variety emphasising law, order, and economic security over individual rights. Ties with Taiwan from the 1960s, and with China after 1978.

Lee Teng-hui (1923–) President of Taiwan from 1988. A former lecturer at National Taiwan University in agricultural economics, he has been widely acclaimed for his efforts in democratising Taiwan politics and introducing social reforms. His visit to Cornell University for an alumni reunion in 1995 caused a serious rupture between the USA and Beijing.

Li Peng (1928–) Prime Minister of the People's Republic since 1989. Zhou Enlai, who was a friend of Li's martyred father, had adopted Li at a young age. Li later trained as an engineer in Moscow. Close to the hardliners, he is known as the man who ordered the crackdown in 1989. He forms the 'mainstream' faction of the Party with Jiang Zemin, to whom he is second in terms of power.

Li Ruihuan (1934–) Chairman of the Chinese People's Political Consultative Conference and member of the Politburo Standing Committee since 1989. The former mayor of Tianjin, a carpenter, he is the only openly liberal reformist in the Politburo. Supported by his late father-in-law Wan Li, the relatively liberal former chairman of the National People's Congress.

Lin Biao (1907–71) Defence Minister after 1959, and named as Mao's successor. In 1971, after allegedly plotting a coup against Mao, he fled in a plane which crashed in Mongolia, en route to the Soviet Union, killing everyone on board.

Liu Huaqing (1916–) An admiral raised to the Standing Committee of the Politburo in 1994, and thus the senior figure in the armed forces. He took Yang Baiping's place on the Central Military Committee. A conventional though elderly figure who supports Deng but gives his best efforts to modernising and depoliticising the armed forces.

Mao Zedong (1893–1976) Co-founder of the Communist Party in 1921, its seniormost leader after 1935 and ruler of the People's Republic 1949–76. Mao at first seemed to embody the very virtues of the Communist hero. People regarded him as a demi-god (and a few still do) even through the disasters of the Great Leap Forward (which led to the death by starvation and malnourishment of millions) and the Cultural Revolution 1966–76.

Qian Qichen (1928–) Foreign Minister since 1988 and Vice-Premier from 1993. He joined the Communist Party at fourteen, and was sent to study in the Soviet Union at the Soviet Komsomolskaya (Young Communist League School). After 1972, he served under Zhou Enlai in the Foreign Ministry. An able diplomat, some tip him to succeed Li Peng as Prime Minister.

Qiao Shi (1924–) The oldest of the Politburo Standing Committee members, and usually seen as the Number Three after Jiang and Li Peng, Qiao has a background of responsibility for security and police matters. In 1995 he moved to head the National People's Congress. He appears to stand neutral between the liberal reformists and the conservatives.

Rong Yiren (1916–) Heir of a wealthy family of Shanghai, his possessions were requisitioned in the fifties. Rehabilitated in 1978, he was made head of a new state-private company with the role of attracting foreign investments. Now one of China's most influential and wealthy men (sometimes called the Red Capitalist), he owns 200 companies, including the only private bank and a private fortune estimated at £540 million. He is the chairman of CITIC (China International Trust & Investment Corporation).

Sun Yatsen (1866–1925) The 'father' of modern China, leading the overthrow of the Qing dynasty in 1911 and establishing a new Republic of China. Unable to maintain national power after the collapse of the Qing, he 'gave in' to Yuan Shikai, who made himself, briefly, emperor. Eventually Sun was able to re-establish the Republic with Russian help but died soon after. Both Mao and Chiang and their respective parties claim him as their forerunner.

Tian Jiyun (1929–) Politburo member and Vice-Chairman of the

National People's Congress from 1993. A liberal administrator closely associated with Zhao Ziyang, his career was held back by conservative veterans. He has been characterised as 'Deng's ideal of a younger official: well informed, experienced, loyal to the party – and above all a doer rather than a talker.' His strength is agricultural policy, an important matter in China. Recently, he criticised the 'blindness' of single-candidate elections.

Wu Bangguo (1941–) Vice-Premier in charge of industry and enterprise reform from 1995. After graduating from Qinghua University he worked in Shanghai on electrical vacuum devices, his area of expertise, for twenty-seven years. In 1983, he was promoted in the Shanghai Municipal Party, assisting both Jiang Zemin and Zhu Rongji. His work was highly praised by both and also by Deng Xiaoping as he helped to liberalise ideology, promote reform, and develop Pudong, the new industrial satellite of Shanghai.

Wuerkaixi (1968–) Student dissident. The most colourful leader of the students at Tiananmen 1989, he was a Xinjiang Uighur student at Beijing Normal University. He attracted much media attention for his outspoken ways and his brusqueness with Premier Li Peng. Escaping to France via Hongkong in mid-June 1989, he was elected vice-chairman of the Front for a Democratic China in Paris, but his allegedly luxurious lifestyle has attracted criticism. Having lost his place at Harvard University, he is presently living as a teacher in Berkeley, California.

Yang Baiping (1920–) Secretary General of the Central Military Commission 1989–92, Director of the Army General Political Department 1990. A younger cousin (some say half-brother) of Yang Shangkun, whose career he follows. He held the key post of Secretary-General of the Central Military Commission until dismissed by Deng after complaints that the Yang family was gaining control of the entire People's Liberation Army.

Yang Shangkun (1907–) President of the People's Republic of China 1988–93. Educated at the Sun Yatsen University in Moscow in the 1920s, he came into the limelight after 1978. He firmly supported Deng and his reforms while also creating his own faction of loyal supporters within the army. He backed Li

Peng's declaration of martial law in May 1989, and despite his age he may be a powerful contender or broker in the leadership succession in China.

Ye Xuanping (1924–) Former governor of Guangdong province. Now operates at the centre as well as Guangzhou, but still represents a focus for southern interests. Son of Ye Jiangying, a stalwart of the Maoist period. He shares the Cantonese scepticism for ideology.

Zhao Ziyang (1919–) Prime Minister 1980–87 and General-Secretary of the Communist Party 1987–89. He came to Deng's attention in 1980 when he revitalised the Sichuan economy as the province's party chief and pioneer reformer 1975–80. At the centre, along with Hu Yaobang, he was a vital plank in Deng's plans to revive China's economy. After Hu's removal in 1987, Zhao became the General-Secretary. He was also removed from office in 1989 for the same fault of liberalism – in his case in dealing sympathetically with the Tiananmen students.

Zhou Enlai (1898–1976) Premier from 1949, and for much of the time Minister of Foreign Affairs as well. China's adroit and able statesman who represented the Communist government in its early years to the international community. A political 'saint' to many Chinese, he was greatly respected and admired for his many acts of kindness and for holding China together, carrying out the day-to-day matters of state while it went through the throes of the Great Leap and the Cultural Revolution. Educated in Japan and France.

Zhu Rongji (1929–) A successful mayor of Shanghai 1988–91, elevated to the Politburo and Vice-Premier in charge of the economy in 1991. A graduate in engineering from Qinghua University, he was declared a rightist in the Cultural Revolution but then became a popular mayor in Shanghai, deftly handling both foreign investors and student protests. In 1993–95 Zhu was concurrently governor of the People's Bank of China.

A BRIEF CHRONOLOGY

221 BC	First Emperor, Shi Huangdi, establishes empire.
AD1298	Marco Polo's *Travels* published.
1644	The Great Wall completed.
1841	Hongkong Island and Kowloon ceded to Britain after the Opium War.
1894–95	Sino-Japanese War. China cedes Taiwan and Korea to Japan.
1911	Republican revolution. Downfall of Qing dynasty.
1921	Founding of Chinese Communist Party in Shanghai.
1926	Chiang Kai-shek dominates ruling Guomindang party and government.
1927–36 1946–49 }	Civil war between Communists and Guomindang.
1934–35	The Communist Long March.
1937	Marco Polo Bridge incident opens war with Japan.
1937–45	Japanese invasion and occupation of China.
1949	Guomindang defeated on mainland. Chiang retires to Taiwan. Mao proclaims People's Republic of China.
1951	Chinese army occupies Tibet.
1956–57	Hundred Flowers Movement.
1958–59	Great Leap Forward.
1965–76	Cultural Revolution.
1971–72	Henry Kissinger and Richard Nixon visit China, detente with United States.

1972	China's entry into the United Nations.
1976	Death of Mao.
1978	Deng Xiaoping's ascendancy. Economic reforms begin.
1987	Party General Secretary Hu Yaobang dismissed as too liberal and replaced by Zhao Ziyang. Li Peng is Prime Minister.
1989	Student demonstrations. Tiananmen killings. Zhao dismissed as too liberal and replaced by Jiang Zemin.
1992	Party's 14th Congress defines its goal as a 'socialist market economy'.
1995	Jiang Zemin promotes his civilian and army supporters as Deng fades into silence.

PREFACE

It all began with Malee. Malee was by sheer character the leader of the Chinese students on the Berkeley campus of the University of California in 1952–53. Tall and slim, with jet black hair tumbling down her neck and skin like a magnolia blossom, she wore a grave look which with friends quickly melted into an infectious smile. I had never met a Chinese before, and found myself as a fellow-student spellbound by her earnest talk about a country so vast and to me unfamiliar, then the stage for such high political drama.

But in the second semester at Berkeley that year Malee began to withdraw, her face taut and downcast. She would hurry back to her hostel room rather than linger for a chat with us. The Australian forestry student who took a particular shine to her eventually teased the trouble out. She had come to America just before the Communist victory in China, which she had welcomed as a genuine liberation, injecting a breath of idealistic fresh air into the stuffy Chinese scene. She herself came from a bourgeois family which was used to living off the land, off tenant-farmers and city rents. But she knew all these things had to be changed if China was to become modern.

Then in the early 1950s came the Maoist campaigns to dislodge the privileged middle class. Malee's parents were among the many victims, and she cried over the letters they wrote to her about their humiliations and losses, their tortures and beatings and killings – all understated but all too vivid to her. They consistently urged her to stay in America, gain the best possible qualifications and come back only when the nightmare of Communism was over.

When the university year ended and we dispersed to our various home countries, I lost touch with Malee and never did find out what happened to her. I think she did return to China, and I was sure that she was spirited enough to turn on the Communists for being so cruel to people who were not all criminals or villains – indeed, some of them were ready to sacrifice their lifestyles and work their guts out for a clean new Communist government if that would restore China's self-respect in the world.

A girl of such shining idealism and personal obstinacy could surely not have stayed out of trouble in Communist China: Malee must have been one of those indigestible personalities whom the revolution could not use. Her distinctive personality made the newspaper headlines about China human and real to me. Whenever I thought of her I felt the tragedy of a national revolution which needed people like Malee to help carry it through, and yet could not accept their co-operation because of what seemed a senseless stereotyping. China's modernisation was going to be a patchy and long-drawn-out affair.

And so it proved. I then joined a London newspaper, and a few years later alighted on the China coast to edit a news magazine based in Hongkong. At last I was living in a Chinese city, a city that was socially and culturally Chinese. I had a window on the extraordinary catastrophe of the Great Leap Forward, where Mao declared an unwise and costly war against nature. In the years since, I have visited China several times, made many friends there and written several books about it. Now, looking back over a lifetime of that involvement, I have tried to write an overview of what the Chinese peoples – in Taiwan, Hongkong and southeast Asia as well as in China itself – are struggling and labouring to achieve. It is the sort of book that Malee, with her grasp of East and West, could have written – passionately, at the cost of a little lucidity, perhaps. If she has survived, it would be in the front line, whereas I am peering from the observation tower. The one sees immediate events most vividly, the other commands a view over the whole battlefield.

It is necessary to know something of the Chinese past in order to understand the Chinese present, without overestimating the force of tradition in the face of social change. Communism has tried to re-shape personal attitudes and values but without durable success, and some of the old ways are creeping back as Communism becomes discredited. I make no apology therefore for emphasising a little of the traditional China at appropriate points.

This is a book for the general reader. Sinologists learned in the Chinese language and immersed in such disciplines as economics, sociology or political science need read no further. I offer a coherent and thorough-going broad-brush account of the Chinese phenomenon of today and tomorrow, rooted in such academic studies and nurtured by a hundred interviews as well as my own visits to China.

Here is what I judge to be the real story, described with the detachment of an outsider, but nourished by the insights of a lifetime of China-watching and by the reports of the most perceptive experts. China is not like Scotland. You cannot take in China on a three-week tour. The Chinese are 250 times more numerous than the Scots, their ground area 125 times bigger. Going to Beijing and Guangzhou and Shanghai and then pontificating to your friends about 'China' is rather like visiting Paris, Hamburg and Oslo and on that basis lecturing about 'Europe'. None of those who penetrate deeply in one place or on one topic can necessarily generalise, and they usually refrain from it.

Napoleon said that when the Chinese giant awoke, the world would tremble. China has now awoken, its almost inert organism brought back to life by three successive princes, not all charming – Sun Yatsen, Mao Zedong and Deng Xiaoping. Sun gave it republicanism, Mao socialism and Deng's gift was enterprise. Now the shackles are being untied, the bonds are cut and the long stilled limbs have begun to stir. Before long the great frame will stand and move and walk. Should we tremble then? No, not if we consider the length of time it will take for China to 'catch up', not if we become meanwhile more serious about studying the Chinese language and culture, and not if we have the courage and self-confidence to treat China as a peer deserving courtesy, respect and understanding even where day-to-day policies differ.

Since about 1960 an economic miracle has gradually overtaken east Asia. It started with the rapid and sustained economic growth achieved by post-war Japan in the 1960s. A decade later the smaller neighbouring economies of South Korea, Taiwan, Hongkong and Singapore – known as the 'Four Little Tigers' – started to expand at the same dramatic speed. In the 1980s China began to show similar symptoms, starting on its coastline facing the Four Little Tigers. China is so large and spread across such differing geographical conditions that homogeneous progress across the board cannot be expected. But some observers have already cast China as the 'Big' Tiger – a title which it is now in the process of earning.

The forecasting boils down to this: east Asia will lead the world economically and politically in the next twenty years. By then China will be leading east Asia. Everyone should know more about China. And the more we know, the more we will come to respect the Chinese people, who have been through successive hells since 1949. We especially respect the students and professional Chinese men and women who have seen the West, or come to know its achievements and ideas, and can speak to us in our own language – metaphorically as well as literally. The Chinese mind is liquid – swift in motion, light in riposte, heavy with millennial legacies of the spirit of its civilisation. The Western intelligence is more practical in bent (that is why China is still so materially backward), slow but thorough in logical analysis and somewhat awed by the prodigious antiquity of China.

The meeting of the two is a marvellous phenomenon, each aware of the other's superiority in different spheres, each burning with a thirst to learn that other superiority. The 1.2 billion inhabitants of the West now face the 1.2 billion of China in what can only be the most fateful encounter in human history. Instead of worrying about rumours of China acquiring her first aircraft-carrier, we should look at the thousands of Chinese students imbibing the physical and social sciences of the West in our universities, compare that with the paltry number of Westerners studying in China – and ask ourselves what is the consequence of that difference in potential world power terms.

At Berkeley forty years ago all we Anglo-Saxon students fell in love with Malee in some way or other. Now a younger Western generation will try to come to terms with Malee's children and grandchildren. I hope this book will encourage them not only to understand but also to admire the people who will be either our partners or our rivals in the world of the next century.

ACKNOWLEDGEMENTS

Let me drop a few names now by way of acknowledgement. I thank the teachers who took time from busy professional lives to answer queries and comment on some passages of my draft: notably Shaun Breslin, Terry Cannon, Liz Croll, Kimirou Fujita, Tomochelor Hao, Wei-hua Jin, Ellis Joffe, Colina MacDougall, Peter Nolan, Dawa Norbu, Lynn Pan, Keith Pratt, Ian Rae, Tom Stapleton, Steve Tsang, Paul Wingrove, Michael Yahuda and Zhao Liqing. Some others prefer anonymity. Several organisations helped my research, especially the Royal Institute of International Affairs, the Japan Foundation, the Government Information Office in Taiwan, the China Britain Trade Group, the International Institute for Strategic Studies, the School of Oriental and African Studies, Great Britain-China Centre, the Japan Institute of International Affairs and the Rajiv Gandhi Institute for Contemporary Studies. I owe much to the research and word-processing skills of four who provided successive assistance while work on the book was in progress, Matthew Grenier, Tobias Newland, Chao-Hui Jenny Liu and Andreas Wilkes – and also to the computer skills of Ralph Amissah and Lucy Zhao.

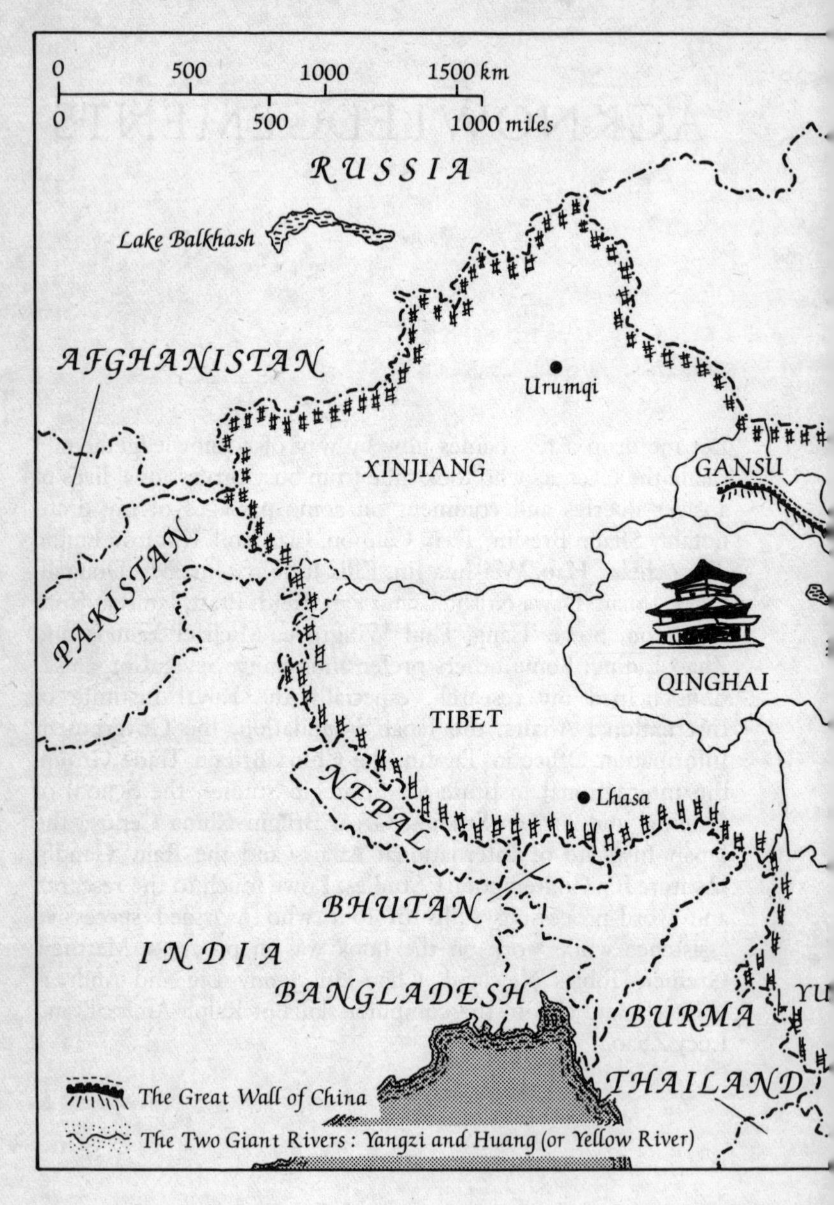
0
500
1000
1500 km
0
500
1000 miles
RUSSIA
Lake Balkhash
AFGHANISTAN
Urumqi
XINJIANG
GANSU
PAKISTAN
QINGHAI
TIBET
NEPAL
Lhasa
BHUTAN
INDIA
BANGLADESH
BURMA
YU
THAILAND
The Great Wall of China
The Two Giant Rivers : Yangzi and Huang (or Yellow River)

China

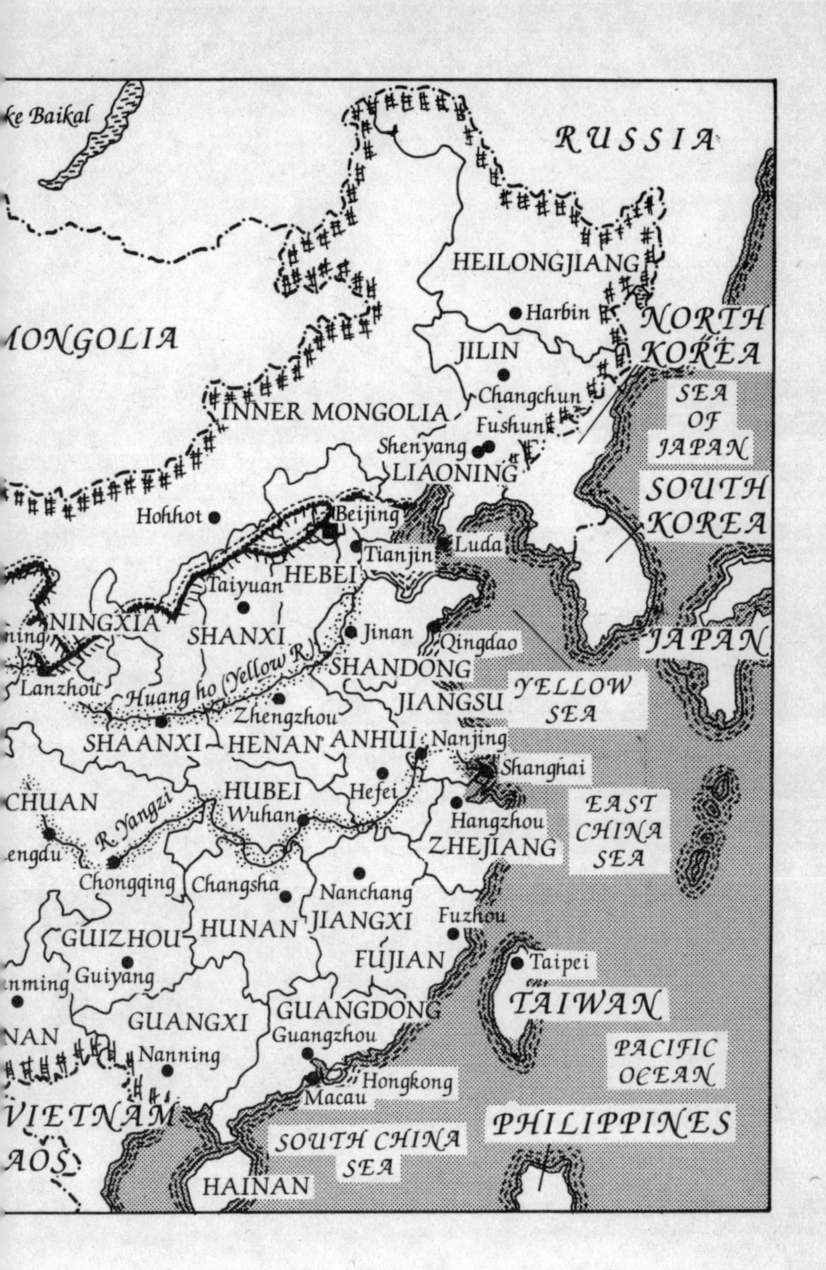
RUSSIA
HEILONGJIANG
Harbin
NORTH KOREA
JILIN
Changchun
INNER MONGOLIA
Fushun
Shenyang
LIAONING
SEA OF JAPAN
SOUTH KOREA
Hohhot
Beijing
Tianjin
Luda
HEBEI
Taiyuan
NINGXIA
SHANXI
Jinan
Qingdao
JAPAN
SHANDONG
Lanzhou
Huang ho (Yellow R.)
YELLOW SEA
JIANGSU
Zhengzhou
SHAANXI
HENAN
ANHUI
Nanjing
Shanghai
Hefei
HUBEI
Wuhan
R. Yangzi
Hangzhou
EAST CHINA SEA
ZHEJIANG
Chongqing
Changsha
Nanchang
JIANGXI
Fuzhou
HUNAN
GUIZHOU
Guiyang
FUJIAN
Taipei
TAIWAN
GUANGXI
GUANGDONG
Guangzhou
PACIFIC OCEAN
Nanning
Hongkong
Macau
VIETNAM
PHILIPPINES
SOUTH CHINA SEA
HAINAN

PART ONE

HISTORY

CHAPTER 1

CHINA'S HISTORY: STRANDS FROM THE PAST

In 1767, the French philosopher François Quesnay marvelled at the pre-eminence of the Chinese empire. 'No one can deny,' he wrote in his *Despotism in China*, 'that this state is the most beautiful kingdom known.' Majestically sweeping from the Siberian forests of the north to the distant deserts of central Asia in the west and the tropical ravines of Mekong and Salween a thousand miles south, China was acknowledged, before the British or the French had even dreamed of world conquest, to be the greatest empire on earth. More books had been published in Chinese than in all the other languages of the world put together, and in every art China excelled. This is why the national pride of Chinese intellectuals is of such a different order of intensity from that of other Third Worlders.

For two millennia the Chinese used the teachings of Confucius and his disciples as their ethos, looking inside themselves for solutions to their external problems. Society, they believed, could be built only from the bottom up, through good men, stable families, contented villages – and humane emperors. Five cardinal relationships governed this process: ruler–subject, father–son, elder brother–younger brother, husband–wife and friend–friend. Except for the last, each of these encompassed a degree of authority of one person over another. 'The foundation of the world lies in the state,' wrote one of Confucius' followers, 'the foundation of the state lies in the family and the foundation of the family lies in the individual.' The disorderly and unpredictable rise and fall of petty kingdoms in his day led Confucius to see the extended family as the saviour of society, avoiding the extremes of dictatorship in one direction and anarchic individualism in the other.

'Here is the way to win the empire,' he continued; 'win the people and you win the empire. Here is the way to win the people; win their hearts and you win the people. The people turn to a humane ruler as water flows downward or beasts take to the wilderness.' To encourage this process, the ruler was advised to surround himself with humane officials, who would act as good fathers of the people. When the ruler acted tyrannically, however, his legitimacy – otherwise called the Mandate of Heaven – was annulled and the people were justified in rebelling (though no institutional machinery was laid down for this and clever but dishonest rulers could get away with murder). This is why today's Communist rulers of China have so few doubts about their right to govern: their Party had led a popular uprising against a corrupt and oppressive regime.

Shi Huangdi, the first Qin dynasty emperor in the third century BC, centralised the government. While Britain fought with primitive Iron Age invaders and Rome and Carthage battled for mastery of the central Mediterranean, Shi Huangdi standardised China's weights and measures and unified the script for official documents. Even now officials administer a society as big as Europe with hardly a qualm, because of the uniformity imposed by an emperor who accomplished in China what Napoleon failed to achieve in Europe.

There was cruelty implicit in all the good works of the Qin. Conscripts secured the military expansion of the empire and built the roads, the emperor's tomb and his 264 palaces. Some of the hundreds of thousands of slaves who erected the Great Wall against potential attackers from the north – today the most celebrated tourist magnet in the world – were killed for slackness and buried inside it. Hence in part Mao Zedong's cavalier attitude to the lives of his subjects, while seeking to promote their progress. The individual must submit to the state's interest.

Huangdi became increasingly absolutist. Departing from the Confucian teaching, and feeling threatened by the discussions of scholars, he proclaimed that all classical books or philosophical treatises criticising him should be burnt (for which Mao Zedong once openly praised him). Private schools and public discussions of politics or philosophy were banned. Like their descendants in the People's Republic, scholars were forced to make self-criticism and find fault with each other. Then they endured the five tortures – caning the soles of the feet, cutting off the nose, branding the cheek, amputating the feet and castration – before being buried alive. After Huangdi's death the dynasty collapsed, there being no Deng Xiaoping figure capable of continuing it with a fine-tuning of ideology.

The subsequent Han dynasty consolidated Huangdi's achievements, however, especially under the energetic Emperor Wudi, so that economic and cultural progress continued unabated even when the empire fell apart in AD220. Chang'an (now Xian), the Tang dynasty capital, was a walled city measuring six miles by five, easily the largest urban conurbation on earth at that time.

The Sui dynasty emperors further strengthened and rationalised China's administration, re-centralising military and civil power and reviving the civil service system in an attempt to break the entrenched privileges of the aristocracy. More work was done on the Great Wall. More than a million men helped construct the long section in northern Shanxi, taking only twenty days. But the human toll, and that of other public works projects like the construction of 1,250 miles of canals, eventually led to popular uprisings in a sequence still discernible in Chinese agriculture.

Under the Tang dynasty a more open and cosmopolitan society began to emerge as trading communities of Persians, Arabs and Jews arrived by land or sea. Yangzhou (on a Yangzi river tributary just downstream from Nanjing) and Guangzhou (Canton) each had foreign populations of more than 100,000, importing a diversity of religions with them – Islam, Judaism, Nestorian Christianity and Zoroastrianism. The most influential was Buddhism, which arrived from India around the second century AD. It enriched and transformed Chinese thought, science, medicine, literature and fine arts.

This revolutionary Indian philosophy, promoted by Bodhidharma, one of the last of a noted line of Indian sages, emphasised enlightenment through insight into one's self rather than through abstruse texts. As with many foreign ideas (including, much later, Marxism), Buddhism was adapted by Chinese intellectuals to Chinese conditions, and those parts which were considered unsuitable were discarded. But, as Franz Schurmann and Orville Schell put it, 'Confucianism taught the Chinese how to live in harmony with the world and Buddhism taught them the secrets of the soul.' Confucianism taught the Chinese discipline, while Buddhism encouraged the sturdy individualism that lay beneath the Chinese skin. It was a good combination, or perhaps one should say a fruitful co-existence.

At the end of the thirteenth century the neighbouring Mongols leapt easily over the much-vaunted Great Wall to conquer China. The process was completed by Kublai Khan, the grandson of Genghis Khan whose exploits were immortalised in Coleridge's poem 'In Xanadu did Kubla Khan/A stately pleasure-dome decree . . .' Age-old Chinese fears of subjugation from the north – fears still operative in the Chinese Communist attitude to Russia – were re-awakened. Mongol rule was military in character and revealed a despotic streak. But maritime commerce with southeast Asia and Indian Ocean ports prospered, as did the caravan trade with central and western Asia. Chinese silk appeared in Europe, and Europeans first set foot in China in 1261. The Venetian traveller Marco Polo was one of the earliest, describing China as 'the richest country in the world', where science and technology were far more advanced than in Europe.[1] Small wonder the Chinese still greet Western visitors to Beijing with a certain condescension.

But China was soon torn apart again by uprisings against the alien Mongol dynasty. Rebels eventually claimed the Mandate of Heaven to become the Ming dynasty. The first Ming emperor's reign marks the high point of China's imperial saga. Local government was honest, the rural economy was rehabilitated, Yunnan was reconquered and the borders fortified. The population doubled from 70 million in 1368 to over 150 million in 1644. Naval expeditions led by that jolly eunuch, Admiral Zheng He, sailed to southeast Asia, India, the Persian Gulf and even the east coast of Africa. No blue water navy ever developed out of these famous fifteenth-century voyages, but today the other Asian countries look with apprehension on China's growing navy and maritime claims.

The emperor ruled from the confines of the Forbidden City in Beijing, where his every need was met by thousands of women and eunuchs. All other adult males were banned. The eunuchs held immense power, therefore, and during the last century of Ming rule over 70,000 of them vied for the emperor's attention. Weakened by popular uprisings caused by subsequent government neglect and economic deprivation, the Ming dynasty fell in 1644, following a successful invasion by the Manchus, a people to the northeast, ethnically and culturally distinct from the Han Chinese, though hardly to be told apart in appearance and today almost fully assimilated. The Ming dynasty was defeated by its conservatism and arrogance, and for the second time the whole of China was again ruled by foreigners.

Not until 1693, with the annexation of Taiwan, were the last remnants of Ming loyalists destroyed and the country fully reunited – a piece of national agenda re-opened at the end of the nineteenth century by Japan's seizure of Taiwan. The new Qing or Manchu dynasty, under the descendants of the tribal leader Nurhachi, proclaimed another Golden Age as the economy boomed and the population soared again. 'The inland trade of China is so great that the commerce of all Europe is not to be compared therewith,' wrote an enthusiastic visiting Jesuit at the beginning of the eighteenth century.

Lulled by the knowledge of their own superiority, the complacent Chinese intellectuals of the Ming had compiled great lexicons of data, but, unlike their counterparts in Europe, applied little thought to new theoretical theses. China's ascendancy in experimental science was upstaged by Galileo and Newton. Scholars worked within predetermined philosophical guidelines, and merchants preferred to reinvest their profits in the acquisition of titles or the education of their sons to gain entry into the scholar class.

European savants paid tribute to Chinese invention, from paper and printing to the magnetic compass,[2] but some two or three centuries ago a chilling deterioration took hold of the Chinese economy. There are many theories about this. One describes a vicious circle of poverty and population growth. Another blames the arrival of rapacious European ships in the destructive imperialist age. Mark Elvin has ingeniously argued that by the eighteenth century the Chinese were so clever at repairing last year's machinery that they lost the stimulus for new inventions. Whatever the reason, China by the early twentieth century ranked among the poorest of nations, and it was this unpalatable fact as much as concern for individual human equality and dignity which had turned the minds of young intellectuals like Mao Zedong and Deng Xiaoping to Marxism in the first place.

The contradictions percolated to the salons of Europe. While Voltaire promoted China as a model of wise administration, because it was theoretically entrusted to the most learned and virtuous men, Montesquieu saw the Chinese as in practice crouched under a brutal despotism, driven by the whims of an arbitrary emperor. These are the two faces of China – plausible theory but errant practice – even today. The arrival of Western traders and European ideas challenged China's preconceptions of intellectual superiority, but the eventual reawakening of Chinese scholars came too late to save the empire.

The most immediate effect of the arrival of the West was on the economy. Western traders were initially rebuffed in the eighteenth century as there was no demand for their wares. The exception was opium, cultivated in India with the encouragement of the British East India Company, and shipped from there to China. By the end of the eighteenth century four thousand chests were imported annually, and by 1820 China was exporting quantities of silver to finance the purchase of even more opium. Since the Chinese monetary system was based on unminted silver traded by weight, the rapid fall in stocks of silver damaged the whole economy. Taxes were not paid, unemployment rose and public relief funds were siphoned off into the pockets of corrupt local administrators (a combination to be echoed in the 1980s).

By the time the Emperor Daoguang came to the throne in 1821, five thousand chests of opium a year were arriving in south China. He prohibited opium smoking, but imports went on rising, to 40,000 chests by 1839. In 1840, angered by his apparent powerlessness in his own country, he sent an envoy, Commissioner Lin Zexu, to enforce his wishes. Lin asked the foreign traders in Guangzhou to give up their unsold opium to Chinese officials and pledge not to bring any more to China. When they refused, he surrounded all the foreign trading houses and again demanded their stocks. The emperor's demands and the seizing of British merchandise aroused the anger of the British government.

The opium trade was not a major issue for the British.[3] But having entered their Palmerstonian phase of scrupulously protecting their own traders in foreign parts, they sent an expeditionary force to China to reassert their authority. The initial demand was for an indemnity to the value of the confiscated opium. But the emperor was the Son of Heaven, ruling the greatest state on earth and leading the most advanced civilisation ever known to mankind. How dare these rude barbarians make such impertinent demands when they should be kowtowing at his feet and offering him tribute as other barbarians from Korea and Burma had done before? 'Isolation,' a British observer later wrote of the Chinese rulers, 'by depriving them of all opportunities of making comparisons, sadly circumscribed their ideas; they thus judge everything by the rules of purely Chinese convention.'

The British expeditionary force blockaded Guangzhou, and then sailed northwards, setting anchor outside the port of Tianjin, where they negotiated with the Chinese governor-general before returning to Guangzhou to negotiate future trading relationships between the two countries. By December 1840, they had lost patience with Chinese procrastination and started to occupy small pieces of Chinese territory. At this the Chinese negotiators agreed to cede Hongkong island indefinitely to the British. Deng Xiaoping was elated at wiping this particular slate clean in 1984 when Margaret Thatcher agreed to surrender Hongkong back to China before the end of the twentieth century.

In a last fling of irritation the emperor sent troops to get rid of the British barbarians once and for all. But his soldiers were outclassed. As the British were poised to attack the ancient city of Nanjing, he finally accepted their demands and signed the Treaty of Nanjing. Foreign merchants now had a legal foothold on the Chinese coast.

The first Westerner to be given permission to reside in Beijing had arrived in China 250 years earlier. Matteo Ricci, an Italian Jesuit, was valued by the imperial court for his scientific knowledge, though disliked for his religious teachings. The Western traders who travelled to China at the beginning of the nineteenth century also had their own religious baggage, in the form of missionaries, and it was from this source that the greatest internal threat to the Qing dynasty was to spring.

In 1836, while walking the streets of Guangzhou, an ambitious young scholar called Hong was handed a Protestant Mission Chinese-language pamphlet, which he looked at without much interest. The following year, after failing the state examinations, Hong lost consciousness, it was said for forty days, during which time he had visions of God and Jesus Christ. Rereading the pamphlet afterwards, Hong imagined himself to be the brother of Jesus, chosen by God to destroy the evil Qing dynasty in preparation for the establishment of heaven on earth. Ten years later Hong and his collaborators launched a movement known as the God-Worshippers. Their followers were initially peasants – Hakka, Miao and Yao – outside the Han mainstream, but they were soon joined by other anti-Manchu elements, including triad or secret society members, in open rebellion against the ruling dynasty.

Preaching equality, the sharing of all property and the transformation of society, the Taiping, as they came to be known, captured Nanjing in 1853 and renamed it as capital of the Heavenly Kingdom of Great Peace. 'It is to be rejoiced,' Karl Marx wrote on hearing of the revolt, 'that the most ancient and stable empire in the world ... is on the eve of a social upheaval which must have extremely important results for civilisation.' Later historians have seen the Taiping as the precursors of the Communists a century later, also riding on the anger of an exploited peasantry. But the Taiping's northward advance towards the Manchu capital of Beijing failed and Nanjing was regained by the combined armies of imperial generals. Traditional Chinese Confucian beliefs prevailed over foreign pseudo-Christianity.

American and European mercenaries – including the well-known Englishman Charles George Gordon – contributed to the victory, advertising the Western powers' imperialist intentions in China. Though initially sympathising with the rebels' Christian ideals, Britain and France feared that a Taiping victory would negate the previous concessions they had gained from the ailing

Manchu dynasty, so they put self-interest first.

The Treaty of Nanjing, which was extended to give further extraterritoriality to the Western powers, had stipulated that a new treaty was to be negotiated within twelve years. When the Chinese consistently evaded that commitment, a second major Western expedition, made up of French and British troops, arrived at Tianjin to enforce it in 1858. Under the pretext of avenging an insult to the British flag, the force defeated the Chinese defenders two years later and retaliated for the murder or detention of European diplomats by burning down the emperor's Summer Palace outside Beijing. 'Thus ended the China War of 1860,' wrote Lieutenant-Colonel G.J. Wolseley afterwards, 'the shortest, most brilliant and most successful of all that we have waged with that country... May its prophylactical effects enable us to trade on freely at every post along the great seaboard of the empire, and so open out new channels for our commercial enterprise.'

For the British, this was all in the interests of trade, the focus for which was the treaty ports, which numbered more than eighty by the end of the century, with their extra-territorial jurisdictions. They were a constant provocation to Chinese pride, offending the belief in the superiority of Chinese civilisation. Not until the Sino–Japanese war at the end of the nineteenth century, when the Japanese navy trounced the larger Chinese fleet and walked away with Taiwan, were these assumptions shattered. Japan, like China, had also been forced to open her ports to the West. Unlike China, however, Japan had undergone a swift transformation, adapting Western ideas to her own advantage.

The nature of the Chinese imperial court, based on tradition and the absolutism of the emperor, stifled any possible transformation from within. The scholar Kang Youwei, whose brief attempt to institute reforms following the débâcle with Japan was hampered by political wrangling within the court, still believed in the essential truth of Confucianism. The emperor, he maintained, should continue to rule, overseeing a gradual transformation of society. But he borrowed from the West the concepts of evolution and change, arguing that the Confucian classics sanctioned institutional reforms which could lead China out of its current disorder into a period of harmony.

The imperial court was less enlightened. It merely sought to maintain the Confucian way of life and organise military opposition to the West. A case soon arose with the Boxer Rebellion. Initially an anti-dynastic revolt marching under the banner of 'Overthrow the Qing and expel the barbarians', the Boxers were co-opted by the opportunistic court to attack foreign enclaves. Early in 1900 the Boxers burnt and looted missionary settlements in the north of China, slaughtering thousands of Chinese Christians, and then marched on the foreign legations in Beijing. While the Chinese government looked on passively, an allied force of foreign powers arrived from Tianjin to lift the siege, and took revenge on the Chinese. The final humiliation was the Boxer Protocol of 1901, which forced the Chinese to pay indemnities of £67 million.

From his base in Japan, Sun Yatsen, the father of the Chinese republican movement, watched the decline of his country with dismay. In 1894 he had formed the Revive China Society, which was dedicated to overthrowing the ailing Qing dynasty and adapting Western scientific and technological skills to strengthen China. Forced into exile, Sun spent years travelling in the West, reading in the British Library and marvelling at the material progress of Hongkong. Unlike Kang, Sun believed in the importance of social revolution (and was thus later sympathetic to the Communist Party). He agitated amongst the Chinese overseas, many of whom had been forced to leave their country because of its harsh economic conditions.

The revolution finally came in October 1911, when the imperial authorities in Wuhan executed two military officers for plotting a mutiny. A Chinese soldier retaliated by killing his commanding officer, and rebellion spread. Sun Yatsen returned from exile to be appointed Provisional President of the new Republic, and the infant Emperor Puyi was forced to abdicate. Effective military power, however, still rested with one man, Yuan Shikai, a former adviser to the imperial court. Sun Yatsen's proposed policies – of nationalism, democracy and improving the people's livelihood – put him on a collision course with Yuan. Yuan had the military power to enforce his wishes for continued autocratic government, and he coolly dissolved the fledgling parliament – China's first. Sun's Guomindang Party took up arms against Yuan, but was swiftly defeated. Yuan became President of China instead.

Once again foreign powers were to play a decisive part in China's internal political development. When the First World War broke out, the Japanese, aligned with the Allied Powers, occupied the former German concessions in Shandong province. In 1915 they presented 'Twenty-One Demands' to Yuan, effectively claiming China's subordination to Japan's will. Yuan's acceptance of even a watered-down version of these weakened his power base in the country. When he then attempted to assume the vacant imperial throne, he lost all support, and province after province, especially in the south of the country, declared independence from the central government. Following Yuan's death in 1916, China split into semi-independent military states. Thus began the warlord era, in which indecisive military campaigns were followed by politico-military manoeuvres between, and within, the tenuous governments in north and south. In the south, Sun Yatsen gradually lost ground to local military leaders.

During the First World War, China had aligned itself (like Japan) with the Allied Powers, sending about 175,000 Chinese labourers to serve behind the lines in Mesopotamia, Africa and Europe. When the Chinese delegation left for the victors' Peace Conference at Versailles in 1919, they expected their reward, carrying with them the hopes of the Chinese people that the German concessions in Shandong now in Japanese hands would be returned to their rightful owners, as a precursor to the eventual reunification of China and the removal of foreign extraterritoriality. But the Japanese wanted to retain their newly-won territory, backed by their European treaty partners, Britain, France and Italy. It was the stronger Japanese voice which was heard over weakling China.

The announcement of the Versailles decision against China sparked off widespread demonstrations, revealing a new international awareness and a budding political consciousness amongst the Chinese people. On 4 May 1919 three thousand Beijing students, prevented from demonstrating outside the foreign legations, vented their anger on the homes of government officials. The so-called May Fourth Movement, joined by workers and some intellectuals, spread across the country. In

Tianjin, students were organised by the future Chinese Premier, Zhou Enlai. The cabinet resigned, and the Chinese delegates left Versailles without signing the final agreement. 'Since the dawn of Chinese history,' Mao Zedong wrote later, 'there has never been such a great and thoroughgoing cultural revolution' as the May Fourth Movement.

Mao was born in the village of Shaoshan in the southeastern province of Hunan in 1893. When he saw the poverty of his neighbours, he instinctively turned his back on the wealth of his father, a successful farmer. In 1918 he travelled to Beijing in the hope of furthering his education, but the nearest he got to books was to become a library assistant at Beijing University. He was back in his native Hunan province by the time of the May Fourth Movement, publishing a magazine advocating democracy and social reform. Returning to the capital, he read the *Communist Manifesto* for the first time. Like many other Chinese students, Mao looked to Western philosophers and social commentators for the inspiration to solve China's problems and evict the foreigners.

A Chinese delegate had joined a meeting of the Communist Second International in Brussels in 1909, but it was not until 1921 that the first revolutionary Marxist cell, consisting of seven members, was formed in China, in a girls' school in Shanghai. Many Chinese intellectuals rejected Marxism with its premise of inevitable class struggle, preferring the ideas of the anarchist philosophers. But by 1920 the optimism behind those ideas had waned, and Gregory Voitinsky, the new Comintern representative in China, offered an attractive framework for renewed organised revolution.

Sun Yatsen's writ now extended only to Guangdong and neighbouring parts of south China, and his chances of ruling over a unified country evaporated with the continued military strength of the warlords. Lacking finance, military clout and Western encouragement, Sun turned to the recently successful Russian Bolsheviks for help, signing the Sun–Joffe agreement in January 1923. 'We have lost hope of help from America, France or any of the Great Powers,' Sun explained in a contemporary article in the *New York Times*. 'The only country that shows any sign of helping us . . . is the Soviet Government of Russia.' Comintern representatives helped to reorganise Sun's Guomindang Party along Leninist lines and established a military academy at Whampoa, an island near Guangzhou. They proposed the acceptance of Communist Party members within the Guomindang. In September 1923, Sun launched a Northern Expedition to reunify the country militarily, but it was mistimed. He died a year and a half later, having promised so much but having been continually thwarted by internal wrangling within China.

His place as leader of the Guomindang Party was assumed by the anti-Communist conservative Jiang Jieshi (Chiang Kai-shek), who had been instrumental in the success of the republican military academy at Whampoa. He launched a new Northern Expedition in 1926; aided by the advance propaganda work of local Communist agitators, Jiang swiftly moved to the outskirts of Shanghai, the heart of China's labour movement and left wing, planning to destroy Russian influence in China on his way to smash the northern warlords.

In 1927, with a column of Jiang's National Revolutionary Army waiting 150 miles to the south of the city, the Shanghai Communists, emboldened by the arrival of their leader Zhou Enlai, organised a general strike. Five thousand workers used antiquated firearms to seize the police station, post office and power stations. The last surviving warlord commanders soon surrendered.

During the negotiations which followed, Jiang wooed Shanghai's businessmen for funds to rescue his party from its dependence on Russian aid, and in the end his men surrounded the General Labour Union building, disarmed the worker volunteers and began street executions. Almost 10,000 Communist sympathisers were killed, and Zhou Enlai, the future Premier, was lucky to escape with his life. This was the first of many brutal killings which ensured that when the Communists took power in 1949 many of their ablest and most realistic leaders, who might have prevented the later Maoist excesses, were missing. The vendetta of parties in China left no room for patriotism.

For the next three years, Jiang implacably persecuted potential urban opponents, cleansing the Guomindang of any left-wing sentiments, while manipulating tensions between rival warlords to his own advantage. 'During the last 30 years,' Lu Xun, the famous Chinese author, lamented in 1930, 'with my own eyes I have seen the blood of so many young people mounting up that now I am submerged and cannot breathe ... What sort of world is this? The night is so long, the way so long, that I had better forget or else remain silent.' Jiang made it so dangerous for his opponents that the Communists had to hold their 6th Party Congress abroad in Moscow. The dream of an urban-based revolution, which had seemed so attainable during the early 1920s when workers throughout China had struck in sympathy with their comrades in Hongkong, was shattered.

While Jiang was decimating the Communists in Shanghai, Mao stood fast in the relative safety of the countryside, establishing a base in the inaccessible mountains of Jinggangshan, where the provinces of Jiangxi and Hunan meet. In 1928 he formulated his principles of guerrilla tactics, which would eventually bring his party to victory and also be played out in Vietnam and other countries of the Third World.

> Divide our forces to arouse the masses, concentrate our forces to deal with the enemy.
> The enemy advances, we retreat; the enemy camps, we harass; the enemy tires, we attack; the enemy retreats, we pursue.

Just as the classical Chinese philosophers had prescribed, Mao set out to win the hearts of citizens, ordering the first Red Army soldiers not to alienate the people by raping and pillaging like a warlord army wherever it went. Working alongside the legendary radical military commander Zhu De, Mao gradually expanded the area under his control, and by the end of 1930 commanded 100,000 men. They were soon joined by the battered and bruised Russian-influenced Communists escaped from Shanghai, including a somewhat chastened Zhou Enlai.

In 1931 Jiang launched the first of five encirclement campaigns against Mao's revolutionary base. The first two vindicated Mao's guerrilla tactics, as the Guomindang obligingly fell into the carefully laid Communist traps and could not draw the Red Army out into the open. Jiang led the third campaign in person, and after two months of being easily picked off by Zhu De's soldiers, the Guomindang troops finally managed to engage the Red Army in battle. With only their headquarters left in their hands, the Communists were saved by the unsolicited intervention of a foreign power. At this moment the Japanese army invaded China's northernmost region, Manchuria, and popular pressure forced Jiang to forgo the pleasure of a kill in Jiangxi. He moved his troops away from Mao's base to face the Japanese.

The League of Nations failed to come to Jiang's assistance, and he was forced to give in to Japanese demands, acknowledging their special position in north China and accepting the loss of Manchuria. But once international loans were forthcoming again, Jiang used them to mount a fourth encirclement campaign against the Communist base, this time with the help of experienced German generals. Some 300,000 troops were ranged around the Jiangxi base, methodically constructing roads and fortifications.

After Red Army troops inflicted considerable losses on this slowly moving monolith, Jiang halted the campaign and sought new funds for a fifth and final encirclement in January 1934, fielding a record half a million troops there. They encircled the Communist base and began digging more fortifications. Once the first lines had been stabilised, the Guomindang made slow marches forward, digging in and marching again in an inexorable tightening of the noose. By the summer, four separate belts ran around the Jiangxi base, and whichever way they turned, the Communists ran into one or other of these fortified lines. They somehow had to break out of the snare that was closing around their necks.

In October 1934, with heavy hearts, the Red Army stole out of their Jiangxi base by night on the Long March that would take them 6,000 miles – the equivalent of walking from London to Hongkong – through twelve provinces, over eighteen mountain ranges and across twenty-four rivers. They were bombarded by Guomindang planes, had skirmishes with the enemy on average every day, and came several times within inches of defeat. The narrowest escape was at Anshunchang, in the remote Tibetan-inhabited mountains of southwest Sichuan, as the beleaguered Red Army tried to cross the Dadu river, where the Taiping rebels had met their defeat in the nineteenth century. Mao sent his shock troops up river to Luding, where thirteen iron chains, stretched across the 90-metre gap between the two facing cliffs, served as a bridge for the local inhabitants. The planks which formed a walkway over the chains had been removed by Guomindang defenders. Undeterred, the Communist vanguard swung along the chains, some falling a hundred metres into the raging torrent below but others surviving to rush the planks back into place. In two hours the town was captured, and another legend about the unbeatable Communists was created.

By the time they reached the relative sanctuary of northern Shaanxi province, protected by mountains and desert, only 8,000 were left of the original 100,000 men who had left the Jiangxi base. Many, including an infant son of Mao's, had been lost along the way, others were deliberately left behind, unable to travel because of ill health. The Long March began as a strategic retreat but swelled into a triumphant proof of man's endurance against overwhelming odds. More importantly, it gave the Communists, and in particular Mao Zedong, an aura of invincibility. 'The Long March is a manifesto,' he wrote. 'It has been proclaimed to the world that the Red Army is an army of heroes . . . Has history ever known a Long March equal to ours? No, never.'

The Communists were still not fully secure in their new refuge, and in late 1935 they faced the prospect of yet another encirclement campaign. Jiang assembled 200,000 troops but had to rely on the co-operation of reluctant local warlords. When he ordered these to move in for the kill in April 1936, two refused, insisting that he should deal with the increasingly belligerent Japanese invaders instead of killing fellow-Chinese. A furious Jiang moved another fifteen divisions of his élite troops into the area, and flew to Xian to oversee the campaign personally. But troops loyal to the Manchurian warlord most concerned about the Japanese invasion kidnapped Jiang and held him hostage until he agreed, with Zhou Enlai as the unlikely mediator, to stop fighting the Communists and form an anti-Japanese United Front with them instead.

Mao and his faithful followers were now given a brief respite. They moved into the caves of Yanan, the austerity of which came to be synonymous with their fighting spirit and high ideals. The Red Army was reorganised under the command of Zhu De, who 'lived and dressed like the rank and file,' Edgar Snow, the American author, discovered. 'He shared all their hardships, often going without shoes in the early days, living one whole winter on squash, another on yak meat, never complaining, rarely sick. He liked to wander through the camp ... sitting with the men and telling stories, or playing games with them. Any soldier in the army could bring his complaints directly to the commander-in-chief. Zhu De took his hat off when he addressed his men.'

The tense truce between the Communists and the Guomindang was prolonged by the worst invasion of Chinese sovereignty for several centuries. In July 1937 the Japanese launched a full-scale attack on China proper: in only three weeks they captured the ancient capital of Beijing. Shanghai fell in August, scene of the 'the bloodiest battle since Verdun', according to a Chinese military historian. In December they marched into Nanjing, Jiang's former national capital, and began an orgy of violence against the city's inhabitants that lasted for a month. Over 50,000 people were killed and more than 20,000 women were raped. Once again, the Chinese found themselves defenceless in the face of naked foreign aggression.

By 1938, China was divided into three. The Japanese maintained a puppet Chinese government in most of the coastal cities. Jiang moved his administration inland to Chongqing, while the Communists expanded the area under their control in the north and created pockets of 'Free China' within the Japanese-occupied zone. Despite its greater military potential, the Japanese army was increasingly thwarted by the resistance of the Chinese people and was unable to unite the country under the puppet government. Chongqing, where Jiang's business associates and military colleagues flocked, became a hotbed of corruption, fed by American aid hand-outs. Students preferred to join the Communists at Yanan in order to prosecute the patriotic struggle against Japan.

The entry of the USA into the Pacific War, after Pearl Harbor was bombed in December 1941, officially allied Jiang's government with the most powerful nation in the world. By the end of the war, however, there were at least fourteen Communist bases spread fairly evenly throughout China, and there could be no prospect of peace without the involvement of the Communist Party.

As the two sides hastened separately to accept the surrender of the Japanese and thus gain territorial advantage over each other, the Americans tried to play the conciliator. But their close association with Jiang made it impossible, and the two sides soon drifted back into the civil war which Japan had interrupted. In the cities, inflation spiralled upwards; 'in those days,' a bank employee remembered, 'a 100-yuan note was worth less than a sheet of toilet paper.' Buoyed by the stories of Red Army heroics, and antagonised by the sagging value of their pay packets, the urban middle class began to welcome the prospect of a new government, even if it was Communist.

The Guomindang armies still maintained superiority of numbers over the Communists. But they were demoralised by bad leadership and ravaged by the effects of two decades of continuous squeeze on finances: the troops had often gone without pay while their superiors lived in luxury. The Communists, on the other hand, had a remarkable sense of duty – to one another, to local farm workers and to the Communist cause. Controlling most of the rural countryside, they gained friends by redistributing land to the farm workers.

In early 1949 the Communists finally engaged Jiang's troops in positional warfare at the battle of Huai-Hai, and won. Jiang resigned as President of China. The commander of the Guomindang garrison in Beijing handed over the keys of the capital to the Communists without a shot being fired, and Jiang retreated with his main force to the island of Taiwan.

When Mao Zedong stood proudly at the Gate of Heavenly Peace in Tiananmen Square on 1 October 1949 to announce the establishment of the People's Republic of China, he stated that the Chinese people had 'stood up'. After so many years of decline and humiliation at Western and Japanese hands, China saw a new and apparently idealist party that preached equality of men and women, the common ownership of property and an end to imperialist privileges, claim the Mandate of Heaven.

Mao, who took his Marxism rather literally at first, went so far as to say that the Chinese people were a sheet of blank paper on which beautiful words could be written. In other words, ethics and a progressive outlook could be hammered into them by a creative author. We have sketched three thousand years of Chinese history in a mere nineteen pages, but enough has surely been said to suggest that the strands of that illustrious history are still enlaced in the Chinese personality and were arguably to foil Mao's grand design for a regeneration of the race.

CHAPTER 2

MAO: THE COMMUNIST WHIRLWIND

China has long ceased to deserve Marco Polo's accolade as the world's 'richest country'. Its Gross National Product is among the top six in the world, but it also has the largest population, which puts its average annual income per head among the lowest in the world. After the elimination of foreign colonialism, this low standard of living has been the major target of every thinking Chinese, every intellectual, every politician for the past hundred years. When Mao proclaimed his Party's rule over China in 1949, Communism seemed to many apolitical Chinese to be not so much an extremist arm of European dogma as the best available modern recipe for economic growth with social justice. Since then the Chinese economy has indeed advanced by about 6 per cent a year – better than most industrialised countries, and much better than most developing countries. But it has been erratic growth from the lowest of bases, all too often interrupted by turbulent political campaigns.

Although the Communists had years of experience of government in some northern parts of rural China, they were fully aware that ruling over farmers in the countryside was no preparation for the complexities of governing a partly urban country the size of China. As the old Chinese proverb stated – and almost every imperial dynasty could confirm – 'It is easier to seize power than to maintain it.'

The People's Liberation Army soldiers returned to their native villages to aid economic projects and extend highways. But in the cities the workers' expectations were gradually scuttled as the Communists, intent on resuming production, arbitrated disputes between disgruntled employees and their bosses. It was not to be an immediate workers' state, nor did Mao pursue the idea of export-led development or trickle-down economics. The critical factor in economic growth was human consciousness. 'China cannot attain true equality with other powers by depending on the good graces of foreign governments and foreign peoples alone,' he argued in his influential tract, *On New Democracy.* 'She must depend on the effort of her people to build up, politically, economically and culturally, an independent, free, democratic, united, prosperous and strong New Democratic nation.'

Evil foreign influences were targeted. Corporations were told to divest themselves of foreign ownership. In Guangzhou, wheeled pedicabs symbolically replaced rickshaws. Opium smoking was outlawed and rehabilitation centres opened for thousands of addicts. Venereal disease was soon eradicated and brothels closed, while films like *Our Fallen Sisters Have Stood Up* documented the liberation of prostitutes to become working women. The Party's commitment to a better status for women was seen in the 1950 Marriage Law, which confirmed the sanctity of marriage while for the first time permitting divorce. Almost a million couples took advantage of the new law in its first year.

But there were not enough suitably trained administrators dedicated to the Communist cause. A crash Party membership drive in 1945–49 brought in over three million new members, mostly young farm workers. One senior Party member warned in 1949, 'now that we are moving from the countryside into the cities, the greatest difficulty is in the backward, conservative, agrarian socialist thought of some people who have worked for a long time in the countryside.' You cannot instil socialism through the instrumentality of teachers who are not themselves genuine socialists. This was to be Mao's Achilles heel.

While the farmers' loyalty to the Party could be depended on, the Communists in the cities had to fall back on the existing bureaucracy to help them govern. They ran an early campaign against counter-revolutionaries, aimed at old Guomindang members, social non-conformists and foreign workers. A Thought

Reform Movement followed in 1951, and then the Three-Antis campaign against corruption, waste and over-bureaucratisation, and the Five-Antis campaign against bribery, tax evasion, fraud, theft of government property and theft of state economic secrets. The easygoing Chinese of an earlier era had to learn that suffering, hard work, self-control, constant study and unswerving compliance with the commands of state and Party were needed for the great cause of building a new and ideal country.

Like all the later political campaigns of the Communists, the Three-Antis and Five-Antis were distorted and manipulated to meet Party ends. At Yenching University in Beijing, for example, the Three-Antis became a campaign to eliminate the 'Befriend U.S., Worship U.S. and Fear U.S. sentiments' elements on the campus. The University's President, Dean of Divinity and Professor of Philosophy were criticised, stripped of their posts and branded 'U.S. imperialist elements'.

In April 1950, as part of the government's spending cuts, Mao announced plans to demobilise a third of the People's Liberation Army. Two months later, however, the Korean War broke out, and the Chinese found themselves embroiled in the Cold War. American support for the Guomindang during the civil war had led to China's 'leaning to one side', i.e. towards the international Communist fraternity in world affairs, and Mao had signed a treaty with the Soviet Union. As North Korean troops poured over the demarcation line dividing the Korean peninsula, American warships moved to protect the Guomindang's island haven of Taiwan, dashing Chinese hopes of a period of peaceful reconstruction and early reunification of all of China's former territories. UN troops under General MacArthur checked the North Korean advance and slowly began moving towards the Yalu river, which forms the Sino–Korean border.

'To Mao's mind,' Peng Dehuai, the Chinese Commander in Korea, explained later, 'if China stood by when North Korea was in peril, then the Soviet Union could also stand by when China was in peril, and "internationalism" would be empty talk.' That summer and autumn, after heavy bombing of towns along the Yalu, including accidental hits on the Chinese side of the river, Chinese 'volunteers' entered the fray. They forced the UN soldiers back to the original demarcation line along the 38th parallel. There they dug in and built a line of fortifications from coast to coast, while peace negotiations dragged on for almost three years. Although the war provided a patriotic focus for China's new régime, the economic and human costs were high. Mao lost his only remaining son in the fighting, grieving afterwards that 'there are no parents in the world who do not treasure their children.'

Western opinion at the time blamed China for having encouraged Kim Il Sung to invade the South. This was not Mao's initiative, however, but Kim's and Stalin's. China was badly damaged in reputation and goodwill, as well as losing decades of potential reconciliation with Taiwan. The Korean War was a huge disaster for Mao, and partly explains China's later coolness to both North Korea and Russia (Russian aid to China was extremely parsimonious).

Khrushchev's denunciation of Stalin and his policies in 1956 confirmed the Maoists in their distrust of the Kremlin. The idea that Mao was an earnest camp-follower of the Russians was a fiction of John Foster Dulles' invention that suited his over-simplified world picture, but under-rated the vigour of nationalism. The Chinese were not blind followers of the Kremlin: their system of governing in coalition with smaller parties, of military administrative regions and of a strong Chairman with a weak Prime Minister were significant infractions of Stalinist advice. Mao had been practically forced to beg for Soviet aid, cap in hand, on Stalin's doorstep in Moscow in 1950. Now the Chinese belief that Soviet economic policies were the most suitable for their country's particular conditions was undermined. Mao looked for economic theories of his own. He turned to the countryside, and to the farm workers, his most loyal supporters, for the special home-grown ingredient in China's development recipe.

The Communists were seasoned in rural matters, learning for example to implement land reform by choosing a key village which could later become a model for the surrounding area. Here the farm workers would be educated, encouraged to 'speak bitterness' about their previous experiences of being exploited, and to demonstrate publicly their pent-up frustrations – re-enacting Mao's guilty anger with his land-owning father? By the end of 1951, the old rural order had been comprehensively changed, although there was still no ban on the private ownership of land. Land redistribution at the expense of landlords was then enacted gradually, when the majority of farm workers were in favour and the necessary economic support networks – transport facilities, for instance – were in place.

At this point Mao decided to quicken the pace by transforming co-operative agriculture into collective farms. By 1956 some 90 per cent of the farming population belonged to collectives, enabling them, as the following extract from a novel by Zhou Libo illustrates, to contribute their full energies – Mao's special ingredient – to the revolution. The speaker is a young secretary of the local Youth League in a mountainous region.

> After the co-operative is established, I'm going to propose that we do away with all the ridges between the fields, and make small plots into large ones... When we've built a reservoir, all the dry fields in the village will be irrigated, and even after paying tax we shan't be able to eat all the grain we grow. We'll send the surplus grain to help feed the workers in industry. Won't that be wonderful! Then they, all smiles, will come in their jeeps to the countryside, and say to us, 'Hello peasant-brothers, would you like to have electric light here?' Yes, paraffin lamps are really too inconvenient and wasteful. 'Very well, we'll install it. Do you want the telephone, lorries and tractors?' We shall live more comfortably than they do in the city, because we have the wild fruit, more than we can eat.

While the collectivisation campaign gathered momentum in the countryside, Mao launched one of his most famous urban campaigns, to 'Let a hundred flowers bloom, a hundred schools of thought contend'. He invited artists, teachers, writers and scientists to give their verdict on the Party's performance after seven years in office. From petty grievances over dishonest Communist officials and minor bureaucratic peccadilloes, the criticisms crescendoed into full-scale questioning of the Party's role in society and the suitability of Communism for a backward agrarian state. Wu Ningkun, who had returned from studying in the United States to join the teaching faculty at Yenching

University, overcame his initial reluctance and complained about his treatment during previous political campaigns. Like thousands of others, he fell into the trap which Mao afterwards revealed had been the sole purpose of the campaign – to expose the urban intellectuals as enemies of the Party who preferred capitalism to Communism. 'The next day,' Wu Ningkun recalls in his book *A Single Tear*, 'the great victory of the anti-rightist struggle was celebrated in Tiananmen Square and throughout the land, and I was one of the hundreds of thousands of victims on the sacrificial altar. I had been turned into an untouchable.'[1]

With the intellectuals' criticism ringing in his ears, Mao turned once more to the farm workers to provide the impetus for economic development. In 1958 he launched his Great Leap Forward. By combining farm collectives into even bigger units, the people's communes, the Great Leap sought to free surplus rural labour for the production of basic industrial goods. But within three years the Great Leap Forward policy was reversed, acknowledged as a catastrophic failure. More than 40 million people died from malnutrition or sheer starvation after unusually bad weather compounded the man-made follies.

Reckless experiments were made without prior testing, such as deep ploughing which lowered the water table. Village steel furnaces sprang up all over the countryside producing metal of such low quality that it could not be used. Typical of the madness of the Leap Forward was the suggestion of two young engineers that Russian cranes at their foundry could be made to lift 30 per cent more than the specified weight. The Russians and the senior Chinese engineer said that was impossible, and warned that the cranes would break. But the local Party Secretary went ahead with the suggestion, and both cranes collapsed. The two young engineers were later commended for their inventive spirit, and only told mildly to be more accurate in future, whereas the senior engineer was publicly criticised for his 'negative attitude and lack of faith in China's potential'. Meanwhile the cranes could not be replaced. The incident showed not only the depth of irrationality to be overcome in Chinese society but also the strong nationalist contempt for foreign ways.

Mao's confidence that farm productivity would increase was wildly over-optimistic, and, rather than appear negative or sceptical about government policy, many middle-ranking officials grossly overestimated the harvests. A campaign was run simultaneously against the 'four evils' – rats, flies, mosquitoes and sparrows; even prisoners banged on pans and pots along with their fellow-citizens at certain hours of the day throughout China. Panic-stricken by the deafening noise, the sparrows flew until they dropped dead from exhaustion. Mao had not realised that the insects on which the sparrows thrived were now free to destroy crops at will.

Peng Dehuai, the military leader, challenged Mao's authority at a famous meeting of the Politburo at Lushan in 1959, but Mao weathered the storm and Peng was dismissed. In 1960 Khrushchev pulled out all the Russian technicians from China and abruptly stopped work at all the industrial projects on which the Soviet Union had been helping. Since Stalin's death in 1953 differences of opinion over revolutionary tactics and economic theory had become increasingly testy. The technicians, along with Russian equipment and blueprints, and the training of Chinese students in Russian universities, had given a priceless lift to China's infant heavy industry. Overnight the influx halted, along with the main source of China's export earnings, the Sino-Soviet trade. The combination of all these factors – inadequate planning, waste of resources, political over-optimism and loss of international assistance – added to the nation-wide famine of 1960–61 to cause a deep recession. Mao concluded that the Russian leaders had become infected by capitalism, and that China would escape the same fate only by undergoing a *cultural* revolution, political changes not being enough.

A railwayman, who started junior middle school in Lanzhou about that time, recalled:

> The whole country had been having a terrible time. After the Great Leap Forward, trees had been stripped of leaves and bark for food, and all the edible grasses had been gathered, too. People started making coarse buns from husks and elm bark. Later they just ate the husks . . . Our teachers took us looking for all kinds of edible things. Sometimes we found beancake crumbs by the railway tracks in the marshalling yards. We used

> to get down on the sleepers and the roadbed to lick up those crumbs . . . Once I picked up a goat's tail, a hairy great thing, in the goods yard and took it home. It seems incredible now, but my father insisted that I should take it back, even though I hadn't eaten any meat for a year. He even forced me to confess it to my teacher. I still have a very clear memory of taking it back to the meat train.

With Mao's pretensions to economic expertise dented, a new moderate leadership headed by Liu Shaoqi, Deng Xiaoping and the theorist Chen Yun took control of economic policy, letting individual farmers decide their strategy and looking to Western Europe for technological assistance, an anticipation of the more permanent shift after 1978. This gear change could have come sixteen years earlier but for Mao. Mao was made to take an unaccustomed back seat in the decision-making process, but he used his leisure to plan a new campaign to vindicate his long-held belief in the latent power of the Chinese people, to remove Liu Shaoqi and other colleagues who contradicted his ideas, and incidentally to plunge the whole country into chaos for nearly a decade. This was the infamous Great Proletarian Cultural Revolution of 1966–76.

The first target of the new campaign was within the Party leadership itself, especially those comrades whom Mao believed had gone soft on Communism. Liu and Deng had both emphasised economics above politics to further China's development, so Mao turned instead to leftists within the Party, notably his secretary, Chen Boda, and his wife, Jiang Qing. The latter with her three confederates Zhang Chunqiao, the Shanghai Party leader, Wang Hongwen and Yao Wenyuan were later labelled the 'Gang of Four'. Mao presided over the mass meetings of Red Guards, his shock troops in vindictiveness, in Tiananmen Square, and shouted that Liu Shaoqi, the President of the Republic, was the 'number one capitalist roader' – his deadliest insult – within the leadership and the target of the campaign. Liu was humiliated and harassed literally to death by the pitiless young Red Guards. Luckily for China, Liu's chief follower, Deng Xiaoping, was let off lightly with rural exile.

Loyally pinning their Mao badges masochistically through their skin and waving the *de rigueur* 'Little Red Books' of Chairman Mao's sayings, the Red Guards were mainly impressionable teenagers. Almost a million of them would cram into Tiananmen Square to be spurred on by Mao before fanning out across China to recreate revolutionary events and undertake house searches for the 'four olds' – books, money, documents and antique art treasures – all deemed decadent and counter-revolutionary. When the Red Guards came to his house, the musically minded En Shao was twelve years old. They spent ten hours there, smashing his father's record collection, the largest in Tianjin. Another band of Red Guards arrived and found nothing left to smash, so they put En on top of a tall cabinet and beat his parents, shaving his mother's hair and pouring paint over her head. The distraught boy burst into tears, so the Red Guards toppled the cabinet and he broke a finger in the fall. Because his father was branded a counter-revolutionary, the boy was refused medical treatment and his hoped-for career as a pianist was spoiled. But En had enough of the renowned Chinese resilience to win the Budapest International Conductors' Competition twenty years later.

The rationale behind the Red Guard attacks could be ingenious. The Minister of Culture denounced Beethoven's Fifth Symphony as 'fatalistic', and the Third because it celebrated Bonaparte, who was an 'imperialist aggressor'. Many, however, managed to foil Red Guard missions. Jia Lanpo, author of *The Story of Peking Man*, documenting the discovery of *homo erectus* near Beijing, burnt his manuscript page by page rather than let it fall into the hands of the Red Guards. After the Cultural Revolution was over, he rewrote it from memory.[2]

As revolutionary fervour spread from students to disaffected workers and dissident officials all over the country, the Party appeared to lose control. The establishment of the urban Shanghai Commune in 1967, based on the Paris model of 1871, was vetoed by Mao as anarchistic.

Factional fighting was everywhere. Power was seized by those who could mouth the most loyalty to Chairman Mao. In China's only leper colony in Anhui province, rival factions, each claiming a higher loyalty to Mao, accused each other of being counter-revolutionary. 'Looking back now,' a former worker recalled, 'it was all wrong. But the whole country had gone red. Not many people kept their heads. Nearly all of us were taken in. We made complete fools of ourselves.' Cases of ritual cannibalism were reported in Guangxi in which youngsters ate the hearts, livers and genitals of their victims. 'Because he was a class enemy,' a researcher later concluded, 'it wasn't enough to kill him. You had to eat him. It was a symbol of loyalty to the Party.'[3] By then events were beyond Mao's control. His bewildered colleagues persuaded Mao that the time had come to rein in his 'little generals', as the Red Guard leaders were called.

'I am issuing a nation-wide notice,' he announced in 1968. 'If anyone continues to ... destroy means of transportation, kill people, or start fires, he is committing a crime. Those few who turn a deaf ear to persuasion and persist in their behaviour are bandits, or Guomindang elements, subject to capture. If they continue to resist, they will be annihilated.' But the central idea behind the Cultural Revolution, that Chinese youth needed to imbibe the Yanan spirit which had facilitated the Communist victory in 1949, was retained and even re-emphasised in the decision to send students to the countryside to experience the everyday realities of rural life.

Between 1968 and 1976 over 12 million youths were sent to the farms. One later reminisced, 'We former Red Guards met to exchange our experiences. We agreed that our stay with the people in the country had taught us the value of things – and of life itself. Looking back dispassionately, whatever motivated Mao to launch the Cultural Revolution, some of the ideas which emerged from it are still valuable. The "barefoot doctor" and "barefoot teacher" system are certainly good for a country like China ... Basic things like how to read, write and calculate can be taught very cheaply if they are organised by the local people themselves.'

While students went to learn from the farmers, the People's Liberation Army restored order. The army had been indoctrinated politically and was led by loyal Maoists, but, as he found with his Cultural Revolution advisers, Mao soon discovered that those who rose to the top could be sycophants, desperate for power whatever the cost. In 1970, Chen Boda was dismissed as a 'sham Marxist political swindler'. A year later, Lin Biao, who had been the youngest and most daring of the military commanders during the civil war and had actually been named as Mao's chosen successor in 1968, allegedly plotted to overthrow Mao. Lin became a victim of his own unconcealed ambition and vanity, and also of Mao's vindictiveness. Liu died in an air crash as he was apparently fleeing to Russia.

The man to whom Mao now turned to restore the Party's control over the country had been the number two target of the original campaign. Deng Xiaoping had been born in Sichuan province in 1904 and became a brilliant and precocious student. He travelled to France, where he worked briefly at a rubber overshoe factory. His personnel office noted when he left that Deng 'refuses to work – not to be rehired'. After a sojourn in Russia, Deng had rejoined the Chinese revolution, working in the Communist Party underground movement in Shanghai at the end of the 1920s. In 1931 he fought his way from Shanghai to the Jiangxi base, where he quickly proved his ability and his loyalty to Mao in the political power struggle that consumed the Party leaders. By the 1950s, Deng was considered one of the seven captains of the revolution, after Mao, Zhou Enlai, Zhu De, Chen Yun, Liu Shaoqi and Lin Biao. He headed the Party's administrative arm, the secretariat. In 1957, Mao had told Khrushchev not to underestimate 'that little fellow' who had destroyed a Guomindang army of one million, predicting that he had 'a great future ahead of him'.[4]

In the Cultural Revolution, Mao had nevertheless branded Deng a 'capitalist roader', despatching him to live in an ill-heated abandoned schoolhouse in Jiangxi province. Deng's political loyalty was not in doubt – he had, after all, been stern in handling the purge of the northern separatist Gao Gang in 1954 and relentless in bringing intellectual malcontents to book after the Hundred Flowers movement (his harsh report on them was one speech he never allowed to get into his *Collected Works*). But Mao correctly sensed in his zealous lieutenant an economic pragmatism similar to the vogue in Moscow, which could eventually usher in a capitalist restoration in China. Deng Xiaoping's most famous remark was that 'it doesn't matter whether a cat is black or white, as long as it catches mice', a philosophy which came to underlie his economic reform policies in the 1980s.

In Jiangxi Deng was escorted every day to a factory to work as a bench fitter, a trade he had learnt in France. Contact with the other workers or the local farmers was banned. This method of isolating political opponents was described by the famous writer Ding Ling, who was similarly imprisoned for five years in Beijing during the Cultural Revolution, and was not allowed any visitors. 'I had no pen, I had no paper. If I had anything that I wanted to say to someone, there was no one else in the room but myself. It was isolation, complete and absolute from nighttime to daytime; one had the choice of sitting facing the wall or of pacing about between the walls. That loneliness was like a poisonous snake, gnawing away at my heart.'

There was worse to come for Deng. His eldest son, Deng Pufang, was held blindfold by Red Guards and repeatedly interrogated about his father's 'conspiracy' against Mao. In despair the young man threw himself – or was pushed – out of a fourth-floor window of the Beijing University physics building and snapped his spinal cord. He was rushed to hospital by merciful classmates, but the doctors refused to treat him because, as the Cultural Revolution slogan put it clearly, 'If the father's a hero, the son's a good chap; if the father's a reactionary, the son's a bad egg.' Paralysed from the waist down, he joined his father in Jiangxi, where Deng senior massaged the boy's legs and helped to bathe him, while petitioning the authorities in Beijing for suitable medical treatment.

In 1973 the permission arrived along with – a sign of the declining influence of the ultra-leftists in Beijing – an invitation from Mao for Deng to resume his post. The economy had not suffered in the Cultural Revolution as badly as it had in the Great Leap Forward, but the Party's organisation was in tatters and Mao's colleagues demanded Deng's return. Deng quickly immersed himself in the day-to-day running of the country, stepping into the shoes of the ailing Premier, Zhou Enlai, who had done much to limit the damage during eight years of political struggle. Deng consolidated the ping-pong diplomacy which had brought President Nixon to China in 1971 and pursued stability and economic growth as best he could against the resistance of Mao's Gang of Four.

The succession question, however, remained unanswered. When Zhou Enlai died in January 1976, the Gang of Four stepped up their opposition to Deng Xiaoping, while simultaneously playing down the recently departed Premier's role in the Chinese revolution. On 4 April, when Chinese traditionally honour their dead in the Qingming festival, thousands of Beijingers flocked into Tiananmen Square and left wreaths eulogising Zhou Enlai at the base of the Monument to the People's Heroes (later to become the focal point for the 1989 student demonstrations). 'He left no family,' read one of the tributes, 'he had no children, he has no grave, he left no remains. It seems he left us nothing, but he shall live for all time in our hearts. The whole land is his. He has hundreds of millions of children and grandchildren. All China's soil is in his tomb. He left us everything. He shall live in our hearts for all time. Who is he? Who is he? He is our Premier!'

That night, Public Security officers, obeying the Gang of Four, took the wreaths away, provoking thousands of angry citizens to gather outside the Great Hall of the People and demand their return. After several violent incidents in the Square, over two hundred people were arrested by militiamen, often with brute force. The Politburo's reaction was to appoint a compromise figure as Premier – not one of the Gang of Four but a relatively unknown though loyal Maoist, Hua Guofeng. Deng Xiaoping was accused by the Gang of Four of master-minding the pro-Zhou Enlai demonstrations and suffered his third and last fall from grace, being dismissed from office.

For the moment, the Gang of Four appeared to have gained the upper hand, but, the exiled teacher Wu Ningkun recalled, 'the mood of the university and the country was perceptibly different from that of the earlier years of the Cultural Revolution. Most people were simply fed up with the endless political upheavals and the increasing hardships of life ... The talk of the town was about the slogans that appeared on a college wall, supporting Deng and denouncing Jiang Qing as a demon.' A joke that went the rounds at the time centred on three inmates of a Beijing prison asking each other how they came to be there: 'I am here because I supported Deng Xiaoping,' said the first; 'I am here because I *opposed* Deng Xiaoping,' came the second's reply; the third man simply said, 'I *am* Deng Xiaoping.'

In September 1976, at the age of eighty-three, Mao Zedong died, leaving Hua Guofeng as his anointed successor. The Gang of Four had other plans, claiming that Mao had actually wanted them to assume considerable, if not total, power. Already unpopular, and with their patron, Mao, gone, they were politically outwitted by the moderates in the Party. Within a month they were arrested. In 1981 they were tried for their involvement in the Cultural Revolution and given suspended death sentences.

Deng Xiaoping's supporters had helped Hua to act against the Gang of Four, and now he skilfully manoeuvred himself back into the limelight. More and more of the 'counter-revolutionaries' who had suffered in the Cultural Revolution returned to their jobs in the government.

Chen Yizhi had joined the Party at the age of eighteen on starting university, but was sent down to the countryside in 1963 because he defended a fellow-student accused of rightism. On his return to the university in 1966, he was again targeted as counter-revolutionary by the Red Guards, and his girlfriend was made to watch as he was beaten nearly to death on three occasions. 'I lay in a coma for six days,' he stated later. 'There were times when I knew how easy it would be to give in to death. If only I had recovered earlier, I might have been able to stop my fiancée from killing herself.'

In 1970 this same Chen was sent to Henan province and rose to rural prominence there as the Cultural Revolution petered out. At the Agricultural Economy Research Institute he produced a seminal report entitled 'Down in the Countryside: China's Hope', analysing the experimental agricultural responsibility system in Anhui. This came to the attention of the reform leader Zhao Ziyang, who used it to consolidate the position of the economic reformers within the political leadership, even though, as Chen admitted, their political direction was often unclear. 'We are trying to build a Chinese-style socialism which is neither feudalistic nor capitalist, modelled neither on the Soviet Union, nor on the West,' he explained. 'Sometimes we feel as if we are groping for stepping stones to cross the river' – a graphic image that came to be used in the reform period after 1978 as a metaphor for incrementalism. That was only one example of the human resources released through Deng Xiaoping's policies for application in China's development.

The original verdict of the 1976 Tiananmen incident (that it was counter-revolutionary), influenced by the Gang of Four, was formally reversed in November 1978 and that was an endorsement of Deng's reinstatement, confirmed by the launch of his ambitious economic reforms at the Party Central Committee meeting a month later. Hua Guofeng relied on an uninspiring policy summed up in the mindless slogan, 'We will resolutely uphold whatever policy decisions Chairman Mao made, and unswervingly follow whatever instructions Chairman Mao made' – known derisively as the 'Two Whatevers' policy. Deng's supporters also voiced allegiance to the departed Chairman, but insisted that, as Mao had also stated, policy should 'seek truth from facts'. 'You can't just take what Mao Zedong said about one problem,' Deng argued, 'and apply it to some other problem, or take what he said at one place and apply it to some other place, or take what he said at one time and apply it to some other time! . . . There's no such thing as one man being absolutely right.'

Hua was replaced as Premier and Party Chairman, and a new liberal leadership headed by the reformer Hu Yaobang took control in 1981. Although the 'Seek Truth from Facts' faction won the day in 1978, Mao's role in history still had to be reassessed – and so did the faction's own involvement in the Party's catastrophic mistakes. 'Mao Zedong Thought,' Ye Jianying, who had overseen the arrest of the Gang of Four, observed, 'is not the product of Mao's wisdom alone, it is also the product of the wisdom of his comrades-in-arms.' The official verdict in 1981 was that Mao had been 70 per cent correct but 30 per cent wrong, enabling the reformers discreetly to unburden themselves of the blame for the Great Leap Forward and the Cultural Revolution. Deng Xiaoping took no office, ruling behind the scenes and sometimes called the 'paramount ruler.'

For many faithful Chinese, however, Mao's memory was still sacrosanct. 'I'm still hoping to get the money together for a trip to Beijing to have a look around,' Zhang Yuxi, a fifty-four-year-old Shandong farm worker, told visiting Chinese sociologists during the 1980s. 'Before I die I want to see what Chairman Mao really looks like. I know about his mistakes in his last years. But they weren't his mistakes. Sitting there in his dragon palace, he couldn't possibly have known what was happening to us farm workers. It was the people under him who were bad. Chairman Mao had wealth and greatness written all over his face. He had the look of a real emperor, but he was better than an emperor. No emperor ever saved the poor. Chairman Mao was the saviour of the poor from the moment he was born.'

For many of those who wrote the wall posters which aided Deng's return to power, however, Mao represented all that had gone wrong with the ideals of the revolution. 'We had beautiful ideas,' Liang Heng wrote. 'Mao became our first father, especially when our own fathers were disgraced. We dreamed about giving ourselves to the communist cause. But the revolution, for me, for my family, for my friends, for the farm workers, for all the persons I know – was a tragedy.'

Not all the public criticisms supported Deng. 'I thought our superiors were working hard,' lamented a poster in Beijing entitled *A Very Frightened Person Who Loves Life*. 'I thought that they were trying to bring about a better life for the people. I had no idea that in their eyes the people counted for nothing – nothing at all. Their first priority is to protect the status quo. They want to hold on to what they've got – and then get more. They use smiles to get it. Their attitude is "Democracy is something we can give you out of our own generosity" . . . They carry out their reforms, but if you want to participate and if those reforms develop to the point where their interests are in danger, what do they give you? I'm afraid . . . I'm still afraid. It's really tragic.'

Deng did end the ultra-leftist control over culture. Shakespeare, Mark Twain and Dickens came back on the shelves of libraries (though still under lock and key). But he would not allow any move towards popular political participation. In 1980 the privilege of writing wall posters – *dazibao* – which Mao himself had originally introduced, was withdrawn from the constitution, and Democracy Wall, where they had been permitted by Deng, was scraped clean of its offending messages. Deng adopted Zhou Enlai's programme of Four Modernisations (of agriculture, industry, national defence and science and technology), but he arrested Wei Jingsheng for daring to add a fifth modernisation – democracy – to the agenda. The prosecutors explained:

> Our constitution clearly stipulates extensive democratic rights. However, our democracy should be a democracy protected by law. It does not mean absolute freedom for one to do as one likes... Freedom of speech of the individual citizen must be on the basic principle of insisting on the socialist road, the dictatorship of the proletariat, the leadership of the party and Marxism-Leninism-Mao Zedong Thought. The citizen has only the freedom to support these principles and not the freedom to oppose them.

The wall which had been covered with Democracy posters was later overlaid with billboards advertising commercial products. It was a fitting symbol of the effects of Deng's policies on Chinese society. Under Mao, physicists had been told to undertake manual work for political reasons; under Deng, they were enticed to do commercial work for economic reasons. Yet it was to the countryside that Deng turned for the spark to ignite China's economic growth, with the nation-wide introduction of the responsibility system. Farming contracts were extended to fifteen years, and by the end of the 1980s, the farmers had once again asserted their leading role in the Communist drive towards prosperity. 'Last year,' a woman farmer observed in 1987, 'we earned RMB 11,000 and harvested 13,000 lb. So we've really made it. Townies are useless. We poor and lower middle peasants are ahead: we've left the working class behind.'

These freedoms were then extended to factory managers, who were allowed to choose their own workers and pay them accordingly, although the managers were also responsible for losses and could face charges of bankruptcy. Party committees were retained within the workplace to 'guarantee and supervise implementation of Party principles and politics', but political struggle appeared redundant, and the Party's theoretical beliefs increasingly outdated. 'We're depressed because we care about what's happening to the country,' an instructor in Marxism-Leninism lamented. 'We're not reactionary at all. We all feel a sense of responsibility, but there's nothing we can do... The

Communist Party has been around for over sixty years, and we've been building socialism for a good thirty, but what's the result?'

When senior Party officials, many the personal victims of the Cultural Revolution, began debating the idea of increasing popular participation in politics, the old guard within the leadership, raised on a diet of strict Leninist belief in the omnipotence of the Party, reacted strongly. Hu Yaobang, the erratic and excitable General Secretary, was the first to suffer. On a visit to Inner Mongolia in 1985 Hu, Deng's first protégé, made the mildly revolutionary proposal that 'we should prepare more knives and forks, buy more plates and sit around the table to eat Chinese food in the Western style, that is, each from his own plate. By doing so we can avoid contagious diseases.' (The Chinese custom, of course, is to eat with chopsticks from a communal plate.) This kind of remark incensed the old guard. He was dismissed in 1987.

With near-double-digit annual growth rates throughout the 1980s, the Chinese economy attained its healthiest state for decades. 'Chinese leaders,' Robert Delfts of the *Far Eastern Economic Review* argued, 'have concluded that capitalism works, but this does not mean that they believe socialism or Marxism does not work. On the contrary, there is a certain resentment that "Westerners tend to think of the market as something peculiar to capitalism." Why should the West have a monopoly of the market?' Nevertheless, to many of the old conservatives, and especially Chen Yun, who had also criticised the Great Leap Forward, the reforms incorporated too many other unwanted elements of capitalism which had been the original targets of the revolution. Deng Xiaoping replied that bourgeois pollution was like flies buzzing into a room when the window is open. 'We can put up with the flies,' he crisply commented, 'but we cannot do without the fresh air.'

The student demonstrations in 1986 provided the excuse for which the ageing conservatives had been waiting to reclaim some of their lost influence over policy. After Hu Yaobang's dismissal, the economic reforms were to some extent reined in, but the next wave of student demonstrations in 1989 led to the tragedy of the Tiananmen killings.

In order to satisfy the conservatives, Deng was constrained to sack the liberal General Secretary of the Party, Zhao Ziyang, his second protégé and leader of the reformers who had wanted to use softly-softly tactics with the students. Discussions within the Party about further democratisation were put on ice until a new generation came to power, but the economic reforms continued. Today over one Shanghai family in five owns shares, and there is one former steel worker who earns $70,000 a year from his investments. The whole country took literally Deng's slogan to 'get rich quick', showing more enthusiasm than it had shown for Mao's earlier political rallying cries.

Along with the new sense of economic achievement, there was also a resurgence of the old society's ills. Corruption soared as Party members used their position to get rich as quickly as everyone else. Opium addiction was officially admitted to be once again a major problem, favoured by the *getihu* – the first generation of stressed businessmen with the money to indulge. Spending on bribes and traditional ceremonies seriously undermined potential investment in the economy, with typical newlyweds splashing $3,000 on their marriage celebration. One Shanghai couple rented forty-four cars to take their guests to a restaurant to which they could have walked in fifteen minutes. Funerals in Hunan province alone cost RMB 1.5 billion in 1990.

Traditional demeaning attitudes towards women also resurfaced, especially in rural areas, because of the government-imposed one-child policy. One couple beat their daughter to death when local officials would not allow them to try again for a son. The return of the traditional desire to continue the family line was mirrored by a revival of superstitions about women, which Mao had begun to counter. 'I'm not going to let my old woman touch the tickets I've bought today: women's hands stink,' one thirty-two-year-old remarked while queuing to buy a lottery ticket. 'And I only buy lottery tickets from the windows where men are selling: I won't buy them from women.'

The media are still used by the Party to promote its policies, but there are increasing signs of freedom of expression, most notably in the cinema. Chen Kaige, the most Westernised of the film directors who entered the Beijing Film Academy in 1978 and are known as the Fifth Generation, was a teenager during the Cultural Revolution and had betrayed his father. 'I knew it was wrong to do so, I can't forgive myself. I had the choice of saying nothing but I was selfish. I saw my father's face go white.' Now his father works with him on his films, many of which, including *Farewell My Concubine* and *Yellow Earth*, have won international awards. His philosophy is shared by many of his contemporaries. 'The minds of our generation have been washed clean in the torrents of life. Our generation is determined to create our own lives through our own efforts.'

After forty-five years of power, the Chinese Communist Party has kept the Mandate of Heaven, bringing both positive and negative changes to society. The feelings of some conscientious Chinese people after all those movements to the left and right of the Marxist political spectrum were well expressed by Yue Daiyun. In spite of the nationwide suffering during the Cultural Revolution, she said, she could not forget the martyrs who had been sacrificed for Communism's liberation of China from the feudalistic tyranny of previous regimes. 'Even as I recalled the disappointments of my own life and the tragic loss of my friends, I realised that some flame still burned in my heart . . . Surely the hardships, the losses suffered together, would not be redeemed unless we strove to keep that flame alive. I would join in the efforts to rebuild the Party, convinced that whatever its past mistakes it alone could lead China forward. I was far less confident of success than in 1949 and far less certain that I could contribute, but I knew I had to try.' Many more Chinese would probably say in all frankness that Communism has failed in China, and that its proponents are able to stay in power only by borrowing the clothes of capitalism.

PART TWO

POLITICS

CHAPTER 3

POLITICS: HE WHO ARGUES...

In 1941 I received a letter from Clementine Churchill, thanking me for collecting a little money from friends and neighbours for her Help China Fund. As a thirteen-year-old I felt proud to be of assistance to a brave and worthy nation stubbornly resisting Japanese invasion at great sacrifice. That was the general Western perception of China then.

A residue of that good feeling prompted some observers to overlook or minimise the subsequent excesses of Mao Zedong, and the final spin-off may be the general Western assumption today that China wants and deserves – but is tragically denied – the democracy which the West has developed into such a formidable and, it believes, universal method of modern government. My thesis here is to show that while democracy in a very general sense is indeed desired by educated Chinese, many specific aspects of the democratic system and procedures in the West simply do not fit the national character, making it futile for outsiders to promote them.

How people behave in Chinese society is a variable amalgam of two distinct modes. One is dictated by tradition, handed down from one generation to the next and nourished by the relative isolation of so many Chinese from the outside world. The other is the modern mode, dictated by recent advances in science, technology and the economy, and also by greater access to more modernised societies elsewhere. The modern mode is broadly similar in all countries, and may need no significant special knowledge to understand it. But the traditional mode does take some explaining to those who are not Chinese.

An article published in Beijing in 1988 defined the perennial Chinese social values as understood by the Chinese themselves:

> It is a tradition of hard work and patient suffering; respect for teachers and elders; it is belief in . . . the virtues that emphasise relations such as those of ruler to subject and father to son; it is great concentration of power and authority in the centre under the belief that there is no piece of earth beneath the sky that does not fall under the jurisdiction of the king; it is a class system of gentry, farmers, workers and merchants; it is a system of employing in the government those who excel in learning; it is a value system that puts learning at the top; it is a psychological attitude of being attached to one's native land and being unwilling to leave it; it is a style of living and a style of production that uses the family as the basic unit; it is the way of thinking that puts the ethics and morality of human relationships in the primary position; it is a modus vivendi based on dependence on parents inside the home and dependence on friends outside the home.[1]

The culture of compliance has been instilled into Chinese society over many centuries. Not only Chinese: every other East Asian state which came under the historic influence of Chinese civilisation is today ruled, to the apparent satisfaction of most of its people, in an authoritarian manner, though sometimes behind a democratic façade, and changing faster than China.

In colonial Hongkong the few elected representatives of the people never enjoyed real power: the place was ruled by gubernatorial decree, although many of the British traditions – the rule of law and independence of the judiciary – manage to prevail there. Singapore is outwardly democratic, but a single ruling party under Lee Kuan Yew has managed to retain power for three and a half decades by operating in a highly paternalistic way. The same was true of Japan's Liberal Democratic Party until 1993. South Korea now boasts a large middle class, partly because of its excellent education system, inherited from Japanese rule in the early part of this century, and that class has at last developed active democratic politics – but only in the last ten years or so. In

Taiwan too, the earlier authoritarianism of Jiang Jieshi and his son has recently opened up to accept a little pluralism. But this has not happened in Singapore or in China.

China follows the authoritarian model during these early phases of its economic modernisation. Why is this? The Chinese have never adopted a religious faith requiring them to treat all other people as equals, and a universal ethic is a core foundation of democracy. Confucius and his successors taught the Chinese to behave well, but their teachings were mostly concerned with relations within the family – and a hierarchical family at that. The younger members of the family must obey their elders. Chinese parents usually indulge their children in infancy but then discipline them strictly after the age of about five, and that usually makes them grow up obedient, unassertive, dependent and unaggressive.[2] In classical China the family, which could be very large, or the clan, which is a family of families, were the most important units of society, even forming the lowest rung of government.

One of the most difficult things the Communists set out to do when they came to rule China was to make schoolchildren 'tell' on their fathers and mothers. It would be shocking in any country, but in China it was the highest form of personal treason, to renounce those who have done everything to give you life, in exchange for an unstable membership in your own age group. The tradition of obedience within the family still exists, and remains an important force in social relations.

When Frank Ching, a Chinese journalist in Hongkong, was a child he used to be told the story of the boy of eight, Wu Meng, who exposed his skin to mosquitoes every night in the hope that they would be satisfied and spare his parents. 'Such stories,' says Frank, 'made me feel unworthy, since I knew I could never be so selfless.'[3]

But life cannot be confined nowadays to the small ambit of one's family, and tradition extends these family relations to such new contexts as the factory, the military unit, the Party branch etc. The drive to gain things from society is channelled through the group. A Chinese does not grow up under pressures to assert his individuality. From the beginning of his consciousness as a baby he will share a bedroom with brothers or sisters. When his parents go out for the evening, even to a restaurant or nightclub, he goes with them, however young he may be. As a child he will eat at the circular dining table preferred in China, because it conveys the feeling of being part of a group much more than the square or rectangular table of the West – which affords more privacy but discourages people from joining together. Life presents itself as something dependent on other people in the group. A Chinese is mostly conditioned to take a passive role, first in the family and then in the society outside.

The Sichuan radical of the 1900s, Zou Rong, concluded that China needed to abolish servility before attempting a revolution, and Fang Lizhi, the astrophysicist and doyen of the contemporary dissidents, meant the same thing when he called on Chinese individuals to seize democracy in their own spheres by 'straightening their bent backs'.[4]

A line from the ancient Chinese classics runs, 'A good man does not argue; he who argues is not a good man.' The man to whom you are thinking of being rude may be tomorrow's boss, after all, and it is safer to be tactful with everybody. Western farmers, if pestered by local officials' unjustified fees, would probably take an individualistic stand in order to protect their own interests, challenging those officials and even suing them, with or without the support of neighbouring farmers. In China, however, the farmers are mostly claimed by the old cultural system which requires them to view those in authority as right, or at least to treat them with respect. They may give in without organised protest, at least until the impositions become intolerable.

'In China,' a Chinese lecturer says, 'if the state doesn't stifle you, then society will. We don't like it when someone protests openly... In the West you say "this is right and that is wrong". Here, you can't do that. If you come out and protest, people are surprised and suspicious.' Social pressure makes the individual a collectivist in the end. Truth has a low value in China, subordinated to the cult of successful relationships. As a Beijing headmaster observed: 'Telling the truth can bring no benefit, only harm.' The system means a gain of efficiency by the group, but a loss of efficiency from individual initiatives.

Liu Binyan, the author and editor, recalls a newspaper report he wrote in his early days about an extreme case of two men working to build a bridge on the Yellow river. They were caught unawares by flooding. The first one waited for orders, watching the work they had done wash away downstream. The second man acted on his own initiative and saved the pier. But the result was that the first man was promoted for his obedience, while the second was punished for his breach of discipline.[5]

The traditional Chinese has an inbred sense that taking advantage of individual rights is selfish. People in a factory do not pursue vigorous competition among themselves. The traditional Chinese expresses his individualism only when he is alone or with a very close friend, whereas a modern Chinese might show it off on all occasions. Liu Binyan joined the Chinese revolution in order to liberate himself, as did many others. He felt something inside him which was waiting to blossom so that one day he could do something very special. 'Nobody could ever explain to me,' he mused, 'where natural self-interest ends and selfishness begins.'[6] Yet it is that distinction which enables Western societies to carry out a large amount of communal work while still allowing the individuals concerned to monitor their behaviour themselves through their own individual consciences.

In America it is considered a regrettably wimpish lack of initiative if a son stays under his parents' wings. But in China it is the other way round. The one criticised is the one who leaves the family and goes out into the world, forgetting his family obligations. Individualism begins to flower in boarding schools and universities, where students mostly live in dormitories away from their parents. Two Beijing university students wrote an exchange about it. 'Mankind!' the first wrote. 'Why can't he understand his brother?' To which the other replied, 'It is very difficult for man to understand his brother, not to say impossible. I, however, have decided that I don't need understanding. Those who beg for understanding are childish. A strong, mature person who is not understood can walk forth from his own loneliness.'[7]

One incident will illustrate the low value placed on individuality. One young Chinese will never forget the day when, at the age of nine, he joined thousands of schoolchildren parading on the occasion of Mao Zedong's funeral. Because of the numbers, the boys and girls had to assemble very early, and waited for four or five hours, standing in the sun, before the official procession went past. Having been up even earlier than that to make sure they had the right school uniforms and accessories, and to rendezvous at their school, they were tired out long before the mourning big shots went past. This boy happened to yawn, apparently the only one to commit such a discourtesy. He was dragged out of the ranks, taken away, and severely chastised. For three weeks he wrote letter after letter of apology, until one considered sufficiently contrite was accepted by the local officials. When he went back to school, where he had been reckoned one of the best students, his friends and teachers boycotted him as a 'bad element'. The individual may transgress in minor ways, but if his mistakes set a bad example to others present, or might encourage a slackening of discipline by them, then the group's interest is placed squarely before the individual's and punishment will ensue. Organisations routinely reject membership applications from an individual labelled a 'bad element' (usually because his or her parents were on the wrong side politically in the past) regardless of whether that person might technically be better qualified than other applicants. The group organisation always gets priority.

The new generation of intellectuals is very keen to change the classical system of family or group loyalty. A singer with a nationwide following has a song with the lines:

> Listen to me, Dad, give me the freedom to grow up.
> I don't want to listen to all that you've arranged for me.

'I want to emphasise individualism,' said the principal of China's first private boarding school in Chengdu. 'I want these students to change and reform society.'[8] But it will take a long time.

The beginnings of a retreat from the family may be seen in recent opinion polls suggesting that Chinese students respect film stars and world statesmen like Margaret Thatcher more than they respect their own parents. The two preceding generations witnessed considerable damage to the old values, grandparents because of the Cultural Revolution, which lessened their respect for authority, and parents because of the reforms by Deng Xiaoping which are loosening respect for authority in a different way by putting money first. All that is compounded by Western influence in the cities, by legal reforms, by the mushrooming of corruption, by unemployment and internal migration. The greater freedom in literature and the cinema, although it still has a long way to go, also buttresses the self-confidence of the individual.

The opinion polls indicate that almost every other Chinese student now believes the individual will to be sacred and inviolable, while almost two-thirds feel that each person should be considered as an individual rather than submit to rules and authority applying to everyone.[9] They say that, but they do not always act on it. In practice, since China lacks a universal code of conduct, who you are determines what you can individualistically get away with.

One consequence of the orthodox social system is that once the traditional Chinese moves out in the world, he tends to look for father figures or superiors to follow. Conditioned by his formative years as a junior member of a family, he seeks out a similar source of authority in bosses, heads of department, commanding officers, editors and political superiors. Just as a father would protect the younger traditional Chinese from sometimes unruly brothers, sisters and cousins, so the traditional Chinese expects a personalised political authority to impose order in society and give a clear guidance for all to follow. In psychological terms, it is hard to induce the traditional person to internalise the commands of the high authority – to become autonomous and independent, acting on his own judgement and moral sense. With this concept of authority, and given the hierarchical structure which accompanies it, one could say that China is a society in which the traditional Chinese would like there to be an emperor to tell him what to do.

That is not hyperbole. During the last few years there have been signs that reverence for emperors has not died. The most recent one was the boy emperor Pu Yi, who was portrayed from a Western viewpoint in Bertolucci's film *The Last Emperor*. He died in obscurity at the beginning of the Cultural Revolution. Yet a memorial meeting was held to restore his reputation in 1980. He left a nephew as his heir – the 'dragon pretender' who works in a bank in Beijing.[10]

More surprising is the fact that in 1993 over 10,000 Chinese, including the provincial governor, assembled to worship the legendary Yellow Emperor, the sixteenth-century BC founder of the civilization, at his supposed burial ground in Shaanxi province. Overseas Chinese came from Hongkong, Taiwan, Singapore and America to join this remarkable tribute, and US$300,000 was raised to refurbish the tomb.[11] That kind of thing had been banned under Mao Zedong. Now it is allowed to play its part in a society which is officially Communist but is drifting steadily towards nationalism – of which the Yellow Emperor is the symbol.

Another feature of the primacy of the family is that the traditional Chinese show a particularly strong preference for older 'fathers' in authority. When Mao elevated the youngest member of the Gang of Four, Wang Hongwen, then still in his forties, to be Vice-Chairman of the Communist Party, critics privately mocked him as 'a baby still smelling of milk'. Reverence for age makes for a relatively strict seniority system in most organisations. An outstanding candidate for an important position in his thirties will be passed over in favour of one twenty years older even though less qualified. It would be said that if the older man were not promoted, he would never have another chance, whereas the younger one had years ahead of him in which to be promoted. 'This is how the seniority system squeezes out excellent young cadres,' a Beijing journalist commented. 'The Chinese way of dealing with the generation gap', said the psychologist Sun Longji more severely, 'is to demand the complete surrender of the younger generation to the elders.'[12]

The extension of submitting to father's rule is the tradition to defer to authority at large. It may sound sheepish, but it is practical. It normally keeps you out of trouble, and allows the ruler to remain largely free of distractions and wasteful argument while getting his policies implemented. ('He who argues is not a good man.') The family experience also leads the traditional Chinese to be fearful of anarchy, or, one might say, of losing the main benefit of autocracy. All these feelings combine to ensure a relative passiveness.

Deference to authority can easily go to extremes, of course. A Harbin dance-hall, for example, was once playing a melodious waltz for its patrons when the music abruptly stopped, to be replaced by a vigorous tango. The manager explained that a very high official, Mr Qiao, had arrived, and he liked to tango. Most of the dancers coolly changed their step, used to such boorishness and ready to pander to the high-up's rudeness rather than be marked down as a disrespectful troublemaker. But one man's inquisitiveness ran away with him, and he aimed a conspicuous stare of curiosity at the new arrival. The VIP's guards began to beat him up, and when his wife came forward to help, she was struck so violently that she lost not only two front teeth but also the baby she was carrying.[13] The dance-hall manager's action was a routine deference to authority, of the kind that happens every day. A traditional Chinese does not question the orders of his superiors, otherwise he would be singled out for punishment and loss of access to favours.

Meek compliance with a cruel father or ruler may in the end explode into angry mutiny. The Taiping rebellion in the nineteenth century sent 20 million Chinese to their graves. Mencius, who was second only to Confucius in fame as an ancient philosopher, declared that tyrannicide was legitimate when the monarch broke his social contract with the people. But for most of the time the traditional Chinese does not expect to have much control over his own destiny, something which makes him a less effective democrat and a less effective rebel. Deferential to father, employer and 'emperor', he hopes that others better informed and more capable of power than himself will lead the nation or enterprise in the right direction. He may thus appear a somewhat ill-armed player on the Chinese chessboard.

But there are two compensatory institutions which do much to put the balance right. One of them is 'face', or the preserving of someone's self-respect in the eyes of others. 'Face' means that a traditional Chinese very rarely criticises another person in public, or draws attention to that person's mistakes and deficiencies when other people are present. If he has to put a subordinate in his place, he does so privately and not in front of the whole office. The subordinate can then go away with his self-respect and the good opinion of his colleagues intact, even with the reprimand.[14] That is something which some modern Westerners may perhaps do instinctively, seeing it as the humane way to maintain discipline – the difference being that the traditional Chinese would do it more systematically as a matter of custom. It is the same in Japan: Morita Akio, the co-founder of Sony, attributed some of his industrial success to letting juniors get the credit for his own ideas – thus giving them 'face'.

You may say that the thin-skinned softness of the Chinese in needing such treatment is something to fault. But a modern Chinese would probably reply that the Western custom of publicly giving a piece of one's mind to one's juniors makes for a bad atmosphere in the group and could drive the man criticised to slacken his work or even take some kind of revenge.[15]

The second useful institution to mitigate the disadvantages of deference is something for which the Chinese word – *guanxi* – has no satisfactory English translation. With the weak universal ethic and the strong sense of hierarchy discouraging notions of equality, the traditional Chinese obviously needs to have another way of dealing with other people, a means of manipulating them and advancing his own desires and rights as in every human community. *Guanxi* is the highly material way of performing this function. It is a complex network of reciprocal obligations.

If you need an operation, you give a present to the surgeon. If you want to escape a fine, you give money or food to the policeman. If you want your child to do well at school, you give presents to the teacher. Whenever a gift is made, it creates a reciprocal obligation on the other side. It can be much more sophisticated than that, but this is the essence of it. Gifts are not unknown in Western society and the Chinese system is perhaps a formalisation and extension of that – magnified by the relative lack of trust between Chinese from different families. The magazine *China Youth* of Beijing described *guanxi* rather well in a 1993 interview with a soldier, who said:

> If you don't have *guanxi*, do you think anyone would help you if you wanted to transfer to volunteer soldier status, if you wanted to enter the Communist Party, if you wanted to go to school, if you wanted to be an official? No way! What *guanxi* do you have if you're a hayseed from some backwater place? None. If you've got none then you'll have to go looking for it. You call on hometown cronies, you call on acquaintances, you

> call on friends and relatives. And how does one call on such people? By giving gifts and spending money . . .[16]

Lee Kuan Yew, the former Premier of Singapore, predicts that it will take China twenty years or more to develop a rule of law system with transparency of rules and regulations, and *guanxi* connections will make up for the lack in the meantime. They depend on affinity of language and culture, which is why Hongkong and Taiwan businessmen were so successful in exploiting the trade and investment opportunities offered by Deng Xiaoping.[17]

These are the major constituents of the traditional social system, presented rather baldly, shorn of the lengthy reservations and qualifications they deserve. Tradition tussles with modernity inside every contemporary Chinese mind. Sometimes one wins, sometimes the other. Much of the time it is a compromise. Tradition will mostly lose out to modernity in the long run, but

千曲百弯路难行

***The motorcyclist 'economic and social efficiency' stares in bewilderment at the maze of roads to his goal labelled* guanxi (People's Daily, *5 September 1993*).**

meanwhile an acquaintance with the tradition will help our understanding for the next several decades. There are many ways in which tradition is being infiltrated by foreign ideas and examples, and the pace of modernisation in China also erodes the old-fashioned system. But every Chinese living in China, however Westernised, bears some marks of traditional values, and it is these values which sometimes lead Westerners to misunderstand their Chinese partners or friends from time to time. Let us now see how these Chinese characteristics affect politics.

To begin with, it must be apparent why law is such a weak concept in China, when appeals for support are commonly addressed not to the lifeless pages of old law tomes or new statute books but to the persons in authority – with whom, if you are lucky, you may have some connection, or with whom you may be able to set up at least some form of *guanxi*. An impersonal Chinese law will eventually emerge, containing elements of Western law, but that may take a very long time, except in the narrow area of commercial and contract law where foreign business is involved.

An alternative for the Chinese supplicant is to take matters into his own hands. Qiao Shi, who was then responsible for public security matters across China, complained in 1991 that 'in some areas, secret societies and clan organisations have formed armed public security forces to deal with civil and criminal cases in the countryside.'[18] In other words, people at the grass roots are trying to get justice done, not through unfamiliar institutions like law so much as through the trusted channels of the Chinese tradition. In one county thirteen officials, including the head of the very important grain office, were found guilty of bribery and corruption. Four of them were sent to prison. But then a higher rung of local officialdom reviewed the case and released the four men on bail for medical treatment, so no one went to jail at all.[19] A case of *guanxi*? Yes, it was probably local connections that led to that result.

The officials who are meant to enforce the theoretical law have to live in the real world of *guanxi*. A legal newspaper complained recently that some of them 'make private use of the power they hold to sponge off everybody in sight. They get free food, free drinks, help themselves to whatever they want free of charge. They put on the squeeze. They extort money and goods. If they don't get what they want, they make all kinds of trouble.'[20]

The rather open-minded *China Youth* magazine tried in 1993 to spell out the rationale of the rule of law for its readers.

> Western countries have established the system of democracy and rule of law... in order to guarantee long-term social and political stability and free and equal relations between people... Under such systems, the power of state leaders is not unlimited but is bound by the constitution and the law, and is constrained by the legislature ... and the judiciary and by public opinion ... The leader cannot abuse power and thus gravely damage legality. If he acts in this manner he will be driven out of power. The socialist countries adopting the Soviet model, however, pursue a highly centralised system in which the Party leader holds ultimate power, and... has the final say in deciding everything or changing policies haphazardly. In this sort of system, when leaders exert absolute power which is not restricted by any control, socialist democracy becomes an empty slogan.[21]

Well said! At least some people in Chinese public life are aware of the Western system. But the voice of power sings a different tune. The man in charge of the judiciary, Ren Jianxin, President of the Supreme People's Court, showed no such understanding when he laid down in 1990 that 'the People's Courts must self-consciously accept Party leadership. It is a mistake to think, because there is the law, that justice can be executed without the guidance of the policies of the Communist Party. Separation of powers is bourgeois.'[22]

In practice the courts still defer to higher political authority, either by order or by the exercise of self-restraint, just as journalists employ self-censorship. When Wang Meng, a former Minister of Culture, wanted to sue the editor of a newspaper for publishing a letter implying that he had criticised Deng Xiaoping, he could not get a single court to hear his suit for libel. A Nanjing professor dared to file a lawsuit against the Communist Party itself, challenging its legal right to stop him travelling abroad to attend an academic conference. He became an exile in the United States. Now litigation is beginning to grow in popularity, indicating a mounting interest in law. But when a high official in the judiciary wrote a newspaper article arguing the case for independent judges and less administrative intervention, he was immediately criticised by the Party.[23]

Some conservative Chinese intellectuals say that democracy is neither needed in China nor suitable for it. They go on to argue that if the Chinese are released from the control of a strong authority, they will go wild and abuse their freedom, acting with extreme selfishness and no patriotism. If the repressive function of the Communists were relaxed, it could cause an explosion of political demands. Some believe that the result would be an uncontrollable 'man-eating beast', spreading 'yellow peril' throughout the world. 'Do not open this Pandora's box, please, world!' they plead.

This is not just dictatorship, it is dictatorship on top of a tradition of political submission. Robert Elegant concluded that Western democracy is 'unworkable – technically and psychologically – in China'. A Western political scientist makes a good case for what may seem an extreme point of view. China, he explains, has no concept of citizenship, no assembly, no Senate, no Magna Carta, no social contract, no immemorial rights of the freeborn subject, no constitution, and nothing requiring any of the people to take part in the legislative process. It is basically contrary to the social values of the Chinese to put their political future 'to the hazard of an election'.[24] Democracy, in this analysis, becomes ultimately frivolous. At the very least, as Gong Xiangrui, a law professor, puts it, 'the machinery of government could not be copied from the West, definitely not, but the principles and ideas might be transplanted.'[25]

The high respect for age resulting from the supreme status of the grandfather in the family not only spawns a generally inflexible seniority system for promotions but also keeps retired seniors in power. Only the deathbed can take away from a leader the personal authority which he has built up in his working life. There is a small group of men in their eighties and nineties, veterans of the Party long since retired – they are sometimes called 'the immortals' – who still exert a strong influence on affairs, especially on promotions. Their leader is, of course, Deng Xiaoping, but even he finds it necessary to let the others have their way from time to time. The 'leader of the opposition' within the immortals was Chen Yun, a shrewd former typesetter who managed the economy under Mao Zedong. Chen used his sizeable following in the country and among Party officials to slow down Deng's race to reform. There are five or six other gerontocrat activists, and since they all cut their teeth on Maoist economics it is hardly surprising that most of them act to restrain Deng's enthusiasm. They support the economic reforms only when they are carefully planned and do not precipitate 'over-heating'. Chinese politics, says Brantly Womack, are 'at the mercy of a handful of very old biological clocks'.[26]

Not many countries allow such a semi-formal veto in the hands of political grandfathers. They can become figures of fun when they appear at meetings and ceremonies, tottering on their sticks with young nurses at their side or, alternatively, in wheelchairs. Young wags call them the 'Politburo Sitting Committee', to be distinguished from the (younger) Standing Committee of seven who constitutionally form the Party's highest executive. It is presumed that they are able to achieve their remarkable longevity by taking such traditional Chinese medicaments as Three Whip Pellets – a potion of deer's tail with dog and horse genitalia, which is supposed to arrest cerebral senility – as well as those more common aids to long life, deer antlers, ginger and asparagus.[27] Since the prime purpose of an 'immortal' is to outlive his rivals and thus assure his own followers of power, such nostrums assume political significance.

An immortal may do only an hour's work in a day, but if he can remain vocal when his opponents die, he may be able to achieve a clean sweep of policy and personnel. If the late Chen Yun could have outlived Deng Xiaoping, China would have expected a definite move to the right. But Chen suffered from leukaemia, and therefore depended on blood transfusions and on a magnetic-field therapy machine invented by a Shanghai doctor. His relatively conservative views were shared by Deng Liqun, another immortal, and by Li Peng, the Prime Minister. Liberals in China prayed that Chen would go first. 'Is God listening?' one asked desperately. He did!

It may sound unreal that a geriatric ward should figure as a fount of power, but each old man has dedicated younger followers below. 'They may not have a position,' the dissident professor Fang Lizhi complained, 'but their secretaries and their aides now are in positions of power, and these old guys just get on the phone and say "do this".' Deng Xiaoping's authority largely derived from the fact that he was the Secretary General of the Party for a decade, during which time he approved thousands of appointments and promotions, the beneficiaries of which are eternally grateful – not to the system, but to the man.

Equality is an important feature of Western democracies, but little observed in China. In the socialist market economy which Deng Xiaoping has done so much to create, genuine competition is needed between enterprises, and competition is unreal without social equality – which China never had, and which even the Communists were not able to impose. Chinese democracy, when it comes, is likely to be burdened with a hierarchical character.

The transparency and open spirit of Western-style democratic elections would not find it easy to co-exist with Chinese 'face'. Take one small example from local council elections in 1990. Mrs Yao Chunlan, a member of her street committee, stood for her council. Asked by a reporter whether she was canvassing the electors, she replied: 'We avoid voters during election time: it is embarrassing for voters to talk about the elections in our presence.'[28] To give even slightly critical opinions of candidates is felt to be at the least bad-mannered, and at the worst insulting. For one voter to talk in privacy with one candidate is fine. But add to the picture a third person, or several people, and both the candidate and the voter become embarrassed, and the latter will not talk about which candidate he plans to vote for. So this candidate is sparing the voters' feelings by not meeting them face to face, and the voter is protected against the practical discrimination he may have to endure afterwards if he allows a winning candidate to know that he voted for someone else (the secrecy of the ballot is not always strictly observed and votes become known through word-of-mouth from the voter's family and cronies). All candidates, of course, have to be treated with kid gloves, because one of them (you may not know which) will be elected to fill the position of authority – and you may at a later date need the protection of that authority.

Similarly, officials cannot stomach fault-finding from below. Vice-Premier Tian Jiyun complained in 1995:

> Some comrades still find even mild criticism unacceptable. They do not know that they have to force themselves to listen to criticism, harsh though it might be.... We Chinese tend to find the multi-candidate electoral system unacceptable. If five candidates are nominated for four vice-governorships, one candidate will have to lose the election. The defeated candidate will then feel too ashamed to show his face. I think this tradition must be changed.... If only five persons are allowed to run ... and you are one of them, you should feel glorious. Even if you fail in the election, you can still take pride in it. In your personal file, you can write in big characters, 'I ran for vice-governor once.' In my view, this is a glorious page in your history.

He added, significantly, that 'candidates should speak about their

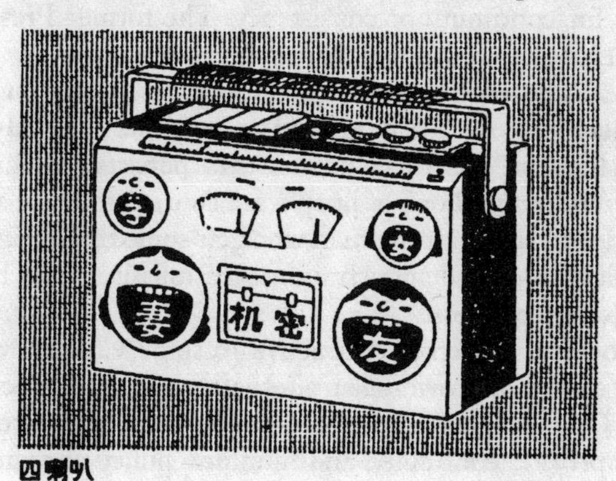

Secrets can't be kept, the* People's Daily *cartoon (5 January 1992) is saying. The 'secrets' radio has four 'speakers' – wives, friends, sons and daughters – who all too often become channels of disclosure of senior officials' confidential information.

ideas and policy so people can judge.' (At present it is status and connections which voters look for.)

This east Asian authoritarianism is not as generally harmful as Westerners imagine. The other east Asian states have mostly seen more benevolent, constructive and public-minded single-party rulers than awful or catastrophic ones in modern times. Even with superficial democracy, the east Asians still appear to prefer solidarity and consensus to the apparent antagonism that characterises Western democratic politics. The Japanese Liberal Democratic Party has always preferred to do business in the legislature not by mathematical majorities but by near-unanimous consensus obtained by acceding to some opposition demands in a compromise. In Singapore the energies of the ruling party concentrate on damning the reputation of any opposition politician who dares to be elected to the legislature, and relegating him as soon as possible from active political life.

East Asia's rulers gain their authority not from policies but from sheer personality and the exercise of power itself. Ideas for policies can be picked up from many sources, and need not detain the political boss overmuch. A review of the past policies of the Japanese and Singaporean ruling parties does not bear long scrutiny for continuity or consistency. The former President of China, Liu Shaoqi, rather charmingly described how running China was 'like piloting an aircraft. You go left, then you go right – and there you are! You've arrived at socialism.'[29] If only he had had a navigator! Personalistic rule still persists in China, and several hundred millions of people are content to leave affairs in the hands of a single strong man who gets some things right, even if a modest student demonstration occasionally panics him into unnecessary repression.

Democracy, perhaps, is attractive to some Chinese voters in the limited role of providing an alternative system for deciding on leaders. Once a leader takes office, people want him to settle into the job, provide continuity, and minimise policy arguments and policy upsets. If the leader turns out to be a bad lot, however, there is no way in the existing Chinese system to get rid of him, indeed he will probably end up in the geriatric ward still laying down the law with the other immortals.[30] The spectacle of a Winston Churchill being seen out by the British electorate after the war was noted by Chinese with a certain frisson – but also with a certain envy. There is no machinery in China for unwanted leaders to reconcile themselves to a spell in legal opposition. They are attuned in the Chinese tradition to playing every card they can, legal or not, to retain or recover power. This is what Mao did in the 1960s, unleashing a violent nationwide movement which resulted – at the cost of millions of innocent lives – in most of the other leaders being put out of the reckoning in the Cultural Revolution. It is what Deng Xiaoping did more softly in the 1990s, with better results.

That Cultural Revolution was a nightmare. How could such a big population stand aside and allow the misdeeds of the Cultural Revolution to take place? One intellectual wrote, 'If there had not been a certain national culture and psychological foundation, or if our nation had not had some common weak points, the Cultural Revolution would not have become a fact.' Liu Binyan's comment was that the Communists had been able to carry out their Cultural Revolution 'only because the people of China had allowed it, and even welcomed it'. When Stephen Spender encountered a professor who had swept floors and confessed the sins he was accused of in the Cultural Revolution, he asked if he had hated confessing. 'Oh no,' came the reply. 'There is always a lot to confess.'[31]

So the Chinese are divided about what they see of Western democracy. Some say that China should not be denied democracy, should not be cheated of its modern political development, should not appear as unworthy of what Western countries take for granted. 'We cannot accept the absurd view,' leading political liberals said in a joint manifesto on the eve of the Tiananmen killings in 1989, 'that democracy must be delayed because the quality of the Chinese nation is too low.'

Yet many Westerners who have lived in China believe that Western-style democracy is unworkable there, and many Chinese would agree. A book circulating in the summer of 1994 in Beijing put a strong argument against democracy. The time was not ripe: 'eight hundred million peasants are like a living volcano, which could erupt at any time'.[32] The repressive screw would have to be tightened further, at the cost of restricting freedom, in order to guard against turmoil.

It is an irony that more autocracy should be argued as an assurance of more individual freedom, but it is so. A few eager intellectuals aside, most Chinese have shown little real interest in democracy and have not seriously campaigned for it. As Conor Cruise O'Brien said in a letter to *The Times*, if democracy were introduced in China, Deng Xiaoping would probably sweep the board.[33] This is what deference to authority, and strong dislike of authority changes, mean. Deng himself explained to George Bush just before Tiananmen: 'There are so many Chinese people, and each has his own viewpoint. If there's a demonstration by this one today, and that one tomorrow, there would be a demonstration every day, 365 days a year. In that case economic construction would be entirely out of the question.'[34]

Young intellectuals expect too much of democracy. One of the student leaders at Tiananmen who is most admired by Chinese intellectuals is Wang Dan. Still in his twenties, he has a mature and balanced way of writing which contrasts with his personal experience of suffering in prison. When he wrote, therefore, about political reform for the *Mingbao Daily News* of Hongkong, his views attracted much attention. But what does he say in that keynote article? He says that 'The democratisation of policy-making and open, direct elections will guarantee that the choice of reform strategy is more wise and comprehensive.' The separation of powers, he goes on, freedom of speech and plural party politics 'can all resolve the problem of corruption at the root.'[35]

These statements are to be doubted, though they may perhaps be excused by the strength of Wang's frustration with Dengist politics and his enthusiasm for new institutions. But what do Wang and his co-writer Yang Ping cite as their best specific example of where democracy would score? It is over the question of wages being allowed to rise faster than the rate of economic growth, worsening inflation. Our two Chinese champions of democracy blame the Communist government for raising wages in order to win over public sympathy, thus sacrificing long-term economic development to short-term political goals, and treating the symptoms instead of the disease.

But where is there a democratic government anywhere in the world which, facing re-election in a few years' time, can resist the temptation to serve short-term objectives, and to give in to workers' demands at whatever cost to the economy? Thatcher is a rare phenomenon in Western politics. Democracy is actually the political system least able to steer a steady course of long-term economic policy. Many people would argue precisely the opposite to Wang Dan, namely that neo-authoritarian or autocratic governments are more likely to be able to cope with the wage-inflation problem. If the Communist government in the 1980s pampered workers because of their long-standing connection with the Party, would not any successor democratic government feel a similar urge – and have fewer institutional means to repress it? China has no use for such misty-eyed idealists for at least another quarter-century!

The late Hu Qiaomu, a lifelong conservative, could be counted upon to tag democracy as one of those bad things which China could do without. He once criticised bourgeois liberalisation, then a target of Communist attack, as taking on board 'the bourgeois parliamentary system, two-party system, election system; bourgeois freedom of speech, assembly, association, bourgeois individualism, and a certain degree of anarchism, bourgeois thinking and behaviour models that put profit above all means . . . bourgeois profiteering, speculation, corruption and theft, graft and extortion, abuse of public wealth for personal gain or use, and the idolisation of and cuddling up to the capitalist world'.

Even liberal thinkers have their doubts about shifting from culturally comfortable dictatorship to a more personally demanding democracy. Wei Jingsheng, China's senior dissident (his imprisonment, for the crime of writing the wrong wall-posters, goes back to the late 1970s) concedes that 'democracy would not be realised even if the Communist Party were overthrown today . . . the situation in China could then become even more dangerous and autocratic.'[36] Others say that village elections would easily become an arena for resurgent clan feuds, and would create more corruption through the bribing of voters – a complaint heard in Thailand, Japan, India and many other Asian countries.

Yet the spread of education and the growth in economic activity must gradually work against the ancient values. The future must belong to the modern, not to the traditional Chinese.

It is encouraging that officially registered social groups – harbingers of pluralism – are now increasing in the cities, especially in Shanghai where they trebled in only three years. Political factions, which used to build around personalities, increasingly focus on common policies.[37] Once people begin to organise themselves in groups to pursue a shared interest, the ground becomes fertile for new political parties and a modern attitude to political procedures. The Peace Charter group recently formed by pro-democracy activists is an indication of what may happen on a larger scale. Its intention is to press for a multi-party system.[38]

But a *social* liberation of the individual from feudal-family mindsets that restrict both his freedoms and his exercise of responsibility is a necessary precondition for the arrival of *political* liberation from single-party élite rule. Architecture is durable when the foundations are well and truly laid before the superstructure is erected.

The Western impact on this development will not be decisive, and may not even be very substantial. There is a psychological influence of the West on intellectuals, for example in the acclaimed film *River Elegy* of 1988. This sent out the powerful, if somewhat exaggerated message to Chinese intellectuals that 'only the wind that blows in from the deep-blue-coloured sea can . . . be transformed into rain to once again bring moisture and nourishment to this parched and dry yellow earth.'[39] The blue sea is, of course, the industrial civilisation of the West.

There is thus an incipient serious Western influence at the élite level of Chinese society, and for a few months in the mid-1980s it seemed to be operating on the heads of government and Party – Zhao Ziyang and Hu Yaobang. But it remains a minnow in the stream of Chinese life. For most Chinese intellectuals, the opening to Western culture offers an alternative mind set with which they can relate to Westerners and Western life, but which must run parallel with the deeply embedded Chinese values that govern their actions within Chinese society. Like dragonflies, they watch in two directions at once. A Chinese does not behave to his compatriots in China in a Western way. Neither the modern nor the traditional mode, co-existing in the Chinese personality, is conceding defeat.

But the farm workers and urban proletariat are also contributing to the onward march of democracy. The excesses of Mao made them sceptical and cynical. Such attitudes can be socially harmful, but they could also prove a blessing in disguise if they weaken the grip of conformity. Against that background, the reforms may hasten the dismantling of the dependency on authority that has held social change back for so long. There are thus seeds of democracy across all social classes.[40]

The official Communist Party reaction to all this is mostly negative. Its spokesmen usually say that, yes, we must practise democracy, but democracy means meeting the deepest needs of the people (i.e. food, clothing and public order) rather than yielding to its wildly extravagant whims. Wang Dan, the dissident, blames the Party for not being honest about the political timetable. He accepts that democracy does not necessarily bring immediate progress or prosperity. 'If,' he goes on, 'the Communist Party, as a ruling party, had set out frankly the reasons for its opposition to fairly large-scale political reforms ... then the free media both at home and abroad might not have unanimously condemned it.' Similarly forty-five scientists and intellectuals wrote an open letter to President Jiang Zemin and Qiao Shi in May 1995, asking them to tolerate all political and religious thought, and 'never again regard individuals of independent thought and independent views as "hostile" elements and submit them to repressive attacks, surveillance, house arrest and even detention.' But Jiang runs – and depends on – a Party with little stomach for sharing power.[41] The Communist Party is a giant organisation trying to control one-fifth of mankind, and its actions and policies now need to be examined at more length.

CHAPTER 4

THE PARTY: STAYING IN POWER

In the very early years of his reform administration, Deng Xiaoping sounded optimistic about political reforms. He urged a 'systematisation and legalisation of democracy so that it would not change with a change in leadership, so that it will not change with a change in the opinions and tensions of the leadership.'[1] Democratic institutions, he said, should be non-partisan. Dongzhen in eastern Beijing was the first district to pursue such liberal new ideas: in November 1979 it voted between three candidates to fill only two seats, the first time that such a choice had been offered in the People's Republic.[2]

In this liberal mood of the early reforms, the Communist Party created a little space for its political opponents in the 1980s. At the 13th Party Congress in 1986 Party Secretary Zhao Ziyang took as his themes the division of authority and the dispersal of power. The conservatives in the Party were not then ready for such an advance, however, and little came of it. But when elections were held for the Party's Central Committee that year, for the first time in over thirty years there were more candidates than seats, though only by the small margin of 5 per cent. This introduced a degree of 'negative democracy', as Stuart Schram, the Harvard sinologist, has called it, whereby the voters could at least get rid of those candidates they did not want to see in power at any cost.

When the Guangdong province People's Congress had to elect a president of the province's high court during this period, neither of the two Party candidates, lacking legal qualifications, could win a majority of the votes. New nominees were therefore listed for a second round of balloting – which was also a kind of negative democracy. In Beijing a son of the senior 'immortal' Chen Yun was voted out of the municipal Party standing committee, while the Henan Provincial Congress in 1988 elected a vice-governor standing against the official Party candidate, which was unheard of. In various parts of China in the 1980s it became clear that when, for example, farmers were given the chance, they would happily vote unpopular village heads out of office. Secret balloting was introduced at the National People's Congress in Beijing in 1988, and the number of votes cast against candidates became a public measure of their popularity or unpopularity with voters. A few tentative steps were thus taken in the direction of democracy.

There was also more democracy in the conduct of meetings. It had been the Communist custom for nobody to stir when the chairman asked, after some piece of business, for those objecting to 'please raise their hand'. But at the Guangdong Provincial Congress in 1988 an argumentative woman deputy from Hongkong, Ms Priscilla Lau Pui-king, a lecturer in business studies at the Hongkong Polytechnic University, did raise her hand, to the astonishment of all present. She said it would be wrong to pass the draft in question as satisfactory, since there had been so much dissatisfaction voiced during the group discussions. The chairman adjourned the meeting for ten minutes to allow the presidium to resolve the matter, and Lau found herself supported by the Party Secretary himself. In the end she was voted down, however, by a majority including the provincial governor. A senior provincial politician commented approvingly: 'Although the fostering of a democratic atmosphere cannot be achieved in one stroke, there has to be a beginning somewhere along the road.' Ms Lau's intervention was regarded as a daring move to expunge the rubber stamp image. A local Communist newspaper grumbled that the congress had in the past been reduced in some ways to a 'powerless sham by the relentless pursuit for "unanimous"'.[3]

In a multi-candidate election in Xiamen, the sitting mayor won fewer than half the votes of the 300 delegates and only nine more than his rival, a notable put-down after he had steered the city out of its isolation to become a booming economic centre. 'Some people were shocked,' it was said. 'They are not familiar with this kind of election.' Since he did not gain the required minimum of 50 per cent of the vote, there had to be a second ballot on which he just scraped through.[4] The wife of the dissident Fang Lizhi was elected in the Haidian district of Beijing as a candidate for higher-level bodies but was screened out by the indirect election system at that level.[5]

Another doughty woman from Hongkong had caused consternation at the National People's Congress, the nearest thing that China has to a parliament, in 1988. Dorothy Liu Yiu-chu, a renowned lawyer and scourge of British colonialism, abstained on the votes to elect the committees. 'Abstention,' she explained afterwards, 'was my only way to express my opinion . . . I didn't know how the lists of candidates were drawn up, nor did I know the criteria for their nomination. Besides, all deputies should have the right to nominate, but we didn't have a chance to do that.'[6] The *Dagongbao*, the Hongkong Communist newspaper, acknowledged that 'credit is certainly due to Hongkong deputies for winning the right to abstain, and to Taiwan deputies[7] for ensuring the confidentiality of the secret ballot.'[8] (When electronic voting was later introduced, delegates were unhappy because others could look over a delegate's shoulder to see which button he would press – and they preferred the former system of secret ballot.) The mainland slowcoach was thus being vigorously prodded along the road to 'creeping parliamentarianism', in Brantly Womack's phrase, by the representatives of the Greater Chinese communities outside. Yan Jiaqi, then Director of the Institute of Political Science, though later an exiled dissident, proposed that the National People's Congress should be based on open direct elections, with people free to choose the candidates, but he was well before his time.[9]

A Taiwan delegate, Huang Shunxing, a defector from Taiwan in the 1970s, also made Congress headlines. He angrily shouted objections to the voting, and on the controversial ballot on the Three Gorges Dam project, Huang said that he was upset to be the only deputy ever to stand up and be counted for opposing the dam – although it was well known that a fairly large number of people also opposed, but were not prepared to say so in public. In the end two-thirds of the deputies voted for the dam, 177 against, and a remarkable 664 abstained, revealing the widespread doubts about the project.[10]

One deputy of the National People's Congress defended the system in the following words:

> Deputies fully discuss and consult with one another on resolutions and decisions before they are submitted for voting. . . . When two draft laws were submitted to the Congress' standing committee earlier, most members felt they were not practical. The standing committee decided therefore not to put them to the vote, but to put them to the next meeting after revision. Even then, in the next standing committee, members felt further inputs were needed. Again, they were not put to the vote. This process was repeated several times. Finally the committee reached consensus, and the two laws were ratified by the standing committee with majority votes.

That does not make the congress democratic, perhaps, and we have seen examples of objections to the voting procedure from Hongkong and Taiwan delegates, but it explains why many delegates accept the degree of participation that is offered them, and do not actively lobby for changes in the procedure.

In one case where a provincial people's congress voted out the sitting governor and other Party-approved candidates, officials were so horrified that before announcing the results they telephoned Beijing to ask what to do. President Jiang Zemin ruled, to his credit, that the result must stand. 'We must respect the people's opinions and their votes.'[11] One delegate said he had heard that during a National People's Congress, 'when the new Vice-President found that 200 votes had been cast against him, he promptly and thoroughly wet his pants.' Such is the evacuative power of partial democracy.

The most substantial change came lower down, in the counties, where representatives have been directly elected since the late 1970s, weakening Party control over county congresses. Under the Village Organic Law of 1987 varying degrees of democracy have hit the rural areas. Sometimes the ballot is secret, sometimes candidates are elected by open acclamation. There are informal ways of deciding nominations. The long-standing mayor Yan Qinxue was beaten by a new face, and he blamed 'putting everything up on a blackboard like that for all to see'. The new faces may be young businessmen, professionals, religious leaders or even persons not members of the Communist Party.[12] But all delegates for provincial congresses are still designated, to ensure Communist Party control. Students and trade unions, which might be expected to give a lead, usually ignore the election niceties of their own organisations.

One problem plagues such reforms. If village government is handed over to local voters, the state loses the ability to balance local leadership by making special provision for women, for example, or for minority competing clans. Village democracy hands power over to the mathematical majority, the 51 per cent, and in some instances could signal the green light to the tyranny of the majority clan. The tyranny of wealth can also take the field. One businessman reportedly gave US$115 to each voter to ensure his election as head of a city assembly. But the new village councils are apparently strong on transparency and accountability. Mr Wang Zhenyao of the Ministry of Civil Affairs aims to spread the election system from the villages up to the county level. 'After that,' he enthuses, 'the process becomes irreversible.'[13]

Deng Xiaoping stated a far more cautious view in the later 1980s in these words: 'Great democracy is avoidable. We should have small democracy... we should let the masses express their views constantly. Whether the Communist Party is qualified to exercise leadership or not is decided by our party itself.'[14] But younger leaders were less discouraging. A Politburo member, the carpenter and former mayor of Tianjin, Li Ruihuan, assured the National People's Congress in 1994 that 'democracy will certainly develop along with the development of society.' A Politburo middle-roader, Qiao Shi, told the Congress that in order to promote the national economy, China would have to 'promote socialist democracy with Chinese characteristics'. That did not mean mindlessly imitating foreign models, he added, drawing a distinction between socialist 'democracy' on the one hand and capitalist 'anarchy' on the other. With three members of the Politburo Standing Committee – Tian Jiyun, Qiao Shi and Li

Ruihuan – all favouring more liberal elections, there is hope for the future.[15]

Zhao Ziyang, then Prime Minister, was responsible for many of the electoral advances. Not satisfied with introducing multi-candidate elections for certain posts, he also proposed civil service appointments by examination, another innovation under Communist rule.[16] When spelling out the case for examination, Zhao put weight on the fact that it was the custom of Britain, France and other modern Western countries – not mentioning, or not realising, perhaps, that the impetus for this reform in eighteenth-century England had been precisely the *Chinese* imperial example, one of the instances where Europe had borrowed from China. Zhao also started to abolish Party organisation in government ministries and departments. By 1989 he had achieved his aim in about a quarter of all government departments, but his colleagues did not like it and they

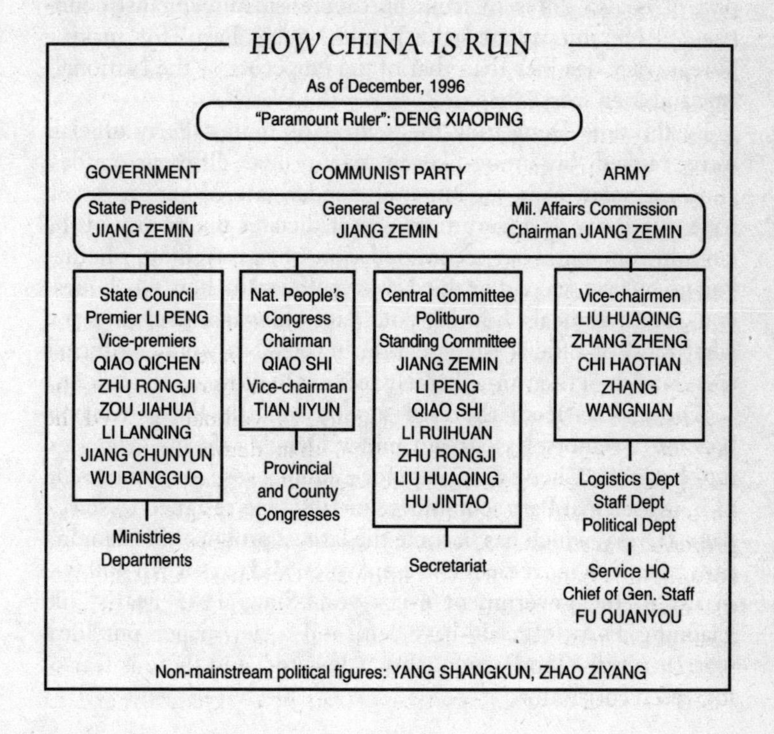

reintroduced the Party network after his fall from power. Most leaders did not wish to make a clean separation of government from Party in the Anglo-Saxon style.

It is one of the failings of the Communists that they have never been able to control the bureaucracy. The old Communist leaders, including Mao and Deng, hated bureaucrats, and ran campaigns to reduce them. But they also needed them to rule the country and pass down government wishes. Both the Communist Party and the government soon became thick with bureaucrats, and today that is one of the major complaints of the people. Deng put the problem at the head of his list of obstacles when he told the Politburo in 1980: 'with respect to the system of the country's leadership and the cadre system, the chief weakness is our bureaucratism, excessive concentration of power, patriarchy and life-tenure ... the bureaucratism we suffer from is not only different from the type of bureaucratism China has had in the past, it is also different from bureaucratism in capitalist countries.'[17] He thus pinned the blame on his Party for making bureaucracy deadlier than that of the emperors or the Nationalists, and even worse than in Russia or the West.

By the time Deng took the helm, Communist Party officials were ranked byzantine-like in twenty-five different grades, almost as many as in the imperial mandarinate. What grade you have as a Party or government officer dictates the quality of the cloth in your suit, your accommodation when travelling, whether you go by first, second or third class on the train, how much meat you can eat at meals, how big your flat is, how many servants and what kind of official car you ride in, etc. No wonder officials spend much of their time fiercely seeking to move up the ladder.

The exodus from the civil service and the Party has now become a remorseless stream under Deng's reforms. Many go into business. Cheng Xiaoping, for example, rose to membership of his municipal Party committee in 1985. He resigned to start a paint factory, which has become the largest producer in Liaoning province, with more than 200 employees, and pays RMB 400,000 in tax to the government every year. Since 1985 nearly 700 Liaoning Party officials have left, and a newspaper put local worries pithily: 'So Party quality is lowered, and there is fear of increased corruption.'[18]

Bureaucratism is something we can actually measure. The medieval Han emperors maintained only one official for every 8,000 people. The Tang doubled that, and the Qing emperors doubled it again. When Mao Zedong stormed into power in 1949 the ratio was one official to every 290 persons. Today, for all the Communists' efforts, it stands at about 1 to 34, an extraordinarily heavy concentration of talent in the work of bureaucracy.[19] Beijing alone hosts two million of them – a quarter of the city's total population.

The Party leaders have tried to thin out this carpet of implementers. A significant advance was the creation in 1988 of a new Ministry of Personnel, accompanied by a vigorous study of foreign administrative systems with the help of the United Nations Development Programme. Communist Party officials were actually briefed by Margaret Thatcher's Conservative Party headquarters in London and Ronald Reagan's Republican Party headquarters in Washington on how to run a successful political party.[20] At that point in the mid-1980s the Chinese were taking their institutional modernisation very much to heart, but it lost momentum after Zhao Ziyang was sacked in 1989.

There are a few non-Communist parties active in China, usually referred to as the 'democratic parties'. Technically they

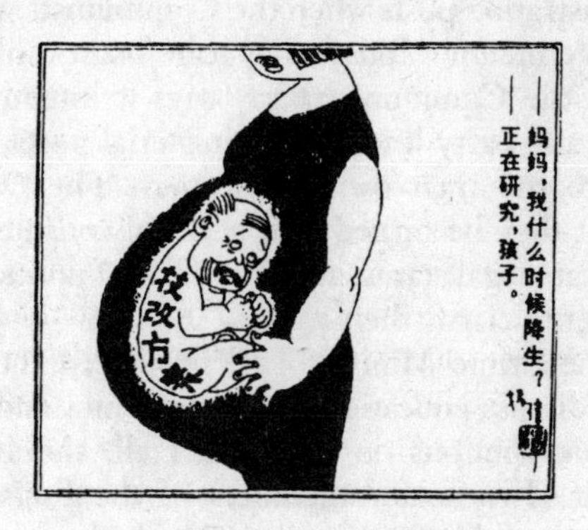

The delayed baby labelled 'technological transformation plan' plaintively asks when it is going to be born. The mother's answer, typical of the bureaucrat, is 'We're looking into it, child' (Economic Daily, ***Beijing, 2 September 1992).***

are in coalition with the Communist Party, and when it suits the Communists' purpose they may be invited to meetings or discussions. Although they have no power, some people hope – against the odds – that they may in the end provide the pluralism which the Chinese system needs, and that the Communists will allow them an increasing role.

During most of the Maoist period these parties were utterly sidelined. Deng brought them back to the fringe functions which they now perform. They include the Democratic Alliance (whose chairman, the elderly sociologist Fei Xiaotong, appears on a number of official platforms and foreign missions), the Association for Democratic Progress, the Association for Democracy and National Strength (which attracts businessmen and entrepreneurs), the Public Welfare Party (patronised by Overseas Chinese and their relatives), the Taiwan Democratic Alliance (comprising people who have lived in Taiwan, and their relatives, especially from Fujian and Guangdong) and the Revolutionary Committee of the Guomindang (a remnant group which has lost all links with the ruling party in Taiwan).

These parties have small memberships and minuscule funds. Their leaders are basically hangers-on, dummies in the political window-dressing. Their representatives once filled a third of senior administration posts when the Communists were new and green in government. Today they can boast only one vice-minister, but the Communist Party says it intends to appoint more democratic party leaders to ministerial posts, and even to allow them to run their own newspapers. The *Dagongbao* has proposed that they be turned into political consultation groups with appropriate legal status, and that a law of political parties be passed in order to clarify their role.[21]

In 1993 the Prime Minister Li Peng called the democratic parties in to discuss education policy with him and his experts, soliciting their opinions on what, after all, should be a non-partisan affair. Two senior members of the Fujian provincial government raised the question in 1994 whether a nationalist or republican party could legally be established as a step not only towards political reform but also towards peaceful reunification with Taiwan. If the ban on new parties were lifted, it is said that one-third of that province's Communist Party might move over.

But the Fujianese who raised these futuristic questions were investigated and demoted, after which they left the Communist Party.[22]

The real impetus for political reform can come only from within the Communist Party, and although Zhao Ziyang is in disgrace, and many of his friends, as well as many of Hu Yaobang's advisors, are now out of office, there are still men of importance in the party – though in the second or third rank – who regard the eradication of Stalinism as an important item on the future Party agenda. One of Zhao's acolytes, Chen Yizi, who used to be the Director of the Research Institute in the State Economic Structural Reform Commission but is now in exile in the US, foresaw the creation of a 'grand coalition of democratic reform elements within the Chinese Communist Party', as well as in every sector of society and among the Chinese in Taiwan and Hongkong and elsewhere, which between them would transform the Chinese mainland polity. 'The likelihood of this happening in the next five to eight years is very high'.[23]

Another dissident, Liu Binyan, carries the scenario further. One part of the Communist Party, he forecasts, 'will separate to make itself into an independent opposition party that may win a majority of the vote some day'. He feels that such a potential opposition party has already 'vaguely emerged'.[24] This is precisely what has already happened in two other countries with strong single-party rule struggling to match democracy with Asian culture, Japan and India.

The older generation has latched on to the concept of neo-authoritarianism as a rationale for single-party rule. This serves the double purpose of reassuring rulers about their continuing in office, and also reassuring intellectuals of all stripes that anarchy is not going to snatch away the fruits of the economic and social achievements which China has already made.[25] Two thinkers, Wang Xiaoqiang and Li Jun, identify four policy choices for China. The first is 'tough' or interventionist government and 'tough' economics, which was the Stalinist model, now rejected in China. The second is 'soft' or permissive government with 'tough' economics, which India has pursued with some difficulty. The third model is 'tough' government with 'soft' economics, as practised by South Korea, Taiwan and Singapore. The fourth model is 'soft' government and 'soft' economics, for which one would look to the Western democracies. The third model, say Wang and Li, has been the only successful one for the developing countries in the post-war years, and it is this model to which Deng Xiaoping's policies come nearest.

Democrats argue that China has been authoritarian for centuries, and needs a radical change in order to modernise effectively. Only democracy, they insist, can begin to curb official corruption. But the platform of neo-authoritarianism, which so interested Zhao Ziyang and his followers in the mid-1980s, is likely to be used by the Communists when they need to win the middle ground, because it appeals to intellectuals who are neither Communist nor totally democratic.

It is thus hard for Chinese politicians to sink their differences and collaborate. The Communist Party is remarkable in being able to contain extremes of attitude, but that is because so many members are either ideologically uncommitted or else opportunistically following the sole party in power. One does have a difficulty in regarding the reformer Deng Xiaoping on the one hand and the conserver Deng Liqun on the other as belonging to the same party. Disunity is even more marked among the opponents of the Communist Party. During the Tiananmen clash the more mature 'students' like Hou Dejian and Liu Xiaobo were appalled by the failure of student leaders to follow democratic practices. When these two tried to persuade the students to elect their leaders conscientiously, they were given the brush-off by the self-same leaders in the words: 'What if we are not elected?'[26] Leaders like Chai Ling and Li Lu became locked in power struggles to be head of their respective student groups. One faction of students tried to kidnap Chai Ling and boot her out of the square on the charge of embezzling student funds.

So tough ruling Party politicians can retain power because their opponents are divided, and the people impassive. Lu Xun, the most brilliant Chinese writer of the century, had abandoned his medical training for literature because he believed that would enable him to change China. The trigger for him was watching a documentary wartime film in Japan which showed Japanese soldiers beheading a Chinese in front of a large Chinese crowd – which gazed with apparent indifference. In most countries such a situation would lead to an outbreak of emotional nationalism, but the Chinese have a slow fuse. The individual's fate is not the concern of the others, especially others who can do little to alter events.[27]

An airline pilot once spotted a shoplifter in the act, and brought him down. But the thief flashed a knife and left his assailant lying bleeding in the street. No one in the crowd tried to stop the thief, passing cars would not halt to take the pilot to hospital because of the bad luck his death in their vehicle would bring, and in the end he died on the street, lacking a Chinese Samaritan. You could find such stories in Western newspapers, but not as frequently or as unrelievedly heartless.[28] In another well-known case a girl in Jiangxi fell into a canal. About a hundred people were watching, but none of them helped. One offered to save her for cash, and while her mother haggled over the price the girl drowned.[29] China is a passive society which will not reach out impatiently for a share of political power. Democracy and serious democratic reforms are not necessarily going to get exuberant support.

In spite of these advantages, the fifty-million-member Chinese Communist Party finds itself today in deep trouble. A confidential report by ex-President Yang at the end of 1994 revealed the paralysis of two-thirds of its bodies at the basic rural level, the village Party groups being 'in a state of feebleness and laxity' not observed for more than sixty years. 'It seems,' said Yang, 'that socialist ideology, communist ideas and the Party's objectives have become outdated and are no longer suited to the present day of reform and opening, and the people will no longer accept and maintain their belief in socialism and Communism.' The then General Secretary, Jiang Zemin, said in an internal speech that only a rescue operation for grass-roots party organisations could save the Communists 'from going under'.[30] An opinion survey also in 1994 showed that almost half of the young officers and workers in the Party do not believe in either socialism or Communism any more. Of research personnel workers in science institutions, 88 per cent no longer believe, and of students 77 per cent.[31]

If the Party had intellectual respectability, it might be different. But in seventy-five years the Chinese Party has not produced a single original Marxist thinker of truly international note. Mao's homely style of writing has attracted many people, but his pretensions to international theory were exploded long ago, and other leaders have not penned anything more than time-serving texts for the latest ideological scrape in which the Party finds itself.

Deng and his colleagues know very well the basis of their appeal to politically aware non-Communists. It is because the Communists on the whole keep the peace and punish the guilty – and until recently at least, as Deng himself claimed in 1987, 'because only socialism can eliminate this greed, corruption and injustice which are inherent in capitalism and other systems of exploitation'.[32] Deng is said to have been offended by Mao's catty remark that Deng had 'never been a Marxist'.[33] But Deng's selected works have drawn little interest in intellectual circles. Marxism is in fact in leisurely retreat. The octogenarian 'Immortal', Li Xiannian, told the Central Committee after the Tiananmen massacre that the dismissed Zhao Ziyang 'did not use Marxism as thought guidance; he feels Marxism is obsolete.' The People's University has actually dropped Marxism from its curriculum, replacing it with the more popular subjects of property management, marketing and taxation.[34]

So there are defections from Communism. A former vice-president and close aide to Mao, Wang Dongxing, applied to leave the Party in 1993, citing its violations of Party goals and theory, its loss of cohesion and leadership, and its violation of Marxism in favour of revisionist capitalism.[35] In 1993 more than 30,000 officials left the Party, many of them by simply failing to turn up, moving home without leaving a forwarding address, or failing to pay their dues – but three thousand of them asked to leave on their own initiative.[36] What do they believe instead? A play was staged in Shanghai in which God sent Jesus, Confucius and John Lennon successively to rescue China from its mind-numbing Maoist conformity. None of them succeeded, although Lennon came the closest.[37]

The most popular alternative ideology now is the worship of money. A young man in Shenzhen told officials from Beijing, 'We will never listen to what you have to say. We are here to make money. There is no such thing as ideas or making contributions to the state.'[38] A common thing which the Chinese now say to each other is, 'Make your money while Deng is around, and while you still have the chance, because who knows what will happen in the chaos after he dies?' A good part of the current economic success is the desire of so many capable people to build up enough money to enter the middle class before the economy flattens out. A conversation expressing this was reported in the *Washington Post*:

> 'I hear you are not dating Jiang any more.'
> 'Yes, my feelings towards him have changed.'
> 'Then you will return his watch to him?'
> 'No, my feelings towards the watch have not changed.'[39]

One Party member explained the new phenomenon in this way. 'Before, there were no markets, and the world was like a closed room with nothing in it. Suddenly you open the window

***Why does an engaging young lady marry an unattractive old man? 'I married him for the convenience,' she explains to her friends while withdrawing another amount from her inexhaustible private cash dispenser* (People's Daily, *20 June 1994*).**

and everything is there – women, cars, television, refrigerators, restaurants. It is no surprise that some people cannot resist using their power and influence to get these things.' A twenty-six-year-old taxi driver spent more than six years' wages on his wedding. 'These days,' he explained, 'we have a wealthier life, and we want to enjoy ourselves.' A senior journalist who had been an ardent Red Guard in the Cultural Revolution and had seen her best friend die in her arms in Tiananmen Square, has reacted by developing an obsession about money. 'That is all I am interested in now.'

The addiction to money-making and the elevation of material values to the forefront of life may be an inevitable phase in the speedy modernisation which China is undergoing. But the ethical void is something else. 'There's nothing left,' one intellectual finds. 'We feel an emptiness.' A woman student says, 'Our generation believed in many good things, but now we have stopped believing in anything.' More sadly, a widow of a senior Communist official disclosed that 'He stopped believing all that long ago, but what could he do? The only person he could admit it to was me.'[40]

Behind these doubts lies serious questioning of the very basis of Chinese life. After Hou Dejian, hero of the Tiananmen democracy movement, returned to his native Taiwan, he sourly commented, 'If civilisation is supposed to be a living thing, I don't think the Chinese have it any more.'[41] The replacement of Communist ideology by consumerism was visually illustrated at Tiananmen itself, where on one side of the square you see a giant calligraphy of Mao Zedong saying 'Serve the People', while opposite it, until very recently, were the plate-glass portals of McDonald's bearing the legend, 'Billions Served'. The contrast was provoking.

The downside of this sudden switch of values to a moral vacuum filled by materialism is an unprecedented outbreak of crime, nepotism and corruption. Robbing graves is a profession with a long history in China. Now it has become an epidemic, organised and skilled. The robbers use cars and explosives, detonators and electric chainsaws. A Hunan farm worker who failed at business got his friends together with their tools, and spent a night plundering a tomb to make RMB 5,000. He became the leader of a sixty-man grave-robbing organisation, stealing from more than seventy tombs a year.[42]

Even respectable people can become involved in this. The Communist Party branch secretary of a village robbed a Ming grave and confessed at his trial: 'After thinking it over and over, I came to the conclusion that this was the only way to get rich quick.' It was Deng Xiaoping, after all, who exhorted his people to get rich quick. There is a little jingle which sometimes goes around now:

> Want to experience a personal boom?
> Rob an ancient tomb.
> Become a millionaire overnight.
> If you want to make a fortune
> Open a coffin,
> The treasures will flow and flow.[43]

A variant of this anti-social activity is the growth of vandalism across China. One example may suffice. The Yellow river flood control system depends on communications and facilities out in open country. In one of the riverine provinces, more than 200,000 metres of copper wire have been cut down. Thieves also cut away the steel hydrological survey towers, using gas-welding tools. A junior engineering official had his right hand cut off at the wrist by two thugs when he tried to stop them vandalising.[44] What can one expect in a society where, researches suggest, the average monthly income of beggars in cities like Beijing and Shanghai can exceed that of university professors or army colonels?

The demoralisation of the Communist Party is compounded by something that has vastly increased over the past decade, namely nepotism. According to estimates in the Chinese press, more than 3,000 relatives of high officials are holding top positions in the Chinese government, and 900 of them are managing directors of foreign trade companies. Another estimate is that 4,000 of the children of high officials have prominent posts in the military and in state industry. Zhao Ziyang refused to prevent his sons from taking up commercial posts. 'The offspring of senior cadres,' he insisted, 'are also human beings. We cannot deny them the right to do business.'[45] But the slow march of the law in China, never catching up with the fast-changing need, put great temptation in the way of the princelings, as they are sometimes called.[46]

The Immortals in particular cling firmly to their offspring because they cannot trust others. 'With our children,' said Chen Yun, 'our hearts are at ease. At least they will not totally deny their own fathers.'[47] As a result of these attitudes, death squads of students have been reported, with the self-appointed mission of assassinating insufficiently liberal leaders or their children. Some of the children whose fathers were involved at the highest level in the decision to attack the students in Tiananmen Square in 1989 went into hiding to avoid trouble, paying the price of family notoriety.[48]

There are four categories of Red 'prince'. The good ones

'Kill the chicken to frighten the monkey' is the old saying about punishing offending junior officials in order to frighten senior ones from straying. Nowadays, the Popular Tribune *cartoonist suggests, the monkey is no longer so impressed.*

behave as commoners, not aspiring to anything ambitious, and often plead the people's cause. Peng Zhen's lawyer son Fu Yang is an example. The second type have vision and ideals, and try to use the name and its fame in order to promote reform. Some of these set up an informal political group called New Conservatism, with the idea of creatively re-interpreting Marxism and drawing on the Confucian tradition for an ideology more suitable to China. In 1992 six sons of the famous bid for election to the Central Committee of the Communist Party, but Deng's own daughter, Deng Nan, and Chen Yun's son, Chen Yuan, both failed, indicating a healthy sense of discrimination among the Party rank and file voting. The remaining two princely categories can only be condemned. One takes personal advantage of the famous name, and uses the privilege it conveys for personal gain. The fourth category is even worse, acting in blatant defiance of the law and public opinion, and using the name to get round the law.[49]

One of the sideline activities of the Tiananmen students in 1989 was to post a list of twenty-seven relatives of leaders in important positions, covering almost every leading family. But the story should perhaps start with overseas education, something for which every élite family yearns on behalf of its sons and daughters but is in short supply. The princes and princesses were among the first to benefit from the wave of studying abroad which began in the early 1980s. Deng Xiaoping's younger son Zhifang was in the United States for ten years, and returned with his wife only to avoid the threats by pro-democracy Chinese students at Rochester University, New York. Zhao Ziyang's daughter attended a Texas college, and Jiang Zemin's son Mian studied engineering at Drexel University in Philadelphia. Two daughters of the former President Liu Shaoqi went to Boston and Bonn Universities respectively. Bo Yibo's children were educated at Brandeis and Massachusetts Universities. Qiao Shi's son went to Cambridge, England. So the list could go on, and it is very obvious that the princes have done rather better than 'commoners' in getting this priceless experience of overseas education.[50]

At a lower level, nepotism can arrive by intent. The personnel office at a university may post an advertisement for a position, one qualification being precisely that a candidate should be a child of a university employee – and that may actually be the most important qualification. In this way relationships between members of enterprises and organisations develop inexorably towards consanguinity, kinship ties and nepotism. It is not wrong, and it is not illegal, and it perhaps makes for a more efficient organisation, but it is unfair and it does hinder the goal of keeping private and public interests separate.

A newspaper in Guangzhou concluded after investigating this problem that, 'for enterprises and large work organisations, nepotism and consanguinity are the beginning of a long, slow suicide.'[51] More than fifty work units under the provincial administration were surveyed in 1992, and it was shown that 18 per cent of the 4,000 individuals concerned were related to members of the same organisation. In another province the even higher proportion of 37 per cent was found.[52]

A novel on family ties in China, published in 1992, had a deputy mayor making dance-floor acquaintance with a pretty young textile worker, who starts making frequent visits to his official residence and is soon promoted to the post of accountant in the foreign trade bureau with a much larger salary and, even better, membership of the Communist Party. This woman's parents and two young brothers are also given better jobs with higher wages. Gradually the good fortune stretches out to her uncle's family in the far countryside: one by one they get jobs and residence permits in the city. The popular comment was, 'Perhaps raising a daughter isn't so bad after all!'[53]

Another famous – and true – family story from Shanxi is about the county official who is promoted to be deputy secretary of the city committee. His son gets into trouble in his unit for gambling, so the father succeeds in getting him transferred to a knitting factory, where he joins the Party and gets bigger wages. Eventually the father pulls more strings to place his son, in violation of regulations, in a garment factory as director. The factory loses money year after year, and the son is obviously not up to the job. There is a second son who is called 'a garden variety hooligan', who with his friends strips a girl one night of every stitch of clothing. The father transfers him, too, into another office. The third son is a hardened thief, but he rides the wave of his father's authority to become an official in the foodstuff bureau. Needless to say the daughter and daughter-in-law also benefit, with better status jobs and higher pay.[54]

When nepotism is mingled with theft, the effect is deadly. There was a meat factory in Kaifeng, in Henan province, which experienced widespread inside theft. When it sent a shipment of frozen meat to Beijing for the Asian Games, six tons mysteriously disappeared en route. The greedy deputy secretary's wife was discovered pilfering one day by a vigilant woman worker from the packaging department, who reported her to the security. Next day the wife slapped the woman's face, shouting that her son would 'get you'. The deputy secretary himself barged into her home later to browbeat her, so she reported him to the municipal government. By then the two families were so furious that the deputy secretary's wife very nearly bit off a piece of the informer's breast.[55]

The preference for family employees extends to Chinese everywhere. Jack Chia, the Singapore industrialist, declared, 'I have made it absolutely clear to all my key people that only where my children are almost, let me repeat *almost* as good as the others, would they be given priority. I would give my children priority because I have no question about their loyalty.' But this can be carried to the reverse extreme, as in the case of the Oversea-Chinese Banking Corporation, also in Singapore, whose outstanding chairman, Tan Chin Tuan, made a point of not allowing his son to join the bank, even though the son wanted to. He felt a better impression would be given, and a better morale would prevail among the staff, if he did not have a son working underneath him. He is a rare exception to the rule.

The number of princes who have joined business organisations where their family connections help is immeasurable. Deng Xiaoping's elder son Pufang was reputed to have used the charity funds which he ably solicited, being himself disabled, to bring watches and electronic goods from Hongkong to resell at a profit, and the paramount ruler's son-in-law became vice-president of the National Non-ferrous Metals Company which was active in the south China ports and Hongkong. It was rumoured that relatives of Li Peng, the Prime Minister, were behind Huaneng International, a new company selected for overseas listing. The son of the 'Immortal' Wang Zhen was said to collaborate with a relative of Deng's in running a company in Macao. A son of the key 'Immortal' Bo Yibo was described as displaying dubious conduct while with a handicraft mission to Europe. Both of Zhao Ziyang's sons, Dajun and Erjun, were active in the import-export business, and it was said that Erjun went abroad in order to avoid an investigation.[56]

Several of the princes turned out to be bad lots. Hu Yaobang was brave enough to execute the degenerate grandson of Zhu De, who had been second only to Mao in the early years of the Party. He was accused of thirty rapes! Li Xiannian's great-nephew was also accused of rape and murder. Another villain was Hu Qiaomu's son, arrested for irregular business moonlighting. Then there was Li Guo, the bad hat son of a bad hat father, Lin Biao, who allegedly maintained a harem and had *Playboy* and *Penthouse* brought in from Hongkong for his amusement.[57]

Even Mao's grandson Xinyu had to be cautioned by the Party because he was always convening student meetings about his grandfather's legacy. He was a good student at the People's University, and popular, but it was felt he was cashing in too much on the Mao nostalgia.[58]

Shenzhen, the new Special Economic Zone adjoining Hongkong, was an obvious draw for the princes, being a place where business could be conducted with international companies with relatively little regulation. Sons of Hu Yaobang and Zhao Ziyang were said to be involved in the Shenzhen City New Technology Development Company, and a grandson of Ye Jianying was also said to be there. Again, the list is endless. All of these cases cited here have been discussed in the Chinese press, but some are denied by the government. It is not possible to be sure about all of them, but the stories in this chapter are typical and have considerable plausibility.[59]

The government has acted against the bad behaviour of the princes. Hu Yaobang in particular was relatively fearless in trying to deal with delinquent princes in spite of their heavyweight fathers sitting on the Politburo. Investigating teams sent out by the centre to the provinces to check their adherence to national economic policy complained that they were balked in some of the projects, because 'the sons or assistants of important central figures' were behind them.[60] In 1988, however, general approval was expressed for them to take high positions, and it was pointed out that princes had their good points, being mostly more open than their parents, and more favourable to reform. Deng Pufang, the crippled prince, worked actively to prevent the repression of the students at Tiananmen in 1989.

Two success stories are the Immortals' children, Bo Yibo's son Xicheng and Nie Rongzhen's daughter Nie Li. The young Bo had three years of labour reform in the Cultural Revolution. In 1986 he became Director of Tourism in Beijing, in which position he boldly removed troublemakers, put his enterprises under the guidance of economics and law and trimmed the number of employees. His brother became a very successful Mayor of Dalian. Nie Li, daughter of the 'Mr Science' in the Party leadership, was another achiever. After studying precision mechanics and optical instruments in Leningrad, she became Deputy Director of Industry with the Defence, Science and Technology Commission, and also Deputy Director of the All-China Women's Federation.[61]

But overall there is still the envy and dissatisfaction that one would expect when the boss promotes his own son above others. It may be a universal phenomenon. But in China things have gone to extremes, building on the general high regard for the family bond, so that the striking workers of Shenyang in 1994 could shout, 'Down with the newly emerging nobility!' A workers' organisation called them 'China's future privileged monopoly capitalist class.'[62]

Not all the blame should fall on the princes' shoulders for the profitable business deals in which they are involved. The Hongkong and overseas Chinese tycoons who are investing such vast amounts in China are delighted if they can find as a partner someone who is the son or nephew or son-in-law of some very important political leader like Deng Xiaoping, Li Peng or Jiang Zemin. It is a form of insurance that any political problems that arise with the business project can be satisfactorily resolved.

That Hongkong business giant, Li Kashing is a case in point. He took Deng Zhifang, Deng Xiaoping's son, as a partner with the Shougang Corporation to take over a big Hongkong property company. He also allied with the National Non-Ferrous Metals Corporation, whose vice-president is Hu Jiancheng, Deng's son-in-law, to take over Oriental Metals. Finally, not wanting perhaps to put all his eggs in one basket, he joined China Venture Tech, headed by Ms Chen Weili, daughter of Chen Yun, to take over Public International. Li was rather embarrassed by the resignation of the Shougang chairman, an old crony of Deng, who had grown decadent, it was said, in his old age, and the arrest of the chairman's son on corruption charges.[63]

The actions of the princes should also in fairness be seen in the context of a general lapse of honesty and plain-dealing in contemporary China. Here is what a young reader of *China Youth* writes about Party officials: 'It is obvious that what they smoke, eat, drink and inhabit is not obtained by legitimate means. And when you know that the means are not legitimate you start to get angry inside. But you can't stop these people, and you can't catch them in the act, demanding and accepting bribes and being corrupt.'[64]

It may be almost innocuous, like the municipal officials of Quanzhou who have the habit of inviting provincial-level officials to cut the ribbon of new projects, and who provide for the purpose a RMB 30,000 pair of gold scissors which the official is invited to keep.[65] Another young man writing on the same topic in *China Youth* told the story of the bank he works for in Guangdong. Anyone who visits is given very special treatment:

> First, go to a private bathhouse for a sauna; second, go to a local luxury hotel to 'work' for a while; and when the guest is leaving everyone must present him with two cartons of Tazhonghua cigarettes. The part about the sauna is, of course, not limited to bathing, but rather includes seeing some of those girls from outside Guangdong who come here in search of work. Although 'work' during sauna time isn't always of such a carnal nature, instances of hanky-panky are certainly not few . . .[66]

We are not here talking of colossal bribes, but are at the level almost of traditional hospitality in pre-modern times, considered a courtesy or a service rather than a bribe. But small gifts can arouse great emotions. There is a sad report about a woman farm worker in Hubei who could not afford a gift for the wedding in her village chief's family. She thought she would get away with filling two empty wine bottles with plain water. Unfortunately the aides of the village chief spotted the deception. Believing that she had completely lost face, the woman went home to kill herself by swallowing fertiliser.[67]

One estimate is that 'abnormal' earnings by political leaders made up a quarter of the national income, and that half of the assets of state enterprises had found its way into their pockets. Such figures cannot be confirmed, but illustrate public perceptions of the problem. The official estimate of entertainment money spent by companies for food and drink is RMB 100 billion a year, which is a quarter of the government's annual budget. It is a well-known routine for an official to purchase receipts from restaurants, which he can then show as a legitimate expense, although the restaurant usually charges about 5 per cent for that service. In Inner Mongolia, officials were found spending four-fifths of their entertainment allowances on themselves.

Much of the lower-level corruption has to do with the police, whose behaviour has in many places become arbitrary and vicious, so that more money is spent by citizens to buy them off. A Guangdong man went shopping with his girlfriend, and a uniformed policeman for no reason hurled abuse at him. He responded in kind, so the policeman called colleagues to assist. The man was hauled off to the public security office for a vicious beating, and when he remained defiant the policemen actually stabbed him to death.[68]

In another case in Wuhan, police looking for illegal vendors had an argument with a farmer who was running a small business. Reacting quite out of proportion, the patrolmen took him to an upstairs room in the local public sanitation office where they hit him and kicked his balls so hard that he died in the ambulance on the way to hospital. These days about 7,000 law enforcement officers are penalised for breach of discipline or illegal behaviour every year.[69]

If it is not the police, it may be one's fellow prisoners who do the damage. The son of a senior public security man drove his motorcycle over some lotus roots belonging to a vendor, triggering a quarrel which ultimately involved the vendor's father and uncle. The motorcyclist got the three men taken into custody and

HOW CARTOONS EXPOSE CORRUPTION

***A transaction which should have been finalised at an official's desk mysteriously migrates to a banquet table: public funds are thus used for officials to wine and dine while settling business at the public expense* (People's Daily, *5 April 1994*).**

***While the front doors to state coffers are well protected, the side doors are wide open to those with* guanxi, *or with the money to bribe* (People's Daily, *20 April 1994*).**

***The 'seeking personal gain' hand greedily swipes at the heart, representing an official disaster relief fund for flooded areas* (People's Daily, *5 February 1992*).**

Four government officials greedily talk about how they will spend the illegal fees and bribes they expect to get from the public (Outlook Weekly, *Beijing, 7 March 1994).*

The official guides the chicken about to lay an egg, labelled 'public funds', to his own basket, labelled 'personal savings' (Legal Daily, *Beijing, 27 November 1992).*

locked up in the local detention centre, where they were brutally beaten by their cellmates at the prodding of the guards: the vendor's father died from his injuries.[70]

The police and public security officers can also cash in on their new freedom to start enterprises. One bureau opened a fireworks business, and licences for all other sales points in the city were suspended. The bureau could then monopolise the local market without lifting a finger.[71] But the smart swindler will collude with the police and share ill-gotten gains with them. As Frank Ching, the Hongkong columnist, recently wrote, 'The tentacles of the underworld stretch into every nook and cranny. Sometimes they are indistinguishable from the long arm of the law, because, very often, the two are one.'

Yet the powerful Beijing municipality Party boss, Chen Xitong, was dismissed in 1995 for misusing US$24 million of public funds and keeping six mistresses in luxury, and at one point it looked as if the finger of suspicion was pointed at the Prime Minister, Li Peng, himself.[72]

What can the Communist Party do about corruption? From time to time an envious look is officially taken at the anti-graft experience of Hongkong and Singapore, where things are done rather better. One suggestion is to organise a system for leading officials to declare their assets. Another is for impeaching transgressors, but investigations do not seem to be fruitful. The Shenzhen Commission in charge of inspecting discipline complained that 80 per cent of the cases defied its probes.[73] Those who benefit from a corrupt or illegal practice very often regard it as their right to do so, their right by custom and their right by common sense. In that kind of atmosphere, it is easy to see how anybody getting in the way of such practices becomes vulnerable. One factory head who stopped his women employees from stealing fabric had his leg broken for his pains.

The gravity of these social diseases – crime, corruption, nepotism – is potentially alleviated by spiritual antibodies in the Chinese system which could in the long run begin to fill the vacuum, but they would also take China further away from Marxism. Communism is on the decline.The old tradition is one candidate for filling the vacated space.

For one thing, tradition is a beneficiary of the new wave of nationalism. Li Shaolian of the Henan Academy of Social Sciences urges his readers to cultivate 'pride in being Chinese, a member of one of the world's ancient civilisations with a magnificent and brilliant culture ... no matter what nationality you are, as long as you are Chinese ... you have not forgotten your roots.' All descendants of the Yellow Emperor should unite, he says, in the struggle to revive Chinese culture. This can sometimes verge on racism, as when a pro-Communist newspaper praised Hongkong voters for backing pro-China candidates who said, 'I am Chinese and I have yellow skin and black eyes.' That may be forgiven because British officials were running the election, but the paper called it 'a great trend'.[74]

A good example of the new importance of scholars of philosophy is a 1994 article by Ma Zhenduo of the Chinese Academy of Social Sciences. He calls it 'The Position of Confucianism in Future World Culture'. One passage runs as follows:

> Western culture lies in the incompatibility between science and the religious form taken by its morals and its value of life. If Westerners' morals and their value of life were based on another humanism rather than on Christianity, the above contradiction would not arise. The right solution is Confucianism, because it is a non-religious humanism that can provide a basis for morals and the value of life ... The culture that results from combining Confucianism with science will enable people to seek truth, while also advising the public to

Like the woodpecker, which lives on harmful insects and parasites, the investigatory and disciplinary officials are supposed to root out corruption. But when the traditional coin with its square hole is slammed onto its beak, the bird – and the officials – are paralysed (*Perspective*, 18 April 1994).

> do good work. It could explore the outside world and yet show concern for the value of life. Because Confucianism with science breaks free from the contradictions which plague Western culture, it is far better than it. It will thrive well in the next century and will replace modern and contemporary Western culture.[75]

Here we see the missionary strand in Confucianism magnified as a contribution to nationalism. But there is a long road to tread: the astrophysicist Fang Lizhi concedes that 'all those who have been to foreign countries must admit that discipline, order, morality, culture and civilization in those countries are superior to what they are in China ... In general terms, these countries are more civilized than we are'.[76]

So the tradition is likely to supply social backbone by absorbing some Western ways. Some experts claim to discern already how the compromise is being forged. Dr Michael Bond of the Chinese University in Hongkong pinpoints the confluence of these two mighty streams by commenting that the Hongkong Chinese, who are caught exactly midway in this tussle, 'retain their traditions of respect for authority, but discard its fatalism; they adopt modern competitiveness but reject its sexual promiscuity.'[77] In the jargon of political science, China is changing from vertical to horizontal authoritarianism, like South Korea and Taiwan before.

There has been some official recognition of Confucianism at the highest level. When Mao Zedong revisited his birthplace in Shaoshan in 1959, he surprised his colleagues by walking up a hill to an old graveyard, where he bowed at the tomb of his parents. 'We Communists,' he noted, 'are thoroughgoing materialists. We do not believe in ghosts or deities. But still we must acknowledge that we owe our birth to our parents.'[78] Lee Kuan Yew is blunter. 'The day Chinese lose their Confucianness, that day we become just another Third World society.' Or, as a Chinese Academy of Social Sciences report put it, Confucianism, having powered the economic development of Taiwan, Korea, Hongkong and Singapore, would ensure Chinese culture its place in 'the forest of world culture'.[79]

The missionary side of Confucianism has been taken up by

Chinese scholars in Taiwan and Hongkong since 1949. Mou Zongsan and three other philosophers published a declaration 'Offering Chinese Culture to the World', and founded the New Asia Institute for the purpose.[80] Gu Mu, then a senior minister in Beijing, opened China's first international conference on Confucius at Qufu: a hundred and twenty scholars came from many countries, and Gu told them that Confucius crystallised Chinese culture and belonged to the whole world.[81] One scholar declared that practical Confucian ethics has a stabilising effect on Chinese society, claiming it as a moral code based on kindness and also an active philosophy of involvement stressing individual concern for the fate of the nation and people.[82]

These Chinese intellectuals called for the utilisation of traditional Chinese culture to enrich and develop Marxism, countering earlier Maoist efforts to use Marxist theory to reject traditional Chinese culture. Actually, Confucianism – or neo-Confucianism – does not by itself generate economic dynamism, for all the efforts of modern scholars to associate it with economic development. It emphasises stability but shows contempt for trade. It was the overseas Chinese who first demonstrated the economic power of family solidarity, raising the question whether Confucianism becomes dynamic only in an open environment, and when hybridised with other cultures. The Toynbee theory of societies being toughened by challenge may also apply.

Religion in general was revived under Deng Xiaoping, especially in the coastal south.[83] An intellectual basis for renewed interest in the spiritual side of life was provided by Liu Xiaofeng, a philosopher who used Christian theology as the entry point into the elevation of morality in the process of Chinese modernisation.[84] The Chinese have never really succumbed to religion, but the new generation of students, turning away from Marxism, is showing a surprising interest in Christianity and Buddhism. More students go to church on Sundays. Students are also keen on convergence theory, arguing where and how socialism and capitalism will eventually converge. Some 12 per cent of senior students in eight big universities claimed to believe in or to have begun to have contact with a religious creed. That was three times more than the avowed hard-core believers in socialism. Those who still follow the socialist or Marxist banner nowadays constitute only 4 per cent of students and Party officials, a survey claims.[85]

But the fifty million Christians are still subject to persecution. The Protestants in Shanxi saved up to build a church, but during a service it was raided by armed police and destroyed on the spot, and one woman died from the trauma. Bishop Fan Xueyan, who refused to be disloyal to the Pope, was imprisoned for decades and died in jail. When his corpse was taken back to his diocese, it could be seen that his torso and half his face was severely scarred, and his legs broken. Another bishop also died in prison in 1992, his body thick with scars and bruises, and several other bishops have been detained. Archbishop Dominic Tang, the Catholic Archbishop of Canton who now lives in Hongkong, has described how for twenty-two years he was 'a guest' of the Chinese Communist Party in a variety of its prisons. His crime was to refuse to submit his conscience to the Party's control.[86]

During 1992 more than a thousand Protestant believers were arrested by the Public Security, more even than democracy activists! (A high proportion of arrested dissidents turn out to be Christians.) Late in 1992 more than a hundred worshippers attended a service in Henan, with three overseas Chinese Christians in the congregation, when they were interrupted by a group of forty police officers carrying guns and ammunition. All the participants were arrested, and another forty believers later. The overseas Chinese were released through the intervention of their embassy, and were deported. But the others were kept in prison.[87]

According to one Hongkong newspaper, Christianity is rapidly becoming 'the sole movement with broad social support able to wage organised resistance to the Communist Party'.[88] Its popularity is certainly spreading. A woman of twenty-one worshipping in a Beijing church explained: 'Everything is changing so fast now, at work everything is high-pressure, things are very complicated. Individuals don't know how they should act, so they are interested in anything which gives them guidance.'[89] The dissident Yan Jiaqi went into a church for the first time in his life to hear Billy Graham preach. He commented that Graham's point about 'how to help people love each other has value in society... science can't solve all the problems in the world. Religion has use too.' Religion satisfied psychological needs, and people's behaviour needed to be regulated not only by law. 'It must also be influenced by their consciences, and this can be based either on religion or ethics.'[90] Billy Graham's sermons in China are not wasted.

Buddhism perhaps has slightly less to offer in the busy life of the contemporary Chinese. The Buddhist monasteries were just as badly hit by the Cultural Revolution as the Christian churches. The Xilin monastery with eighty-eight monks was ravaged by more than seven or eight different groups, differently named, of Red Guards. They put up posters and banners, sealed the monastery, assembled the monks to listen to Mao's works, told them not to believe in Buddhism and castigated them as parasites, vampires, reactionaries and foreign agents. Now things have returned to 'normal', and there is some new interest by the young in Buddhism, but to meet their individual needs rather than their communal thirst.[91]

'There's nothing left. We feel an emptiness,' is a characteristic comment in China. A few turn to Christianity and Buddhism, others opt out to become one of the 400 daily suicides in China. An Oriental Moral Research Institute was set up, hopefully, in Beijing in 1994 to promote traditional moral standards.[92] Communist ideals have collapsed for most members of the largest Communist Party in the world, struck down by dictatorship, cruelty, turbulence and injustice. Li Tzu Ching in *Cheng Ming* says that people have adopted 'individualism, hedonism, liberalism and other non-Communist ideologies' instead. But these are small maps of the complex human mind, and China will probably have to travel a route similar to that of the West, via nonconformism, rationalism, nationalism and socialism to attain a satisfactory and efficacious modern relationship between its individuals, the world and its own society. The difference is that China must probably complete the journey to the harmonious co-existence of these various beliefs in about one-tenth the time it took Western people, and that the accretive process starts with the Chinese tradition which is so distinct from the West's. China's role will be lonely and late.

Meanwhile one can at least say, with Professor Andrew Nathan, that the Chinese people 'have no rights, but they are

The* Beijing People's Daily *cartoonist (5 June 1993) mocks those who argue over ideological correctness and adherence to Marxism-Leninism, so meaningless to the man in the street.

allowed some space'.[93] Similarly Fang Lizhi said that under Deng, people had no freedom of speech, but they did have 'the freedom of silence'. Liu Xiaofeng talks of the 'reprivatisation' of the individual in China, which is an apt description of the transitional process now beginning.[94]

The Chinese Communist Party today remains the world's largest party of any colour, run on bureaucratic Leninist lines but having to operate with its main ideology blown away by the winds of economic change. Shamelessly adapting all kinds of capitalist procedures and techniques in order to develop the sluggish economy, its leaders cannot bring themselves to say in public that the entire philosophy which their founders and great leaders like Mao had so eloquently articulated as the only way for China, has been guiltily thrown out of the window. Many excuses were made. Certain market practices of capitalism as practised elsewhere were in fact non-ideological, it was explained, and could usefully be borrowed in China without apology. The Party would first like to push the economic development onto a self-generating level so that almost no one need fear poverty, before attending to political change. It clings to majority state ownership of the big industrial corporations, but that is wearing a little thin and the proportion of state ownership in the economy is steadily declining. What is left for the Party to do?

It can try to keep 'dangerous' Western bourgeois phenomena out, and it can try harder to stem the flood of corruption. Tragically, many of the men and women of ideals whom the Party was able to drive in the direction of social change in the early years of Mao and the early years of Deng are now giving up the game and retreating to business offices where they can see results for their individual efforts. The quality of the Party has declined, and so has its reputation and its capacity to harness people's energies. It may take quite a long time for the Party to bow out, and there may well be splinter groups leaving beforehand ready to form alternative governments.[95]

With the death of Deng Xiaoping the Chinese Communist Party loses its most eager and powerful reformer, and what kind of leadership will follow in the middle to long run is uncertain. There were three men in harness at the top of the Party and government long before Deng faded away, and they were responsible for the transition. Jiang Zemin, a genial but hardly charismatic state President from Shanghai, was nominated by Deng as the leader of the new team. He tried very hard to build up a following in the army and Party, but the allegiance to him hardly goes skin-deep.

Li Peng, a quiet but determined Russian-trained engineer, has not had outstanding success as Prime Minister despite his advantage of being an adopted son of Zhou Enlai, and his efforts to manage the economy have been frequently upstaged by Vice-Premier Zhu Rongji. Above all, Li Peng is regarded as the man most responsible for the inept handling of the Tiananmen students in 1989. The army is still smarting from popular disapproval of its shooting civilians in Beijing on that occasion, and resents being under political orders. The military would like the whole incident to be re-assessed, and in that event Li Peng would inevitably become a scapegoat.

The third figure is the less well-known Qiao Shi, who runs the National People's Congress and therefore has a constituency of politically articulate Party members across the country. He is a reformer, but only a cautious one, and he has good connections in both army and Party, having abstained on the vote among the leaders at Tiananmen whether to use force against the demonstrators. *The Times* called him a 'natty dresser'. Qiao Shi could well prove the kingmaker, and if Jiang Zemin and Li Peng fail, he might even take the crown himself. Li Ruihuan and Tian Jiyan might back him.

Another figure sometimes mentioned in the leadership stakes is Zhu Rongji, a Shanghai man who is a little arrogant because he is so clever about the economy, of which he is certainly the most capable manager in the senior leadership. But the Party would probably try to avoid having another Shanghai man alongside Jiang so high up in the hierarchy, since that would lead to resentment in the populous interior.[96] One or two of those recently dismissed may also jockey for a come-back, including Zhao Ziyang, the former Prime Minister, and Yang Shangkun, who is the most powerful military figure though 'demoted' by Deng to be state President. They are both keen reformers.

In the medium term new and younger figures who have not yet made their mark may come to the limelight. The army also will be active, though since it is not united on policy its efforts will be divided between candidates. Younger leaders are more in favour of reform, and even conservatives actually have little choice: there is no stopping economic reform and economic growth. That in turn will reduce the Party's overall control and surely lead in the long run to some kind of political reform including democratic features.

Theoretically the Chinese government could lay the groundwork for the transition to a more modern form of government, but the Chinese leaders hesitate. Extending the franchise means empowering people who have no experience of or social preparedness for political participation. Impostors, intruders, charlatans, cheats and frauds would grab the opportunity to ride on democracy's back for their personal gain. Will that make it more difficult or easier for genuine political institutions to take shape afterwards? Nobody knows. The most significant benefit from a rapid shift to democracy would not be urban gains but the greater protection of farmers and farm workers from the demands of local bureaucrats.

It would be comforting to think that individual provinces could decide on their own political reforms, because this would produce many different solutions from which the Chinese public could eventually choose. Some experts in Taiwan, observing the situation in nearby Fujian and Guangdong, believe that federalism and opposition parties will begin not at the centre in Beijing, but in the provinces and regions, perhaps beginning with independents standing against the local Communist candidates. This would be in parallel with the new mood of nationalism sweeping over China.[97]

Or will the source for alternative leadership be found among the political and intellectual dissidents whom the Party cannot handle? Could they provide the substitute for Communism, the successor to Communism, which China will badly need in a few years?

CHAPTER 5

TIANANMEN: THE OBJECTORS

The whole world knows about China's bad record on human rights.[1] The government says that the first right which an inhabitant of China needs to have recognised is the right to subsistence (little enjoyed under previous régimes), and this is being addressed by economic reforms. Human rights are of little use, after all, when people are starving or living at a very low level.

Premier Li Peng told Vice-President Al Gore at the Copenhagen Human Rights summit in March 1995, 'You say human rights are the loftiest convictions of the United States. That is your business in which we have no intention of interfering. But it would be intrusive if you also want Chinese citizens to accept your loftiest convictions ... as far as China is concerned, its loftiest conviction is to develop its economy, improve the people's living standards, and maintain long-term peace and stability in the country.' Foreign ministry spokesman Shen Guofang had said earlier, 'The Chinese people would enjoy more rights in various fields along with the deepening of China's reform, the wider opening of the door to the outside world, further economic development, the popularization of education, and improvement in the people's cultural qualities...' (a tacit admission of the unsatisfactoriness of human rights in China?) To China's delight, the conference turned down the draft US-led resolution criticising China's human rights.[2]

The Chinese leaders want to achieve their economic miracle first, and then attend to political reforms, as other east Asian states did before. Westerners might reply that driving for economic improvement does not necessarily preclude the simultaneous observing of human rights. They forget or ignore the Chinese suspicion that, whether consciously or otherwise, nationalists in the West would like to slow down China's economic development by imposing a weak government unable to discipline its workforce. There is some truth in both of these opposite statements. The reaction of the Chinese man in the street to violations of human rights, as long as they do not affect him directly, is to be rather satisfied that the government is keeping law and order. There is no tradition of human rights in China in the sense of individual rights vis-à-vis the government.[3]

Those who try to measure these things have put China fifth lowest in the world league of human rights, better only than Iraq, North Korea, Burma and Sudan. There are a breathtaking fifty-five capital offences which include smuggling, bribery, theft and drug smuggling. Publicised executions reached 1079 in 1992, and in one recent year there were more Chinese executions than in the rest of the world put together. These official figures do not include those from reliable but unofficial sources, which would suggest an actual total of possibly 20,000 a year. The executions are typically carried out within public view by a shot in the head.[4]

Some Westerners argue that violation of human rights is not as serious in China as it would be in the West, because of the difference in tradition and the different popular attitude towards authority. Governor Chris Patten of Hongkong rebuts this view by saying, 'If you're beaten by a policeman, it feels the same in Asia, in Africa, in America, in Europe'.[5] He adds that the UN Declaration on Human Rights made one country's respect for the rights of the individual a legitimate international concern.

Strictly speaking, Patten is right. No one would seriously value a Chinese life differently from a Western life. Fang Lizhi put it accurately: 'Like all members of the human race, the Chinese are born with a body and a brain, with passions and a soul. Thus they can and must enjoy the same inalienable rights, dignity and liberty as other human beings.' But it is true all the same that the popular tradition and attitude to punishment *is* different from that in the West, if only because so many instances are tolerated by the general public in China. Han Dongfang, the dissident trade union leader, puts a considerable restriction on Chinese human rights when he warns: 'Nobody has the right to place his individual "human rights" above the overall interests of a country or a nation.'[6] Patriotism comes first!

What is certainly unacceptable is the widespread use of torture. Although China has signed a United Nations declaration outlawing torture, and although its security officials have been told that the eradication of torture is a key priority, detainees are still routinely tortured with electric batons, even before they are interrogated. In a recent year it was officially reported that there were 30,000 illegal detentions and more than two hundred cases of the police raping detainees, beating them to death or seriously injuring them.[7]

Liu Gang, one of the protest leaders in the 1989 Tiananmen confrontation, was abused from his first day in prison with beatings and electric baton shocks. The torture and maltreatment continued: he had been listed by the government as one of the twenty-one most-wanted participants in Tiananmen. His account of his ordeal was smuggled out of prison and given by relatives to the foreign press. A physicist, now thirty-three years old, he ended up with a prolapsed anus, psoriasis, facial swellings and prematurely whitening hair. His prison commander told him during torture sessions, 'This is the dictatorship of the proletariat. If you refuse to bow your head, we'll grind you slowly to death.' The truly appalling thing to learn is that people tend to regard Liu's case as an improvement, because at least his family was not tortured as well, as would probably have happened earlier in the Communist régime.[8]

It must also be counted an advance that the government admitted in 1990 for the first time that some prisoners had been tortured or injured and had died in custody. Qiao Shi, the senior leader then responsible for security, told Han Suyin: 'There have been cases of beatings and torture. It is not our policy, but it does happen.'[9]

The inmates of labour camps, where over a million political prisoners work out their reform-by-labour sentences, live at the whim of often sadistic guards. When they created disturbances in Liangyuan Motor Vehicle General Assembly Plant in 1991 – refusing their co-operation, going on hunger strike, etc. – prisoners suffered the standard kicks and electric batons.[10] That plant plays an important role in the economy. Unofficial estimates of the population of these camps go as high as twenty million, or one to every sixty population, but this seems strained (the comparable ratios for America and Britain are one in two hundred and one in a thousand respectively). An unexpected site where prison labour is used at extremely low cost is the Sino-French Winery near Tianjin, which exports 400,000 bottles a year of its palatable Dynasty and other wines. It also produces Chinese 'medicinal' remedies, such as Dragon and Phoenix Three-Penis Wine, for export to Hongkong.[11]

As if this were not enough to defeat so many of the worthy objectives which the Chinese government seeks to pursue in the international arena, it has only recently come out that the kidneys of executed prisoners are sold, especially to overseas Chinese who travel to China for a transplant operation with anything up to $15,000 in their wallets to pay for it. The permission of the prisoner's family is not necessary. The police notify hospitals ahead of an execution, and they will fire into that part of the prisoner's body which is not required, aiming at the skull if a retrieval of the kidney is envisaged. Nanfang Hospital in Guangzhou specialises in such transplants, performing roughly one a week, and it advertises its services in Hongkong. Its representative in Hongkong finds nothing unethical or shocking about this, and the Chairman of the Hongkong Society of Kidney Specialists, Dr Man Kan Chan, confirmed that kidneys came from executed criminals. 'What do you want to ask their consent for, when you are going to execute them? They might as well do something for other people before they die.'[12] The Chinese have little time for pointless sentimentality. Even Buddhism is invoked to back up the argument, because Buddhism teaches that you lessen your crimes if you die benefiting other people.

Judging from the freedom allowed to visitors of the labour camps, and the general level of publicity about them, China's rulers feel little guilt or embarrassment about them. Zhang Bingcheng, a specialist in autopsy, was pulled out of his re-education camp in order to join the team that was embalming Mao in 1976.

So who are these courageous men and women, the dissidents or objectors who risk all this to criticise the government and

Communist Party? To put it the other way round, why do government and Party leaders pay so much attention to dissidents working on relatively minor parts of the national canvas? One answer is that the Chinese leaders lack the legitimacy of having been freely elected by the people, and therefore feel insecure vis-à-vis the dissenters, so they persecute them. Western leaders almost automatically enjoy the cachet of having been elected by their people, so they do not have the same need to persecute opposition spokesmen.

But it goes deeper than that, because Chinese and Western leaders are operating in two completely different situations. The primary goal of Chinese leaders is to persuade opponents round to the official view. 'We don't want you to die,' they will say placatorily. 'We want you to become a model socialist.'

No wonder the exiled poet Liu Hongbin lamented, 'China has been a prison for free speech for thousands of years.'[13] China has no genuine tradition of personal non-conformism or independent media. The thousands of democracy demonstrators in many Chinese cities who took to the streets in the middle of 1989 for various good causes found their options pitiably narrowed after the government cracked down. 'I did not spend eighteen years getting educated in order to have guns pointed at me,' said one angry activist a couple of days after the confrontation. 'There are only two ways out now – go abroad, or go into business.'

Nien Cheng, writer and widow of a former Guomindang diplomat, reveals why a sister would turn in her own brother, giving him away to the authorities to be taken to prison. 'In urban areas in China,' she explains, 'living conditions are very congested. His presence must have been known to her neighbours. If she didn't turn him in, the neighbours would have. And if the neighbours had reported it instead of her, she and her husband and all her family would be arrested for shielding him.'[14]

There are naturally great shades of difference among the intellectuals, who are the most individualistic group in China today. There are conservative dissidents like He Xin, an economist who published a book under a pseudonym accusing Deng Xiaoping of leading China into a 'trap' of too rapid growth, and calling for less freedom and tougher government.[15] The American-trained scientist, Qian Xuefen, who helped to make

China's H-bomb in the 1960s, publicly praised the Communist Party for crushing the pro-democracy demonstrators in 1989. He particularly attacked Fang Lizhi for his lack of patriotism. Qian was born into a rich Shanghai business family, and is the darling of the Party because in 1950 he brought back from America almost a ton of useful scientific documents. But large numbers of intellectual dissenters have gone abroad, including Fang Lizhi, who offered from exile a counter-Deng slogan for the opposition: 'No matter whether the cat is black or white, neither is good at catching mice.'[16]

It is the student leaders at Tiananmen who were so telegenic on Western TV screens in June 1989 who are lionised by the Western media. Han Dongfang, who led the Workers' Federation Group on the Square, has been called China's Lech Walesa. He was arrested after Tiananmen, but released two years later on grounds of health. He was told not to see foreigners or discuss his experiences in prison, but he cheerfully disobeyed these instructions. His aim in life is to create an independent labour movement. He was force-fed in prison, and made delirious. Soon after returning home, Han asked permission to hold a one-man demonstration passing out leaflets about workers' rights. It was refused, but the request created the needed result of publicity: everybody knew about it. 'If the law allows me to do something I'll do it,' he says cheerfully. 'If it doesn't allow me to do it, then I'll press for a new law.'[17]

The duo of Chen Zimin and Wang Juntao has a longer pedigree of protest, having supported Wei Jingsheng at Democracy Wall in 1979.[18] When Wei later changed his ideas in favour of promoting reform within the Communist Party, they parted ways with him. They were harshly treated after Tiananmen, being given thirteen-year jail sentences. Wang attracted particular attention from the Western press because he had liver and heart trouble. The German Foreign Minister, Klaus Kinkel, secretly met Wang's wife and then asked China to transfer Wang to a better hospital, offering treatment in Germany. Wang was duly transferred to a civilian hospital, released and allowed to go to an American hospital in 1993. The release of Chen Zimin followed soon afterwards.[19]

Another difficult customer from the point of view of the

Communists is 'Harry' Hongda Wu, who has actually spent nineteen years in Chinese prisons. The guards responded to his hunger-strike by force-feeding him through a rubber tube to his stomach and wrecking his nasal membrane in the process. He escaped to America but daringly returned with a US passport, new name and an American companion who was able to take surreptitious film footage at the many prison camps which, surprisingly, they were permitted to visit.[20] Wu has since become a kind of one-man exposer of the prison-camp scandal. The authorities naturally declare that the prison camps are all legal and above board, and nothing could be objected to. But they arrested Wu again when he came back a second time.

Dissidents who find their way into business get a better deal. The Party apparently finds their progression salutary. Muo Qizhong was sentenced to death in the Cultural Revolution for writing a big-character poster which said 'Where is China Heading?' He was rehabilitated, released, detained and re-released. Then he became Chairman of the Nande Economic Group which has bought airliners from Russia and is capitalised at more than RMB 100 million.[21]

The big day of the dissidents was 4 June 1989, when demonstrators almost forced the government to back down in its policies, but were instead violently repressed by the Chinese army. All the major strands of Chinese politics were bound up in the Tiananmen affair, from which no one emerged with much credit, and to understand it properly needs a little detail.[22]

The incident around Tiananmen Square in the heart of Beijing in 1989 is often called a massacre, though the deaths were relatively few and scattered in time and place. It was a crucial event for China, but foreign impressions of it were distorted. What went out to TV viewers in the rest of the world for those few evenings was graphically true and accurate in the sense that the camera never lies, but much of the background to the event, and the actions of others in different parts of the city (and in other cities as well), did not appear on film. Foreign reporters were concentrated at one end of the square and mostly failed to get the larger view until much later. Meanwhile the world, remembering a few violent and harrowing images, presumed that it was all like that, and wondered why the government and army were being so extraordinarily brutal towards their own unarmed people. Afterwards Beijing put out its own film version which was, of course, quite different, showing (and the camera cannot lie) ordinary citizens provoking soldiers into violence against them, for example, or students protecting soldiers threatened by the crowd. These different versions must be integrated if the truth is to be unearthed.

To find the origins of the Tiananmen crisis, one must go back to 1976, to the memorable events on the same square when citizens were prevented from laying wreaths for Zhou Enlai, the long-time Prime Minister who had just then died, on the Martyrs' Memorial, as was the usual custom for the dead. Deng Xiaoping, who was then a Vice-Premier, was blamed by Mao and his clique for the disorder.

Then things changed around. Deng established his position as paramount ruler after Mao's death, and the verdict dubbing the 1976 Tiananmen incident as 'counter-revolutionary' was reversed. The students had more to say, however. Led by Wei Jingsheng, they massed again to put up big-character posters on what became known as Democracy Wall in Beijing. The protests went on through the winter of 1978–79, until Deng got so exasperated with them that he stopped them – proving, for the first time under his own rule free from the shadow of Mao, that he too was an autocrat who would not stomach demonstrations against his government.

The next big student demonstration in 1986–87 was also against Deng. Some of the freest open political debates were carried on uninhibitedly in 1986, and some liberal conclusions were echoed even by some of Deng's lieutenants. But Deng, whose power rested partly on the conservatives, clamped down again and dismissed the liberal and popular Party Secretary Hu Yaobang. It had seemed to many intellectuals that Hu Yaobang was the best thing that ever happened to Communist China, because of his modest democratic demeanour, and his new ideas about opening up the Party to more free discussion.

And then came the penultimate step in the Tiananmen story, in September 1988, when the Central Committee voted for a programme of economic retrenchment, finding that the economic reforms had run away with themselves and the fast growth which Deng had encouraged in the economy was now hurting the ordinary man through the rise in inflation. It was the grievances and resentments which arose out of this 'stop-go' economy, where people suffered first from rising prices and then from shortages, with all that meant for students and their families, that created the climate for Tiananmen itself in 1989.

There were two ways for the authorities to handle student demonstrations. Some leaders like Xiao Yang, the Governor of Sichuan, or Zhu Rongji, who was then mayor of Shanghai, dealt cleverly with hotheads from the campuses. They would send police cars, for instance, to clear the way for the students when they marched, which had the effect of preventing them from clashing with other members of the community, keeping them out of trouble. But the more common attitude was unthinking toughness, treating the students as if they were stupid (which they were not) and lawbreakers (which they sometimes were, but for good reasons).

In the middle of April 1989 Hu Yaobang died, in a kind of semi-disgrace, with the bitter taste of rejection by his colleagues still in his throat. As was the usual custom, a memorial meeting was mounted, like that for Zhou Enlai thirteen years earlier, and once again there were thousands of students milling in Tiananmen Square to lament a dead leader's liberalism, his modernity and his example. Hu's posthumous political rehabilitation became the first of a rather long list of student demands.

The students went on to call for an end to the repressive political campaigns against spiritual pollution and bourgeois liberalisation. They wanted Party and government leaders' incomes to be published. Next came free speech and no censorship of news, followed by better pay for intellectuals and freedom to march in the streets.[23]

Beneath these lofty aims lay the usual petty student grievances, which began, according to a Beijing University survey, with not enough pocket money, and proceeded to higher prices (especially for meals), isolation and 'not knowing what to do with one's life'. What particularly hurt many students was the ritual insincerity which they were asked to show in speaking about events, being expected to parrot the official line, or 'speak against your heart', as many described it.[24]

It would be a fair verdict on these demands to say that there were rather a lot of them, and that they were very heterogeneous, smelling strongly of having been squeezed together from different groups, colleges or universities joining in the demonstration. Notably, there was no mention at this stage of democracy, despite the meetings of the weekly democracy salon at Beijing University every Wednesday afternoon.

Now the big student armies began to manoeuvre. Some four thousand of them tried to break into the Zhongnanhai, where most of the political leaders and 'Immortals' live. The first mass demonstration at Tiananmen came on 18 April, mostly of law students. The spacious and imposing square of Tiananmen – 'gate of heavenly peace' – had for centuries served as a popular gathering place at the entrance to the Forbidden City where the emperors lived and worked. It had first gained fame as the site of political protest on 4 May 1919, when the younger generation led

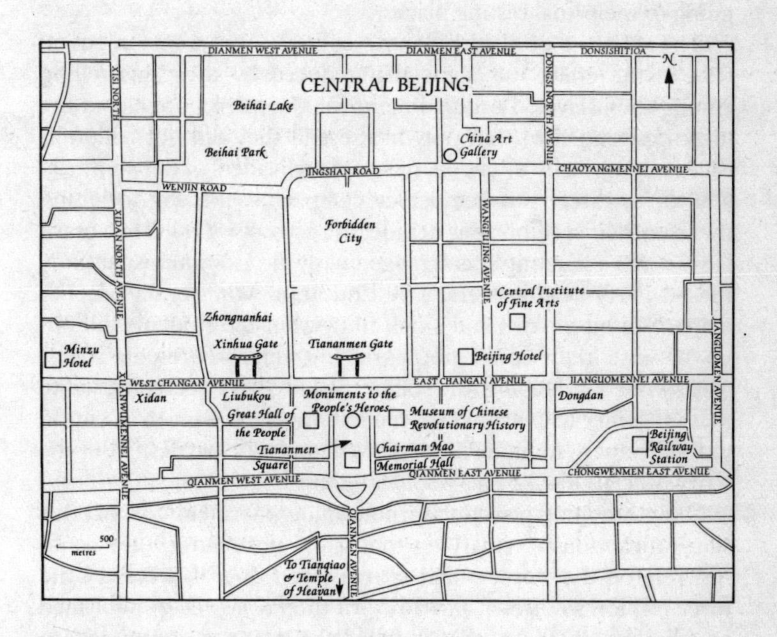

Tiananmen

by Zhou Enlai and other students protested at China's weakness in accepting the bullying of the big powers at the Versailles Peace Conference. Mao chose the square in which to proclaim his People's Republic in 1949, and the Red Guards used it actively in the 1960s. It became a springboard for Deng Xiaoping's leap into power after 1976.

Since then a new 'temple' of Kentucky Fried Chicken has been established at the southwest corner of Tiananmen Square, and was used by the student leaders for many of the meetings they had to hold during this conflict. They set up a broadcasting tent with a jerry-rigged public address system. For faxing or telephoning they went to the nearby Beijing Hotel, and the student leaders met in the hotel lobby coffee shop for late-night tactics sessions.[25]

On 22 April Zhao Ziyang read the memorial speech for Hu Yaobang in the Great Hall of the People, near Tiananmen, and a million people watched the cavalcade of Hu's mortal remains going to their final resting place.

The students of all the Beijing colleges now went on strike, though the effect was somewhat reduced by their quarrelling among themselves. Leaders fought for the microphone, and the meetings tended to thin out. In the end they did not ballot, as they had originally intended, to select the leaders of the unofficial council to direct pro-democracy campaigns, thereby forfeiting much of their credibility as democratic activists.[26] It led to a grave lapse when a meeting was arranged with the Communist authorities at Party headquarters. The Education Minister and deputy mayor waited for two and a half hours, but the students did not go because they could not agree on their representatives.[27] Meanwhile Hu Deping, the son of the late Party Secretary, wrote that his father had wanted special attention to be given to youth, to intellectuals, to minorities and to democratic parties.[28] But the Party officials blocked his publishing this filial testament.

Deng Xiaoping played the whole student ferment down at this stage, incautiously remarking that it did not matter, they could still rely on the workers and farmers, and then if necessary the three million soldiers.[29] On 26 April the *People's Daily* published an editorial attacking what it called the 'planned conspiracy' to overthrow the Party, something for which the students had never called: they added the retraction of this charge to their list of demands. An even bigger demonstration followed of 150,000 democrats – students now supported, in a crucial escalation, by the general population.[30] In fact, workers surrounded the troops who were fielded by the Party, in order to prevent a clash. Deng waxed even more hard-bitten, saying that blood could be spilt if necessary, and repression of these demonstrators would not harm China's image abroad.[31] The reformists in the State Council, however, sent conciliatory messages to the demonstrators.

The fatal month of May now arrived, and forty-five students had a three-hour meeting with Communist leaders. The Party representatives would not recognise the legality of the new Independent Student Council which had at last been formed, nor would they respond to the main concerns of these students, lecturing them instead of listening to them. The next day the Shanghai students joined the marching and protesting. 'We are more patient than people in the West,' claimed one student, 'but when we explode, nothing can stop us.'

At last a senior leader broke through Party orthodoxy. Party Secretary Zhao Ziyang – Hu Yaobang's successor and just as liberal – addressed the Asian Development Bank, which was holding its annual meeting in Beijing, saying that the student demands were reasonable and would not cause instability, and that the two sides should meet peacefully. Unfortunately Zhao had chosen to visit North Korea during the crucial preceding days when attitudes towards the students were hardening among his Politburo colleagues – a strange misjudgement. On the same day 60,000 students massed in Tiananmen Square, now including representatives from the provinces and, significantly, the Chinese University of Hongkong. Jonathan Mirsky wrote in the *Observer* that it was an indictment of the politically stagnant preceding years that these students 'know who they want to get rid of, but have no idea who should replace them'.[32]

On 8 May Deng chaired a meeting of most of the 'Immortals', two of whom, Chen Yun and Bo Yibo, had to be pushed in on wheelchairs. Only one, Peng Zhen, spoke in favour of the students.[33] At this point the students would have done well to consider who were their friends and who were their enemies in power, and to take note of their friends' warnings. They could have gained many of their demands. The news of their stand, and sympathy for their goals, had by now spread all over the country and overseas. Radical staff members of the All China Federation of Trade Unions donated RMB 100,000 to the student cause, and there would be many such donations in the days that followed, notably from Hongkong. There were marches in Changsha, Chengdu, Chongqing, Xian and numerous other provincial centres.

The director of the Party's United Front Department, Yan Mingfu, invited a dozen intellectuals to discuss how the students' hunger-strike in Tiananmen Square might be ended. One of them was Dai Qing, a journalist and foster daughter of the 'Immortal', Ye Jianying. She told students afterwards that if they ended the strike their requests would be met, and she warned that the strike was not helping the reformists in the Party leadership. The students decided, however, that they would not give up until the government accepted their demands in full. The irony was that Dai Qing's own daughter was one of the hunger strikers, one of many families to be divided by the politics of Tiananmen.[34]

By 15 May there were half a million in the square, including teachers, scientists, journalists, even disenchanted Communist Party officials, and, of course, workers and students. Yan Mingfu tried again to persuade them to call it off, and Zhao offered to retract the *People's Daily* editorial of 26 April which had caused such anger on the campuses. He offered to establish an organisation under the National People's Congress to investigate corruption of the 'princes', and also to publish the financial situation of senior officials. But the Student Council now had the bit between its teeth, and rejected all these overtures as inadequate and unsatisfactory. They hardly seemed to sense the warning note of Premier Li Peng who called for 'swift remedial action'. A million people were congregated in the square, and Li Peng duly proposed martial law. Zhao Ziyang and Hu Qili voted against it, so the leadership was badly split. Deng despairingly appointed a small leadership group consisting of Li Peng, Yang Shangkun and Qiao Shi, thus easing Zhao Ziyang out of the central core leadership.[35]

By 17 May the demonstration in Tiananmen Square had taken a remarkable form. There were three concentric circles. Three thousand hunger strikers sat in the middle sipping their fruit juice. Many had fainted, but most returned after medical treatment. Around them ranged the student supporters, officious and disciplined, clearing paths for ambulances and checking special passes for visitors wanting to see the hunger strikers. Finally around the very outside were rows and rows of workers and university teachers. All in all, there were more than a million, drawn from twenty-four other cities besides Beijing, with civil servants joining in, even from the State Council itself, not to mention business organisations like China International Trust and Investment Corporation (CITIC).[36] A provincial student could usually twist the conductor's arm to let him travel free on the railways to Beijing for such a big occasion. A thousand soldiers expressed solidarity with the students, as well as sports teams and farmers: Tiananmen took on the character of a whole city by itself, with toilet arrangements, traffic rules and twenty-four-hour broadcasting. The students were at their best in this kind of specific, almost military, challenge of organising a million people to live in such a small space.

The last chance, as it turned out, of face-to-face negotiation came on 18 May, when twelve student leaders were invited to talk to Li Peng. The encounter was dominated by the curious behaviour of Wuerkaixi, the most charismatic of the student representatives, a bubbly Uighur from Xinjiang, winning friends with his rough good looks, his air of authority, his spirit and energy. He, more than anyone else, galvanised the entire student body. Now he found himself face-to-face with the Prime Minister. Appearing in hospital pyjamas, with an oxygen tube in his nose and visibly weak after six days of hunger strike, Wuerkaixi began aggressively. When Li apologised for being late for the meeting, Wuerkaixi startled the others by shouting, '*Very* late'![37]

Wuerkaixi then put two propositions to Li Peng: firstly to repudiate the earlier editorial in the *People's Daily* about the students being 'troublemakers' and Party-overthrowers (which Zhao Ziyang had already offered to do), and secondly to hold meaningful negotiations with the students which would be broadcast live. Li Peng shifted marginally to the extent of grudgingly conceding that the students' concerns were 'patriotic', but he did not accept their demands. The meeting lasted for only seven minutes initially, at the end of which Li asked them to vacate the square without preconditions. Soon afterwards the meeting resumed, this time for an hour. Wuerkaixi appeared fainter than ever and Li Peng condescended to shake hands with two or three of the students.[38]

One of the Prime Minister's remarks showed how defensive the national leaders felt on the allegations of corruption and nepotism. 'I have three children,' Li told the student leaders. 'None of them engages in official profiteering.' Another menacing remark of Li's which the students seriously underestimated was 'We will protect the students' lives, factories and the achievements of socialism as well as our capital – whether you like this or not.'[39] This contrasted with Zhao Ziyang's remark to the Politburo Standing Committee, 'I do not believe that a handful of bad elements would be able to mobilise such a large number of people.' There was a genuineness in the students' motivation, Zhao was saying, which the Party would be wise to take note of. The sole 'Immortal' to take the students seriously was Peng Zhen, who said that 'The motive for the students' rallies is good, pure, wholesome and constructive.' He warned Deng Xiaoping to lower his political ambitions, because China 'must aim for the rule of law, not the rule of personality'.[40] Many posters attacked Deng Xiaoping's senility, or made fun of his televised clumsiness with chopsticks at dinner with Gorbachev. Some posters derided him as 'shorty' Deng.

Zhao Ziyang was obviously on the losing side of it all. When he visited the hunger strikers who were in hospital, he could not restrain his tears. But Deng Xiaoping, who made no attempt to see any students, was swinging to the tougher view of Li Peng. Law and order was paramount in Deng's mind. What government in the world would allow its university students to occupy and block off to normal traffic, for days or weeks at a time, its capital city's main square – its Parliament Square or Times Square? The Politburo Standing Committee voted by four to one to call the army in, and the other two were said to be considering resigning.[41] But the army was not necessarily on Deng's side. At least seven leading generals wrote to the *People's Daily* opposing the proclamation of martial law. They included many well-respected commanders.

The message of these liberal soldiers was that the People's Liberation Army belonged to the people: it should not confront the people, much less oppress them. Most important, it should never fire on the people, and should not enter the city at all. Another 150 senior commanders declared that the army should not be used to spill blood. The army would have to live with the demonstrators after it was all over – and supposing (they did not say this, but they thought it) those same demonstrators came to power afterwards?[42] The crack 38th Army in the western outskirts of Beijing refused initially to obey the government's order to intervene. It was said that some of its officers had daughters among the student demonstrators. For twelve days the Communist Party suffered the humiliation of commanders refusing to obey their political superiors' orders: all the armies found the prospect of acting against students and citizens thoroughly distasteful.[43]

By now the student leaders, still at sixes and sevens, were admitting that they could no longer control the situation in the square. As troops began to converge on them, they shifted their tactical focus away from the vulnerable three thousand hunger strikers to a sit-in by tens of thousands.[44] Li Lu, a Nanjing University physics student and deputy under Chai Ling of the hunger strike committee, arranged a distracting piece of theatre at this point. He had asked his girlfriend from Nanjing to join him on the square. She duly arrived on 21 May and the couple were informally 'married' in the square.[45]

A couple of days later, getting no response from the government, the ten-person group of student leaders decided to carry on with the sit-in. But they expelled Wuerkaixi for advocating evacuation to his followers against the majority wishes, and for having dealings with Deng Pufang, the disabled son of Deng Xiaoping, who was trying to be a channel of communication between his father and the students.[46] The leaders of the students were almost as disunited as the leaders of the Party and the government. Already there were allegations and rumours about some student leaders using for themselves the considerable public donations that were received. Some disillusioned students drifted away.

But the students were heartened when the Standing Committee of the National People's Congress endorsed their movement almost unanimously, and called for the removal of military force from Beijing. The Congress has little power, but it does constitute almost the only legal arena for the expression of grassroots public opinion. When its then chairman, Wan Li, returned from a visit to America on 28 May, however, he made his colleagues do an about-turn and support the government. By then Deng had carried out a dramatic purge of the senior leadership, the centrepiece being the dismissal of Secretary Zhao Ziyang.[47] Meanwhile students installed in the square a model of the Statue of Liberty, something which irritated Deng more than almost anything else. The Goddess of Democracy, as it was called, became a cult object for students and other liberals.

Now came a fateful moment. The original group of student leaders decided they had had enough, and wanted to end the occupation of the square, with the last demonstration to take place on 30 May. By then, however, more students from other institutions all over China had come, eager and expectant, to join the event in Tiananmen Square. A new group of student leaders, who had not experienced the early phases of the campaign, proposed to continue the demonstration in the square until 20 June, when the National People's Congress was due to meet – and hopefully might be persuaded to give them some support.[48]

For the first time there were fistfights and conflict, not between the students and the government, but between the Beijing student leaders and the provincial student leaders. That damaged the student image, and made it even more difficult, as if it were not hard enough, for the reformists to support and protect them. Meanwhile Deng Xiaoping's language became even more lurid, his analysis of the situation at the end of May being, 'We need to quickly use a sharp knife to cut the tangled reeds in order to avoid even greater turmoil.'[49]

Another warning to which the students did not pay sufficient attention was the holding on the last day of May of a government rally in the outskirts of Beijing. Its participants, who were rumoured to have been paid RMB 20 each, burnt the astrophysicist Fang Lizhi's effigy. That doubtless afforded some satisfaction to Deng Xiaoping, but Fang was already an exile, far removed from the ebullience of a new generation of students. It was said now that about a third of the staff of the *People's Daily*, mouthpiece of the orthodox voices in the Party, had joined in. But the workers, professional people and disobedient officials who attached themselves to the students were also joined by a dubious element of 'riff-raff', as both sides called them, possibly including *agents provocateurs*.

On the night of 2 June more than 10,000 soldiers armed only with clubs and knives marched at a trot to Tiananmen from different directions, their orders being to clear the square and enforce martial law. Some came through underground tunnels. Many were stopped by civilians, who persuaded them not to proceed. By now the larger part of the students had left the square, but Deng intended to punish their supporters, especially the ordinary citizens of Beijing who had dared to flout the government's orders. In the early morning of 3 June fighting broke out on Changanjie, one of the main roads leading to the square, where the remaining students sat quietly in the darkness. Two armed personnel carriers (APCs) trying to proceed along Changanjie had crushed people as well as bicycles in their way, so the crowd dragged the soldiers out and lynched them. Students tried to protect the troops, but were too few. This attempt by the government and army to retake the square with foot soldiers failed. Now tanks and armoured personnel carriers were sent in.

At 4.25 in the morning of 4 June, Hou Dejian, the young Taiwanese pop singer who had defected to China and now mysteriously emerged as one of the leaders of the demonstrations and hunger-strikes, negotiated with the soldiers, but without the approval of the other student leaders, a peaceful student retreat. The officers whom he contacted consulted their headquarters, and then said that the demonstrators should withdraw from the southeast of the square. Hou conveyed this on the microphone to the demonstrators in the square, adding that enough blood had been shed. 'We should all live on,' he implored, 'for the country, for the race, for democracy – and not die in the square.' Some of those in the square questioned the strategy and morality of giving in. But the soldiers closed in, repeating the message that they should leave or die. Some people dispersed, others stayed in the square, only to be beaten with thick wooden sticks.[50]

The whole confrontation had now become an intricate quadrille between the students, the citizens, the soldiers and the politicians – all with different goals. By six o' clock in the morning of 4 June most students had walked out unharmed, persuaded by Chai Ling, the brave psychology student who became commander-in-chief of the Tiananmen students, and Liu Xiaobo to evacuate. In Hou's account, the four remaining hunger-strikers had decided to lead the students' supporters also out of the square. The sound of gunfire came closer and closer. But some students resisted, 'How can we account to those who have already been killed, and what about the possibility of retaliation afterwards?'

Premier Li Peng told a French visitor, Alain Peyrefitte, that what Hou Dejian had said about the incident so far was true. He listed three main causes of discontent: price rises (triggered, he said, by the erroneous policies of Zhao Ziyang), corruption and the unjust sharing of resources or polarities of income. Li seized the opportunity to blazon his own virtue, adding that he himself used to have two Mercedes cars, but now economised with a Chinese-made Audi 100. He added that the Chinese word *jieyan* is not correctly translated as martial law. It merely means that when the police are insufficient for the job, the army lends a hand. Peyrefitte asked the Chinese Premier why the government could not handle it better, to which Li's bitter reply was: 'To be honest, we were unable to impose martial law in the small section of Beijing where it was necessary. We had become a clandestine government.'[51]

A foreign correspondent asked one of the crowd how unarmed men could stop tanks, as they had done on Changanjie? 'First you take a thick iron pipe,' came the reply, 'and shove it in the tracks. Then you put petrol-soaked mattresses under the carriage and over the bay, hold a torch over your head and negotiate with the soldiers inside.' The correspondent said, 'Where in the world did you learn that?' The delighted reply came, 'In the army!'[52] But it was impossible for the army not to hit anyone. When one soldier shot a child, the crowd hanged and burnt him.

In the early morning of 4 June the army launched its infamous final all-out assault on the square. APCs and tanks crashed through the barricades, firing to disperse almost a million people. There were still three thousand students in the centre of the square, and the army secured all four corners of it by dawn. The diminished band of weeping undergraduates held hands and sang the *Internationale*. During the night two APCs entered the square from the east, but were set on fire.

The 27th Army was led in from the north by President Yang Shangkun's step-nephew, Yang Jianhua. This was Yang Shangkun's own army, tough and ruthless, equipped with T-69 tanks and French helicopters. About seventy tanks and APCs were deployed for this operation.[53] But from the south it was an ill-prepared peasant-recruited army of a rather different calibre. Just as there was fighting between the student leaders at one point, so now the rival armies found themselves exchanging shots at the airport, the 27th Army versus the 16th. The 38th Army was also supposed to join the manoeuvre, but it was so reluctant to get into a situation of fighting students and other civilians that the implementation of the orders to clear the square had to be carried out by Yang Jianhua's 27th Army instead. The 38th Army had traditional ties with students, and its commander, Xin Qinxian, was afterwards sacked for his disobedience.[54]

During that last night many students were shot in the back as they left the square. They had agreed to leave and obey the orders of the army, but some who took their time, fell.[55] Kate Adie of the BBC was grazed by a bullet which killed the man behind her. The Beijing Hotel, where some of the protagonists and correspondents had argued and talked, could not serve breakfast that morning because the chef had been shot. It emerged that the crowd of civilians in Changanjie threw bottles at the troops, who fired back. The tents in which people had been living during the demonstrations were levelled by army vehicles, allegedly with their occupants still inside.[56]

The image which millions of viewers all over the world vividly retain in their memory was the sight of a single unarmed man with a carrier bag of shopping defying a tank. He was a nineteen-year-old student named Wang Weilin. The BBC footage taken by Philip Cunningham from Room 1413 of the Beijing Hotel must be one of the best known sequences in history. Wang Weilin was foolhardy, but he succeeded in stopping the tank and in engaging the driver and crew in argument. His sangfroid is still marvelled at. Li Lu, one of the main student leaders at Tiananmen, commented that the driver of the tank who refused to drive on and kill the man who would not get out of his way was also a hero.[57] This was a fight in which there could be no victors.

There were scenes of ugliness and needless cruelty when the crowd clashed with soldiers: sometimes the soldiers were nervous and uncertain what to do. The civilian crowd would not take attack lying down, and retaliated against the troops, sometimes successfully. On the day after 4 June there could be seen several disembowelled bodies of soldiers hanging on the railings. When it was all over, the students sent round China a travelling exhibition of the corpses of five students who had been crushed by APCs. Wreaths and white paper flowers were placed on the square by people coming forward to mourn their dead.

The number of deaths is a matter of keen dispute, the students tending to exaggerate, while the government side tries to minimise. The best estimate is that rather less than a thousand were killed in Beijing, roughly two hundred students, twenty soldiers and the rest civilians.[58] One thousand dead is not a colossal loss in the course of demonstrations involving more than a million, or in a national population of 1,200 million. That is not to excuse the deaths, but to keep them in a perspective – no bloodier than some riots in Rangoon, Bangkok, Seoul, Kuala Lumpur, Manila or Jakarta in recent decades. Transient foreign visitors or TV viewers have usually seen the affair as much bigger than it really was.

Some foreigners who were there blame the students for illegally occupying the square.[59] They defied martial law, usurped the power of the city authorities and provoked conflict. In the process they probably upset the political prospects of the best peaceful reforms in years. If the students had not demonstrated, Zhao Ziyang might have continued as General Secretary, and the weight of the reformists might have prevailed in all the major organisations and councils. After June 1989, opportunities for peaceful reform had to be surrendered with the change in the political climate. Deng Xiaoping, who had previously been open to liberal ideas, and showed himself as relatively innovative and pragmatic, increasingly turned to his conservative colleagues, who were more concerned about law and order and ideological orthodoxy.

Premier Li Peng explained afterwards that the Chinese security forces did not possess enough tear-gas, rubber bullets or water cannon, and were untrained in crowd control as developed in Western countries. There was no hydrant at the edge of the square which could have been used for water jets.[60] Lacking Zhao and his followers, the Central Committee and State Council issued a joint vindication to the Chinese people on 5 June. 'The People's Republic, a nation created by the sacrifices of tens of millions of martyrs, would have been subverted: the construction of socialism and the achievements of ten years of reform would have been destroyed in one stroke, and the entire country would have been engulfed in a white terror. These decisive acts of suppression, then, are totally justified.'[61] But a Hongkong periodical rephrased Li Peng's arguments about the lack of gas and rubber bullets, sarcastically putting his argument this way: 'If one lacks a feather duster at home, then can't one just use a butcher's knife to discipline the children?'

President Jiang Zemin admitted that there were 'different opinions within the top Chinese leadership'.[62] The real tragedy is that divisions of opinion among the students got in the way of their safe evacuation (a few hours would have made all the difference), while differences of opinion in the Party and government leadership seemed to create a vacuum in which official decisions were taken too late, and with insufficient precision. There seemed to be nobody in Zhongnanhai, where the leaders are, to take the issue by the throat and deal with it without hesitation and without interfering emotions.

Never was there such a haplessly mistimed visit as that of Mikhail Gorbachev to Beijing in the midst of this student turmoil. It was the first visit by a Soviet President for thirty years, and promised to be the most important diplomatic event for China since Richard Nixon's visit in 1972. Three days before his arrival, the students began their hunger strike on the very spot where China's top military brass were due formally to welcome him. Cheekily, the students asked the Soviet embassy to arrange a meeting for them with him.

In Tiananmen Square there were banners for Gorbachev welcoming him as 'the initiator of *glasnost*'. But Gorbachev's itinerary was disrupted. His motorcade had to use the back streets, and many of the visits in central Beijing had to be cancelled entirely. Even when dining in the Great Hall of the People (entered by the back door), Gorbachev's view of Tiananmen Square was blocked by curtains.

Prophetically, the Russian leader saw Zhao Ziyang's troubles as a possible harbinger of his own. Only with Zhao did he feel at ease. Zhao actually sealed his own fate in a talk with Gorbachev, with the remark that, on the most important questions, Deng was still needed as the helmsman despite his lack of office, something formalised in a resolution two years earlier that had never been published.[63] And that ended the encounter between the two brilliant reformers of the Communist world who both lacked the political skill to realise their ideals. The onlooker of it all was Deng, doubly angered by Zhao's seeming disloyalty and the ease with which the students could rob him of the control of his own streets when he most needed them for his most auspicious guest.

The poor timing of the students, hoping to take advantage of Deng's humiliation at not being able to receive the Soviet President in a fitting way, actually angered Deng to the point where he could never have been persuaded to parley and compromise with the students. This is what he said after it was all over: 'It should not have been supported, but shots should not have been fired.'[64] Deng was evidently disapproving of the way in which the military operation had been conducted, but he said, with utter finality, 'No mercy or even an iota of forgiveness' should be shown to the 'enemy', i.e. the student leaders.[65]

Those student leaders lost none of their bombast and rosy vision afterwards. Wuerkaixi and Yan Jiaqi called for a hundred days of mourning, and for the Nobel Peace Prize to be awarded to the students. Li Lu delivered a stirring address to the United Nations Subcommittee for the Prevention of Discrimination.[66] Wuerkaixi himself was smuggled out of China under a load of timber. Chai Ling went to Princeton, stopping to give an interview to foreign media in the Beijing Hotel on the way, Li Lu to Columbia, where they were all received as heroes of the modern age. Virtually all of the student leaders escaped to be fêted abroad. But Chen Zimin and Wang Juntao who refused to confess the charges were each given thirteen years imprisonment. Hou Dejian spent two months in asylum in the Australian embassy before escaping in a fishing boat to his native Taiwan.

At home, a thousand vengeful students travelled to Deng Xiaoping's native village in Sichuan province, intending to dig up his family graves. One can think of more rational and productive things for a thousand students to do, but this is a deadly means of insulting a person in the Chinese tradition. In fact the police were forewarned, and blocked the young people from getting at the graves.

In the inevitable general crackdown on journalists and others who supported the student movement in 1989, some 400 were arrested in Beijing, and tortured in order to implicate others. A Central Committee directive laid down that 'counter-revolutionaries' would be suppressed for one year, and that one Party member in ten was either bourgeois or corrupt and would therefore need to be eliminated. 'Those with serious offences and poor attitudes will be killed, those with relatively minor offences who show repentance will be exiled for labour reform, those with good performances will be reformed, struggled against and utilised.'[67] That is surely the most chilling sentence that one could read in modern Chinese history. It is accurately grounded in the national tradition, overlaid by Stalinist-Maoist brutality. That hoary old maxim of Chinese dictatorship, 'Execute one to warn a hundred', still lived in the China of Deng Xiaoping's reforms.

Yet it was a strange feature of the aftermath of Tiananmen that the government and Party seemed to prefer the erring student leaders to leave China rather than stay behind for punishment. While Chen Zimin and Wang Juntao received heavy prison sentences, the government did not appear to be overly embarrassed or put out at the activities of the student prima donnas in Washington and Paris. The Communists seem to be relieved at not having the burden of dealing with them at home, where they would either have to be kept in prison, which is bad publicity for China abroad, or else be treated seriously in the political arena, which they do not want at all. When the first returnee, Shen Tong, came back in 1992, he started organising again in Beijing, trying to set up a human rights group under the Chinese law. He was duly arrested, then re-expelled. Han Dongfang was also re-arrested. Wei Jingsheng himself, the original perpetrator of the subversive posters on Democracy Wall in 1979, was released after fourteen and a half years behind bars, on the eve of the Olympic Committee's meeting to decide the next host city for the Olympic Games. He was re-imprisoned after Beijing's failure a few months later.

The favourite site of exile was, of course, the United States, where the students formed a Chinese Alliance for Democracy. But many went to Paris, where the Federation for Democracy in China was launched. Paddy Ashdown, the British Liberal Democrat leader, gave its initial meeting an address in Cantonese, and Yves Montand and Henri Cartier-Bresson attended. After arguing fiercely into the small hours they elected Yan Jiaqi as president and Wuerkaixi as vice-president. It had become apparent that financial support from abroad had been a big factor in the Beijing demonstration, and continued to be a source of support for these exiled organisations. HK$27 million was said to have been contributed by people in Hongkong, and there was a Taiwan subvention. Money was also raised within China, notably from Wan Runnan's Stone Group, which had identified itself with the student movement.

Neutral figures in the community of exiles tried in vain to make the two organisations in Paris and the United States merge, to be more effective. Liu Binyan, who started from the ground that Marxism is still valid, led a group called Future China Society. Shen Tong launched a Democracy for China Fund in the United States. All these divisions, personal animosities and rivalries mean that the Chinese exiles have no power and no realistic chance of acquiring it.[68] They keep the West interested, but usually fail to transmit an understanding of the real problems in China. They would possibly come into their own again in the event of another mass student uprising, but the chances of that seem slim in the near future. The country of 1.2 billion seems unable to provide an alternative leadership to the Communist Party, but then the Chinese tradition works against the role of objector.

Something with which their Western sympathisers have to come to terms is that the political dissidents do not usually present constructive ideas for change. When a very distinguished group of a dozen political opponents of the government lobbied the National People's Congress in 1995, they did so under the officially fashionable guise of ideas to combat corruption. Only at the end of their document did these worthies, including Chen Ziming, Wang Ruoshui and Liu Xiaobo, urge the ending of the ban on free association, and provision for voters to restrain Communist power through free elections. The National People's Congress, they suggested, should be transformed into a legislature independent of the Communist Party. An independent constitutional court should punish breaches of the constitution by the ruling party and other bodies. Media censorship should go, and private property be given a clear legal status. The future depended on whether 'the ruling party continues to carry out reform from the top downward, and whether the civilian political forces organise reform from the lower level upwards.' The taming of the Communist Party is the clear priority, and only after that will the field be open for detailed political reforms.[69]

These brave dissenters rarely face the likelihood that changing the leading party will not necessarily change the defects which they identify in the political system. Unless 1.2 billion people are educated to abandon the submissive attitude to authority, a new party or coalition may come to rule as arbitrarily as the present one.

Wang Juntao told Chinese students at London University in June 1995 that whereas American democracy proceeded from a popular belief in the people's right to pursue life, liberty and happiness – leading to the toppling of tyrants and finally a constitution to guide the process – China could not follow such a path. Where the West makes laws to shape reality, China makes laws out of reality. So the democracy movement would do better to address social problems. When social group interests become organised, they will come to share with the Communist Party a need for rules, and that is when real democracy, motivated by mutual benefits, will begin.[70]

Two major groups of actors on the Chinese political stage are thus hamstrung by their own weaknesses – the intellectuals by uncertainty about the forms of democracy suitable for China, the Communist Party by its lust for continuing power and deep acceptance of China's need for authority. Neither group is united. Can a more disciplined force, like the army, become a more incisive instrument of change, as is common in Asia?

CHAPTER 6

THE ARMY: OUT OF A GUN BARREL

Many armies, especially in Asia, have taken the plunge into politics. China might appear to be an exception, and yet its People's Liberation Army, three million strong, has close interaction with the Communist Party and notably bailed the civilian leaders out at Tiananmen Square in 1989. Actually its role is unique. It is the largest army in the world and although it is rapidly being professionalised, it has in the past been a very political army. The Communist Party and the Red Army, as it was first known, were like close brothers in a family rather than rivals. Mao Zedong and his colleagues were as much military politicians as Marshal Zhu De and his high command were political soldiers. Power, Mao said in his most memorable utterance, 'comes from the barrel of a gun' – such is the debt felt by the Party to the army.

The generation of civilian leaders which is just now fading out in China used to don military uniform and participate in battles – normally, it is true, as political commissars, but they often showed an aptitude for military campaigns. Deng Xiaoping himself was at various times an army commander, a political commissar and a leading Party official. Ranks and insignia were not formally introduced in the army until 1955, and were abolished just before the Cultural Revolution ten years later, to be re-introduced only in the 1970s, so the army's 'democratic' history is almost as long as its 'professional' one.

In those circumstances, there was bound to be little jealousy between the Party and the army, and even today the Party does not regard the army as a problem in political terms. Though the

Defence Minister Lin Biao led units loyal to him against Mao in 1971, the Chinese army as such has never taken power from the political leadership, in the way that has happened in Indonesia and Burma, or from time to time in Thailand and South Korea. There is much trust between the two institutions in China, much shared history, and the Party has naturally had more opportunity to indoctrinate its army politically than was possible for most other civilian governments in Asia. The armed forces account for a quarter of the Party's Central Committee, and one soldier in three is a Party member.[1]

Now that the army is being professionalised, there are some hints of possible future friction, for example over the growth in power and prestige of the rival uniformed service, the People's Armed Police (PAP) – and even the military police. The PAP has gained an annual budget which is almost 80 per cent of the army's.[2] In 1994 there was an extraordinary battle between the army and military police in Guizhou. An army vehicle lost control on the road, and happened to smash into a military police station on the roadside, immediately killing three and wounding two. The MPs confiscated the car and took the soldiers as hostages, demanding RMB 15,000 in compensation. From there it escalated to involve 700 military and police personnel, 60 army vehicles and armoured personnel carriers with machine guns and flame-throwers. There were 150 casualties.[3]

A new factor with huge political consequences is the noticeable lack of enthusiasm in the army for the way in which the Party handled the student demonstrations in Tiananmen Square in 1989. The army units which were called out took their time before intervening, causing the Party to lose about two weeks in seeing its intended repression take place. Army people are surprisingly liberal in their political opinions, and have mostly backed the Deng Xiaoping reforms. They saw the Tiananmen action as a deviation from that policy, and in any case many officers have children or grandchildren in the student ranks, and many other ranks have younger brothers there. Some even called for the reinstatement of Secretary General Zhao Ziyang.[4]

The Communist Party seeks to keep the army under control by promoting army leaders who would favour the group or coalition of factions in the Communist Party which is running the government. For a long time Deng Xiaoping took the chair of the Central Military Commission which controls senior appointments. Indeed, that was the post to which he held on longer than any of his other appointments.

In 1987 he created the office of First Vice-Chairman of the Military Commission, in order to insert Zhao Ziyang under himself at the number two position and thus allow him to gain some authority over the army. Apparently Yang Shangkun, the senior military figure, was angry at a civilian being appointed. It seemed like a downgrading of the military's voice, since Zhao, being from a younger generation, had no significant military experience. When Zhao was politically disgraced during the Tiananmen affair, a potentially damaging competition to succeed him on the Military Commission broke out between Yang Shangkun and Qin Jiwei, the Defence Minister. Yang was then the junior Vice-Chairman of the Commission, and also its Secretary-General.[5]

Yang, who was later made President of the People's Republic, headed an unprecedented family group at the top of army leadership. He and his half-brother General Yang Baibing had played a role earlier as key supporters of Deng in all the reforms and military changes he had undertaken. Yang Shangkun had been of great assistance to Deng in realigning military commands in the late 1980s. Yang Baibing was made a full general, promoted to be political commissar of the Beijing Military Region and placed on the Central Military Commission. He seemed to be rather liberal in the freedom with which he permitted writing and publishing in the army, and the two Yangs with Deng seemed to form a solid pro-reform group in the highest leadership. But other veterans in the army were irritated by the fast promotion of the Yangs. A group of senior officers including Qin Jiwei, Yan Dezhi (formerly Chief of Staff), Yu Qiuli, Chen Xilin (Commander of the Beijing Military Region), and Zhang Aiping, who had given critical help to Deng Xiaoping earlier, opposed the Yangs.[6]

It did appear as if the Yang family was taking over the army. There were persistent rumours that Chi Haotian, of the General Staff Headquarters, was Yang's son-in-law, but he has denied it. Meanwhile Yang Shangkun's step-nephew Yang Jianhua (son of

Baibing), headed the 27th Field Army which belatedly led the assault on the students in Tiananmen. Then there was Yang Shaojun, said to be a son of Yang Shangkun, who commanded the 27th Army. Yang Shangkun's loyalties were with the old 2nd Field Army and all its famous campaigns in the past, but the new members of the Central Military Commission now appointed by Deng were mainly from the old 4th Field Army. Civil war Field Army loyalties from the 1930s are an important determinant of present commanders' political alignments, though the Party has tried to muddy the water by routinely rotating the commands.

Deng's solution after Tiananmen was to move Yang Shangkun sideways to the relatively powerless post of President of the Republic, and to prise his nephew out of his influential army post, in exchange for something of less professional value to him, namely membership of the Party Politburo. Deng felt forced to jettison his old allies in order to stem a rising resentment among other senior officers at the domination of the Yang brothers, who were trying to promote their supporters to key posts and even to manoeuvre for the coming political succession struggle.[7] The result was to leave the army in a three-way state – units broadly loyal to Yang, units broadly hostile to him, and younger commanders who regard themselves as professional, and do not wish to enter into the government of the day in any way. Time is on the side of the third group.

Probably the army has more political influence as a result of Deng's changes, and will be seen to support the reformists in the Party. The awkward thing was Deng Xiaoping's having to choose between personalities and groups all loyal to him, some of whom had to be disappointed.

When Jiang Zemin was appointed Party General Secretary to succeed Zhao Ziyang in 1989, Deng put him into the Central Military Commission chair as well, succeeding Deng himself. It was a necessary effort to keep the army under the Party and consolidate Jiang's position, but Jiang was another complete civilian, with no military experience whatsoever, and there were murmurings about that from some officers. He had the support, however, of the old 4th Field Army veterans now dominating the Commission, including the late Li Xiannian and Zhang Aiping. More politically ambitious senior officers were retired, and trusted professionals promoted, at the Fourteenth Party Congress in 1992. Admiral Liu Huaqing, though seventy-eight and said to be in poor health, was brought in as Vice-Chairman of the Military Commission and was also put on the Politburo Standing Committee. Liu guides the armed forces into acceptance of Jiang Zemin as Deng's successor and propels it relentlessly towards professional standards and values. With the eighty-year-old General Zhang Zhen, Liu is seen as a military power-broker after Deng's death.[8]

There are military princes, who do not all go down well in the ranks. He Pengfei, son of the 'Immortal' He Long, became a general and, one has to admit, a popular one. Ye Xuanping's son Xuanning became Director of the General Political Department's Liaison Section. Marshal Fu Yu has a son who is Director of Military Affairs in the Department of the General Staff.[9] But the problem is not quite as bad as it is on the civilian side, except perhaps for the Yang family itself in the 1980s.

The army has many grievances which in another country might well provoke intervention in politics. To begin with, it is badly under-equipped. There was visible shock in the Chinese high command when the Gulf War against Iraq revealed such an effortless superiority of Western military technology. The fact is that China supports 10 per cent of the world's armed forces on only 0.6 per cent of the world's military spending. Wages are lower in China than in the West, it is true, but there is more to it.

Morale is slightly diminished by the four successive streamlining programmes launched by the Party. The most recent of these sent about 300,000 soldiers back to 'civvy street', closed a number of military colleges and merged some specialised units.[10] The army budget was reduced, from 17 per cent of the total national budget in 1978 to only 8 per cent in 1987,[11] but its upward path was then restored. For ordinary soldiers, 20 per cent inflation along with cuts in pay spells dangerous dissatisfaction. The army is forced into a posture of self-funding, similar to that which other Chinese institutions and services have to take up, notably the civil service and education.

The soldiers, it is sometimes said, have to beat their swords into name-cards and develop business incomes to make up for government parsimony. One of the biggest sources of income is to rent out unused barracks to new entrepreneurs, or to be used as warehouses. Army units are today expected to stick to their budgets and make sure that both sides add up to the same total. *Guide to Securities*, *Introduction to Stocks*, *Investment Primer* and other business 'classics' are now seen on officers' shelves. A recent Central Military Commission circular actually contains the order that units should not, in the endeavour to produce creditable financial results, 'beat your auditors'.[12] It goes without saying that the army is after the profits to be made from manufacturing and services for the civilian market.

Today the army controls more than 20,000 enterprises with several million employees, run mostly by the General Logistics Department and also the General Staff Headquarters and the General Political Department. The original purpose was to promote the self-sufficiency of the army, but in the 1980s the goal

CHINA'S ARMED FORCES

PERSONNEL

Army 2,200,000 active personnel in
- 72 regular infantry divisions
- 11 tank divisions
- 5 artillery divisions

Navy 265,000 personnel
Air Force 470,000 personnel
People's Armed Police 600,000 on border and internal security duties

TOTAL 2,935,000 (43% conscripts) with 1.2 million more on reserve.

CONTROL

Chairman of Central Military Commission: JIANG ZEMIN

Vice Chairmen: LIU HUAQING, ZHANG ZHENG, CHI HAOTIAN, ZHANG WANGNIAN

Chief of General Staff
FU QUANYOU
Navy Commander
ZHANG LIANZHONG
Air Force Commander
CAO SHUANGMING

EQUIPMENT

Army
- 9,850 tanks
- 4,500 armoured personnel carriers
- 14,500 towed artillery

Navy
- 63 submarines
- 55 cruisers
- 18 destroyers
- 36 frigates

Air Force
- 420 bombers
- 4,000 fighters
- 485 transports
- 190 helicopters

FINANCE

The official 1996 defence budget was US$8.4 billion or 1.5% of GNP, but Western analysts estimate total defence-related spending at around $32 billion. The PLA owns, administers and partly mans some 25,000 farming/industrial/commercial enterprises additional to regular defence industries which employ more than 3 million people.

OVERSEAS

The PLA had some 36 observers with UN peacekeeping operations in the Middle East, Iraq/Kuwait and Western Sahara.

Source: **The Military Balance 1996–97**

became profit, so that the army now operates as a kind of subsidiary economy in China, exporting and importing, running hotels, holding patents for civilian products and owning foreign subsidiaries. Some of these enterprises absorb demobilised soldiers: the navy, for instance, runs a maritime transport enterprise in which half of the workers are expelled servicemen – and it produces a RMB 50 million profit for the navy. The taxation rules were amended for the benefit of the military enterprises, to allow some tax exemptions and other privileges. A similar picture is found in Indonesia, Thailand and other Asian countries.

The major arms exporter for the army is Polytechnologies, founded in 1983 and regarded as the most aggressive of China's arms dealers. The army also has a very large transnational corporation, which made profits in 1992 reported to be US$162 million, most of which was turned over to the army or re-invested. The manufacturers in this group, mainly of pharmaceuticals, are located in Germany, Thailand, Russia, the USA, etc. There is even one army firm reported to be into currency futures in Guangzhou. Estimates of the total profit from all these enterprises vary, from $3 billion to $6 billion, compared with the official army budget in 1995 of $7.5 billion, and estimated actual expenditure in 1992 of $22 billion.

The temptations to smuggle, bribe and defraud are obviously high. One general was recently arrested for smuggling. Yet officers and men are now familiar with the ways and advantages of the market, and regional commanders can be observed urging an affiliated industry, maybe an automobile company, to use the share holding system in order to finance product development and upgrade technology. The military now has a stake in a more streamlined and efficient defence sector, in which advances in military and civilian technology go together. The Foreign Ministry is left finding difficulty in controlling Chinese arms exports and maintaining adherence to China's international commitments.[13]

The army now produces more than three-quarters of China's pharmaceuticals. The air force has set up a new civilian airline, and the army has its own economic development zones in Guangdong. Army companies are very active commercially in Hongkong.[14] The army had a raw deal in the 1960s when the government directed a massive relocation of electronic and other defence installations away from the strategically vulnerable coasts to Sichuan and other interior provinces, in the so-called Third Front policy of Marshal Lin Biao. It is the coastal areas today which are the most economically dynamic, and the army has faced an expensive re-relocation process under Deng Xiaoping.

One of the jewels in the army's crown is the China North Industries Corporation, known as Norinco, a super-conglomerate which succeeded the former Ministry of Ordnance. Its artillery and tank plant had to convert to civilian use. The government gave Norinco the exclusive right to make minicars, and lent RMB 800 million for it to start operations in Hunan. It is into optics and chemicals as well, though there is some question over the soundness of all its products. It used to export to Iraq, Iran, Pakistan and Thailand, but this trade tailed off after the Iran–Iraq war, and some clients expressed disappointment at the quality. There were joint ventures with companies from France, Britain, Italy and the USA to produce tanks and armoured personnel carriers, but that halted after Tiananmen. Norinco collaborates with Izuzu, Suzuki, Charoen Pokphand and Benz for various items of transport equipment.[15]

About two-thirds of the output of Chinese army factories is now destined for civilian markets. In the five years to 1992 arms exports by army factories have been estimated at US$8 billion, which was 5 per cent of the world total, just below the British or French level.[16] A recent exhibition in Hongkong of army industrial items included nuclear, astronautics, aeronautics, ordnance, electronics and shipbuilding equipment.[17] Recently the centre has tried to restrain the business role of the soldiery, but it is probably beyond curbing. Inevitably it increases corruption within the army.

China has formed an attack force centred upon complete series of guided missiles: shore-to-ship, ship-to-ship, ship-to-air, air-to-ship and submarine-to-ship. The guided missile known as the Chinese Flying Fish has impressed some potential foreign buyers.[18] China is thus shifting from a passive territorial defence posture to one capable of engaging potential enemies outside China, although this is limited at present to the South China Sea and the nearer parts of southeast Asia. The navy and air force are moving away from solely defensive capability.

'People should not be surprised,' a *Liberation Army Daily* reporter wrote, 'if one day in the future the silhouette of an aircraft carrier appears in China's navy fleet.' It was said officially that there are no current plans to build or buy an aircraft carrier, but that China had never promised that it would not have one. Such a development would, of course, allow China fully to control the strategic Spratly Islands in the South China Sea, including the oil and sea lanes so vital to many east Asian countries. It would also facilitate a naval blockade of Taiwan. In 1995, the Chinese fleet had only one nuclear-powered ballistic-missile submarine, and five nuclear attack submarines which some Western experts say are not operational. The forty-odd diesel-powered submarines and more than seven hundred fast-attack craft are defensive in character, but there are fifty-four destroyers and frigates and over forty amphibious craft with offensive potential.

The navy is now getting priority.[19] Moscow Broadcasting Station reported in 1993 that China was negotiating for a Ukrainian aircraft carrier then under construction, which Ukraine no longer needed. But the discussions broke down on the price. Now, the Russian source continued, China would like to buy two 38,000-ton light carriers which were currently in Russian service.[20] Another report in the same year said that future aircraft carrier captains had been trained in secret classes from 1987, by the order of Admiral Liu Huaqing, who is now the most senior armed forces officer.[21]

But there is still fear of inefficiency affecting the quality of the army's work. Communications between army headquarters and the North China military zone once went down for twenty-five minutes, because four soldiers who were on duty went to buy wine just before the shift changed. The two who were left switched off the equipment at the time the shift finished, left the room and locked it, so that when the four returned just afterwards they could not get in.[22]

Gradually the Chinese armed forces will become more powerful and better equipped. Already the largest armed force in the world, they may become the strongest during the 2010s. This does not necessarily constitute a threat to other nations in the near future. For one thing, the army cannot be regarded as fully united. For another, the Chinese leaders have vital foreign policy goals to pursue which could restrict the army's room for external manoeuvre. What draws the military together is the emotion of nationalism, together with the burgeoning sense of professionalism, and the fact that they all subsist on the same military budget voted by the government and supplemented by the army's own economic activities.

But regional loyalties among units are becoming more open, along with the general trend in China for decentralised provincial power and decision-making. It came out in the Tiananmen confrontation in 1989, for example, how different armies in China had different attitudes to what they were asked to do, so that the centre had to manipulate in order to get the result it wanted. Each military region in China roughly corresponds to a handful of neighbouring provinces, and in the years to come we may see increasing identification of the local armed forces with those provincial authorities, on the basis of sharing ideas about policy and priorities which may differ from those of other regions and of the centre. Economic factors may also disturb the army's unity, because vital economic installations are usually in one region or another, and cannot necessarily be replicated across every region.

But the most effective source of divisiveness is personal factionalism. Civilians tend to take up political heroes or gods like Mao or Deng to follow, enjoying a life where they defer to such high authorities and do not want to be consulted or need to be convinced about every single policy change. The degree of deference is even more striking in the armed forces, where obeying orders is the primary duty, lines of authority are distinct and rewards are more obvious. And this can extend beyond the authority of a single commander. The Yang family, as we have seen, actually controlled, it could be said, more than just one army, with more than one family member at the highest rank. If units comprising different personal factions are required to co-operate in any campaign or exercise, it is possible that the personal factor may affect the result, making it less good than it could have been, politically if not militarily.

The Chinese People's Liberation Army began its new post-liberation role in the new People's Republic in 1949 with a rich reputation. It had defeated its Guomindang rivals over the length and breadth of China in swashbuckling style, like a combination of Genghis Khan and Robin Hood. In the middle of the protracted civil war, it had helped considerably to defeat the Japanese army on the battlefields of north China during the closing stages of the Pacific War. After the People's Republic was established, it went on to win laurels in the Korean War, which the Chinese saw as a Western attempt under General MacArthur to invade northeast China and destroy much of its industrial potential. General Peng Dehuai succeeded brilliantly, against many odds, in forcing the American and other United Nations allied troops back to the 38th parallel dividing North Korea from South Korea. Indeed Peng was so praised for his success that he was later emboldened to challenge Mao Zedong in the Central Committee, criticising both his disastrous Great Leap Forward policies and by implication his leadership. Peng's career was very brief after that.

The Chinese army maintained its good reputation in a number of smaller skirmishes or border wars, notably at the Russian frontier on the Amur–Ussuri river, and on the Indian Himalayan border in the 1960s. In each case the Chinese military tactics were well chosen, well timed and well carried out, however gauche the diplomacy that accompanied them. But then came the little war with Vietnam in 1979 which was Deng Xiaoping's introduction to supreme responsibility for important foreign policy matters.

The purpose of the Chinese incursion was to make clear to the Vietnamese Communists that they could not harass China's protégé, Cambodia, in its hour of weakness in the south, and leave their Chinese flank unguarded in the north. China, not Russia, was to be seen to be boss in southeast Asia. China was a principal backer of Cambodian independence, and the Chinese invasion gave notice of its intentions to try and stop Vietnam from turning Cambodia into a colony of its own. But the campaign was not well planned. The equipment used by China was largely outdated, some of it going back to the Pacific War, while ironically the Vietnamese used newer weapons which they had purchased more recently from China.

This left the Chinese armed forces at the time with a complaint. They badly needed to update their armaments, and have spent more in the past five years or so than they had earlier, explaining to foreign enquirers that this was because of the once-for-all opportunity of purchasing cheap surplus materiel from post-Soviet Russia. Deng Xiaoping took pains in the later 1980s to see that the military budget was increased year by year. It has doubled since 1988, and went up by a further 21 per cent in 1995, though that was less than the anticipated inflation.[23] The politicians saw in 1989 in Tiananmen Square how much they must finally depend on soldiers to maintain their authority in the event of a severe challenge. But China has no record of expansion beyond its pre-claimed territorial frontiers in modern times.

Indeed the frustration of the Communists has been precisely that they took power at the lowest historical ebb of modern Chinese territorial extent, and therefore felt obliged to recover pieces of 'lost' Chinese territory. That list includes Tibet, Taiwan, Hongkong, Macao and a few small unstrategic and largely uninhabited stretches of land on the long Indian and Russian frontiers. Those stretches have mostly been occupied by China for many years already, though approval from the other side is still awaited. That is largely a question of prestige: the other country does not seriously want the territory back, but feels humiliated at 'losing' it by force.

Tibet has been recovered, to become a major focus of Western criticism of China. That is a political rather than a military matter, however, and there is always the hope that a future Chinese régime, succeeding Deng Xiaoping's, would recognise the advantage of taking a lower profile in Tibet and shepherding it towards a substantial degree of autonomy. Taiwan, Hongkong and Macao are in a quite different category from the interior border questions. They are undeniably Chinese societies, though they happen for historical reasons to be governed by Guomindang, British and Portuguese authorities respectively. Deng achieved an agreement for Hongkong to retrocede to China peacefully in 1997, and then won a similar arrangement for Macao to follow in 1999.

It is Taiwan which remains the difficult question for China. So far China has never been able seriously to threaten Taiwan militarily. The Chinese are well aware of the desirability, for both sides and for world opinion as well, of effecting the adhesion of Taiwan to the Chinese People's Republic peacefully. But now the government in Taiwan is becoming more liberal, presiding over a pluralistic political system where a big opposition party in the legislature has openly opted for a policy of independence from China rather than reunification. Nothing could be more calculated to stoke the fires of Chinese anger, particularly in a situation where China has for many decades been simply unable to launch any kind of attack on Taiwan. That would require a larger and more powerful fleet, and the backing of a larger and more powerful air force,[24] to be sure of vanquishing the substantial Taiwan army.

The Democratic People's Party, which leads the Taiwan opposition, has since toned down its independence policy, saying that it is not an urgent issue and does not call for immediate implementation. China is unlikely to launch an invasion, even if seriously provoked, because it would not care to be seen by mainland Chinese or, indeed, by foreigners as capable of killing its own fellow-Chinese people on a large scale in order to achieve political objectives – although it was able to alarm Taiwan with missile practice held near the Taiwan coast during the presidential elections of 1996. The military will steadily increase its capacity in order to acquire the capability for such an invasion and thus lend plausibility to Chinese pressure. Yet for the time being China has to confess its technical inability to manufacture jumbo jets or large naval ships comparable to those available in the West.

The Chinese army will also react to a number of other likely developments in east Asia. For one thing, there is the possibility of China, Hongkong, Taiwan, Macao and Singapore forming a loose network of ethnic Chinese states, collaborating with each other economically and culturally. China would wish to dominate such a grouping, as it would be expected to, and to be ready to act for itself and the others in the event of any outside interference. The army might thus secure a positive role in an emerging Chinese sphere of influence.

Such a development would cause some unease in the non-Chinese states of east Asia (led by Japan and Korea but also including Indonesia, Malaysia and other southeast Asian countries) and might lead them to band together to counter what they may perceive as a Chinese threat. Alarmed by China's use of air and naval power to assert its perceived rights in the multi-claimed Spratly Islands in the South China Sea, the southeast Asian countries have recently begun to discuss their security and military co-ordination.

China's growing weapons trade will also affect these power equations. China, if it holds together, will emerge as a global military superpower, although that would be many years ahead. Who can tell how Europe and America, as well as south, central and western Asia, will react to these remarkable changes which would modulate the global balance of power?

At home, Deng and his followers have done much to keep the army and its generals on the straight and narrow path of staying out of politics. They have begun the process, always difficult, of slimming a bloated army in the interests of efficiency. There is less chance than before of a bold general successfully intervening in the political life of the country.

Only if the post-Deng administration reveals itself as disastrously inept and indecisive might the army strike to instal new leaders – but that would be through political, not physical action favouring alternative civilian, not military leaders. Abroad, it will be decades before that same army can fight effectively on foreign soil, save for border skirmishes. China maintains its army for general duties and for two specific purposes: to keep the pressure on Taiwan to reunify, and to deal with border problems of which the knottiest now is the Spratly Islands.

These are the political realities which any party or group seeking leadership must face. But there is one other challenge, and that is to maintain a good pace of *economic* development without a painful loss in the value of the currency.

PART THREE

ECONOMY

CHAPTER 7

ECONOMIC REFORM STRATEGY: IVY ON THE WALL

Mao Zedong, son of a successful peasant farmer, led the decisive liberation of China from feudalism in 1949 and offered a stringent strain of socialism in its place. Though never himself trained in Russia, he broadly trod on Stalin's heels, dispossessing landlords, collectivising farmers and fostering factories behind the protective stockade of state ownership. Disappointed with the resulting rate of economic growth from a baseline – 1949 – which marked the nadir of China's material fortunes, Mao tried in the later 1950s to quicken the pace. In the Great Leap Forward of 1958 he mobilised 'people power' to substitute for the new technology China could not afford. When that misfired, leading tragically to mass famine which claimed millions of lives, Mao had to yield to his more orthodox colleagues, including Deng Xiaoping. For five years Mao sulked in the wings, and then he wrought a terrible revenge on most of those colleagues, humiliating and physically tormenting them in the Cultural Revolution of the late 1960s, while the economy faltered.

This was the inheritance of Deng Xiaoping, son of a small landlord, when, having been spared the worst punishments in the Cultural Revolution, his turn for supreme power came in 1978. He and his friends had stood helpless on the sidelines during the shattering failure of Mao's Great Leap Forward, and had personally suffered in the Cultural Revolution of the 1960s. Determined to avoid such excesses again, they looked for new recipes for material development. Mao had two achievements to his credit. He had initiated a society of farmers into the idea of industrialisation, and he had managed to concentrate resources for the big dams and other construction projects which those farmers needed. To that end he succeeded in raising investment and centralising the control of the economy, but he failed to galvanise the productivity of China's workers or convincingly lift their standard of living. The World Bank counted 300 million people living in absolute poverty when Deng took power. Mao's growth strategies had no more relevance.

Deng was only one of seven or eight veteran Party hands who had served the state with distinction in the more orthodox periods of Mao's supremacy, but were tormented, exiled – or worse – for their pains in the 1960s. In 1978 they were left holding the wheel with some uncertainty where best to steer. They nursed a sense of personal demoralisation, along with a certain dissatisfaction, in some cases, with Marxism. Only the irrepressible Deng, taking the leading position in the new ruling group, kept his self-confidence intact.

Too much damage had been done by Mao for these survivors simply to return to the policies of family farming by contract which had briefly prevailed during the Chairman's few years of disgrace in the early 1960s. That was the right direction, but something more thoroughgoing was now called for. Deng was able to explain better than his colleagues the market reforms and the Open Door policy which he believed could do the trick. He won the crucial support of Chen Yun, the self-educated typesetter who had become the acknowledged economic theorist in the Politburo though lacking Deng's political flair. The two of them set the guidelines for the new era, though Chen subsequently took issue with Deng for going too fast and succumbing to the charms of a younger group of technocrats with little respect for Marxist ideals.

The elders' motive was not simply material. They did not seek economic growth only for its own sake, or merely to satisfy their people's yearnings for a better life. Economic achievement was to them also a road back into the respect of the world, the kind of international power and self-respect China had enjoyed before the nineteenth century. The GNP was a benefit to the nation as well as to the people, and this perhaps accounts for a certain unexpected note of passion which may sometimes be detected when Chinese talk about their economic development.

When Deng and his colleagues looked at the world around them in the late 1970s, they saw for the most part higher standards of living and better technology based on the system of capitalism. The palpable success of an ideology they had shunned all their lives obviously disturbed them. Despite the apparent intellectual inconsistency, Chen Yun, anchor man for the early ideals of socialism, often spoke in a conciliatory or ambivalent manner about capitalism. He once told financial officials that China would lose out in world markets 'if we do not make a study of capitalism'.[1] On another occasion he observed that 'capitalists possess an ability which could be utilised to the advantage of socialism, outweighing the disadvantages'.[2] Another veteran Communist, Li Xiannian, told a visitor in 1979 that there was blindness in both capitalism and socialism: 'in China we sometimes produce blindly without knowing what the customer really needs.'[3] Deng Xiaoping echoed these ideas, and embroidered them with the comment that 'if capitalism has something good, then socialism should bring it over and use it.'[4]

Some of the younger officials and intellectuals were even more outspoken. Xu Jiatun, the former provincial boss who became China's representative in Hongkong in the 1980s but was so sympathetic with the Tiananmen demonstrators that he chose exile in California when they failed, lyrically described modern capitalism just before his defection as 'a masterpiece of human civilisation, with a relatively comprehensive legal system, an environment of free competition, and hard-working managers and middle class'.[5] Hu Sheng, President of the Chinese Academy of Social Sciences, invoked the famous tract of Mao Zedong, *On Coalition Government* (1945), for the quotation that 'it is not domestic capitalism but foreign imperialism and domestic feudalism which are superfluous in China today: indeed, we have too little of capitalism.' Hu's gloss on the Chairman's words was that China had lost out by not having a capitalist legacy in between pre-1949 feudalism and post-1949 socialism. The Chinese should therefore study the industrial experience of capitalism, and Mao had been wrong to ignore this or to think of it as contradicting socialist principles.[6]

A certain degree of capitalism had been biding its time all along in some towns, ready to spring out and resume business as soon as the reformers in Beijing waved the starting flag. Wenzhou, just 250 miles from Shanghai, is such a town. It used to be a haven of capitalists before the Communists came to power, and even after 1949 it demonstrated the cohesiveness and spirit effectively to defy the Communist Party. Jiang Qing, Mao's widow, had remarked during China's ultra-left period, 'if you want to see capitalism, visit Wenzhou.'[7] A more recent description had it as 'this flourishing city of Dickensian capitalism', where private factories hire labourers to work twelve hours a day, seven days a week. When soldiers fired at Wenzhou's democracy protesters in June 1989, local 'capitalist' tycoons sent donations to the men who fired the shots, thus shrewdly ensuring that Wenzhou would not be punished by hard-line leaders in Shanghai or Beijing.[8]

There were many former capitalists in China who had lain low during the reign of Mao, in Wenzhou and elsewhere, and were now quite ready to begin again from where they had left off – if the Communist Party permitted them. And there were many younger well-educated officials prepared to act literally on the new call for entrepreneurs who would raise money and take risks on the basis of their own assessment of the market.

Deng initially declared, cautiously, that while market forces provided 'a useful supplement', and one that was 'not harmful on the whole' to planning, it was central planning that should still predominate. Whether he said such things sincerely, or was seeking to lull his remaining socialist comrades into acceptance of his reforms, is debatable.[9] But the mood changed over the 1980s. When a journalist on the *Economic Daily* in Shanghai learnt that the non-state sector was now producing 47 per cent of China's industrial output, he could write quite openly, 'This is not just "supplementary" to the state sector, it is an equal partnership.'

Deng himself was quite innocent of economics, of any variety. In order to decide what reforms to introduce, and in what order, he surrounded himself with younger officials and economists, including many who had studied economics in Western universities. Except when he felt they were going too far or too fast for comfort, or for squaring with the veteran conservatives, Deng boldly backed his tyros and gave them the necessary political support to implement their ideas. Sadly, he was not able to find senior political leaders ready to take up the lead of the reform movement after him. Zhao Ziyang and Hu Yaobang were both dismissed from office in the 1980s (and Hu has since died). These two had remarkably open minds, but the reformers could also be more impulsive, sometimes even reckless, in trying to push reforms before they had a reasonable chance of acceptance.

If the reformers were happy to release the forces of individual private enterprise, other leaders were less sure. One might have thought that bureaucracy would drag its feet on the reforms. But civil servants soon saw how rich the pickings would be for them, as had already happened in capitalist Singapore. Everyone professes to support reform, and they all accept the initial reforms in agriculture, but some resist the rapid introduction of new reforms, and some have particular constituencies to protect. Deng might have to bow to the conservatives on social policy, for example, or treatment of political dissidents, in order to save an economic reform.

The Tiananmen killings in 1989, where reformers, including Zhao Ziyang, interceded on the students' side, was a setback for the progressive group. In the mid-1990s, with the help of Deng, they started to come back into public life. Much to the annoyance and fierce opposition of veterans like Chen Yun (and even with the disapproval sometimes of Deng himself) they have publicly forecast China's need for more political parties and democratic politics.

The co-existence of reformers and conservatives in the Party and government is explained by the fact that the conservatives need to make the economy more efficient so that they can reward their own constituencies. Everybody in China would like to be better off, and if his political mentor or patron does not arrange it, he may defect to another. There are enough instances of the wives and children of senior politicians and bureaucrats in both camps, for and against reform, being able to make money out of the market reforms, and senior generals in the army doing the same, to make it clear that this is another force that binds the reform coalition. William Overholt, the American analyst, describes China's power élite as enlisted in reform through a combination of 'idealism, expedience and corruption'.[10]

Some of China's veteran planners debunked the new ideas. A market economy may be practical in small places like Hongkong and Singapore, they argued, but how could it possibly lead to anything but chaos in a country of China's size? In the West there are indirect controls to restrain the excesses of capitalism, but China has no such machinery. Goh Keng Swee, the long-time Finance Minister of Singapore, noted that central banks can influence money supply in the West, and national taxes are used to influence the demand for goods, but in China these levers are either very weak or non-existent.[11]

A huge lacuna in China's system from the point of view of free-enterprise capitalist operations is the rule of law. The traditional legal system is arbitrary, politicised and geared more to conciliation than adjudication. It is widely flouted, and Qiao Shi, one of the three or four most powerful men in China, has explained rather apologetically that the government would make special efforts to ensure that laws which are promulgated are observed.

The capacity of lower officials to effectively ignore orders from higher up is illustrated by one mouse (junior official) telling the other not to worry as the cat (senior official) is only going through the motions of some new directive (*Popular Tribune*, no. 4, 1994).

'If a law is not observed,' he said, 'it will mean nothing.'[12] There could be no truer testimony to the unreadiness of Chinese society for modern Western-style life. Under Mao state enterprises, for example, were treated as bureaucratic extensions of the government, not needing any separate legal framework. The transition now is arduous.

Having substituted a new market-enterprise system to correct the Maoist economic mistakes, Deng also reversed Mao's isolation of China in the world. Dazzled by the electronic achievements he saw in the USA in 1973, Deng proclaimed an Open Door through which China could import the latest technology and managerial skills. These were to be the twin pillars of Deng's new-look China after 1978 – economic reform at home, and the Open Door to the West. He was not alone in this. Other leaders in the regions marked by Chinese civilisation had already come to the same conclusion. Lee Kuan Yew was elected Prime Minister of Singapore as a strident socialist, but soon recognised the value of the market if carefully tempered by government. Park Chung Hee also began life as a left-winger but actually guided South Korea to prosperity through controlled free enterprise, while Chiang Ching-kuo, President of Taiwan in the 1980s, ultimately forsook the Leninist ideas he had imbibed as a student in Moscow in favour of a more sophisticated approach, bringing Taiwan almost to a European standard of living.

All three of these east Asians were moulders of their country and pioneers in uncoupling them from inappropriate foreign ideologies. Deng Xiaoping, the diminutive chain-smoker from China's interior regions, now joined these ranks of pathfinders. If he could extend the benefits of the market to China's hundreds of millions without plunging them into anarchy, returning to the mixed economy ideas of Sun Yatsen in the 1920s, history would rank his achievement even higher than that of those pioneers. The initial steps showed all the hallmarks of Deng's practical peasant wisdom. His reforms were gradual, introduced after experiments in some locality or other. The old familiar ways of doing things went on in the background, allowing the new ideas time to gain acceptance. The market, said one of Deng's best technocrats, should 'overgrow the planning, like ivy on a wall'.[13]

Two kinds of prices co-existed, for instance, in a two-tier

structure, one planned, the other varying with market supply and demand. Critics were quick to point out what absurdities this could bring about. A factory might deliver a third of its output of rubber gloves to the buyer designated by the bureaucracy at a low planned price, as agreed. If that buyer wanted more, another third might be sent on to him additional to his 'entitlement' or quota, with the price adjusted to the market rate. The remaining third could then be sold to another customer 'outside the plan' – at market prices, of course. Surprisingly, Chinese factory managers took all this in their stride.

It is easier to defend such gradualism, or what economists call incrementalism, when a reform proves self-reinforcing. The first farm reforms, for example, abolished the Maoist people's communes in favour of first group and then family farming. That encouraged more savings by individual farmers, but also threw up some unemployment. Rural processing factories were obviously the way to mop up both these surpluses, and such enterprises were therefore encouraged to the point of being freed from local authority control. Eventually these vigorous new town and village enterprises did so well that they began to compete with the bureaucratically hampered state factories, which responded by pressing the state authorities to relax their controls and allow them more freedom. That in turn stimulated the state to reform its public finances. One good reform leads to another. There is no master plan.

The State Commission for Restructuring the Economic System wrote fourteen reform blueprints in the first decade of reform, and yet none – for various political, economic or technical reasons – was actually implemented. The whole process was piecemeal rather than gradual.

The dual-track character of Deng's reforms first revealed itself in the price reform, but it has also extended to the reform of foreign exchange, labour, housing, social security and ownership, so that the whole Chinese economy is, in a sense, evolving into a dual-track economy. The reformers take refuge in the truism that 'nobody can design a market economy'.

The market price proved to be a very strong contender in economic transactions, as the story of the price of matches shows. Before the reforms a box of matches sold at the fixed price of 2 cents, as a result of which all the factories were making losses. When the reforms started, the government tried to increase the price to 3 cents, but held back because of the complaints that would be voiced by consumers. The factories had to do something to survive, so they began putting fewer matches into the box (selling it at the same price) and designing new boxes to be sold at higher prices, which was permissible because new products need not abide by the old prices. At this point there were two prices for matches. The official price of the old kind of box was not changed, but it became harder to find in the market and eventually disappeared. The result is that all matches in China now sell at the market price.[14]

Behind such apparent irresolution lies a leading canon of Chinese psychology, whereby change is effected peacefully through allowing the losers some retained position or 'face'. Deng softened the resistance of powerful bureaucrats by arranging for them to enjoy better opportunities and even larger earnings from the reforms. One Chinese economist goes so far as to say that the reforms 'have not stripped any major interest groups of their vested interests, but just changed the ways in which these vested interests are materialised'.[15] The dual-track idea allows those who run the old system to have their status quo respected. If the reforms transfer economic power from bureaucrats to entrepreneurs, why not let the bureaucrats *become* entrepreneurs – and if they are not qualified, or not willing to take the risk, why not at least let them become 'shareholders'? President Jiang Zemin has recently put the matter with commendable clarity. 'Reform,' he declared, 'must be carried out under a stable situation, within the tolerance of the vast number of staff and workers and with their support, otherwise, the desired goals of reform will not be achieved.'[16]

The same leader placed the burden on the 'planners' to salvage any chaos that ensued. 'With the imperfect development of the market system, the incomplete transformation of enterprise operating mechanisms and the incomprehensive growth of enterprise groups, it is still difficult for the fundamental role of the market in material resources distribution to be totally effective for the time being.'[17]

The Chinese economy emerges, in a World Bank economist's

description, as 'half-reformed', leaving China without any one single economic system prevailing, so that the defects of both are magnified, leading to high levels of corruption, inefficiency and imbalance of production. Yet this is a rather short view. Economic reforms must in the end change not merely the system, but also the people, their habits, their behaviour and their value judgements. Under Mao's command economy no one needed to show initiative, innovation or creativity. That has now changed, but how many years or decades does it take for a national entrepreneurial class to emerge, after thirty years of heavy suppression?

A crucial consequence of Deng's reforms was a decentralisation of economic power far more sweeping than anyone at the top had intended. When conservative bureaucrats in the central ministries in Beijing obstructed Premier Zhao Ziyang's reform measures, he resorted to winning the support of provincial governments which were much more in favour of his programme, and in the end it was the local governments which dismantled much of the planning system and came to dominate the reforms. Zhao Ziyang himself had been picked out by Deng Xiaoping as a likely reform-minded local government leader to be promoted into the centre, and the same could be said of Wan Li, the former Governor of Anhui province.

A less admirable characteristic of the reforms came to be the frequent changes of gear, whereby a reform drive was usually followed by a setback and only later by another push. In a 'two steps forward, one step back' pattern, important reform measures may be implemented in the 'push' period, but partly withdrawn in the setback period. The result is a gradual accretion of small and half-hearted reforms, accumulating into radical change only over a period of time. A political advantage of this procedure is that conservatives and reformists can take it in turns to appear to be in charge of economic change.

Not all the reformers were happy with this way of doing things. In a government structure as big as China's it was only to be expected that there would be many differing personalities, many individual biases from training, many schools of thought about economic reform. Some of the ideas implemented by Deng Xiaoping had been hinted at twenty years earlier by economists in the various institutions of the Chinese Academy of Social

Sciences, and they were augmented in the 1980s by younger Chinese economists trained in the West.

In the end these varying views settled down into two broad camps. One was headed by Li Yining, an economics professor at Beijing University and close adviser to Zhao Ziyang. He argued that the ownership of state factories was the first thing to be reformed, before changes needed to be made in the price structure. The big state enterprises should become joint-stock companies, with the autonomy and incentive to operate efficiently in the competitive market environment which the freeing of prices would later create. But a rival school led by Wu Jinglian, adviser to the State Council, urged that all the major reforms – of prices, enterprise ownership and management of the economy – should be quickly introduced in an integrated and co-ordinated manner. Otherwise the individual reforms, undertaken one by one, could not be effective.[18] After some fifteen years of faltering and piecemeal reform, many of the impatient younger reformists were ready for a 'big bang', to get all the major changes effected swiftly – with pain all round, but pain that would rapidly fade.

Deng eventually pulled the scattered pieces of reform together into the kind of theoretical framework which the Chinese always appreciate. In 1984 the Party's Central Committee explained that 'we must draw upon the world's advanced methods of management, including those of developed capitalist countries, that conform to the laws of modern socialised production.' Ownership would be separated from management, enterprises would be made independent and responsible for their own profit or loss. The Party and state would be left merely to formulate general strategy. The freeing of prices would essentially replicate the way in which capitalist economies organised their decision-making. At last the programme began to acquire a plausible coherence.[19]

The most detailed conceptualisation of the reforms came three years later, at the Thirteenth Communist Party Congress in 1987. Zhao Ziyang, then Premier, gave the main report. The goal, he said, was to build 'socialism with Chinese characteristics', transforming China into 'a prosperous, strong, democratic, culturally advanced and modern socialist country'. Class struggle would continue, but would no longer be the main contradiction in Chinese society: that would be the contradiction between people's needs and low production. China was already a socialist society, but one still in its primary stage, and the Chinese must accept the logic of that (i.e. in not expecting rapid wealth or nation-wide welfare).

Zhao spurned the notion that China would have to go through a stage of fully developed capitalism in order to win through to the further stage of socialism. That, he said, was a mechanistic way of looking at things. But he also thought it wrong and utopian to believe that China could jump over the primary stage of socialism during which the forces of production were to be developed. The capitalist road, he said firmly, was 'a blind alley' for China, but China would need at least a hundred years to go through this primary stage of accomplishing the industrialisation and economic modernisation which so many other countries had already achieved under capitalism.

'We are not in the situation envisaged by the founders of Marxism in which socialism is built on the basis of highly-developed capitalism,' Zhao noted. China would try to go through its 'capitalist' phase under a socialist umbrella, hoping the more quickly and effectively to swing back to the advantages of a socialist society once the economic wherewithal was in place. With poverty and backwardness abolished, socialism in its fullest sense would begin. Socialism may have been found wanting as a conqueror of poverty, but using alternative means would not rob China of its socialist reward in the end.

Having proclaimed a new orthodoxy, Zhao went on to explain what it would all mean immediately for China. A fully-developed commodity economy would now have to be introduced, but with public ownership playing the dominant role. And if some comrades worried about reconciling the commodity or market economy with socialism, they should know that socialism had never required absolutely perfect egalitarian ownership and distribution of goods.[20] Other leaders followed Zhao in embroidering these remarkable proposals at the 1987 Congress, surely among the most innovative by any Communist leaders in this century. They explained that some of the measures being introduced to China, including stocks and bonds, were not unique to capitalism, but were bound to make an appearance with large-scale industrial production and a commodity economy.

'Socialism can and should make use of them, trying at the same time to minimise their negative effects in practice.' The use of the market mechanism to regulate the economy did not mean that China would be practising capitalism.

The private sector, it was said with a certain defensiveness, was now to be a 'necessary and useful supplement' to the public sector, promoting production, stimulating the market, providing jobs and helping to meet people's needs. Owners of private enterprises would, it was true, gain some income that did not arise from their own labour. But they would do so under socialist conditions; wage labour under private ownership would be subjected to the constraints of a powerful public sector and would have to abide by state promises and laws. It was therefore 'different' from the exploitation of workers in capitalist countries.[21]

Actually, the gravity of economic production has gradually shifted towards the private and collective sectors, which now have a larger share than the state. A reformist newspaper wrote in 1993 that the predominance of public ownership had been abandoned. It was no longer necessary to talk about public ownership being the mainstay, or to set limits to the relative proportions of various components of the economy. But free competition between the sectors was not yet on the agenda. The old habit of constructive social hypocrisy kept socialism in people's mouths. 'In public,' said a successful Hunan trader, 'we still must talk socialism. But in private we all talk capitalism.'[22] When the energetic Vice-Premier Zhu Rongji spoke about socialism in Shanghai in 1993 he quoted Deng's definition. 'The socialist economy has two essential features. One, high efficiency in resource allocation and labour productivity. Two, social justice and common prosperity.' Not a word about public ownership.[23]

But when the stop-go aspect of market economics became more apparent in the later 1980s, and leaders had to choose between slowing down the rate of growth or allowing runaway inflation and wasted resources, the senior leaders gathered around Deng Xiaoping began to lose a little confidence. If they had been more restrained in freeing prices and ending price controls in 1988, the students might have been deprived of one of their major grievances – rising prices. There might conceivably have been no Tiananmen killings in 1989, because workers and citizens might not have rallied behind the students, and the Party might not have considered the students alone as such a threat, and Zhao might have kept his job. At odds over the timing and handling of reforms, the leaders had to reach awkward compromises about the central programme of letting prices and wages find their own level. The academic debate among the economists whether prices should first be freed to create a competitive market, or whether ownership reform should take priority, grew more heated.

Chen Yun, keeper of the socialist conscience among the 'Immortals', gave the reformers pause by telling Deng Xiaoping that throwing the economy into the 'filthy pit of free competition' had led China into chaos: 'it is no different from the early stages of capitalist development.'[24] Zhao Ziyang and the reformers tried to shoot holes in Chen Yun's case, but Deng felt it politically necessary to take a midway position, agreeing with Chen Yun that measures should be taken to curb corruption, and to re-centralise the economy to some extent, but throwing his weight behind Zhao, in a typical Chinese compromise, in opening up the coastal areas and exposing China to the outside world.[25] No one tried to fling aside the slightly tattered banner of reform. But the enthusiasm for waving it was patchy.

Disproportionate political energy began to be spent on the 'stop-go' problem. While cautious conservatives like Yao Yilin and Song Ping cried 'overheating' at the slightest sign of significant inflation, Deng and his reformers would deny it. Supporting Deng's view, the Beijing University professor Li Yining argued that inflation was a feature chiefly of the belated reform in the structure of companies, and also in the financial sector which had long operated under a planned economy. In these circumstances, the national economy could not be said to be overheated as a whole, only in certain sectors. Retrenchment would not solve the problem, therefore, but would lead to the reimposition of administrative controls and spoil the unfolding reform picture.[26]

Inflation, Vice-Premier Zhu Rongji once declared, 'is more terrible than unemployment'. Li Yunqi, a People's Bank of China economist at Stanford University, explained that inflation redistributes income, but also worsens the inequities of income distribution. In a full-blooded market economy the central bank can adjust the cost and availability of funds for business through interest rates and money supply, but China's reforms had given autonomy to provincial governments and enterprises without altering the basic economic system. The cure for inflation was for the central bank to slow down the increase in money supply, raise interest rates and reduce the currency in circulation but the People's Bank lacks independence. It is surprising perhaps to find that inflation in China is modest compared with Latin America or Russia, and that the Communist government has generally succeeded in keeping it down.[27] It registered 15 per cent in 1995, and only 7% in the first half of 1996.

During the overheating of the early 1990s it was Zhu Rongji, assuming the governorship of the People's Bank as well as being Vice-Premier in charge of the economy, who had to court unpopularity by rushing round the country telling provincial leaders to restrain their spending – pulling the firewood, as the Chinese say, out of the stove. In the 1993 episode, Zhu issued a long list of austerity measures, but three months later Deng Xiaoping called for accelerating growth again. In his closing years, Deng could not restrain his impatience with any interruption of the fast growth he saw as China's salvation. Zhu was rebuked, and the provincial governors and bosses of state enterprises whom he had been urging to slam a foot on the brake could openly reproach him for misjudging the problem and overdoing austerity. Yet a few weeks later he resurfaced to argue the case with provincial bosses for more tax discipline. He was particularly concerned that the imminence of tax reform had led some provinces to collect next year's tax in advance. During these exhausting provincial rounds, Zhu complained – or boasted – that he lost more than 5 lb in weight, but he kept Deng's confidence.

In the last resort, Zhu would appeal to the socialist consciences of local people, pointing out that the future of the Communist Party depended on them. 'Since we are Communists,' he told leaders in Shanghai, 'we cannot just have the title. We must make more contributions to the people and to the state. Otherwise we cannot call ourselves public servants of the people.' At a central political meeting he described the overheating of 1993 as threatening a collapse of banks, in which case the impact on the economy would be enormous, 'and we will have to step down'.[28]

Outwardly the coalition in Beijing kept ranks. Li Peng, the conservative Russian-trained engineer who succeeded Zhao Ziyang as Prime Minister, continued to support the reforms through all the difficulties of the late 1980s. He called them a way of achieving 'the socialist system's self-improvement and self-development', and 'designed to demonstrate the superiority of the socialist system.'[29] The language was not all that different from Zhao's, though in other ways Li Peng demonstrated his more cautious approach to reform. In the end words themselves become weapons of politics. As a senior Shanghai official said of a new joint venture, 'our main aim is to help the Shanghai economy grow and make lots of profit for both sides. Of course we use another term to describe it . . . we call it economic result. But it actually means the same thing . . . profits.' A further refinement in vocabulary came at the Party's Fourteenth National Congress in 1992, where Jiang Zemin, now doing Zhao Ziyang's old job as Party Secretary-General, defined the goal as a 'socialist market economy' – an ingenious marriage of the two systems, or a blatant contradiction of them, according to one's viewpoint. Observers guessed it was Deng's idea and wondered what would happen to it after his death.[30]

When the Commission of State Economics and Trade says that the purpose of reforming state enterprises is 'to further liberate and develop the productive forces, and fully bring into play the superiority of the socialist system', one wonders if what is being so energetically preserved is simply the socialist name for an economy which is in reality changing.

There is another factor in all this. In the early 1980s many, perhaps most, politicians and economists still believed in the planned economy and public ownership. But they recognised that it was inefficient, and their concern was how to make it more businesslike. It was common ground among such people that China's economy had let the country down because of the ceaseless political movements interfering with it. The basic economic structure itself was surely sound, but it needed to be fine-tuned. So they went along with the early reforms, thinking that planning could be improved with such imports from Harvard as 'input-output analysis' and computers, and perhaps by introducing some elements of the market at the margin of the economy, not changing the whole system.

The younger economists capable of providing such fine-tuning were less interested in ideology, though they had ideals, and they were pragmatic enough to study how other economic systems actually worked instead of such academic issues as whether a particular institution or mechanism belonged to capitalism or socialism. The American economist Jan Prybyla concluded that the Chinese reformers were making things worse, because problems that had been suppressed in the past, like inflation, unemployment and differentials of income, were now brought out into the open without any means of mastering them. He advocated a new revolution against Communism.[31] But that was perhaps an over-dramatised short-term view.

The problem of decentralisation was a very real one. Relinquishing control of industrial development to provincial or municipal authorities did not always mean more market freedom for those factories, because some local governments, being physically closer on the ground, could stifle them with more planning regulations than the centre had ever decreed. It also meant a lamentable waste of investment funds and industrial resources. Within a few years of these reforms, for example, China boasted a hundred uneconomic low-capacity car assembly plants. The same thing happened with TV set production. Indeed, the mid-1980s inflation which caused the reformers to waver so disastrously, and without which the Tiananmen massacre might never have happened, was also the result of newly de-centralised state factories having a field day of over-consuming, over-investing and over-paying their workers. There was nothing to hold them back.

In Fujian province, two international airports were built simultaneously only 190 miles apart, and two more were planned only fifty miles away. A Shanghai factory making TV sets issued shares to foreign investors, but instead of using the foreign capital for TV manufacture as promised, it speculated in property. One of Zhu Rongji's jobs was to track unnecessary golf-course projects. Eight were initially approved in Shenzhen alone, and the Finance Minister came across a plan to build ten golf courses in a single coastal zone! Such extravagance and duplication weakened the economy, but the centre had no institutional means of preventing it.

During the 1980s an entirely new class and interest group of rich private businessmen began to form. Hu Dapeng of Beijing may be taken as a case-study. After working in a radio factory, he left in the early 1960s to become an individual radio repairer. This made him in the Party's eyes a private entrepreneur outside the socialist system, so he was a second-class citizen with no work card. If he parked his bicycle in a lot and lost the key, he could not get the bicycle back. But he earned enough to cope with all this until the Cultural Revolution closed his little business down and the Red Guards began to harass him. His daughter wanted to join her peers in the Red Guards, but was refused because her father did not have the correct class credentials. The pay-off came, however, in 1979 when the tools the Red Guards had confiscated were returned and he was given a licence to re-open his business. Now he has bought a Suzuki motorcycle, a refrigerator, a TV and a washing machine. His son has joined him in the business, and he has been honoured by the state.[32]

Today there are more than 30 million men and women working in the individual or private sectors, and a new monthly magazine was produced for them in 1994 called *Guangcai* (*Splendour*). The first Communist Party branch for individual entrepreneurs opened in Shenzhen; the announcement explained patronisingly that such people may vary in morals, but are mostly honest and law-abiding. In Shanghai there are 200,000 credit cards in circulation, and by the end of the century there are expected to be 200 million in the country (but these will please Zhu Rongji because they will involve a deposit of RMB for future drawing, and will thus contribute to the fight against inflation). The city of Tianjin has reported that three-quarters of its households have colour TV sets, refrigerators and recorders, while 83 per cent had washing machines: these markets were considered saturated.

A recent survey showed that four million Chinese are earning the equivalent of $2,900 a month, which is eleven times the national average. Among these, pop singers, film stars and fashion models are the leaders. China's favourite actress, Gong Li, was paid one million RMB for a TV commercial for air-conditioners lasting only one minute, and she did not have to speak a word (within three days a gullible public bought 100 million RMB-worth). Popular singers can ask RMB 10,000 for a performance. A second category of *nouveaux riches* is, naturally, the entrepreneurs, and third come the senior government officials who until recently could get documentation to import foreign goods and sell them in the domestic market at a profit. Fourth come the scientists who can make money from patenting their inventions, especially in the field of computers. Finally the Chinese yuppies, mostly working for joint ventures with a foreign employer, can earn up to $2,000 a month and used to be able to profit from the former dual-track foreign exchange system.[33]

Within the past two years a new phenomenon has been observed outside China, namely the arrival of children of rich Chinese to attend schools in the West and Japan. Huang Wei, aged fourteen, arrived in Britain to take an English language course, after which he hoped to enrol at either Eton or Harrow. The headmaster of a well-known British public school received a hundred replies when he advertised in Beijing. There are now about 2,000 Chinese students at British universities and colleges, Jung Chang, author of *Wild Swans*, being a pioneer in taking a PhD at York University in 1982. If a grant is not available, this kind of expense can be undertaken only by the very rich.

The Beijing leaders respond to this unwelcome offshoot of their reforms by puritanical homilies which must simply fly over the heads of their intended hearers. Consider this passage in a speech by Li Ruihuan in 1993 in Hebei province:

> Tens of millions of people have yet to solve their food and clothing problems. We must make arduous efforts over a long time in order to have China catch up with developed countries. Our generation is destined to do pioneering work and to bear hardships. The practices of wheeling and dealing, extravagant drinking and eating ... the ideas of money worship, egoism and hedonism; and the admiration of those who make and spend money in a big way – an admiration which now

> prevails among people in society – are quite incompatible with the conditions of our country. These are inauspicious.[34]

Inauspicious it may be, but conspicuous consumption has spread all over China, and in the absence of an effective income tax or other organised social restraints, it will go on being indulged whether the central leaders like it or not.

One should not exaggerate the rifts in the reform coalition. After the overheating crisis of 1993, when Deng Xiaoping and Chen Yun were in virtually open disagreement over the speed with which the credit squeeze should be lifted and the reforms pursued again, Zhu Rongji and others of his generation brokered a compromise between the two Immortals rather than putting their weight fully behind Deng, which might have risked a debilitating stand-off at the highest levels of power.

Looking back on Deng's statements, one can see two basic concepts. On the one hand he sought to cut the ground from under the feet of the old-fashioned conservatives who disliked his reform programme because it promoted social inequality. 'We oppose egalitarianism,' he roundly declared in 1983, 'because it is not beneficial to development.' That effectively underpinned the reformists' arguments. But then Deng also said on another occasion that 'we shall persist in the socialist principle of distribution, and reject polarisation.' China would follow the 'socialist principle of distribution according to labour input', and this would mean that, even when Chinese industry became developed in another twenty or thirty years' time, 'there will be no polarisation'.[35] Yet it is common ground among the younger reformists that there would have to be some private incomes not earned by labour but accruing to owners of factories. Another consistent theme of Deng's has been to back the Special Economic Zones of the coastal areas, and he continued to do this even after the departure of their patron, Zhao Ziyang, and even after other elderly leaders had bitterly criticised them.

Behind all the debating points lay, of course, much deeper matters to do with the role of the individual in Chinese society and the future political structure most suitable for the economically advanced population that should emerge at the end of the reforms. Liu Zaifu spoke for many intellectuals at the humane end of Chinese scholarship when he wrote in 1986 (*On the Composite Aspects of Human Nature*) that the Chinese individual had traditionally been 'appendaged to a fixed position in the feudal and patriarchal framework', so that individuality had been 'drowned in the sea of common attributes' and effectively stamped out. Now, as the twenty-first century looms over the horizon, state, government and Party should not interfere with a person's individuality, Liu went on, but should rather respect whatever role he or she chooses to play in society – as long as the rights of others are not endangered.[36] The Oriental Moral Research Institute recently established in Beijing with the mandate of promoting traditional moral standards recognises this question.[37]

These are the political questions which the reform arguments must ultimately encompass. But for the moment the issues are the more mundane ones of when and how to control credit and money supply, when and how to let prices follow the market, when and how to compel managers to make their own decisions and stand by the results in terms of profit and loss. These innovations were first broached among China's 900 million farmers.

CHAPTER 8

THE FARMERS: BACK TO THE FAMILY

Farmers do not often form the shock troops in campaigns for modern reform. But China is different. Its agriculture is underdeveloped, its economy under-industrialised, its people devastated by decades of war. There was a yearning for change. Mao's answer had been the people's commune, strong on irrigation, good at managing the rural environment, making a start on health and education facilities and giving farmers more alternative employment to become more self-sufficient in simple processing and manufactures. But none of these boons could compensate for the fact that farm output per head actually stagnated during Mao's rule.[1] Collectivised farmers had no incentive to harvest more, and during the appalling famine of 1960–62 at least 20 million people died of starvation or malnutrition.[2] Some of those died because of freak weather conditions, but the tragedy was mainly the fault of Mao's amateurish policies.

China's farmers face a daunting challenge from nature. Their land is more mountainous than any other major state, with 60 per cent of the country lying more than 3,250 feet above sea-level, and a third of it over 6,500 feet – almost as high as the Urals or Mount Kosciusko in Australia. Two-thirds of China in the west and north is semi-arid desert or wasteland, and only one-tenth of China's land is fit for cultivating. Chinese farms have to feed 22 per cent of the world's population on only 5 per cent of the world's arable land. This is not like the lush tropical agriculture of southeast Asia or the temperate farming of Europe – it is backbreaking and impoverishing.

Even before Mao's death in 1976 some farmers were venting their anger and frustration. In Fujian province, notoriously good at flouting central control, thousands of farm collectives disbanded, dividing the land among their individual members.[3] In other parts of the wayward south, private farming reappeared, using underground warehouses safe from the prying eyes of Communist officials. Farming in the south is quite different from that in the north of China. Wheat and other cereals are the main crops in the north, where relatively flat land makes large-scale cultivation with tractors and other machinery possible. In the south, by contrast, the main crop is rice, requiring more complex watering arrangements and frequently grown on hilly terrain where tractors are not much use. The north lends itself better to planning, whereas southern agriculture is more personal and idiosyncratic. It is no accident, perhaps, that the momentum for reforms has come from the south, the historical centre for rebellion.

So when Deng Xiaoping gave the signal to dismantle the collectives, the first village actually to do it was Xiangyang in Sichuan, though local experiments with family farming had already been conducted in Fengyang County in Anhui province. Encouraged by the Sichuan Party Secretary – none other than Zhao Ziyang before his elevation to be Prime Minister – the county around Xiangyang tried out a new contract farming system in 1978. You could control your own little piece of land, on condition you provided a fixed amount of the crop to the government.

It worked, producing more grain from more satisfied farmers, and Xiangyang was made the test site for further reform trials. Today that pioneering pocket of interior Sichuan runs about 90 per cent of its economy by the market mechanism. Only a quarter of the farmers are still on the land, the others working in village businesses. Over fifteen years, Xiangyang village has built eight elementary schools, a secondary school, an old people's home, a technical school, community centre, library, theatre and dance hall for its 10,000 inhabitants. Farm incomes quadrupled, harvests climbed by 6 per cent a year and county revenues by 15 per cent a year.[4] Zhao sold his ideas to Deng Xiaoping and was brought into the central government as Premier to see them implemented across China.

Deng made China's farmers draw lots for individual plots of former commune land, to hold on lease for between fifteen and twenty-five years. At one stroke, at the start of the 1980s, 180 million farming families had their own farms of more or less equal size and equal value, and China had 180 million farms that were to prove too small. The average farm unit changed from being a 1,500-acre estate worked by 13,000 labourers to a three-quarter-acre garden farmed by a single family. Bangladesh's farms, it was pointed out, are bigger.

Technically the village community – or the otherwise defunct collective – held the freehold ownership, but the leases were long enough for farmers to invest labour and money in their fields. A percentage of each crop was to go to the government, and farm prices were raised generally by 25 per cent. Later they went up by 50 per cent, and were doubled for grain. These measures led to a surge in rural incomes by an annual 15 per cent, at least into the mid-1980s. The resulting rise in farm savings naturally found its way into rural enterprises, whether processing, basic manufacturing or servicing. Some of them replaced what had formerly gone on in the collective communes but on an independent commercial basis.

As the lease terms ran on, some economists saw the farmers' interest in infrastructural work falling off, and the gains from the reforms wavering. 'Agriculture,' a State Planning Commission economist concluded after ten years, 'has about reached its limit of development on the household basis. The household responsibility system, though successful in the past decade in promoting farm production, has dispersed farmlands, technical knowhow and capital and made large-scale and comprehensive investment impossible.'[5]

The late 1980s and early 1990s saw modifications of the household contract system. In many places, farmers are now allocated two or three different types of plot. One is the kind allotted equally to everybody, as in the original reform, which is fixed and cannot be reallocated by the authorities. Here a farmer can grow what he likes, and has only to pay tax to the state. A second type of plot is the 'responsibility' plot, which *can* be reallocated, and which is contracted to farmers in return for their providing grain to fulfil government quotas as well as contributing to collective expenses which are administered by local officials. Sometimes there is a third kind of plot which ambitious farmers may bid for, and their income from that would be a major source of revenue for the collective expenses in the village.[6]

This is one way for the authorities to ensure that the irrigation ditches and dams are maintained and, where necessary, extended. Even in China's imperial days, farmers had co-operated to control water and maintain defence against intruders, distributing the financial burden among themselves, and indeed, the people's commune of Mao Zedong was in some sense a natural, if over-coercive successor to the nineteenth-century market town with its satellite villages and system of internal collaboration.[7] The Communist Party might well have recollectivised in the late 1980s, in order to achieve the best long-term infrastructural and environmental conditions for farming, but instead it authorised a more complex and more sophisticated version of household farming which encouraged responsibility for better rural management. One series of local experiments was with a kind of co-operative, to develop specialised infrastructure services on a share-capital basis, funded through village taxes and thus side-stepping the need for recollectivisation of the land. Reluctant farmers were not press-ganged into undertaking the dirty work beyond their fields which is necessary for the common good.

In Mao's communes thousands of farmers had been organised in large units of land to utilise the off-seasons for digging ditches and building dams for the common good. The acreage served by irrigation, especially powered irrigation, was decisively expanded. Western economists dismissed this at the time as resulting from an unacceptable coercion of the farmers by the Communist authorities. Yet Deng's reforms left farmers with an average of nine separate small fragments of land – and with less powerful social organisations to maintain, repair, renew or extend those vital ditches, the precious water from which is needed for their crops to grow tall and rich. Now this unpopular but necessary work can be done for a market wage by men and women who are not forced into it politically but cannot find other work.

The government used to intercede in the distribution system by procuring from farmers grain and other vital crops, such as cotton, sugar and tobacco, for onward sale to urban consumers.

Only very recently have some areas – led, as before, by the county around Xiangyang in Sichuan – taken full advantage of the ending of quotas, while paying income tax instead, with city dwellers receiving cash payments from the government instead of subsidised grain rations.[8] The money economy asserts itself, and farming falls in line with the market mechanism. Prices of these staple products have been allowed to move nearer to the market price (and for a few months in 1993 were actually decontrolled altogether). The conversion of the state subsidy into what amounted to supplementary wages for city dwellers laid the groundwork for important price reforms for grain and oilseeds in the 1990s. Procurement contracts for grain, sugar and oilseeds are abolished, leaving only cotton under official controls.

These new freedoms invigorated the farmers' sideline activities: so-called rural Township and Village Enterprises flourished in the 1980s and set a lead even for the more experienced city industries. This is a kind of corporate organisation which has not been seen before in China. Its ownership varies, and may be extremely informal, governed by the traditional, pre-Communist network of reciprocal obligations or *guanxi*. Some are owned by local governments, others are private enterprises in all but name. They do not compel, they compete fiercely with each other and with outsiders, they do not observe political correctness, they are not significantly subsidised by their local governments and do not have easy access to bank loans, so they depend on their own savings and are therefore heavily profit-motivated.

Because urban factories are so inefficient, and have been feeling sorry for themselves during this period of unwelcome change, these rural Township and Village Enterprises have rushed into the light industry export limelight, selling US$12 billion of goods overseas annually.[9] Many of the basic consumer goods like textiles and simple electronics now exported for sale in American or European high streets originated from these villages or small towns. These rural enterprises came to account for 40 per cent of China's industrial employment and a quarter of its exports. To the more conservative central politicians they represented the sudden arrival of an undisciplined and unruly player in the economy, and when those conservatives had a chance to dictate a policy of austerity in 1989–90 they made sure that the deflation measures hit rural enterprises hard, hoping to benefit the ailing state factories. In three years almost 400,000 rural enterprises had to close, while the survivors laid off almost three million employees. But the state enterprises fared even worse, so that rural enterprises were able to gain the respect of government economists by increasing their share of industrial output.

Linking these successes to the new freedom from regulation, a county entrepreneur and vice-president of a clothing factory in northern China noted that his factory paid its technicians RMB 15 more than its salesmen, to convey a respect for knowledge. 'This would be impossible to implement in a state enterprise.' These rural enterprises can act quickly to profit from market trends. A rural cement factory converted its standing kiln into a revolving one, more than doubling its productivity, in only eight months. 'Any technology that I can use,' said the director, 'can be implemented right away with the factory's approval. This contrasts with state enterprises, where everything has to go through layers and layers of requests and approvals.' As another county enterprise leader gleefully put it, in a state enterprise 'You submit an application one year, the second year the proposal is evaluated, the third year you still haven't heard anything.'[10] (In the city of Guangzhou alone there are more than a hundred government departments directly administering state enterprises.)

But if the rural enterprise responds well to market signals from the outside, internally it might be said to resemble a miniature planned economy. It relies on the natural leaders which rural society throws up (often people of former landlord or money-lending families who have inherited some drive and panache, and also former grassroots leaders from commune days) and does not insist on a high level of democracy. Its overheads are few. Villages have a natural social security mechanism which lets the enterprise off the hook when it comes to welfare benefits for employees. If some workers have to be laid off, they can simply go home and tend their crops. Managers of state industries in the cities facing lay-offs must be green with envy.

The physical side of farming is in fairly good shape. Spectacular gains were made with new high-yielding rice hybrids introduced widely in the early 1980s: they now cover almost two-thirds of the total irrigated rice-fields. President Ferdinand Marcos of the Philippines gave Chinese visitors a bag of the new high-yield rice developed by the International Rice Institute outside Manila, and the Chinese put it to good use. Now China grows six tons of rice to an acre, more than three times the yield of Indian farmers.[11] But economists predict that the problem of the population growing faster than the grain harvests will hit China hard in the years ahead. There has actually been a fall in the area of farmland cultivated during the 1980s, mainly because of low prices of outputs and high prices of inputs, although this has been partly offset recently by more multi-cropping – growing two or more crops a year on the same piece of land. Harvests per head are expected to rise by only 1 or 2 per cent a year in the 1990s, and affluent farmers are eating more grain themselves. One consequence is that higher meat consumption is blocked by the shortage of grain needed to feed the animals. The Chinese proverbially love pork in any form, but in 1987 rationing had to be reintroduced in the big cities because the price of pigfeed rose so high. Not only meat but rice, flour and edible oils were rationed in Shanghai and several other cities in 1995.[12]

So what will happen? Will China's consumers go hungry, or will fashion and improved diet gradually wean them away from wheat and rice? Or will there have to be substantial imports, which would be of great interest to the cereal-producing countries around the Pacific, especially the USA, Australia and Canada? American wheat is not much dearer than Chinese, and some economists in China argue that a modest import programme would be better than aiming for self-sufficiency. China did for many years import wheat for city consumption, finding it cheaper than transporting domestic grains from the interior, but now the quantities involved will become much bigger. A vice-premier, Li Lanqing, recently warned that 'since China is a very large country and has a huge population, it is impossible to rely on foreign countries to feed us.' When Lester Brown, director of an American think-tank, rhetorically asked a ministerial-level forum on sustainable production and conservation in Oslo in 1995: 'Who will feed China?', the Chinese delegation indignantly retorted that they could feed themselves. The government used to defend its wheat imports by saying that on trade in all agricultural goods as a whole, China was in surplus. That was when rice used to be exported in modest quantities to Japan and southeast Asia. Now the pendulum has swung the other way: China is importing about 10 million tons of rice a year from Burma, Thailand and India. But selective imports should not break the Chinese bank, given the general level of exports which the country should then be generating.[13]

The great achievement of the Chinese farmers is to have decisively disproved the Communist economic philosophy and thus to have fundamentally changed China's beliefs.[14] The Communist Party and its leaders can no longer present Marxism as the infallible key to utopia. No one believes that any more. Because state-owned industry was cocooned in antediluvian regulation, so regimented that it had no room to breathe, let alone produce goods efficiently, a vacuum was left in which farming communities could flourish as manufacturers, exporting synthetic garments and transistor radios all round the world, from Europe and North America to the Pacific Islands, in open defiance of Marxist teaching.

The exploits of the farmers who made their fortunes became legendary. When Sun Guiying, a suburban chicken farmer outside Beijing, bought a new Toyota out of his egg profits and became the first farmer to own his own private car, a whole political theology crumbled into dust.[15]

Another legend built up around Daqiuzhuang, a village of 4,400 rich farm workers enjoying an average income per head of about US$8,400. The place has more than 150 Mercedes and other luxury cars. Every resident receives housing, electricity, hot water, gas, medical care and education free of charge. 'Here,' says Sun Guiqi, the senior official, 'we have reached the perfect form of socialism, i.e. Communism.' Is he mischievously provocative, or does he merely echo what Deng Xiaoping has often said about the unattractiveness of the socialism of poverty? Perhaps both. The Daqiuzhuang phenomenon is partly explained by the villagers keeping their incomes low on paper in order to avoid tax. Much of their success is owed to *guanxi*. Mr Yu, the village head, sat on a Central Committee body in Beijing, and when his son married a few years ago one of the wedding gifts was a house valued at US$275,000. Some of the houses in Daqiuzhuang have eleven rooms, two or three colour TV sets and several telephones.

Mr Yu poured funds into manufacturing industry, using the profits of one venture to capitalise the next. The factories pay annual wages of US$800 to $900, and one construction company manager earns $9,300. Most remarkable of all, Mr Yu sent a hundred local youths to foreign countries as exchange students, and offered them a bounty if they married a daughter of a foreign capitalist. But four people of Daqiuzhuang were recently accused of beating to death an insubordinate migrant suspected of embezzlement, and this has darkened the picture. Mr Yu tried to keep the higher authorities out of the matter, insisting on investigating it himself, but his cover-up failed and he was himself jailed for twenty years on a charge of obstructing justice.[16] Reform and wrongdoing sometimes go hand in hand, but that does not necessarily undermine the reforms.

At the other end of the scale there are farmers who are still miserably poor. Ironically, the area near the Yanan base from which the Communists launched their successful bid for power in the 1940s is one such locality: in the village of Yangzhuang in northern Shaanxi the average annual income per head is only $74. This is such a backward community that the local Party secretary does not know what the term 'joint venture' means, and most of the villagers do not know the name of the Communist Party chairman. When the former Prime Minister Zhou Enlai returned to this area, legendary for the Communist guerrillas, and saw the poverty that still existed after fifteen years of Communist rule, he burst into tears.[17] There are even a few interior stretches of China where the 'one-pants' family, sharing garments, is the rule rather than the exception, and there are mountain villages in Yunnan province which still lack water or electricity, and where children have to walk many miles to get to school.[18]

The most recent feature of Chinese rural life is a disturbing backlash by local Communist officials who have lost both income and status because of the decentralising aspect of reform. No longer able to order the farm workers about or tell them where to go and what work to do in the people's communes, low-level Communist officials invented a way of thwarting the farmers' use of their new freedom, by which they claw back income for themselves. They did this by manipulating taxes, levies and special charges for the various services and permissions which the farmers need. Under the agricultural reforms, many services formerly provided free of charge or at a subsidised price by the state now have to be paid for by farmers, including levies for building toilets and rat-catching, as well as for building schools and providing electricity. A farmer will be asked to pay so much towards local highways every year, so much for school costs, for social insurance and welfare, for development projects. What used to be met from collective income may now be charged to each individual, with a larger scope for abuse.

Farmers in Anhui were told to pay nine different kinds of fee before they could build their own houses. If a rural town builds a police station and has no funds, it will levy the farmers, after which the policemen will knock on the farmhouse door for a contribution towards their wages, uniforms and motorcycles. Other ways of squeezing the farmer were discovered. Local officials held up the bank drafts which are sent home by farmers' children toiling in distant cities as migrant labourers. Officials delayed paying farmers for their crops, dishing out IOUs instead, and when bumper crops depress market prices, and when the government withdraws its subsidies on some crops, farmers could find themselves left in the end with no money at all.[19]

The State Council in Beijing responded to these complaints by setting a ceiling on charges, at 5 per cent of annual incomes, but the real level on the ground was said still in the press to be more than 10 per cent.[20] There were cases where higher officials came to the villages to investigate farmers' complaints and were warmly welcomed, but the farmers were then presented with the bill for their investigation report – RMB 2 per farmer, and a further RMB 7 to meet the investigators' office expenses.[21] The problem was expected to improve when the State Council eventually cancelled altogether thirty-seven kinds of levy on farmers and severely rebuked local officials for imposing them. Fees for rat-catching, film screening, water supply improvement, public toilet refurbishment and building police stations were specifically prohibited in 1993. This proved the good intentions of the government, but China is large enough for officials on the ground to get away with much disobeying of central orders.

▲ 卖粮记

***The hopeful farmer drools over the money he will get for selling 2000 catty (1.25 tonnes) of grain to the state, but the official informs him that he still owes RMB 38 after various fees are deducted* (Legal Daily, *14 May 1993*).**

In one rural town in Sichuan the local authorities collected RMB 15 from every farmer for the high school. But the town also planned to build an auditorium, and the higher authorities have a plan to build a hospital, so that the cumulative levy on each farmer came to RMB 27. Some officials enforcing these payments were so brutal that farmers avoided them by going into hiding. Some officials overestimate the prosperity of the farmers and therefore set their fees too high, but others are simply opportunist or put the interests of their own organisations before that of the agriculture they are supposed to serve.

The farmers were not quite helpless. In three counties of Sichuan province they sued the officials responsible in the local court, winning not only the return of their fees and charges but also damages. This is a locality where fees were reaching about 15 per cent of farmers' incomes, and even in the worst cases 30 per cent. But most farmers across the country did not know how to seek the protection of the law. They submitted to illegal levies until their anger could no longer be contained, and in 1993 a wave of riots spread over the farming areas.

How serious this unrest could be, and how even more serious it might become, was demonstrated by the farmers of Renshou county in Sichuan, ironically one of the localities which had led the reforms in the first place. The farmers clashed with county government officials for more than two months, but when the harvesting season began they went back to their farms. A few days later they were aroused again by a local newspaper article describing how the county had collected funds from the farmers once more for highway construction, and how one farm worker who objected had been handcuffed and trussed to a tree. The furious farmers all around reacted by kidnapping a senior official, beating him and injuring him. After that they smashed up a vinegar factory and a rabbit farm, beat up a policeman and held him in a bus for ten hours. The mayhem was so fierce that the pusillanimous public security men did not dare to rescue him, sending in some local hooligans instead to bring him out at knife-point.

Then came another article, this time in the *People's Daily*, explaining in a somewhat detached fashion that rural officials were not allowed to grab farmers' grain, drag away their animals or remove their furniture. This contrast between high-level official homily and low-level official non-compliance made the farmers even more angry, and many village officials refused to work. In the course of all this the farmers' demands had escalated: they wanted the illegal taxes and fees which they had paid over the years to be returned. In the end, officials decided to arrest the ringleaders, sending in over a thousand armed policemen (some of whom had actually fought in the Indian and Vietnamese border wars!) By surprise attack they succeeded in capturing most of the leaders, except three who were not at home. The police surrounded the houses of these three, but were in turn surrounded by hundreds of farm workers. It became a battle of tear-gas versus bricks and stones, and within a couple of days there were 15,000 farm workers surrounding the government office, holding up traffic, blocking the streets and closing shops. By now the publicity was such that Renshou students in various urban colleges were sending messages of support, and 10,000 students in Chengdu, the provincial capital, also publicly backed the farmers.[22]

From its relatively humble beginnings, the farm workers' riot in Renshou almost triggered a student rising. The grievances on the farms are serious and widespread, although it would take much more petty oppression for them to develop into a movement politically threatening the central government, or even provincial governments. But they make life uncomfortable for the leaders. When President Jiang Zemin went to unveil a statue of Mao Zedong in his birthplace of Shaoshan at the end of 1993, he was surrounded for almost an hour by petitioning Hunanese farm workers.[23]

The story of illegal fees brings home two fatal weaknesses of China's rural life: the gullibility, timorousness and habitual dependence of many farmers, and the callous venial dishonesty of a minority of local officials, all of whom have been hit in the pocket by the rural 'privatisation'. Between them, these two factors go far to explain the feeble prospects for democracy.

Unjustified fees and charges place an unbearable burden on China's supposedly free farmers, but now they converge with a second and greater problem. It is hardly profitable any more to grow food grains. Many farmers can no longer afford modern agriculture, because prices for seed, fertilisers, pesticides, insecticide, diesel oil and tarpaulins as well as fees for power tilling and irrigation have soared. The production materials which farmers need cost about 15 per cent more each year, whereas the price they are paid for their grain grows very much more slowly. The low fixed price for staple crops on which the government insists in order to please its urban citizens makes it more and more difficult for farmers to scratch a living. They have begun to leave land uncultivated and to desert the fields. To put a figure to it, one economist reckons that 250 kilograms of rice are now worth only the price of a carton of cigarettes. 'The only thing left to do,' farmers were quoted as saying, 'is to sit at the end of the field and cry.'

The *Farmers' Daily* found one locality where it cost RMB 100 for the production inputs to cultivate an area capable of producing 500 kilograms of rice, which would fetch RMB 180. The profit of only RMB 80 is then eaten into by fees, charges and taxes.[24] Farmers can make a reasonable, even good, living from their cash crops like sugar or cotton, or, even better, vegetables and flowers for city markets. But the grain farmers have come to the edge of despair, so much so that even Prime Minister Li Peng has warned that the conditions for a farmers' revolt now exist in China. The grain harvest has been virtually static for the past ten years, and was weak even before then. The exceptional bumper crops of 1990 and 1993 kept the supply side going, but punished the farmers with even lower prices. The polarity of income and wealth both within the countryside, and between the countryside and the cities, is widening.

One of China's experts on village reform, Lu Zixiu of Anhui, argues that the pace of urbanisation in China is too slow, and the shifting of excess village manpower too sluggish. China's level of urbanisation, he says, lags far behind that of India or Pakistan.[25] Rural industry has mopped up many of the landless or jobless farm workers, but millions of them have also migrated either to richer areas or to the cities. More than 100 million people who were full-time farm workers in 1978 are now under-employed. During recession time the flood of work-seekers swells in the better-developed areas around Shanghai or Guangzhou, and over a recent New Year holiday period five million migrants passed through the centrally located Nanjing railway station.[26]

The disincentives to migration are considerable: you cannot claim food rations in another place and depend therefore on free markets, and a residential permit in a new place is difficult to get: without it you must expect some inconvenience. Yet rural people migrate. With their numerological fixation, the Chinese talk of farming being left in the hands of 'Army Unit 3861' – to decipher which you need to know that 8 March is International Women's Day and 1 June is Children's Day: it is the women and children – and now the elderly – who hold the fort on the farm while the able-bodied men go to work elsewhere.

Apart from labour deployment, Lu Zixiu finds a second major weakness of rural policy in the uncertainty over farmers' rights of ownership and use of land. Beijing has not given a clear signal whether contract rights will be renewed, and if so under what conditions. Agricultural investment is thus discouraged.

Deng's reforms at first brought bigger harvests, but after about six years, the all-important grain crop started to hover around its 1984 peak before edging up in the 1990s to reach 447 million tons in 1994: the terrible floods of 1995 cut the figure again. The overall performance over fifteen years was worrying, because by the end of the century the harvest needed to keep the growing population fed at a minimally reasonable level would be over 500 million tons. The annual food grain harvest (rice and wheat, etc.) rose by an average of 3.3 per cent during the 1980s but is expected to show an average increase of only 1.2 per cent in the 1990s. To wrest 20 per cent more grain from China's farmers in only five years sounds impossible,[27] and yet there is no consensus yet about spending big sums of foreign exchange on large-scale imports. What can be done? One proposed remedy is to boost the farmers' price incentives. The government procurement price for most crops was substantially raised at the beginning of the reforms. In 1993 the government lifted the controls on grain prices altogether, but felt it had to restore them a few months later and reassert its monopoly over grain purchases from the farmers.[28] In

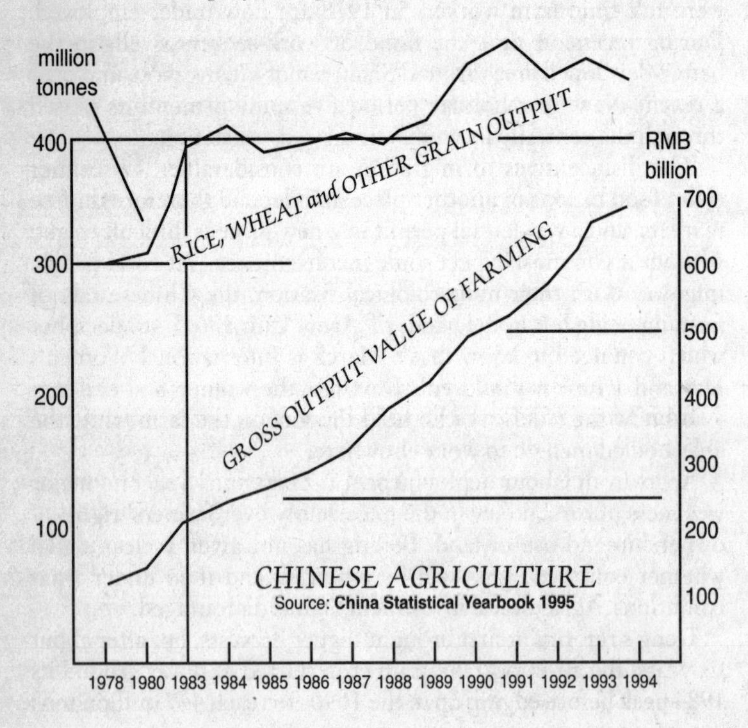

CHINESE AGRICULTURE
Source: **China Statistical Yearbook 1995**

any case the quick march of inflation seriously eroded these agricultural incentives.

Another view is gaining ground, therefore, that it is more and more urgent to improve irrigation and other large-scale works which the individual farmer or his family cannot undertake alone. It may sound retrograde, but some Chinese economists are now suggesting a return to the commune with its high capacity for mobilising labour, but in a new version stripped of coercion. Day-to-day farming, under a proposal of Liu Minquan, a Chinese economist at Cambridge, should be contracted to individual families, as now, but instead of being paid the price of their output, they should get work points to that value. Work points used to be given to commune members for the various jobs they completed, and were totted up at the end of the year to decide what share of the collective annual income each member should receive. That does not have to be coercive unless its leaders choose to make it so.

This *baochan*, as Liu christens it, would combine the respective advantages of the present system and the discredited commune while avoiding their shortcomings, providing high incentives for group members to participate in (remunerated) collective work, without the element of force.[29] There is at least one village – Nanjie in Henan province – which has already re-collectivised itself in a semi-Maoist fashion and claims to have retained thereby the old spiritual values and discipline.[30]

Improving irrigation and big farm works cannot be guaranteed under any system. Tales of wastage on an extraordinary scale used to be told about the communes. Liu Minquan was himself in the early 1970s involved in a commune programme to reclaim land from Lake Tai in rural Wuxi. The grain area was duly extended, but at the cost of raising the water table so high as to threaten the waterlogging of more land than had been reclaimed – and some of the reclaimed land was later dug out in any case, and replaced by water to breed fish in! But an enormous amount of necessary work was completed under the communes, and since 1978 there has been no dependable means of maintaining that work.

Baochan would not involve changes in the ownership of land or farm animals. It may not be necessary at all in areas like southern Jiangsu, perhaps, where the infrastructure is already in good shape. William Hinton wrote a best-seller about a farming co-operative which he assisted in Long Bow County, Shandong. He later vented his anger on the Chinese Communist leadership when it successively decreed a blanket abolition, first of co-operatives and then later of communes; he argued that some of the co-operatives, like Long Bow, were both popular and successful and could, suitably modified, have held open an alternative strategy for Chinese agriculture.[31] But political leaders did not favour them.

Now the government talks of a double-tier management system which would give a larger role to village-level and former commune organisations, evidently recognising that it might have swung too far against the communes in 1978. Shaoxing County has pioneered a flexible way of putting household plots which are abandoned or no longer cultivated into the hands of 'commercial' teams of farmers, with greater village autonomy in how it is done.[32] This will be the rural wave of the future. A case of two steps forward, one step back!

CHAPTER 9

POPULATION: THE MISSING GIRLS

China has too many people for their own good. The population is officially 1.2 billion, a figure which towers 30 per cent above India's, the runner-up in this dubious world championship, and saddles its rulers with the unenviable task of governing 22 per cent of the human race. Every fifth person in this world is Chinese. The heavy weight of people can be felt in terms of a labour force expanding by 2.5 per cent a year, and unemployment exceeding 200 million. Some of the jobless hang about in the rural areas, others pester the rich coastal zones and cities for jobs which are mostly no longer there. A third of Sichuan province's farm workers are idle, and migration to better-off areas is now a permanent feature of Chinese life. This is the job creation challenge of China's government.

Every Chinese wants – demands – a son to carry on the family name, a son to be responsible for his aged parents at the end of their lives and see to their proper funeral rites and burial. It is more than a religious faith, it is a fierce concern to protect and continue the ancient family line which for a traditional Chinese male imparts meaning and legitimation to his own life. The Confucian ideal was always to have as many descendants as possible, to 'crowd the hall with sons'. A Sichuan proverb puts the point crisply in its farming context: 'Early sowing, early harvest; early fatherhood, early retirement.' Chinese individuality is immemorially sacrificed to the historical collective of the family. One does not say this lightly. When the American Chinese journalist Frank Ching sought to discover his antecedents from faded archives and weathered tombstones in China, he was able to trace his ancestors back almost a thousand years. A less palatable illustration is the peasant couple with four daughters who, desperate for a son, bought a baby boy. But its 'genitals' fell off a few days later – it was a fake![1]

Frank's interest in his family tree was sentimental, and modern Chinese no longer dance automatically to the summons of the family line. They have entered into the beginning of a new era of unabashed individualism and preoccupation with the short-term present. Many who live in China's cities today are slightly detached from their groups, and the round of urban life makes children seem less of a necessity, so large families are out of fashion there. But in the countryside, where four in five Chinese live, those traditional feelings for family still throb in people's hearts.

> 'I've borne nine children,' an embittered southwestern farmer's wife told a reporter in the late 1980s. 'The first was a boy, but he died. Then I had seven girls . . . only the ninth time did heaven send another son. Girls are no use. They can't inherit your house or your property. Having sons is what women come into the world for. What's the point of it all if you don't have a son?'[2]

It took four thousand years of recorded history for China to reach its first five hundred million in population. The second five hundred million, born since Mao proclaimed the People's Republic in 1949, took only thirty years. The marathon has become a sprint. The current rate of increase is officially 1.1 per cent, which means adding new babies almost equivalent to the entire population of Holland to China's masses every year. Some independent experts put the growth higher, at nearer 1.5 per cent.[3]

Mao himself did not believe that a big population was dangerous. Western warnings on the subject were politically motivated, he said, designed to reduce China's importance. In the 1950s the Chinese were forbidden to study demography, and the Beijing University president who urged population control in the interests of economic development was dismissed and disgraced. Eventually advisers expressed alarm that, despite a doubling of the grain harvest in the first thirty years of Communist rule, grain output per head of population had been virtually static. The policy was changed to encourage family planning and restrict the number of children, initially to two in each family but later to only one. 'The immediate, primary task,' said Chen Yun, China's economic theoretician, at the end of the 1970s, 'is to advocate each couple to have just one child. The resultant problems are secondary.'[4]

To bring the population growth rate down, the government brings pressure on young people not to marry early: at one point the permitted age was twenty-eight for men and twenty-five for women. Large families were not allowed to have bigger private plots of land. In the cities, parents limiting themselves to one child were given cash bonuses and earned priority in schooling and housing. Baby quotas were fixed for different localities in each year, and neighbourhood committee officials were even told

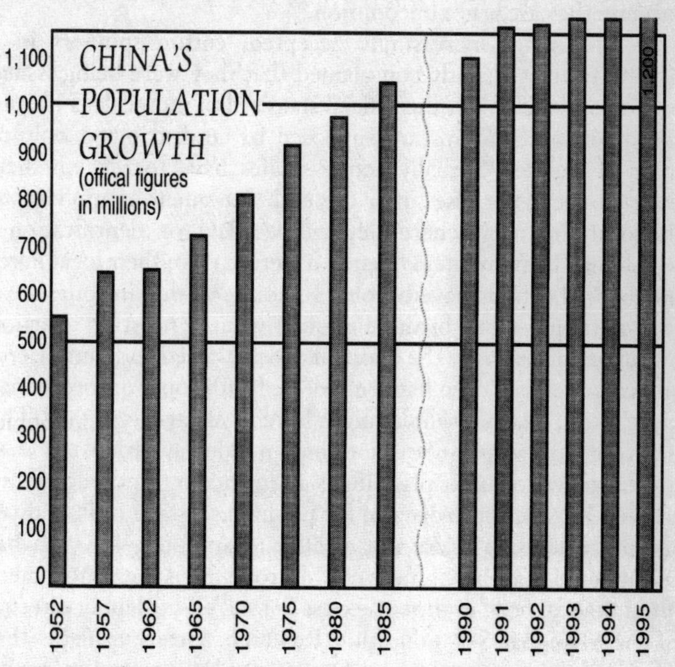

to monitor each woman's menstrual cycle. They were punished if the quotas were not met. This was the government's strategy from the 1970s on. There was a chilling story by an American correspondent in China about a woman, seven months' pregnant at the end of the year, who had her labour induced on New Year's Eve at the bidding of local officials who wanted to include the child in that year's quota rather than the next. The baby died, the woman was crippled for life, but the government later denied the story.[5]

The accepted Western means of contraception were promoted, along with such traditional Chinese prescriptions as swallowing live tadpoles. Intra-uterine devices became very popular, as did sterilisation, abortion and tying the fallopian tubes. One woman in Guangzhou was so frightened at the prospect of this operation that her husband searched for a gynaecologist who would give her a fake certificate without the surgery: the case is not uncommon.[6]

Condoms are increasingly accepted: cotton spinners in a Beijing factory recently complained that they were being issued only two a week.[7] But the official standard of morals lags behind social reality: condoms are supposed to be distributed only to married couples. Sexually active singles have to rely on their married friends or else suffer the embarrassment of applying to the local pharmacy, where they will be asked for identification – which may later lay them open to a lecture from their local Party official.[8] Abortions have become so common that in some areas they outnumber live births. Pregnant women resisting abortion for pregnancies above the quota may be harassed and humiliated, and in some cases even handcuffed, tied with ropes or forced into pig-cages. Their household might have its electricity cut off. The birth control campaign was nothing if not deadly serious.

Resistance to family planning is intensified by ignorance about sex in China, and the distaste for public discussion of it, and yet social attitudes to it are not at all puritan. Lung-kee Sun has commented that the Chinese can 'de-romanticise sex into a mere physiological need in the same class as food'. The deputy director of the Shanghai Sex Education Research Society explains that 'You cannot just regard masturbation as unhealthy. In fact, we no longer refer to it as masturbation. We call it self-comfort.'[9] Yet the story is often heard – and told by parents to their sons – of the boy who masturbated so hard that his penis burst into flames.[10]

Now the government has tried to cure some of the myths with a radio programme called 'Pillow Talk', covering such topics as 'the harm of one-minute love-making' or 'what to do if children find their parents having sex'. It is undoubtedly ignorance, together with the new affluence of many people, that caused a reappearance in the late 1980s of venereal disease after it had been stamped out earlier.[11]

Rational attitudes are not helped by the rising circulation of pornography. An army poll revealed that two out of every three soldiers and officers read pornographic books and magazines. One publisher of *Playboy*-type books and calendars was sentenced to death in 1989, but the trade goes on.[12] Homosexuality is officially regarded as criminal, and Dr Gao Caiqin was thought courageous when she set up the first gay clinic and research centre at Harbin in the far north near the Russian border. She accepts the official view that homosexuals disturb the social order, and treats her patients with electric shock therapy and herbal medicine, claiming a high 'cure' rate.[13]

Superstition plus sex drive was a familiar combination only yesterday in many European societies. But the story of Chinese women slaves and wives for sale is appalling. Hundreds of girls from backward areas of Henan province were paraded in 1988 in their underwear in the local market town with their names and prices on their backs, and local farmers paid up to £700 – ten years' earnings – for their choice of wife.[14] The sale of women or children were two of the 'six evils' against which the government waged war in the late 1980s, others being gambling, drug trafficking, swindling and con games exploiting superstition. One Sichuanese twenty-seven-year-old was executed for selling his wife, daughter and mother into slavery as well as eighteen other women.[15] All these reports originated in the Communist press.

Sometimes this problem is created by the authorities themselves. The 250,000 temporary women workers in Shenzhen, abutting on Hongkong, had no residence cards and therefore could not marry in a situation where they greatly outnumbered men. 'They strongly desire satisfaction from the opposite sex,' a local official noted. 'Providing women with sexual satisfaction,' he found, 'is even more difficult than reducing conflict between management and labour.' The outcome was prostitution, pregnancy out of marriage and lesbianism.[16]

Marxist social ideals much improved the status of Chinese women in the earlier years of the Communist government, but the older tradition of female inferiority is now reviving a little. Women face discrimination in jobs, in the inheritance of property and in entry to higher education.[17] There are notable cases of breaking through these barriers, like Wu Yi, the Minister of Foreign Economic Relations and Trade, who negotiated with Mickey Kantor of the USA on their trade and intellectual property dispute in 1995.[18]

As for men, their concerns seem the same all over the world. Chen Kai, President of the Male Sexual Functional Rehabilitation Committee, is making a fortune in Shanghai with his machine, invented by himself, for enlarging penis size by up to 2 centimetres and curing premature ejaculation. Members of the public can also patronise a handful of sex shops of which the Adam and Eve Health Centre in Beijing was the pioneer in 1993.[19]

These pre-modern social attitudes explain why the backlash to the official birth control policy can be so terrible, far beyond the limits of Western experience. When a school teacher in Anhui province became pregnant for the sixth time, her husband locked her up out of public sight until the child was born. He then carried the baby to a remote spot and tried to pretend it had been abandoned by someone else.[20] Another couple in Sichuan had two daughters already, but wanted a son, so the wife became pregnant. To keep it secret from officials, the man sealed his pregnant wife into a cavity behind the wall of their home.[21]

But the most horrible depth of degradation and despair in this awesome contest between ancient superstition and imposed rationalism was reached in the town of Wenzhou, which has already featured in these pages as the epitome of capitalism. A local official there insisted that women who became pregnant again after their first birth must abort. One couple steadfastly refused. Threats to reduce their income and inconvenience them were ignored, and finally the official assigned the woman to heavy farm work. When her labour began, she went out to the fields to have the child there: the official followed her and strangled it. She then went to his house and strangled his three children with a piece of wire.[22] Anger is whitest-hot where the officials enforce on others policies which they do not observe themselves. In one county thirty-five Party officials and staff with more children than the quotas allowed were dismissed, and some were fined.[23]

The scars from such struggles disfigure individual lives and communities long after the event. There are said to be a million children who do not have residence permits because they were born, as officials put it, outside the state birth control target. Their parents did not register their births for fear of punishment, or else were refused if they tried to register. That makes these children a kind of outcast group unable to receive rations of food or cloth during times of rationing, ineligible for schooling, jobs or housing.[24] So far these 'black children', as the locals call them, are mostly under sixteen. Their plight is only now showing up in society. The lucky ones may be adopted, at home or abroad. Chinese children are popular among the Americans and Scandinavians, and the Chinese government facilitates this process. They are almost all, of course, girls: a solitary boy in one group of such adoptees going overseas was asked to dress as a girl at the airport so that the Chinese onlookers would not be upset.

Even the families which co-operate with the one-child programme face problems. No one is so spoiled in China as the only child, who tyrannises the household and never learns to share with brothers or sisters. These *xiaowangdi* – 'little emperors' – will in time create a society of inconsiderate self-willed citizens

▲ 小祖宗值日

***How the one-child policy spoils the child. Here a 'little emperor' goes to school attended by a retinue of parents and grandparents* (Beijing Farmers' Daily, *22 March 1993*).**

with a lusty demand for material things. Such a future generation may have lost the spirit of helping other people (so much for socialism), and a rising crime rate is expected.

The worst sufferers of all, though they are unable to complain, are the unwanted infant girls. A pattern repeated by couples all across China is to await the last permitted birth (the first or second, depending on locality) and, if it is a girl, to kill it and try again for a boy. Chen Muhua, the senior woman in the Beijing leadership hierarchy, has admitted that millions of baby girls were killed for this reason in the 1980s.[25] Female infanticide is now the subject of numerous learned studies and reports on China, and an American demographer, John S. Aird, wrote a book about Chinese policies under the title *Slaughter of the Innocents*. Infanticide is frequently pre-empted nowadays by abortion, because the ultra-sound scanner has hit the paddy fields, allowing a woman to foretell the sex of the child in her womb. The scanner has been manufactured in China for the past fifteen years, and is therefore affordable: more than 100,000 are in place. It has been said officially that one female foetus in eight is being aborted after such scans, and that is probably an understatement. The National People's Congress has called for a ban on scanners.[26]

The government's birth control policy was intended to control the total numbers of the population, but the side-effect is thus for boys to outnumber girls. In 1992 new-born boys were 18 per cent more numerous than new-born girls, and the press is speculating that many of these infant boys will not easily find marriage partners in twenty years' time. 'An army of bachelors,' said the president of the All-China Women's Federation, 'now 20 million, will number 50 million by the end of the century.' A Shanghai newspaper predicted 'a great army of hoodlums' by 1999. Even now a young man complains, 'Women are so hard to find now. And I just want one.'[27]

Recent population counts seem to indicate two million or more 'missing girls'. Were they aborted, killed in infancy or brought up surreptitiously without being entered into the official statistics? Will the new sex ratio lead to polyandry (several men sharing a wife), a higher valuation of women as a 'scarce commodity', homosexuality or a splurge of male hostels? One thing seems certain: the shortage of women of child-bearing age will enable the number of new births to be reduced, and that will vindicate the original policy of containing China's population growth, though by a process the planners never intended. Possibly this development may throw the official policy into disarray because of popular indignation, and China may have to relax its guard on family planning. After all, as a newspaper comment recently put it, China 'cannot just have men left'.

To add to its difficulties, the government has now caught the eugenics bug. Some experts suggested that intellectuals in the cities should be allowed to have a second child. A Draft Law on Eugenics and Health discussed the problem of inbreeding in the 'idiot villages' of China's remote areas, and the desirability of upgrading the quality of the population in future generations. One baby in twenty is born either mentally or physically disabled. The idea of preventing disabled prospective parents from bearing children in China was hotly criticised in the West, especially the United States, revealing the chasm between Chinese fatalism and the American obsession with the individual. Soon afterwards the Chinese government changed the English name of the new draft law to 'Natal and Health Care Law', but the Chinese title remained the same.[28] Lee Kuan Yew of Singapore has also introduced eugenics into his government's programme.

Another 'chauvinistic' tinkering with the birth control policy came after projections suggesting that the national minorities would reach about a quarter of the total population and continue rising when the mainstream Han population was stabilising. Rather than see the minorities attain such enhanced proportional importance, the government has now sought to extend birth control to them for the first time.[29]

With a death rate below 0.7 per cent, and life expectancy reaching seventy-one years (both figures putting China 'ahead' of India and other Third World countries), a new problem arises about the mounting proportion of old people in the population. It is, of course, the reduced death rate, caused by improvements in health, water supply, sanitation and medical care, that mainly causes the population growth. There are now more than 75 million people over the age of sixty-five, and this will swell to 90 million by the end of the century – even more when today's parents of single children pass sixty-five in about forty years' time. International experts say that China has the world's fastest-growing population of oldies. Germany took seventy-two years for its over-sixty-fives to jump from 10 per cent of the total population to 20 per cent. Japan took thirty-two years. China will do it in only twenty-one years.[30]

How will society accommodate these old people? The one-child family is not equipped to look after the parents when they become elderly, particularly when the one child is a daughter, who will marry and go away to live with her husband's family. The burden of pensions will weigh more heavily as the number of retired workers swells rapidly. Today is something of a golden age for workers as far as disposable income is concerned: and they can spend on their dependants. Young couples with only one child to spoil and relatively few elderly dependants should not have to scrape and save.[31] The next generation may find it tougher. For this reason the experts have discussed allowing urban couples to have two children again, but their earlier work had succeeded only too well in the sense that when such a new policy was carried out in Shanghai on an experimental basis, only twenty-three couples applied for a second child in the first year.

Nation-wide pensions are now the largest single item of welfare spending. Compulsory retirement insurance does operate in some localities, but farm workers find it difficult to contribute from their small budgets. The story was told in the press of a villager who had one child more than he was allowed, so his house was torn down and he had to move to a small hut. An official came to collect his social insurance premium, but the villager had no money. The official gave him two days to pay, and then came back and took his bicycle. On complaining to the village officials about this, he was beaten, locked up and further fined.[32] It was in this sort of atmosphere that a village retirement social system was introduced in Jiangsu province in 1992. Guangdong has announced that it will experiment with an endowment insurance system in the rural areas.

During the first decade of reforms under Deng Xiaoping the government could congratulate itself on bringing China's average population growth rate down below 1.5 per cent a year. But there was evidence that it was climbing again towards the end of that decade. The smaller increase of the early 1980s was partly attributable to the fact that relatively fewer mothers were available in the shape of women surviving from the 1960s famine. Now the same shift in ideology which put in train faster economic growth, free enterprise and decentralisation has also begun to weaken the ability of the state to control its citizens' behaviour, whether by means of command or incentive. The discipline of the one-child family is beginning to relax. A recent anthropological visitor reports that 'peasant resistance has in fact forced the state to move considerably on the one-child policy, so that the policy is now more generally a two-child policy in the countryside.'[33]

Those who believe that China's population problem can be solved only under an authoritarian régime are usually those who like the idea of authoritarian government anyway, and are therefore disliked by liberals. But they are probably right. The relative success of earlier decades in keeping the growth rate down resulted from the ability of the government to impose tough and unpopular policies. A spokesman for the State Family Planning Commission promised in the mid-1980s that the one-child restriction would be imposed on only one generation, or for twenty to thirty years. Ten years later, in 1994, Mrs Peng Peiyun, Minister of Family Planning (though herself the mother of four), warned that these tough family planning laws would have to be continued 'over the long term'. Yet over the long term means running into a period when restrictions can no longer be so widely and uniformly carried out.

Western experts believe that the Chinese population will peak in about fifty years from now, to reach about 1.5 billion or a little more by the middle of the twenty-first century. Professor Song Jian, Chairman of China's Science and Technology Commission, puts his reputation on the line to say that the population will stabilise at the end (not the middle) of the twenty-first century at 1.6 billion.[34] Such an increase will be well below the anticipated experience of several countries at a similar stage of economic development, such as India. It will represent a drain on the benefits of economic progress, but if the economic reforms are allowed to work out steadily over those decades during which the population will approach its peak, there may be just enough resources and enough social organisation not only to give most of the additional persons satisfactory employment, but also to provide a minimal cushion of social security for those unable to earn.

Solving the population problem in this manner will, however, reduce the government's options in two respects. It will not be able to alter the pace or direction of economic reform, and it will have to allow the economy to become much more interdependent with the outside world and integrated into the world economy, on which it will depend for food supplies to meet the needs of larger population and to which it must export manufactures and commodities to earn the price of those foodstuffs. China will be interlocked with the rest of the world for the first time in its history.

CHAPTER 10

INDUSTRY AND FINANCE: FACTORIES CHANGE COLOUR

Industry was small, scattered and decidedly old-fashioned when the Communists won power in 1949. In the 1970s the Shougang Steel Corporation, now one of China's thriving giants, was still using a turbine dating back to the Empress Dowager's time around 1900, and one of the games that foreign visitors play when touring Chinese factories is to spot the oldest machine still in use. In 1964, I went to see a textile mill in Shanghai which was still using spindles made by Howard and Bullough of Accrington, England, in 1911.

Mao Zedong's wild swings of industrial policy and his damaging mistakes are well-known, yet his rule from 1949 to 1976 saw industry's share of national production jump from less than a fifth to almost half – though it was biased in favour of heavy rather than light industry, and cripplingly bureaucratic. In Shanghai's hot summers people wanted to buy electric fans, but the factories needed permission to increase their production at will, and by the time the necessary authorisation was received from a higher level, the summer had gone.

The Communist Party itself controlled both factories and trade unions. The factory manager was more than a glorified technician: he headed a miniature welfare state and behaved like a small-town mayor. The verdict of an expert from the Organisation for Economic Cooperation and Development even as late as 1992 was that 'unambiguous evidence paints a picture of widespread technological stagnation, high costs, low efficiency, poor management and low skills in most industrial sectors.'[1]

Deng Xiaoping therefore had his hands full trying to modernise this unwieldy sector of the Chinese economy. He waited until the reform of farming had made a firm start, not introducing limited and experimental urban and industrial reforms until 1984. The two-tier price system, where prices were partly determined by the market and partly by the planners, was launched then. So was an industrial responsibility system making managers legally responsible for meeting the factory's targets. (Before that, they were accountable to their local Communist Party.) The government made formal contracts with state factories clarifying the arrangements regarding responsibility, authority and profit. It did not always work, because, for example, state enterprises did not own their own assets, and could not necessarily meet all the losses that might arise. This contract system gave managers valuable autonomy, but the mere fact that a contract was required underlined the fact that in the last resort power still resided with the bureaucrats. It is they who choose the managers.

A provincial Party Secretary, Li Changchun of Henan, has called for more democracy in factory appointments. Better, he said, to 'choose horses at the horse track' instead of from far away: democratically elected factory directors would be able to 'share ups and downs' with their employees.[2] Another way of freeing managers to run things independently is where the government leases the fixed assets of the enterprise to the manager, with full right to use and manage them in exchange for a fixed payment. This was found a useful formula for small state factories.

For small state-owned but privately-operated enterprises, Beijing organised a system where the land belonged to the state, the equipment was leased, operating capital was self-raised and each business was individually run. It was in effect an adaptation for small urban businesses of the rural responsibility contracting system. It was said that the philosophy was to 'pay enough to the state, reserve enough for the collective, and keep what is left for oneself.' The privatisation drive led eventually to over three-quarters of these small state-owned enterprises being sold or leased to private owners.

Zhang Weiying and Gang Yi, two Western-trained Chinese economists, argued that the state enterprises have also helped to bring about an 'implicit privatisation' by subsidising the admittedly small private sector.[3] To persuade a worker to leave a state enterprise and try his luck in the labour market, the enterprise may give him 'unpaid leave' – to reduce his risk and protect his *status quo*. If that worker joins a private enterprise or joint venture, the enterprise may allow him to continue to stay in his old flat, in which case the new employer does not need to provide housing and can afford higher wages to attract quality employees, being in effect subsidised by the state enterprise. One estimate of government spending on industrial subsidies was equivalent to 10 per cent of the GNP.

Real privatisation on any scale would create massive unemployment. To keep that unemployment within the state sector allows better conditions for the private sector to expand. Zhang and Gang therefore urged that privatisation should wait until conditions are smoother. Besides, there is still prejudice against privatisation. A column in the *People's Daily* in June 1994 concluded, 'we should never take the road of privatisation in reforming state enterprises today or in the future.'[4]

One pathfinder for the new policies was the geographically isolated town of Wenzhou in Zhejiang province, a town with, as we have seen, a history of rebellion. When the Communists conquered China, Wenzhou was taken over by an independent local force of guerrillas who formed a 'Communist' administration of unusual solidarity capable of resisting many of the new central state policies. After 1978 Wenzhou became the first place to be dominated by private entrepreneurs. Private industry quickly became more important than the state sector, a local capital market was fostered, and interest rates were floated long before such measures were sanctioned by Beijing. The Wenzhou farmers and industrialists were always a step or two ahead of the government in Beijing. Their joint public-private ventures or partnerships became popular, with local Communist officials acquiring vested interests in them and protecting them from state interference. In 1994 Wenzhou pioneered cable TV broadcasting in China, and its new mayor came to England in search of finance for a power station, water control plant and bridge – and a partner for a yellow cling peach cannery.[5]

The older and bigger heavy industrial plants were also given more autonomy, with power to make their own investments, recruit and supervise their own personnel, and administer their own finance and foreign trade. Shougang, the steel leader, took particular advantage of these new freedoms. It joined the Hongkong entrepreneur Li Kashing in purchasing a Hongkong steel trader, and it bought up an entire steel-making plant from California to be dismantled and shipped to Shandong province. Shougang also acquired Peru's state-owned iron producer and actively planned to buy a bank and set up an international headquarters in Hongkong.[6]

Shougang, formerly the Capital Iron and Steel Works, made ambitious plans to become the third largest steel works in the world early in the twenty-first century. It hired more than a hundred Russian, Japanese and American experts and swallowed up more than twenty military-industrial complexes on the verge of bankruptcy. It reinvested its profits, built housing for its workers, promised substantial pay increases and doubled pay for passing an exam. It acquired Deng Xiaoping's son Deng Jifang as a partner in one of its companies. It was the first Chinese corporation to start looking like an international conglomerate. Its chairman, close to Deng Xiaoping, and his son lost their jobs in 1995 in the preliminary moves for the succession to Deng, but the corporation business did not suffer.[7]

Another fate for an unhealthy big enterprise might be a sale to a private company. This happened to the Wuhan Match factory after it accumulated debts of $2.7 million. The attraction here was the valuable site of four and a half acres of prime land in the centre of Wuhan. Seeing the many acquisitions by private enterprise, one factory director said, 'We are like a big elephant being eaten away by ants.' Sometimes the non-state sector is sold a pup. The government handed the Number 541 Military Tank Factory in Shanxi to China International Trust and Investment Corporation (CITIC), to steer it round to civilian production. But CITIC was not allowed to dismiss the 20,000 workers, and it turned out that renovation of the obsolete machinery would not be financially worth while. CITIC is landed with an open-ended economic burden which it now wishes it had refused.[8]

Selling to foreign interests is worth while, if only for the access to foreign exchange, as the Jiangan Jingxi Chemical Factory of

Wuhan found when it negotiated a sale to a Hongkong company for RMB 6 million. The city of Quanzhou in Fujian province sold 60 per cent of the assets of its thirty-seven state enterprises which were in trouble to Hong Kong China Strategic Investment Company, after which there was a great improvement. The chairman explained why: there was now a clear distinction between management and ownership, foreign exchange could be obtained for technical transformation, and the enterprises could explore the international market.[9] Asset-stripping has a bad sound, perhaps, but the World Bank has given its cachet to the view that asset-stripping in China is not as damaging as it has been in many other countries, and has led to a reallocation of resources to more productive enterprises.[10]

There is an element of idealism in this process of transforming the state enterprises. Harbin, the northeastern industrial city, claimed to be pioneering in selling state enterprises 'to society', making some of them non-government enterprises, or joint-stock companies, or leasing or selling them to workers or citizens. After the Central Committee meeting in late 1993 active consideration was being given to workers holding shares in their enterprise. Hong Hu, Vice-Minister of the State Commission for Restructuring the Economy, proposed that such shares would be managed and represented by a special committee under the trade union in the enterprise.[11] The union, as a legal person, would buy the shares on the workers' behalf. Workers would earn dividends, but would not be able to negotiate, trade or bequeath their shares. It is a curious thought that while these revolutionary ideas were being discussed round the table in Beijing, Governor Chris Patten in Hongkong was seeking to enlarge the constituencies for elected industrial representatives on his Legislative Council in a manner that almost smacked of syndicalism.

Bankruptcy, outlawed by Mao, was now recognised again as an instrument of reform and as the last remedy for sustained inefficiency. Provisional legislation was enacted in 1988. Companies unable to pay debts or agree with creditors would be declared bankrupt and the officials in charge would be punished. But the status of debt incurred before the reforms was not clarified. The Prime Minister, Li Peng, preferred merger, telling the National People's Congress in 1992 that, 'For the sake of the workers and administrative staff, we should try to have unsuccessful enterprises shift to a different line of production, or merge with others, rather than suspending operations or closing down.'[12] The psychological revulsion against bankruptcy is still strong, and the reluctance to throw large numbers of people out of work remains for many Chinese another indispensable Chinese characteristic of socialism. In 1994 the government was driven to give workers at bankrupt state enterprises a golden handshake of RMB 20,000, on condition they severed ties with the firm and gave up their claims on it.

The Sichuan Dyeing Factory went bankrupt in 1994 with RMB 100 million outstanding debt, but very few others were willing to renege openly, finally and impersonally on their obligations. In 1995 Fujian Electronic Computer, Shantou Sodium Hydrosulfate and Shantou Huaqiao Rubber Plant all went to the receivers, but the number of bankruptcies reached only 1,625 in 1995, despite much larger targets, and the law was revised. The result, of course, is a continued misallocation of resources to many uncompetitive factories.

Zhu Rongji, then Deng's economic 'tsar', said in 1992 that the efficiency and profits of Chinese factories would increase if 70 million state enterprise workers were sacked.[13] But no more than one and a half million employees of industry have lost their jobs since the reforms began. The popular solution was the case of Bailan ('White Orchid') Electrical Company, which was taken over by its more successful competitor, Baiju ('White Chrysanthemum') Electrical Appliance Company. Baiju was run by a skilful manager who had borrowed large amounts of money to pay Toshiba of Japan for a twin-tub washing machine technology licence. The new combined company was expected to absorb the labour force of both companies. It was, the personnel manager said proudly, the 'superiority of socialism, that we look after our people and the government looks after us.'[14] Others were less lucky. Wuhan Steel Corporation had to carry out an 'orderly' layoff of 70,000 workers in 1992–93.

To take a man's job away means depriving him not only of work and social respect, but also, in the state sector at least, of a whole parcel of benefits including health, housing, education and pensions. The Shanghai Petrochemicals Enterprise, which employs 60,000 people, is committed to educating its workers' children (for whom it runs several schools and a college), and to giving them medical care (employing for that purpose 2,000 health workers). It pays a pension to its retired workforce, employs police to guard the houses where its employees live, and counsellors to help them resolve their marital disputes. Before the reforms it used to have quotas to buy raw materials cheaply, but now it is supposed to pay something nearer the full market price and compete for its customers. To reform such an enterprise fully is beyond the capability of either politicians or bureaucrats.

It is claimed that more than 200 million people are now covered by social insurance, of which 70 million are on the dole. Most provinces now have a system of official unemployment relief, where factories withhold up to 1 per cent of employees' wages. The total premia for all types of social insurance represent 5 per cent of national income. But the benefits are small by comparison with the need.

The reforms have thus created new problems in the course of addressing the old ones. One consequence of devolving authority to individual enterprises, and taking decisions away from bureaucrats at the centre, is to duplicate effort, especially in glamorous industries like motor cars or electronics. The investment in automobiles has been double what the state wanted or what the nation needed. In Japan and the West a motor-car plant must turn out some 300,000 vehicles a year to achieve efficiency of scale. In China there are only two enterprises which reach even the 100,000 level and some of the other 200 plants are making only a few dozen cars a year.[15] Again China now has seventy-six colour television factories producing 20 million sets a year, but the market needs only half of that, leaving the other half of production unused. Many of these companies are losing money.

Of the two hundred manufacturers of refrigerators, only four are operating at scale efficiency. There are eight separate makers of Ariston refrigerators, mostly operating below capacity. There are one hundred elevator manufacturers whose average yearly production is one-200th that of major Western producers. Even in textiles, a traditional industry, the market in China can take up the yarn from 250 million spindles every year, but production has now reached the level of 400 million. Communist Party researchers conclude, 'we must determinedly eliminate those enterprises which sprang up as a result of overheated economic expansion; otherwise we are unlikely to make any real progress'. Meanwhile billions of yuan are frozen in the shape of overstocked goods.

There are more direct disappointments. One factory processing metals spent over RMB 40 million to acquire the most advanced copper foil production line from the USA, and sent personnel there to train. But two of the four vital rollers had to be sent back to America for repair before they were even used, and the other two broke down within a month. This particular American supplier was unqualified to produce such equipment: the Chinese side had been cheated. The Jinbei Automobile Company of Shenyang bought 580 pick-up kits from General Motors, its joint venture partner, but was so disorganised that it refused to assemble all of them because they were found too

CHINESE INDUSTRY AND FINANCE

Industrial Production
Selected Items

	1992	1993	1994
Motor vehicles ('000s)	1,067	1,298	1,400
Crude Oil (m. tons)	142	145	146
Steel ('000 tons)	81	90	92
Electricity (10 m.Kwh)	754	839	920
Coal (m. tons)	1,116	1,151	1,120
Cotton cloth (b. metres)	19	20	20
Cigarettes (m. cases)	33	34	34

Leading Exports 1993
US$ billion

Garments	18
Metals	17
Electrical equipt.	14
Textile fabrics	8
Minerals	5
Shoes	5
Veg, fruit, cereals	4
Others	21
TOTAL	92

Monetary Indicators
billions

	1994	1995
Money supply (M2) (US$ b)	34	29
Foreign exchange reserves (US$ b)	52	74
External debt (US$ b)	93	n.a.
Govt. spending (RMB b)	579	681
Govt. tax revenue (RMB b)	522	619
Bank deposits (RMB b)	4,582	5,386
External trade balance (US$ b)	+5	+17
GDP (US$ b)	549	704

Source: **China Statistical Yearbook 1995**

expensive and unsuitable for Chinese road conditions, and the market now preferred four-seaters to two-seaters!

In another case a washing machine manufacturer bought a fully automatic assembly line from Japan, the first of its kind in China. But having spent this money it neglected to make its technicians familiar with the equipment, and during a test run the micro-processor and deceleration clutch developed such problems that the washing machines produced from this line could not be sold and were left to gather dust, entailing losses of RMB 140 million and debts of RMB 420 million. As a Party member sourly commented, 'our plant has enough debt to go bankrupt twice over.'[16]

There is a kind of 'national' face which can impede progress. I met in the billiard room of my hotel in Beijing in 1964 a bored Rolls-Royce engineer from England whose technical services were available to the Chinese for six months as part of the contract for a fleet of Viscount aircraft. The Chinese never called on him, finding it distasteful to confess their ignorance or inexperience before a foreigner. They coped themselves with engine problems as best they could, with results that later let the Chinese airline down.

Pilfering is a habitual contributor to inefficiency in Chinese industry. When a new manager taking up his job at a metals processing plant commissioned the first inventory for seven years, he found that nearly a thousand tonnes of copper, worth some RMB 10 million, were missing, nobody knew where or how. A small tractor factory ran an inventory after a six-year gap, and found 182 tractors unaccounted for. It had recently sent twenty tractors to a customer, but never received a cent for them, and there were no records to support the deal. The comfortable old Chinese concept of socialism was that materials used in production could be freely taken by workers. As a reformer complained, 'it is like having a wolf guard a baby's crib'.[17] As for sleeping on the job, playing poker on the shop floor and ragged arrivals after the supposed starting time, these practices were rife and are still common.

Never having experienced a full-scale market environment, Chinese managers find it difficult to adjust their ways to the new reform era. Even now, fifteen years on, businesses can continue producing goods simply to prevent losses in their books, though they know that the product is massively overstocked and not selling. In situations like this, Party officials may order factories to 'loosen their bowels', by releasing stock to the market at discount prices.

China needs to alter the role of government in industry, and to have institutional mechanisms which would separate the government functions – hitherto entwined – as regulator, owner and manager of factories. But the reform of ownership is still ambiguous. A company law defining the relative rights of the parties involved, and regulations to standardise accounting and auditing procedures, did not appear until 1994.[18]

Chinese managers are just beginning to feel independent of their owners. Excellent, the outsider may say, but the upshot is that managers, cut off from their cosy partnership with bureaucrats, are easily tempted to find themselves a new ménage with their workers, doing everything to please them in pursuit of an easy life in the short term, at the cost of uncompetitive wage levels and inefficiency. Privatise, say some (especially foreigners). But that would lead to a fragmentation of shareholding which would not necessarily ensure better management either. Dong He, a Chinese economist at Cambridge, makes this an argument for turning all state industries into joint-stock companies with a limited number of institutional shareholders – such as insurance companies, pension funds, companies holding government assets, banks and other industrial firms.[19]

The state enterprise share of industrial production has now fallen from two-thirds in 1985 to just under half. Cyril Lin of St Anthony's College, Oxford, calculates that only 7 per cent of industrial output is planned, the rest being 'free'.[20] But only a third of those are profitable (chief losers being the coal mines and small-scale factories), and their average pre-tax net profit is only 10 per cent of the sales revenue.

The Township Enterprises are themselves a new model for industry, a novel institutional arrangement to provide corporate governance for factories. Their managers have a role similar to those of private firms, but they are controlled by the local community. The Township Enterprises have been growing at about 14 per cent a year recently, and the fact that they exist in small communities, usually with a close link to neighbouring villages, makes it possible for the local community to have more control, with a considerable ownership stake and a capacity for close scrutiny. They are not state, not private, not co-operative but a new type of enterprise altogether.

It has been suggested that all the 104,000 state industrial enterprises be turned into Township Enterprises eventually, taking the legal form of joint-stock companies with control rights handed over to individual investors. Another imaginative scheme is to choose a hundred of the best state factories and transform them into enterprise groups which would be relatively free from restrictions or controls. Shougang, for example, has about 170 subordinate plants. If successful, these élite firms would set a conglomerate vanguard at the head of Chinese industry. Typically centred on a 'core' enterprise, they may come to be seen as Chinese versions of Japan's *sogo shosha* (trading companies) or Korea's *chaebol*, although there is a distinctive underlying individualism in the Chinese personality which makes sustained intimate collaboration with others in an industrial enterprise less popular or feasible than in Japan or Korea. There has already been an experiment with comprehensive trading enterprise groups in Suzhou and Shenyang, utilising the joint stock company structure. But it is not easy to make such groups compete with each other effectively (as Japan's pre-war *zaibatsu* did), and the government still remains the largest shareholder.

Experiments with the joint-stock system began in Shanghai in 1984. Two years later the State Council allowed some state enterprises to issue shares to employees and to affiliated companies. At first that was not taken up with enthusiasm, but interest quickened after the opening of the two Stock Exchanges in Shanghai and Shenzhen. Several younger economists believe that the joint-stock system, which was, they point out, invented even before capitalism, is useful in a socialist society. China's state enterprises should, in their view, have been 'corporatised' into joint-stock companies long before the other reforms: they are moving in this direction.[21] Already the first boardroom challenge, unprecedented in China, was noted at the China Vanke Company, a sleepy office-equipment importer in Shenzhen which was transformed into a predatory real-estate acquisitor through the pressure of shareholders angry over the slipping share price.[22] It is, of course, no easy matter to take on the new corporate garb. The Company Law finally published in 1994 requires an inventory and evaluation of assets, a clarification of debts receivable and payable and the establishment of standard internal management and accounting organisation and procedures. Many state enterprises which have ambled along in their own sweet way all these years may well fail at this last hurdle.

There are thus three challenges which the ownership reforms must now address. The first is, after separating ownership from management, how should state ownership of the enterprise be expressed? The second challenge is to diversify state ownership to lower levels such as provinces or sectors. Every board meeting does not have to be in Beijing. The third is to promote alternative ownership forms. The State Investment Corporation set up in 1988 is a first step towards rationalising the state role. But it does not yet act as an investment agent for the central government, seeking merely to check the assets of state enterprises and define their property rights and financial responsibilities. Some larger state enterprises may become holding companies, allowing their transformation into investors capable of crossing sectoral and provincial boundaries.

Given all these problems and changes, it is understandable that some foreign experts would like China to embark on a round of comprehensive and concentrated reforms over a short period – a 'big bang'. This was the position taken by a World Bank study of China in 1992.[23] But the Chinese instinctively prefer to act incrementally, and although the gaps may seem glaring, an enormous amount of change has in fact been put in train during these fifteen years of reform.

The financial side of factory operations was slower to reform. Experiments began in the 1980s to make state factories pay taxes first before repaying loans or remitting profits. State-owned enterprises no longer remit their profits to the central government, but pay income tax instead and share the profits with local authorities. But much of the small-time industrial financing is still unsatisfactory. Companies customarily raise funds from the public or other enterprises at 20 per cent annual interest and on two-year maturity, issuing a receipt stamped with a red seal called a 'red slip'. These red slips would be worthless if the enterprise fails, but they are now very widespread and the government would like to stop them. They follow the example to some extent of the 'white slips' which are the IOUs given to farmers to pay for crops, and the 'green slips' which workers away from their native province use to send money home through the post – but which the post offices at the other end sometimes lack the cash to honour.[24]

The very big and successful companies like Brilliance China Automotive Holdings controlling the Jinpei Auto Plant of Shenyang, which was the first Chinese company to list its shares on the New York Stock Exchange, naturally have to adhere to higher standards of accounting and corporate behaviour. But most of China's smaller enterprises simply do not know how. Some managers routinely arrange not to make too much profit, because that would encourage the government to bump up its tax demand. Books are easily cooked, often in two separate sets, one for internal use and the other for higher authorities.

The core of the industrial dilemma is the role of the manager. A Maoist factory was at bottom a political alliance. Managers were members of the Communist Party, and consulted the local Party committee on all important matters, especially senior appointments. If a manager tried to break ranks, the local Party could strong-arm him through the trade unions which it also controlled. The local Party had connections with the bureaux or committees at a higher level with which the manager had to deal, and the almost universal result was – and largely still is – an obligatory harmonious working relationship between the factory manager and the Party secretary. This cosy partnership is still the root of much inefficiency.

Now, in the second decade of reform, government ministries are beginning to select managers of state industries more on commercial than on political grounds. They may be asked to sign contracts with specific performance targets, and even post a performance bond of half a year's salary. Some of the most responsible industrial jobs in the state sector are actually auctioned. But there is no mad rush for such responsibility, with its concomitant risk of disgrace in the event of failure. A Chinese economist comments that 'many enterprise managers do not really want independence as defined in the reform documents, because such independence, without the funds, simply means they lose the protection of the state.'

The official attitude to that key figure in capitalism, the risk-taker, is surprisingly commendatory. Here is the *People's Daily* pontificating early in 1995:

> Successful entrepreneurs are high-quality, talented people, outstanding elements in the working class, pace-makers in creating the material and spiritual civilisations, and valuable assets under the market economy.

No wonder China welcomes the EU initiative in setting up a 50/50 China-Europe International Business School in Pudong, Shanghai.

The overall picture is by no means dark. Successful modernisation is spreading out from the smaller factories (especially those outside the state sector), from the Township Enterprises which brought to industry some of the canny instincts of rural business, from the more go-ahead coastal regions of the south, and from the better state giants in steel, petrochemicals and the like to permeate slowly to the weaker sections of the industrial economy.

The corruption and malpractice which privatisation and industrial decentralisation have encouraged is now the most worrying problem. In 1989, stung by the depth of feeling among the students in Tiananmen Square about government cadres profiting from the economic reforms, Deng Xiaoping demanded a crackdown on illegal profits, especially those of the big state corporations. Those included CITIC, China Kanghua Development Company (in which his own disabled son Deng Pufang was involved) and Everbright Industrial Company. Almost US$13 million in fines and confiscation of improper profits were taken from five of these corporations after allegations of buying and selling foreign currency without permission, reselling production materials at a profit and evading tax.[25] That was only the tip of a very large iceberg.

As a result of this investigation, two children of members of the Communist Party Politburo, one said to be the daughter of the then President of China, Yang Shangkun, were dropped from CITIC. But an exception was apparently made in the case of Deng Xiaoping's other son, Deng Zhifang, who continued to work as Deputy Chief Engineer in CITIC's New York office. Those who know him say he is knowledgeable, capable and experienced, and not to be treated as an irresponsible 'princeling' unworthy of his job.[26]

But corruption can bring down the innocent as well as the guilty. The head of a company in Shenzhen asked a young woman employee to help him forge contracts for the sale of steel, with which he conned his bank manager into giving him a loan. Using the money to buy a forged passport instead, he disappeared abroad. The girl reported his crimes, whereupon gangsters went to her house and, not finding her, beat her brother to death. At their trial one of them explained to the court that the head of the company had ordered the attack on this twenty-three-year-old 'whistle-blower'.[27]

Profit is now the official goal, but it is not the end of a manager's problems. A successful result would involve him in many congratulations, rallies and meetings, and everyone involved will press for profits to continue, and become even bigger – while he finds himself spending more of his time on unproductive public relations. Officials will press him to make a killing with his new profitability, and he may be swamped with new orders and higher quotas, producing burnout. Meanwhile unprofitable factories and small businesses will seek to hang on to his coat-tails. All kinds of people emerge wanting a little piece of the well-advertised success – 'You go ahead and eat your meat; I just came for a little soup.' A deluge of requests for funds and donations floods in.[28]

In the same vein managers will complain that their authority to hire what labour they wish vanishes in practice, and that influential higher officials can still dictate, largely for political reasons, the establishment, development and even closure of an enterprise. Exercising the manager's right to autonomy may put him at odds with some departments and units whose support he will eventually need.

'The moment they put out a recruitment call for workers,' said a provincial reporter about the factories of Anhui, 'orders forcing people on them fall like snow from the sky – orders from the local labour department whom it is wise not to thwart, since they have authority over you, so don't tie your own feet together. Even if you don't want new staff, you may have to take them. Every year the planning committee sends graduates, the civil affairs sends deactivated soldiers, and the labour department sends technical school trainees.'[29] The social expectation is that these overtures will be accepted out of community solidarity, not spurned because of considerations of profit.

Class can even now win the day. Xu Xingsheng founded a construction and building company employing more than 240 people in Hubei province. Because he hailed from the old pre-1949 feudal aristocracy, he found difficulty in getting land, credit and labour. When people saw him on the street they would jeer, 'The poor and middle class peasants will settle accounts with you some day.' He lamented that his company was 'just like me: it suffers from a "bad class background".'[30] Changing Party policy or state laws does not of itself change people's attitudes, prejudices or priorities.

If China's factories are to be put on a fully efficient footing, they need to be able to buy their materials and sell their products at the market price rather than at a price arbitrarily decided by some blinkered bureaucrat. Yet the change from fixed to market prices hurts many producers and consumers, especially the latter because they were benefiting in the past from subsidised products. The Chinese technocrats cannot agree about this problem. Professor Wu Jinglian of one of the State Council Research Centres argued for a blanket reform, including not only the rapid relaxation of price controls but also deflation, plus appropriate changes in taxation, wages and investment. That is a kind of 'big bang' approach which is not generally favoured. Professor Liu Guoguang of the Chinese Academy of Social Sciences preferred the strategy of taking only one step at a time, and then looking around before taking another. Prices should be reformed gradually, one by one, and this is more popular.

As a reformer told students in Beijing, 'You cannot have it both ways. We have only two options, one is to have the government impose strict price controls. Then ... production will shrink, income will stay where it was before, and there will be supply shortages, long queues and coupons ... The other option is to lift the price controls to give greater incentive to production. This means that everybody will earn a little bit more. Things will be a little more expensive, but you could buy what you want to buy.'[31] Price reform brings two risks in its train. One is inflation, to which the politicians make a knee-jerk response if only because of China's hideous memories of it in the 1940s. The second is throwing the government budget out of kilter, and both are politically risky.

Prices are sensitive matters, especially for a socialist economy in the course of changing its colours to be a market economy. In 1986 Beijing ran out of toilet paper. The factories had found their profits declining, so they cut production. The local government did not want to offend public sentiment by raising the price of this 'precious commodity', so initially it subsidised the manufacturers with several hundred thousand RMB, only later announcing a rise in the price.[32]

The freeing of prices has in fact gone a long way under Deng's reforms. It is reckoned that perhaps two-thirds of the transactions in the economy now take place at the market price. The big exceptions are energy, transport and grain. In 1992 controls were lifted on almost 600 commodities, from soda ash to electrical machinery, reducing the number directly priced by bureaucrats to 89. This was creditably less than the 737 in 1991, but it is still a big rent in the market economy.[33]

What will happen to workers when the market reforms really take hold? Can the government smash the 'three irons' (iron armchairs meaning secure management posts, iron rice bowls meaning lifetime employment, and iron wages meaning fixed salaries unrelated to performance)? Since 1986 new workers hired by the state-owned industries have very different terms from their predecessors'. About a fifth of the state industrial workers are now on contract, which means that they may theoretically be fired. There is a similar development in factories not owned by the state. It remains to separate the worker from the social benefits traditionally provided by big factories, and to arrange for him to enjoy these from another source, such as the state or the local authority. This is tricky ground because the state, for political reasons, has always valued its control over labour mobility from one place to another.

The importance of these benefits may be gauged from the long-established Shanghai Radio Factory, producing TV sets, radar and radios with almost 4,000 employees including over 630 engineers. It is efficient enough to export to Malaysia, Britain and many other foreign countries. Annual bonuses here have represented as much as ten months' salary in the recent past, and there are additional bonuses geared to productivity. Subsidies for soap, transport and inflation boost take-home pay to well over the average.

But the workers get much more than money. They are given chopsticks and rice bowls with the factory logo, as well as umbrellas. They may buy products of the factory at discount prices. At the autumn moon festival they receive orange juice, tea, sugar, green beans and mooncakes. In the summer they get subsidised ice cream, and in the winter padded cotton shoes and a coat. All medical costs are paid by the factory, and a full wage is paid for the first six months of illness, going down to 70 per cent of the full wage thereafter. Children of workers have their medical expenses partly paid. The factory provides a free day-care centre for children, and if the home is too far away it will pay for outside day-care. It pays maternity leave. It organises clubs for singing, painting, model aircraft, football, basketball, volleyball, ping-pong and swimming and there is a well-stocked library. Every worker has two days off a week, and the factory closes for one week a year. Newly married couples get three to ten days off depending on their age. When retirement comes, at fifty for women and fifty-five for men (intellectuals go on till sixty), the pension is usually three-quarters of the final salary. This paternalistic factory is highly successful, a credit to socialism and, needless to say, popular with its employees.[34]

The Shanghai Machine-Building Factory goes even further. Here work groups of fifteen or twenty compete with each other, and individuals compete within the work group. A 15 per cent bonus is given to 40 per cent of the workers chosen by democratic consensus. But if a worker is late he loses a third of his monthly bonus, and if he is late three times he loses the whole bonus. Quality circles have been introduced and it will not surprise those with some knowledge of Chinese society to learn that fellow-workers have a say even in an individual worker's marriage, children and travel.[35]

The Qingming Automobile Company in Chongqing is another variant of this kind of success. One of China's 500 most profitable enterprises, its rules are even stricter. Workers must attend in their work clothes ten minutes before work starts each day, ready for the ten-minute morning meeting. They are not allowed to be late for it, or to leave it early. The men wear the same uniform, from the manager down to the canteen cooks, but in different colours to distinguish departments. This factory employs no cleaners. Each worker has to clean his own machine at the beginning and end of the shift – and clean the washroom as well. There is no shortening of working hours in the summer, and no bonus system. The company has introduced advanced Japanese technology, but strictly forbids moonlighting (something which workers at other companies are allowed to do, much to their profit). So here at this Chongqing car plant there is some dissatisfaction when employees compare its regulations with those of other factories in the city. But intrinsically it is a well-organised concern capable of earning profits and paying good wages.[36]

Compare that with the Shanghai Toothpaste Factory, responsible for one-third of the national output. Here lateness is frequent, workers doze with their legs crossed, and three workers are assigned for a post which only needs two (the third acting as a reserve). One worker comments, 'I worked really hard when I first came to this factory, but as time went by I discovered that lazy people received the same bonus and no less pay. Why should I work so hard?'[37]

The reforms have not always been popular. The manager of a shirt factory, Bu Xinsheng, abolished egalitarianism, slimmed the workforce, and paid piece-rates instead of fixed wages, as a result of which profits soared and state tax revenues increased. Take-home pay was doubled, but no more slacking was allowed. Some of the dismissed workers sued the manager: 'You are just like a capitalist boss, and we are just working like slaves in a labour camp.' But success eventually went to Bu's head. Overwhelmed by the honours he won, and by his new closeness to the Prime Minister, Zhao Ziyang (whom he personally advised to make China into a share-owning society with simplified taxes), Bu saw his once-renowned factory come to the brink of closure and he was dismissed.[38]

Many workers, forced to cut their pay packet or be dismissed, took revenge on their managers by beating them up or even killing them, as one redundant chemical factory employee in Hefei did by running his manager over twice with a truck. He was sentenced to death. Even Party officials themselves resorted to violence. A Communist Party secretary who was made to accept early retirement at the Shanghai Number 17 Bleach and Dye Factory, reverting to a traditional form of protest, spread manure on his factory manager's door, a gesture that would be understood in every country.[39]

Because a Chinese factory is traditionally run as a big family, employees expect favours, as they would from a parent. In a freezer factory in central China the gateman's brother got married, so he asked the factory to provide a bus for the guests. The manager explained that their bus was for use at work, and if the employees didn't have it, they could not work. He offered to lend two sedans instead. Who would have thought that this would cause offence? Yet for the next three days the factory vehicles could not leave the grounds without being harassed by the guards.[40] Even with the surviving degree of Communist Party control over industry, that kind of revenge by employees who have become used to the perquisites of the former era could not be prevented.

Some labour is forced, as in the labour reform camps to which thousands of criminals and dissidents are condemned and the products of which are targeted by the USA as unacceptable imports. This is a standard punishment designed to 'create a new man' through the discipline of work. It also provides the state, as one Chinese commentator put it, with an army of 'obedient, expense-free, mostly young, male labourers'. In Guangdong province alone their output is thought to exceed RMB 156 million. They are particularly important for the car industry, where one in seven of the factories making vehicles or parts, including the Hunan Heavy Truck factory, is a labour reform enterprise. The B 6050 shaping machine exported to Hongkong and Singapore by the Xiangyang Machine Tool Factory was made by prisoners. The *Nineties Monthly*, the well-informed Hongkong magazine on Chinese affairs, naughtily commented that these prisoners should actually be envied because they enjoy the privilege of secure jobs when millions outside are unemployed.[41]

The West usually thinks of Chinese workers as diligent and dedicated. That is not the general experience of foreign visitors or investors these days. 'Basically they do not care about productivity and profitability as we do,' said a textile investor from Taiwan. A Japanese expert criticised the lack of attention to detail of Chinese shirtmakers. But similar comments used to be made about the early stages of industrialisation in Taiwan itself – and Japan, for that matter. China's workers today often came fresh from the slower pace of rural life, infected by the monolithic paternalism of the Maoist period. That will change. What may not change is a certain lack of taste and indifference to standards. Dr Terry Ginty runs the Shanghai Yaohua Pilkington Glass works on the bank of Shanghai's Huang Pu river. 'There is no natural Chinese concern for quality and appearance,' he complains. 'People say, "Why do we have to scrap this lovely large piece of glass just because of that tiny flaw?"'

Chinese chauvinism makes it especially legitimate to complain against a foreign employer. The two thousand workers, mostly women from north China, at the Mitsumi Electric Plant in the Special Economic Zone of Zhuhai struck for higher pay in 1993. It was found that not only pay levels but conditions of work at many of the factories owned by Taiwan and Hongkong businessmen were very poor indeed. One joint venture in Shanghai did not allow its employees, housed in company dormitories, to date with the opposite sex for the first three years.

Japanese visitors at a hotel with Japanese management had some of their belongings stolen, and two Chinese women staff came under suspicion: the managers ordered an illegal nude body search. The hotel apologised later, and a *People's Daily* article affirmed that enterprises were not allowed to beat or curse workers at will, to make body searches, to confine workers or encroach on their personal freedoms or damage their personal dignity. 'Some foreign businessmen ... believe that since the workers are hired hands, the boss and managerial executives of an enterprise can do anything they want to the workers. This is an extremely incorrect concept.' When a Taiwan-owned textile mill in Shenzhen dismissed a woman worker, she set fire to the factory and in doing so killed sixty-one of her fellow-workers.[42]

All this gave the trade unions the chance of much-needed publicity. A leader of the All-China Federation of Trade Unions cast his members working at foreign enterprises as 'masters of the country', with status and rights protected by law, though he added that the unions must 'support foreign-funded enterprises in their legitimate management and business operations'.[43]

The worst cases were in Xiamen and in Guangdong, where Taiwan managers used to rougher justice often mistreated their workforce. One woman in a Taiwan shoe factory in Fuzhou tried to steal two pairs of shoes. When the Taiwanese managers caught her, they tied her up and beat her, hanging the shoes around her neck in front of the other workers, and then locked her up in a dog cage where two big dogs barked at her. Next morning the Taiwanese manager was said to have told the six hundred women workers: 'I have treated you as humans in the past, but now I am going to treat you as dogs.' Safety in the Special Economic Zones was not usually given a high priority, so cases of electrocution or lost fingers and even severed hands and arms were not infrequent (one Taiwan factory in Xiamen had forty-three cases of severed parts of the body). A foreign manager in Shenyang noticed that a glass product had not been properly cleaned, so he made the worker concerned lick it with his tongue.[44]

Foreign investors were eventually told at the highest level to clean up their act. President Jiang Zemin warned Taiwan investors in Xiamen that 'we have drafted the law to protect Taiwan compatriots' investment . . . but there is one condition. You must protect the workers; only then will workers be motivated.'[45] Beijing also set a minimum wage for the first time, at half the average wage in each province, thus tightening up the conditions under which foreign investors can operate.

Unrest was not confined to foreign enterprises, though it was more publicised there. Some laid-off workers from state factories took to the streets. When the industrial city of Shenyang could not pay wages to the workers of more than eighty enterprises in 1994, workers applied to hold rallies, demanding that the government cease factory closures. They chartered trains to take petitioners to Beijing and protested under such slogans as 'Down with the newly emerging nobility', and 'Eradicate the new bureaucratic bourgeoisie'.[46] This was getting too near the bone for political leaders. It was found that there are now 800 unofficial trade unions in Guangdong alone, trying to protect the interests of migrant workers from other provinces.

In the spring of 1994 some sixteen people were accused of forming an underground union. They included five intellectuals (a former language lecturer, a former hospital doctor, a former Beijing University law student, a former law teacher and a former science researcher). The government accused them of forming a 'Liberal Democratic Party of China', a 'Progressive Alliance of China' and a 'Preparatory Committee for the Chinese Free Trade Unions'.[47] This kind of collaboration of professional intellectuals and unofficial workers' leaders struck a chill in the hearts of the Communists who expect to control the trade unions. Tiananmen had advertised the incipient danger of an intellectual-proletarian alliance.

China undergoing reform has, however, thrown up an remarkable number of capable – often brilliant – entrepreneurs. A carpenter called Liu Xiang loved to race motorcycles, but wondered why crash helmets were not made in China. He took an imported one home to dismantle, and designed a new one. By selling his motorbike and cashing in his savings he raised enough in his twenties to buy an electric drill to make his own helmets. Now he employs over sixty workers, has an American joint-venture partner and exports helmets to the USA at a fifth of the price of the American article. His assets are put at over a million RMB, he swaggers around in a leather jacket and plays the stock market with his profits. 'If you don't fulfill your quota in this company,' his sales manager flatly warns the employees, 'you're fired.'[48]

Students were eager to try their luck. An undergraduate at Oxford raised £1.5 million from state-owned firms to launch a development company. Another pestered all his fellow-students and friends for pictures of European dogs. He was sure his proposed calendar for the imminent Year of the Dog would be a winner. A Tianjin student quickly earned his million. Indeed most of the new tycoons were very young, and the old school – and college – tie has become important again after thirty years of egalitarian neglect.

A carpenter who carved an astonishing fortune for himself out of the reform economy was Zhang Guoxi of Jiangxi province. After school he joined a small collective repairing farm tools, and later won an order to make carved wooden chests for Shanghai. So he sold his mother's house for £200 and used that to hire a master carver from the next province. He was in business, and never looked back. Without taking a penny from the state he went on to organise singlehanded a network of over 2,000 workers carving Buddhist house shrines for the Japanese market. Today he is worth at least £300 million. Small, almost bald and bursting with energy, he runs over thirty different enterprises and eight joint ventures including a bank in partnership with the Bank of China. Still in his early forties, Zhang smokes 100 cigarettes a day, drinks cognac, collects antiques and hunts pheasants: he could almost fit into the England of P.G. Wodehouse. His disappointment is that the government would not let him have his own aeroplane, though he could easily afford it. One reason for his industrial success is that he hires workers in their twenties who never knew the old factory routine of tea-breaks and gossip, and actually work hard.[49]

At the other end of the millionaire spectrum are the old dogs of pre-1949 capitalism who were lucky or smart enough to wait out the Maoist period, ready to stage a dramatic come-back under the Deng reforms. An early case was the Mingshen Industrial Shipping Co. of Chongqing which had been nationalised under Mao but was leased back to the founder's son in the 1980s. In form Mingshen became a collectively owned company with all the workers co-owning, but since they were still loyal to the family, the new boss ran the business as the family used to run it – only more diplomatically.

Capitalists came out of the closet all over China. Seven thousand of them were declared 'reformed' and were solemnly rehabilitated. Since Deng had introduced his new policies on the platform of rejecting the Cultural Revolution, it was natural for him to restore to the capitalists the money, homes and bank interest which the Red Guards had grabbed from them. That was their 're-starting' capital.

The star of this revival hailed from a very old capitalist family. Rong Yiren, once the biggest businessman in Shanghai and its deputy mayor, king of textiles and flour milling and much else besides, was on the face of it an unlikely ally of the Communist Party. While the Cultural Revolution raged, Rong quietly planted flowers in his garden and studied books. Deng, who had got to know him, gave him millions of RMB in compensation for what had been confiscated, and Rong used that to become the most famous 'red capitalist' of them all. Within a decade, at seventy-two, he headed a commercial empire conservatively estimated to be worth $1 billion, centred on the China International Trust and Investment Corporation. Through CITIC Rong controlled 200 other firms including Communist China's first private bank, with branches and assets world-wide including American timber forests and Australian factories. Wisely perhaps, when offered a slice of London's Canary Wharf development in 1988, he declined, finding it 'too big and ambitious', though his company lost heavily on the London Metals Exchange in 1995.[50]

Rong climbed politically to be Vice-President of the People's Republic. He claimed that his salary from the company was little more than £60 a month, but his benefits and perks were unprecedented – villas crammed with works of art, eight servants, three cars. He liked to tell visiting correspondents, 'I am not a capitalist: call me an entrepreneur. I work for the state, not for myself. Our company gives all its profits to the state.' If you ask likely-looking old boys at official receptions whether they are capitalists, they are apt to pale and clear their throats nervously and say, 'We would rather you call us industrialists. We may have a lot of money, but you see we don't exploit people any more.'

Sometimes the son or daughter of a senior Communist turns out to be a gifted entrepreneur. Now that Rong Yiren has 'gone international', the richest man in Shanghai is probably Ren Baizun, son of a diplomat who soaked up capitalist ideas while he was a teenager in his parents' house in Tokyo. Currently he employs 11,000 people in the hotel and tourist business and is also worth about $1 billion.[51] More distinguished is Wang Guangying, the brother-in-law of China's former President and Deng Xiaoping's former ally, Liu Shaoqi. As a kind of compensation for Liu's tragic death in the Cultural Revolution in 1969, Deng gave 'Big Wang' US$ 50 million and told him to build an industrial and trading company in Hongkong that would compete with the capitalists there. This was the Everbright

Company, owned by the Chinese state with headquarters in Hongkong and assets of about $500 million. In the first two years of his new assignment, 'Big Wang' negotiated $40 billion-worth of foreign investment capital or technology for China in all kinds of manufacturing. His star waned somewhat when he burnt a finger in Hongkong's treacherous property market, and Everbright is now run by Chinese technocrats. But in the meantime Wang drove a Mercedes, joined the Rotary Club, played golf, drank champagne and ran a luxury apartment in Hongkong as well as a Beijing villa. All on an official salary of £72 a month.[52]

If he cannot claim a family relationship with political leaders, the next best thing for a businessman is to be very close friends with one. The outstanding example of that was the electronics wizard Wan Runnan, who hobnobbed so enthusiastically with Premier Zhao Ziyang that when Zhao fell from power in 1989, Wan's position collapsed too. Wan had originally launched the Stone Group on its meteoric rise to international fame with six other computer specialists and only RMB 20,000 in his pocket. He claimed that his creation was a co-operative rather than a private company, with workers holding shares. Stone became the first Chinese company to contribute technology as equity, in a joint venture with Mitsui. For a Chinese company, it was unusually aggressive in developing and marketing new products. One of its 900 employees invented a novel typesetting process which the company was able to develop in a joint venture with Unisys, though Stone was then caught in an angry legal battle over patent rights.

In 1989 Wan found himself on the government's wanted list for having supported too enthusiastically the student demands leading up to the Tiananmen killings. Armed soldiers occupied his factories after Zhao's ousting. Business and opposition politics do not mix in China. Wan fled, first to Hongkong, then to the United States and France, where he became an exiled dissident. 'If the political system is not changed,' he warned Chinese students in Paris, 'we cannot have economic development.'[53] Gorbachev would have agreed, but not Deng Xiaoping or most other Chinese leaders. Stone itself survived under another leader, while hundreds of other high-tech companies mushroomed on the ground Wan vacated.

The re-labelled capitalists and the new post-Mao entrepreneurs soon got together. A hundred Shanghai businessmen put up RMB 57 million to launch the Patriotic Construction Corporation (Patco) which paid them fixed interest and re-invested the profits from various factories and housing developments. One of the founders called it a people's organisation. 'The state,' he explained, 'has not put one cent into it. But the state has exempted the company from taxation for the first five years.' The vice-president had trained at MIT and London's Imperial College. Before 1978 his technical knowledge had been utilised only in working on a lathe in one of his father's factories, and he was not allowed to inherit his father's wealth and holdings. Yet he was one of the very few in China with any pretence to practical business experience. At Patco he was once again in his element.[54]

Another throw-back to capitalist days was the opening of a new entrepreneurs' club in Shanghai in 1985. Guangzhou followed suit a year later with a 'millionaires' club' open to the sixty enterprises earning more than US$1 million a year. That idea came from Ye Xuanping, the provincial governor and son of the respected old Communist Ye Jianying who had been one of the Party's economic overseers in earlier years. Club members get preferential treatment for foreign exchange, tax payments, import credits and export market surveys.[55]

The new business élite is clearly making up the ground it had lost under Mao. But will it be sensitive enough to avoid a flamboyant show of wealth? Two recent developments make one wonder. In Wuhan a private fee-paying school has opened, funded by local traders. In Guangzhou the first batch of schoolchildren from rich families has flown privately to Japan for education there. It is a very old Chinese tradition to value schooling, and parents will still sacrifice to shoulder their offspring up the educational ladder. But too much social privilege may provoke political opposition and hamper the economic role of these 'pink' capitalists.

Foreign managers are a different bowl of beansprouts. No one seriously believes they could take over the Chinese economy, topple national institutions or subvert Communist ideology. They could simply be expelled, against China's background of mild xenophobia, if they became a nuisance. Yet many of them have left a deep mark on Chinese industry, typically those joint ventures where the foreign partner sends a manager to get the enterprise going.

Hongtex of Hongkong, for example, bought up 51 per cent of the Wuhan No. 2 Printing and Dying Works, which was in deep trouble, losing almost US$2 million a year. Mr and Mrs Cheung of Hongtex, two energetic Shanghainese from families which had opted out of the Mao turmoil by fleeing to Hongkong, found it a tricky acquisition. The government allowed them to fire two-thirds of the workforce, but hundreds of angry redundant men and women surrounded the Cheungs all the same, shouting 'Down with capitalism' and stealing TV sets and tools from the factory. In the end many of those dismissed got work in canteens and guesthouses affiliated with the company and qualified for tax concessions, while others were sent home with municipal hand-outs of two-thirds the former wage. Mrs Cheung, who was in day-to-day charge, paid the lucky survivors three times their old wage. But she also put them on short-term contracts with incentive schemes, withdrew their former perks, and raised their working hours to ten. The plant was soon in profit.[56]

That was a case of a Chinese disciplining Chinese. What happens when a European or American tries it? A former Nike manager showed that he could pull it off without injury. Howard Shaffer started a partnership with the suitably named Long March Leather Shoe Factory in 1985. He decreed no more sleeping on the job and no more lateness at work, and four years later Shaffer was running three profitable factories making 7 million pairs of shoes a year for the American market.[57]

As an owner, Shaffer had some clout, but there were also cases where a naturally chauvinistic labour force found itself working for a foreign manager hired by the Chinese company, for a salary, to lick its workers into shape. Werner Gerich, a German engineer, was the pace-setter here. Invited to China as a volunteer consultant for the Wuhan Diesel Company, to help them introduce new equipment, he liked the place and enjoyed the professional challenge. If he were put in charge, he told city officials, he could make the plant's diesel engines last three times as long and sell them abroad. The Wuhan Municipal Communist Party Committee agreed to the experiment, giving him the power he asked for to fire not only workers but even Communist representatives at the factory.

Gerich imposed high standards from the start. On his fourth day an inspection team, finding that holes had been wrongly drilled in water tanks, recommended a smearing of glue. Gerich insisted that this was not enough. The tanks should be reworked. In the end he dismissed the head of the inspection team and the chief engineer, and demoted the men responsible for the faulty work in the first place. He also demanded prompt starts and no early shut-downs, to get full production for each shift, and he had the temerity to restrict the number and length of the Party officials' factory meetings. The pay-off was a big increase in output and profits.[58]

Wuhan liked the result, and the next to be hired was Ken Hayes of Australia. Under the new contract system he was given full management authority at the Changhong Mould Factory on the basis of keeping 70 per cent of the profits for himself but paying a penalty if the annual profit target was not met. When he replaced seniority wages by technical ability grades, the older workers took everyone out on strike – but they shuffled back within an hour. Many employees liked the new pay system. The Party Secretary who wandered about 'doing nothing', or 'sat in his office drinking tea and reading the newspaper', was asked to retire.[59]

The Japanese are renowned for revitalising old factories, but they were not outstandingly successful in China. The extraordinary technical mistakes made at the Japanese-funded Baoshan steelworks near Shanghai cast a long shadow over Japan's reputation. The site proved unsuitable for the foundations, and the nearest deep water port able to take iron-ore carriers was a hundred miles away. Economic overheating forced the Chinese government to seek cancellation of Baoshan's second stage at the last minute, when Japanese firms were already committed. It was, an economic journal unkindly wrote, 'a case of the ill-advised asking the insensitive to finance the unneccessary'. It went ahead eventually, after Japanese protests, with a reduced role, and today the plant, though late completing, is profitable.[60] In the later 1980s and early 1990s, Japanese investment picked up. Japanese managers found Chinese workers more money-conscious than status-conscious, unlike their Japanese counterparts, and many joint ventures with Japan paid 60 per cent or so of employees' earnings in the form of basic pay, with the rest in bonuses.

Some Chinese enterprises did without the foreign managers, only using the capital involvement of an overseas company as a means of modernising themselves. Such was the experiment of the Shanghai Construction Machinery Factory, a nationally strategic group making crushers through a large network of smaller companies. In the early years of industrial reform it introduced promotion by merit, followed by open management, and in 1989 the company entered a joint venture with a Hongkong firm which injected cash and sent executives in twice a year to help make management decisions and distribute profits. The result was more autonomy, a greater concern about getting a return on assets and an internal production management system capable of adapting to changes in the market. Only one worker was struck from the payroll. The benefits quickly flowed. The managers did not have to seek approval for purchases or fund allocation. Sales were no longer contracted or guaranteed by the government. The Hongkong investor insisted on a minimum level of profits (higher than interest rates on bank deposits in Hongkong), and although it had only a minority ownership, that proved to be a powerful lever in propagating the ideas of capital expansion and capital returns.[61]

In 1994 the Chinese government felt it could become more discriminating, and it limited the influence of overseas models by putting a ceiling of 35 per cent on foreign investors' proportions of a listed enterprise's equity.

Drawing the lessons from it all, the *Liberation Daily* of Shanghai noted that the first requirement for such transformations was a new structure for the enterprise, severing ownership and management rights and creating 'an autonomously run, financially accountable, self-accumulating, self-developing, self-restraining producer and handler of merchandise'. Secondly, the owners must take clear-cut stands, especially on the return from assets. Revolutionary words from a Communist daily!

A bleak picture of the actual situation was painted in 1995: 'State-owned enterprises are now facing many difficulties ... including their traditionally heavy burdens, unduly high asset-liability ratios, small shares of working capital, large numbers of surplus personnel, excessively heavy social responsibilities, outdated technology and equipment, failure to separate government administration from enterprise management, lack of clearly defined investor responsibilities, extensive losses and serious interlocking debts.' These were not the words of a domestic critic or pessimistic foreign analyst, but part of a speech by Wu Bangguo just before his promotion to be vice premier in charge of industry – a sober economic leader and touted by some to succeed Li Peng as Prime Minister of China.[62]

If it all seems early days for China's industrial revolution, the progress so far should be put into a perspective. Taiwan began forty years ago with the state owning 90 per cent of industrial assets. That was steadily reduced, at a rate of about 2 per cent a year, to 20 per cent. China is moving faster than that, and should reach Taiwan's level in under forty years. But the infrastructure is poor. Every kind of transport is under-developed, as anyone knows who has tried to travel in China. The amount spent on infrastructure per head of population is only half what Korea or India lays out.

Scientific research and technology is also weak, slowing down China's industrialisation programme. In some ways it should not be. China produced an atomic bomb and constructed a second-generation electronic computer thirty years ago. But Mao's Cultural Revolution swept scientists out of their laboratories just as the West was making its own leap forward in computers and electronics.

Coincident with the Cultural Revolution came a tragic error in industrial policy which proved even more economically destructive than the Cultural Revolution itself. The military leader Lin Biao suggested that China protect its industries from possible American, Taiwanese or Soviet invasion by setting up a 'Third Front' in the interior, especially Anhui and Sichuan, behind the more vulnerable first two fronts on or near the coast. Like Stalin's shift of Russian production to the other side of the Urals during the Second World War, this was an incredibly expensive exercise. Railway track in other areas was torn up in order to construct new railway lines to this interior region, where Third Front defence industries, especially electronics, were by the late 1960s eating up more than half of the national investment. A few years later many of these costly factories, wrongly sited from the point of view of the civilian economy, were declared useless.[63]

The more down-to-earth Deng Xiaoping sensibly shifted the focus to developing the naturally favoured coastal areas first. A few Third Front factories managed to keep afloat, including the Number Two Auto Plant in Hubei, but that was only on the basis of moving much of its production out of the mountains into the small nearby city of Xiangfan. Zhenhua Electronic Corporation relocated to Shenzhen where it now makes printed circuits and colour TV sets for export and the domestic market. About a thousand of these rusticated military-electronics factories have now resumed their natural place in the cities, while others merged or closed. But Lin Biao's legacy lingered on. Many Third Front workers had been summarily taken from coastal cities to work inland, and could hardly be simply abandoned by the government, and the inability of Third Front factories to cope with the rise in raw material costs was one of the factors inhibiting price reform in the 1980s.

The reformers tried to introduce their famous contract responsibility system into the scientific research institutes in the 1980s, and there have been several successes, including the completion and testing of the Beijing Electron-Positron Collider, and a number of space launches. Shanghai built a micro-electronics park. In 1983 Zhao Ziyang, the first truly forward-looking leader to emerge in China, read Alvin Toffler's *The Third Wave*, and instigated the creation of twenty hi-tech zones, including Beijing's 'electronics street' which has 150 private electronics firms employing more than 4,000. The Stone Group was, of course, a big initial player in the new drama.[64]

But the problem is how to link research and development systematically into actual commercial use. Most of the 9,000 research institutes have no direct connection with companies. They are collaborations between industrial ministries and universities. Horizontal links in Chinese society being always poor, there is much duplication, along with under-utilisation of resources.

At least China has taken its first steps on the controversial road to nuclear power, as one would expect from its earlier military

***The stout horse called 'scientific research expenditure' has to pull a heavily loaded wagon crammed with people, most of whom are administrators bunched in front while the few genuine scientists teeter at the back on the brink of falling off* (Popular Tribune Monthly, *September 1991*).**

applications. A 3 MW experimental reactor was built at Qinshan, near Shanghai, mainly using indigenous designs, although two French companies were contracted in 1992 to help design two new 600 GW reactors for the plant. A second nuclear power station was built at Daya Bay close to Hongkong, opening in 1993 amidst considerable protest from the people of Hongkong who judged it far too near to their urban concentration of six million people, especially after the admission by Chinese, French and British engineers of some apparently minor mistakes in construction and a later hiccup in energy production. Local Guangdong province officials, worried about their own communities' future safety as well as the impact on Hongkong opinion, had wanted the plant to go up at Yangjiang, much further away from the populous coast, but the site would have been more expensive.[65]

The economic arguments for nuclear power in China are persuasive. Nuclear waste is no problem: 'We have very good storage facilities,' said Liu Zongtang, vice-chairman of the National People's Congress Environment Protection Committee, 'in the Gobi desert.'[66] Two bigger reactors are now to be added at Daya Bay, and a third, very large nuclear power station is planned in Jiangxi. The Prime Minister, Li Peng, himself an electrical engineer by training, has taken a personal interest in the Daya Bay project and visited it at least nine times, while his wife plays the part of agent for the company.

The national nuclear power goal is 6,000 MW, to fill the huge gaps left by traditional energy sources. Coal is the biggest conventional source, meeting about two-thirds of the nation's energy needs, but it enters the market mostly unwashed, with a consequent loss of efficiency. Finds of oil and natural gas have been made, but not yet of a size to make a dramatic difference. Oil exports may have to be controlled, and imports have resumed. Power cuts or shortages are frequent in Chinese factories, making up to a fifth of their production capacity idle. The government plans to have more wood burnt to produce energy, even though the forest-management record is bad. As with the major industrial materials, price policy worsens the problem. Energy prices are kept low to help industry and consumers, as a result of which the energy producers operate at a loss and have to be bailed out with enormous state subsidies. The concept of efficiency goes up in smoke.[67]

Many Chinese hopes are placed on new hydro-electric power, for which there is a potential although it currently contributes only about 12 GW. The Sanxia (Three Gorges) dam on the Yangzi river would alone add 18 GW and create a new reservoir the size of the Republic of Singapore. This is a breathtaking scheme. It would be the world's largest dam, much larger than Aswan in Egypt, and it fascinates China's political leaders as a symbol of how their deep hunger for rapid economic development could be satisfied. The idea of a giant dam near the Hubei–Sichuan border was first advanced by Sun Yatsen seventy years ago, since when many teams of engineers – Chinese, Russian and American – have surveyed the site and recommended construction.[68]

The Communist government took an interest after bad flooding caused much damage in the area in 1949 and again in 1954, and Chairman Mao wrote an approving poem about Sanxia:

A stone wall in the Western Yangzi

Cuts off the turbulence of Wushan Mountains
Forming a placid lake among proud gorges.
The Goddess can rest at ease
When such distinction appears in the world.

The downstream provinces (especially Hubei and Hunan) approved of the proposed Sanxia dam. Just below the dam site the river bed runs higher than the surrounding fields, so that no amount of dykes or embankments can protect farmers indefinitely. The local planners, who would benefit from flood control, also backed the dam, along with the central planners and the Ministry of Water Conservancy. Opposed to the project were Sichuan province, which would bear the brunt of upstream flooding and silting while receiving only a tenth of the power, and also the Ministries of Electric Power and Communications.

Proposed starts were repeatedly postponed until serious flooding struck again in 1991, when over 3,000 people died and damage was estimated at the equivalent of a quarter of the annual national budget. Yet opposition – and caution – are still in evidence. One of Mao's smaller dams, completed in 1960, had lost much of its hydro-electric potential because of silting, and it was feared the same might happen to Sanxia. Conservationists reminded everyone of the works of eighth-century poets extolling the natural beauty of the area and warned of the possible extinction of the Yangzi sturgeon, Chinese sucker, grenadier fish and Siberian crane. A third of the National People's Congress delegates refused to vote for the scheme, and it was not helped by the 1993 collapse after only eight years of the Gouhou dam in Qinghai province, killing more than 240 people and destroying 3,000 buildings.

Deng Xiaoping resolved to end the arguments and go ahead with the dam and Premier Li Peng became personally committed to it. Westinghouse, Siemens and Hitachi were poised to supply equipment. What tipped the scales was the prospect of protecting Wuhan and many other places against flooding, generating additional electricity, and providing new access for 10,000-ton ships to the inland river port of Chongqing for half the year. Wuhan was readying for its mega-container port in which the Hongkong Chinese capitalist Peter Woo – called by Wuhan's

Communist mayor 'a visionary' – wanted to invest on a big scale.

But Sichuanese leaders still demanded more research, because 'the consequences of any errors ... are terrifying to contemplate.' They believed that silting would kill Chongqing harbour navigation and its client industries, and that Wuhan's freedom from floods would be purchased at the expense of more flooding in Chongqing, parts of which would be submerged. Dai Qing, the writer and daughter of a Communist Party elder statesman, wrote passionately: 'We only have one Yangzi. We've already done enough foolish things to her. We can't afford further foolish mistakes.'

Speaking independently, much to Deng's vexation, at the UN Earth Summit in Brazil in 1992, Dai voiced the critics' deepest fears. 'Nowhere else on earth can one find an enormous hydro-electric power station built on a river which has high silt deposits and is needed for shipping.' The planners had specified an expensive shiplift system to raise large ships 370 feet through five consecutive locks, but the risk of mechanical failure seemed a real one.

To the list of threatened species Dai, a dedicated conservationist, now added the *Lipotes vexillifer* and Chinese paddle-fish. She stubbornly asked questions about the resettlement of over a million people living in the reservoir site – and its cost. If anything went wrong, six provinces and municipalities would be inundated and the lives or livelihoods of several hundred million people would be put in jeopardy. It would be 'a burden on our descendants and a target ... for our enemies.' (Sanxia's vulnerability to nuclear attack had been another opposition argument.) But other independent-minded critics eventually saw that Li Peng, backed by Deng, had made up his mind and that further opposition was pointless. Only a few others continued the fight, and Dai herself was arrested, jailed and had her emotive book *Yangtze! Yangtze!* banned.

Meanwhile, lower down on the Chinese coast, another kind of flood was being kept at bay. A million would-be shareholders from almost every province descended on the virgin Stock Exchange at Shenzhen, across the river from Hongkong, on 9 August 1992, scrambling to apply for a new share issue. So keen were they to join the share-holding élite that the police had to use leather belts, bamboo poles and electric cattle prods to bludgeon them into keeping order. More than 200 people had to be treated at the local hospital. At one point, officials at the local branch of the Bank of China were forced to barricade their doors with filing cabinets to stop the hordes from pressing their way through. Windows were broken and cars smashed.

By evening all the application forms for shares had been sold (for RMB 100 yuan each), and disappointed applicants went on the rampage, accusing officials of corruptly giving forms to their friends. The mayor of Guangzhou dismissed talk of chaos. 'It's just like a baby learning to walk,' he insisted. But there had been a similarly undignified fracas over an earlier stock issue in Shanghai, whose unanticipated demand led to stock being sold at a premium six times its face value.[69]

China's age-old love of gambling was being resurrected. Had not China agreed to allow betting on Jockey Club races to continue in Hongkong after 1997? Was not horse-racing introduced in Shenzhen? The share market may reassure Western businessmen that China is serious in permitting free enterprise, but its contribution to the economy remains controversial. When Zhao Ziyang was Prime Minister he told the Thirteenth Party Congress that shares were 'one means of raising money for socialist enterprises', and would be experimented with on that basis. Professor Li Yining of Beijing University argued eloquently for using the share market mechanism and assailed the reservations expressed by such political leaders as Tian Jiyun.[70] Towards the end of the 1980s it frequently came to be commented in the Chinese press that Chinese people were not psychologically prepared for the risks they would encounter on the Stock Exchange.

An unlucky bus driver who had speculated on the Shanghai Exchange jumped off the Nanpu bridge, and another killed himself after hearing of his losses. 'The government told us,' a sophisticated loser complained, 'that investing in stocks would help China's economic development by providing capital for industries that need to modernise in order to compete. But the government and newspapers did not educate investors to the dangers of the stock market.'[71] The Chinese are learning capitalism the hard way. Even the international experts are having second thoughts. A recent World Bank report says that the emphasis placed on stock exchanges in China is 'misplaced'.[72]

The gambling instinct is ingrained all the same, and the Chinese may well in the end become more eager practitioners of the skill of share-holding than Westerners. Already Beijing offers lessons in basic finance and advanced Wall Street techniques at a private night school hopefully named the Wanlong (Ever-Prosperous) Securities School. At US$33 for a three-month course it sounds a bargain.[73] Keynes may have despaired of the longer-term rationality of the stock market, wanting the buying of a share to be as 'permanent and indissoluble' as marriage. But the Chinese prefer the excitement of short-term investment affairs with frequent changes of partner. A former Red Guard, who made a fortune on the Shanghai Exchange and is now known as 'Millions Yang', advised a desperate woman whose stock was descending fast: 'You must be willing to take a loss. If it's going down, sell it and accept the loss. Otherwise you'll be stuck with a bigger loss.'[74]

The first unofficial stock market in Shanghai opened early on, dealing mostly in government-controlled stocks: it was officially recognised three years later. Now it has a well-trained man in charge. Wang Poming holds a higher degree in international finance from Columbia University and worked on the New York Stock Exchange. His dream is to preside over a fully-fledged 'Great Wall Street' bourse which would stand comparison with the big Western exchanges. For the moment the Shanghai Exchange is housed in the old Astor Hotel. Its electronic quotation board was, most appropriately, a gift from the Taipei Exchange, along with clearing and settlement software. So the Shanghai Exchange is influenced by Taipei, just as the rival Shenzhen Exchange grows in the shadow of big brother Hongkong. When it comes to speculation, political borders melt.

The rivalry between the two Chinese exchanges is intense. In 1995 the pioneering Shanghai International Securities gambled on the bond market and almost came to a Baring-like crash: the government set up a new supervisory committee to avoid recurrences. Eventually other cities will open exchanges, but for the time being those two will be the laboratories for 'share-holding with Chinese characteristics'. Hainan tried to climb aboard the enticing bandwagon with its own exchange in 1992 but Zhu Rongji soon closed it down. 'He swatted us like a fly,' they complained, because 'if we could launch a stock market on our own, soon they would be sprouting up all over the country.'[75] Given teething problems to be overcome, the securities and companies law of 1994 should regulate the industry better and keep temperatures down in Shanghai and Shenzhen.

Shanghai is hoping with official encouragement to regain its former pre-eminence as an international financial centre. The first step was to allow foreign bank branches to take deposits and make loans. The second ambitious stage would see Shanghai rivalling the regional facilities of Hongkong and Tokyo, followed by the city's début in the middle of the next century as a major international player with a convertible RMB to back it. This is what the senior Communists linked to Shanghai, like Vice-Premier Zhu Rongji and President Jiang Zemin, would like to see, for reformist reasons as well as local pride. They are deafeningly supported by the people of Shanghai themselves. Of course such ambitions may prove a little too capitalistic for the Party as a whole, and are in any case best denied in the presence of competitors.

When Zhu led a team to Hongkong in 1990 as mayor of Shanghai he downplayed such grand designs. 'We do not see Shanghai as a financial centre,' he assured Hongkongers. 'We are not your competitor, we just want to enliven the business environment. We have come here to learn from you. Developments in Shanghai will only make Hongkong even more successful.' He knew that whatever ambitions the Shanghainese truly nursed would have many hurdles of bureaucracy and inexperience to overcome, and that most observers would put Shanghai about twenty years behind Hongkong in financial development. Foreigners agree that the longer term should favour Shanghai. Whereas Shenzhen is a satellite of Hongkong, says one, 'Shanghai has the potential to be a real national market. The companies are weightier, the participants have a greater vision.'[76]

Shanghai had fallen back tangibly during the Mao period. One statistic makes the point: during the decade officially occupied by the Cultural Revolution, 1966–76, no new housing was built in the entire city, and yet its population grew by millions. Now it is a magnet of investment, domestic and foreign. At the beginning of the 1990s it recorded economic growth of 15 per cent a year, and in 1992 it increased its incoming foreign investment twelve times to exceed $3 billion. But note that half of the $14 billion accumulated investment in Shanghai over the first twelve years of the reforms came from Hongkong. Superhuman efforts were put into Shanghai's new industrial zone across the river at Pudong,[77] partly designed by the British architect Richard Rogers.

A high Shanghai official has recently promised that the 'dying embers' of the city's underworld – kidnapping and prostitution – would not be allowed to glow again.

> We still cannot have things like horse racing . . . casinos or betting companies. Some friends in Hongkong and Macao have written with a good intention to me telling me the merits of those things. However, we have, after consideration, decided not to have such things. We cannot have girls accompanying customers in drinking and other activities. We cannot have pornography in any disguise . . . Because Shanghai was infested with foreign adventurers in the past, we will find it difficult to deal with them if they develop as a result of inappropriate management. For example, those who maintain order in casinos are actually hired ruffians. They would form an underworld, then corrupt our judicial departments, turning policemen and bandits into one family and it would be impossible to stop them.[78]

If the puritanism sounds heavy, it should be remembered that the West had the same problems when it was administering parts of Shanghai under various antique treaties. The pre-war missionaries, who had a more detached view than most, used to say that if God allowed Shanghai to survive, He owed an apology to Sodom and Gomorrah.

Banking has begun to break out of its red fetters, and not only in Shanghai. Gone are the days when a Bank of China official, asked about changes in the foreign exchange rules, could reply, 'Yes, there are new regulations, but I am not allowed to tell you what they are.'[79] One of the first private banks to be established under Communism came in 1985 when a group of young economists in Zhao Ziyang's old stamping-ground of Chengdu formed the Hui Tong Urban Co-operative Bank. Wenzhou could not be left behind. In the recession of 1985 the Wenzhou branches of the state banks would not allow companies to withdraw money, so that some were faced with bankruptcy. When credit was withheld from a new electrical goods entrepreneur, he responded by founding a rival Wenzhou-Lincheng City Credit Co-operative. A British visitor at the time found it offering investors a 32 per cent annual return on their shares![80]

On paper the reformers made impressive improvements in the sphere of public finance, reorganising the banking system, creating a national insurance company, introducing such new concepts as commercial bills, bonds and certificates of deposit as well as stocks and shares, and setting up markets for them. In the first ten years of reform total deposits of state banks grew on average by over 20 per cent a year, and the average individual savings account jumped by a third each year.

Yet the monetary authorities found it difficult to keep the economy on a steady keel. Their control over money seemed to veer from the very loose to the very tight. They could not ensure that funds went to deserving efficient enterprises rather than politically-connected wastrels. Quick-profit industries like TV sets, refrigerators and washing machines secured more credit than others with a longer-term future.

Presiding over these problems is the People's Bank of China, which in the days of Mao used to share a building and have equal status with the Ministry of Finance. Only in 1984 did it become the official Central Bank, surrendering its former commercial functions to the Industrial and Commercial Bank of China. But the old leopard does not change its spots. The People's Bank still hangs on to its branches, sub-branches and staff in every province and municipality and tries to assert its old authority in a new 'moral' guise. The branches, however, are fully caught up in China's favourite game of 'centre-versus-province'. Their heads are appointed in Beijing but their other officials and staff are mostly local, and are expected to be loyal to the province.

When times are bad, a provincial government leader will take leaders of the local branches of the People's Bank and the commercial banks to Beijing to lobby the central authorities for funds, and the People's Bank branch officials will adopt a completely local stand. Their housing, rations and discount-price goods depend, after all, on the local authority, and they can do nothing without that authority's goodwill. If the provincial government is thwarted on some funding matter by the local branch of the People's Bank, it may humiliate it by appealing directly to the central government – where political factors will decide. One such People's Bank branch leader in Sichuan committed suicide in 1986 because of these pressures.[81]

For ten years the People's Bank was under non-professional captains. Chen Muhua was a forceful Party veteran but rather at sea on monetary matters. Her successor, a Moscow-trained chemical engineer and former provincial Party secretary, Li Guixian, was also without any financial background. He took the blame for the failure to control the inflation of 1992–3 and allegedly turned a blind eye to various malpractices. So Zhu Rongji, the multi-talented technocratic Vice-Premier, took the job as President of the People's Bank until 1995 while simultaneously running the rest of the economy.[82]

The People's Bank's capacity to control inflation is hampered because it has no effective control over money supply, is powerless to stop state banks lending (at the order of the State Planning Commission) to unprofitable state enterprises, and has no authority to prevent other financial institutions (such as leasing companies, which are under the Ministry of Foreign Economic Relations and Trade) from pouring money into speculative investments. Rather than lender of last resort, it is actually lender of first resort. 'It is a printing press,' was a Western banker's verdict. 'It is the government cashier.' The banks between them were said to have lent twice the amount planned in 1992, and money supply rose by a third. Banks lend for policy reasons dictated by higher authorities and do not worry about creditworthiness, statutory reserve requirements or similar constraints of banking found in capitalist countries.[83] And yet in spite of all these handicaps inflation has mostly been held down to below typical Russian or Latin American rates until early 1995, at least, after which it climbed to the 20 per cent level.

Vice-Premier Zhu took a stiff-bristled broom to the Bank,

halting irregular inter-bank lending, banning rises in interest rates and cutting the Bank's further links with the businesses it had already funded. The Industrial and Commercial Bank and the Bank of China were ordered to recall high-risk interbank loans and cease lending to leasing, property or securities firms. Such necessary medicine is painful. It is also slow to work. These free-market mechanisms are novel to China, and crude use is only to be expected at first. Until tax reforms are in place and working, there are no fiscal weapons to fight with.

A new tax system was introduced in 1994, imposing a uniform 33 per cent tax on all enterprises, though preferential rates for foreign enterprises and joint ventures were given a temporary reprieve. Personal income tax was standardised to range between 5 and 45 per cent, and value-added tax was fixed at 17 per cent on all goods – with additional excise tax on certain luxury items such as cigarettes, alcohol and petrol. The centre assumed responsibility for collecting taxes directly, but provinces are holding back on what they should remit to Beijing.[84]

Managers do not see paying taxes as a duty to be honoured. In the earlier years of reform when the respective virtues of capitalism and socialism were being ardently debated, Gordon Wu, the Hongkong engineer-developer, used to tell his friends in China that capitalism also incorporated some socialism in the form of income tax, whereby the rich and successful subsidised the poor and needy. Such an idea has not yet taken hold in China. Ge Yale is perhaps typical. A former city planner who rescued an unprofitable state bicycle factory and fired 1,500 workers to keep it going, Ge describes himself as a Communist Party capitalist. Like many other successful managers, he is good at negotiating tax exemption from the local authorities, and he is taken aback by the suggestion that he should pay tax to help the authorities subsidise other workers. Why should he? Did he not relieve the state of a drain on its resources, thereby doing the government a favour? Is he not contributing to society by ploughing profits back into the business?[85] Neither individuals, nor companies, nor, for that matter, provinces are shy about dodging their responsibilities over tax.

Although the People's Bank is not in the commercial banking business any more, it remains a provider of funds to other banks, and to certain high-priority projects and enterprises. The People's Bank was actually ordered by the government in 1990 to make 'debt-clearing' loans to the commercial banks. When it becomes preoccupied with this funding function, the other role of monetary control over the economy can suffer, fanning inflation.

Judgements should not be too severe, however, on the Central Bank's use of bank credit creation to finance investment. It may not be neo-classically correct, but, as Dr Goh Keng Swee, Singapore's former Finance Minister and more recently adviser to the Chinese government, has noted, Japan did the same thing during its economic miracle – though it also controlled inflation, avoided budget deficits and would not use Central Bank money to finance government spending. China is less disciplined, but then its long-term growth prospects are so evident.[86]

The 'big four' commercial banks – Industrial and Commercial Bank of China, Agricultural Bank of China, Construction Bank of China and Bank of China (the trade and foreign exchange bank) – used to keep strictly to their respective parishes. They have only now begun to compete with each other. When Moody's of the US downgraded its credit ratings for the Chinese commercial banks in 1995, it was for administrative uncertainties rather than financial weakness.

It would be impossible to have a totally independent Central Bank in an even partly government-controlled planned economy like China, but reform of the People's Bank role is freely advanced in Beijing. The ideal would be to remove the fund supply function (to another state agency or bank) and encourage the People's Bank to use more diverse instruments, such as the reserve requirement and the interest rate (usually kept too low at present), for monetary control of the commercial banks. The network of provincial branches of the People's Bank could then be reduced. But this will not be achieved easily or quickly.

China's provident rural savers balance the nation's soaring credit and money supply. Some economists believe there is US$200 billion stashed away under those country mattresses. If an attractive and efficient rural savings bank were in place it could soak up much of these savings and make them available to industry, leaving farmers with a tidy income from interest. A financial market in bonds has already emerged; secondary market trading in government bonds and negotiable instruments of deposit by securities firms and trust and investment companies is carried on in more than fifty cities. Enterprise and bank bonds were launched in 1990 with a world-class nation-wide computer network, and foreign currency bonds are available. But co-incident with Britain's Baring disaster in 1995, a big loss on the Shanghai bond market led to closure of the bond futures market and stricter regulations.[87]

The grass-roots pioneer in this sector is a Mr Yang of Shanghai, who made a million RMB in one year by humping a suitcase of bonds and cash all round the country, buying government bonds cheap, for instance in Shenyang, and selling them at a profit in Shanghai where demand is stronger. Worried about his legal position, he hired a lawyer to confirm that there was no law or regulation against what he was doing – and no capital gains tax either, so the tax men did not know what to do with him! Most recently a futures market for various crops has opened in the big agricultural provinces.

All these new opportunities are manna from heaven to young bankers and officials, many of whom now speak the language of Western economics – 'something,' as William Overholt of Bankers' Trust puts it, 'akin to a religious conversion among China's educated younger élite.'[88] The Chinese have never really gone for religion before, but Mammon is currently eating their heart out.

CHAPTER 11

TRADE AND INVESTMENT: THROUGH THE OPEN DOOR

The Chinese, as everyone knows, are consummate traders. 'Nobody', boasted a wise old Beijinger, 'has to teach the Chinese how to trade. We are like the Jews; we are born with it.'[1] But this particular light was hidden under the Communist bushel until the arrival of Deng Xiaoping who, while setting in train the reforms of China's domestic economy, was also introducing his second iconoclasm, that of opening China's door to the outside world. Thirty years of closure under Maoist self-reliance, with limited Soviet help during the first decade, had not produced the desired economic results. This was a dramatic reversal of policy, a bald and honest recognition that China's own resources were simply not enough to secure the speed and quality of economic advance for which every Chinese yearned. It was also a preparatory corseting of nationalism, a considered first step to full membership of the world system.

Obsolete attitudes to foreign investment were brusquely buried. Maoist economists had complained in the 1970s that 'capital export is an important tool used by monopoly capitalists to exploit and plunder the peoples ... of the developing countries.' The *Red Flag*, then the Communist Party's bible, pontificated: 'we have never allowed, nor will we ever allow, foreign capital to invest in our country. We have never joined capitalist countries in exploring our natural resources, nor will we explore other countries' resources.'[2]

Deng replaced all that with the simple formula, long familiar to grasping foreign capitalists if not always honoured by them, of mutual benefit. As one of Deng's sophisticated officials told the

Asian Wall Street Journal in 1980, 'In order to . . . develop the socialist economy, we'll allow exploitation to a certain degree. What investors want is profit. What we need is modernised socialist construction. Well, we'll each take what he needs.' When the National People's Congress debated the draft Foreign Enterprise Law in 1986, one provincial Party secretary even wanted it to be more lenient. 'If you don't consider the foreign investors' interests,' he argued, 'how can you expect them to come and set up such enterprises?' Foreign investment brought money, technology, jobs, tax revenue, skills and foreign exchange earnings to China, so 'what have we to lose when the country's sovereign rights are in our hands?'[3]

China now participates in the international division of labour. Honda parts are brought in from Thailand to make motorcycles in Henan province. Huan Xiang, a senior economist, denies the traditional Stalinist concept of there being two separate markets in the world, one socialist and one capitalist. 'There exists,' he now writes, 'only one integral market in the world. Capitalism dominates the market, and China is an integrated part of it.' Another economist, Wang Jian, argued that China should absorb its rural unemployed in the countryside in labour-intensive industries, and then export the products in order to earn foreign exchange which could be spent on upgrading those same industries – and that is precisely what is now happening. China follows in the footsteps of the successful export-oriented industrialisers in Hongkong and Taiwan: indeed Premier Zhao Ziyang based his coastal-area economic development strategy of the 1980s on them.

Once the floodgates were open, capitalist boardrooms round the world remembered Rockefeller's adage about a billion Chinese all wanting to buy a kerosene lamp. The McKinsey consultancy has worked out that 60 million Chinese already earn more than US$1,000 a month, constituting together a market bigger than Korea or Malaysia. The number could triple by 1999, though the individuals are geographically scattered and it is not a unified market. After thirty frustrating years of being sidelined, Western and other Asian corporations raced to get a toe in the door. It was 'like taking the cork out of a champagne bottle'.[4] In seventeen years the Chinese accepted US $60 billion of direct

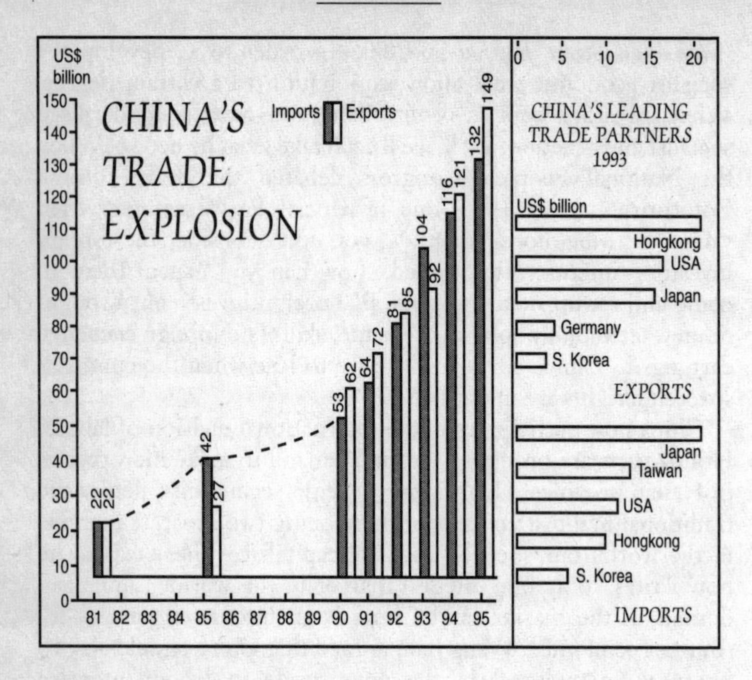

foreign investment ($10 million on an average day), a flow matching what China borrows commercially from abroad. China became the most favoured Asian destination of foreign direct investment after Singapore, taking about one-eighth of all such investment in developing countries world-wide.

The twist was that it was Chinese who mainly invested in China. Two-thirds of the total came from Hongkong, and a further amount from other Chinese corporations outside the People's Republic of China, especially in Taiwan and southeast Asia. So there is a nationalist, ethnic or cultural ingredient in those investment agreements which gives a special motivation to both sides – patriotism for the investor and an assurance of cultural compatibility in the enterprise for the Chinese host.[5] And this led logically to the 'one country, two systems' formula, which underpinned the 1984 agreement to give Hongkong autonomy when it is retroceded to China in 1997.

Some of the early investments from abroad were just what Deng's critics had feared, businesses seeking a slice of the

Chinese domestic market without trying seriously for exports. The computer giants – IBM, Hewlett Packard, Unisys – set up in order not to lose out in the world's biggest potential market. They at least had some skills to pass on. But the Coca-Cola plant aroused real passion. Chinese people who patronised Coca-Cola, a group of novelists and poets alleged, 'lose their national pride, succumb to capitalist decadence and harm China's basic national interests to satisfy the profit motive of foreign capitalist groups. They willingly fulfil the role of slaves for the foreign sellers. This is not only shameful but criminal.'[6] Could the same go, perhaps, for the apple pie investment by Bama Pies of the USA, or Daiwa's golf investment?

Further inquiry revealed that the Coca-Cola equipment had been supplied free from the USA, and that the cost of imported syrup was outweighed by the foreign exchange earned by selling the drink to tourists in China. So the plant manager made a spirited rebuttal. 'Can we say that because foreigners like to drink Chinese tea, *maotai* liquor and Qingdao beer, they have no national sentiments, are not patriots?' In any case the Chinese consumer was the final arbiter. In 1992 Coca-Cola sold more than 75 million cases in China.

McDonalds ('Maidanglao') opened in Beijing that same year to little criticism, though some of the arguments used against Coca-Cola could have applied. The government had already subscribed to the equity of the predecessor in hamburgers, the Good Earth Development Corporation, a joint venture between Kanghua (the company then run by Deng Xiaoping's son) and a New York firm represented by a Chinese who had fled Communism for the United States at twenty-three – one of tens of thousands of prodigal sons who now brought home foreign know-how, sometimes of a more essential kind.[7]

Cigarettes might have been the difficult case, especially after the opium wars of the nineteenth century. Rothmans and R.J. Reynolds took care to form joint cigarette-making ventures with Chinese partners in Shandong and Fujian provinces respectively (the former was opened by Sir Edward Heath). 'We're not encouraging the Chinese to smoke,' Lord Swaythling, Chairman of Rothmans International, insisted defensively. 'They have been the world's biggest consumers of cigarettes for forty years. They all smoke like chimneys here anyway, we just want them to smoke our brands.'[8] It was true: with one in five of the world's population, the Chinese appear to smoke one in three of the world's cigarettes. Deng Xiaoping himself chain-smoked until he was eighty-four, and his government obtains 20 per cent of its revenues from the tobacco tax. Only in 1990 did professional medical people form a Chinese Smoking and Health Association to publicise the risks, and their lobby is ineffectual.

The variety of foreign investment in China is now legion. Not all of it takes the form of joint ventures, although most foreigners prefer to have a Chinese partner to help deal with the local bureaucracy. The Seattle restaurateur Tommy Qwan, another refugee from Communism at the age of fifteen, found his patriotism stirring in the 1980s and decided to try growing oranges, the business of which in the American Northwest he knew a little. He bought a few acres in China and hired 160 people to tend 12,000 trees for exporting oranges to Canada and Hongkong. 'This is not a joint venture,' he insisted. 'This is our own. It has nothing to do with the government. They always like to participate in a business, but I wouldn't do that. They always want to hire their own people, their sons and daughters. If they're not doing the work, you're in trouble. How can you fire them?' Michael Parry, who ran the Hua Dong winery in Shandong, had another solution for the same problem. He sited his business a long way out of the nearest city in order to minimise the interference of bureaucrats. 'They don't have the cars to get out this far too often. It makes for a quieter, less complicated life.'[9]

Now the field has broadened to umbrella investments like venture capital firms. China Assets (Holdings) Ltd is an example, a joint venture between Standard Chartered Asia, James Capel Far East and China Venturetechno International, with US$39 million placed by institutional investors outside China. It looks for enterprises on the Chinese coast with a profit track record and foreign exchange income, ready to take 25 per cent of the ownership to make them into joint ventures. Another flourishing development is the business won by foreign architects, planners and engineers. Shanghai backed the proposals of Richard Rogers (with Ove Arup and London New Researchers) to develop a master plan for a business centre across the river Huangpu which

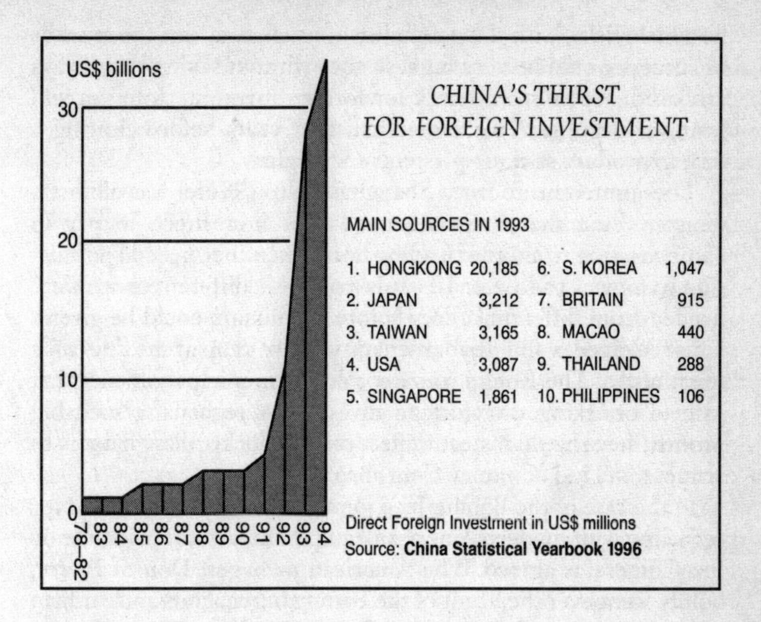

would be eight times bigger than Canary Wharf in London.

Another breathtaking project in Shanghai illustrates the all too frequent problem in China of competing ministries, departments or organisations which can spoil each other's plans and yet will not collaborate. Li Kashing of Hongkong agreed with the Shanghai Harbour Bureau to acquire some of the city's container terminals and to build new ones, investing more than US$1 billion over eight years. Zhu Rongji had visited Li Kashing's terminal complex in Kwaichung in Hongkong in 1990, and was impressed. The Shanghai partner said that the joint venture would enter the cargo agency and inland trucking business, sectors of the local economy on which Sinotrans, a giant state agency operating cargo ships, had a stranglehold.[10]

The key to the apparent puzzle was that whereas Sinotrans was controlled by the Ministry of Foreign Economic Relations and Trade, the Harbour Bureau came under the Ministry of Communications. Li Kashing was effectively assisting one bureaucracy in Shanghai to compete for the first time against another. It could be a little risky, with the possibility of retaliation, but the rewards of success would be very high. It goes without saying that delays are another pain in the neck for foreign investors. Johnson and Johnson negotiated for more than four years before clearing a deal to produce sticking plasters in Shanghai.

The joint venture for a Shanghai Hilton Hotel was almost a disaster. First the partners argued over how much to pay in compensation to another leading hotel, then they needed permission to move a gas meter 10 yards (thirty-six different chops were needed from different offices before permission could be given). Their Mercedes and Toyota sedans were held up at the docks for ten months. Zhu Rongji roundly told the municipal officials that instead of asking why foreign investors were making such big profits, they should instead reflect on how lucky Shanghai was to attract that kind of money from abroad.[11]

In the case of the Beijing Jeep joint venture, money needed for retooling with modern American equipment was not paid over by the Chinese as agreed. The American manager, Don St Pierre, boldly went over the heads of the Beijing bureaucrats and car firm officials and wrote direct to Prime Minister Zhao Ziyang, threatening to close the plant. Zhao put Zhu Rongji in charge of the matter, and a compromise was agreed. 'Too many guys doing business in China hang on just too long,' St Pierre reflected, 'they put too much of a personal stake in the project, their entire career may be committed to it and they are reluctant to go out and raise hell when it is necessary. What went wrong with the Jeep project was not my fault. It was not the fault of the American side. I felt that if it did not work, I would pull the plug.'[12]

Many foreign investors came near to packing their bags and leaving China, but the Chinese usually managed to dissuade them. When an Italian investor in a spectacle-making joint venture threw up his hands because his Chinese partner pirated the product to sell domestically, an official reproached him with advice straight out of Confucius' *Analects*: 'When a son is sick, you shouldn't hang him.'[13] Occidental Petroleum did pull out of a giant open-cast coal mine in Shanxi province. Personnel problems occur at the highest level. The Construction Ministry arbitrarily dismissed the chairman and general manager of an elevator joint venture with Schindler and Jardine, without consulting its foreign partners. This was one of the largest joint ventures in China, with annual output of over US$200 million. The authorities backed the foreign partners in calling it a violation of the agreement, but no redress was forthcoming.[14]

The most publicised example of a joint venture that failed was the Ramada Renaissance Hotel in Guilin. Here the local China Youth Travel Service teamed up with an Australian Chinese called Tony Fung who had run a successful textile mill in Hongkong. But the Youth Travel Service supplied incompetent managers, made high charges for services and utilities, and suddenly required 267 per cent duty to be paid on imported limousines. There was widespread pilfering by the staff. When the foreign managers ordered hotel staff lockers and pockets to be searched, the Youth Travel Service denounced the three foreigners concerned for violating human rights, and had their passports impounded so that they could not leave the country. This was a region of China where the Cultural Revolution had been particularly violent. Fung said of his partners, 'They know nothing of business, only politics.' But Fung retained sufficient hope for the China market to sign another deal later to set up a steel mill in the same province. Another hotel project, the Holiday Inn in Xiamen, was the centre of scandal when the Singapore owners were squeezed for bribes by city officials.

The saddest experience was that of the Briton, Richard Gosling, who put £150,000 into a joint venture in Tianjin for the export of printed electronic circuit boards. Everything went wrong. Samples came late, and were different from the ones he was originally shown. They were of indifferent quality, and British retailers who had placed orders made legal claims. Gosling's Hongkong associate resigned and when Gosling flew from London to Tianjin to try and sort it out, officials would not even discuss the venture with him. He won an £18 million judgment in the British courts, but could not enforce it. He and his lawyers and accountants trying to trace assets in China were followed by the Public Security Bureau, and the flat of an English associate working for the joint venture was entered. Gosling was familiar with China, and his wife was Chinese. 'I have a strong feeling for the Chinese,' he said, 'but there are no rules covering the enforcement of law.'[15]

That is why Chinese investors from outside China, who instinctively understand the Chinese way of doing things, are so much more successful. For the most part they tread the road back to their fathers' or grandfathers' home towns. Most of the Hongkong investment, for example, gravitated to neighbouring Guangdong province which was the origin and main headquarters of most of the families which had sent offspring to find a better life in Hongkong during the last hundred years.

There is, of course, a significant minority of Shanghainese business families which emigrated to Hongkong at the beginning of the Communist regime and is therefore more interested in investing in the Shanghai area. A good example is the family of Zhang Jian, who had travelled in the West and was educated there a century ago but returned to his hometown of Nantong, across the Yangzi estuary from Shanghai, bringing experts from Japan and Holland to help modernise it. He set up textile mills, a teachers' college, a shipping college and many other useful institutions. One of Zhang's nephews, Zhang Shengwei, became a prominent businessman in Hongkong who now invested, under Deng's Open Door policy, in a hotel in Nantong. That branch of the family which had remained in the country under Communist rule produced Zhang's grandson, Zhang Xuwu, who became a deputy governor of the province and a very good friend, incidentally, of the Communist 'ambassador' in Hongkong during the late 1980s, Xu Jiatun. Zhang took a team of potential Hongkong investors to visit Nantong at the Chinese New Year in 1988.[16]

The next biggest Chinese investor from abroad is Taiwan, whose total stake in China exceeded US$4 billion by 1992. There are two distinct groups of population in Taiwan, the mainlanders who had crossed with Chiang Kai-shek in 1949, and the Taiwanese whose forefathers had emigrated from the coastal provinces facing Taiwan in earlier centuries. When it came to investing in the Chinese mainland in the 1980s, their respective preferences were quite distinct. The mainlanders went to Shanghai, the Taiwanese to the more culturally friendly environment of Fujian. To the Taiwanese the growing business link with the facing ports of Xiamen and Shantou is a natural convergence of their *liangan* – 'two shores'.

The overseas Chinese scattered in the more distant outposts of

Singapore, Bangkok and Jakarta also booked their flights to their original hometowns in China at various points along the coast, from Hainan in the south up to Shandong further north, to satisfy that strong Chinese family urge and to place funds where they would receive the most careful treatment. The Srifuengfung family of Thailand, for instance, enlisted in the Pilkington Glass joint venture in Shanghai, while Mr Kitty Dumnernchanwanit, whose father had emigrated to Thailand at the beginning of the century to build up a small rice-milling business which became a diversified giant, is putting US$1 billion into a forestry and pulp mill scheme in Guangdong province, planting eucalyptus and acacia trees. 'I have been persuaded by Chinese authorities,' Kitty explained, 'to invest in the reforestation project... and other industrial projects in Shanwei. I am Chinese, but was born in Thailand. I always realise that for a human being it is a must to bring progress and prosperity to his country of origin... It is my great hope and that of my family to contribute to the success and development of Guangdong as the "head of the dragon".'[17]

Japanese and Western investment in China is still vital to China in terms of higher technology, even though the value may be smaller than the overseas Chinese. British companies, for example, are investing £128 million in bottling plants in Shanghai and Guangzhou, and a GEC subsidiary has helped set up the largest private telephone exchange in the world, connecting Guangzhou with Tibet, over 2,000 miles away.

The preponderance of investment is from Hongkong all the same, and this brings its problems. Deng opened China's door just as Hongkong and Taiwan were beginning to feel the discomfort of economic middle age. They had passed beyond the stage of full employment to experience serious labour shortages, leading to soaring wages and ugly labour disputes, while industrialists suffered from the high price of land, an appreciating currency and greater pollution. The manufacturers had to look for alternative production bases, just at the moment when China changed its policy.

China had everything that Hongkong lacked – abundant labour, ample space for industry and low costs. A survey of Hongkong's factories in 1990 showed that almost 500 had set up production in China, mostly in Guangdong. It was essentially outward processing, where materials or samples are imported to China from Hongkong for processing in the Chinese factory. In the end the Hongkong manufacturers came to employ more than two million people in the province, or a quarter of the entire workforce in secondary industry there. It was said that in the first decade of reform, Guangdong brought in more than a million production facilities through the open door.

But Hongkong also relocated some of its international trade problems in China. Hongkong is a natural port for the Guangdong region of China, having been selected by the British for that natural advantage in the first place. It is hardly surprising that about 45 per cent of China's exports worldwide go to Hongkong, of which almost half are exported onwards to the USA, much of it in containers. It has now reached a point where Hongkong exports world-wide an annual US$12 billion worth of textiles and clothing produced in China. Textiles and clothing have for many years been restricted under an internationally agreed régime set up under the old GATT, to which each of these two suppliers subscribes. By physically manufacturing in China, the Hongkong industrialists are able in effect to 'borrow' some of China's quota in the US market. Yet the Chinese naturally regard deliveries of textiles and clothing from Guangdong factories to Hongkong as an export to Hongkong rather than to the USA.

The problem will not go away in 1997, because Hongkong has been accepted by China and its trading partners as a separate Customs territory with continuing membership of GATT or the successor World Trade Organisation in its own right. The whole question will provide fuel for dispute in the future. The Americans and Chinese are also at odds over calculating the whole trade balance between their two countries, which boils down to whether the indirect trade through Hongkong should be included or not. Bitter American complaints of 'quota-dodging' fall into a chasm of statistical discrepancy, under-invoicing and label-switching.

The Americans claim that US$2 billion-worth of low-cost garments are coming from China via Hongkong every year, and since they are made in China they should therefore fall within the China quotas. At one point the Americans cut China's textile quotas by 8 million square yards, costing China US$18 million in sales. From China's point of view this is a disadvantage of Hongkong's investment in China. Even within China there are different versions of the trade picture, because the Customs count one way and the Ministry of Foreign Economic Relations and Trade another. The Chinese Customs figure for China's trade showed a US surplus in 1992 of US$306 million. Yet the US statistics showed a quite different result, a US trade *deficit* with China of US$18 billion. (China's foreign trade world-wide was in surplus to the extent of US$17 billion in 1995: $149 billion exports, $132 billion imports.)[18]

The worst hazard to China's export trade has temporarily evaporated, namely the annual threat of the United States' cancelling China's Most Favoured Nation status. That would lose China about US$10 billion in exports, or roughly a quarter of its total world-wide. Hongkong too would lose a similar amount, as well as perhaps 20,000 jobs and a 2- to 3-point drop in its economic growth rate. But President Bill Clinton wisely decided in May 1994 not to withhold MFN for the following year and not to make it an annual cliff-hanger as a means of pressing China on human rights issues. Those would be pursued by other means.

The Chinese are dilatory in improving their statistical service and making it more transparent, and also in not beginning to take the various steps which Japan had undertaken in the past to deflect this particular kind of American criticism. China can punish its quota-riggers when it wants to. When the Shankou Company of Shenyang made cowboy shorts and ladies' pyjamas with 'Made in Fiji' labels and sent them to the USA, the Chinese government confiscated its earnings, cut all its quotas and suspended its business activities. In 1994 it claimed to have confiscated over 2 million pirated compact discs and over 1½ million pirated books.[19]

The Chinese skill in smuggling also robs the trade figures of some usefulness. About US$1 billion of consumer durables arrive illegally from Hongkong alone every year. Hongkong officials say that about one-sixth of Hongkong's exports to China are bootlegged. The loss in tariffs and duties is incalculable, and the Chinese officials often connive. A Public Security Bureau Chief's home was raided near the border and a cache of imported liquor, foreign cigarettes and several hundred thousand RMB were seized. The goods are legally imported into Hongkong by the smuggling syndicates and loaded on to motorised sampans after dark to sail with the fishing boats at dawn. Once international waters are reached, the mainland partners are contacted by cellular phone, and the goods landed and trucked to 'safe' Chinese villages – Jiujiang, for example, which specialises in smuggled luxury cars.[20]

At least China has not fallen into the trap which snared so many developing countries in Asia, of running up too large a foreign debt. The Communist Party has always treated external debt as a potential danger to the country's national independence. The reforms from 1979 have opened the gates a little, but the additions to debt have been gradual and conservative. At the end of 1994 the total was US$93 billion. A fifth of that was short-term trade finance, which is a different matter, leaving a real debt of some US$70 billion. China has also been prudent in building up gold and foreign exchange reserves, to a level of over $70 billion, leaving a very small gap and even a surplus. The reserves are bigger than either Britain's or France's. China's debt servicing can be met with about one-eighth of export earnings. Even at times of political crisis and factional competition China's external finances have been handled conservatively. It should be noted that China has the most open economy of all the world's large countries, in the sense that trade represents over 30 per cent of Gross Domestic Product – more than twice the Indian, American or Japanese ratio.[21]

China's imports from the West used to be restricted by the so-called Cocom export controls operated by Western countries to prevent items of strategic importance from reaching Communist states. Sometimes the Chinese were able to get their own back. Thwarted in trying to buy sophisticated optical sensors from the West, the Chinese worked on the fact that for some crystal formations the human eye is a more effective monitor than a sensor, and so they observed the growth of their crystals 'manually' around the clock. Today they lead the world in developing new non-linear optical materials.[22] China is good at making the most of its resources. But import policy is much influenced by political motives, for example smoothing the way to entering the WTO, or avoiding further restrictions on exports, rather than by the potential of imports for stimulating China's efficiency and exposing its own producers to more competition. At the beginning of the Open Door the Chinese had a spree of buying complete second-hand factories or production lines, for example a bankrupt timber works in Manaus halfway down the Amazon river in Brazil for only US$2 million cash, or the Vetlanda Nordiska Piano works for $750,000, destined to produce China's first high-grade pianos in Liaoning.

For its exports, China began with traditional commodities based on farming. The Meishan pig from Lake Taihu in eastern China has a hide like a rhinoceros, and its sow sprouts up to twenty teats, far more than European varieties. It reaches puberty in half the time taken by the more languorous swine of Europe, and it regularly delivers sixteen piglets per litter. On all these grounds it is a most desirable farm possession, and is exported to Britain and the United States for cross-breeding to increase litter size.[23] The British get their own back by selling UK ducks, which are less fatty than the Chinese, and duck-processing equipment to help China meet its domestic demand for Peking duck.[24] China's manufacturers can often surprise and annoy Western competitors with their export scoops, such as making the Union Jack flags and the John Major ski caps which were handed out at the Tory party conference in Brighton in 1992.

A new entrant to the export game is the People's Liberation Army, a small economy by itself set apart from civilian enterprises. It exported 2 million guns to the United States in 1989–91, to become the largest foreign supplier of small arms to the American market. The army also sells pig iron, basketballs, bicycles, car jacks and negligés to American importers. More worrying to Western governments, China's now diverse and specialised defence industries can make advanced weapons, some of them, notably the 'M' short-range ballistic missile series, explicitly for export. The Americans object because this increases instability in the regions to which China exports, whereas China feels it is merely joining the established arms sales club.[25]

The commercialisation of China's trade is illustrated at one end by the new millionaire Muo Qizhong, well known because he looks like Chairman Mao. Now fifty-five, he was once a political prisoner under sentence of death, but on managing to escape that fate he became a middleman putting deals together. His sensational achievement was to barter 800 train cars full of Chinese consumer goods for four Russian TU-154 passenger planes, clearing a profit of US$18 million.[26]

Despite the politics, the disputes and misunderstandings, old hands in the China trade were often full of praise for the way the Chinese honour their contracts. Bernard Buckman bumped into his old friend Dr Chi Chao-ting, the Chinese scholar-banker, at a trade conference in Moscow. They decided to duck out of the conference and talk business together instead, negotiating a £20 million trade deal on the products which China wanted to sell to and purchase from the West. 'The Chinese,' Buckman remarks, 'are the most marvellous people to do business with. In the early 1970s I was selling nickel to them, three months forward. There was a strike in Canada. The price tripled to £600 a ton . . . But the Chinese – unlike other people – honoured the contract.'[27] Other Western traders are less commendatory these days.

The long-term gain in keeping a trade relationship warm and good for both sides can over-ride the lure of a short-term coup. Desmond Wong, the man who brought hamburgers into China, says that handshakes are more important than contracts, and since the Chinese have no tradition of contract law, or of any impersonal law governing contracts between two parties, that is still true.

Foreigners mesmerised by the Chinese market can take comfort from the fact that the distribution system is beginning to loosen up and become more efficient. The heroine of this development is Guan Guangmei, who grew up on a farm in her local commune and then worked in a grocery store in her hometown of Benxi in northeast China, rising to be assistant manager. In 1985 the grocery was put up for lease under the new reforms, and she bought the lease, going on later to take seven more shop leases at public auctions to control a profitable chain store supplying a third of the town's 680,000 inhabitants with their groceries. Efficient and short-spoken in her sober grey pantsuit, Guan liked to say, 'This is reform. I have the power to run this enterprise.' She cut out waste, set targets for the staff and slashed their wages if they were not met.

A Communist who had worked for twenty-five years in the shop criticised Guan for being an exploiter who downplayed the role of political education and disliked Party supervision. Her reply was a classic one. 'Some people think socialism means everyone should have rice to eat, whether they work or not. This kind of thinking is a real problem.' Guan was unpopular, and something of a martinet. She never learnt the trick of persuading people how they would personally benefit from more efficiency. Yet, now in her early forties, she has a personal income of US$12,000, or twenty times the average of her 1,000 employees.[28]

Most stores probably live in the pre-reform days still. A foreign visitor to a Chongqing department store found the assistants beginning to tally up their sales slips a little before closing time, and some of them went home before the customers had all left. They would not deal with a purchase query near to closing time.[29] This goes to underline the importance of investments like that of Jardine's Dairy Farm of Hongkong in a US$25 million joint venture to develop sixty supermarkets in Shanghai.

Advertising has already made a bold start after being virtually banned as capitalist-consumerist under Mao. Rejustified as a practical link between producers and consumers, it was taken up at first by foreign cigarette-makers. They were soon restricted, as was the total quantity of foreign advertising of all goods. *Red Flag* refused to run Coca-Cola advertisements. But the numbers employed in advertising quickly reached 70,000. China requires a certain literalness in being truthful, so that Toyota's slogan, 'Where there is a road, you will find a Toyota', was criticised. Where is the Chinese imagination?[30]

The most dramatic of the early reforms in 1979 was the creation of Special Economic Zones where normal rules would be suspended to tempt foreign investment. 'Foreign capital and advanced technological and managerial skills' would be induced, it was said. The real innovator here was the China Merchant Steam Navigation Company, an outward-looking Hongkong-based Chinese firm originally set up in the nineteenth century in Shanghai to compete with British shipping along the Chinese coast. The company asked the Chinese Communist government for permission to develop an industrial park at Shekou in

Guangdong province, and it was granted in 1979.[31]

Chinese economists were already then studying different forms of export processing zone in the Third World. Soon Special Economic Zones were formed on the Guangdong coast (Shenzhen, Zhuhai and Shantou) and in neighbouring Fujian province (Xiamen, the former Amoy). Now the list has lengthened to include Hainan (the new island-province in the deep south), fourteen coastal cities (including Guangzhou, Shanghai, Tianjin and Dalian) and Open Economic Zones in the three deltas of the Zhujiang (around Guangzhou) and Changjiang (around Shanghai) rivers and the Golden Delta around Xiamen. In effect, economically active areas along the entire Chinese coastline have been excused from unnecessary regulation in order to hasten their development.[32]

Sometimes Beijing's judgement seems to falter, as when a joint venture to build a 50,000-grave cemetery in Shenzhen was given a financially preferential blessing. But then much of the incoming capital is from Chinese abroad who yearn to be buried in their original homeland. For the same reason tourism facilities have been built up, especially in Zhuhai, adjoining Macao on the opposite side of the Pearl river estuary to Hongkong, to cater for the returning sons and daughters.

There is, incidentally, another meaning to Shenzhen, whose skyscrapers now tower over the undeveloped borderlands of Hongkong: it assures both Hongkongers and Taiwanese that reunification with the People's Republic will not necessarily spell a cut in living standards or a painful adjustment in systems. Shenzhen stands more or less midway between Hongkong and the rest of China in prosperity, wage levels and industrial sophistication. It has become an entrepôt, importing for onward delivery to the rest of China, as well as exporting Chinese manufactured products. Shenzhen has even reached the point where high wages and rents are driving resident companies inland, e.g. to Dongguan, bequeathing to Shenzhen a 30 per cent factory inoccupancy rate.[33]

The Zones have not had a trouble-free passage through the politics of the past fifteen years. One of the conservative leaders in the Communist Party dismissed them as foreign enclaves like the nineteenth-century treaty ports. The reformers, he said, had 'given way too much to the inordinate demands' of the foreigners. 'Why should the Communist Party be prohibited from public activities in foreign investment enterprises in the Special Economic Zones? Foreign businessmen even forget the laws of their own countries when they come to the Special Economic Zones.'[34] More potentially damaging is the criticism of an academic economist from Fudan University in Shanghai who pursued research at the University of Sussex, Dr Zhang Jun. The Zones, he argues, distort economic activity and serve a merely relocationary function without adding to wealth. Investors go there to benefit from artificially lowered rentals, not because of the physical location. Chinese firms go there to trade rather than to learn new technology. State firms in the Zones are protected by easy access to foreign exchange and low taxes – yet a third of them still lose money. It is a formidable indictment.[35]

An equally loaded critique was made by David Wall of the University of Sussex. The Zones, he says, may superficially appear successful, but the investment actually involves only limited modern technology giving limited net value-added and little modern skill. It tends to dovetail into the Chinese tradition. The import content is high, and at the end of the day there may be a net outflow of foreign exchange with various payments to be made abroad. In sum, the Special Economic Zones failed to develop the market-style economy which China's leaders intended. The incentives attracted those who already controlled resource flows in China and sought to exploit them for their own ends, through the *guanxi* system.[36]

Some of the more spurious Zones have been abolished under the rational régime of the 1990s associated with Zhu Rongji, and a gradual phasing out of tax incentives for foreign investors is now promised: they are inconsistent with the WTO and promote provincial polarities. Their role will decline.[37]

Shenzhen was the first Zone, chosen specifically to compete with, and be a bridge into China from, Hongkong. It became a kind of capital of the various high-tech industrial parks and zones which form the Pearl river delta Open Economic Zone along with the two nearby Special Economic Zones of Shantou and Zhuhai. These various special areas now take up a fifth of Guangdong Province's territory, a quarter of its population, 40 per cent of its production and half its industrial output. If that is not creeping liberalisation, what is?

The people of Shenzhen like to echo, poetically, the aphorism of China's outposts, that 'the mountains are high, and the Emperor is far away.' Close control by Beijing is difficult. Yet the latter-day emperor, Deng Xiaoping, did grace Shenzhen with his presence in 1992 in the course of campaigning for more reforms, and he heaped praise on it. These days the Shenzheners, caught between two worlds, have graduated from being the sweatshop behind Hongkong's shopfront and dream of becoming an integral part of the Hongkong marketing network. Forgetting Beijing's purpose to develop hi-tech manufacturing, they aspire to form a free trade zone like Hongkong, with no duties or controls. Shenzhen's border fence with the rest of China is actually better fortified and more secure than its border fence with Hongkong. Some Shanghainese already write Shenzhen off as merely a satellite of Hongkong. 'They structure their deals for the Hongkong players, the participants are mostly from Hongkong and there is a daily back-and-forth that connects the two completely.'[38]

One of the Politburo members less enchanted with the Special Economic Zones was the late Yao Yilin. In 1991 he accused Shenzhen of surviving only because of transfusions from the state treasury. Maybe, he suggested, it was time to 'pull out the syringe'.[39] Three years later, after visiting Shenzhen, he again expressed anxiety, saying that instead of following the plan, Shenzhen relied on foreign investment, backing from the centre and land sales. How could it survive when these were no longer available?[40] However, Deng went out of his way to patronise and justify the Zones and the most common attitude towards them is that the stimulus they provide is worth a great deal of misuse.

The Chinese certainly took the Open Door policy seriously. Nicholas Lardy, the American economist, concludes that China's economy has become, as a result, more open than those of Korea or Japan.[41] The Chinese are well aware that their openness is abused. One journal asked, 'Are we using foreign capital, or are we being used by foreign capital?' Many examples are cited of misdemeanours, irregularities and fraud on the part of foreign businesses engaged in joint ventures in China. From there it is

THE OLD LEADERS AND THE NEW

Above: Chairman Mao Zedong (centre) ruled China 1949-76, with the help of Premier Zhou Enlai (on right) and Party General Secretary Deng Xiaoping (on left), all seen here at a Central Committee meeting in 1962. (Xin Hua)

Below: The new post-Mao leadership Mark I is seen here at another Central Committee meeting in 1987. Hu Yaobang (on right) was General Secretary during the early post-Mao reform years and Zhao Ziyang (on left) was Prime Minister, succeeding Hu as General Secretary at this meeting. The man in the middle is Li Xiannian, then President of China and one of the 'immortal' veterans. (Magnum Photos)

THE NEW LEADERSHIP MARK II

Above: The seven men who now run China form the Standing Committee of the Politburo. Left to Right: Hu Jintao (at 54 the youngest member), Zhu Rongji (economic czar), Qiao Shi (head of National People's Congress), Jiang Zemin (State President, Party General Secretary and overall supremo), Li Peng (Prime Minister), Li Ruihuan (a liberal carpenter) and Liu Huaqing (armed forces boss). Their average age in 1996 was 68. (Frank Spooner Pictures/ Gamma)

Right: The two men responsible for the economy, Vice-Premier Zhu Rongji and Premier Li Peng, consult before Li gives a keynote speech to the National People's Congress in 1994. (Popperfoto/Reuter)

REFORMERS

Right: Qiao Shi is a lesser figure but may tip the balance for the reformers after Deng. The most intellectual of the Politburo Standing Committee (on which he ranks third), he is a law and order specialist and head of China's 'parliament', the National People's Congress. (Frank Spooner

Below: The steel thread that runs through successive leadership groups is the diminutive chain-smoker Deng Xiaoping, seen here in mid-career addressing a Party meeting with characteristic enthusiasm and resilience. In 1978 he carried China into its momentous phase of market reform. (Xin Hua)

TIANANMEN KILLINGS

Above: The world held its breath when a student carrying his shopping stopped in front of a tank, daring it to mow him down, during the military suppression of the demonstrations at Tiananmen Square in 1989. (Popperfoto/Reuter)

Below: General Secretary Zhao Ziyang was the only senior political leader to visit the student hunger strikers, and he lost his job immediately afterwards in consequence. The students defied the government for weeks before the army was sent to remove them. (Xin Hua/Sygma)

FLOWERING OF ARTS

Artists and writers are more free than before – except in criticising the government! The better climate has thrown up a wealth of cinematic talent to produce, for instance, Farewell My Concubine *and* The Blue Kite. *Here Gong Li and Leslie Cheung (a Hong Kong actor) appear in Chen Kaige's* Temptress Moon. *Ms Gong is China's most popular film star and is thus a millionairess. (Patrick Zachmann/Magnum Photos)*

HONGKONG'S RICHES

The spectacular harbour view of Hongkong advertises the wealth and economic clout of Britain's last important colony, due to return to Chinese sovereignty in July 1997. The tallest of these elegant skyscrapers is that of the Beijing-owned Bank of China. (Camera Press)

HONGKONG: THE THATCHER PACT

In December 1994 Margaret Thatcher went to Beijing to seal the retrocession of Hongkong to China in 1997. Here she toasts the then Premier Zhao Ziyang and the 'paramount ruler' Deng Xiaoping on their Joint Declaration about Hongkong. But stormy times lay ahead as the two governments came to open and angry disagreement on interpreting their pact. (Camera Press)

THE LITTLE (OFFSHORE) CHINESE TIGERS

Left: Ethnic Chinese politicians offshore are not always approved by Beijing. Martin Lee, a Hongkong lawyer, seen here at the climax of the 1995 elections, is the most popular local political leader and yet China brands him unpatriotic and disloyal. (Popperfoto/ Reuter)

Right: Lee Kuan Yew of Singapore on the other hand has won the admiration and trust of the Chinese government. Over 35 years, first as Prime Minister and more recently as 'Senior Minister', Lee has transformed Singapore economically while preserving Chinese values. (Topham Picture Point)

only one step to condemning the bad habits that come in with foreign investment.

The governor of Hainan said, 'We cannot afford to discard the traditional culture and ethical sense of the Chinese nation, and we cannot afford to let in the spiritual garbage of a Western society.' Material development, he explained, helps to develop spiritual civilisation, and people who are well-clothed and fed will tend to pay attention to honour. 'But they will also tend to be obsessed with carnal pleasure.' You can pass legislation in Beijing permitting foreign companies to set up and invest and produce in China, but you cannot legislate that they will behave properly or that their Chinese workers will also behave properly. The delicate machinery for dealing with these problems of foreign interface hardly exists in China.

China's international trade under the reforms has been conducted without the benefit of membership of GATT, and it was only in the late 1980s that the government began to seek the resumption of its status as a contracting party to the GATT. The political problems were readily cleared, through China's acceptance of separate GATT or World Trade Organisation membership for Hongkong, and its agreement to seek membership for China in parallel with a similar application from Taiwan. The WTO, after all, deals with economies and not with sovereign nation states. But the negotiations ran into enormous difficulties because China lacks the legislation and institutional means to regulate trade and trade disputes in the way the WTO expects. As Long Yongtu, one of the leading negotiators for China, has admitted, China does not have a foreign trade law, an anti-dumping law or a countervailing law.

If and when China does claw her way into the WTO, the composition of her exports would alter slightly. Chinese corn, soybeans, fruit, fish and meat would become more competitive, at the cost of wool, rubber, milk products and prawns becoming less competitive in world markets. Long Yongtu argues that China has a major advantage as a socialist country: 'in case of a sudden import surge that could spark possible social consequences, our system possesses bigger flexibility to absorb, cushion and resolve these problems.'[42] But social discipline and cohesion may not last forever in China, whether they spring from socialism or from the

Chinese tradition. China will inevitably become even more open in future.

Now there is a trademark law in place, and already some 3,000 cases of infringement involving foreign companies have been found. As an author I can testify that a book of mine has been pirated and sold in two separate Chinese translations with no royalty paid, but then even Deng Xiaoping's daughter had the same experience. Her biography of her father was also pirated. There is now at long last a law of copyright and there are theoretical grounds for recovering compensation for these thefts of intellectual property, but it is all very new and unfamiliar, and no one can yet be certain of getting fair treatment. It is, of course, the Americans who are the biggest complainants of intellectual property violation, especially concerning films, video tapes and computer disks, and in early 1995 a threatened trade war was defused by China's agreeing to be more thorough in acting against domestic violators of intellectual property law.[43]

Although Shenzhen and the other Guangdong special areas dominated the early publicity, Shanghai soon got into its stride with an economic zone extending into five adjacent provinces, and started to build up its own industrial zone in the trans-riverine suburb of Pudong. Pudong is much favoured by the pro-Shanghai personalities in the leadership, including the reformist Zhu Rongji and President Jiang Zemin. Pudong will be massively served with foreign investment to become the industrial powerhouse of the Yangzi river basin. Vice-Premier Zou Jiahua, China's planning head, told the Royal Institute of International Affairs in London that Pudong would be a 'window, bridge and launching pad of China's opening to the outside world'.[44]

The territory accorded the most liberal treatment of all on this lucky coastline is the tropical island of Hainan in the deep south. Until a few years ago hardly anyone had heard of Hainan, but in 1988 it was not only designated a province in its own right (it is almost as big as Taiwan or Switzerland) but was also made a Special Economic Zone. Beijing labelled it a 'laboratory for system reform', experimenting with a 'small government and large society', and pioneering changes which might ultimately spread across the whole of China. A senior official described its future as '*laissez-faire* island' – by inference on the Hongkong model. The Communist Party, it was said, would act as governor of Hainan in the same way that the British governor ruled Hongkong. Investors in Hainan could take out leases of up to seventy years and enjoy a free market in foreign exchange.[45]

Predictably this drew an Alaska-like avalanche of speculators, Chinese and foreign, seeking their fortunes in this favoured outpost of the Chinese market system. Hongkong bars were full of eager entrepreneurs hoping to catch the next plane to Hainan. Equally predictably it threw up amazing cases of embezzlement, smuggling and fraud. A group of smart local government and Communist Party officials were found to have imported 89,000 vehicles and three million TV sets, paying the island's preferentially low Customs duty (half the mainland's), and calmly re-selling them, at considerable profit, to customers in other parts of China. Perhaps they should have been promoted for resourcefulness, but in fact they were dismissed for irresponsibility.

The island's natural resources bubbled into an almighty boom. A quarter of Hainan is covered with rubber plantations originally developed to beat the US trade embargo in the 1950s and now responsible for about two-thirds of China's domestic production. The island also boasts China's best iron ore reserves, exploited by the Japanese in the 1930s, as well as good deposits of titanium and zirconium. Tourism has a golden future here. The beach at Yalong Bay was hailed by some as 'the Chinese Hawaii', and by Zhao Ziyang as 'better than Hawaii'.

Irrigated rice was not grown, surprisingly, until the 1930s. The dams and canals of that era have now decayed, and the Hainan government went ahead of the rest of China in giving incentives for farmers by rationalising the grain trade more thoroughly, letting grain prices float within a 10 per cent margin and allowing a larger retail price increase than on the mainland. For its next step Hainan proposes to encourage voluntary farm co-operatives on a non-profit basis, with investment incentives, land use controls and training for the market – all to increase commercial tropical crops, shellfish aquaculture, forestry and paper mills.

Many reservations were voiced about these ambitious plans. Higher-yielding rubber clones and better protection against typhoons will be needed if competitiveness with Malaysia is to be achieved (and why not attract the rubber-using industries from the mainland?). There is still a heavy government hand in many of the proposed new arrangements, and not all agreements are conscientiously honoured. But at least this provincial government has broken the mould and devised its own innovations.

Hongkong investors were the first to jump at the new opportunities in Hainan, and they now account for about three-quarters of total foreign investment there. Mainland firms have also moved in, taking advantage of the more liberal rules about retaining foreign exchange earnings, to route their exports through the island and create a re-export business which is now five times larger than the export of local products.

Chinese bureaucracy can still frustrate the investor. It took four years for one development project at Yangpu in Hainan to get official approval, because officials jibbed at the length of the lease and the possible speculative profits. The Macun Thermal Power Plant, financed by Hongkong companies with guaranteed 9 per cent interest, though controlled by government ministries in Beijing and built (without the requirement of international competitive tender) by a Chinese constructor, illustrates how far Hainan will go to attract investors in the weak sectors of transport and power. The province has a mind of its own and will not necessarily bow to foreign advice. The island is building twenty-two vocational secondary schools, for example, though the World Bank insists that more flexible general secondary schools would give better value. Hainan has allowed George Soros to buy half of the new Hainan airline.[46]

When Hainan's new status was being discussed in Beijing in 1987, the central government considered making it a special Customs Zone with a separate convertible currency, like Hongkong. That was dropped, though the necessary powers are there if Hainan should decide to go in that direction. However, the central government still controls, as a matter of history, the rubber and sugar plantations and the iron mines, while the island's public finances depend heavily on Beijing subsidies and support.

Hainan has been described here at some length because it demonstrates what the Chinese economy might be like with even more deregulation than now. If it were not so geographically peripheral to the Chinese heartland, so vulnerable to mistakes and abuse and so under-developed, Hainan might prove a powerful example for Chinese progress. As it is, Hainan, being the province institutionally one step ahead of everyone else, can show on what sector the torchlight of national reform might fall next.[47]

China is so large that it used to be thought of as potentially self-sufficient. Yet even under Mao's autarchy, millions of tons of wheat and maize were imported to feed the big cities. China very obviously needs today to import technology and capital as well as grain, and that will continue for many years, though imports of consumer goods will doubtless be progressively restricted to protect domestic producers. That is already happening with cars.[48]

Meanwhile China's exports are bound to improve in competitiveness. China will become the world's largest trading nation

——对不起，我们只收高“财”生！
Sorry, We Only Accept "Financially" Gifted Students

*'Sorry, we only accept "financially" gifted students here.' Talent used to be the criterion on the education ladder, but money is often substituted these days (*People's Daily*, 20 August 1994).*

and will gradually shed its reputation for cheap, inferior goods. That has already happened in telecommunications equipment (China's third best export after clothing and toys), while domestic electrical equipment, sound recording equipment, electric power machinery and watches and clocks have all passed the US$1 billion a year export mark. In the end most Western homes, offices and factories will be rich in Chinese goods made with Western machinery.

Trade, driven by home development demand, will bring China into greater contact with the West and the rest of the world, and increase the pressures on China to adhere to world norms, laws and practices – with a softened landing on the world stage.[49] In 1997 Beijing's first British-style pub will open, for which barman Ping Yuan has been learning how to pull pints at the Horniman in Bermondsey, to take small example of the new interchange.[50]

China's modernisation is at the cost of the kind of independence and detachment from outside forces and events which the Emperor used to practise. This time, despite the size of population and territory, the Chinese must perforce rub shoulders with other quarters of the world whose technical superiority they must now recognise. Trade and investment are the keys to China's acceptance of interdependence.

CHAPTER 12

ECONOMIC OUTLOOK: CAT ON THE LOOSE

What verdict should we return on the Chinese reforms? The statistics give them a resounding vote of confidence. Since Deng Xiaoping inaugurated his daring programme in 1978, China has raised its economic growth rate by 50 per cent, doubled the consumption of goods by its population, and rescued some 160 million people from below the poverty line. Average housing space doubled, the number of bicycles quadrupled, colour TV sets in urban households increased sixty-fold. Productivity grew by 4 per cent a year, and the Open Door trebled the proportion of national production going to foreign trade. Never have the Chinese experienced such a sustained lift in their living standards.[1]

That still leaves China with one of the lowest incomes per head in the world, but an Australian economist, Ross Garnout, with a Chinese colleague, Ma Guonan, have salved the wounded feelings of Chinese sensitivity by measuring China's Gross Domestic Product (GDP) in international prices instead of domestic Chinese prices. The result is a GDP per head of more than US$1000 a year, much more respectable – and realistic – than the conventional $500 or so.[2] A Chinese can buy as much rice on his low income as a richer European can on his higher income, because Chinese prices are lower. In terms of real life, away from the artificialities of exchange rates, most Chinese people enjoy a level of food and basic consumer goods supply not very different from that of Taiwan or Hongkong. Their life expectancy, at seventy, is nearer to the Newly Industrialising Economies of Korea and Taiwan than to the poor developing countries of, say, south Asia.[3] So the real purchasing power of the Chinese was clearly higher than the earlier system of calculating GDP allowed.

The International Monetary Fund thus altered its estimates of China's GDP per head in 1991 to reflect what it called Purchasing Power Parity (PPP), and arrived at $1,450. The systematic suppression of 'real' prices by China's socialist bureaucrats had combined with international differentials of prices to paint a falsely low picture of China's living standards in the past. Now the comparison is more honest. Those who question the new basis of calculation consider revaluing a Chinese farmer's income at the price of his Oregon counterparts to be also unrealistic, so a golden mean between the two unrealities might be $900 to $1000.

Putting the results of Deng's reforms against the earlier period of Maoist economics, one can see just how far China has come since the devastating decades of civil strife and Japanese attack before 1949. At the beginning of the Communist régime the majority of national production came from the farms. By 1990 that proportion had fallen below one-third. Industry filled the gap, its share moving up from less than a quarter of GDP to over half. That is the kind of change that happens only once in a nation's experience. Britain saw it at a slower pace in the first half of the nineteenth century. Japan went through a similar transformation between 1880 and 1920. One might imagine that such comparisons would not interest the Chinese, but they do. Chinese are aware of, and care about the way that the developed industrialised countries – especially Japan, which used to be a kind of satellite of China – have outrun China so far in economic terms.

A wall-poster in Guangzhou a few years ago noted indignantly that Japan's steel, car and rice production were 300 per cent, 100 per cent and 60 per cent respectively higher than China's. 'Does this mean,' the anonymous critic thundered, 'that the Chinese people are less intelligent than the Japanese, that we are less diligent? Does it mean that Chinese natural resources are inferior to those of Japan, or that our social system is somehow lacking?' Those questions had also been posed by Deng Xiaoping, who, unlike Mao, had seen Detroit and Osaka for himself and had the practical sense to discuss with trained professional intellectuals how this 'social system' of China could be changed in order to achieve that kind of prosperity.

Chinese consumption today is comparable in broad terms with Japan's in the late 1950s or Taiwan's in the late 1960s. The average Chinese now ingests more calories than the Japanese then, but less protein (especially animal protein). In housing floor space the Chinese do better than Japan or Taiwan at that time, with about 18 square metres on average in the rural areas, 5 in the cities. Of course the quality is not up to Japanese standards, with fewer toilets and less piped water. But Chinese clothing is better.

It was the first seven reform years, 1978–84, that showed the best results, with higher living standards up an extraordinary 9 per cent a year for almost everybody equally. After that the pace settled down at a still creditable 4 per cent or so, but income differentials began to widen again. The increase in life expectancy slowed down, though average height still increases at about one inch every decade. Illiteracy started to rise again after its low point of 23 per cent in 1982. But the underlying improvement in Chinese life is unmistakeable and irreversible. A young Chinese economist points out proudly that the initiation into 'capitalism' Chinese-style is more humane than it was in England. Working conditions and wages are much better than they were for the pioneer European countries undergoing the industrial revolution. A Japanese commentator puts it differently. 'China,' he declares, 'is practising nineteenth-century capitalism, without an effective trade union movement or a responsible concern for the environment.' Both comments are legitimate, though exaggerated. China lives in the twentieth century like the rest of us, but is in a great hurry to make up for lost time and claim a seat at the table of world power.

China is of course trying to quick-march from paternalistic labour relations where unions were regimented to the Communist Party drum and workers' jobs were guaranteed, to an impersonal Thatcherism with Chinese characteristics where workers must suffer the whims of the market. Wang Zhicheng of the Beijing Labour Bureau recently summed up the new philosophy. 'Being fired, picking jobs, having choices, jumping into the labour market: these are all new concepts that people must accept. It is time to break the iron ricebowl.' With the army of unemployed officially estimated at 200 million, it could hardly be otherwise.

What virtuously separates China from the free enterprise market economies of the West, its leaders claim, is the retention of public ownership as a dominating force. Enterprises may cut each other's throats in business competition but they are owned in large part by the state or its organs – unlike in Eastern Europe, where privatisation became a vogue. The Chinese believe that Russia threw the baby of public ownership – the mainstay, they claim, of socialism – out with the dirty bathwater of industrial inefficiency. China still has too much dirty bathwater swilling about in the economy.

Prime Minister Li Peng catalogued the shortcomings in a speech to the National People's Congress in 1991. Everywhere, he lamented, he found 'excessive consumption in production, inferior quality, enormous waste in construction, slow capital turnover, low labour productivity and serious enterprise losses'. One state factory won a US$22 million order from a developed country, for which it had to sign a penalty clause for payment if the shipment were late. It took six months for the manager to negotiate the initial capital out of local and central bankers and bureaucrats. Raw materials were not easily obtained even then. A deal was made with a steelworks, but at the last moment its parent firm insisted the order be placed through itself, which the Chinese, to whom this is an all-too-familiar phenomenon, charmingly call 'pulling the feathers off the passing goose'. It meant another large commission added to the original factory's costs.

The counterpart to the story about the Shanghai factory not getting permission to make fans until the summer was over is the story of the factory which waited a whole year to get permission to stop making an item for which there was no longer any demand. Both are true. This is why the state sector is crumbling.

The bureaucrats may require more than 400 chops on a foreign investment application. The Nomura China Investment Company needed only forty-five chops for its joint venture to build the Garden Hotel in Shanghai, but when it brought in a Japanese construction company, Obayashi, the local government's Construction Bureau made it pay the Chinese building workers the same rates as Japanese workers. Obayashi could not get co-ordination between the workers putting up walls and those installing electrical fittings. The chef refused to train apprentices, so he had to be replaced by a more modern-minded Hongkonger. Not only did workers steal, the 300 security officers stole as well. Local staff were recruited for the hotel, but most were quickly dismissed. This provoked threats of physical violence to the hotel and its management. The Japanese appealed for help to the mayor, then Zhu Rongji, but the city's Cultural Commission jumped into the act with a demand for 6 per cent of the revenues from the hotel's music-playing areas. Nomura had to ask itself if its deal – an investment of *yen* 17 billion for twenty-five years of expected profitability, after which the hotel would revert to the Chinese partner – was really worthwhile.[4]

Party leaders in Beijing are set on keeping heavy industry in the state pocket, though their younger comrades are less doctrinaire. But medium and small enterprises will probably be privatised, and some large ones may be partly privatised, perhaps on the model of Singapore Airlines in whose fate the Chinese are taking much interest. The government will still control them and hold the primary ownership, but minority equity is already being sold not only to foreign investors but to other domestic enterprises and even to the public. Some form of co-operatisation of enterprises through collective ownership may also develop. But young economists say nothing will improve until ownership becomes transferable.

The state is not quite as dominating as Beijing pronouncements make it appear. Of the national economy as a whole, including farms as well as services and industry, the state owns only a quarter, the balance being shared between collective owners, individuals and joint ventures with foreign investors. The two minor sectors of foreign and privately owned enterprises are growing fast – by about 50 per cent and 20 per cent a year respectively. 'A few more years of expansion,' concludes William Overholt, 'will make foreign and independent enterprises the predominant force in the economy.'[5]

The state's strength is in industry, of which it owns under a half, though that is expected to fall to a quarter by the year 2000.

Being used to the all-pervading power of the state in the past, but seeing now a vigorous private sector challenging a constricted state sector, the Chinese, who like animal metaphors, describe it as 'tying up the tiger and letting loose the cat.' Government revenues as a proportion of GDP have fallen from about a third at Mao's death to about a fifth today.

The World Bank and other Western economic advisers tell the Chinese government that its new role will be as challenging as the old, if not more so. Instead of setting production targets, allocating resources or controlling investment funds, as it used to, the government now needs to set the economic framework for producers, correct market failures and plan for bottlenecks and for its own diminishing state sector – an agenda resembling that of the Korean and Japanese governments in the 1970s.

But there is plenty of time for adjustment to the new role. The transition to the market mechanism via the law of supply and demand is painfully slow. The lingering traits of the old economy, characterised by state-owned enterprises mired in inefficiency and labour rigidity, prevent demand from ruling the economy as in theory it should. One county in Inner Mongolia claims to be an exception: Zhuozi may be the only true free market in the whole country, with a bankrupt county government selling its assets to its staff and workers. But Zhuozi is the exception that proves the rule.

One source of misunderstanding is the meaning of the key words 'market' and 'planning'. The Chinese government defines planning not as the mandatory allocation of resources (as was the case in China's command economy, 1949–78), but the broad regulation of the economy to ensure balance and stability. Similarly 'market' means a way of allocating resources at the lower level, not private ownership with democracy. When the eighth Five-Year Plan was announced in 1991 it called for setting up a 'new system based on the socialist planned commodity economy, and an economic operating mechanism which integrates the planned economy with market regulation.' The tortured compromise allows central politicians and economists to believe that they can rescue 'socialism' while building a free enterprise economy – perhaps on the lines of the socialist parties which have occasionally come to power in Western countries to introduce more controls on management and more benefits for workers.

Beijing intends that command planning and administrative allocation of resources will still play a big role in large projects vital to the national economy. And its solutions for the existing state enterprises focus on more effectively separating the state's ownership function from its regulatory and management functions, and carrying out those functions in a more rational and arm's-length way. The state will remain the owner. In a sense China is saying it could implement socialism in a capitalist economy better than Harold Wilson, François Mitterrand or Felipe Gonzalez.

How far was this a temporary sop to the veteran leaders like the late Chen Yun or Bo Yibo, to keep them quiet while other reforms were put in place? Criticism by Chen Yun centred first on the extent of the Open Door and the amount of 'garbage' that blows in through it along with the needed technology. Many things went wrong under Mao, but at least China had its pride. Sometimes Chen's school is called that of the 'restorationists' because it harks back to a 'golden age' of China from 1949 to 1966 (the Great Leap Forward is forgiven, the Cultural Revolution is not).

Chen Yun explained his concept of the economy in a famous image, that of a bird (the economy) in a cage (government control). 'You must not hold the bird in your hands too tightly or it would be strangled. You have to turn it loose, but only within the confines of a cage, otherwise it would fly away.' Keeping caged birds is one of the less attractive Chinese pastimes, but the metaphor is a good one and carried some weight with older Communists who worried about 'spiritual pollution' by the West.

In fact the market is held back by the government's failure to organise and control money effectively. That kind of control used to be exercised by the Central Bank, but reform of the banking structure has left it weakened. China has decentralised economic decision-making without strengthening those central monetary controls which would give decentralisation the fullest revitalising effect. The provinces now rule over the Central Bank, and the bars of the birdcage look frailer. Some would say that fixed asset investment is already out of control, because the centre has no way of stopping the localities' demand for investment funds from passing up through the banking system to drain the money supply. The money supply jumped by a quarter over the central planned amount in 1994, but fell back again in 1995.[6]

'If this is Marxism,' a Russian visitor to Guangzhou reflected in the late 1980s, 'I must re-read Marx.' We do not have to go that far, but at least it is clear that while China has at different times applied both socialism and capitalism to its problems, it has never taken them undiluted. The Chineseness always shows.

Why did the reforms succeed relatively well in the China of the 1980s? China was luckier than Russia or Eastern Europe in a number of respects. First of all, the two national disasters of the Great Leap Forward in 1958–60 and the Cultural Revolution in 1965–76 convinced many Chinese that the Marxist system did not work for them, and everyone accepted the need for change in economic policy. Secondly, the farmers, who formed 80 per cent of the population, were depressed and ready to make changes the moment central control was relaxed. Thirdly, the Chinese outside China, especially in Hongkong, were supportive of the reforms, especially the Open Door, as were Western merchants. All of those factors, so potent in the 1980s, continue in the 1990s, though with lessening force.

One consequence of these policies was the widening of the economic gulf between the better-off coastal provinces and the poorer interior ones. Farmers outside Shanghai have average incomes three times those in Gansu, on the edge of the Central Asian deserts. The gap began to narrow in the early reform years, but most Chinese officials and many Western observers believe that regional disparities began to increase again after the mid-1980s. The hope is that inland areas and the northeast will in future retain more profit from the commodities they produce, and thus begin to climb back in the provincial prosperity stakes. Henan, for instance, should have its own mills in which to process its cotton instead of sending it to the Shanghai mills. A westward relocation is beginning, with some Shanghai textile mills, for example, emigrating to low-cost Xinjiang. The trickle-down has started.[7]

It is expected that coastal centres, starting with Pudong and Hongkong, will generate surpluses for interior development. This has begun to happen in the case of Hongkong investment in Wuhan container facilities. Some provinces are already taking their own action to get a better place on the economic bandwagon. Henan is thus forming a trading zone with five neighbouring provinces to cut down the barriers to inter-provincial trade.[8]

Before Deng's reforms the goal of the typical Chinese family was to own a bicycle, a sewing-machine, a radio and a watch. Today the status symbols for which everyone saves and strives are the six *da jian* – 'big things' – video-cassette recorders, TV sets, washing machines, cameras, refrigerators and electric fans. Dreams of material wealth have been elevated to an altogether loftier level. China's average living standard, it should be stressed, is higher than that of many other developing countries. China is at the high end of the Third World league in literacy, life expectancy, school enrolment and infant mortality. Only the GDP value figure, based on the old calculation system, is lower.

The Communist leadership recognises the unevenness of development but spiritedly defends itself from critics. 'The discrepancy in prosperity in the present-day countryside,' the *Workers' Daily* editorialised in 1983, 'is only a matter of "some get rich first and others get rich later". In no way can this be considered polarisation. We adhere to the road to general prosperity. But it is illusory to think that early one morning over 800 million peasants could find themselves all in affluence.' This should be seen in perspective. In Taiwan, so admired by international economists, urban incomes were 30 per cent higher than rural ones even in the 1980s.[9]

Meanwhile another kind of polarisation is that between rich and poor in each community, and this is not yet effectively checked by means of the income tax so familiar in the West, though farmland and much of industry are in community ownership. It took Deng seventeen years to get an effective national income tax on the books, largely because of arguments with the provincial governments about how it should be divided, and it still has teething problems. There is a village in Sichuan where one family earns RMB 1600 a month but some of its neighbours earn only RMB 165, mainly because the first family has two grown-up sons, and all four of them work in a Village Enterprise.[10]

The young man in Guangzhou who bought 999 roses for his girlfriend's birthday could have been congratulated for his charm, gallantry and good taste instead of being criticised for extravagance.[11] The elders see a 'me-generation' coming into public life. The young reply with: 'money is not everything, but having no money is worse.'[12] What do the very rich do with their money? Golf is gaining popularity among the male élite, with Zhao Ziyang a keen player in his enforced retirement. There are at least nine golf courses in China, not counting the nine-hole course outside Beijing, though only one of them is owned by Chinese.[13] Another twenty are planned with US$500 million of foreign investment, especially in the areas favoured by Taiwan, Hongkong, overseas Chinese and Japanese businessmen, i.e. Guangdong and Fujian. As for well-to-do women, suffice it to say that there were at a recent count more than 18,000 Avon ladies selling Western-style cosmetics door-to-door in Guangdong province alone.[14]

With inequality, the other grave threat to long-term development is damage to the environment. Hua Sheng, a Chinese economist at Cambridge University, reports a disturbing feeling among entrepreneurs and would-be businessmen from the bureaucratic ranks that they have perhaps twenty-five years of relative freedom ahead of them in which to build a durable business or a fortune or both for their families, after which the government will be forced to take ecological considerations more seriously and impose restrictions on economic activity in order to protect what remains of the environment. A book called *China on the Edge* telling the story of neglect sold 430,000 copies until it was banned, along with other honest criticism of the government, after the Tiananmen Square killings. It detailed the loss of 40,000 acres of arable land to desert every year, the pollution of air and water, soil erosion and deforestation – all made worse by the decentralisation of power to the provinces which was the centrepiece of Deng's reforms.

Some of the details are horrifying. Soil erosion is now estimated at 620,000 square miles a year, especially along the Yangzi river and particularly in Sichuan where the affected area has more than quadrupled since 1975. China's rivers carry a mind-boggling 2.5 billion tons of silt into the sea each year. The

Yellow river further north has the dubious record of transporting more silt than any other river in the world. China's forest cover is below the world average and sinking fast. Grassland is receding and the desert expanding, threatening cultivated fields and railway track: by the year 2000 another area twice as big as the island of Taiwan will have been made barren. The much-praised rural industries are partly to blame. They manufacture electric cable, chemicals and even heavy metals, all most competitively, but the pollutant waste is uncontrolled. Village Enterprises making sulphur in southwest China use only a part of the material, releasing the rest to poison the soil outside. This is one reason for the new interest in creating some commune-level authority in the countryside.[15]

An expert reporting on the pollution problem for the Chinese Academy of Social Sciences, Hu Angang, had harsh words to say in 1991. 'Today,' he warned, 'we continue to struggle for personal profit, sacrificing everything to immediate gain, exchanging short-term economic prosperity for wasted resources and ecological damage. We congratulate ourselves on our rapid economic growth, and revel in making arbitrary demands on the natural world and in achieving cheap victory. Yet we still run against the tide of history, wilfully squandering the achievements of our ancestors, in desperation borrowing what belongs to our children while running up an even greater ecological debt.' A vigorous indictment, but the political-economic vested interest in continued fast growth – constantly put forward by Deng Xiaoping – shows no sign of faltering. It may indeed take twenty-five years to dissipate, particularly when the government treats every foreign criticism as an insulting interference in the nation's domestic affairs.

The Chinese concede that they produce almost one-tenth of the gases which contribute to global warming, the third biggest amount after the USA and Russia. But in per head terms China does not rank even among the fifty worst offenders, while Americans bear much more responsibility. Furthermore, Western countries have been polluting the atmosphere for longer. 'It's not good enough,' complained another Academy of Social Sciences specialist, Wang Mingting, 'to calculate total emissions of one year... If you calculate the emissions for two hundred years,

China's concentration is very small.'

The Director of the Environmental Engineering Institute at Qinghua University put the problem squarely in north–south terms: the greenhouse effect was 'not created by the developing countries but by the industrialised ones'. It is a theoretically appealing argument, though hardly relevant to the need for action today. The Worldwatch Institute in Washington concludes that the current increase in China's carbon-dioxide emissions is far bigger than any other major emitter's. As with human rights, one may conclude that external pressures on China do not work in the short run, though the defensiveness of Chinese statements on the environment suggests that there is a nerve there to be struck.

The third casualty of the economic reforms is the moral level of public life. Commercialisation is on the march. Chinese schools, for example, now go into business, opening shops and factories to raise the funds they can no longer get from the state. There are at least 700,000 such school-businesses making textiles or TV sets, selling books or fish-farming. A forty-six-year-old history master running a clothing store admitted: 'It took a while for me to get adjusted because, well, traditionally Confucius simply does not think highly of commerce.' In Beijing in 1993 ten private schools opened their doors, charging US$4,000 a year in fees. Mostly boarding schools, they pay teachers three times the national average salary.[16]

Not only teachers but many other state servants must now throw their entrepreneurial hat into the ring and expose themselves to the mud of the marketplace. The process is called *xia hai*, or plunging into the sea. Bureaucrats now have many opportunities to benefit from trade. They can buy scarce commodities like cement or coal on the state-controlled distribution network at low fixed prices and then sell them on the free market at decontrolled inflated prices and make a tidy profit – for their department, for themselves individually or a little of each, though the further freeing of prices will make it more difficult for them. In Anhui one bureaucrat in five was found corrupt in 1993, mostly siphoning public funds to pay for their children's schooling. So the whole tone of public life is lowered. Stern measures are taken, including the execution of guilty officials, but a common comment is, 'They'll swat the flies but leave the tigers.'[17]

Misuse of funds is widespread, and legitimate money-making is often indistinguishable from the other kind. When the veteran Communist Bo Yibo inscribes his new book for US$100, he is not breaking the law but he may be contributing to the general moral decay. When an intelligence agency establishes a bakery to eke out its budget, it seems an unusual but unexceptionable way to fund its spying. When the People's Liberation Army runs, through its travel agency, a commercial brothel and when the Chinese Women's Federation brings in eight luscious Russian masseuses for its hotel in Guangzhou, one is taken aback by the shrinking of puritanism in what is still nominally a Communist state. As the poet-journalist Dai Qing observed, 'People are transforming power into a commodity for sale.' A businessman in Hubei province put it succinctly of his bureaucrat ally: 'I used my money to buy his power, and then used his power to make myself more money.'

Philip Bowring, a former editor of the *Far Eastern Economic Review*, believes that the families of some Chinese leaders are acquiring personal assets on the scale of Chiang Kai-shek or Ferdinand Marcos. Much of the US$35 billion capital outflow in 1990–92, he alleges, represented corrupt deals to salt new wealth away in Swiss or Hongkong banks. This is not easy to verify, but some Chinese believe it.

The most famous relative of the great is Deng Xiaoping's crippled son Pufang. He attracts universal sympathy because he was maddened by Mao's Red Guards into throwing himself out of a fourth-storey window in the Cultural Revolution, and was thus condemned to a wheelchair for life. After his father became China's paramount ruler, Pufang started a trading and investment company called Kanghua ('Healthy China'), the profits of which were earmarked for the Welfare Fund for the Handicapped. It was widely suspected of speculation and various irregularities, and Pufang's father soon withdrew Kanghua's tax privileges and restricted its activities, acting swiftly to rescue his son's reputation.

Many sons and daughters of China's élite have opted for a business career for which their name and family connection is an enormous asset, even if no undue influence or bribe is involved. People regard deals with 'great' families as the best kind of insurance. Not all of the so-called 'princelings' are venal money-grabbers. Some, like Chen Yun's son Yuan, hold senior jobs in the bureaucracy – in his case as a well-thought-of modern-minded vice-president of the People's Bank of China. Others have dived into the exhilarating sea of business, like Wang Zhen's son Jun, the number two executive at CITIC, a colourful hard-working buccaneer not linked with corruption.[18]

A heartfelt condemnation of China's political philosophy and a cry of pain at the corruption it has induced came from Qian Jiaju, a one-time eminent Marxist economist who has taken refuge in California. In an open letter to Chen Yun, Qian wrote: 'In the deep night I clasp my heart and ask myself, could this corrupt, degenerate China in which official graft runs amok be the new China I sought after? We opposed the bureaucratic capitalism of the Guomindang and ended by replacing it with an even more corrupt bureaucratic socialism.'

In case the reader feels that Qian's rhetoric may outrun his facts, here is a random sample of the practices he refers to. The *huang niu* (yellow cows) openly sell forged railway tickets at the station. 'How many tickets do you want?' they say. 'I can get you as many as you want. The police won't interfere. They know us. In fact they buy their tickets through us too.' In 1992 it was found that seven train passengers out of a hundred travelled without a ticket, and RMB860 million were recovered in uncollected fares.

Or consider the coup of the Guangzhou Tax Auditing Bureau in 1990, when it received a tip-off from a rival miscreant that a forger from Zhejiang was about to arrive in Guangzhou carrying two boxes of forged receipts to sell. In one year 400 million counterfeit receipts were confiscated nation-wide. Some accountants will sell genuine tax office receipts to black marketeers for a profit. Official investigators once dug six feet underground to uncover four tons of counterfeit pharmaceuticals and 14,000 counterfeit trademarks of a factory in Henan.

The lingering ethical influence of Confucius on public life has apparently almost vanished, and the Communists were not able to supply an alternative ethic. They are, after all, materialists. All one can say, perhaps, is that the Chinese now have a more realistic idea of the country they live in. In the early 1980s somewhat naïve utopian ideas prevailed about equality, freedom and prosperity. Hu Yaobang and Zhao Ziyang associated themselves with those new currents. Today, after Tiananmen and after the settling down of the economic reforms, people recognise that they must live with China's imperfections. That perhaps means more stability. To put it at its bluntest, people now see that Communists and businessmen can both be corrupt.

As far as the economy is concerned, the highest priority is clearly the reform of the state-owned enterprises, to nudge them into actual competition, professional management and profit. Fear of agitation by workers has held enterprise back. The implementation of the pilot scheme for a hundred 'model' bankruptcies in eighteen different cities has been repeatedly put off. The second priority lies in the financial sector, where the commercial banks must be brought to lend on a more rational basis according to creditworthiness. That in turn leads to the fiscal reform which is needed, to replace the old system of generating revenue for the government with a diversified national tax system: some advance was made here in 1994 but implementation was ragged. It remains to be seen how effective it will be. Fourthly, external reforms are needed of the kind which will reduce the risk of American retaliatory trade measures, including more transparency, *yuan* convertibility and opening up the Chinese market to imports on a broader scale. There are still price reforms to be made for farm products and raw materials, without which the market in China remains distorted. Finally, in the social sector, labour mobility needs to be improved by converting housing, pensions and other factory benefits to wages, and that leads back to the reform of state enterprises.

These are things which the government must do if the reforms already introduced are to have their full effect and benefit the economy. A Gladstone or a Kemal Ataturk might pale before such an agenda of reforms, and Deng's successors will surely find it impossible in its entirety: they will be judged by how near they can get to the full agenda.

Scenarios for China's future growth are legion, and it is not all that useful to make arithmetical extrapolations for a country of doubtful statistics facing such enormous domestic and external problems. In its 1992 study of the Chinese reforms and plans, the World Bank put as a base case the assumption of 7.5 per cent average growth in the 1990s, supposing reasonable progress on the state enterprises and public finance fronts.[19] A faster growth would risk a return of the stop-go cycle of the 1980s, with retrenchment every four years or so. The two major weaknesses to watch, said the Bank, would be the lack of fiscal or banking reforms, and the inefficiency of the state enterprises. But all of these future logical exercises will be affected by the rate of inflation and the tendency for the political leaders to go for rapid expansion and accelerated growth even when their experts are telling them to slow down.

The Economist flatly forecast in 1993 that 'if history is any guide, China's explosive economic growth is about to give way abruptly to stagnation.' That is a remarkable warning against making definite predictions, and a reminder not to extrapolate rashly from the bad examples, of which many are retailed in this book. However bad the individual cases are, the aggregate picture is never quite so awful. China will somehow muddle through, responding pragmatically to the crises as they come along. It is almost too big to fail, since the size, extent and compartmentalisation of the economy cushion it against severe shocks.

Ideological strictness has never been a feature of Chinese leaders. For the foreseeable future, planners with a cooling bent will co-exist in an intellectually disunited central leadership with reformers demanding to keep the economic heat up. This arrangement, necessary for political reasons, allows periodical escapes from doctrinal blind alleys and energetic changes of emphasis, though gradually the reformers will gain the upper hand in the 'post-Immortal' era. The Chinese economy may surprise us yet, as long as the political climate is minimally congenial.

Calculating from projections of relative labour productivity in China and the USA – her best economic partner – the City University of Hongkong lecturer, Shuhe Li, predicts a potential annual growth rate of around 9 per cent until the end of the century, falling to 8 per cent in 2000–03 and 7 per cent in 2004–10, then 6 per cent in 2010–20 and 5 per cent in 2020–24.[20] This sounds more plausible than some other guesses, and can be recommended as a good starting point for futurologists. It means that China's Gross Domestic Product would increase eightfold over the next thirty years. Such gradual convergence to the average world growth rate would mean China's overtaking the US economy in absolute size in about the year 2040.

The ninth Five-Year Plan for 1996–2000 aims at 9 per cent annual growth, the consignment of 99 per cent of state-owned enterprises to sink or swim in the market, a shift from production to fairer distribution of wealth – and the creation of 58 million new jobs.

So China is likely to grow at about 8–9 per cent for the rest of the 1990s, and should be able to continue at a little less breathless a pace into the twenty-first century – the century when the Chinese will at long last catch up with the West. Perfection in economic policy and popular democracy will not be completely necessary for this result, but a moderate effort on ecological and industrial ownership questions is a pre-condition.

William Overholt called China the next economic superpower. That is true in the sense that China's population, area and foreign trade loom so large on the world's game-board. In individual terms, however, China's men and women are still pawns on the world chessboard compared with the higher-value pieces of the West. Year by year the pawns will get bigger, but we will all be dead before it can be known whether – and when – China will match the individual wealth of America or Europe. Meanwhile China's sudden prominence in international trade shows how a pack of pawns, sticking together under a strong and purposeful leader, can harass a plump Queen or Bishop.

The Chinese know they are on an upward escalator. There is a new spirit and determination afoot which are not evident in most other developing countries, and which call for cautious optimism about the country's future economic prospects.

The discussion so far has been about China's vast heartland. But the fringes of China present problems of their own, involving borders, religion, ethnic minorities and the millions of Chinese who live outside the People's Republic of China – and these now call for discussion.

[illegible] the Church's [illegible] would [illegible] [illegible]

[illegible] 2000 [illegible]

[illegible]

[illegible] in the way the Church [illegible] contrasted with [illegible]

The Church [illegible]

[illegible]

PART FOUR

THE FRINGE

CHAPTER 13

RESTLESS PROVINCES: THE DRIFT TO FEDERALISM

The unity of China, to which most Chinese passionately subscribe, cannot be taken for granted. The Chinese state appears to be heading gradually towards greater provincial autonomy and weaker central government, at the same time as the communities forming the various branches of the ethnic Chinese tree, from the Chinese provinces to Taiwan and from Hongkong to the overseas Chinese, appear to be converging and networking for mutual support and possible future common action. A restructuring of the Chinese world is in progress which may or may not see a strong centre preserved.

Take first the status of the thirty-one provinces, autonomous regions and municipalities which make up the People's Republic of China. Westerners usually think of China as a united elephantine power dwarfing all others on earth, containing 22 per cent of humanity. Governing China is a tough assignment, however. The thirty-one provinces are restless and frequently at odds with each other. They are experienced in avoiding or ignoring the *diktats* of the central government. It is a loose union, not a tightly cohesive one.

The three cities which rank with provinces as municipalities – Beijing, Shanghai and Tianjin – are great industrial and commercial centres with populations of over 5 million each, which assures them of economic clout. Among the provinces Guangdong is the economic leader because of its good fortune in standing next to Hongkong, source of apparently limitless investment capital. But Jiangsu, behind Shanghai, is almost as well off as Guangdong and has better chances of future growth, perhaps, having developed a most successful brand of collective rural enterprise underpinning a balanced industrial structure. Jiangsu is poised to serve Shanghai rather as Guangdong serves Hongkong.

The most glaring contrast is that between mostly rich coastal provinces and mainly poor inland ones. The governor of Hebei province, Cheng Weigao, endorses Deng Xiaoping's slogan that there is nothing socialistic about poverty, but punctures the official line by adding that 'poor-rich disparities are also not socialistic'. Indeed they are much resented. Shanghai is eight times wealthier than Guizhou, and Guangzhou is three times wealthier than Guizhou. Within the single province of Guangdong, Zhuhai city, favoured by outside investors, is thirty-four times richer than the province's poorest county.[1]

The sometimes artificial provincial borders are not the last word. The veteran sinologist, Professor William Skinner, sees river basins as the basic framework for regional economies. The go-ahead counties are invariably at the heart of the big river basins, while those with disappointing levels of development are mostly high up on the watersheds. Skinner's research showed a consistency in these regional economy boundaries going back at least eighty years.

On this analysis the real division in China is not between coastal and inland regions but between the centre core of each river basin and its periphery areas. The Middle Yangzi core is as affluent as South Korea, but at its edges the standard of living falls to that of Nepal. Similarly the core of the Lower Yangzi basin is better off than Taiwan, whereas some people on its periphery must live at Nepalese or Bhutanese standards. It is a further lesson in not treating China as just another nation-state: it has patterns of its own which do not always mesh into Western categories. Even within provinces ethnic divisions appear: the Cantonese and Fujianese are increasingly self-aware, but so are the Hakka, Min, Swatow and other minorities in those two provinces.[2] Any future democratic domino effect from Taiwan and Hongkong would, incidentally, first bowl over these two coastal provinces.

Ethnicity is not enough to unite China. It is the same Han race which peoples every province (the minority nationalities having their own autonomous regions, mainly at the Western fringes).

Northern provinces

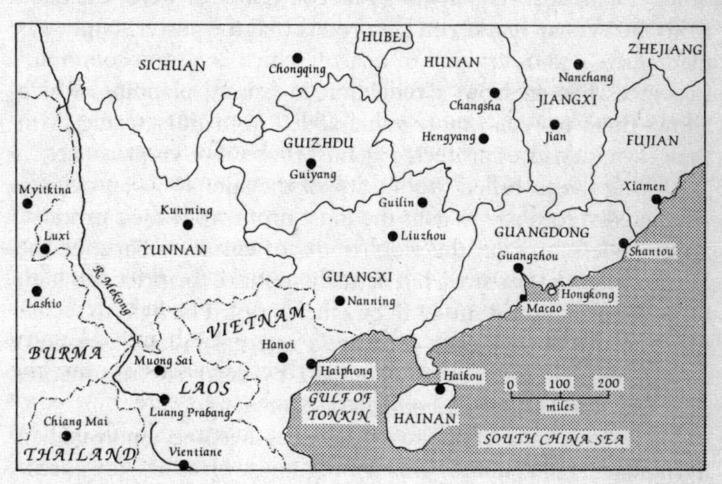

Southern provinces

But that is not sufficient to counteract differences of geographical and economic interest between the provincial units.

Guangdong province has switched from rice to more profitable cash crops and manufacturing industry, so it all the more needs a reliable outside supply of rice. Hunan is an obvious source, but its officials exploited their bargaining advantage by asking for a high price. Guangdong officials responded by directly offering Hunan farmers a price below what the Hunan authorities demanded from Guangdong but more than those same Hunan authorities paid their own farmers. Hunan's rice-growers naturally welcomed the chance to earn more for their crop. Infuriated, the Hunan government put armed militia on the provincial border in order to stop rice shipments crossing, and there was almost a small 'rice war'.

Such roadblocks became a regular feature of inter-provincial commerce, and a similar tale may be told of the Sichuan–Guangdong silk trade. Not only Hunan but Guangxi and others imposed small-time protectionism in this way for pork, rice and other foodstuffs. Guangdong air-conditioners were excluded from the Wuhan market on the pretext that the power supply was inadequate – another kind of quarrel which is all too common.[3] Provinces benefit from a reduction in central planning, which allows them to retain more value-added in manufacturing, with their own industries protected against those of other provinces.

During the so-called 'wool wars' of the later 1980s, provinces competed vigorously to gain the most profit from their product. Some levied taxes on the wool trade, ostensibly to finance the improvement of pastures, but actually to make the price too high for other provinces wanting to buy their wool. The fight to secure the wool needed by each province's internal industries was so disorderly that the government had to drop its free market aspirations and slap price controls back on wool.[4]

Sometimes more than two provinces become embroiled in triangular trade disputes. Guangdong housewives like the succulent meat of the Sichuan hog, so the jealous Hunanese, who also supply pigs to Guangdong, impeded the Sichuan hogs' transport through Hunan, knowing there was no other available route. Jilin forbids cheap beer to enter from Liaoning or Heilongjiang. Xinjiang prohibits the import of colour TV sets, soap or sorghum. When one northeastern province needed thousands of diesel pumps to prepare for an expected drought, its agriculture department ordered pumps, better and cheaper than the locally manufactured ones, to be rushed from another province. At the last minute, pressed by indignant local manufacturers, the provincial government decreed that only locally-made equipment was to be bought. In the traditional way an eventual compromise – half imported, half local – was agreed.

Most provinces help their domestic industries with low-interest loans and other financial incentives, so it is only natural for them to be protectionist. In Hubei and Hunan you can buy only local beer, soap powder or bicycles. Even Guangdong, supposed champion of 'free trade', used to keep out liquor, cigarettes and electrical appliances from other provinces. Some provinces producing raw materials issue 'shipping permits' to regulate 'exports'. Under the national plan, Hebei and Shandong should send cotton to Shenyang, but they block it as part of a campaign to acquire their own value-added cotton-processing industries.

The city of Shenyang experienced a different kind of economic provincialism when its representative went to collect a debt in another province and the creditor agreed to pay, but on going to the bank to collect the money, the representative was told that loans outside the province could not be repaid because funds were short![5] Some areas of Henan printed their own currency, and a truck of grapes once had to negotiate a hundred roadblocks and pay US$250 in charges between Shandong and Fujian – where the fruit was found to have rotted.[6]

Guangdong is the province now accused of over-reaching the others, getting too big for its boots and asserting a wilful degree of independence from central directives. Other provinces also hope to wrest more freedom from Beijing. Guangdong is already the butt of northern jokes about its alleged 'unintelligible' language, with more tonal variations, not to mention vocabulary differences, compared with Mandarin, and its lack of refinement, coarse manners and outlandish cuisine. The neighbouring Fujianese say with a condescending smile that a Cantonese will eat 'anything with four legs – except a table'!

Yet these same Cantonese produced the founder of modern

China (Sun Yatsen) and the initial support for his military campaigns to unite the country into a republic. They went on to build first Hongkong and then Guangdong into the most economically advanced parts of China, all through native enterprise and hard work. But they are practical. When the Cantonese students rallied in support of the Beijing students in May 1989, just before the Tiananmen confrontation, they did so after dark during hours when the industrial production which was taking their province to the top of the Chinese league would be least interrupted.[7] Their provincial Communist leaders nevertheless seriously considered withdrawing from the People's Republic at the time of Tiananmen, so angry were they with the centre's mishandling of it.

Deng Xiaoping dispensed an imperial blessing on Guangdong's economic feats by visiting it in January 1992 and lauding what he saw as a 'fast growth' model for the rest of the country. The local leaders were, an observer noted, 'euphoric'. Guangdong had been in the front line of the battle for fast growth for some time, playing on its strong connections with Zhao Ziyang, who had worked in Guangzhou for thirteen years before becoming Premier and Party Secretary-General in the 1980s. Guangzhou in turn was pushed by its outlying towns throbbing with the financial overflow from Hongkong. When the centre was trying to rein in the national economy to avoid over-heating, a vice-mayor of one of these towns argued indignantly that 'the slowdown should not apply to us ... We started from a low base, so 30 per cent to 40 per cent growth is quite normal.'

The key to Guangdong's rise in the 1980s is, of course, the response of Hongkong to the central government's Open Door policy. Hongkong now supplies a major part of the province's capital investment, new technology, new jobs and modern management. Thousands of Hongkongers cross the border every day to work in Guangdong factories. Ten years ago Cantonese leaders saw Hongkong as an economic role model. Now they view the British territory as more of a partner, since Guangdong itself has developed to a higher stage. At one point they wrote economic union with Hongkong into their draft five-year plan.[8] By the same token Hongkong businessmen who used to look down on Guangdong as a mere export-processing zone now seek local partners for joint ventures. Shenzhen, the Special Economic Zone adjoining Hongkong, intends to adopt Hongkong's legal system more or less wholesale.

In the result Guangdong's provincial income, 90 per cent of which in 1978 came from farming, now comes 90 per cent from industry and only 10 per cent from farming – a neat reversal of ratios. During the 1980s the province more than trebled its output from industry and agriculture, from US$14 billion to $44 billion, an average annual growth rate of 12.5 per cent. (Thailand, which would like to be Asia's 'Fifth Tiger', registered only 7.5 per cent during that period.) Guangdong now accounts for a third of China's total exports. Guangdong lacks oil, but when the centre threatened to hold back oil supplies in order to bring the province to heel, the local authorities calmly chartered a tanker themselves and got it to bring imported oil bought by them on the international spot market.[9]

The rising affluence is clearly visible. Nine out of ten households in Guangzhou have colour TV sets, and the local élite has begun to send its children to study abroad, even at the primary level. Vast projects of infrastructure – superhighways, railways, ports, power plants, a cross-river tunnel – have been completed or are under way. The province will almost certainly be as rich as the southerly members of the European Union by the end of the century, and could already qualify as a Newly Industrialising Economy like Taiwan, Korea or Singapore, if only it were an independent state. The income per head is about US$3,500.

The tensions which this creates with less fortunate neighbouring provinces reached a peak in the recession of the late 1980s. Guangdong relies on Hunan not only for pork but also tungsten, while more Hunan products are exported via Guangdong than Hunan can export directly. This provokes border 'wars', as we have seen, which sometimes escalate into violence. Another contentious import from neighbouring provinces is human labour. Up to a point, immigration is welcomed to keep the factories going. Beyond that number, the wretched job-seekers become unwanted vagrants who doss down in railway stations and drift into crime.[10]

In 1991 the central government tried to make migrants carry

'identity cards' with details of their birth, marital status and records of birth control methods used, hoping to plug a gap in the population policy.[11] The nationwide total of these migrants is about 70 million, and a large proportion of them are in Guangdong, which seeks from time to time to 'repatriate' them, with inter-provincial altercation that is easy to imagine. The problem goes all the way up the coast. An absurd rumour spread that new enterprises in Xiamen were recruiting 6 million labourers at 1,000 *yuan* per month. Hopeful candidates arrived on every train, at the rate of 11,000 a day, from provinces shattered by natural disasters.

The Cantonese are said to stand in fear of the 'tall pugnacious migrant workers' who come from the northeast, calling them 'Manchurian tigers'. One Guangdong town organises a vigilante team round the clock to check incoming vehicles and 'encourage' migrant workers to 'return to their home provinces'.[12] The sensible thing is for steps to be taken at the source, and this is what Guangdong has finally done, in the shape of a co-operative pact with Hunan, Sichuan, Guangxi and Henan whereby the latter provinces promise to curb migrant workers heading for Guangdong. One may doubt its full efficacy, but it goes in the right direction.

From the national point of view, these commercial quarrels may seem rather less important than various other pressing problems. But they demonstrate feelings of provincial identity and concepts of provincial self-interest which would become important if stirrings for political autonomy were to rise later. Like the Central Bank, the Communist Party perpetuates its power by permitting its provincial representatives a certain degree of *de facto* straying from the Party line on matters of great local importance, but we do not know how wide the area of tolerance can be stretched without caving in.

The big issue in inter-provincial relations remains that between the coastal and the inland states. Twelve coastal provinces won about half of state investment funds during the 1980s, and the east–west gap in living standards widened towards the end of that decade. This is a crude measurement, because there are wide variations between coastal provinces and between interior and coastal provinces. The special treatment of the coastal provinces is over but most people believe that the coast, led by Guangdong, is still advancing at a quicker pace than the interior, widening a gap which is already the source of envy and unrest. William Overholt shows from official figures that this is not actually true.[13] Xinjiang and Yunnan, two of the poorest provinces, have been achieving rates of economic growth higher than any of the rich coastal provinces (with the exception of Fujian). Starting from a low base, the inland regions are inching nearer to the prosperity of the coast, but it will take a long time to catch up, if they ever do so, and it will be easy to slip back into the slow lane again.

The provincial Party Secretary of Guizhou province, which has lagged lamentably behind the others, could still say at the end of 1993: 'today, the gap between eastern and western regions is widening. A poor region like Guizhou province should have a sense of urgency. We must adopt and firmly establish in our minds the idea of macro-agriculture, and develop the rural economy in an all-round way. While not relaxing grain production, we should vigorously develop diversified economic operations, Township and Village Enterprises, animal husbandry and courtyard economy.' A Guizhou official visiting Shanghai was much impressed by the fact that it took nearly two hours to travel the ten miles from Hong Qiao airport to Shanghai City Hall because of the traffic jams. 'I hope some day my province will have such a traffic problem,' he told his apologetic host. 'In my provincial capital,' he explained sadly, 'it takes only seven minutes.'[14]

There are signs of trickle-down to the interior. The Ministry of Agriculture revealed that the gross output of Township Enterprises in central and western provinces was growing 10 per cent faster than the country as a whole.[15] The government has prodded Anhui province to sign contracts for over 3,000 projects with neighbouring provinces, and Anhui's economic growth in 1992 was almost 5 per cent higher than the national average. Similarly, Xinjiang concluded over 4,000 contracts, receiving 200,000 spindles from Shanghai's textile industry. Gansu, another backward province, sent hundreds of people to Zhejiang and Fujian on the coast to learn management expertise, and they came back with more than a hundred projects in their briefcases worth RMB 50 million. One cannot say definitively, therefore, that the great divide gets worse in every way.[16]

Apart from deliberate central pressure to develop projects in the inner provinces, natural balancing factors are at work. Guangdong has reached virtual full employment, so foreign investors are beginning to look instead at Hunan or Guangxi, where many of the migrant job-hunters come from. Taiwan alone had at a recent count invested US$275 million capital in 345 projects in Hunan for export manufacturing.[17]

When Wuhan, China's Chicago, opened its doors to outside business early in the 1980s, the Guangzhou textile and other light industrialists negotiated to exhibit their products, and a bicycle factory in Wuhan placed orders for components with manufacturers in other provinces. The main benefit of the Sanxia Dam, if it is ever built, will be the supply of cheap electricity to the manufacturers of Wuhan and inland Yangzi provinces downstream from Wuhan.

One of the State Council think-tanks recently reviewed this problem and listed measures which the government could take to solve it. Inter-provincial blockades, it said, should be made illegal. Tax reforms should be implemented to make local governments less dependent on revenues from their local producers, and the price-setting mechanism for those commodities which are still centrally regulated should avoid provincial differentials.

The provinces still complain that 'free trade' will force their enterprises into bankruptcy. It is a big challenge to Beijing, where the reformers hope that the exercise on which they are engaged, of disentangling government from business, will eventually weaken local governments' identification with their local producers and at the same time strengthen their role as regulators of the local economy.[18] But there is little the government can realistically do to dissuade scholars like Wang Huming of Fudan University from concluding that 'the sense of local interests has gradually overwhelmed the sense of national interest.'[19]

Some Chinese academic analysts claim to detect an alarming rise of economic 'warlordism', matching a decline in the power of the central government, particularly in its capability of drawing revenues for the national treasury from the localities (though its situation was improved by tax reforms in 1994). Wang Shaoguang and Hu Angang (one a political scientist, the other an economist) wrote an influential report in 1993 warning of a future 'weak-centre, strong-localities' China leading to a national collapse and inter-regional clashes on the model of Yugoslavia. The authors called for an urgent halt to decentralisation, a US-style federal system to regulate centre–province tensions and recognition that 'economic warlordism' is threatening China's break-up. The modern champion of federalism is Yan Jiaqi, once an important aide to Zhao Ziyang, leading political scientist, mentor of the Tiananmen democracy movement and now an exile. In July 1989 he proposed a Chinese federation, elaborating the idea in a book entitled *A Design for a Federated China*, as a means of both reforming Chinese politics and also dealing with the Tibet and Taiwan problems. Some intellectuals agree, but still lie low in the aftermath of Tiananmen.[20]

There have been short-lived secessions even in this century, as well as in earlier periods. Sichuan, Hunan, Zhejiang and Shanxi all briefly declared their independence and a government of Fuzhou was actually formed in the 1930s. Cantonese leaders were ready in the 1920s to assert Guangdong's independence if the British in Hongkong had given backing, and Heilongjiang secessionism had to be nipped in the bud in the early 1950s. But unified central government came to a peak, at least in modern terms, under the Communist Party in the 1950s. Since then the unitary state has technically held. Nobody believes the Taiwan novelist Bao Mi's book *Yellow Peril* which predicts that the Third World War will be triggered by the secession of China's south coast provinces.[21]

Provincial character varies greatly. Paul Theroux was told by the Chinese that, in the north, they are 'imperious, quarrelsome, rather aloof, political, proud noodle-eaters', while below the Yangzi they are 'talkative, friendly, complacent, dark, sloppy, commercial-minded and materialistic rice-eaters'. Subvarieties of these two strains could be sketched, one being the conversation-stopper by a vice-mayor of Guangzhou: 'We're all Chinese. We're just a little more creative down south.'[22]

The most serious issue between the centre and the provinces is the tax take. In the mid-1980s a new budget contract system was brought in, requiring the provinces to pay a fixed amount, or a fixed proportion of their revenues to the centre.

It used to be argued that the new system would lead to inefficient provinces like Innner Mongolia ceasing to supply their raw materials to efficient provinces like Shanghai, choosing rather to build their own uneconomic factories to process the materials. But then if Shanghai were more efficient in processing materials than Inner Mongolia, it was counter-argued, it should by the same token be able to afford to pay higher prices for the materials.[23]

Poor inland provinces benefited hugely from the new tax system, able to retain incremental revenues for their own use without any responsibility for shortfalls. Henan, for instance, recently collected RMB 8.4 billion in tax in one year, and should contractually have handed over about one-sixth of that to Beijing. But by the time extra payments for Henan from the centre were calculated for enterprise losses, disaster relief, additional capital construction and grain subsidies, it turned out that the central government not only received no tax revenue at all but actually owed Henan RMB 400 million *yuan*.[24]

The tax system was altogether reformed in 1994 under Zhu Rongji's eagle eye, to yield two-thirds of revenues to the centre, one-third to the provinces. We wait to see how the provinces will fare under this, whether they accept it as equitable between themselves, and whether Zhu Rongji and his successors can continue to enforce it. The World Bank estimates that the centre will be creaming off about half of total tax revenues by the end of the decade and will have more leverage over local governments.[25] That presumes efficiency: a general once defended China's need for spending on arms by telling a foreign diplomat that even tax-collectors needed to be armed!

One highly effective economic weapon which the centre can use to hold the provinces together is to ensure that urban incomes remain reasonably uniform throughout China. The average city-dweller gets roughly two and a half times the income of the average villager, which is similar to the experience of many other countries in Asia. But whereas the villager's income varies considerably according to the weather patterns and agricultural richesse of his area, the city-dweller has a broadly similar standard of living whether he lives in a rich coastal province or a poor inland one.

The system of subsidies, tax apportionment, and state employment on standard wage scales facilitates this inter-provincial equality of urban incomes, which lessens the enthusiasm for separatist sentiments. The cities are, as it were, bought off.[26] But this is unlikely to survive the reforms under which the market will take over from the central government the task of deciding wages and prices in each city. Greater provincial autonomy would thus be one of the major prices which China may have to pay for its modernisation.

The economic and other practical interests of individual provinces strongly suggest a trend towards autonomy. 'Rapid growth,' the *Strategic Survey 1992–93* of the International Institute of Strategic Studies of London observed, 'might require so much regional diversity that China might not be recognisable as a centre-driven, single state by early next century.'

Kenneth Lieberthal, the US sinologist, wonders why so many observers in the West go on assuming that China should be unitary rather than federal. We on the outside do tend to be swayed by the conventional views of idealistic intellectuals in China who see their national unity as a priceless shield against Western intellectual, cultural and political imperialism. But there is little practical reason why a federal state, or something approximating to it, could not meet the needs of the Chinese people as satisfactorily as any other kind. The Communist Party proposed a federation as early as 1922, and both Mao and Deng supported the idea at one time or another. Deng's reported view was that federation or confederation should be seriously considered after Taiwan's reunification.[27] The likely non-democratic nature of the constituent partly independent provinces might threaten the effectiveness of the autocratic central government, it is true. One relatively cohesive dictatorial group may be more efficient than thirty such groups trying to work together in harness. But a conclusive appraisal of that is not yet possible.

We are also over-impressed by the public exercise of power over provincial leaders by the central government and Party leadership. A dramatic instance came in 1994 when Vice-Premier Zhu Rongji, on an inspection tour of the state-owned industries, supposedly under reform, abruptly dismissed the governor and Party Secretary of Heilongjiang province because of their alleged inefficiency and sluggishness in reform. That certainly made the country aware of how seriously the central government took its industrial reforms, but it may not make the task of Zhu and his colleagues easier when dealing with provincial leaders in future.[28]

The Chinese emperors in their final decades took it for granted that China had to be a unitary state, although it was (and still is) too large to be governed really effectively from Beijing. In the past century no Chinese leader has seriously addressed the laws and regulations which would be needed to equip China with a federal system assuring it of both decentralisation and stability.[29] Fast progress in federalisation is not to be expected even if a majority of leaders were to decide to pursue it.

The technique of inserting leaders from one province to senior positions in another is well known in China, and conscientious efforts have been made to mix people of different provincial origins together in the Communist Party and some state organisations. For example, all seven of the senior commanders of the military region based in Guangzhou are northerners.[30] While undertaking economic decentralisation as part of the reforms of the 1980s, the government under Deng Xiaoping also continued the old practice of drawing key provincial leaders into the central leadership, to be assured of their loyalty and to deflect separatist tendencies.

An interesting case was that of Ye Xuanping, a governor of Guangdong province and son of a particularly powerful elder in the former generation of leadership. He once reportedly spurned the conventions of 'face' by openly disputing with Premier Li Peng at a meeting. Ye was offered a post on the Politburo, but obviously preferred to stay at home in the south, and only after a period of pressure and persuasion did he finally submit to what was generally interpreted to be the superficial 'victory' of the centre over its richest province. In Beijing Ye was subject to stronger central pressures, but could also more efficiently protect his province's interests during the debates and intense lobbying with which the capital fills its days. He once told an Indian Ambassador: 'Beijing pretends to rule, and we pretend to be ruled.' Guangdong is now ruled by a governor and Party Secretary, one of whom is Cantonese. The other should have been transferred, but the province would not accept the centre's nominee to take his place. Similar situations prevailed in Sichuan and Shanghai in 1995, proving that provinces now enjoy more bargaining power.[31] One of the tensions created by the succession to Deng Xiaoping is the possible emergence of a Shanghai clique dominating the Party leadership under Jiang Zemin, aided by Zhu Rongji and Wu Bangguo. Most of the provinces have a palpable dislike for Shanghainese.[32]

The centre has the advantage of knowing that the provincial leaders, being fierce rivals, would hardly ever collaborate among themselves, leaving room for Beijing to play one off against another. On the other hand the provincial leaders do have certain common interests, for example relating to inter-provincial trade and the apportionment of taxes, and on these matters they could conceivably present a united front to Beijing – all behind the scenes, naturally. So there are contradictory indications about the likely direction of China's internal state structure – federal or centralised politics. Gerald Segal is probably right in noting that there can be 'informal variants of federalism', which could in the end lead us to the situation where 'in practice, if not in law, there is more than one China to deal with.'[33] Another scholar counter-argues that any federation acceptable to Beijing would inevitably be dominated by Beijing.[34]

A cautious conclusion would be that the forces making for provincial autonomy and a more federalistic structure in China are more weighty and likely to be more constant in the future than those against. The progress in that direction may not be steady, and may proceed by two steps forward, and one step back, with incessant jockeying for short-term advantage by the actors involved, but in the end China is likely to become, some time in the twenty-first century, a country with a weaker centre and a gaggle of very healthy autonomous provinces, many of which are, after all, as large as France, Italy or Spain. They would share a Chinese cultural identity, and might leave important defence and foreign relations questions to the centre and even accept continuance of the People's Republic umbrella. A strengthening of provincial autonomy does not necessarily undermine the centre, which has many instruments of pressure at its disposal.[35] The precise delineation of central and provincial responsibilities will not follow western definitions but rather novel constitutional hybrids unfamiliar to Western political scientists.

CHAPTER 14

MINORITIES: TIBET AND OTHERS

The people of China are not racially or culturally homogeneous. About 95 per cent of the inhabitants of the People's Republic are Han Chinese, sharing Chinese culture and ethnicity, but the remaining 70 to 80 million are people forming the national minorities. The three biggest are the Zhuang of Guangxi, the Miao of Yunnan and Guizhou, and the Manchus in the north. Little is heard of them, living as they do mostly surrounded by Chinese. Tibet, Xinjiang and Inner Mongolia on the contrary pose very difficult problems for China. Vast in area, rich in minerals, not traditionally carrying a Han Chinese population and strategic in location, these interior regions display a dislike for Chinese rule which the Communists find deeply frustrating. The problems of these far western domains are also involved with bordering independent states, India, Mongolia and the formerly Soviet states of Central Asia, and their future may well be influenced by those countries. The best known case is Tibet.

The concept of a clearly defined national boundary was never part of the traditional Chinese world view. The Han-dominated areas directly administered by the Chinese emperor formed the core of the imperial Chinese state, but the status of the areas surrounding this inner political core was always ambiguous. Many territories which were effectively self-governing would still recognise the power of the Chinese empire and pay regular tribute to the emperor. This penumbra of Chinese influence used to embrace Manchuria, Mongolia, Korea, Muslim Central Asia, Tibet, Burma and part of what is now Vietnam.

Tribute was a personalised and loosely hierarchical system of international relations. It collapsed in the nineteenth century with the arrival of Western colonial powers which, in the course of seeking control over large slices of territory, divided competing claims by arbitrarily drawing European-style state boundaries. Many former Chinese tributary states were completely taken over by Britain, France or Russia, which also demanded commercial and territorial rights in small coastal enclaves of China proper. In the first half of the twentieth century when power in China itself was divided between warlords and a weak nationalist government, it seemed as if the old united China was finished.

When the Communists seized power in 1949 they said they would reunify China and claim back lost territories. But they realised that the old system of tribute and loosely defined buffer states could not be resurrected. Unless China took full economic, military and administrative control of these territories they would either become independent or else fall under the wing of a neighbouring power. In the new system of later twentieth-century nation-states the Chinese had to make hard-headed strategic decisions as to what regions they would claim control over.[1]

In many areas the choice was limited. Just as Western imperialism had crystallised Chinese nationalism, so it produced a similar effect in many of China's former tributary states. Korea, Burma, Vietnam and Outer Mongolia all emerged as independent states. In Manchuria there was no contention: the Manchurians themselves had forged their claim to be Chinese in the course of forming the ruling élite of China's last imperial dynasty.

China's potential successes were thus confined to Tibet and Central Asia, a region which had been seen by Western powers as having only marginal strategic and economic value, and had therefore escaped serious colonial intervention. The sheer size, small population and inaccessibility of these territories made nationalism a weak force there. The Chinese Communists grasped the opportunity to make up for the loss of other former tributary states, with little opposition either from the native inhabitants or from outside powers.

The feeling that Tibet is part of China is not mere governmental posturing but a widely-shared view among China's Han majority, including intellectuals. The plight of the Tibetans was not highlighted by the students demonstrating in Tiananmen Square in 1989, for example, in spite of the Dalai Lama's message of support for the democracy movement.

Behind the official line of tolerance and co-existence lies a deep-seated animosity among China's intellectuals towards Tibet and Tibetans. A neurosurgeon from Beijing refused to accept that China 'invaded' Tibet in 1951. 'Tibet has no culture ... The spread of Han Chinese culture to outlying regions is not an aggression because it is the spreading of civilisation.'[2] Literacy today in Tibet is still only 27 per cent compared with rates of over 80 per cent in Beijing.

One revealing report described the reactions of two Beijing-based artists in their mid-thirties who toured Tibet in 1986. They belonged to the so-called 'lost generation' of China whose education had been wrecked by the turbulence of the Cultural Revolution. These avant-garde artists, attracted by the exotic and virgin wilderness of Tibet, were as a rule extremely sceptical of the beliefs of the Beijing government. Considerably more broad-minded, tolerant and cosmopolitan than most Han Chinese in their attitude towards other races and cultures, they were

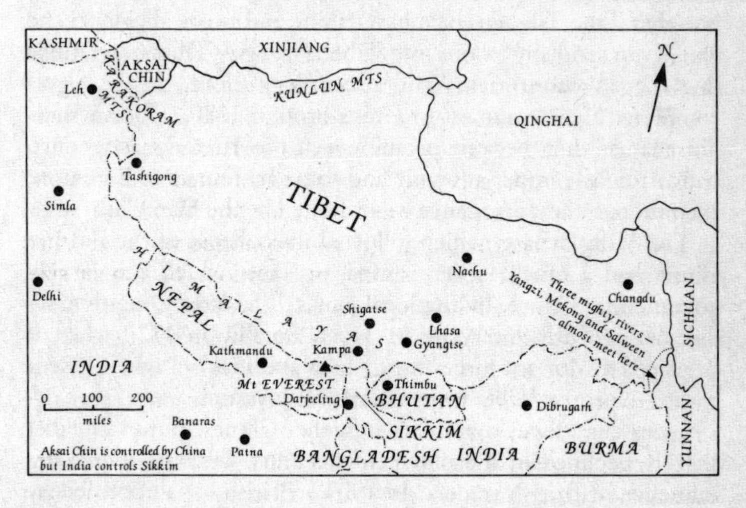

Tibet

nevertheless surprised and shocked at encountering Tibetan nationalism. They were stung by a monk's cry that he was not Chinese but Tibetan: 'Tibet has always been part of China,' one of the artists replied. 'We have done so much to develop Tibet. The central government built roads and schools, freed an entire class of slaves – how can you be so angry?'[3]

Although China has problems with other national minorities, Tibet is unique in being the only region inhabited by an overwhelming majority of a single nationality (of about five million) with a wholly non-Chinese culture and a tradition of virtual independence stretching back over a thousand years. The core of Tibetan culture is a form of Buddhism, known to Westerners as Lamaism. The word *lama* (Sanskrit *guru*) signifies a religious teacher or monk of high standing. Buddhism is said to have reached Tibet simultaneously from India and China during the seventh century AD. By the twelfth century it had become the national faith of the Tibetan people. Successive Dalai Lamas were both the spiritual and temporal rulers of Tibet until 1959.

Apart from some earlier incursions into China, the Tibetans' first contact with a Chinese dynasty was with the Mongol Yuan emperors. In 1206 Genghis Khan, offering to be converted to Lamaism, invited lamas to preach in Mongolia. Genghis promised that if the Tibetans paid him tribute and swore allegiance, he would not send any troops into Tibet. Mongol–Tibetan relations thus began more than half a century before the Mongols completed their conquest of China around 1280. Tibetan Buddhist lamas then became prominent at the Yuan dynasty court, converting the imperial family and some aristocrats to Lamaism, even though their arrogance was resented by the Han Chinese.

The Ming dynasty which followed the collapse of the Yuan in China had a much looser control of Tibet which was largely governed, as before, by the local lamas. The later Qing dynasty did subsequently intervene in Tibet, notably in 1720 when it displaced a Mongol force from Lhasa and in 1792 when it sent troops to protect Tibet from a Nepalese invasion.

From this apogee of military influence Chinese power in Tibet sharply declined in the nineteenth century with the increasing influence of British traders. In 1903 a British expedition led by Colonel Francis Younghusband forced its way into Lhasa, compelled the Dalai Lama to flee, and imposed a treaty on Tibet. Imperial China's last fling in Tibet came in 1910 when the Qing emperor sent a ruthless general equipped with modern weapons to invade Lhasa. It was the first time the Chinese had entered the capital against the Tibetan will. But the collapse of the Qing only two years later enabled the Tibetans to drive these invaders out, killing the commander in the process.

At Simla in 1914 Britain and China loftily discussed dividing Tibet into a western autonomous region and an eastern Chinese-administered region. At the same time a boundary between China and British-ruled India (known as the McMahon Line) was defined. The Chinese government refused to ratify the treaty, but the British had effectively prevented the Chinese from asserting control in Tibet. The thirteenth Dalai Lama declared the independence of Tibet in 1912, although the Chinese never accepted it. With the increasing chaos in China, Tibet could maintain its *de facto* independence until the Communists took power there in 1949.[4]

Until then the Chinese Communists had remained ambiguous about Tibet. Mao had told Edgar Snow in 1936 that 'when the People's Revolution has been victorious in China ... the Mohammedan and Tibetan peoples will form autonomous republics attached to the China federation.' He assumed that the Tibetans would welcome this.[5]

In the event it took the Communists' 2nd Field Army to incorporate Tibet into China in 1950. An agreement was signed with the fourteenth Dalai Lama in 1951 allowing the existing system dominated by a theocratic élite to continue, but under Chinese control. Tibetans refer to this as the Chinese 'invasion' of Tibet while the Chinese, always publicising the cruelty and inequity of Tibet's traditional feudal society, call it a 'liberation'.

The archaic features of Tibetan life were now rapidly eroded. The northern Tibetan province of Amdo was incorporated into China's Qinghai province, while large areas of eastern Tibet became part of Sichuan province (which is why the Dalai Lama's new call for autonomy of the 'Greater Tibet Area' caused such a furore in Beijing). The government in the reduced Tibetan Autonomous Region, nominally under the Dalai Lama, was then pressed to introduce reforms. The feudal élite of Tibet, joined by discontented Khambas from the east and, it is alleged, marginally helped by American and Taiwan sources, rebelled in March 1959. The rebellion was easily suppressed, but a 'government-in-exile' under the Dalai Lama in India challenged the legitimacy and acceptability of Chinese rule.

Tibet was now rapidly reformed along Communist lines. The systematic cruelty of Tibet's former rulers, including slavery and unimaginable tortures, was stemmed. During the nationwide famine of the early 1960s, Tibetan grain was seized for delivery to Han Chinese provinces, effectively spreading the famine to Tibet. Although Tibet became one of the most heavily subsidised regions of China, the material conditions of the Tibetans did not improve. In the countryside they were forced to abandon their traditional barley for other grains unsuited to the conditions of the high plateau. In the urban areas economic and social conditions were skewed heavily in favour of Han Chinese immigrants.

The Cultural Revolution was an unmitigated disaster for Tibet. The religion which is the heart of its culture and society was desecrated. Some 5,000 monasteries were totally destroyed, and for the ten years 1966–76 all religious practices were banned. In 1980 the liberal General Secretary of the Chinese Communist Party, Hu Yaobang, visited Lhasa to apologise to the Tibetan people for their maltreatment: 'We feel very bad. We have worked for nearly thirty years, but the life of the Tibetan people has not notably improved. Are we not to blame?' As a mark of good faith Hu ordered a tax amnesty for the benefit of rural Tibetans.

Despite some changes for the better, evidence from foreign visitors suggests continued discrimination against Tibetans and their culture. Some put the number of Tibetans who perished in the famines of the early 1960s and the violence of the Cultural Revolution as high as 1.2 million.

But the Communist newspaper for Tibet unwittingly illuminated a major source of tension between the Han Communists and the Tibetan Buddhists by commenting, 'Communists are atheists and regardless of their ethnic origins, they should uphold materialism and atheism ... Communists have a duty to propagate atheism among the people and to help the latter gradually cast off religious influence. They may not believe in religion and participate in religious activities, nor may they engage in matters that increase religious influences.'[6]

Tibetan nationalists feel that the biggest threat to their culture now comes from Chinese immigration. The proportion of Han Chinese in Tibet is hotly debated. The total number of Tibetans is usually put at five or six million, of whom only about two million live in the Tibetan Autonomous Region itself. The rest are scattered through various parts of four or five adjoining provinces of China. The Chinese census in 1982 put Tibet's population at 1.9 million, of whom only about 5 per cent were Han Chinese. That excluded the many Han Chinese who work and live temporarily in Tibet, such as the Chinese soldiers garrisoned there, some for seven years. On top of this there is a seasonal influx of Chinese traders into Tibetan cities during the summer months. According to the Dalai Lama's government-in-exile the Chinese now outnumber Tibetans in the Autonomous Region by 2.5 million to 2 million – and in the capital Lhasa they outnumber the Tibetans by two to one.[7]

Is the influx of Han Chinese into Lhasa a deliberate government policy, or does it partly reflect the broader trend of urbanisation in China? Chinese traders who are refused residence permits in Han Chinese cities can get them more easily in Lhasa. By 1993, trading licences in Lhasa were said to be exchanging hands for as much as RMB 8,000. An unemployed peasant from Henan province now repairs bicycles in Lhasa, for example. Many new Chinese graduates have to accept an eight-year 'hardship' posting in Tibet before being allowed to work in a Chinese city.[8]

Tibetan fears at being swamped by Han Chinese were heightened in 1990 when a plan came out to limit the number of children in rural Tibetan families to three or four. Till then rural Tibet, along with other minority regions, had been exempt from China's population restrictions, although Tibetans in towns had been allowed only two children – or three if the first two were both boys or both girls. Contraception is not readily available in Tibet, and sterilisation is the main method used for family planning.[9]

The existence of so many Tibetans outside the borders of the

Tibetan Autonomous Region makes Han incursions into Tibetan areas more difficult to trace. The Qinghai village where the Dalai Lama was born, for example, used to be predominantly Tibetan, but by 1981 only eight out of forty families in the village were Tibetan, the rest being Chinese.[10]

The impact of Han Chinese on the Tibetan way of life is seen most vividly in the Tibetan areas of eastern Sichuan. Markham, a Tibetan village in the Tibetan-Qiang Autonomous Prefecture of Aba, used to be a small yak-butter trading centre, but now 40,000 Han people live there in seven-storey concrete apartment blocks and only a few thousand Tibetans are left. The village is very prosperous with spotless streets, restaurants boasting a wide range of dishes and shops bulging with consumer goods. The area is also made more attractive to Han Chinese settlers by the local population policy which allowed them until recently to have two children instead of only one.

The local Tibetans benefit from the new prosperity. They can sell their barley, apples, wheat and vegetables on local free markets, and extend their mediaeval two-storey Tibetan houses up to three or four storeys. But the Tibetans do not find it easy to participate in the new urban and industrial culture. Sherab, a high school student, complains that 'in the few factories that are operating here, the workers are mainly Chinese. You have to be able to speak Chinese to work in these factories. We want our own factories.' There is also a feeling that the flourishing local timber industry is plundering Tibetan resources, with ethnic Tibetans getting very little compensation for the destruction of their traditional way of life. Where is the Tibetan entrepreneur?

There is more than a hint of fatalism in the Tibetan attitude. 'We sit here every day,' says Tenzin, a Markham Tibetan, 'and we watch the logging trucks go by, down to Chengdu. I've watched it for years. In the time it takes me to drink one cup of tea, I count an average of fifteen trucks loaded with timber passing by. I see the wealth of our land being taken east every day and I do not think that is right. We are getting nothing from it. What can I do to stop this happening?' Forest cover in that valley has dropped to 18 per cent from 30 per cent in 1949, a pattern repeated all over Tibet. The Chinese bring in concrete and take out timber. The government wants to attract foreign investment to the region to further the exploitation of resources which include uranium, gold, iron, manganese, titanium, tin, tungsten, lead, zinc, coal, marble, diamonds and peat.

Asked about the Tibetans' relationship with the Chinese, Tenzin is guarded. 'It is very good. What we eat, what we wear and everything else we buy – Thermoses, bicycles, even chopsticks – all are bought from the Chinese. Yes, our relationship is very good. If I said any more they would chop off one of my ears,' he says, laughing.[11] There is support for Tibetan independence in Sichuan too: in 1990 two Tibetan businessmen were jailed there for distributing such leaflets and posters, showing that Tibetan nationalism is not confined to Lhasa or to monks.[12]

In the ghetto of whitewashed Tibetan houses clustered around Lhasa's Johkang Temple, which forms the old Tibetan quarter of the town, the increase in the number of Chinese-owned shops is particularly provoking. The proliferation of discos, pool halls and bars, alien to Tibetan culture and nearly all owned by Han immigrants, causes disquiet. One monk recently complained that China was strangling Lhasa not so much with its army and police, but by ringing the city with pool tables.[13]

In 1987, 1988 and 1989 demonstrations in Lhasa were bloodily suppressed. Tibetans armed with slingshots made out of yak hair attacked policemen and destroyed Chinese shops and bicycles. In 1989 the Chinese declared martial law, preceding the 1989 Tiananmen martial law in Beijing and outlasting the Beijing clampdown by almost six months. Foreign tourists and journalists were expelled. As a result of the clampdown, twenty-four Tibetans were given long prison sentences. Major-General Zhang Shaosong, the political commissar of the Tibet military region, admitted in 1989 that over 600 people had been killed or injured in twenty-one riots over the space of eighteen months.[14]

The Chinese are quite determined to hold on to Tibet. The Dalai Lama's proposal for a referendum on Tibet's future was indignantly rejected in March 1995. The Communist government, like its Nationalist predecessor, has always insisted that Tibetan independence is not negotiable. Apart from Tibet's rich mineral resources and the historical claims of Chinese suzerainty there is also a military or strategic motive for the Han Chinese presence in Tibet.

The southern border of Tibet forms China's international frontier with India, Nepal and Bhutan. The border with India, one of the largest military powers in Asia, is disputed in several places. The McMahon line to the east delineates a border dating from the days of British colonialism in India, which the Chinese dispute but which the Indians were only too happy to inherit. The Chinese claim territory extending down to the valley floor of the Brahmaputra river, while the Indians want to keep the frontier up in the mountains.

To the northwest of Tibet lies the disputed Aksai Chin plateau through which runs China's only road connecting Tibet with Xinjiang. In 1962 the Chinese and Indians fought a brief but bitter war over these sparsely inhabited tracts of land. Tensions have eased since then but the borders remain an unresolved international issue. The high altitude and thin air of the Tibetan plateau also make Tibet an ideal launching-site for missiles, and Tibetans in exile have claimed that the Chinese have established two ICBM launch sites in Tibet. The Chinese themselves acknowledge that Tibet has the world's largest uranium reserves.

The West has questioned the legitimacy of the Chinese presence in Tibet, but since China's rapprochement with Western countries in the 1970s, most other governments have come to accept China's legal claim. What really keeps the Tibetans on the international agenda is their charismatic exiled leader, the Dalai Lama.

Lhamo Dhondrub was born in 1933 about the time of the death of the previous, thirteenth, Dalai Lama. At the age of two, as a candidate for the reincarnation of the old Dalai Lama, he was successful in picking out the latter's eating bowl, spectacles, pencil, walking stick and drum. Other qualifications for becoming a living god included impressive ears and tiger stripes on the legs. He was renamed Jetsun Jamphel Ngwang Lobsang Yeshi Tenzin Guyatso (Holy Lord, Gentle Glory, Eloquent, Compassionate, Learned Defender of the Faith, and Ocean of Wisdom) and on 22 February 1940 he sat for the first time on the Dalai Lama's Lion Throne in the Potala Palace in Lhasa. After the Chinese invasion of Tibet in 1951, he accepted Chinese rule, and after meeting Mao Zedong he even spoke in praise of Mao's sincerity.

At the suppression of the 1959 rebellion, however, the Dalai Lama fled to India with several thousand compatriots and set up a government-in-exile in Dharamsala. Wearing the patched and threadbare dark red robes of a monk, he receives Tibetan pilgrims there, and asks them for the latest news from Tibet. He eats *tsampa*, the traditional Tibetan food made of barley and butter, and drinks black tea grated from blocks. He listens to the BBC World Service.

Inspired by Gandhi's teaching, the Dalai Lama advocates a peaceful struggle for the Tibetan cause. He was awarded the 1989 Nobel Peace Prize, which was widely celebrated in Tibet. A *People's Daily* editorial fumed that 'the Dalai Lama is not an ordinary religious person, but a political gangster who has for a long time carried out activities aimed at destroying racial unity and splitting the motherland.'[15]

The Dalai Lama is indignant at the Chinese claim that Tibet is part of China. 'Of all the powers which ruled Tibet, China did so for the shortest time. The Mongols and the Manchus never made such claims, even in their imperial heyday... this perversion of language is yet another trick to deny our deep identity... fostering the illusion that Tibet has been Chinese for centuries.'[16]

In 1988 the Dalai Lama floated the compromise of China's retaining sovereignty and control over foreign and defence policy in return for discussions aimed at creating genuine Tibetan autonomy and an end to Chinese immigration into Tibet. He later argued that the principle of 'one country, two systems', the formula used for the retrocession of Hongkong, might be a fruitful starting point for dialogue.

The Chinese would not bite. They continued to insist that the Dalai Lama renounce any claim for Tibetan independence or semi-independence, as a precondition for talks. They offered him a vice-chairmanship of the National People's Congress should he do this. But the Dalai Lama is extremely wary of Chinese offers. 'If I returned,' he surmised, 'I would have a lavish house, lavish food – and a lavish big seal on my mouth.'

The possible fate of a lama in China is shown by the case of the Panchen Lama, who ranked second to the Dalai Lama in traditional status; he played a useful intermediary role with the Chinese government, but was criticised by many Tibetans as a stooge or 'Chinese chopstick'. After many years in prison following the 1959 revolt he was rehabilitated and married a Chinese girl. After his death in 1989 the selection of a boy successor became a dispute between the Dalai Lama and China.[17]

Several Tibetan missions went to Beijing from India, led by the Dalai Lama's brother, Gyalo Thondup. In August 1993 'frank and cordial' talks were held with Chinese ministers and senior officials. The Dalai Lama also keeps in regular contact with the Chinese ambassador in India. But radical young Tibetans were bitterly disappointed by the Dalai Lama's compromise offer. 'Nobody has the right to give up the struggle for Tibetan independence,' said Lhasang Tsering, the fiery president of the Tibetan Youth Congress. 'Tibetan lives have been sacrificed. We cannot just abandon the cause.'[18]

Conservative Tibetans were alarmed by the Dalai Lama's plans to democratise the government-in-exile through elections for members of his cabinet instead of their being appointed by himself. Shock was also caused by his announcement in 1973 that he might be the last Dalai Lama. He is aware of the weakness of reincarnation as a method of political succession – because of the long gap between the death of one Dalai Lama and the coming of age of the next – and he is toying with other means of succession. At the same time he has stated that the next reincarnated Dalai Lama will not be born in Chinese hands.

The international community, which in the 1950s questioned the legality of the Chinese occupation of Tibet, has long since accepted its integration into the People's Republic. The Indians are wary of supporting the cause of Tibetan independence, knowing that they themselves have many ethnic minorities campaigning for self-rule. Despite their former involvement in Tibet, the British are loath to irritate the Chinese for fear of repercussions in the fate of Hongkong. Until the collapse of the Soviet Union, the Americans were restrained in criticising the human rights record of such a strategic ally. In any case, what outside power could effectively intervene in this remote mountain fastness of central Asia?

But from the late 1980s Western governments increasingly complained of China's violations of human rights. The collapse of

Communism in the Soviet Union and Eastern Europe, and the worldwide coverage given to the suppression of the student democracy movement at Tiananmen in 1989, accelerated this process. The Dalai Lama's constant lobbying of Western governments and requests for meetings with prime ministers and presidents are designed to keep Tibet on the international agenda. Since 1985 the Dalai Lama no longer speaks softly and accommodatingly about China. The tone is combative. Tibet is now a fashionable issue in the West, and show-business celebrities such as the film star Richard Gere are active in supporting the Tibetan cause. In 1992 the Dalai Lama accepted an invitation to act as the guest editor of *Vogue*, the well-known fashion magazine. And 'Free Tibet' stickers are now a not uncommon sight on car rear-windows.

The Chinese are alive to the fact that military occupation is not sufficient for them to gain political legitimacy in Tibet. For the fortieth anniversary of Chinese rule in Tibet, they undertook a US$7.4 million restoration of the Potala Palace in Lhasa.[19] The repairs were partly a gesture to show that the Chinese would not destroy Tibetan culture, but they also attracted tourists.

The tax concession made by Hu Yaobang was reversed in 1990, but Chinese economic policy in Tibet has become more positive. A billion yuan was recently invested in the expansion of Gonga airport in Lhasa, and direct flights to Beijing, Katmandu and Hongkong are planned. Nearby is a US$127 million hydro-electric scheme. New resort hotels are being constructed. In 1992 the Chinese created a Special Economic Zone in Lhasa and tried to attract foreign investment there. They promised that the preferential policies for Lhasa's economic zone would be more favourable than many of those in China, with freedom to retain all foreign exchange and customs duties. Tibet's foreign trade reached $100 million in 1993 and the Tibetan government is setting up joint venture factories to process Tibetan raw materials in China's coastal provinces. These include an eiderdown factory in Shenzhen, a goat-down processing plant in Hebei and a bonded warehouse in Tianjin.[20]

Within Tibet the number of private businesses is now growing. More than 40,000 have been listed, employing 66,000 people. There are over ninety-nine free markets, among which the Chongsaikang market in Lhasa boasts the highest business volume.[21] The annual per capita income of Tibet was only RMB 521 in 1993 and the Chinese target for the year 2000 is RMB 1,200. In other words Tibet's economic growth rate, which averaged 7 per cent in the 1980s and early 1990s, is planned to accelerate to about 10 per cent – faster than the rest of China.[22]

In September 1994 the Chinese announced another big investment programme for Tibet, including 62 major capital projects and 113 science and technology projects. The total investment in agriculture, energy, industry, telecommunications, transport and social projects was put at RMB 2.3 billion. Young Tibetans increasingly see the advantage of going to Chinese universities to take engineering or medical degrees over shouting slogans for an independence China will not grant – and this generation tends to be sceptical about the Dalai Lama. Tibet is moving into its post-religious phase.[23]

But the Tibetans' involvement in economic development does not wholly blunt their political aims. Protests by Tibetan traders against inflation in 1993 quickly developed into a political demonstration with shouts of 'Chinese out of Tibet'.[24] As one Tibetan recently put it, 'We don't want their economic projects. We want our land.' Until now development in Tibet has lagged behind the rest of China. If the Chinese now decide it is worth their while to concentrate some resources on Tibet, they could conceivably accelerate Tibet's development to a point where Tibetan separatists might be mollified.

But the situation in the next twenty years may become more complex. Development may open up divisions within Tibet over the priority to be given to political issues. Private Chinese investors and overseas Chinese will become involved. In the case of the latter, Tibet could find itself linked with broader trends within the Chinese-speaking world, such as the possible emergence of federalism or the so-called Greater China. Until recently one of the few matters on which both the Chinese Communists and Taiwan's Guomindang agreed was that Tibet should remain part of China. But now President Lee Teng-hui of Taiwan has stated, on meeting the Dalai Lama's brother, Gyalo Thondup, that the Dalai Lama's proposals for Tibetan self-rule were 'totally consistent' with Taiwan's policy. In return, the Tibetans supported Taiwan's application to join the United

Nations.[25] The question of Tibet's future political status thus appears deadlocked, but economic development and the internationalisation of the Chinese economy may eventually offer a source of hope for the Tibetans.

The next most difficult minorities for China are the Muslim Uighurs and Kazakhs. Xinjiang, where they mostly live, has an area of 650,000 square miles, and is the largest administrative unit in China, comprising one-sixth of the country's total territory. It is important in China's historical links with Central Asia; various branches of the 'Silk Road' run through it.

Xinjiang has been more successful than Tibet in developing its economy under Chinese rule. The building of a railway line and large-scale Han migration were instrumental in this. Much of Xinjiang is uninhabitable desert or gravelly ground but oases are fed by snowmelt from the surrounding mountains. Like Tibet, Xinjiang is rich in minerals. It borders on four former Soviet republics: Tadjikistan, Kirghizstan, Kazakhstan and Russia, as well as four other countries: Mongolia, Afghanistan, Pakistan and India.[26]

In 1949 the Han population of Xinjiang was estimated at less

Xinjiang

than 6 per cent. Uighurs were by far the largest ethnic group, and the Chinese maintained their dominance only by skilful alliances and manipulations. In 1933 and 1944 two attempts had been made by Xinjiang's Muslims to establish an East Turkestan Republic. The leader of the second was Saifudin, a Russian-educated Uighur and a member of the Soviet Communist Party.

After 1949 the local leaders realised that in a military struggle they would be no match for China's Red Army, but Russia was then the Chinese Communists' most important ally, so China's incorporation of Xinjiang had to be handled delicately. Burhan, an ethnic Tartar appointed governor by the Guomindang, was kept in his post by the Communists, and Saifudin became deputy governor. However, after being sent to the Party school in Beijing, some Uighur army officers returned to find their posts taken over by Han soldiers, so they were relegated to minor positions. Many of the remaining Uighur officers were purged during the anti-rightist campaign of 1957.

China made a concerted effort to reduce Soviet influence, a task made difficult by exchanges across the 'friendship border' where the Soviet side boasted a higher standard of living. The Chinese built barriers along Xinjiang's borders, reclaimed land, established new state farms, built highways, railways and factories and constructed entirely new cities – providing in the process an important conduit for Han migration into Xinjiang.[27]

This migration was helped by the rustication of dissident intellectuals (many from Shanghai) and by the setting up of labour camps in Xinjiang. Han areas in the new towns were kept separate from quarters where the minorities lived. To reduce the possibility of conflict, the Hans in Urumqi (the provincial capital) had separate restaurants, market-places and cinemas.

The Hans now make up just over a third of Xinjiang's population, and Uighurs almost half. Next largest are the Kazakh and Kirghiz pastoral groups, both Turkic-speaking and, superficially at least, Islamicised. The Kazakhs (numbering about 1 million) follow a nomadic life in the north along the slopes of the Tianshan mountains. The Kirghiz follow a similar way of life on the southern slopes of those same mountains near Kashgar. The Hui, or ethnic Chinese Muslims, number about 633,000. Altogether there are an estimated 40 million Muslims living in China, which is more than the Muslim population of all the former Soviet Central Asian states put together.

In 1955 Xinjiang became an autonomous region of China, with Saifudin as governor and Wang Enmao as first Party Secretary. But Han-minority relations soon came under strain with the anti-rightist campaign and the Great Leap Forward. Prominent writers and the mayor of Urumqi were declared guilty of 'local nationalism'. The starvation of the early 1960s intensified bad feelings and after an abortive revolt in 1962 some 70,000 fled to Kazakhstan. With Soviet encouragement (Russia by then being disenchanted with China), they wrote letters and broadcast radio messages about how much better life was on the Russian side, urging friends and relatives to follow.

Beijing responded by giving way to some of the minorities' demands, while also speeding up Han migration. The concessions were quickly reversed, however, when the Cultural Revolution set in and army units loyal to Wang Enmao fought pitched battles with units under the control of Red Guards.

In their spare time the Red Guards directed their youthful energies to destroying mosques, wrecking other showpieces of ethnic identity, and force-feeding Muslims with pork. The minorities, heavily armed with stolen Chinese and Soviet weapons, fought back, and tried once more to re-establish an East Turkestan Republic. Wang Enmao tried desperately to persuade Beijing to call off the Cultural Revolution in Xinjiang, because of its 'special situation'. One of his deputies met Russian officials in Mongolia to seek Soviet help.

Eventually the government did stop the Cultural Revolution in Xinjiang, but Wang Enmao found himself demoted and a host of Han Chinese outsiders were brought in to occupy senior official posts. Many of these new leaders were disliked, and further large groups moved across the Soviet border. Saifudin was sacked in 1978, charged with collaborating with the Soviet Union. But his strong support base in Xinjiang protected him to some extent, and he remained an alternate member of the Politburo in Beijing for some years. He even became a vice-chairman of the National People's Congress.

In 1981 another famine led to a demand for the recall of Han cadres. Uighurs planned an uprising, triggered by a fight between a Uighur and a Han youth in the southern city of Aksu. The dispute developed into an anti-Han pogrom, but, realising that minority feelings were running high, the local military chose not to intervene, leaving many Han migrants feeling scared and unprotected by their own military.

Because of this fear, and to take advantage of Deng Xiaoping's ending of rustication policies, many Hans applied to return to China proper. Xinjiang issued exit permits but the government of Shanghai (whence many of the migrants had originally come) refused to honour them. More than 60,000 Hans demonstrated in Aksu, taking over government offices, and the protests spread to other cities. The local Han bureaucrats and soldiers sympathised with the grievances of the demonstrators and refused to intervene. The central government had eventually to bring in troops from Lanzhou.

The problems the Chinese have in ruling Xinjiang were highlighted by an incident where a military truck ran over a Uighur in Kashgar. To pacify the Uighurs, the local government sentenced the Chinese driver to death. The Chinese troops were in turn outraged at this, and rescued their colleague from jail, overturning his sentence. The spectre of a People's Liberation Army mutiny loomed as large as the threat of a Uighur revolt – and was more feared by Beijing.

With a string of bumper harvests in the early 1980s Xinjiang regained the self-sufficiency in food which it had lost in the 1950s. Relations with the Soviet Union revived, and the borders with the Soviet Union and Mongolia were reopened after twenty years. The newly opened Karakoram Highway eased access to Pakistan and Afghanistan. There were major new discoveries of oil. Things visibly improved.

Wang Enmao returned to prominence in the 1980s, appealing for foreign investment and noting that the planned railway from Urumqi to the Soviet border would facilitate trade with the Middle East. In 1984 China's first Muslim stock company was founded. Backed by the Urumqi Islamic Association, it proposed to set up printing houses for scriptures and books, as well as food-processing factories and a construction company for traditional-style buildings. Direct air flights to Mecca were established for the first time and pilgrimages were officially allowed.

In June 1988 population restrictions, from which Xinjiang had hitherto been exempt, were introduced for the first time, limiting the number of children allowed in cities to two and in rural areas to three or four in exceptional cases. The 1980s also saw the rise of a new kind of protest. In December 1985 students demonstrated in Urumqi with a shopping list of grievances. They demanded an end to nuclear testing in the province, the replacement of Han cadres with democratically elected minority candidates, an end to coercive family planning, more support for education, political self-rule and an end to the sending of Han criminals to Xinjiang.[28]

There was more to come in 1989. Demonstrators took to the streets of Urumqi in support of the Tiananmen students – one of whose leaders, Wuerkaixi, was himself a Uighur. Fundamentalist Muslims later joined in the demonstrations with a different agenda, protesting about a new book which claimed that Muslims went to Mecca to indulge in sex. They attacked the Communist Party headquarters with rocks and steel bars, reducing forty vehicles to scrap metal and injuring 150 police. The Beijing government then banned the offending book.[29] Even more turbulent riots came in 1990, when hundreds were killed and at times the confrontations were said to have resembled military battles. The Chinese described the affair as an 'armed counter-revolutionary rebellion'.[30]

The collapse of the Soviet Union in 1991 brought new worries. Illegal immigrants swarmed in from the neighbouring former Soviet republics, destroying border barriers, felling trees, opening up mines and hunting animals. Some of them had left China in the 1960s but now wanted to return. The Chinese, unsettled by these developments, transported thousands more Han, many of whom had lost their homes in the severe flooding in central China that year, into the border areas. To prevent the politics of Central Asia from spilling over into China, the Chinese also tried to keep the refugees from the Russian side in designated settlement areas.[31]

The break-up of the Soviet Union has created new foreign policy problems for China with the creation of five new and not fully stable republics over the border from Xinjiang. China has established diplomatic relations with all of the new Central Asian states, three of which (Kazakhstan, Kirghizstan and Tajikistan) share a frontier with China.[32]

In April 1994 Premier Li Peng toured Uzbekistan, Turkmenistan, Kirghizstan and Kazakhstan, seeking to strengthen commercial ties.[33] There has been initial success: the Chinese state oil company has established a joint venture with Japan's Marubeni to build an oil refinery in Bukhara, Uzbekistan. Xinjiang Airlines leased four passenger planes from Uzbekistan Airlines. Another key transport project is the completion in 1992 of the railroad link between Xinjiang and Kazakhstan, a scheme which has lain on the planners' tables since the 1950s. It completes the direct link from Rotterdam to Lianyungang on the Yellow Sea coast.

The Bukhara refinery is not the only investment from Japan involving China. A high-powered economic mission headed by the Chairman of Mitsubishi has drawn up an ambitious 'Project for the 21st Century Silk Road'. This centres on a huge gas and oil pipeline linking four Central Asian states with China's Tarim basin and the Mongolian oilfields – and ultimately with the south China coast to supply Hongkong, Taiwan and Japan. South Korea is also interested in investing in Central Asia with its Korean minorities there (part of Stalin's grandiose resettlements) providing an impetus. Daewoo's truck factory in Uzbekistan is already under way.[34]

All these initiatives from Japan and Korea lend urgency to China's proposed role in this Asian hinterland. The Chinese have the advantage of being land neighbours, and the growth of cross-border trade is seen, for instance, in the large number of traders from Uzbekistan and Kirghizstan to be seen in Kashgar market. China has much to gain from the economic development of the region but will have to play its cards carefully because an economically strong Central Asia could conceivably threaten China's grip on Xinjiang. The boost given to ethnic nationalism in Xinjiang by the establishment of sovereign states in Muslim and Turkic Central Asia is a new worry for China. Any call for a pan-Turkic federation of Turan or Turkestan, echoing the several attempts in this century to establish an East Turkestan Republic in Xinjiang inside China's borders, would alarm Beijing, especially its military leaders.[35]

Already the Uzbeks and Tajiks claim Tamburlaine, the

fourteenth-century empire-builder and Central Asia's equivalent of Genghis Khan, as their own national hero. There are embryonic stirrings of pan-Turkism, for example, in the verse of the Uzbek poet Nusrat Karim:

> Wake up and unite, you generation of Turan!
> You, man, born between the two rivers,
> People of Turan, the motherland calls you
> Uzbek, Tajik, Kirghiz, Kazakh, Turkmen,
> Give your hands to each other as five fingers.

Fortunately for China, these ideas do not have universal appeal in Central Asia. Many see them as a cover for Uzbek chauvinism. The fact that they tend to be based on Turkic nationalism rather than Islam also gives China some relief, since Tajiks are mostly repelled by these ideas. The Islamic Renaissance Party, which is active all over Central Asia, has had some electoral success, but Islamic fundamentalism has so far caused more trouble in Afghanistan than in Xinjiang or Central Asia.

In Tajikistan an Islamic-democratic coalition government was overthrown by parties dominated by former Communists, causing many Tajiks to flee across the border into Afghanistan where they joined their Islamic co-religionists, the Mojahedin, in fighting back across the border. Russian troops were then called in by the new Tajikistan government to defend the border. China, Tajikistan's eastern neighbour with a substantial Tajik minority, has been lucky not to be drawn into this conflict which threatens to involve Uzbekistan and Turkmenistan.

Or perhaps it is not all luck. The Chinese have 1,000 years of experience in playing off the different Central Asian minorities against each other. The Russians with only 150 years' presence in the region are relative newcomers who seem to have had their fill of the region's tribal complexities.

The Central Asian states also sometimes feel threatened by China. China has territorial claims to parts of Kazakhstan and Kirghizstan, although these are currently in abeyance. Kazakhstan's President Nursultan Nazarbayev is seeking help from the West in guarding its borders in return for giving up its nuclear weapons.[36]

China, of course, shares with Russia a strong interest in the maintenance of political stability in the region. Ironically China, after years of condemning Russian military operations in Afghanistan, now supports the presence of Russian troops defending Tadjikistan against the Mojahedin on the Afghan border. Li Peng on his 1994 tour of the region was careful to calm Russian suspicions by stating that Beijing 'has no interest' in filling the 'so-called vacuum' left by the break-up of the Soviet Union.[37]

The new Central Asian states will make China's balancing act in Xinjiang more difficult. Would increased autonomy reduce demands for separatism, or lead to demands for something more? Many minorities still feel alienated from China's political and economic system, and trade with fellow Muslims abroad strengthens centrifugal forces.

As in Tibet, the Chinese now count on lively economic development as the best strategy for keeping Xinjiang in the fold. But this has not yet quelled demand for separatism. A 1993 report admitted that Xinjiang was falling further behind the coastal provinces and losing out in the competition for Central Asian markets. The new rail link from Rotterdam to Urumqi has not yet led to the anticipated surge in traffic between Xinjiang and Kazakstan. Local opinion believes that oil and mineral resources could make the province economically self-sufficient – even wealthy – were it not for a perceived siphoning off of those resources by Beijing.

The army in Xinjiang is an overwhelmingly Han organisation, unlikely to side with ethnic minorities in any struggle for independence, but unless there is a direct clash with military interests it does not always side with the Han Chinese settlers either. So far uprisings have mainly been in reaction to specific events. There is little co-ordination among anti-government groups and no evidence so far that fellow-Muslims outside China have been assisting their co-religionists to any significant degree. The Central Asian republics are too occupied still in clarifying their relations with each other and with Russia to offer united support for separatists in Xinjiang.

Recent oil and gas discoveries help to link China with Xinjiang, and will reinforce Beijing's desire to keep the region under close financial control. There is also investment and business dealing by Xinjiang residents, both Han and non-Han, in other areas of

China. The widespread and highly profitable illegal smuggling networks, which reach as far south as Yunnan and as far east as Guangzhou, are apparently controlled by resourceful Uighurs.

The percentage of Xinjiang's population which is ethnic Han has now risen to over 40 per cent. The Uighurs who made up 75 per cent of the population in 1949 now constitute less than half. Chinese is taught as a foreign language in Uighur schools, but the Han do not learn Uighur. 'It's for the minorities to learn Chinese,' one Han official explained disapprovingly.[38] The Chinese had earlier attempted to romanise the Arabic script, but it did not work.

The third big interior area of ethnic minorities where China faces problems is the Inner Mongolian Autonomous Region, not as hot a potato as Xinjiang but possibly more threatening in the long run. The new and unexpected sight of Mongolians running their own government without supervision across the border in the Mongolian People's Republic could be seriously unsettling. The Mongolian People's Republic was founded in 1924 with Russian help, and it became Moscow's most faithful satellite. Mao Zedong told Edgar Snow in the 1930s that 'Outer' Mongolia, as it was once known, would return to being part of China after the revolution. But Stalin wrung recognition of Outer Mongolian independence from the Guomindang government in 1945, and after 1949 the Chinese communists, needing Russian aid, decided not to challenge Mongolian independence.[39]

For the thirty years of the Sino-Soviet split the Mongolian People's Republic was completely cut off from China's Inner Mongolia. With *glasnost*, however, the Mongolians are coming out of their shell, travelling more and widening their trade and cultural contacts. Both China and Mongolia are involved in the Tumen River Development zone which would provide an important new seaport for landlocked Mongolia's trade. But Mongolia's economy, still recovering from the loss of Soviet aid, has a limited attraction to Mongols within China benefiting from China's sustained boom.

Despite its official name, Inner Mongolia has little autonomy. Prey to Chinese settlement for 200 years, the Mongols today are swamped by ethnic Chinese settlers totalling about 15 million. There is no real chance of closer union with Mongols over the

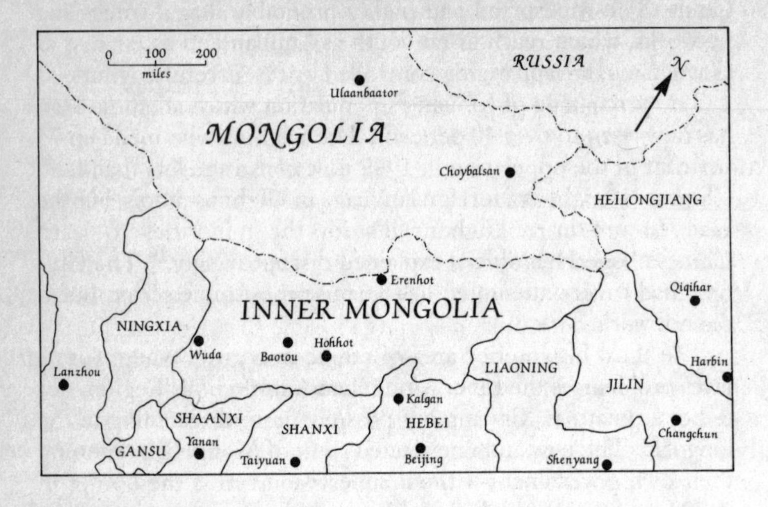

Inner Mongolia

border or even of genuine autonomy – but realism is not always the arbiter in nationalist movements.

There are about three and a half million Mongols in Inner Mongolia and only one and a half million in the People's Republic of Mongolia. Siqinbeilige, a Mongolian official who spent forty years in the Chinese army and can hardly speak Mongolian any more, claimed, 'There is not one Mongol here who would want to join up with Mongolia. Mongols and Hans are now equal under the leadership of the Chinese Communist Party. We are using Communist ideas to liberate them.'[40] Yet some Mongols have been sent to labour camps for the crime of 'Mongolian nationalist chauvinism'. Red Guards murdered up to 100,000 Mongolians during the Cultural Revolution, claiming that they were trying to subvert Chairman Mao's revolution.

At the height of their power the Mongols ruled an empire that stretched from the Danube to the Yellow river and the Ganges. Now the Mongolian language is no longer widely taught in Inner Mongolian state schools and may be dying out. Since 1966, Mongolians no longer hold most of the high government posts in Inner Mongolia.

Inner Mongolia's natural resources do not benefit the Inner Mongolians. 'We would like to be more defiant,' a Mongolian confesses, 'but the will to resist is not in us. We are too passive.'[41] China claims that its relations with the Inner Mongolians are better than those of other minorities. The sinification of Inner Mongolia's economy has accelerated during the reforms of the 1980s, with Han Chinese capital coming in from outside to buy stakes in Inner Mongolia's state industries.[42]

In the Mongolian People's Republic across the border the international fortunes are somewhat reversed. Russia has lost almost all its former influence and is unable to affect developments there, whereas China is on an economic upsurge and can at last implement the old imperial device of instituting buffer states as a first defence against potential attackers. The new Treaty of Friendship and Co-operation signed by Prime Minister Li Peng in Ulan Bator in 1994 formally precludes the reassertion of Russian influence, declaring that neither signatory would permit a 'third country' to use Mongolian territory in order to hurt the other side's sovereignty and security. China thus assures itself that Mongolia will not become a base for subversion in Inner Mongolia. Mongolia has a poorly equipped army of only 20,000, and so the Chinese, backed by a strong army, can call the shots.

The economic links will grow and grow, particularly with the opening of the railway between Ulan Bator and Tianjin in 1992. Mongolia is landlocked and must look either east or west for its trade outlets but it will not become another satellite, and the resurgence of Lamaist Buddhism there makes it a potential source of irritation for China not only in Inner Mongolia but in Tibet as well. Once there were almost a thousand Tibetan Buddhist monasteries in Inner Mongolia. The Chinese are reviving Tibetan Buddhism in Inner Mongolia by inviting monks from the Taer Monastery in Qinghai to train new lamas, but are aware of the possible political connotations of Buddhism. Beijing was angry, for instance, when the Dalai Lama was given such an enthusiastic welcome in Ulan Bator in 1991.

China launched a crackdown on Mongolian nationalists in 1991, arresting two leaders and putting twenty-six under house arrest: the Inner Mongolian League for Defence of Human

Rights made an appeal to world opinion. When the Ih Ju League and National Modernisation League attempted to register legally with the government, with the aim of studying and promoting traditional Mongolian culture and identity, they were branded as separatists aiming at uniting with 'Outer' Mongolia. Demonstrations were reported in six cities in the winter of 1991–92. Wang Qun, Secretary of the Inner Mongolia Autonomous Region Communist Party, warned of the dangers of Pan-Mongolism and 'Westernisation'.

China is politically vulnerable in all three of these Western interior regions. Beijing veers between sensitive understanding of the cultural and national aspirations of the 75 million minority people (a population bigger than Britain's) and a brutal, sometimes callous way of making them conform to Chinese ways and targets. Never will a Chinese official – and rarely a Chinese intellectual – concede that the dilemma is a characteristically colonial one, though the situation in these three regions seems very reminiscent of that in the former colonies of the West.[43]

'Colony' in the Western lexicon now leads logically to independence. That is an unthinkable solution for the Chinese, who still have not been able to see the back of British colonialism in Hongkong. It might not sound so impossible for the Chinese to accept, however, if China itself loosens up politically to become eventually a state with many autonomous provinces and regions – 'one country, five nations'? Whether such autonomy is any longer satisfactory to the minorities, one may doubt. In its western interior China faces challenges of an entirely different order from those in China proper – Han China – and there is no indication that Chinese leaders or intellectuals have grasped this. In the end instability is more likely to come from China's 'Far West' than from within the main body of China.

Han China senses the growing pride and assertiveness of its many minority cultural and linguistic groups. Provinces like Guangdong are behaving more and more independently, and yet within Guangdong there are many small minority populations considering themselves distinct from either the Cantonese or North Chinese. Instead of tut-tutting, Beijingers are enjoying 'ethnic chic', reading minority novels, eating at minority restaurants and adopting minority dress styles and home decorations.[44]

'Ethnic chic' is fashionable, and perhaps that is the first faint sign of hope for future political generosity and sensitivity in China's attitude to these peoples of the interior.

CHAPTER 15

HONGKONG: THE FRONT DOOR

Far-fetched though it may seem in a world which has turned its back on colonialism, Hongkong was still a British colony in early 1997. Six million Chinese, mostly from Guangdong, have inherited Lord Palmerston's 'barren rock' which their forefathers had transformed over a century and a half into a comfortable if overcrowded home – and also into a manufacturing, trading and financial centre famed (and feared) across the globe. They have turned that rock into the urban miracle of the twentieth century, to earn *Fortune Magazine*'s accolade as the best city in the world for business, and to carry on a foreign trade which, at £26 billion turnover a year, ranks eighth in the world.

Yet at midnight on 30 June 1997 British administrators led by Governor Chris Patten will pack their bags and fly home to London. Hongkong will then come under Beijing's rule. Will that rule be light enough for intellectuals and professionals to bear? Will the Communists succeed in managing such a thoroughly capitalist enclave? Will Hongkong be swamped by corruption and nepotism from China? Or will China learn the secrets of capitalism from Hongkong?

Most Hongkongers (or their fathers or grandfathers) went to Hongkong to escape oppression or commercial frustrations at home, or to take up work and profit opportunities which the British *laissez-faire* régime offered by only minimally regulating the economy or people's work. The result of their several labours is an average income per head of almost £10,000, more than their former British 'oppressors' in Britain. The Hongkong Chinese are tickled by their achievement, but quickly focus their attention on the price they have paid for it in terms of population density, environmental pollution and the psychology of stress. Hongkong may be the top city for business, but it has also become the world's most expensive city to live in, toppling Tokyo for that unwanted distinction. Hongkong also boasts the world's biggest public works project in its Chek Lap Kok airport, now under construction against a background of squabbling between the British and Chinese governments over the £70 billion bill. It is about 35 per cent bigger than the recently completed Channel Tunnel project linking Britain and France.

The Hongkong and Shanghai Banking Corporation is still regarded as a Hongkong bank, even though the British authorities made it move its legal headquarters to London as the condition for acquiring the Midland Bank – which the Hongkong Bank did for growth as well as to avoid the future risks of legal ownership in Hongkong. That produced another economic 'trophy', because the newly enlarged Hongkong Bank has become the biggest single company in Britain – greater than Shell, greater than BP, greater than British Telecom. Its stock exchange capitalisation exceeds £20 billion.

Rising costs and bigger pay-packets are making Hongkong's manufacturing industry uncompetitive, so the thrust of the economy comes now from the services side. Yet a small company like Johnson Electrical Holdings can still hold the title of second biggest manufacturer in the world (and the largest outside Japan) of micro motors for toys. Having got rich on manufacturing and trade in earlier decades, Hongkong's tycoons now act out big investment roles, in China and other Asian countries, in the Indian subcontinent and in Europe. In 1994 a powerful consortium of Hongkong companies formed a joint venture with Donald Trump to develop apartments and commercial buildings on a huge 75-acre tract at Riverside South on New York's Hudson River.

The serried skyscrapers skirting Hongkong's once-fragrant harbour stop the breath of every visitor. The Bank of China building by I.M. Pei draws all eyes with its clean line, simple concept and dizzying height. Princess Margaret described the Hongkong Bank building, in the equally modern 'show-it-all' style, as looking like 'the back of a refrigerator'.

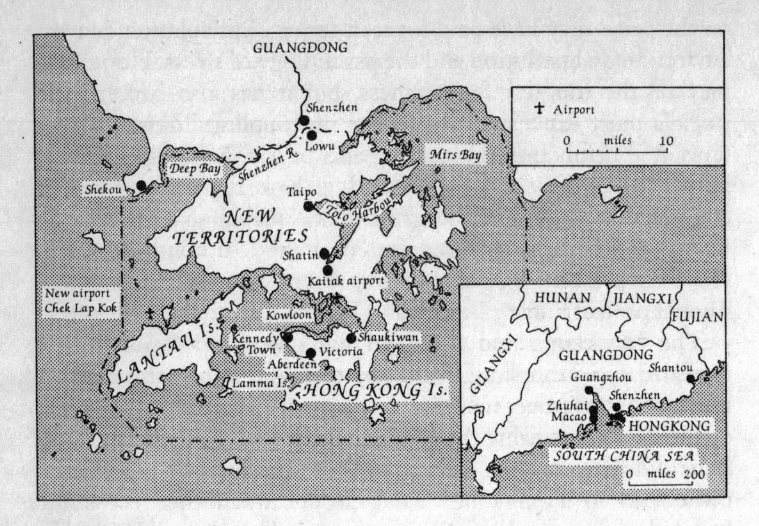

Hongkong

Some Western enthusiasts have for many years called Hongkong 'the Pearl of the Orient'. Hongkong lies at the mouth of the estuary of what Europeans used to call the Pearl river. But the Chinese joined the club in 1993 when a Communist newspaper, used to labelling the colony a sink of iniquity, conceded that Hongkong was 'known to the world as the Pearl of the Orient'.[1] (Only a few years earlier, a European writer had published a catalogue of Hongkong's faults under the title *Hongkong, Mouldering Pearl*.)

In earlier periods Sun Yatsen, Zhou Enlai and probably even Deng Xiaoping all came to Hongkong for life-preserving asylum during periods of warfare and mayhem in China, so a little gratitude has been mixed with China's negative feelings.[2] Similarly when Hongkong donated £33 million for south China flood victims in 1991, Zhou Nan, the official Chinese representative in Hongkong, revealed that it was 80 per cent of all foreign aid offered, proving that 'blood is thicker than water'.[3]

It may come as a shock to learn that these achievements, which China itself would be proud to emulate if it could, have all occurred in a British colony rather smaller than Surrey, or about half the area of Rhode Island. London has sent its plume-helmeted governors every four or five years to look after the place, but all they did was hold the arena for fiercely energetic and astonishingly enterprising Chinese workers and businessmen. The successful executives of Hongkong follow the ideas of Friedrich von Hayek and Milton Friedman rather than Marx or Engels or even Keynes. One curious result is that the British Conservative Party has found itself until very recently indebted to Hongkong Chinese billionaires for donations dwarfing those from the British themselves. (The same entrepreneurs donate to various Chinese Communist funds and causes as well, of course, the motive being identical, namely to ensure a political hearing when their business needs it.)

To the Communists, Hongkong presented a dilemma. From about 1950 onwards it was clear that Hongkong was not only useful but actually profitable to China. The Red Army stopped at the Hongkong border in 1949, taking over the frontier posts previously manned by Guomindang forces, because the Chinese Communists were by then over-stretched and did not wish to provoke British or American intervention at the tail-end of the civil war. Then came the Korean War, for which Hongkong businessmen provided strategic items which China could not have obtained elsewhere. From the end of the 1950s onwards China was earning a substantial trade surplus with Hongkong in convertible currency, some of it for merely pumping water through pipelines or herding pigs into railway wagons. So post-war Hongkong's survival and success were built on China's poverty.

The colonial status rankled all the same. One of the first actions of China in the UN in the 1970s was to strike Hongkong off the list of colonial territories whose political future needed to be debated and negotiated in the UN. Anything drawing attention to the British role in Hongkong was anathema. The kind of independence which the British dispensed throughout their empire in the post-war years was never applicable to Hongkong. China could just about stomach a discreetly low-key British colonial rule in Hongkong, but not an independent sovereign state preachifying to the rest of China, encouraging provinces to follow the same path of self-determination and stealing some of the Communist Party's political and moral authority.

For patriotic Chinese, whether Communist or no, it was a moral and national imperative to send the British packing. 'After the reversion of Hongkong,' said one of the most liberal members of the Politburo, Li Ruihuan, in 1995, 'we will have avenged the wrongs committed against our ancestors; we can console their spirits in high heaven and teach our descendants to learn from this lesson that China must be strong or she will be bullied, beaten up, occupied or carved up.' Throughout the run-up to the restoration in 1997 the Chinese suspected British motives. Yang Shangkun, still a force in Chinese politics though long retired as state President and army head, accuses the British of trying to maintain their influence in Hongkong to upset the new government to succeed them in 1997, and of plundering the colony of its riches before China can reach them.[4]

Once the post-Mao leadership had settled down, at the end of the 1970s, the British sought to discuss their colony's future with Deng Xiaoping's more liberal régime. The Joint Declaration signed by Prime Ministers Margaret Thatcher and Zhao Ziyang in 1984 settled the British retreat and the Chinese assumption of rule in 1997. Thatcher tried hard for the continued right to administer Hongkong for many years ahead, whilst surrendering sovereignty to China immediately. But in the end Britain had to give it all up – the leased New Territories whose term expires in 1997, as well as the more important parts of Hongkong which had been ceded in perpetuity to London in the nineteenth century under what the Chinese call unequal treaties. (These ceded areas were not deemed viable by themselves, without the water, food, industry and space of the New Territories.)

Britain thus gave up her rights beyond 1997, but had thirteen years' grace in which to wind down the British role. Equally, China expressed patience for thirteen years in return for getting the whole package of Hongkong, Kowloon and the New Territories. In order to win this agreement, China promised to allow Hongkong to continue with its own system of government, way of life and capitalist economy under the formula of 'One Country, Two Systems', which Thatcher declared to be 'an idea of genius'.[5] Hongkong would be given a high degree of autonomy as a Special Administrative Region of China, ruled by Hongkongers themselves but under Chinese sovereignty.

Deng and Thatcher congratulated themselves, the one because he had been able, unlike any predecessor, to wring a surrender of territory out of the imperialist Britons, the other because she had won, against all the odds, a commitment for freedom and capitalism in Hongkong to survive the retrocession of 1997. Their agreement initially created much goodwill between Britain and China. But misunderstandings were bound to arise, if only because of the ambiguities of language in the agreement.

British enthusiasm cooled somewhat when the Chinese published their Basic Law for Hongkong. This set out in detail how the retrocession would work, and how the new institutions or arrangements after 1997 would be formed. Subversion against the People's Republic, theft of state secrets, and creating party political ties with foreign organisations – all crimes in China – will be strictly repressed after 1997.

Part of this unwelcome reality was China's insistence, hardly surprising for a sovereign state, that the government would intervene in Hongkong if a 'state of turmoil' came about. In terms of riots or mass internal strife of some kind, that was understandable. But British and Hongkongers alike were chilled to learn of the People's Liberation Army's demands for a premature seizure of Hongkong in 1993–94 merely on the grounds of Sino-British misunderstandings. President Jiang Zemin was portrayed as restraining these military hotheads, but the military representatives at the National People's Congress in 1994 obviously felt themselves quite democratic and liberal in proposing an earlier end to colonial rule in Hongkong, and were backed by many important regional commanders in Guangdong, Beijing and elsewhere. These generals saw their government's policy in Hongkong as pro-capitalist, though one of their motives may have been to consolidate their own 'military-industrial complex' business empire headquarters in Hongkong. It was said that only the superior diplomacy of the then Prime Minister Zhou Enlai had deterred the Gang of Four from attempting a military invasion of Hongkong in 1967.[6]

Some leftist industrialists in Hongkong went to Beijing at the end of 1993 to petition the Chinese government to take Hongkong back in advance of 1997, because it was 'out of control'.[7]

The unlikely alliance of restless generals and Hongkong businessmen expecting to profit from Chinese rule did not prevail, but supposing similar circumstances were to occur in 1997, or a year or two after? If such irresponsible actions could be seriously mooted in China, and if strong civilian leadership at the top is going to be lacking, then Hongkongers have every right to be worried about their future. Many people in Hongkong assume that China is going to make a mess of Hongkong because of its Communism, its lack of skill in management, and its lack of enthusiasm for preserving British institutions and guiding what some American scholars describe as the most capitalist economy in the world.

The Chinese too became a little disenchanted with the Joint Declaration when they saw Britain using its thirteen years' grace to strengthen its influence within Hongkong and make it capable of withstanding the change of sovereignty. China saw how grooming of British-educated politicians and civil servants might perpetuate pro-British loyalties and values after 1997.

The new airport became a symbol of these misgivings: everybody agreed that Hongkong needed a new airport, and the best judgement and expertise available to Hongkong went into the choice of Chek Lap Kok,[8] but it is a highly expensive project, and Chinese doubts have made it more so. Beijing complains that too much money is being borrowed to build the airport, the repayment of which would inevitably become the final responsibility of China after 1997. The British assure China that it will inherit some £23 billion of reserves in 1997, far more than it had originally asked for, and more than enough for the need, but the Chinese believe that the clever British will find ways of milking their colony of money before they leave. The involvement in airport construction work of Jardine Matheson, the company that they least love, seems to confirm this in their eyes.

But the British are not clean of prejudice either. They did not bank on so many hundreds and thousands of Hongkongers preferring to leave Hongkong rather than to stay on under Chinese Communist government – and seeing Britain, the 'mother country', as the natural target for emigration. Some Hongkong Indians may become stateless after 1997, lacking either British or Chinese nationality and without a right of abode anywhere except in India itself, where business prospects are not so good.

The policy of John Major and Chris Patten to engineer a little more democracy in Hongkong before 1997 was one way of assuaging their guilt at not being able to accept large numbers of Hongkong citizens as immigrants in Britain. The social tension within the UK over its immigrants from Asia, Africa and the Caribbean, as well as the tension in Britain's bilateral relations with those countries because it has drawn the line on further immigration, makes it politically impossible for the British government to treat the Hongkong Chinese as the deserving exception they can demonstrably claim to be.

Instead of the recent governors from the ranks of the diplomatic service, used to 'kowtowing' to China, Major put in a political governor in Britain's last innings, someone who would shake up Chinese ignorance and complacency about democracy and its value. The Hongkong Chinese had never expressed serious political ambitions, and had so far appeared to understand that non-participation in politics was a condition of China's leaving them alone. As an earlier British governor had put it after the mass immigration of the 1940s and 1950s, the Chinese in Hongkong had already 'voted with their feet' for the Hongkong system. They didn't have to go to Hongkong, but they chose it. Was further democracy necessary, at least for the time being?

Some British journalists like Edward Mortimer of the *Financial Times* asked why the people of Hongkong themselves should not be allowed to decide how to handle China: why not hold full UK-style elections as soon as possible? There have been few more certain recipes for turmoil in Hongkong and pre-emptive Chinese invasion. Michael Jones of the *Sunday Times* was more circumspect. If, he argued, the Hongkong Chinese only want to make money, they will surely elect protectors of the *status quo*, so why does anyone fear election results?[9] The logic is unassailable, but Jones underestimates the large number of ordinary people who avoid contact with Westerners, do not talk to foreign correspondents about what Hongkong needs, and lack the polish to put it accurately across the cultural-linguistic gulf. Their judgement is not so sophisticated as that of the articulate English-educated élite who will happily bore the pants off a visiting scribbler from London on these matters.

In 1966 three young civil servants wrote an official report on the potential for political reform in Hongkong. One of them was a British-educated Chinese, Paul Tsui. He wrote a separate note elaborating his own ideas, which has become something of a classic text in Hongkong political debates. In the typical Western democracy, he pointed out, election from among several candidates is the accepted way of finding representatives of the people. A potential candidate does not normally refrain from standing because he fears loss of face in the event of failure. Pretty well everybody accepts the elective principle, and so its abuse is minimal. 'In Hongkong, the position is entirely different, and it is doubtful whether popular representation ... will be successful in bringing forward the best qualified and most widely accepted citizens to participate in local administration. Ballot box elections in Hongkong could quickly become controlled by unscrupulous or corrupt power-seekers.'[10]

There are two facts that Tsui highlights here. One is the social system of the Chinese in Hongkong which sets store on letting everybody retain their self-respect and not be submitted to unsettling and damaging loss of face. The second point is about the unusual way in which the society has been formed from recent mass migrations, and its highly temporary and transient character in Hongkong. This society has not fully settled down in a way which would make elections produce a genuinely desired political result.

Tsui's comment was thirty years ago, and his analysis is being gradually eroded: face is not so important, though it is still a factor. Hongkong society has begun to settle down, though still aware of its internal constituents. Beijing is a city of the northerners, Guangzhou and Shanghai are cities of the Cantonese and Shanghainese respectively. Hongkong is more mixed than that, and the mixing is still relatively recent in China's modern history, the Shanghainese having mainly come into Hongkong in the late 1940s and early 1950s. There are still enough differences of speech and character – sometimes matching differences in the economic status – to keep everybody reminded all the time that they live in a polyglot city. Inhibitions about publicly revealing your politics lead to low election turnouts. A successful candidate may find himself put there by only 12 per cent of the entitled voters because half of those qualified may not register, half of those registered may not vote and almost half of those voting will have voted for the loser. Better turnouts were observed in the 1995 elections, but it is not encouraging ground for Patten.

The Tiananmen Square killings in 1989, which brought a million Hongkongers out on the streets in protest, slightly deepened the average Hongkonger's political interest. More people in Hongkong now say what they would like to happen politically in China, or in Hongkong, and that is another step forward on the democratic path. Yet the Tsui analysis still has enough validity to make a sensible Chinese – or Briton – give pause. The politically glamorous Briton who now came forward to occupy the hot seat in Hongkong was, however, ideologically driven towards more democracy.

Chris Patten, one of the most attractive and skilful British parliamentarians of his generation, found himself in 1992 running a general election as Chairman of the Conservative Party. In that capacity he had to go and speak for Conservative candidates in a large number of constituencies. He won the election for his party, but his own constituents in Bath repaid his absences by voting him personally out. Prime Minister John Major offered him the Hongkong governorship. The Chinese Communist leaders observed all this from afar with perplexity. Why should Britain, five years from handing over, suddenly upgrade the Hongkong governorship, from run-of-the-mill colonial official or ambassador to someone who could easily have become Prime Minister? The suspicion formed in the deep-seatedly sceptical Chinese mind that Britain, as usual, was up to no good. Patten was going in to up the ante, and salvage more for Britain from the Joint Declaration.

For his part, Patten disarmingly confessed his ignorance of the Chinese mind. He soon complained that negotiating with Chinese was like 'playing darts blindfold in the dark'.[11] But he immediately set about showing Hongkong how a democratic ruler could behave – introducing governor's question time in the legislature, going on walk-abouts, glad-handing, kissing babies and generally making himself accessible. This part of his act surprised and delighted the people of Hongkong, and certainly moved the preconditions for democracy a little further forward. Chinese authority, by contrast, is exercised behind the scenes, and the public appearances are stage-managed. Hongkongers actually began to say that they would prefer Patten to rule them than Li Peng or Jiang Zemin (nothing could be more calculated to infuriate Beijing).

Patten negotiated an increase in one-way-permit entrants from China, greater co-operation in combating cross-border crime and smuggling, training for senior Hongkong civil servants at Qinghua University in Beijing, agreement on the disposal of military sites in Hongkong, agreement on land for the new airport and airport railway, and on increasing the land supply to halt runaway property prices. The Chinese co-operated on a committee to co-ordinate cross-border infrastructure.[12]

Patten's political plans were helped by the Hongkong economy, which forged ahead in the early 1990s in spite of some assaults on confidence following the Tiananmen killings and the occasional endeavours of the Chinese leaders to cool their economic growth. The worst thing would have been for President Bill Clinton to withdraw Most Favoured Nation treatment in trade with China: that would have hit Hongkong disproportionately. Instead Hongkong's trade continued buoyant, more and more of it serving China, though manufacturing fell back because of high costs.

Hongkong garments and textiles exports were restrained under the so-called Multi-Fibre Arrangement under the old GATT, but since the restrictions were on volume rather than value, Hongkong textile and garment mills were able to upgrade quality and thereby increase their earnings very nicely every year under the shelter of the MFA quotas, without which they would have faced more competition from other lower-cost countries. But in electronics there was almost a mass stampede of manufacturers across the Shenzhen river to set up subsidiary ventures in Guangdong at something like a tenth of Hongkong's labour and land costs. Being themselves mostly Cantonese, these entrepreneurs were much shrewder, and their industrial operations usually more successful, than those of Japanese, European and other investors. What remained in Hongkong was the high-tech end of manufacturing, and the making of high-cost goods.

As if to compensate for that, Hongkong's service industries made a mighty leap forward during the early 1990s. Hongkong became a bigger financial centre, despite the relocation to London of the jovial Scot, Sir William Purves, chief executive of the Hongkong and Shanghai Banking Corporation, in order to consolidate his bank's acquisition of the Midland. The banks and other financial companies rapidly boosted their investment into China, funding a wide variety of projects especially in Guangdong. As Gordon Wu, the Princeton-trained engineer-developer who built key power stations and roads in Guangdong, explained: 'We believe that the only way to help Hongkong and secure its future is to help China.' This was by way of refuting the simplistic notion that Hongkong people should not invest in China in case that made China more powerful – and therefore more likely to interfere in Hongkong. Gordon Wu's reverse logic is sounder. The more Hongkong can serve China, the more

HONGKONG IN THE 1990s: ECONOMIC INDICATORS

	1992	1993	1994
Gross Domestic Product US$ billion	100	115	131
GDP per head US$1000	17	19	22
Total exports, domestic & re-exports US$ billion	119	134	150
Imports, US$ billion	122	138	160
Two-way trade with China US$ billion	81	95	109
Education spending US$ billion	2.4	2.8	3.2
Population millions	5.8	5.9	6.1
Registered Motor Vehicles ('000s)	471	504	524
Telecommunications licenses ('000s)	84	90	97

Source: Hongkong 1995

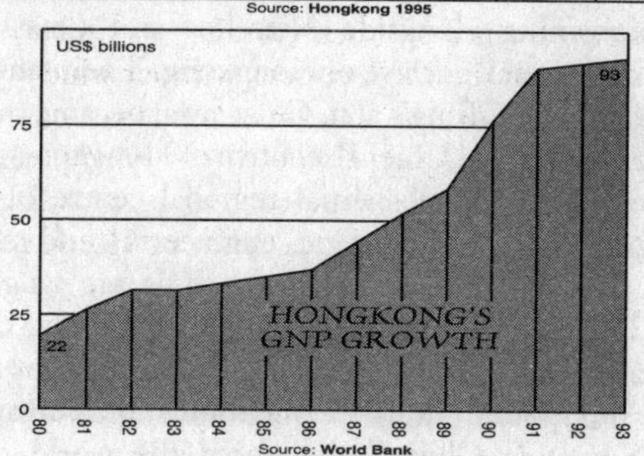

Source: World Bank

China will hesitate to upset the apple cart.

But there was some change of heart in China in 1994, when provincial and central authorities professed concern over the disadvantages of bringing foreign capital in. The consequence was that even efficient and sympathetic Hongkong investors like Gordon Wu and Peter Woo (architect of a stunningly useful container terminal development for Wuhan) became progressively frustrated by delays in the Chinese bureaucratic process. Given this new lukewarmness towards foreign business, Hongkong investors are now going into the Philippines, Thailand or India where the returns are just as good and Hongkong efforts are more appreciated and rewarded.[13] They will return if it comes to be seen as a cyclical phenomenon in China.

Banking is the leader of the Hongkong economy, but other service industries are also more important now. Tourism is a steady performer, since many American and other travellers cushion a visit to China with a few days in the more relaxed and unbureaucratic atmosphere of Hongkong. Aviation has now come to the fore, and hence the need for the new airport. Cathay Pacific Airways is one of the most successful Asian airlines, and Dragonair is following on with its own routes centring on China. Both have taken in some Chinese equity capital.

Shipping was the *fons et origo* of Hongkong in the 1840s, and Hongkongers now control the fifth largest merchant fleet in the world; three giant shipping groups were formed by the Shanghainese refugees – the late Sir Yue-kong Pao of World-Wide Shipping, C.Y. Tung of Island Navigation Corporation and T.Y. Chao of Wah Kwong. Each of these three climbed into the world class of shipowning alongside Niarchos and Onassis, while co-existing in the small enclave of Hongkong. Their families have continued their work. Tung's son, Chee-hwa, became the leading candidate for the post of Chief Executive of Hongkong in 1997.

Hongkong is now a substantial regional centre of the professions, especially law, accounting, engineering and publishing. Managerial and technical or scientific skills are taught at the Hongkong Polytechnic University and the Hongkong University of Science and Technology. Queen's Counsel resident in Hongkong may be spotted in the courtrooms of Singapore and Malaysia. Now that China has entered the world of private enterprise and professional management, there are constant streams of Hongkong practitioners entering China to teach, negotiate or investigate, with a reverse stream of Chinese coming into Hongkong for in-house training of various kinds. All this service activity makes up for the diminution of manufacturing. In any case, of course, the profits from manufacturing in Guangdong mostly devolve on the owners in Hongkong.

The apprehension of the professionals is that circumstances in China may lead to the Chinese government restricting various freedoms in Hongkong after 1997. The experience of Xi Yang, a journalist with the *Ming Pao* of Hongkong (a newspaper not unfriendly to China), has alarmed the colony's scribes. On a visit to China, Xi wrote a story for his newspaper saying that the Chinese government would not raise interest rates over the coming months, but would sell off some of its gold holdings. Beijing regarded these modest scoops of classified information as state secrets, and after being detained for six months, during which he was allowed to see only his father, and him for less than an hour, Xi was put through a secret trial and sentenced to fifteen years in prison. His family were only notified of the sentence four days afterwards.[14]

The obsessive Chinese secrecy about state finances is replicated in Singapore, whose government is also highly repressive on matters which in Western countries would be considered legitimate, if annoying journalistic scoops. For China to make such a fuss of Xi Yang's harmless peccadillo, at a time when it was seeking to reassure Hongkong opinion about Chinese sovereignty, was extraordinary.

This threatens Hongkong's future role as a window on China. Perhaps that was going to be difficult to retain anyway, given Chinese sensibilities and the irresponsible attitude of many Hongkong journalists. Talk has begun among the foreign-owned or foreign-connected 'serious' press, whether to change the content or leave Hongkong (but for where? There is no other town in the region offering both freedom and efficiency). *China News Analysis* has gone to Taipei and the *Far Eastern Economic Review* (which is not just a China-watcher but needs quick access to all of Asia) is now considering its dilemma.

The issue of free opinion goes wider than the media.

Overruling his education director in 1994, Chris Patten reinstated references to the Tiananmen killings in a school textbook. Hongkong should err on the side of openness and truth, he ruled. The official Chinese position is liberal. Qian Qichen, the Foreign Minister, told the Hongkong industrialist, Alex Wu, that the Chinese position was: 'You are innocent if you swear at the Chinese Communist Party, but you are not allowed to violate the law and make trouble.' Some industrialists and businessmen who are proud to be Chinese, are not particularly pro-Guomindang, and do not have particularly close ties with Britain, nevertheless rebel in anticipation against the short rein on which China holds its intellectuals and professional men. Jimmy Lai, of the Giordano retail chain in Hongkong, is one of the many who say that they cannot exchange the political and ideological free-and-easy atmosphere of British colonialism for the tight leash and mental rigidity of even the reformed Chinese Communists. The British governors have been autocratic, but at least it is an 'open autocracy'.[15]

Governor Chris Patten fired the first shot in his substantive political campaign in October 1992, three months after his arrival in Hongkong. During those three months he had made a close study of the Basic Law which he read, he confessed, more often than the Bible. It was not too difficult for his probing legal mind to find a few lacunae in the Basic Law which would allow him to make Hongkong a little more democratic before 1997. He was thinking in terms of convincing other lawyers like himself, briefed by Beijing, and how he would counter their rebuttals.

Patten devised a programme of democratic reforms for the local elections of 1994 and the legislative elections of 1995. He believed he had a watertight case. The agreements with China so far had provided only a modest degree of democracy based on direct elections before 1997. But the question of functional constituencies had been left somewhat open, to be finalised at a later date. The functional constituencies originally represented the British government's hopes of retaining an appointed element in the legislature, and allowing the 'special interests', which were so much more vital to Hongkong's well-being than would be the case in many other countries, to have an assured voice in public policy debate and decisions. China went along with that.

It was already in place when Patten arrived that the lawyers, for example, had voted for their own representative on the council, the Democrat leader, Martin Lee, though he later 'graduated' to become a directly elected member.

But some gaps in the functional constituency system had been left which were open for Patten to fill, and his stroke of genius, as he thought, was to have a functional constituency representative for an industry like the steel industry, for which not merely the board of directors and managers but every single worker would have a vote. By doing this with enough industrial categories, Patten was able to create on paper what virtually amounted to universal suffrage in Hongkong – the very thing which the Chinese were seeking to resist or at least postpone.

Having perfected the scheme, Patten had two choices open to him. He could have flown to Beijing, preferably without publicity, and discussed his plans with his Chinese counterparts, arguing that the gaps needed to be plugged in the elections, and would it not be a good idea to extend the net of voters in these functional constituencies to make them a little bigger? No harm would be done, and people would feel that they were given a little more representativeness in the Legislative Council.

No doubt the Chinese would have thrown cold water over his plans. But Patten is a tireless negotiator, who can pull out a lot of charm, and if he had been allowed to spend a few hours with those people he might conceivably have been able to get their agreement, not necessarily to the whole scheme, but perhaps to a more modest version of it. Patten might then have been able to return to Hongkong and to announce his programme of reforms in the knowledge that they were not going to be entirely opposed by China. Or he might have returned and buried his blueprint, or gone ahead with it alone. The Chinese had made it clear much earlier that unilateral British changes in the democratic structure would be unacceptable.

The alternative was not to go to China at all, but to announce his plan publicly in Hongkong, making it clear that they were only proposals, subject to discussion against other people's ideas. Later Patten could have gone to China and said, 'Well, you have seen the Hongkong reactions to my published ideas, which I sent to you through a secure channel a week or two beforehand, so what do you think of them? Do you agree? If not, what would you like to see done? And then between my idea and your idea we can work towards something in the middle on which we both agree.'

That second scenario was Patten's choice. Maybe he never believed in the possibility of a 'secret' visit to Beijing. Perhaps he did not trust the Chinese enough to be sure that they would honour the secrecy. Patten's fiercest detractor was Sir Percy Cradock, the Foreign Office sinologist who had been ambassador in Beijing and had virtually composed the Joint Declaration in 1984. Drawn out of his normal professional reticence by what he saw as Patten's amateurishness, Cradock said that the successful way to deal with China was confidentiality.[16] Patten retorted, 'I don't think you can treat a community like Hongkong in a "hole-in-the-corner" way.' Hongkongers were not irresponsible children, they were not people who could not be trusted.[17]

The *Guardian* put the criticism in the kindest possible way when it wrote on 25 February 1994 that, 'with hindsight, it seems naive of Mr Patten to have imagined that he could persuade China, by a public demonstration, to accept more than it would in private talks. We shall never know whether, if he had not chosen this method, China might have been more willing to accept the "through train" arrangement.'[18]

Patten and Cradock have gone on needling each other ever since, to the glee of Beijing. On the question of Patten's handling of the negotiation, Cradock must win. The question of substance is a little more balanced. Patten's sarcasm on the question of democracy sounded more convincing than his remarks on the Chinese government's behaviour. Was it not extraordinary, he said, to argue 'that the tenth most successful trading nation in the world contains a population who are not capable of deciding who should collect their dustbins?'[19]

Well, if it were only a question of dustbins, one might agree. Even the British in the old days used to see the ideal for Hongkong as having an elected 'town council' to deal with all the intimate challenges of urban life including dustbins, under a strong executive of people whose background and qualifications made them especially aware of the many international considerations to be taken into account in matters of higher policy.

The gnawing unease of the British at handing over a political structure in 1997 obviously not measuring up to the English-language version of the Joint Declaration is evident. Yet the British must face the fact that a high level of parliamentary democracy cannot be sustained by Hongkongers on their own – and if anyone tried, China would make things very difficult for Hongkong.

Governor Patten saw his reform package get through the Legislative Council by only a whisker, despite his busy lobbying. The vote was 32 to 24 after amendments which he defeated by only a single vote. Triumphantly he gazetted his reforms a week later, looking back on seventeen fruitless rounds of negotiations with the Chinese, and having to look forward to a continuing agenda of acrimony and bitterness with China. Once the Chinese decide to be unco-operative, they can become unpleasantly obstructive.

Patten was now like a goalkeeper defending against two teams simultaneously, one at the front of his goal, one behind. The Liberal Democrats under Martin Lee and their international well-wishers in America and elsewhere nagged at him for not being liberal enough. Meanwhile the Chinese threatened that Britain's trade with China would suffer, and in the end, when the unrepentant Patten implemented the reforms, the Chinese stated flatly that all councils, from the Legislative Council down to the Urban Council and District Boards, would be abolished on 1 July 1997 and replaced by institutions devised by China and filled by a process of selection or election also arranged by China. The cosy little Legco with the first products of Patten's expanded functional constituencies would simply be dissolved after only three years. The precious 'through train' so laboriously negotiated by Patten's predecessor, Sir David – now Lord – Wilson, to allow Council members elected in 1995 to sail past 1997 and see their terms out under a new flag, providing much-needed continuity, was de-railed almost without a second thought.

Was it worth while to gain a slightly more democratic (though still largely appointed) Legco just for three years at the cost of such upheaval? Many Hongkongers felt that it was, because it would give Hongkong politicians more experience of how to run elections and use an elected Legco. Besides, as Patten insists, China would find it embarrassing for its world image to abolish elected legislatures – and the more elective, the more the embarrassment.

But China has risked that kind of response before in other international situations, and is thick-skinned enough simply to smile through such moments. Patten and his supporters underestimate the domestic pressures on the Chinese government to slow democracy down at home; China's threatened abolition of Hongkong Councils in 1997 is as much to do with discouraging democracy at home as anything else. China will eventually build its own road to modern government without benefit of foreigners, even the brilliant Chris Patten.

One of the Chinese reactions to Patten was to set up a Preliminary Working Committee to decide on the institutional arrangements which China would need to make before 1997 and afterwards. It consisted of many leading Hongkong personalities, not necessarily political but including businessmen, lawyers and other professionals. It included the Indian leader Hari Harilela, and a former acting governor, who is one of the few top British officials to be fluent in Cantonese and other Chinese languages and has lived in (mostly rural) Hongkong for over thirty-five years – Sir David Akers Jones. It organised a Preparatory Working Committee to handle pre-1997 arrangements, including the choice of the new Chief Executive, and to supervise the 1997 handover.

China might not insist on a completely new slate on the Legislative Council in 1997. The only individuals to whom China would strenuously object are Martin Lee and Szeto Wah, the two leaders of the Liberal Democratic group, and possibly Emily Lau. These have been frequent and fierce critics of Chinese Communism, and they were prominent in their march through Hongkong streets in protest against the Tiananmen killings in 1989. If they had behaved in China as they have behaved in Hongkong in recent years they would be in prison. China is most unlikely to tolerate these democrats on the legislature after 1997, and it must be even doubtful whether they could stay in Hongkong, or would want to stay on condition of giving up politics, so they will probably be early victims of the Chinese takeover.

The climate between China and Britain began to improve again at the end of 1994, enough to relax slightly the Chinese attitude to Hongkong. If the mood were right, China could in 1997 re-appoint most existing members of Legco minus a few sacrificial lambs. That would create continuity of benefit to Hongkong, and allow China more room to get used to its new responsibilities. But the Chinese will not allow Hongkong to be used as a base for political goals outside Hongkong. Autonomy does not stretch that far. Most Chinese in Hongkong are now aware of this and are prepared to accept it. The Legco votes on Patten's reforms and the election results in 1994–95 suggest that the pro-Beijingers are going to be in contention, possibly almost evenly matching the liberals.

Interestingly, the Preliminary Working Committee, which became a kind of shadow government or 'second stove' in the Hongkong run-up kitchen, has opted for proportional representation to decide twenty of the elected Legco seats, another advertisement of the Chinese cultural preference for providing safety valves at various stages of the electoral process. Hongkong's Liberal Party urged smaller electorates for the functional constituencies, adding up to only 120,000 voters against Patten's 2.7 million. David Shu, a Hongkong industrialist who stood for his industry, commented on Patten's reforms that 'the floor sweeper, everybody, will be voting in my construction constituency. They will out-vote me, but they will not represent me. Indeed, my interests are likely to be misrepresented.'[20]

A Communist view of the functional constituencies was expressed indirectly in an editorial of the *Wenweibao* of Hongkong in October 1993. It complained that when the appointed Legco members disappeared, to be replaced by directly elected members under the British plan, 'people with professional knowledge will not be allowed to provide constructive opinions in the fields of urban and rural administration, recreation, environment protection, transport and other social services.'[21]

The question of a bill of rights has become involved in the Sino-British controversy. Hongkong is weak in this area: police can stop and search people on the street without a warrant, emigration officers can detain witnesses for months, and revenue officials can stop suspected tax-evaders from leaving Hongkong. A bill of rights came into law in 1991, but it is a minimal document, needing a new independent commission to give it teeth. Beijing says it will make Hongkong more of a haven for law-breakers. China prefers tough laws to keep its people in order. Britain, with stronger collective self-confidence and individual autonomy, opts for law that is weak, or even absent altogether, to allow individualism its scope.

So China will roll back British reforms, such as they are, in 1997. Will they really allow free and fair elections? Sir David Akers Jones gave a famous reply to this question, when someone asked if the Chinese would rig the elections. 'The Chinese style,' he answered, 'is not to rig elections. But they do like to know the result before they are held.'[22] This may run into semantics, but there is murky ground between criminal rigging of elections on the one hand and extra-thorough lobbying and canvassing so that you can predict the outcome, on the other.

If the Chinese wanted to, they could and would use their tried and tested United Front tactics in Hongkong to ensure by repeated propaganda, in that self-important tone which Chinese authority can always assume, that their candidates, or the candidates supported by them or supporting them, will win. If necessary they will offer an influential hesitant voter some goodie or service not tied to the voting, but they will come to know one way or another if he lets them down. All this will operate within the traditional Chinese respect for authority and in communities where neighbours, family and colleagues often come to know a person's voting intentions – or, afterwards, the out-turn – and where privacy is hardly known. Few Chinese voters would risk upsetting an authority, even at one remove, which has the power and will to make their lives unbearable. The March 1995 local elections, in which the Communist-backed candidates made a relatively poor showing, were a trial run for China; greater efforts will be made next time.

The Chinese caricatured Patten and his British supporters as anachronistic colonialists. 'Patten and his like ... think that they are still facing the decadent Qing government and that the Western system and values must be imposed on Asia,' said the Communist-inclining *Wenweibao*.[23] More relevant to Hongkong's dilemma, Allen Lee, an industrialist and Legco member inclined to support China rather than Britain on the current issues, alleged that Patten had destroyed the relationship between

Hongkong and China, and therefore destabilised Hongkong on the eve of its retrocession. Allen Lee is a candidate for the chief executive position after 1997, for which he must please the Chinese side, but these are his own thoughts.

Sometimes Patten won a rare accolade from the pro-Chinese press, suggesting divided opinions in the Chinese camp. In December 1993, for example, the *Xinbao* newspaper of Hongkong said that Britain's moves towards transparency, openness and moderate democracy in government were not unreasonable. 'Because the National People's Congress is a puppet apparatus,' it went on, 'and the Chinese government is an autocratic government in nature, it is impossible for Hongkong people to make their opinions known to the central authorities directly. Even if they can do so, there is no political culture in China which subjects the central authorities to public opinion.'[24] (Somebody at last understands the basis of the British system.) But the *Xinbao* went on to imply that democratic elections easily become corrupt, as Paul Tsui had warned more than a quarter of a century before. Patten, the newspaper concluded, had directly challenged China's wisdom, by saying that Legco, although not recognised by China, had more credibility than the Preliminary Working Committee. Patten had here 'hit the nail on the head'. The comment concluded: 'The fact that the Chinese side hates Chris Patten to the very marrow of his bones shows that his tactics are successful.'

There are two types of supporter in Hongkong for the coming Chinese takeover. One is the staunch Communist, the other is the staunch nationalist – and sometimes they overlap. Tsang Yok Sing, leader of the Democratic Alliance for the Betterment of Hongkong, a pro-Chinese political party in the Legco, put this viewpoint very clearly. 'I had an unpleasant impression of white people, especially British people,' he confessed. 'They belonged to the upper class ... When I was growing up it was impossible to have equality between the English and the Chinese ... For better or for worse, China is our country.' Since speaking those words, Tsang's commitment to Hongkong has come under doubt. But many others have the same viewpoint.

Another honest vote for China comes from Dr H.Y. Lee, who admires the British emphasis on justice and keeping Hongkong relatively uncorrupt. He agrees that the rule of law is better than the rule of personalities. But these intellectual judgements in no way diminish his cultural identification with China. 'It's not that I like the Communists,' Dr Lee observes, 'but they've got the same colour skin.' He hopes that some of the British elements of the Hongkong structure will influence future Chinese development, rather as a child can influence its parent. But he sees no room in all this process for more British rule.[25]

One irreplaceable advantage enjoyed by Hongkong is the number of long-standing high-level cross-border friendships. Henry Fok, the property magnate, is a good friend of the army chief and former state President, Yang Shangkun, while the late Sir Y.K. Pao became very close to Premier Li Peng. Such links are normally inherited. Fok and Pao's daughter and two sons-in-law (Edgar Chang and Peter Woo) are all in China's panel of Hongkong advisers, and Fok was also vice-chairman of the crucially powerful Preliminary Working Committee. His sons 'shadow' him, though one was charged in the USA with arms-dealing. Both Fok and Pao donated brand-new universities, among other things, to their Chinese motherland. Li Kashing, Hongkong's richest businessman, is another case.[26] They and hundreds like them will see their families and hence Hongkong's interests protected. But the political parties in Hongkong are weak, inexperienced and divided, and do not impress for fulfilling a difficult role after 1997.[27]

A host of practical matters need to be decided in or after 1997, things like the time differences or whether Hongkong traffic will continue to drive on the left, when China drives on the right. On most matters there will be give and take. Yet Chinese leaders have many times promised an independent system for Hongkong. 'We practise our socialism, you practise your capitalism, and the well water will not mix with the river water.' That is a standard refrain from Beijing, and Li Ruihuan, a Politburo Standing Committee member, expressed this reasonable view in a March 1995 speech.[28] Hongkong will in fact be more democratic than China, and the only arguments come over the extent of that difference, and whether Hongkong people will be allowed some minor role in encouraging China as a whole to follow that political path.

One worry used to be the sense of isolation which Hongkong

people developed because of being cut off from China for all those decades. It will take some time for them to acclimatise to the new prospect. David Tang is a rich young Oxford-educated Hongkong Chinese from a family that goes well back into the nineteenth century in Hongkong. He is a liberal, but he is not hostile to China, and would prefer that Hongkong in the future will go on providing him with an arena for capitalism and for the international contacts that add so much spice to life on a small Chinese island. Soon after the Joint Declaration sealing Hongkong's ultimate fate, David Tang's curiosity took him to Beijing University for a year. He returned with his Mandarin idioms much improved, with less fear of China and with a greater sense of ultimate Chinese unity. To begin with, 'I felt a complete foreigner', but today he can go all over China and feel confident of being accepted and understood. Currently the number of visits to China on the part of Hongkongers is something like 23 million a year – and since there are only six million residents, it means that each one is travelling on average every three months.

Greater contact will enrich the mixture, and already Hongkong Chinese sociologists are tentatively predicting how Chinese society might develop, possibly along Hongkong lines. Professor Lau Siu-kai of the Chinese University of Hongkong, one of the many eminent intellectuals helping to brief Chinese scholars about the Hongkong system, believes that the modernisation of Hongkong is leading it away from what he calls its 'utilitarianistic familism' to a utilitarianistic individualism.[29] He means that Hongkong people still put their family interests above those of society at large, or of the state or of other individuals as the Chinese tradition dictates, but the family bonds are now part of a wider set of modern relationships which reach upwards to the state and allow of more individual autonomy – and are therefore more suitable for contemporary life as well as more easily lived with by modern individuals. There are far more personal options.

Family interests have become complex and sophisticated. Family members interact in different ways with society or with the state or with other individuals – in factories, offices and schools – so that the simple dichotomy of family and non-family is no longer useful. Family loyalties no longer challenge the state in quite such a direct manner. The individual is not yet fully liberated by this process, and continues to subordinate his interests to those of others including other individuals and social organisations. But the ground is perhaps being cleared by these means for enjoying more individuation without losing the family base – the best of both worlds.

China will presumably follow a similar path in the longer run. China has not undergone the same intensity of Westernisation that many Hongkong people have, so we may have to wait a long time for the answer. Meanwhile scholars like Lau Siu-kai on both sides, in Hongkong and to a lesser extent China, are thinking about the questions and the answers. There are telling examples of China's deliberately borrowing from Hongkong, as when Vice-Premier Tian Jiyun told Hebei provincial leaders to copy Hongkong's practice of selling land for revenue.[30]

The Western method of adjudicating disputes and keeping law and order on the basis of equality before the law are not indigenous to China, yet many of the Chinese refugees who swarmed into Hongkong in the 1940s and 1950s have come to form a very high respect for these institutions and values. T.K. Ann, the Shanghainese textile magnate who has led the ranks of industrialists to assist in China's new role in Hongkong (perhaps on the basis stated by British leaders after their nineteenth-century Reform Bills, that 'now we must educate our masters') speaks warmly of the legal process observed in Hongkong. 'There is judgement by argument,' he elucidates, and in just those few words one can catch a glimpse of the arbitrariness and uncertainty of Chinese law when it is applied. The Perry Mason TV series watched in Guangdong as well as Hongkong educate while they entertain.

If Hongkongers' 'conversion' to Western values could be measured, the 'liberty' institutions would weigh considerably above the democratic ones. The lack of experience in democracy may be one reason for that, but certainly the non-political legacies are likely to be more durable than purely political ones. The composition of the forthcoming Final Court of Appeal which has been long disputed between Britain and China is a case in point. The cosmopolitan Hongkongers would like to be able to invite several foreign judges to sit on the court, but China would allow only one. In some ways it is a pity that Patten threw all his prodigious energies into the political reforms and has not given equal effort to the legal and human rights side.[31]

Will the Hongkong economy continue to enhance its usefulness to China? Professor Klaus Spremann of the Hongkong University Business School advocates a mutual peg between the Hongkong dollar and the Chinese *yuan*, which would further open Hongkong to Chinese enterprise, though critics fear it would destabilise Hongkong. Already China does one-third of its total foreign trade with Hongkong, making it China's largest partner. Hongkong provides two-thirds of the foreign investment flowing into China. Such figures suggest a strong grounding for heightened economic reciprocity. The Hongkong Stock Exchange organises seminars in Beijing for would-be Chinese exchange officials, investors and regulators. The first of these at the end of 1992 brought 200 such Chinese 'apprentices' to listen to sixty Hongkong experts over a two-week seminar. Similar courses will be held in other areas of the economy. It is perfectly true, as Philip Bowring once wrote, that the political officials who run the Bank of China, for example, 'do not understand that so-called speculation and free markets are inseparable'. Such matters will take up much of the next few decades of the Hongkong–China interface.

Little has been said so far about Guangzhou's possible relationship with Hongkong after 1997. The economic link is already clear, and there is a suitable division of business functions between the two cities. Hongkong controls three million industrial jobs in Guangdong and has fingers in every pie. As the process of Hongkong's integration into China, and especially into the south China network, gathers pace, more political links will form. In matters ranging from housing, education and legal affairs to modern literature and art, there must be some convergence of interest between Hongkong and Guangdong.

If the efficiency and attractiveness of Hongkong's institutions gradually outweigh the peasant-based conservatism of the more traditional inland areas, it would be logical to expect that Hongkong would eventually become not merely the commercial but even the social and political centre of south China – as would be the case if there were no politics. Hence the idea floated in the 1980s that Hongkong might become the 'tail that wags the dog' instead of China's poodle. If that unlikely point were ever reached, of course, Guangzhou would be jealous, and skilful diplomacy would be needed by the new Chief Executive.

Hard-line attitudes to Hongkong may still be found at high levels of China's military and civilian government. Xu Huizi, head of Hongkong Affairs in the General Office of the Central Military Commission, takes a very strong position on Hongkong. He argued in 1994 that China needed to pander to Hongkong only as long as it had no 'other Hongkongs' to substitute. The Chinese interest was only economic, he added, and so Hongkong should not imagine that it will get away with special privileges and soft treatment indefinitely.[32]

Shanghai would be the first such rival of Hongkong, and is cultivating facilities and economic activities similar to those in Hongkong. But you do not construct such a delicate organism in a week or a month, and it may be twenty years or more before Shanghai can match all of Hongkong's skills. By that time the economic development of the entire coastal region, and a good swathe of the interior as well, will be so developed that one single centre would not be able to cope. There will be specialisation, both regional and sectoral, between the two centres. Hongkongers do not need to fear Shanghai.

All this presupposes that Hongkong can be clever enough to escape China's economic diseases, from inflation to corruption. Hongkong's symptoms of these ills are much milder than those in the People's Republic. As one small-time Hongkong industrialist airily explained, 'that's how China works . . . You just have to pay a little more money, then get some senior official to clobber someone.'[33]

After 1997 Hongkong will become a microcosm of China's accommodation to the West. It will be the major meeting place between China and the West, and both have much to transmit. With almost 100,000 Filipino residents, 26,000 Americans, 23,000 Thais, over 17,000 Australians, over 20,000 Canadians and 14,000 Japanese, there will be no disputing Hongkong's role as China's major place of contact with foreigners.[34] The British companies will not be forced out because of Patten's parliamentary proselytising. China wants the British firms to stay in Hongkong. It needs a variety of options in dealing with Hongkong.

Jardine Matheson has delisted from the Hongkong Stock Exchange, and moved its legal and operational headquarters to the Caribbean and Singapore, but Hongkong remains its biggest single source of business and income.[35] The Chinese will accept that, even as they mouth cheap jibes against Jardine's historical connection with opium and nineteenth-century colonialism. Han Suyin said of Hongkong that it was a borrowed place living on borrowed time,[36] but the term of the lease is about to end in 1997, when the place goes back to its rightful owner. Jardine, which was in on the first act of the Hongkong drama, has grown rich on the proceeds. The Keswick family which is the main shareholder in Jardines is worth well over £500 million. But it has also used the time since 1840 to create networks of business, with injections of expertise and technology that would be regarded as an asset in any developing country. Whatever the insults, Jardine remains busy in China. Those looking a little longer ahead for Hongkong's future commercial colour might ponder the 6,000 Japanese companies now established in Hongkong, some quite explicitly awaiting July 1997.

What about the Chinese entry into Hongkong business? About forty-seven state-owned enterprises controlling a thousand Hongkong firms are now part of the Hongkong scene (controlling a large proportion of market capitalisation), and they include some 'red princes'.[37] The 1994 report of a Ministry of Supervision investigation into Chinese-funded institutions in Hongkong gives an inkling of some of the issues that may arise in future. Descriptions are quoted there of the people running Chinese factories in Hongkong as from the 'red comprador–bureaucrat class', forming the 'new bureaucrat bourgeoisie', and operating in a 'paradise for the offspring of top-level cadres', who make their fortunes out of reform. Over 71,400 Chinese personnel have been sent to join these companies. By the end of 1993, there were 45,000 permanent residents from the People's Republic. Money from the People's Republic flows to private individuals or accounts in Hongkong at the rate of almost HK$4 billion a year. Vice-Premier Tian Jiyun has said that China has injected more capital into Hongkong than into any foreign country – US$25 billion by one count, more than the USA or Japan though still less than Britain.[38]

Some of the people investigated by this Ministry of Supervision 'live decadent lifestyles, squander money, throw money around in nightclubs and receive private commissions and kickbacks.' Some of them seek short-term gain, and 'do not act in accordance with the established rules. They come to Hongkong to speculate in flats, shares and foreign exchange. They spend money extravagantly without batting an eyelid. If they speculate and lose, they put it down as state "study expenses", but if they speculate and profit, the money goes to themselves.'

The investigators conclude: 'The sons and daughters, sons-in-law and daughters-in-law of Chinese Communist Party figures are well-known faces in . . . Hongkong. Would the Ministry of Supervision dare to be disrespectful to them?'[39] This is a quintessentially Chinese problem, whose solution will eventually be found in China, not in Hongkong. But in such a small community as Hongkong these activities are disturbing and demoralising, and they may well provide the future chief executive with some of his worst headaches.

Vice-Premier Tian Jiyun also said that China would not allow Hongkong to become 'a city where all political forces wrestle with each other'.[40] Will Hongkong become a bridgehead for democracy and perhaps other Western political products in China? In terms of what the Chinese government will officially allow, the answer must be no. In terms of what might slip across the border in ways that are not easy to block and with results that might well be approved by a large number of people in China not hugely concerned about official policy, the answer may be yes. That is already happening with satellite TV, which the government has begun to restrict but with limited results. Only the next century will tell us which force is the stronger.

Much of what has been said here could equally be said of Macao, the tiny Portuguese colonial province just across the Pearl river estuary from Hongkong. But Macao is only about one-fifteenth the size of Hongkong, and therefore hardly figures in the high politics of the south China region. Like Hongkong, it is capitalist and, within its limits, a bustling commercial and industrial city. Unlike Hongkong, a fifth of its Gross Domestic Product comes from gambling and betting, and the local government gets almost half of its revenues from these pursuits. Stanley

Ho, the owner of Macao's five casinos, sports four Rolls-Royces, and is deeply superstitious. He believes that his first wife is the source of all his good fortune, and when she was injured in a car accident in Portugal he bought a whole hospital in order to make sure she had the best care. In 1995 he was under investigation for corruption.[41]

Unlike Hongkong, Macao has a respectable history, having been settled by the Portuguese 400 years ago and then used by the Christian churches as a base from which to proselytise the whole of east Asia. Robert Morrison, the British missionary, composed the first Chinese translation of the Bible in Macao.

A conscience-stricken socialist government in Portugal tried to give Macao back to China in the 1970s, but the Chinese refused it, apparently fearing a knock-on effect in Hongkong, where China did not want to prejudice its control over the timing and terms of the retrocession. But in 1987 Lisbon and Beijing agreed that Macao would return to China in December 1999, on very much the same formula that Mrs Thatcher had secured for Hongkong.

The two and a half year gap means that some Hongkong firms or individuals could shift to Macao just before July 1997, in order to have time to observe the Chinese record in Hongkong at close quarters and only then decide whether to go back there or move even further away. Unlike Hongkong, Macao is small enough for China to control fully. Chinese companies now own half of the financial and property economy, and pro-Beijing candidates made virtually a clean sweep of the 1992 elections. Macao can be a centre for the economic development of its side of the Pearl river estuary, including Zhuhai and other Special Economic Zones.[42]

The Chinese love to use romantic images from nature. The narrow belt of 'miraculous' economic development from Japan in the north through Korea, Taiwan, Hongkong and Macao to southeast Asia is sometimes dubbed Asia's Golden Crescent. Robert Ng, leader of the younger generation of Hongkong Chinese entrepreneurs and chairman of Sino Land, carries the metaphor further, arguing that the entry of China into full relations with these crescent communities 'gives us a full moon at last'. It is a good image, and any schoolboy could supply the next line – 'and Hongkong is in the middle.'

John Hung of Wheelock, a buccaneering old Western conglomerate now revived under Hongkong Chinese ownership and management, makes a slightly different metaphor out of the same fact, saying that in Hongkong 'we are sitting on the ringside of the biggest potential economic theatre in the world.' Even the Communists now join in the oratory. Lu Ping, who heads the Hongkong Affairs Office in the State Council of Beijing, has encouraged Hongkongers to follow the path which the People's Republic now sets out for them, predicting that 'with the Chinese mainland behind and southeast Asia in front', Hongkong has an advantage over all rivals.[43]

CHAPTER 16

TAIWAN: THE OTHER CHINA

Taiwan is Chinese. That may sound obvious. But arguments are now being advanced – and as hotly rebutted – which would virtually deny the island province's Chineseness in favour of sovereign independence. Almost all the 20 million Taiwanese are ethnic Chinese, and therefore share the same written language. Pioneers crossing the eighty-five miles of sea from mainland Fujian and Guangdong provinces a thousand years ago were reinforced by larger numbers over the past two or three centuries. Historians disagree as to what effective authority the Chinese central government of the day exerted over this island outpost. Fights were common between rival Fujianese and Guangdong Hakka immigrants, and both groups laid into the unfortunate non-Chinese aborigines (today numbering 350,000) in a west Pacific rerun of the British–French–Amerindian saga in North America.

Both the Dutch and the Spanish tried to take over Taiwan, but the deepest mark was left by Japan, which grabbed it for half a century after militarily defeating China in 1895. Those fifty years saw striking improvements in the island's infrastructure, schools and administration. Lee Teng-hui, Taiwan's scholarly President, has voiced the opinion that one significant reason for the emergence of South Korea, Taiwan, Hongkong and Singapore as Asia's first Newly Industrialising Economies is their experience of Japanese or British colonial rule respectively.

For four brief years after the Japanese surrender in 1945 Taiwan became a part of the old Republic of China, the entity founded by Dr Sun Yatsen after the collapse of the imperial system in 1912 and led after his death by his brother-in-law, Chiang Kai-shek. Under Chiang's rule a cruel massacre took place on 28 February 1947 of more than 9,000 Taiwan people rebelling against their new government's incompetence and arbitrary justice.[1] Only much later, in the 1990s, did a new generation of Guomindang leaders show remorse and begin to apologise.

After Japan's surrender Chiang faced the growing challenge of the Chinese Communist Party led by Chairman Mao Zedong, and was eventually expelled from the mainland by Mao's better-motivated Red Army in 1949. For the rest of his life Chiang sulked in the tiny island province of Taiwan where Mao's Communist forces, lacking naval or air strength, could not reach him. When the Korean war broke out in 1950, the Americans were convinced that the Communists all over Asia would make a concerted all-out offensive, so they sent their Seventh Fleet to protect Taiwan by patrolling the Taiwan strait.

Chiang used that superpower shield to perpetuate the hollow fiction that he still ruled – or should rightly rule – over the twenty-six other provinces on the Chinese mainland. Chiang had

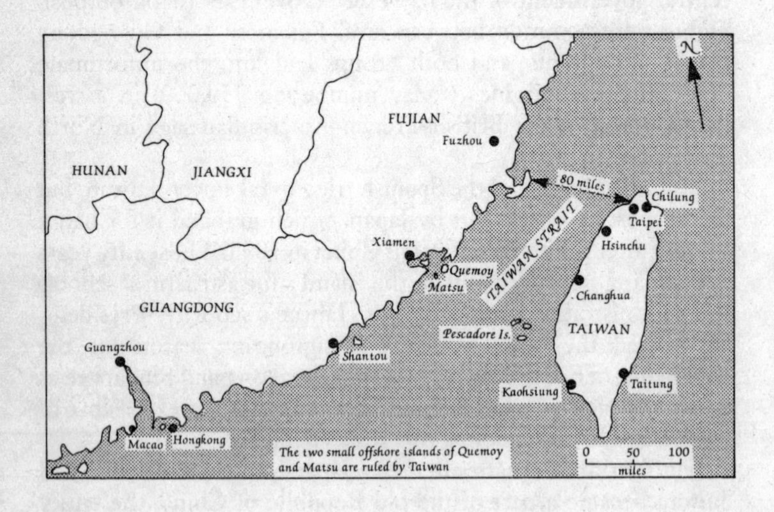

Taiwan

taken 600,000 soldiers and 650,000 civilians with him to Taiwan along with the apparatus of the government and Party originally intended for the whole of China: he expected, after all, to return to the mainland like Napoleon from Elba. Even non-Communist legislators representing the mainland provinces made the passage to the island. It was a case of acute indigestion. By comparison with the Japanese, the Guomindang mainlander soldiers at first seemed to the Taiwanese to be technologically backward, physically dirty and downright dishonest. Yet the Guomindang expected to be welcomed as the restorer of the superior Chinese culture.

The majority of the Taiwanese speak the dialect of southern Fujian, though the Hakka minority has its own language. Both are different from standard Chinese and both have been infiltrated by some Japanese words and expressions. The mainlander minority, on the other hand, are mostly speakers of the standard northern speech which we call Mandarin. The islanders are still developing their Fujian speech, incorporating its local slang into their songs and poems and even inventing new Chinese characters to express their mood, so that it comes to differ more and more from mainland Fujianese. How the Taiwanese feel about their race is captured in the song of Hou Dejian (the adventurous hunger-striker who played a leading role on Tiananmen Square in 1989):

> In the ancient East there is a Dragon,
> Its name is China.
> In the ancient East there is a people,
> They are descendants of the Dragon.
> I grew up under the feet of the Dragon;
> After growing up, I'm a descendant of the Dragon.
> Black eyes, black hair, yellow skin; forever
> Descendants of the Dragon.

The Taiwanese are Chinese, but they are choosy about what kind of Chinese. They also adopted some Japanese ways, instilled through the schools in the first half of this century. Hwang Chun-ming's novel *Sayonara Tsai-chien* vividly depicts the continuing Japanese cultural influence in post-war Taiwan. President Lee went to a university in Japan and speaks 'better Japanese than we do', his Japanese friends concede. Villagers may be found in the distant parts of the island who still speak Japanese, and Japanese familiar with Taiwan sometimes claim fondly that 'the Taiwanese are half Chinese and half Japanese.'

The Guomindang sought to re-sinify its new charges and fill the youngsters with Chinese patriotism, while intermarriage between the Taiwanese and mainlanders has hastened the integration process. After almost half a century it is believed that every other Taiwanese now has a mainlander married into his family. But Professor Fu Hu of the National Taiwan University says, 'We are developing a new and separate Chinese culture in Taiwan. The old Chinese tradition of the one-ness of Chinese culture has gone.'[2]

When a debate surfaced in the 1980s about 'Taiwanese identity', many intellectuals stressed the cultural and anthropological differences between their island and the mainland. Politicians opposing the Guomindang used this new identity to justify not only a new constitution but political independence from China as well. The Guomindang relaxed its official ban on visiting the mainland in 1987, since when some 14 million Taiwanese have made the crossing – though only 34,000 reciprocated from the mainland. Many Taiwanese hoped that the more liberal reformist régime of Deng Xiaoping would reduce the tension.

Then came the bombshell of Tiananmen. The Communists were still capable, it seemed, of the same sort of barbarism against unarmed civilians that the Guomindang had once perpetrated during its forty-year stewardship. How could anyone identify with that? Taiwan was the only population under a government of Chinese politicians which was allowed to demonstrate open support for Beijing's student democracy movement. The 'Taiwan Strait Loving Heart Association' was formed. The graduate students of the National Taiwan University wrote to the students of Beijing proclaiming that 'you are not alone in struggling for China's freedom and democracy.'[3]

A million Taiwan students joined hands in a human chain across Taiwan from north to south, organised by the 'Great Alliance of the Reunification of China under the Three Principles of Sun Yatsen'. That won some support from the Guomindang.

Gaining unexpected advantage from Beijing's mistakes, the ruling party grandly cancelled its forty-year ban on mail and telephone calls to and from the mainland. While Beijing shot its critics, the 'new-look' Guomindang was introducing multi-party democracy, the most far-reaching political reform ever made by a modern Chinese government.

That sweeping change built upon the economic reforms of the 1950s and 1960s which had brought Taiwan by the 1990s to become the richest society per head in Asia after Japan and the non-agricultural city-states of Hongkong and Singapore. They began under a land reform under which farmland was redistributed to the tiller, creating a small-farm system which was economically efficient and socially stable, and which the government fed with high-yielding varieties, fertiliser and new technology.

Another gift which Taiwan owed to the anti-Communist tide flowing over America after 1950 was US$1.5 billion of US aid between 1950 and 1965. Considering that more Western-trained Chinese engineers, economists and scientists also preferred to return to work in 'free' China than in Communist China, one can see how Taiwan got the best of all the worlds and made itself into something of a model for Asia.

The average annual growth of the Taiwan economy was almost 9 per cent during the past four decades. Government strategies were contested by the left wing at the time, but were vindicated by the results and the consensus of the development economists. In 1952, for example, the Taiwan government controlled 57 per cent of industry, but by 1990 its share was down to 19 per cent – anticipating by two or three decades what Deng Xiaoping did in China itself. Even more remarkable was the relatively even distribution of new wealth. In 1980 the highest 20 per cent of households ranked by income had only 4.2 times the income of the lowest 20 per cent, enabling Yu-shan Wu of the University of California to state categorically that 'in terms of income distribution, Taiwan is the most egalitarian of all capitalist countries.'[4] In the later 1980s the ratio rose to 4.6 times, reflecting the emergence of the élite as a propertied class, but the achievement is still remarkable, and most creditable.

Taiwan is a society of individual achievers and conscientious workers who prefer to channel their drive for improvement into small businesses, especially small family businesses. They have never created anything like the interlocking conglomerate giants of Japan (*zaibatsu*) or Korea (*chaebol*). By the same token Taiwan has never developed a serious heavy industry, preferring to live off its skills in light industry, though shipbuilding is beginning to be an exception. Government efforts to make several small car-makers collaborate were not successful. But Taiwan's world class electronics industry is now sending its simple manufactures to be made in China and other countries, while going high-tech at home. If you visit the Tatung electronics plant in Telford, Shropshire, you will see a blown-up calligraphy on the wall blazoning an appropriate Confucian message to the employees –

HOW TAIWAN BECAME RICH IN FOUR DECADES

Average Annual Rates of Increase (%)	1953–60	1961–72	1973–83	1984–91
1. Real GNP	7.6	10.2	8.1	8.6
2. Farm Production	5.0	4.9	3.3	2.4
3. Industrial Production	11.7	17.6	9.6	6.5
4. Consumer Prices	9.7	3.3	10.8	1.8
5. Exports	4.4	27.4	21.4	14.9
6. Imports	6.0	19.5	20.9	15.2

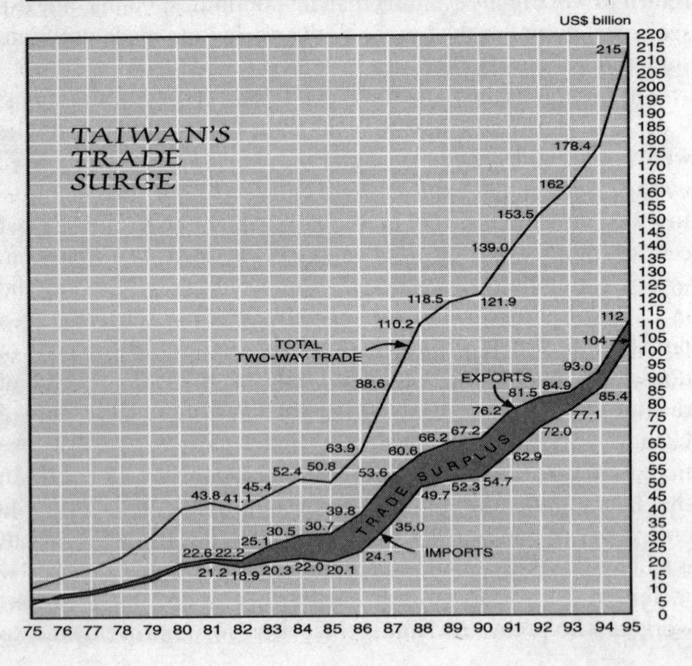

in Chinese! Aerospace with a defence angle and US technology inputs is another industrial success story.

The economy caught the common diseases of industrialisation rather early. With all the new activity and strict rules against further immigration, reflecting the fact that Taiwan has the second highest population density in the world, Taiwan now faces a labour shortage. Illegal immigrant workers come from the Philippines, Thailand and even mainland China itself. Those from Thailand alone number 60,000. Yet the balance of economic achievement in Taiwan is remarkable, and the ambition to become a regional finance centre is not impossible.[5]

When the Guomindang talks about the Three Principles of Sun Yatsen, it is not just lip service. Chiang Kai-shek created a network of Party members at the grass roots and set up welfare stations in villages and farms, so there is a welfare cushion of sorts. His motive, of course, was to ensure support for the Party at all levels of society. Both objectives were met. The constitution adopted in 1947 for the whole of China, but applying only to Taiwan after 1949, was on the face of it a most liberal document. China was to be 'a democratic republic of the people', to be governed by the people for the people. Citizens had not only the right but the duty to undergo education. The President could promulgate laws only with the counter-signature of the Prime Minister (responsible to the legislature) and Cabinet. Elections were to be by universal equal and direct suffrage and by secret ballot.

The whole edifice was undermined by Chiang's declaration of martial law in 1949, when the Communists threatened to capture the island by force to complete their conquest of China. This lasted until 1987, but was not quite as drastic as it sounds, being more like a 'state of siege', with the courts and civil administration continuing their normal functions. Martial law froze politics, however, at the 1949 level (to undergo thaw in 1987) and permitted some drastic action against dissidents.

The Guomindang rule of Taiwan is an unusual case in world politics, a single-party dictatorship which has voluntarily gone on to compete with opposition parties in a plural political system. Dr Steve Tsang of Oxford calls it dictatorship with an 'inhibited centre'. Even before Chiang's far-sighted son Chiang Ching-kuo declared pluralism, his father's Guomindang was not nominating candidates for all the assembly seats (as a result of which opposition candidates typically won some 30 per cent of the seats). In the 1950s only about 15 per cent of the Party's membership was native Taiwanese, but by 1975 its leaders had allowed the ratio to rise above half.

When Chiang Ching-kuo, the dull, unassuming and portly son of Chiang Kai-shek, assumed the Presidency, everyone expected him to carry on with the mixture as before. There was even apprehension because Ching-kuo had spent twelve years in the Soviet Union, graduating from the Central Tomatchev Military and Political Institute in Leningrad. No other Guomindang leader had been subjected to such brainwashing. Yet his actions once in power supported the old Third World adage that if you send your son to Harvard he will come home a Communist, but it you send him to Moscow University he will return a fervent capitalist. Besides, Ching-kuo was known as incorrupt and a good judge of men.

So in 1986–88 President Chiang Ching-kuo, apparently acting on the advice of several local Western-trained scientists, and influenced by the revolution in the Philippines and the violent disorders in Korea, lifted martial law, which automatically legalised the creation of new political parties. He also cancelled press restrictions and announced the phasing-out of the antiquated parliamentary seats for the mainland constituencies. Ching-kuo died within six months of these remarkable decisions, but his chosen successor, Dr Lee Teng-hui, a native Hakka Taiwanese technocrat and intellectual, carried them out.[6] Lee later outlined his own dream of creating 'a great model of political democracy for all times'.

Such sweeping changes could take place only if a majority of Guomindang leaders and army chiefs acquiesced. They did so because of the prestige Chiang Ching-kuo had inherited from his father, and because the conservatives calculated – correctly, as it turned out – that the reform package would win them votes and allow them to retain their parliamentary majority (the same motivation which led their mainland counterparts to back Deng Xiaoping's reforms). By now the political game was no longer between remote mainlander Guomindang politicians versus familiar native Taiwanese headmen. When Chiang announced his reforms, over 70 per cent of the two-million-strong Guomindang membership were said to be Taiwanese.

A younger third generation waits its turn, including secretary-general Lee Huan who masterminded the Guomindang recruitment of Taiwanese, John Kuan, the organisation specialist, and James Soong, President Lee's collaborator. Much influenced by American politics, they will dump the old Leninist-style organisation and turn the party into a machine for winning elections.

The first National Assembly elections under the new rules were held in December 1991. The Democratic Progressive Party (DPP) advocated the independence of Taiwan, while the more prudent Guomindang called for reform, stability and prosperity, warning that independence would bring about a damaging confrontation with Beijing. Its reward was 72 per cent of the popular vote – a heavy blow for the DPP, which won only 24 per cent. It has become a fairly stable pattern since then for the electorate to give around two-thirds of its votes to the ruling party, one-third to the opposition.

A growing sophistication may be observed among these electors, who are returning the younger candidates instead of the traditional Chinese patriarchs, and have filled the National Assembly with educated and dynamic personalities including over a hundred graduates, forty of them holding PhDs.[7] By contrast with their counterparts in Beijing, the very old have stepped down, acknowledging a degree of political mortality. Elections are free from gross irregularities. After much discussion a combination of mechanisms is used, namely a single-entry ballot (which favours the Guomindang) for multi-member constituencies (favouring smaller parties), following the model of Japan and Spain.

The DPP had sprung up even before the younger Chiang's reforms, because in 1986 its leaders were told informally through intermediaries that no action would be taken against them if they founded a party. An early DPP chairman, Yao Chia-wen, explained the Party's links between democracy and independence. 'The reason why Taiwan has no democracy today,' he said, 'is because of the Guomindang government, which is a Chinese government, not a Taiwanese government. That is to say, Taiwan should be independent so that democracy can be achieved.' The

Taiwanese thus sought a resolution of their identity dilemma – Chinese or Taiwanese?

The DPP appealed to the private Taiwan – the middle class, businessmen and industrial workers – whereas the Guomindang's strength lay in the public domain, among farmers, bureaucrats, housewives concerned with the price of food and household goods, and the retired. In the 1991 elections the DPP campaigned for the setting up of a 'Republic of Taiwan'. It conducted a nationwide drive for Taiwan's return to United Nations (of which the Republic of China had been a founder-member but had to give its seat to the People's Republic in 1971). Thousands demonstrated their support, and the DPP went so far as to oppose investment in the mainland or political contacts with it.

But it dawned on DPP leaders that stressing independence under the Taiwan name meant defining who is Taiwanese. What about the children of mainlanders born in Taiwan? Or the Hakka people in Taiwan? Rather than set about excluding people and putting off important potential supporters, as well as the older hands who saw themselves as belonging to the larger and more glorious China, the DPP cooled down its rhetoric. Only one of its constituent groups, the so-called Formosa faction, remained fully committed to independence, while the others took the line that the matter was not urgent, since Taiwan already enjoyed *de facto* independence. So the Party concentrated on the other issues where a real difference could be made, such as full employment, tax reforms, welfare and social security, protection of the environment, civil rights, multilingual education and cuts in defence spending.[8]

John Foster Dulles schemed in 1953 for both Chinas to co-exist in the UN. After all, Mao Zedong himself had conceded the independence of Taiwan when talking to Edgar Snow in 1936.[9] During the Cold War it became *de rigueur* for Washington to support Taiwan, in the name of the Republic of China, as the acceptable non-Communist government of China – until, that is, President Nixon and his emissary Henry Kissinger made their dramatic flights to Beijing in 1971–2. That cleared the air, but the Americans were not about to throw their new China card away in order to back an independent Taiwan and provoke Beijing to furious anger, although George Bush had suggested in 1971 that

Taiwan have a General Assembly seat in the UN. There is still visceral support for Taiwan on Capitol Hill, all the greater now with the Republican resurgence: the USA would be involved if any defence of Taiwan became necessary.

A Taiwan public opinion poll in 1990 supported this analysis. Three-quarters of the adult respondents were for unification only when the Chinese Communists were ready to practise democracy and concede freedom. In another poll two years later more than two-thirds of 3,000 adults voted the same way. The acceptability of reunification to most people is thus a long way off.

China would not perhaps object to 'Taiwanisation' of the island's government and politics if that is all that 'self-determination' is about. But Beijing recognises an independence call beneath all this flurry about democracy and identity, and that is something it could not stomach. 'If they persist,' an article in the well-informed Hongkong monthly, *Cheng Ming*, thundered in 1994, 'in advancing Taiwan independence and creating two Chinas, or "one China, one Taiwan" ... we must resolutely... achieve reunification of the motherland by military means.' Even now China refuses to commit itself not to use force against Taiwan.[10]

Beijing has tried to prove its good intentions towards Taiwan. In 1981 Marshal Ye Jianying, then acting as head of state, issued a nine-point proposal for Taiwan ('China's precious island,' he called it) to enjoy 'a high degree of autonomy' as a special administrative region of China retaining its own armed forces and government. This was similar to the formula negotiated with Britain for the Hongkong retrocession three years later, and the latter was seen as an intended bait to Taiwan. It is probably the best offer Taiwan will ever get, but as long as there is a Communist government in China no one in Taiwan would trust the promises to be kept. More recently President Jiang Zemin made an eight-point proposal with the remarkable undertaking that force, if used, would be used not against Taiwan compatriots but against the 'schemes of foreign forces' trying to push Taiwan independence. But negotiations could only be on the premise of 'one China'.[11]

The Communists did steal some of the Guomindang's clothes and offer them to their own public as 'socialism with Chinese characteristics' or 'socialist market economy'. They did not go far enough to reassure Taiwan, however, and China's human rights record is repellent to most Taiwanese. The confused face of China which Taiwan people see enables the ruling Guomindang to proceed more slowly on its path away from authoritarianism and to mark time on the further democratisation of politics.

Deng Xiaoping sustained the contradictions in China's position over a whole paragraph:

> We insist on seeking peaceful means to solve the Taiwan question, but at the same time we have never renounced the possibility to resort to military means. We cannot make such a promise. What should we do if the Taiwan authorities keep refusing to talk? Does that mean we have to give up unification? Certainly, we cannot use force rashly because our efforts must be spent in economic construction. A little bit of delay in unification will do no harm to the whole situation. But the option for the use of force can by no means be renounced. We must not forget this; our next generation must not forget this.[12]

If it were all left to the businessmen there would be no problem. From only US$47 million in 1978, when Deng opened China's door, the trade both ways between Taiwan and China (via Hongkong) rose to $3.5 billion by 1989. Taiwan investments in China are now estimated at $20 billion, more than half of them in Xiamen and the other cities of Fujian. This coastal province facing Taiwan across the strait is isolated, poor and mountainous. The chief economic activity for which it is famous is emigration. After 1949 the Communist central government did little to help it. Now it is booming, thanks to compatriots across the strait. There are so many Taiwan businessmen in Xiamen that other Chinese provinces send missions there to give investment presentations for Taiwan investors. All in all there are some 100,000 Taiwanese on the mainland running 18,000 factories. There is talk of a joint venture bank in Hongkong owned by mainland and Taiwan banks.[13]

This natural though hitherto repressed trade is conducted largely via Hongkong because the Guomindang banned direct air or shipping links with the mainland. It still bans visits by Communist Party members in principle, though exceptions are made on a case-by-case basis. Mail is now allowed, and about 60 million packages have been exchanged. But in 1991 five mainland doctors were deported back to China during a lecture tour which they had been invited to make. More recently five dissident mainland student leaders showed considerable bravery in reaching Taiwan in a small boat, but instead of being treated sympathetically as refugees from Communism they were beaten, incarcerated and deported to Sweden!

Deng Xiaoping said in 1991 that he was prepared to go to Taiwan to talk to its leaders personally if the situation permitted, and a Taiwan legislator later urged the Guomindang government to invite Deng for a game of ping-pong. Lee Teng-hui has issued a standing invitation to Jiang Zemin to meet in a third country. But no leader on either side is likely to stick his neck out so dramatically without pre-agreement with the other side, and there is no sign of that, given the mutual mistrust.

If the decision were Fujian's, it might be different. Taiwan investors are treated royally in Fujian. They are allowed many privileges and concessions to their own way of life; if one is arrested, for example on a morals charge, such as patronising a prostitute or 'lewd behaviour', he will usually go scot-free. Deng Xiaoping personally authorised a 'super special' preferential package for the Taiwan tycoon Wang Yung-ching's consortium putting US$7 billion into Fujian. 'Give him as many preferential conditions and as much free hand as he wants.'[14] Beijing has authorised the Xiamen Special Economic Zone to make its own rules and regulations.[15]

One rich but superstitious Taiwan investor told important Fujian officials to report for his ground-breaking ceremony of the US$200 million synthetic fibre factory at six in the morning – all except those born in the year of the tiger who would cast bad luck on the occasion. He also demanded a parade of 200 flags to be held on poles by People's Liberation Army soldiers, and if any flag fell, the whole deal was off.[16] The local Chinese did as he said because they desperately needed the investment. How Western investors would envy such bargaining power.

But the Taiwan people involved in such investments can come

away with heightened distrust and distaste. They never imagined that life in China could be so awful. Now the mainland authorities are thinking of not taking visiting parties from Taiwan to poor or backward places any more. But the vivid impression of those four million visitors is of China's inefficiency, backwardness, pervasive state interference, bribery, corruption and contempt for law. Trade exchanges and investments will go on, driven by mutual economic need. But the two sides now know better than before how large a gulf looms between their political, social, cultural and legal systems. Dirty toilets alone have disillusioned hundreds of thousands of Taiwanese who see that they are fortunate enough to live in a style which 'the old folks at home' in the backward motherland could never seemingly attain.

An odd feature of this Taiwan investment is its amazing mobility. Taiwan businessmen arrive at Fujian with their own capital, machinery, raw materials supply and market destinations. Little contact is needed with local banks, suppliers or buyers. The Guomindang has taught them how to get round bureaucrats. So when they complete their three-year tax holidays and ponder the rising labour and land costs due to so many Taiwanese competing (and, some say, ponder also the local crack-down on prostitution), they may up sticks and go to Fuzhou or Quanzhou in other less commercialised, more innocent stretches of the province. But there are also examples of long-term thinking. A small Taiwan electronics firm went to much trouble to persuade its joint venture partner in Guangzhou to take a long view of their personal computer plant there, with local tailor-made designs producing a turnover of more than £10 million. Another Taiwan personal computer manufacturer has started making them in Shanghai, and Taiwan investments now stretch as far inland as Hunan.[17]

The most serious and heartening development is the actual meeting between non-officials from both sides to solve practical administrative problems arising from these trade and capital flows, such as arbitration and the law to be applied to disputes. Taiwan has its Strait Exchange Foundation, China its Association for Relations Across the Taiwan Strait. Formed in 1991 as intermediary groups with the approval of their respective official authorities, the SEF and the ARATS have held several meetings, the first on the neutral ground of Singapore, others in Hongkong and Beijing.

The first conferences appeared to be getting somewhere, but the later ones turned into backbiting sessions. At least the two sides are talking. They agreed on document certification and establishing a registered mail service. The ARATS added a 'one China' clause to the drafts, and a seven-month suspension followed, after which ARATS climbed down. On the other hand the mainland side did respond to a fervent call for joint efforts to stamp out the rampant smuggling and piracy which feed off these trades, so there is pragmatism at work even if political propaganda opportunities are seized by the Communists.

When President Lee made his inaugural address in 1990 he set his goal as 'establishing channels of communication on an equal basis' with the mainland and completely opening up 'academic, cultural and economic exchanges'. Many of his moves since succeeding the younger Chiang were praised in the mainland press. When he adopted a National Unification Programme in 1991 it was greeted in Beijing as a 'move conforming to the historical tide'. Lee's relinquishment of his government's claim to be the sole government of China cleared the air.[18] But the mainland fretted about Taiwan's slow, cautious pace, and its pursuit of 'dual recognition' by international organisations and third states. President Yang Shangkun complained publicly of the 'growing audacity' of the Taiwan independence campaign. This 'dual recognition' actually amounted, a *Xinhua* editorial announced in 1991, to a 'two-China' policy.

Taiwan had to fight hard for its international status – not now as a rival government for the whole of China but as part of China with a separate history that needed, for its economic interest and psychological self-respect, to participate in international life and business without being a mere appendage of Beijing. Taiwan delegations often go to international conferences on trade, the environment or wildlife, for example, only to find that because they cannot agree with Beijing what name they should appear under, they have to sit out the conference in the corridors. This has gone on so long that the Taiwanese, fortified by their new-found wealth (their gold and foreign exchange reserves being the biggest in the world), have become a little belligerent.

In 1989 the Asian Development Bank president, Masao Fujioka of Japan, brokered a pact between Taiwan and China under which Taiwan with Chinese approval took a seat in the bank under the name 'Taipei, China'. Shirley Kuo, the Taiwan Finance Minister, attended the bank's annual meeting in Beijing, becoming the first Taiwan official to set foot on the mainland since 1949. But the name smacked too much of being 'under' or 'part of' China and Taiwan rejected it in other organisations.

With such over-sensitiveness it is not surprising that the Asia-Pacific Economic Co-operation (APEC) and Pacific Basin Economic Council are the only other significant bodies to which Taiwan – here called 'Chinese Taipei' – belongs alongside China. Even there, while President Jiang Zemin breathed benevolence at the Seattle summit of APEC hosted by President Clinton in 1993, Taiwan sent a much more junior figure, thus avoiding any embarrassing encounters at the highest level.

The World Trade Organisation, successor to the GATT, is not such a problem, there being precedents for Customs territories to belong even if, like Hongkong, they lack political sovereignty. But the UN itself will deal blistering rebuffs to Taiwan's self-esteem if the island persists in applying for membership even though it no longer seeks to rob the mainland of its permanent seat and veto in the Security Council but only asks to take part as a humble General Assembly delegation, with some agreed name, to do useful work (and pay a big subscription).[19] Taiwan seems oblivious of the difficulties its UN campaign imposes on China, which might well be seen, if it agrees, as accepting the more or less permanent loss of its eastern island and later of some mainland provinces and regions, possibly. Other member states can be put off by the high moral tone of some Taiwan representatives, as when government spokesman Jason Hu argued the case for UN entry under a title from Confucius – 'The Virtuous Will Not Be Alone'.[20]

The name is itself a stumbling-block. Taiwan officially uses the name Republic of China, and its older generation at least is proud to bear a name that has continued unbroken since Sun Yatsen invented it eighty-five years ago. Yet it smacks of the lingering claim for mainland sovereignty which President Lee Teng-hui has actually disclaimed though in a somewhat backdoor manner.

That title sets mainland teeth on edge. Yet Taiwan, which is the geographically correct appellation for Formosa, the 'beautiful island', and the one generally used outside the ambit of diplomatists, is equally anathema to Beijing because it insinuates the idea of Taiwan independent from China. Dr Bernard Joei has proposed avoiding the complications of the 'China' name by conveying it in the Chinese language – Chung Hua Ming Kuo ('Middle Kingdom People's State') which could ride on the cultural tide of de-anglicisation of world names.[21]

When Taiwan unashamedly peddles economic aid (which it can well afford) in order to secure the diplomatic recognition of small African and Latin American countries, the Chinese are not the only ones to complain of 'dollar diplomacy'. Some of Taiwan's agriculture projects have been beneficial in Africa, and many of the loans well spent. But it is rather crude, and it does not help Taiwan to win acceptance as a serious and worthy state. It meant a constant tit-for-tat rivalry with the mainland, at least until China's priorities switched to domestic development.

When President Lee turned up in 1994 on an Indonesian golf course, or was found chatting with the King of Thailand in his Bangkok palace, he appeared to be getting the best of both worlds. They were 'holiday' visits, so his hosts were not overly troubled by protocol or complaints from China. But diplomatic business cannot be avoided in such circumstances. The upshot is to prod the southeast Asians into not formally kowtowing to Beijing as much as they normally would. Home opinion in Taiwan is reassured that the President is hob-nobbing amicably with his counterparts in southeast Asia, but the suspicions and bewilderment of the Chinese in Beijing are intensified. If that is coherent diplomacy, it needs better explaining. Lee's subsequent private visit to his alma mater – Cornell University – in the USA was an even bigger provocation to Beijing.

Jiang Zemin in 1995 forcefully opposed Taiwan's 'expanding its living space internationally'. The Taiwan Premier, Lien Chan, responded by calling for China and Taiwan to 'face reality, increase exchanges, respect each other and pursue eventual national reunification'. President Lee's first condition was for China to accept the 'reality of two separate governments'.[22] Yet both China and Taiwan seemed to be trying from time to time in

1995 to relax restrictions and keep the dialogue open. Then China staged live missile exercises close to the Taiwan coast in an apparent effort to influence the presidential elections there, upon which the Americans sent a warship to the area. The elections did not seem to be affected by the sabre-rattling, and another period of 'talking softly' ensued.

The West, for its part, would do well to make up its mind about the Taiwan tangle, calculate that reunification will take another twenty to thirty years if it happens at all, and then agree where exactly to place Taiwan meanwhile in the intricate network of international relationships. To take only the trade angle, Taiwan is now the USA's sixth largest trading partner, conducting almost twice as much trade with the USA as the Chinese mainland does. Yet it often sounded in recent years as if Most-Favoured-Nation tariff treatment for China and the copyright questions in Beijing were the Americans' biggest trade issues in Asia. Why should a vigorous, hard-working and conscientious state which has worked wonders in political and economic development be excluded from the world? Suitable stipulations could surely be devised to avoid any unnecessary aggravation of Beijing.

The Chinese target is to achieve a breakthrough in negotiations by 1999, and an actual realisation of reunification by 2004 – or 2009 at the latest.[23] But it may already be too late to unite Taiwan and China into a single state. The conditions were never better than in the 1980s, but those opportunities were not taken. Some wise heads believe that once the old soldiers who fought the civil war have been promoted to heaven, the impetus will go out of the reunification idea. 'The problems concerning the Taiwan issue,' China's former President Yang Shangkun once remarked, 'can be resolved more easily when people who know the history of both the Chinese Communist Party and the Guomindang are alive. If the issue is further postponed, there are many questions the younger generation of the parties do not understand. This is the reason behind our anxiety.'[24]

The best thing that Yang's colleagues could do for their younger generation would be to forget the old quarrels, make a few concessions and bring Taiwan together with China for the great future benefit of both. But the sourness of that desperate struggle to win China in the 1940s and the 1950s left only one surviving statesman of that generation capable of rising to the task, and he (Deng Xiaoping) has shot his bolt.

Taiwan is doomed to match its economic miracle and political freedoms with the deep and frustrating disappointment of being a society that forfeits the full status of independence. It fears what Mother China will do to it, and yet will not entirely abandon the dream of rehabilitation within the Chinese family. Which is a pity, because China could learn from a satisfied, secure and non-combative Taiwan the lesson that economic development leads to increased freedom, more democracy and respect for individual human beings, all safely manageable by a modestly efficient and public-spirited government. China needs all the stimulation it can get if it is to tread this nerve-racking uncharted path towards democracy via prosperity. Taiwan has shown the way, offering China a Chinese model of modernity. China will be the loser if it allows ancient ideological antagonisms to block the road.

CHAPTER 17

THE OVERSEAS CHINESE: OFFSHORE ASSETS

A retired British professor, chatting with a university colleague in China, was asked about declining British power in the world. 'When I was a schoolboy,' he replied, 'we were taught that the sun never sets on the British Empire.'

'We say,' his Chinese host countered, 'that the sun is always shining on a Chinese head. They are everywhere.'

It is true that there is hardly a country without Chinese citizens or residents, and they remain so discreet. How important are they? What is their ambition?

Estimates of their numbers vary, if only because definition is difficult. There has been much intermarriage with host nationalities, and once a Chinese takes up local nationality, his ethnicity may no longer be accurately recorded. But in southeast Asia, where they are mainly concentrated, there are more than 20 million ethnic Chinese, and, taking the world as a whole, the grand total would possibly be around 25 million. One might picture them as equivalent to another Chinese province, sparsely decanted into virtually every other country in the world.[1] To put it in proportionate terms, the Chinese diaspora represents almost 3 per cent of China's present population.[2]

Sometimes these Chinese used to be called the *Nanyang* Chinese. *Nanyang* means southern ocean, the picturesque Chinese term for southeast Asia, and that was their chief destination. More generally writers in China would refer to *huaqiao*, or 'Chinese sojourners abroad', and now some more modern terms are used.

The Taiwanese, Hongkongers and Macanese live in parts of China disputed between different Chinese governments, perhaps, or not quite yet retroceded by colonial powers, but still admitted as Chinese soil, and they should not therefore be lumped in with the southeast Asian Chinese. Chinese governments sometimes call residents of those three wayward Chinese places 'compatriots', a soubriquet denied to the overseas Chinese.[3]

Wang Gungwu, former Vice-Chancellor of Hongkong University, places the overseas Chinese among a new global phenomenon of 'cosmopolitan sojourners'. But the happiest label comes from Lynn Pan, who has recently suggested 'offshore Chinese' (she is one herself).[4]

The early waves of emigrants took great risks, because the emperors in their wisdom made emigration a crime. There had been a moment in the fifteenth century when the Chinese looked like becoming colonialists. They sent seven fleets under the eunuch admiral Zheng He across southeast Asia to East Africa, the Persian Gulf and India. But they began to run out of money, and maritime exploration was victim of one of the earliest budget cuts. China, it was felt, did not need the luxury of either foreign trade or diplomacy. The Chinese city in Luzon, in the Philippines, which could have become the centre of a Chinese empire, gradually crumbled and finally yielded to the Spanish.

It was the slightly later emigration of the eighteenth and nineteenth centuries, when the incentive to flee from economic depression was magnified, that created serious unofficial settlements in southeast Asia (by then under European colonial rule) and also in America. It was not too much to say that in the early decades of this century, Chinese traders followed European flags. Southeast Asia was, and still is, disproportionately rich in natural resources, and the European colonialists had imposed the political, legal and infrastructural conditions for these resources to be exploited. The British and the southeast Asians were not willing to do the hard physical work required: the Chinese were. This is how the Chinatowns found in so many of the world's cities began. A typical case was that of the sturdy inhabitants of the Guangdong city of Tangshan who almost monopolised the staffing of laundries and Chinese restaurants in the USA, as well as building thousands of miles of railway.

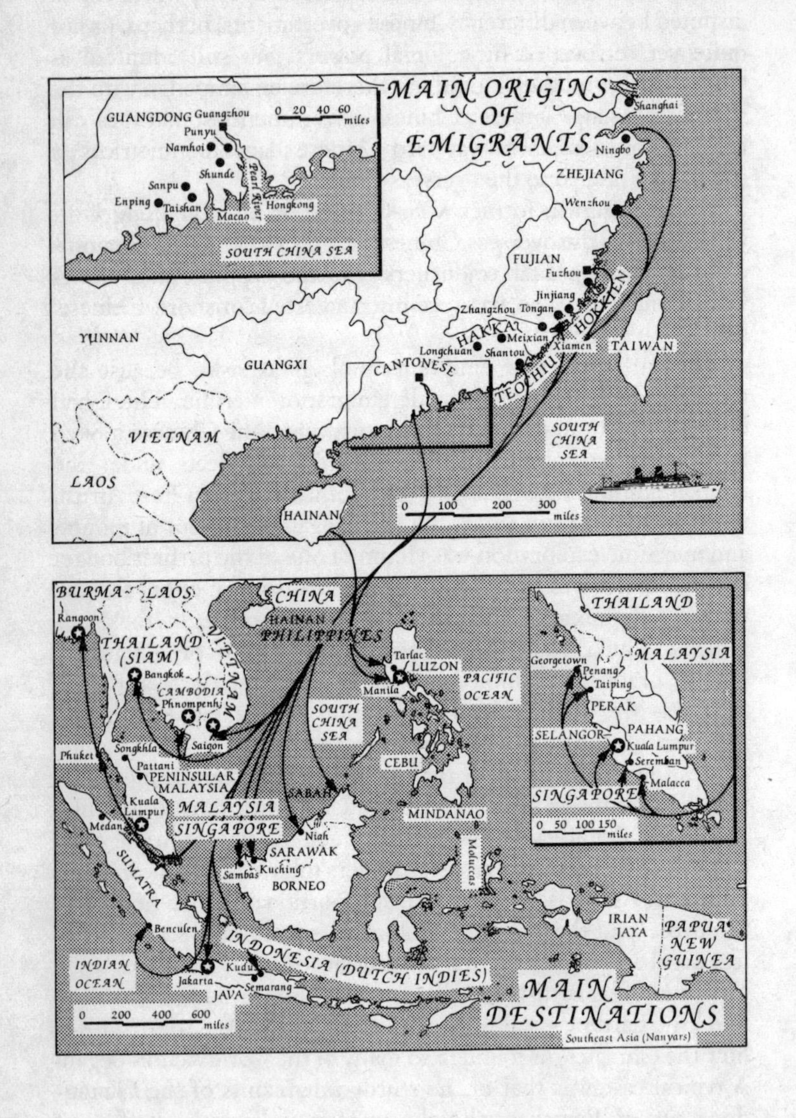

Overseas Chinese diaspora

Now history is turning around: Dewey Yee, whose parents had hailed from Tangshan, now travels almost weekly from Hongkong to China negotiating aircraft leases. He was the man behind the twinning of Washington D.C. with Beijing.[5] Thousands of other Tangshan descendants may be found doing high-level professional work in America and around the world, and they are beginning to return to China.

In southeast Asia the Chinese went on to play the role of middlemen, organising or supervising the hard work of plantations and mines. They often emerged rich in capital, and went on to dominate many sectors of the southeast Asian economies, first under the Europeans and later under the southeast Asian nationalist governments. One king of Thailand in the early part of this century wrote that, where money was concerned, the Chinese knew neither morals nor mercy. Their only god was Mammon. He called his composition *The Jews of the East*.

When local nationalism forced the Europeans out after the Second World War, the Chinese were able to stay put. But the incoming governments of southeast Asian nationalists were understandably envious and suspicious of Chinese business activity, and some plantations, mines and industries were nationalised. The Chinese in Indonesia, for instance, were not allowed to settle in rural areas in any numbers, nor were they permitted to operate their own schools, newspapers or political parties. The Indonesian government actually removed Chinese written characters from the Chinatown shopfronts and blacked them out of photographs in magazines. It made the Chinese take Indonesian surnames. But all that was worth the reward of having even a part of their previous business turnover, and there was always the hope of striking deals with individual rulers.

A role model here was Khaw Soo Cheang, who sailed from Fujian province to southern Siam, made himself indispensable to the Thai king and was rewarded with high office and the tin monopoly. His sons widened the family power by marrying into Thai nobility.[6]

Several decades later another brilliant south Chinese businessman made the same sort of voyage from the port of Shantou in Guangdong province. Dhanin Chearavanont's family had a seed shop which began to lose money in the great depression of the

1920s. It had already set up a branch in Bangkok which was more successful, and when the Communists conquered China in 1949 the family moved to Bangkok, where Dhanin spearheaded the expansion of the small family firm into the chicken-rearing, feedmill and hogmill businesses. The enterprise is now known as the Charoen Pokphand Group and is a multinational agribusiness with subsidiaries in at least six countries. It became the world's fifth largest feedmiller, but has its fingers into industry, property and communications as well.[7]

It left China because it feared Communist policies, but the group went back in the 1980s to invest in new feedmills. Dhanin now presides over a Chinese network of breweries, a petrochemical plant and even factories making motorcycles and cars. The offshore Chinese goes back on-shore with money and technology which his original homeland badly needs.

The other legendary tycoon among the southeast Asian *huaqiao* is Liem Sioe Liong, now the richest man in Indonesia but born a penurious Fujianese in 1916. As a teenager, he ran a noodle stall. Later, he sailed to Java to work in his uncle's peanut-oil venture. There he hacked his way to fortune in the *kretek* (cigarettes spiced with cloves) business, and later through war-time smuggling. He smuggled for the Indonesian army, and found himself dealing with a young officer called Suharto, who twenty years later became (and still is) President of the Indonesian Republic. In the Indonesian style, Liem's companies were then singled out for favoured treatment or monopolies, and those companies began to acquire partners from Suharto's family.[8]

Liem's wealth is now almost uncountable, but his story begins to explain why the Chinese, who account for only 2 per cent of the population of Indonesia, own three-quarters of its private domestic capital. It is the same across the region. Chinese in the Philippines are also only 2 per cent of the population, but they probably control half the capital. In Thailand they are 10 per cent of the population, with 80 per cent of the private wealth. In Malaysia they constitute almost 30 per cent of the population, but control over half of private wealth.[9]

An article in the *Australian* recently calculated the wealth of all Chinese living outside the People's Republic (so this figure would include Taiwan and Hongkong): their liquid assets except stockholdings may be worth up to US$2,000 billion – which is more than those of the Americans and Japanese combined. The growing financial and therefore political clout of these offshore Chinese is clear. Even China itself must need kowtow, as it were, to a population only 2 or 3 per cent of China's own. A meticulous survey by the Australian Department of Foreign Affairs shows these offshore Chinese generating about US$450 billion of Gross Domestic Product equivalent – almost as much as the 1.2 billion Chinese in China.[10]

Such conspicuous disproportion of wealth has sometimes maddened poor southeast Asian nationalists into violence. The worst pogrom was in Indonesia in 1965 when nationalists, including the army, waged war on the Indonesian Communist Party for allegedly attempting a coup d'état. Probably half a million people were shot, knifed, strangled or hacked to death, many of them Chinese whose links with China made them suspected of aiding the Communists. This was where Liem's friendship with Suharto became crucial, because Suharto then succeeded the rejected Sukarno as State President. But Liem Sioe Liong was later criticised by a senior official of Suharto's régime when he spent US$650,000 on a lavish party in Singapore to celebrate his fiftieth wedding anniversary. The money, the official said sourly, would have been better spent on the poor.[11] Even as late as 1993 there have been anti-Chinese riots in Indonesia. A Chinese factory-owner was beaten to death by an angry mob, and many Chinese shops, cars and homes were damaged.

Tensions are also high in Malaysia, and yet the Chinese, because of their numbers, feel able to form their own political parties there. In the 1969 elections these parties did better than expected, so the Chinese held victory parades which jolted xenophobic young Malays into street-fighting in Kuala Lumpur. Two hundred people were killed. This led the government to bring in a New Economic Policy designed to bridge the economic gap between rich Chinese and poor Malays. But the Malays' stake of the corporate economy is still hardly more than one-third. One or two southeast Asian countries have virtually expelled their Chinese communities: most of the Vietnamese boat people who sailed to Malaysia and Hongkong and elsewhere in search of freedom were actually ethnic Chinese.

The guarantee against violent racial tension in the future must be the assimilation of the Chinese into their host societies. This has been a trend all along. As Teresita Ang See of Manila puts it, 'Our blood may be Chinese but our roots grow deep in the Philippine soil and our hearts are with the Philippine people.'

The earliest Chinese immigrants in southeast Asia, invariably males, married local women and began to take up local culture. The Peranakans of Java, for example, saw themselves as Chinese – but as Indies-born they felt different from other Chinese. Many of them lost their use of the Chinese language, or abandoned chopsticks. Their counterparts in Malaya were the Straits Chinese or *babas*, who acquired some Malay blood and English culture, drinking brandy and soda and playing billiards in their exclusive clubs, all the time despising those unacculturated Chinese who remained impervious to the improving Western influence. In the Philippines one Chinese *mestizo*, José Rizal, became the father of Philippine nationalism.

It is almost impossible now to draw a clear line in Thailand between the Chinese community and people of purely Thai descent. Here there has been more assimilation than anywhere else, throwing up a very large élite group of Sino-Thais. The proportion of the total Thai population which has some Chinese blood, including the royal family and all the leading politicians and professional men and women, is very high.[12] Buddhism made a big difference, being shared by the Thais and the Chinese immigrants, whereas Islam, with its lesser status for women and its interdiction of pork, the favourite food of south China, repelled the Chinese in Indonesia or Malaysia.

Whether you are Chinese or not can therefore be a puzzle, not always as simple as working out the arithmetic of the blood. Sino-Thai people with one Chinese grandparent may or may not think of themselves as Chinese, largely depending on whether that grandparent was male or female, but also determined by a complex web of social, intellectual and psychological circumstances.

This leads to what some writers now call the 'double identity' situation, where a person's Chineseness may be hidden in public, and brought into play only in the performing of Chinese traditional rituals, for instance, or in private relationships. A Thai Chinese studying at an Australian university once made friends with another Thai student, but did not realise that he, too, was Thai Chinese until several months later he chanced upon him taking part in a private ancestor-worship ritual for his grandfather.

Language is one measure of assimilation, since overseas Chinese tend gradually to lose their command of the written characters and even the Chinese spoken tongues. Most southeast Asian governments have clamped down on Chinese-language schools, requiring young Chinese to go through the local language streams. Chinese education is still found in Singapore and Malaysia, but elsewhere it is disappearing. In any case, the off-shore Chinese were never homogeneous in language, bringing from China a number of different and mutually incomprehensible dialects and sub-languages.

A final difficulty is that the level of knowledge of Mandarin, the Chinese *lingua franca*, is relatively poor, a southeast Asian Chinese having to cope first with his own dialect (perhaps Hokkien) and then with Malay or *Bahasa Indonesia* and English. Only very recently has there been a market, so to speak, for Mandarin because of the new intercourse with China.

All but a few per cent of the ethnic Chinese in southeast Asia today were born there, so assimilation becomes a natural process. It also creates a cultural generation gap. A first-generation Thai Chinese in a famous novel blamed himself for the loss of his children's Chineseness: 'I could not shelter them from the thousands of experiences which made them another people, another race. There were so many of us here, yet the Thais have won.'[13] (Many Thais, of course, would put it the other way round, that the Chinese have 'won'.) But the beauty of the Thai situation is that nobody seriously complains, and everybody can take some advantage of his or her situation.

'We are ethnic Chinese,' said Senior Minister Lee Kuan Yew of Singapore, 'but we must be honest and recognise that at the end of the day our fundamental loyalties are to our home country, not to China ... After two or three generations away from China, we have become rooted in the country of our birth. Our stakes are in our home countries, not in China where our ancestors came from ... [We] invest in and visit China frequently, but few want to make China their home.'[14]

On that occasion Lee was repeating what a senior Chinese leader, Qiao Shi, head of the National People's Congress in Beijing, had advised. Qiao told a Thai Chinese gathering at the end of 1993 that China wanted them to abide by the laws of their countries of residence, to live in amity with local people and contribute to their economic prosperity. 'We approve of and support the acquisition by the overseas Chinese of the nationality of their countries of residence of their own will. Those who have acquired such nationality should show their loyalty to the countries where they have become citizens and fulfil their corresponding obligations.'[15]

Many offshore Chinese do not need such advice. 'Malaysia is my home,' says Lai Kuan Fook. 'I was born here, I will die here. My children are here. When I go to China, one week is enough. We are committed to Malaysia.'[16] There are Malaysian Chinese for whom the advice grates. When Sim Kwan Yang, a member of the Malaysian parliament, heard Premier Li Peng on a visit to Kuala Lumpur lecture the local Chinese on their duty to behave as good Malaysian citizens, he asked himself: 'Who was he to tell us to be good Malaysians?'[17]

The economic achievements of the Newly Industrialising Economies of East Asia, coupled with the general growth and networking of intra-Pacific trade and investment, not to mention the transformation of China itself, all make it less important for the southeast Asian Chinese to assimilate. Furthermore, the southeast Asian nation-states have grown visibly in confidence, leaving behind the occasionally paranoid anti-Chinese reflexes which were perhaps a necessary adjunct to the intricate process of nation-building. Now the southeast Asian governments are not only more confident in dealing with their Chinese communities, but have also downgraded their instinctive fear of China itself, building better political relationships with Beijing instead. China, for its part, has abandoned support for southeast Asian insurgency and has developed substantial trade and investment with southeast Asia.

The southeast Asian Chinese is no longer the local rural moneylender or merchant who grows rich by exploiting the peasants and then takes his bank balance back home to China to see out his days in his native village in comfort. Instead there is a new type of international Chinese, who may have not just dual but triple nationality, feeling at home wherever the profits are most attractive. His brothers and children may be scattered around the Asia-Pacific region, one in California, one in Hongkong, one in Singapore, and so on. Having so many places of residence is a good way of keeping tax inspectors and immigration officials at bay.[18]

Many of the overseas Chinese are involved in some way with the new economic miracle that is China. Some go out of patriotism, others for sentiment or nostalgia, or for family reasons, but probably most go because they see an opportunity there to make money. An Indonesian businessman says: 'I think the Chinese are tired [of Indonesia]: they will keep their investments here, but profits will go to China. The Chinese are going back to China.' Wong Siu-lun of Hongkong University sees this trend to return home 'in an ultimate sense'. The overseas Chinese have a strong feeling for ancestral roots. 'They want the status that comes with the recognition conferred on them by their birthplace, or the birthplace of their ancestors.'[19]

If southeast Asian Chinese had been found out remitting money to China in the 1960s or even 1970s they would probably have been censured for illegal capital flight. Today the Malaysian Prime Minister and Philippine President take large entourages of their local Chinese businessmen with them on official visits to China in order to demonstrate their confidence in the loyalty of their Chinese citizens, and also to get the best business deals.

Time Magazine reported in 1993 that the southeast Asian Chinese were now for the first time 'bonding with the mainland to create something like a nation with borders ... linked by blood'.[20] To inject the concept of blood into this discussion is not liked by the Chinese or by the southeast Asian governments. But it is common ground that the southeast Asian Chinese are thwarted of their earlier opportunities for profit. There are now ethnic quota restrictions on what a Chinese contractor can do in Malaysia. The big projects must go to *bumiputras* (sons of the soil, i.e. Malays) yet in China that same Chinese contractor 'might get a contract to build a whole town'.[21] What more natural, while remaining resident in southeast Asia, than to seek business in China.

The southeast Asian Chinese come back from their visits to China with differing impressions. Some are starry-eyed after first seeing their ancestral villages. Most are soberly shocked to see how far China still lags behind. 'For me,' says Chote Sophonpanich of the Bangkok Bank family, 'returning to China is a bit like an American returning to his country of origin in Europe. Though my father came from China, I was born and brought up here in Thailand. I have no close friends there. I am interested in China, but no more than that.'[22]

The political and personal spectrum of the southeast Asian Chinese is very wide: some of them welcome China's re-invigoration while others see it as irrelevant to them. China, too, has travelled the spectrum in attitude to its overseas children, from seeing them as deserters or dropouts to welcoming them as know-alls. Whatever the attitudes, China is attracting more direct investment from abroad than any other Asian country, and much of that is from the pockets of the overseas Chinese.

The next step is to have more formal organisation of offshore Chinese businessmen, for example in the World Chinese Entrepreneurs' Conference, the brainchild of Lee Kuan Yew. The second of these conferences, held in Hongkong in 1993, was described by one observer as 'a celebration of Chinese triumphalism'. Actually the conferees were mostly from the more recent destinations of emigrating Chinese, namely Australia, the United States and Canada. These are countries where the arriving immigrant from China usually expects to go straight into a professional or commercial job. A century ago their counterparts would have sweated it out on the railroads, but now their entry is a soft one.

The ancestors of the offshore Chinese led the resistance to the conquering Manchus in the seventeenth century, and then assisted the overthrow of the ensuing Qing dynasty in the early twentieth century, sheltering and financing Republican nationalist leaders. But when the anti-business Communists won the civil war, a disillusionment with China set in among the richer overseas Chinese. Only in the last ten to fifteen years has their interest revived, lured by the new commercial opportunities and comforted by Beijing's restitution to Aw Boon Haw, the Singapore 'Tiger Balm' King, of his property and funds in China which had been confiscated during the years of Mao. Mr Kitty Dumnernchanwanit, one of Thailand's mega-millionaires, put his name in 1992 to a US$ 1 billion forestry and paper-making project in Guangdong province. 'I am a Chinese,' Kitty clarified, 'but I was born in Thailand. I always realise that for a human being it is a must to bring progress and prosperity to his country of origin.'[23]

The Chinese, whether onshore or offshore, never give away a figure or a fact if they can help it, but it is generally believed that about 10 per cent of the foreign-funded enterprises in China are financed by southeast Asian Chinese capital. Singaporean companies alone, encouraged by their government, have invested more than US$ 1 billion. This is mostly praised by the world outside under the heading of patriotism, though in the context of Western coolness after Tiananmen it might be said unintentionally to have helped Deng Xiaoping to stave off a Communist collapse.

Some overseas Chinese, on the other hand, agree with Lai Kuan Fook that 'one week in China is enough', as if it were a painful or boring duty to visit there. They would echo the snide comment of a fellow-overseas Chinese that 'We love China best when we are far away.' Very few active overseas Chinese want to live in China, although some of the sentimental ones would like to die there.

Using European administration and indigenous southeast Asian labour, the Chinese have changed the face of southeast Asia, to place it in the front ranks of today's economically developing regions. Now that energy is partly transferred to China. The example of the overseas Chinese and their apparent success has been a major influence on the recent generation of Chinese leaders, and was probably instrumental in Deng Xiaoping's opening up the Chinese economy to world trade and investment.

The case of Singapore is illuminating. Here is a city-state with a 75 per cent Chinese population surrounded by much larger Indonesian or Malaysian neighbours and yet inheriting a British colonial administrative structure. Singapore is Chinese in the sense that its affairs are decided by a small caucus of politicians of south Chinese stock. But the city-state can always field a minority

Indian face when a negotiating impression needs to be made on outsiders, whether in southeast Asia, the Indian subcontinent or the West. All of Singapore's foreign ministers since independence have been of Indian origin, and it sends big investment missions to India balancing those to China.

Nowadays things have become sufficiently relaxed at ministerial meetings of the Association of Southeast Asian Nations (ASEAN) for it to be difficult sometimes to tell who is who, because they can all look Chinese, such is the successful penetration of the Chinese (except in Malaysia) into the higher political and bureaucratic ranks. When ministers from China and ASEAN met in Hangzhou in 1995 for a regular conference on politics and security, the Chinese Vice-Foreign Minister shared the chair with Brunei's Lim Jock Seng![24]

Casting around the world for encouragement and example, Deng Xiaoping's aides lighted on Singapore with delight. Here was a state, albeit a small one, largely Chinese and run on Chinese lines, which operated a very successful capitalism and followed a parliamentary political structure under an unashamedly strong ruling party which never gave up power, not even in a single constituency, if possible. Here were political leaders who were pragmatic and yet idealistic. In the result Lee Kuan Yew and the former finance minister, Goh Keng Swee, and other ministers became prominent economic advisers to China. Lee Kuan Yew led missions of Singapore businessmen and masterminded huge investment projects, for example at Suzhou. Goh Keng Swee, the man behind the Jurong industrial town which was the pioneer in artificially boosted manufacturing industry in Asia, gave the Chinese advice on their Special Economic Zones in the coastal areas.

More than this, the Chinese lapped up the Singaporean experience of applying Chinese 'Confucian' ideology, whether in tough punishments for crime, unabashed intrusions into private life over matters of eugenics and morality or fudging the line between the state and private owners in the economy. The unalloyed admiration which China shows towards Singapore is enlightening. The normally staid *Legal Daily* of Beijing was over the moon about the Singapore retailer who was fined S$52,000 for not marking the price on a handbag he put up for sale on his shelf. Such rule of law was, the paper extolled, a powerful deterrent which made Singapore 'a place famous for its economic prosperity, good social order, civilization, courteous citizenry, stunning beauty and hygiene'. Another periodical in Beijing waxed lyrical about Singapore's success in beating corruption, and especially keeping bureaucrats on the straight and narrow through the Provident Fund, which put their pensions at risk if they stepped out of line by accepting bribes.[25]

Yet Lee Kuan Yew had been ahead of his time in discreetly cultivating Taiwan in the period before China opened up under Deng Xiaoping. By 1992 he had paid twenty-one visits to Taiwan, and Singapore received in return two Prime Ministers and a President from Taiwan. Soldiers from Singapore have been trained in Taiwan for many years, going for three or six months to army bases in Hukou or near Kaohsiung. So close did the relationship appear, that many speculated that Lee Kuan Yew had been asked to play the role of bridge or matchmaker with Beijing. Certainly the Communists did not object to these visits. Probably the Communists believed that Singapore's dual relations with Beijing and Taipei benefited not only Singapore's survival as an independent state but also China's interests in Singapore. Lee Kuan Yew's policy has always been to achieve a balance of the big powers in southeast Asia, and a 'multi-sustaining' formula for regional security. In this respect, Singapore sees Beijing as a positive factor.

But Beijing also sees Singapore as a base for maintaining and promoting Chinese culture among the overseas Chinese in southeast Asia. Active cultural exchange programmes have been arranged between China and Singapore on Confucian studies, language and art. Finally, China sees Singapore as providing a business springboard for China, not only to southeast Asia, but even to the whole world, including prosperous Taiwan. Singapore's location, and its strong links with Western transnational corporations explain this. Taipei recently announced that it would promote Singapore instead of Hongkong as its main channel of investment into China. The Economics Minister, Vincent Siew, explained that Singapore, which had investment guarantee pacts with both Taiwan and China, was a better base for Taiwan subsidiaries in China.[26] It will of course be more independent of

China than Hong Kong will be after 1997.

One interpretation of what the overseas Chinese are doing in China today is that they are helping to deliver back to China the traditional cultural values which are helpful to economic development but were suppressed by Mao while they flowered in southeast Asia. Professor Gordon Redding of the University of Hongkong analyses overseas Chinese capitalism as having three distinguishing features.[27] The first is paternalism, because the family is pivotal in society, with the father figure at its centre. The second is 'personalism', because people rely not on the impersonal rule of law but on bonding with another person as the basis of any transaction, using *guanxi*. Thirdly insecurity, because the sense of uncertainty under which overseas Chinese have laboured in southeast Asia raised the value of their hard work, intensified their urge to accumulate wealth and strengthened their will to control their environment. Of these three hallmarks, only the third, which is in essence a Toynbeean process of challenge and response, is peculiar to the overseas Chinese: the first two could equally well describe Deng Xiaoping's 'capitalism with Chinese characteristics' in China.

A visit to almost any part of China these days would show factories or other enterprises wholly or partly financed by overseas Chinese whose representatives are unconsciously reintroducing traditional cultural values that had been savaged by Mao and almost driven underground. Today the people who most personify the new amalgam of Chinese tradition and cosmopolitan Westernised modernity are the overseas Chinese investors and managers to whom such synthesis is almost second nature. So they filter modernity for the inward-looking Chinese, making it more palatable than when it comes directly from the West. Even Japanese firms which often have problems dealing with Chinese workers in their joint venture factories in China are turning to overseas Chinese to manage their enterprises or at least be middlemen.

The élite among the overseas Chinese community already has a transnational character, with entrepreneurial families based in more than one country. They will come into their own if and when Taiwan is reunified, and their influence is two-way. The overseas Chinese filter Western ideas for Chinese consumption, but they also stand ready for the successful promotion of Chinese culture, including political and business culture, on the world stage.

From any point of view, whether Western or Chinese, the offshore Chinese have already contributed richly to the life of the world, from the pianist Fu Ts'ong to the architect I.M. Pei, from the American astronaut Leroy Chiao to the creator of 'The Saint', Leslie Charteris. Their success gains them invitations to advise not merely the authorities in their own host state, but those in China as well. Lee Kuan Yew, who lectures all over the world about how to run human affairs, has now been asked by President Nelson Mandela to help decide what to do in a totally different corner of humanity, in South Africa.[28]

In many parts of the world, especially in southeast Asia, the worry was that Chinese culture might prove superior to others by such a margin that the Chinese state would knock the rest of the world politically for six. The living proof of that was thought to be the overseas Chinese. An early assault on such thinking came from Maurice Freedman, who found, to the contrary, that the Chinese in southeast Asia were good at assimilating, perhaps because they had no other choice, but that when they did assimilate, 'their specifically Chinese culture has often been weathered away.'[29]

Chinese culture is certainly strong; it has been matured over millennia, for the most part with less sustained influence from outside societies than other comparable civilisations. If there is a superiority, however, it is a marginal one, and could not compensate the overseas Chinese for being in a small arithmetical minority in southeast Asia. The southeast Asian Chinese have all had to agonise whether to seek salvation from their inner Chineseness, or from their outward southeast Asian-ness.

They solved their problem in different ways. Some feel so fully assimilated and satisfied that they feel no particular pull to China, resist visiting the 'homeland', and readily join Europeans and others in faint contempt for China's deficiencies. Others, perhaps reacting against their early experiences of discrimination and prejudice from their Thai, Indonesian or Malay hosts, feel a definite bond with China, and are willing to join in the upswing of China's reputation in the world. The two attitudes co-exist, not only in each Chinese community in southeast Asia, but sometimes within a family or even within individuals.

For practical purposes outsiders may safely assume that the large majority of ethnic Chinese in southeast Asia have thrown in their lot with their host countries and will not be a destabilising factor – except for their temptation to make an inordinate amount of money and thereby alienate the host country, risking resentment and violence against them (depending on the growth rates in southeast Asian economies).

In the rest of the world the Chinese are answerable for a looser intrusion: past emigration there from China has been small. Europe boasts only about 100,000 Chinese, and the world-wide total outside China, Taiwan and southeast Asia may not be more than a million. Emigration is on an individual or familial basis, so that local interests are hardly threatened and tensions can be minimised. These days, if you organise a student uprising in China which (predictably) fails, you will most likely end up in Los Angeles, New York, Paris, Sydney, San Francisco, Vancouver or London. Your arrival in those places will be hardly noticed in a social sense, although the newspapers may play you up for a while, and you will quickly settle down to a programme of study or professional work, reserving the possibility later of either returning to China under a change of government or of government policy, or staying in the Western country of your choice, especially if your wife and children wish it.[30] That is a loss to China, perhaps a small one, but a real one nevertheless – and a small corresponding gain to the Western country. Both China and the West will benefit in one way, however, in that this new breed of emigrant from China will be an outstanding channel for legitimising and popularising Chinese culture in the Western mind and thus reducing misunderstanding.

CHAPTER 18

GREATER CHINA: ONLY RECONNECT

The key to China's movement towards economic integration beyond its legal borders is what happened at the slow, winding, sluggish and grossly polluted river Shenzhen which divides Hongkong from the People's Republic. Throughout the 1950s and 1960s goods were quietly traded across this little frontier, and gradually others came to realise the significance of this commercial exchange between a tightly controlled Communist economy on the one hand, and an almost totally uncontrolled *laissez-faire* economy on the other hand. Taiwan exporters sent some goods via Hongkong across the Shenzhen river, and importers from other states took delivery of mainland products at the Hongkong railway station after arrival from China. That was as far as things went under Mao Zedong, but when Deng Xiaoping opened China's door and introduced his economic reforms, the way was open for such trans-ideological trade to be replicated across other frontiers.

Huang Chih-lien, a Harvard graduate and professor of history at Hongkong's Baptist College, threw out the idea in the 1980s of a South China Economic Union or trading bloc, to comprise four Chinese provinces (Guangdong, Fujian, Guangxi and Hainan) with Macao, Taiwan and Hongkong. Intellectuals on both sides of the Taiwan Strait were receptive: a Taiwan journal had urged as early as 1979 a Chinese Common Market embracing those territories as well as Singapore.[1]

Some Chinese intellectuals fear the disintegrative effect of a 'Greater China' upon China itself. Yet Chen Yicun and Li Jiaquan of the Chinese Academy of Social Sciences in Beijing both supported Huang's proposition. Yan Mingfu, head of the

Communist Party's United Front Department in Beijing, expressed the hope that Taiwan would co-operate. Deng Xiaoping himself commented that the scheme 'wasn't a bad idea', though he urged Chinese officials not to discuss it in public because if Beijing promoted it Taiwan might suspect an ulterior motive, and other countries might misread into it a new 'yellow peril'.[2]

In 1988–89 this idea was much debated informally, especially in Hongkong where Professor Huang and Dr Edward Chen of Hongkong University were active publicists. Some hoped that Hongkong would become the 'Brussels' or secretariat of the new organisation. The Taiwan economist and publisher, Kao Tsi-jun, was keen, but in the end Taiwan remained officially cautious for the reason anticipated by Deng. The Communists were well known for using trade as a political ploy, and Taiwan needed to avoid excessive dependence on Chinese raw material supplies or markets.[3]

Early in 1992 an international symposium 'On Coordination of the Chinese Economic System' was organised in Hongkong. For three days scholars, officials and businessmen from the four 'Chinese' economies exchanged views. President Jiang Zemin had ordered high-level studies to be made of the Taiwan–Hongkong proposal, and the Chinese now suggested that all of China south of the Yangzi – and even, at a later stage, northwest China and Singapore as well – become involved. The talk in Hongkong during this conference was buoyantly forward-looking. Apart from unnecessary bickering with Taiwan (Beijing's Li Jiaquan observed that co-operation could not be on the basis of sovereign states because Taiwan and Hongkong were both parts of China), the Chinese were at their most positive. A Greater China Trade Community could be formed without tariffs and with a free flow of technology, capital and labour, though the word 'community' was later dropped because it suggested early integration on the European model. Chinese Americans would supply brainpower and capital. The progress would be in three stages, from economic co-operation to economic co-ordination and finally economic integration.[4]

'You Westerners,' a Shanghai economist delegate told foreign reporters, 'are forming your blocs, so the Chinese race will unite to form its own. It is only natural for us Chinese to compete with you.'[5] The tone of that remark suggests that political emotions rather than economics do indeed lie behind the Chinese interest, and that serious homework has still to be done to cost what benefits and losses may accrue to China by opening *all* its doors to its southern co-Chinese neighbours. The institutional framework may be a long time forming, with heavy political implications for both Taipei and Beijing, but the trade and investment are on tall waves which will simply wash away many of the obstacles in their path.[6]

At the end of 1993, Qin Yongmin composed a dissidents' Peace Charter in Beijing which included the rousing summons: 'we urge all Chinese and descendants of the Yellow Emperor all over the world to join us'.[7] The agenda of China's redemption is not merely for the 1.2 billion in China, but also for the 25 million ethnic – 'offshore' – Chinese all over the world. The process begins with a certain continuity of cultural links, but leads rapidly into matters of trade and finance, and then at last reaches the amphitheatre of political institutions. Such developments, if they are ever realised, would alter the power balance of east Asia and heighten China's influence in the world by perhaps a half.

Economic necessity has led China's provinces along an autonomous path. The mutual attraction of cross-border trade has given provincial governments a new role as almost paradiplomatic actors in China's foreign trade.[8] Former parts of China which were ideologically estranged have come together for the exchange of goods, services and funds. A recent estimate of the total cross-investment between China, Hongkong and Taiwan is US$40 billion.

This South China Economic Circle, which has been the leader of the movement all along, driven by the vigorous free enterprise of Hongkong and Taiwan, may be heading in a political direction – though with quite distinct political goals sought by each of the three economic partners. China expects the economic circle to load the future in favour of eventual smooth political reunification with both Hongkong (which is now assured) and Taiwan (which is not). Hongkong hopes for a bigger Chinese stake in the British colony, which will make the transition to Chinese sovereignty in 1997 easier and hopefully lessen the risk of China taking action harmful to Hongkong afterwards. As for Taiwan, it believes that the build-up of economic links across the Strait will provide enough commercial advantage to China to give Taiwan a lever for wresting political concessions from China.

The process by which China's provinces become more autonomous and therefore more capable of conducting their own economic relations with foreign states beyond the Chinese border is linked with the pressure from some intellectuals and professionals for China to become a federal state. Yan Jiaqi, who under Zhao Ziyang's supremacy in the 1980s directed the Institute of Political Science of the Chinese Academy of Social Sciences, but who later chose foreign exile, made a detailed proposal for a Chinese federation based on democracy, in order to reform China's domestic politics and resolve the reunification problems of Hongkong and Taiwan as well as the special

GREATER CHINA
IN THE WORLD

1992	GNP (US$ billion)	Population (millions)	Area ('000 sq.kms)	Trade (US$ billion)
'Greater China' including China, Taiwan, Macao, Hongkong and Singapore	800	1,180	9,635	287
USA	5,905	249	9,156	1,002
Japan	3,508	124	376	573
Germany	1,846	80	366	839
Britain	1,025	56	244	402
Russia	398	147	17,071	68
India	272	844	3,286	45

When the other 'Chinese' states are included, China's performance relative to other powers is enhanced. The GNP is twice that of Russia's and not far behind Britain's. The population is the biggest in the world, and the area second only to Russia's. The combined trade is four times Russia's and six times India's – and 'Greater China' is growing economically faster than any of them.

difficulties of Tibet.[9] The initiative fell on stony ground, but it remains a theoretical option for China of considerable interest.

Taiwan's overriding demand in any new set-up is for equal status with the People's Republic on the mainland, otherwise it would amount to legitimised subjection to Communist Party dictation. Hence the Taipei call for 'one country, two governments'. If Beijing were to devolve more authority to its provinces, and create a federal national government of some kind, this would enormously facilitate the reunification drive. Taiwan is able so far to avoid becoming economically dependent on China: despite the dramatic growth of the cross-Strait traffic, Taiwan's trade with the Chinese mainland remains less than 10 per cent of its global trade. China and Hongkong cannot avoid a higher degree of interdependence: almost one-fifth of China's GNP now derives from Hongkong.

In the longer sweep of history, current moves regarding economic circles could be painted as a partial return to the territorial integrity of the medieval Chinese empire which is now split into five separate parts: China itself, Taiwan, Hongkong, the Mongolian Republic and Macao. This raises in many thoughtful Chinese minds a potential issue of patriotic duty and idealism on top of the commercial base.

The next conference on Greater China was in Hongkong in 1993. That saw much discussion about the term 'Greater China', which many participants considered vague, pejorative and expansionist. Professor Wang Gungwu preferred a lower profile, and put forward 'Lesser China' as a better title for the South China economic zone. But the discussants at the Hongkong conference saw one virtue in the Greater China label, namely its informality. It enables the territories involved to push ahead with their economic relations, and even with certain administrative, political, diplomatic and legal institutional adjustments to smooth the path of commerce, but without forcing political institutions into an uncomfortable harness.

Informal relationships are second nature to Chinese who have to deal with their own public life on the basis of *guanxi*. Never has the task of re-harnessing Chinese outside the immediate Chinese fold with their compatriots at home been less difficult. Chinese societies all over the world, including those in the West as well as in southeast Asia and in the various distinct parts of China, are interacting with one another on an increasing scale. Their desire to do so coincides with the gradual collapse of the political and administrative barriers which used to stand in the way of such intercourse. Having left home, or at least escaped the authority of the Chinese ruler, the offshore Chinese can now begin to reconnect with their original homeland on terms of minimum sacrifice or commitment. By the same token, China is more open to internationalisation through its lost children than ever before.

There is a cultural underlay to this development which is not only to do with traditional cultures, although those obviously play a significant part in the reconnection. The autonomy trend in China itself finds cultural expression in a renewed interest among Guangzhou, Taipei and Shanghai intellectuals in their own local as distinct from national history. They are more engrossed in regional folk religion and culture, there is greater use of local dialect, and less interest in high national culture or the use of *guoyu*, the Mandarin speech. In south China the so-called *gangtai*, or popular culture shared by Hongkong and Taiwan, was acclaimed by many young mainland Chinese in the 1980s, and the cult is still not over.[10] Every other household in Guangdong province probably watches Hongkong television.

There are now so many economic zones of one kind or another in Guangdong province that all combinations seem possible. Wang Cho has urged the Chinese government to make Hongkong, Shenzhen and Daya Bay (site of the controversial nuclear power plant) into an open economic zone to facilitate rural Guangdong's trade with the outside world.[11] By taking in the southern Chinese coast right up to Shanghai, including Fujian, an entity sometimes called Greater South China is identified. A major factor in all these developments has been the pioneering role of the adjoining provinces of Guangdong and Fujian in reforming and liberalising foreign trade, and it was this that gave them so much bargaining power *vis-à-vis* the central government. There will be no way of stopping the spread of Open Door activity along this coast.

The Yangzi Economic Circle focuses on Shanghai although, as Zheng Yong-Nian points out, Shanghai's development has been rather independent of its neighbouring provinces. A Shanghai

Economic Zone Planning Office was set up in the middle of the 1980s to co-ordinate such operations, but has little as yet to show for it. There is a psychological factor at work: 'The leaders and people in Zhejiang, Jiangsu and Anhui always believe that they have been victimised by Shanghai, and they regard it as a colonial centre.' Unwillingness to co-operate with their metropolis is reinforced by the fact that these are relatively rich provinces which do not have to form coalitions for collective bargaining with either the centre or a metropolis.[12]

The Bohai Circle includes the Shandong and Liaodong peninsulas and Tianjin, encircling the Bohai Sea and looking out to the Yellow Sea. These areas look hopefully, and with historical support, to trade and investment from Germany and other European countries but also reckon to attract capital from Japan and South Korea. They are establishing a common market for foreign trade, a series of North China Commodity Fairs patterned on the Guangdong fairs, and an international company for Bohai Sea management.

The four Bohai cities of Qingdao, Yantai, Qinhuangdao and Dalian, all important in their own right and attracting more than US$1 billion a year in South Korean and other foreign investment, have agreed to specialise among themselves in industries and services, and to collaborate in orderly exploitation and conservation of the Bohai Sea. Tianjin is often named as the 'capital' of this region, and in that role would lead the Bohai Zone producers with their Korean partners into the hyperactive Beijing–Tianjin industrial corridor.[13]

Even further up the coast is the very new Special Economic Zone of Hunchun, which the Chinese would like to turn into a river port on the Sea of Japan at the hub of the United Nations-sponsored Tumen River Area Development Programme. This neglected corner of Asia where Russia, China and North Korea meet will flower, it is hoped, with investments from Korea and Japan, and would also offer landlocked Mongolia a badly needed additional outlet to the western Pacific. Whether the necessary international collaboration for this project is forthcoming remains to be seen. The legal, tariff, currency financing and siting arrangements were discussed by the countries concerned in Beijing in 1992, but so far it is just talk, and other countries are not enthusiastic.[14] Meanwhile China is making sure that its territory will be prepared to draw maximum benefit from whatever emerges.

The Chinese have begun their own debate on the larger issue of international collaboration across the entire northeast Asian economy, covering Japan, the two Koreas, Mongolia, Siberia and the Russian Far East – and, of course, China, though it is not really clear whether they mean the whole of China or merely the northern half. 'The diminishing political confrontation in this area,' Zhang Pan, Deputy Director of the State Council's Development Research Centre, told a Beijing seminar in 1991, 'has created a favourable atmosphere for multilateral economic activities and raised greater possibilities in the forming of a regional economic zone.' One of his colleagues predicted that 'this region will probably turn into one of the most economically developed areas on the globe in the next century.' To these dreamers on the grander scale the Tumen project is a mere experimental seed-bed.

A particular feature of the northeast developments is the Korean angle. The Tumen delta is the focal point of the two-million-strong Korean ethnic minority in China, and the place where those Koreans meet counterpart Korean residents of Russia, so that it may not be an exaggeration to talk of Tumen as an outlet for 'overseas' Korean energies. For South Korea the Shandong peninsula lying south of the Bohai Sea is not only a site of traditional links with China but also a heaven-sent destination for its domestic industries made uncompetitive by rising costs at home.

Just as Taiwan ignores political differences in order to relocate in Fujian or Shanghai, so anti-Communist South Korea asserts a disdain for ideology by investing in nearby Shandong. It began in 1990 with ships running between Weihai in China and Inchon in South Korea. After Seoul exchanged diplomatic recognition with Beijing in 1992, hundreds of Korean businessmen descended with blueprints – for an international airport and for scores of automobile, electronics and similar industrial projects, all in Korean-speaking areas full of low-wage ethnic Koreans. In the first four months following recognition more than 440 Korean investment proposals were approved. Korean tourists started to roam through Weihai, local shops began to put up signs in the

Korean language, Korean Chinese found lucrative jobs as interpreters, and Korean lessons for Chinese students in Shandong University were a sell-out.[15]

'We'll be moving all our production over here,' explains Kim Co Duk, a Korean electronics manufacturer. 'The corporate headquarters will remain in Korea, along with our technicians, marketing, quality control and trade departments. But manufacturing will all be over here.' 'Here' means in his case the town of Songchun on the Shandong coast where 180 young farm girls assemble Kim's transformers for less than £50 a month.

Moving now to the other side of China, a southwest China circle is institutionalised in the Regional Economic Coordination Association of Southwest China, which seeks to develop trade with the south and southeast Asian countries. Sichuan, Guizhou, Yunnan and Tibet are the four provinces involved, but because they are all inland provinces Guangxi has been allowed to join, in order to provide access to the sea. They will pursue trade with Burma, Laos, Thailand and Vietnam.

A northwest circle connects China with the Central Asian republics. Ningxia leaders have proposed an Interior Special Economic Zone to attract Islamic investment into China's northwestern provinces, which have already opened cross-border trade. Xinjiang is expected to develop trade with Kazakhstan, and a Sino-Kazakh Joint Development Zone was set up in 1993.[16]

The unexpected success of the Special Economic Zones along China's shoreline where 1.2 billion consumers meet traders and shippers from two hundred nations can go to Chinese heads. Some academics and officials hit upon the concept of the 'gold coast', meaning the whole western Pacific shore stretching from Korea in the north to Malaysia in the south, which would soon claim the attention of the rest of the world – with China's coastline, of course, at its centre.

Beijing drafted Dr Goh Keng Swee, architect of Singapore's pioneer Jurong industrial township, to give advice on the development of these coastal areas (and doubtless to recommend Singapore investors where to go in.) Perhaps the Singapore minister explained to his hosts the virtues of the 'triangle' economic collaboration projects between three neighbouring countries which have been launched in southeast Asia. Certainly

China is now taking up such ideas with enthusiasm, not only in north China, as we have seen, but also in the south.

The Greater Nanyang Circle includes all those territories already named but adding Singapore and the overseas Chinese of southeast Asia. It was a Taiwan journal, *Chang Qiao*, which first advocated a Chinese common market linking these particular territories in 1979. But the extension to Singapore worries many mainland Chinese and some southeast Asian Chinese like Lee Kuan Yew, because of the risk of fanning nationalist fears in Indonesia and Malaysia and possibly triggering new restrictions or new prejudice against the resident Chinese there.

The Singapore Chinese leaders have always warned against becoming too overtly Chinese in an increasingly nationalist southeast Asia, and yet the Singapore élite has now taken the plunge and identified itself more fully with China than ever before, at least in cultural matters. In politics and economics they deliberately distance themselves somewhat.

Singapore has sent very important investment missions to China and committed large sums for economic developments there, but they have done the same to other Asian countries, notably India, and Lee Kuan Yew and his colleagues openly criticise some Chinese policies, respectfully but firmly, in the manner of a younger brother, while defending China on other issues. Whether Singapore can be realistically seen as a future member of a Chinese political family system, as distinct from merely an economic partner, is doubtful. Singapore solicited and won the headquarters of the Asia Pacific Economic Co-operation (APEC), which looks like becoming a major forum for big and little powers on both sides of the Pacific – including China and Taiwan – about their future relations and systems.

Beijing itself is wary of getting closer to Singapore, appreciating the danger of souring relations with the other southeast Asian states, especially Indonesia. Singapore has, after all, had a very strong if discreet relationship with Taiwan during the Maoist period, especially over military training. Lee Kuan Yew used to hobnob with Chiang Ching-kuo in Taipei long before he put a nervous first foot on the Communist mainland, and both the Lees – Kuan Yew and Teng-hui – are of Hakka descent (as is Deng Xiaoping, possibly!).

An even grander Greater China Circle is now talked about which includes all those territories mentioned already plus the overseas Chinese worldwide. This is an awkward concept for Western political theory to handle, because it puts together sovereign states with relatively small ethnic minority communities residing in host states. It is difficult enough to determine who is Chinese and who is not Chinese in Jakarta or Bangkok or Medan, let alone decide how those who could be defined as Chinese would actually operate as Chinese within the meaning of a 'Greater China Circle'.

Western thinking would want them to choose between their rival affiliations. Ambiguity would not be allowed. But the Chinese value ambiguity and use it as a mollifying factor in their political life. They hope that the two kinds of participant in their Greater Chinese Circle – ethnic Chinese and national Chinese – would happily co-exist and support each other in various ways without upsetting anybody else. China will face the reverse problem when and if the two Koreas become reunited and begin to attract, perhaps through economic achievements, the two million or so ethnic Koreans who have lived in northeast Chinese provinces for the past fifty years or more. There is a slightly similar awkwardness about the co-existence of Mongolian nationals and ethnic Mongolians on each side of that particular frontier of China.

The goals of the one and a quarter billion Chinese worldwide are beginning to clarify. Maria Hsia Chang, an impassioned Chinese scholar who loves China but hates Communism, recently wrote from the heart: 'Together, Taiwan and the mainland could rebuild China into a modern world power, restoring it to its historic prominence.'[17] Those who are more circumspect, like Wang Gungwu, avoid using the term Greater China because it conveys to the rest of the world a China with political expansion in mind – or else with a grandiose culture lacking in the humility which adjustment to a world system would require.

One can think of another type of Chinese intellectual who remembers mainly the enforced humility which Chinese had to adopt at the hands of Western political and cultural imperialism over the past century or two. If we are to go on re-fighting history, progress will be slow. But the West should not take fright at the gradual emergence of a Chinese politico-cultural system under cover of which the Chinese of China and their offshore cousins will join together in order to assert their equality with the West and come to live with it on agreed terms.

The Chinese government thus finds itself at some international conferences on current politics or economics able to count on the backing of the 'other Chinas', particularly Singapore but also to a limited extent Hongkong. It can also benefit sometimes from the fact that heads of other delegations, or their intellectually active members, may be ethnic Chinese who sympathise, not necessarily with Chinese ideology or with Communism, but with the Chinese cultural national viewpoint on matters like human rights or intellectual property laws, as the Brunei delegate probably did at the recent Hangzhou China-ASEAN conference. They have sometimes been able to operate as an informal 'Chinese' lobby in such meetings.

Many possible names for the principal collaborations across the borders have been suggested, including South China Economic Circle, Greater China Free Trade Area, Chinese Economic Community, China Productivity Triangle, China Economic Circle, South China Newly Industrialising Economy, Chinese Prosperity Sphere, Greater China Common Market and Cross-Strait Economic Circle. 'Great' or 'greater' was used to qualify 'China' because the concept was obviously bigger than China, extending to other Chinese communities beyond the frontiers. But none of these titles seemed quite right. There are also proposed terminologies that venture beyond the economic realm. The Chinese Federation, the Chinese Commonwealth, Cultural China and Chinese Civilisational Community are not labels for mere commerce and banking.

The most exciting elaboration of the idea of a global Chinese society is the vision by the philosopher Tu Wei-ming of a global 'Cultural China' whose intellectual inhabitants would become profoundly reflective and cerebrally original, no longer pushed around by political line-givers such as Mao or Deng (or foreigners for that matter). That ambition is probably common to many Chinese who have tasted the centres of learning in the world. What is unique to Tu is that he would also include in this favoured band non-Chinese people who are personally or professionally interested in China. His professorial paradise would include 'scholars, teachers, journalists, industrialists, traders, entrepreneurs and writers, who try to understand China intellectually and bring their conceptions of China to their linguistic communities.'[18] He sees the Chinese phenomenon in the future world as perhaps becoming as extensive, influential and taken for granted as the Anglo-Saxon is today.

Membership of the global Chinese phenomenon would thus be defined in cultural rather than ethnic terms.[19] Everyone participating in the international discourse of cultural China would qualify. The corollary is that the intellectual capitals of China's literati would be found not only in Beijing, Shanghai and Hongkong, but also in the overseas dissident communities of Cambridge, Princeton and Paris. China met its cultural Waterloo along with military defeat in the nineteenth century, and its scholarly foot-soldiers today will need every assistance if they are to reverse that débâcle and reinstate Chinese values on equal terms. An array of sympathisers wait in the West for their cultural passports to fight in this campaign – if only it were under the baton of a united and non-ideological leadership.

Arthur Waley, Joseph Needham, James Legge, John Fairbank and Edgar Snow have in the past demonstrated the readiness of 'Anglo-Saxons' to serve under such a banner. John Lewis, Michel Oksenberg, Jonathan Spence, William Skinner, Stuart Schram, Dieter Heinzig and Marianne Bastide are among the many potential warriors for Chinese culture of our day. None of them would enjoy working, even on a cultural subject, for governments such as those in Beijing and Taipei which tread independent spirits into the mud, expect a barren conformism and have in living memory shot their own unarmed students to death. Under a new bright banner of Greater China, with more liberal institutions and leaders, the campaign for new respect for Chinese culture could attract weighty support on Western campuses.

Considering the guarded and overcautious views of Chinese politicians and officials in the past, Beijing's reaction to the imaginative recent suggestions for linking trade and investment with neighbouring states under the rubric of Greater China or various economic circles has been remarkably constructive. The attraction of investment was always the highest priority of Deng Xiaoping when dealing with the offshore Chinese.

A Party document on foreign policy in 1991 was unequivocal in its approval of the offshore proposals. China should try to establish a cultural and economic Greater China, rather on the model of what the US, Europe and ASEAN/Japan were doing in their regions. 'The fact of the matter is that Taiwan, Hongkong, Singapore and China share a common culture, maintaining a strong Chinese economic presence in southeast Asia. The capital, information and technology of Taiwan, Hongkong and Singapore could be allied with the complete industrial network, corps of scientists and technicians and cheap labour force of China, to make a big economic leap forward for the whole region.'[20]

This document described east Asia as 'an untapped emerging market', to be categorised as the soft underbelly of the Asian economy. Indonesia, for instance, needed Chinese light industrial products and consumer goods. The Japanese and American markets were going to be difficult to enter for a long time, so China should develop markets in the receptive Asian countries which have been deeply influenced by Chinese culture.

These days China is appreciative of Singapore and the views of its leaders, but this document had a rap on the knuckles for Lee Kuan Yew. The Singapore Senior Minister had suggested replacing Chinese civilisation with 'East Asian civilisation' as the credo of the new regional arrangements. While accepting that this would still in fact be primarily Chinese, the Chinese Communist authors called Lee Kuan Yew 'quixotic' for casting the cultural net so wide. China will not countenance the soft-pedalling of Chinese culture which the offshore Chinese were forced to adopt.

In conclusion the document warned that China should seize the present opportunity to take a lead in this direction, otherwise it might forfeit the trust of Chinese people around the world. The conditions for success, it added, were no worse now than they had been for Peter the Great when he expanded Russia's borders, or for the Emperor Meiji in Japan. That postscript was intended to make the project sound desirable and respectable for Chinese readers, but had precisely the opposite effect, of course, on

China's neighbours. The circumstances clearly show, all the same, that what is being discussed is collaborative arrangements with other Chinese societies rather than their incorporation into the People's Republic.[21]

A few months later the *Liberation Army Daily* in Beijing reviewed the new economic circles in a detailed analysis by a Jiangsu research director, Sun Dongchuan.[22] He saw China at the centre of eight new economic spheres. The leader and pioneer was, of course, Guangdong–Hongkong–Macao, and the contours of this grouping were becoming clearer. Hongkong was well into the process of becoming integrated into a region of south China which could eventually expand to include Hainan, Guangxi and even Singapore. Another distinctive sphere was that of Fujian–Taiwan, where the initial formative stage had been completed. They could be integrated into an All-China Economic Sphere, South China Economic Sphere or a Donghai–Nanhai (East China Sea–South China Sea) Economic Sphere.

In the northeast there was a Shandong–Korea economic sphere, which could expand, as tension eased between North and South Korea, to the whole Korean peninsula and become a Bohai and Yellow Sea Economic Sphere. Lianyungang and parts of Jiangsu could be added to take advantage of the opening of overland trade routes to Europe. Siberia would participate in a northeast Asian economic sphere which would include these regions, and Heilongjiang might form an economic sphere with the former Russian border areas and Inner Mongolia, involving not only cross-border trade but labour mobility and joint ventures.

Moving to the west, economic relations were developing between Xinjiang and the former Soviet central Asian states as well as Pakistan. Ala Shankou (the Dzungarian gate) was the important passageway for this trade between northern Xinjiang and the central Asian states, while the Khunjerab pass route served the same function for southwest Xinjiang and Pakistan. Inner Mongolia had economic relations with the Mongolian Republic, while Tibet traded with India and Nepal. Yunnan had exchanges with Burma, Vietnam and Laos, while Guangxi has economic relations with Vietnam and Laos. All these links should strengthen and expand. Even such a bald summary of a meaty report brings home the full potential of this peaceful Chinese spill-over into its neighbours.[23]

China is doing exactly what the West would like it to do. It is not retreating sulkily behind its borders, nor is it aggressively expanding its military acquisitions beyond those borders. Instead it is actively engaging in trade and other economic exchange with neighbouring countries, especially those with a Chinese ethnic or cultural connection, to make 'Greater China' a non-threatening reality. But that is not how it always appears to other governments, as a review of China's foreign relations will now show.

PART FIVE

THE WORLD

CHAPTER 19

CHINA AND JAPAN: BACK TO BACK

Visitors to the Palais des Nations in Geneva or the UN building in New York may sometimes observe two orientals spiritedly conversing across a table. Their talk is in English, but they pepper it with incorporeal drawings traced by the index finger on the table-top or even in the air. That is how a Chinese and a Japanese diplomat will often communicate: enough of the traditional Chinese ideograms are shared by the two countries to make a useful supplement to a serious exposition, and both countries are familiar with the device of drawing a character in the air or on a tabletop. However quickly the finger moves, the eye of the other person can take it in.

But this borders on a dialogue of the deaf, supplemented by a third language equally alien to both. Not a single post-war Japanese ambassador to Beijing has been fluent in the Chinese language. The late Premier Zhou Enlai spent eighteen months in Japan without learning Japanese. A Japanese who met Zhou then on a train talked with him for twenty hours: at first in Japanese, but Zhou's Japanese was hardly intelligible, and then in English, but the English of the Japanese was broken, so finally, he recalled, 'We continued to communicate by writing characters on paper.'[1] These two neighbouring countries face a formidable communications gap.

If there are two countries whose actions will determine the future of Asia, these are they. Earlier in the twentieth century Asia-conscious Japanese intellectuals coined for China and Japan the phrase *dobun doshu* – 'same script, same race'. Superficially the scripts do look similar. Japan borrowed China's ideograms as its first written language. Later, however, it added alphabets of its own invention, and the ideograms in China have developed in their own way, so that two intellectuals from either side could now read fewer than half of the other's newspapers. In any case the spoken language is completely different. The Japanese lack tones, and their grammar and sentence structure are quite distinct.

Same race? Similarly, there may be an ethnic resemblance on the surface. Perhaps a half of the Japanese gene-pool did originate in north China at the dawn of history, but those colonists mixed with more or less equal numbers of immigrants from southeast Asia and the southwestern Pacific, and the Chinese find the resulting amalgam very hard to fathom.

Sometimes there is a rare rapport between a Japanese and a Chinese, as happened in the early 1980s between Prime Minister Yasuhiro Nakasone and General Secretary Hu Yaobang. Both were at the modern end of their respective political spectrums, both were innovative and imaginative, both were straight-talking.[2] Deng Xiaoping, by contrast, never made his Japanese hosts or visitors feel at ease. Another prime minister, Kiichi Miyazawa, was also successful in relating with his Chinese counterparts. An aide explains that while the logical construction of his mind is quite Western, his emotions are fully east Asian. Miyazawa is old-fashioned enough to enjoy reading the Chinese classics, and with the Chinese he can drink and sing and dance in east Asia's traditional outgoing way. The old intellectual friendships at the beginning of the century, epitomised by warm-hearted sinologists like Okakura Kakuzo and his seminal book *Ideals of the East*, were mortally wounded by Japan's unbridled invasion of China in the 1930s and then killed off by China's Communism.

The Japanese were thus grateful early beneficiaries of Chinese civilisation, receiving not only the ideographic script but also Buddhism and medieval material technology. Since then, though separated by only a hundred miles of sea, Japan and China have followed separate paths.

Both countries were alarmed by the simultaneous arrival from Europe of acquisitive traders and self-righteous missionaries, but it was Japan which systematically kept them out for two hundred years, while characteristically arranging a narrow controlled safe entry channel for European medical and surgical technology.[3] When those defences were broken down by the American Commodore Perry and his 'black ships' in 1853, the Japanese staged an internal revolution which brought the modernising factions of the nobility into power, and they then organised a steady programme of sending students to train in modern knowledge in the West.

When the two senior leaders of China and Japan, Li Hongzhang and Prince Ito Hirobumi, met to negotiate a treaty in 1896 they agreed to collaborate 'so that our Asiatic yellow race will not be encroached upon by the white race of Europe'. But Ito wondered aloud why China was so slow to modernise. Li did not comment, and Ito was too polite to recall that as a young *samurai* he had undertaken the hardship of a berth before the mast on a British ship from Japan to London in order to learn the language, customs and know-how of the West. That would have been quite beneath Li's dignity.[4] The contrast between Chinese vanity and Japanese practicality still prevails.

After two major wars of aggression by Japan, China rightly attaches priority to keeping Japan on the rails. A Chinese diplomat has said that China and Japan should relate to each other in the manner of France and Germany, standing for peace after the disputes of the past, and collaborating to strengthen the east Asian region in the context of the new post-colonial era. But Japanese diplomats tend to be suspicious still of China's claims to be a world power.

The Chinese concept of world order differs from the Anglo-Saxon idea in which post-war Japan has become caught up. Japanese with some sympathy for China sometimes say the relationship should be like the Anglo–American alliance, where past ties of culture are built upon after territorial conflicts are resolved. Yet a confidential report made for the Chinese Communist Party in 1990 named Japan as the most likely threat to China over the next thirty years, and 'rightists' in Japan having less sympathy for China believe that the two countries are fated to clash for hegemony over Asia.

The late Premier Zhou Enlai once confessed to Japanese leaders that China would not have been able to stand up against the bullying Soviet Union of Stalin and Khruschchev if the Japanese had not invested so much capital in Manchuria during their rule there. China inherited that level of development in Manchuria in the later 1940s, and could for that reason contemplate standing fast against the Russians. Mao Zedong used to confide when feeling particularly truthful that if Japan had not defeated Russia in 1905, the Soviet Union would have inherited Manchuria then and would never have returned it to China. So the Chinese can feel gratitude to Japan for the consequences of its aggressive actions on the north China mainland, though it does not, of course, speak much for China's patriotism or vigilance against invaders at that time.[5]

The Japanese like to put their past aggression behind them, squeezing it firmly out of their minds in order to get on with the life of the present and future. China, on the other hand, 'never forgets', as the intellectuals of Japan sadly agree. The other side of the coin is that, like Count Ito, the Japanese are often contemptuous of China's inability even now to follow Japan's example in zealously pursuing sustained political reforms and smooth economic progress. In the eyes of Beijing traditionalists, however, Japan is an upstart 'outer province' of the original Chinese civilisation. China feels psychologically superior, but economically inferior, to Japan.

A Japanese littérateur claims that the affectation by some Japanese poets to compose in Chinese (rather as English authors as late as John Milton chose to write in Latin) provides the only recent example of the literature of one culture being written in the language of another.[6] But meaningful intercourse between the individuals and organisations of today is negligible. They stand on their respective shores with their backs to each other, looking in opposite directions. Until the Pacific War, Chinese intellectuals looked mostly to America while the Japanese preferred European culture. Afterwards they reversed, the Chinese looking to Russia and Western Europe, the Japanese to America.

When they did engage, it was most violent. The mutual image of being equal members of the 'yellow race' destined to resist and eventually defeat the West under the banner of pan-Asia did not survive the 1910s, when Japan insisted on retaining colonial possessions on Chinese soil. War with Japan led Chinese intellectuals to divide the category of 'yellow race' into a first class, containing themselves, and a second class embracing the Japanese.

There is no mystery about the Sino–Japanese war in the 1930s, except present-day Japan's reluctance to face up to it. The worst incident was the massacre at Nanjing, which Japanese hostile to their own militarists later exaggerated as a horrific atrocity costing hundreds of thousands of lives, many through bayoneting, decapitation and the like (the Chinese did such things to each other at that time). This self-abusing view became established in school textbooks, since teachers were strongly left-wing, and this provoked a reaction from nationalist politicians like Shintaro Ishihara and from the *Sankei* newspaper. They questioned the very fact of a massacre.

In the end the veterans spoke out. 'We believed in Japanese superiority over other races,' confessed Nagatomi Hiromichi, a Japanese soldier who claimed to have killed two hundred at Nanjing. 'We were taught that killing inferior people was an honourable act.' Darwin thus prevailed over Christ.

Hata Ikuhiko, a serious researcher, has gone into all the evidence and found that the most likely total of Chinese deaths was about 50,000, including deserters from the Chinese army who cast off their uniforms and assumed civilian clothes.[8] Even that is nothing to be proud of, but the Japanese never felt able to apologise in the heartfelt emotional way which the post-war Germans, for example, did to the Jews. Instead of apology, Japanese leaders talk of 'regret', 'remorse' and 'contrition'. Prime Minister Murayama's letter of apology to John Major was not repeated for China's benefit. China's horror over Japanese atrocities was well conveyed in Mo Yan's *Red Sorghum*, which became a best-seller.[7]

The Japanese feel guilt, but do not know how to express it without destroying themselves, their emperor (in whose name all these acts were committed) and their imperial system. Their guilt has been diminished since the 1960s by China's apparent aggression in India and Vietnam, and by the barbarism of Chinese against Chinese in the Cultural Revolution. But guilt is still part of the psychology of the relationship. It dictates a lack of symmetry in Sino–Japanese exchanges, allowing the Chinese to take the high moral tone, which comes naturally to them, helping them to twist more economic aid out of Japan, while the Japanese are forced back to a humble low posture. All this is a bait to the Japanese right wing and re-emerging Japanese nationalism, helping to make it stronger than it otherwise would be.

By criticising Japan's war record, China has been able to trump the Japanese cards in many post-war bouts of diplomatic argument. But it is a wasting asset. Kotake Kazuaki, the Japanese analyst, explains, 'as the generation of Japanese with memories of Japan's militaristic past gives way to a younger generation with a weaker sense of historical guilt, China may not be able to continue the stratagem' [of winning concessions from Japan by bringing up the past].[9]

In the 1990s some Japanese writers and scholars began to say forthrightly that Japan should make explicit apologies for its behaviour in China (and in other Asian countries too, it being a wider issue).[10] The big moment should have come when Emperor Akihito made a historic first visit to China by any Japanese emperor in 1992. All his officials would allow him to say was that he deeply deplored 'an unfortunate period in which my country inflicted great sufferings on the people of China'. In many of these attempted apologies the meaning and translation of words has proved an obstacle. The exact words of Akihito on this occasion were *fukai kamashimi*, which may literally be rendered as 'I feel deep sorrow.' When put into the Chinese language this sounded banal and attenuated.[11]

Emperor Hirohito, Akihito's father, could have been held responsible for the war, in spite of his having privately opposed it, because of his constitutional responsibilities as head of state and head of the armed forces. If Hirohito had been deposed by the Americans in 1945, the blame could have been focused on him, but the Americans believed that this would risk making Japan ungovernable and that foreign interference with their imperial system could unleash impossible violence and opposition to the US occupation. This was the kernel of Japan's later dilemma over apologising for the war, and the only possible opportunity after Hirohito's death was lost because the issue was still too big for any one political leader or group to handle. The consensus was still elusive.

In contemporary terms, China's moral superiority enables it to be a constant critic of Japan's 'remilitarisation', although that is a sensationalised label for the gradual growth of one of the smallest (per head of population) and most legally restrained armed forces in the world. The Chinese media still refer to Hirohito as an 'arch-criminal' and 'number one hangman'. On the Japanese side, Nanjing massacre scenes from Chinese war films were said to be censored. It is a running sore which does not poison the whole body of the 1990s relationship but undermines its vigour.

Westerners are often surprised at the degree of Chinese support for the American military presence in Japan, but this is easy to explain. China sees American troops in Japan as a disincentive for Japan to remilitarise.[12] If the Stars and Stripes disappear, there will inevitably be larger Japanese armed forces which will therefore gain bigger domestic influence. If and when the Americans do scale down their forces, as they seem likely to do for financial reasons over the next decade or so, and if this causes Japan to preserve its own security by increasing its own army, China would have to redouble its clamour against Japan's remilitarisation.

The Japanese know how China will feel, because Japan has experienced tension in the last few years over China's rearmaments using bargain-basement Soviet weapons. Tokyo even went so far as to lobby the Russians to be restrained in selling armaments to China.[13] But China's fears of Japan have been somewhat allayed by the record of Japan's peacekeeping forces serving in Cambodia under the United Nations flag. At first China felt this would be the thin end of the wedge of renewed deployment of Japanese troops in Asia, a trial run for a military comeback on the mainland. But the performance of the small non-combatant Japanese group was so good that the Chinese actually congratulated them instead, strengthening the possibility for Japan to repeat that kind of action on UN instructions.

There are still specific disputes between China and Japan which could cause trouble in the future. One of these is Taiwan, about which the Japanese feel motherly, and which they were most upset at having to abandon when the People's Republic of China was recognised in the 1970s. Now that the Taiwan opposition is advocating independence to some extent, it is obvious that Japan would be the major source of support if that were ever to be carried out, and so China is ruffled by the prospect. There have been several recent incidents involving shipping and property, the famous instance being a Chinese government student hostel in Kyoto which was bitterly disputed between Beijing and Taipei, much to Japan's embarrassment.

Take two recent occasions when this China–Taiwan contentiousness has affected Japan. China succeeded in preventing the Taiwan president, Lee Teng-hui, from attending the Twelfth Asian Games in Hiroshima in 1994, in spite of the protests of many Japanese media which insisted that China should not be allowed to interfere with international games held on Japanese soil.[14] Again, when the Bank of Tokyo set up a branch in Taipei, which after all houses the biggest foreign reserves of any country in the world, China crossly refused to give it a licence to operate in Shanghai, which it otherwise could have expected.

There is even a minuscule territorial issue in the East China Sea where five small islands (Diaoyutai in Chinese, Senkaku in Japanese) used by fishermen and held by Japan are claimed by China with possible oil reserve and military implications. More than a hundred Chinese fishing boats armed with machine guns were once involved in incidents here, and an unusual example of the tortuousness of diplomacy in these areas was shown in 1990 when a group from Taiwan tried to plant an Olympic torch on one of the islands as a symbol of sovereignty: the Japanese duly expelled them, whereupon not only Taiwan but also China registered strong protests. A similar clash occurred in late 1996.

Another issue much affected by war-time memories is that of human rights. As an industrialised and constitutionally democratic country, Japan normally follows the Western view on this, for example in deploring China's repression of its students in Tiananmen Square.[15] But no Japanese politician has been able to make an effective critique of China's human rights record because they know that Japan's record in China in the 1930s and early 1940s renders Japan's claim to moral judgement today laughable. The Tiananmen killings of 1989 did damage China's moral authority and prestige in Japan, spoiling the image previously held by defensive Japanese of a China that was almost always 'correct'. The Prime Minister Toshiki Kaifu was self-confident enough in 1991 to talk to the Chinese about their human rights.[16]

However, there is a contrary factor also. Nationalism is slowly rising in Japan, and one of its manifestations is the thought that Japanese do not have to do things exactly as Westerners do, but may legitimately retain their own ways, customs and preferences without feeling uncomfortably ashamed. In future the Japanese will feel less inhibited about resisting Western pressure on human rights in Japan – which are not, after all, bad and are in some respects very good, but have weak spots. So Japan's delegates to human rights conferences in Asia have been ready to go along with the idea of a distinctively Asian platform differing from the West's on matters of individual rights, for example, and that makes Japan something of an ally with China on this matter. Japan will find itself backing China against unjustified Western pressure, while at the same time supporting the West over justified criticism of China's human rights record. It will be a tricky role, the kind of role Japan has not in the past been good at playing. Prime Minister Morihiro Hosokawa agreed with the Chinese premier while visiting Beijing in 1994 that 'it is not proper to force a Western or European type democracy on others.'[17]

Then there are Japan's hopes for promotion within the UN. One element in the perceived superiority of China is its possession of a permanent seat on the UN Security Council, with a concomitant veto. Japan would very much like to have a similar position, and is beginning to lobby governments all over the world to this end. Since China would be able to veto such an application, it must be an essential part of Japan's diplomacy to get Chinese agreement. What price would China exact for such agreement, and what other changes in the UN would China insist on as a part of a general UN reform? That will be another weak card in the Japanese hand against China.

The Franco–German relationship has been cited as a model. But the bones and muscles of the Sino–Japan relationship bear no comparison to those of European partnerships. The Japanese who became involved in pre-war China, either as civilians or soldiers, came home mostly with very little smattering of Chinese culture or speech. Now there are a few hundred Japanese students in China, and probably a larger number of industrial technicians and managers. Since about 1988 China has accepted International Cooperation Volunteers from Japan, the equivalent of the Peace Corps, and that is an excellent basis for long-term understanding. But the average young Japanese professional would like to go to America or Europe for training. China remains low on the list of preferred destinations.

To look at it the other way round seems more encouraging. There are probably 500,000 Chinese people in Japan at any one time. This supports the impression of Japan's China specialists that the policy-makers of Beijing know Japan better than the Japanese know China.[18] The Chinese community in Japan includes many interesting figures, including Yoshio Kou, a promoter who tried to catch the Loch Ness monster and tour the world with it.

But the Japanese regret that Chinese students come to Japan to learn Western sciences rather than the Japanese experience. Lu Xun, the most famous Chinese writer of the twentieth century, was such a one, studying medicine in Japan, and one of his short stories helps to illuminate mutual perceptions. One day, in this story, his Japanese professor talked to Lu after the class and asked for his notebook. Lu had not been able to make a note of all the lectures because of language problems and technical terms, so he hesitated. But the professor snatched it away. Next day he returned it, with all of the gaps filled in with red ink reproducing what he had said in his lectures.[19] It was the core cliché of the conscientious east Asian teacher helping his handicapped pupil beyond the course of duty – neither patronising nor intrusive.

The personal exchanges of trainees and tourists cannot be counted on to undo the past.[20] Economic links, on the other hand, are strengthening fast. In 1993 Japan, on the Chinese customs figures, became China's biggest trade partner (see graph on page 244). China finds itself facing a market large in numbers, and even larger in wealth, with an insatiable appetite for the consumer goods, handicrafts and traditional items that China can supply relatively cheaply.

China meanwhile is a huge customer for Japanese equipment, machinery and technology. Just as Japan is China's biggest market, so Japan is China's biggest single source of capital funds and industrial technology. In earlier years Japan had been a cautious investor in China, and many other countries outdid the Japanese contribution. Now Japan provides one-third of all the economic inputs – loans, aid and exports – which the outside world supplies to China.[21]

There are difficulties, particularly over past Chinese complaints of inadequacy and poor quality of Japanese aid and investment. The Baoshan steelmill in Shanghai, for example, was a Japanese venture which took far longer than planned to get off the ground because it was wrongly sited and the supply of materials was not well organised. Now the last Japanese technicians have left Baoshan after years of struggle, and China is using some German experts instead. 'They are developing products,' a Japanese official says, 'but have not yet been able to produce seamless tubes for the oilfields.'

After all the hesitation of the 1970s and 1980s, Japanese companies are now rushing to invest in China 'like lemmings going over a cliff', a Tokyo analyst said.[22] This investment is mostly to make products which can no longer be made competitively in high-cost Japan. Sometimes that means exporting them back to Japan, sometimes to third countries, and sometimes to the allegedly limitless China market itself. But Japanese companies find management in China difficult, and usually seek a partner to help them. Ironically, one of the most popular types of manager or partner is the overseas Chinese.

This new situation of extensive Japanese industrial experimentation in China allows another old myth to be nailed. Superficial observers from the West may see the concept of hierarchy and deference to authority as common to both China and Japan, which is why they are often put together under the label of 'neo-Confucianism'. There is now a considerable literature in China about what to learn from Japan, and how best to learn it. One management journal, *Modern Enterprise Herald*, wrote in 1987: 'The Japanese sense of hierarchy based on age and experience has nothing to do with authoritarianism. The Chinese also pay attention to hierarchy based on position and experience, but this respect for hierarchy is accompanied by blind faith in authority, a contempt for knowledge and worship of power.'[23]

The contradictions are many, and so interpretations of the Japan–China relationship, for all its compelling importance for the future of both countries and for the east Asian region as a whole, differ substantially. A tempting prediction is that of Robert Taylor in his book *The Sino-Japanese Axis* (1985) of 'a new civilisation built on Chinese culture and Japanese technology'.[24] Facing third countries beyond the sinic ambit (such as the West and India), Japanese and Chinese do indeed feel a certain cultural brotherliness. But how far can one get drawing invisible characters on table-tops, as Zhou Enlai did? Such brotherliness seems shadowy. Now the Chinese are catching up steadily on technology, and the Japanese are becoming prouder of their culture. So the twelve years since Taylor's book have not been good to his thesis.

The opposite point of view was argued by Edwin Reischauer, who believed that the real problem for Asia in the longer term, especially after the American military withdrawal, will be the rivalry between China and Japan.[25] They will certainly compete for influence, obviously in areas like southeast Asia and possibly in other parts of Asia too. In the present balance of power between east Asia on the one hand and the rest of the world on the other, there is room for Sino–Japanese collaboration. They have both suffered for the past 500 years from being at the wrong end of the world, to put it crudely. But now projections indicate that the wealth and power of east Asia will first match and then exceed the power of the West and of other areas of the world within a relatively short time, perhaps fifteen to twenty years.

In that environment, where Japan and China are assured of seats at the world's high tables, they would no longer systematically need each other's support, and could begin to indulge in the old familiar squabbles and rivalries that have marred similar relationships in Europe in the past.

A welcome new initiative came in 1993 when bilateral security talks between private academic institutions in China and Japan blossomed into official discussions between the two Foreign Ministries on a subject which had previously been taboo on both sides. The Chinese Institute of Strategic Studies in Beijing and the Institute of Peace and Security in Tokyo began annual meetings in 1988. That was before Tiananmen, and the Chinese criticised Japan's dependence on the USA. After Tiananmen, however, they became more tolerant.

There were initial problems with the official talks over the participation of the Self-Defence Forces of Japan and the People's Liberation Army of China in the discussions. The South China Sea islands, Taiwan, Korea and future US deployments in the region were the main topics. The Japanese asked why China needed to spend so much money on its armed forces. These regular talks will provide a channel for mutual information on military developments and anxieties, and channels for better understanding of the other's point of view.[26]

Takeo Iguchi, a retired Japanese ambassador, complains that China 'has become a lion, and we are all little rabbits'. Only the development of federalism in China could substantially reduce Japan's fear, expressed or otherwise, of China's growing strength. Many Japanese agree with Yoh Kurosawa, president of the Industrial Bank of Japan, in predicting a united, confident and pro-growth China.[27]

Asked about the development of the concept of Greater China, and the possibility of growing economic collaboration between 'all the Chinas' including Taiwan, Hongkong and Singapore, Japanese nationalists seem baffled how to respond. 'We would have to take the lead in a non-Chinese group in east Asia,' say some of them. But geography, ethnography and history lay down that this region is going to be a Chinese playground. Whom could Japan recruit for such a non-Chinese group? Korea would be the first obvious candidate, but it is almost impossible to imagine Korea ever abandoning a basic neutrality between China and Japan. Korean feelings against Japan and Japan's legacy as a colonialist and conqueror in modern Korean political history simply do not allow of such a switch of allegiance.

After Korea, the Japanese would have to go 1,000 miles south into southeast Asia to find other allies – Vietnam, perhaps, or Indonesia or the Philippines. But southeast Asian countries are very well aware of the rivalry between Japan and China and will not lightly join one camp or the other. Their recent economic development and political self-confidence make it unlikely that they ever would. So Japan may have to fall back, one would think, on a Pacific role (APEC?) based on communication by sea and air and the power of money, or else join the pantheon of east Asian partner states, accepting China as the Asian Zeus. Either way, Japan seems bound to play second fiddle to China in the long run.[28]

Korea will be the testing-ground for Sino–Japanese rivalry, as it was before. The Land of the Morning Calm juts down from the massive Asian continent into the ocean separating China from Japan, as if nature intended it to be a buffer between the two countries. But it can also be a threat. China felt threatened when Japan annexed Korea for the first half of this century, and Japan subsequently felt under threat from the existence of a Communist regime in North Korea patronised by China and Russia. Korea was traditionally seen as 'a dagger pointed at the heart of Japan'. In modern times, Korea has been a constant flashpoint, and despite its relatively small size it has become a major concern for China's foreign policy despite the many other calls around its frontiers.

We have come a long way from the Cold War period when China backed North Korea a hundred per cent, while reviling South Korea as a puppet of the Americans. Almost a million Chinese 'volunteers' – including a son of Mao Zedong – died defending North Korea against UN forces in the early 1950s. The international thaw has proceeded apace since the pioneering of Henry Kissinger and Richard Nixon, and China actually recognised the South Korean government in 1992. The haemorrhage of Russia's influence in Korea since the collapse of Soviet Communism left North Korea with very few friends. China is now counted as the major foreign patron of the North Korean Communist government.

But Chinese support is not unconditional. The Chinese did not defend Kim Il-Sung in his more excessive policies. They urged him to scale down his nuclear programme, as in the end he had to because of foreign pressure. Nor did the Chinese openly support the more extreme demands of Pyongyang about reunification with the South or entry into the UN. Finally, China advised Kim not to name his son as successor, thus making their relations with that son when he became president on his father's death somewhat questionable.[29]

China benefits considerably, on the other hand, from having

normal contacts with the richer southern half of the divided peninsula. Two-way trade has reached the US$10 billion mark, which makes China the third largest trading partner of South Korea after the USA and Japan. South Korean investment into China is extremely important, especially in resource-rich Shandong. Such investments now exceed 500 with a value of more than $400 million. One of the latest agreements is for China and South Korea jointly to lead an international consortium to develop a US$1.5 billion series of airliners.[30] The two economies are complementary, although some Korean economists are warning against technological complacency, reminding their business and government leaders that Korea will still need technical investments at home if it is to stay up in the world competitiveness league in the future.[31]

China thus faces a delicate diplomatic challenge in juggling the two Koreas, keeping both in play and seeking reconciliation while maintaining a fundamental neutrality. Beijing's influence is now benign, as was seen in its contribution to defusing the nuclear crisis in 1994, getting North and South Korea simultaneously into the UN, and persuading North Korean leaders to replace their Stalinist economics with market reforms similar to China's.[32]

Whether China can retain a rapport with the younger Kim now in power must remain uncertain. The older generation on both sides felt a kinship in resisting Japanese aggression and in swimming in to land on the tide of Communism. The generation after Deng Xiaoping and the new generation of Kim Jong-Il have no such common experience. Yet North Korea is more fragile than ever before because of its isolation, and more dependent on China. The most likely outcome is a discreetly increasing Chinese influence over not only North Korean domestic policies but the slow march to reunification or peninsular federation as well. China's interest is to see the peninsula stable, peaceful and prospering.

One should not forget the existence of some two million Koreans on the Chinese side of the border, who are Chinese nationals but ethnic Koreans. Their future role in this region where so many states and nationalities meet is not quite clear. Even the one million ethnic Koreans in Japan, who are mostly

Japanese citizens 'passing' as ethnic Japanese because of the deep-rooted prejudice against Koreans in that country, might also have a part to play in the future of the Korean peninsula and its environs.

China's position is so pivotal that we may in the end see it masterminding a comprehensive settlement in Korea including perhaps an international conference and peace treaty, an acknowledgement of the peninsula as a nuclear-free zone, a non-aggression agreement between North and South, and a phased reduction of arms in which the UN command would disband and American forces withdraw from South Korea. Given the prolonged suspicion and mutual isolation between the two Koreas, that is going to take a long time. What is new is that China is today left as the most immediately and effectively concerned regional power, to begin ushering the two recalcitrant halves of Korea along this path. It may take ten or twenty years, but then China is renowned for its patience.

One final caveat might be that one should not expect China to follow Western models and styles in all this diplomacy. While having broadly similar ultimate goals as the United States, the Chinese refused to appear to bully North Korea publicly over the nuclear proliferation issue, thinking it more effective to press privately on the matter. Yet China refused to veto South Korea's application in the UN Security Council in 1991, despite Pyongyang's request for it to do so.[33] A self-confident Chinese style of diplomacy is emerging where China's interests beyond the borders are most at stake in this northeast Asian region – and where effective non-Asian power is visibly withdrawing.

CHAPTER 20

THE THIRD WORLD: SHIFTING PLATFORMS

China's relations with that ill-assorted caravan of the South – for which the old label 'Third World' is no longer appropriate, but a new one is not yet accepted – convey a certain unreality and fickleness. Here there are virtually no abiding special relationships, no specially favoured states or alliances, only the hesitant shared identity as developing economies qualifying for preferential trade and soft aid from the West.

At the beginning of the Maoist régime there were two clear priorities. The first was to persuade as many Third World governments as possible to recognise the People's Republic of China rather than the Republic of China on Taiwan. The second linked priority was to maximise Third World support for the People's Republic to take the China seat in the United Nations. The 1950s and 1960s therefore witnessed an extraordinary competition between Beijing and Taipei, offering trade, aid and technical assistance to many countries of Africa and Latin America which knew very little about either China, and about which the two Chinas were themselves ignorant.

But once Beijing had won the battle by entering the United Nations in 1971, and once it began accepting trade and investment from Taiwan in great volume from the end of the 1970s, these efforts in Latin America and Black Africa became redundant, as did China's campaign to become a leader of the motley Afro-Asian concourse. For the past fifteen years at least China's policy in these Third World countries has focused on other goals, especially the enduring national interests of military security and supply of strategic materials, notably oil. These preoccupations have reversed the earlier priorities so that Chinese diplomacy in the 'South' now begins with southeast Asia, proceeds to south Asia and then southwest Asia but tails off markedly in Africa and South America.

China's policies in southeast Asia have already been partially discussed in the context of the Greater China economic circles and the overseas Chinese, which just goes to show how many gilt-edged interests China has in a region which used to be called the Balkans of Asia. Broadly speaking, China tries to cultivate the friendship of the southeast Asian states, but with difficulty. The general switch of diplomatic support from Taiwan to the People's Republic was made only fifteen to twenty years ago, and Indonesia, which is the largest southeast Asian country with the greatest potential in economic and military power, still has lingering reservations about China's intentions towards the region. But China has, for example, become the best customer for Malaysia's key export, rubber.

The present leaders in Jakarta remember vividly what they perceived as direct Chinese intervention to support the attempted coup by the Indonesian Communist Party in 1965.[1] In the long run the stresses and strains between the southeast Asian countries may enable China to play one off against another, but for the moment they are joined in a common cause through ASEAN (the Association of South-East Asian Nations), and now that Vietnam is joining ASEAN, it could look like something of a closed shop against China.

Since 1965, at least, China has studiously refrained from involvement in the domestic politics of southeast Asia, whether on behalf of overseas Chinese, Communists or anybody else. Beijing has also extricated itself from Cambodia, where it had supported the Khmer Rouge, in spite of their genocidal record, in order to prevent Vietnam from gaining control over another of China's border states. China even joined the UN peacekeeping force in Cambodia in 1992–93, contributing a 400-man battalion of People's Liberation Army engineers to work on the roads. Generally there are tensions across the land borders on such issues as drug-smuggling and the spread of AIDS, and China has found itself open to criticism for not being able to control activities within its own province of Yunnan. China waged a brief but unsuccessful border war with Vietnam in 1979, a humiliating setback for a vastly larger neighbour.[2]

Another southeast Asian country to which China pays special attention as a potential client state is Burma, whose repressive military régime is boycotted by many countries. China is helping Burma by upgrading the port of Hainggyi on the Bay of Bengal, building bridges and possibly a hydro-electric power station, and conducting trade worth more than US$1 billion a year. Unconfirmed reports say that China has sold US$750 million-worth of weapons to the Burmese government, and is building an electronic monitoring station on Great Coco island. Some of these activities are denied, but neighbouring countries, especially India, profess to be very worried about growing Chinese influence and fear a Chinese beachhead to the Indian Ocean which would threaten India's hitherto unchallenged control there. China gratefully remembers Burmese support in the cartographical struggles on China's southern borders in the 1960s, enabling China to gain some leverage over India. Premier Li Peng's visit in 1994 set the seal on the friendship.[3]

The big issue in southeast Asia is one in which almost all these countries are involved and which carries the greatest threat of armed conflict in future. That is China's claim to territorial waters in the South China Sea based on the sovereignty of the Spratly and Paracel Islands. Chinese maps show the claim as a monstrous curve sweeping southwards a thousand miles or more from the South China coast and then back again, a claim which has been described as 'breathtakingly audacious'. Five other countries, especially Vietnam, but also Malaysia, the Philippines and Brunei (as well as Taiwan) claim some or all of these islands with their surrounding territorial waters.

In themselves, the islands are so small and rocky as not to be of great importance to anybody. Though spanning a thousand miles of sea, their aggregate area is less than ten square miles. Chinese sailors living in makeshift barracks on one reef (Huayang, or Cuarteron) have soil brought in from Hainan to grow sunflowers. But the sea around them has a high strategic value because these are the sea lanes between northeast and southeast Asia, carrying, for example, three-quarters of Japan's oil supply from the Middle East. The islands also sit upon oil reserves which look like being far bigger than anything else offshore in this region. There have already been military clashes: small Chinese and Vietnamese units fought near Lansdowne Reef in 1988; three Vietnamese ships were sunk, and about seventy men were killed. In 1995 the Philippines navy was involved in confrontation at Mischief Reef.

China took the tack in 1990 of offering to leave the question of sovereignty over these islands aside, if all the parties involved

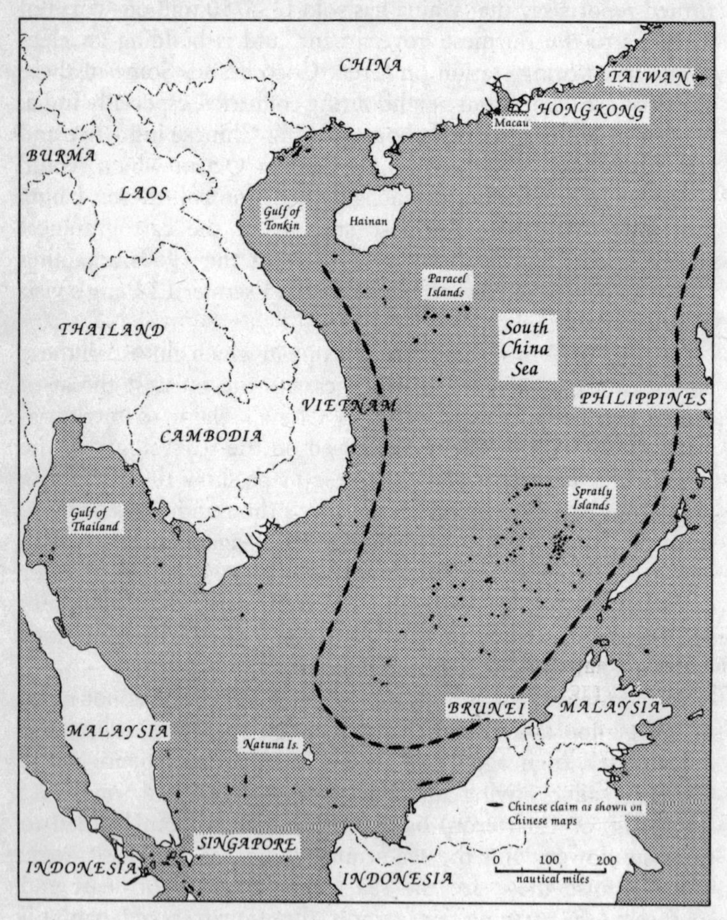

Spratly and Paracel Islands

would agree on their joint economic development. 'China is willing to jointly exploit and share the resources, temporarily shelving the disputes over sovereignty.'[4] This was well received in southeast Asia, but China later awarded unilaterally an oil exploration concession to Crestone, an American company, in waters which were disputed with Vietnam, whereupon the Vietnamese authorised a Norwegian seismic surveying company to prospect in the same area and awarded a consortium of companies led by Mobil an exploration bloc next to the one awarded by China.

Oil may be the key factor for China, because its interior fields are not enough to supply its future economic needs. The China National Offshore Oil Corporation is currently producing only 44 million barrels of oil a year, and hopes to double this by 1997 when other fields come on stream. By contrast Vietnam, with a population twenty times smaller, already extracts 33 million barrels from its sole field in the South China Sea.

The other claimants have also been active. At one point Malaysia arrested Filipino fishermen within its claimed area, and in 1992 the Philippines did the same with fishermen from China. Malaysia published plans to turn one unoccupied reef into a holiday resort, while Vietnam built a fishing port on another. China invited journalists to visit some islands, and set up a weather station claimed to be under the auspices of the World Meteorological Organisation. The Philippines has granted oil concessions. The Chinese claim line overlaps with the large gas field discovered by Exxon off Indonesia's Natuna Islands, which is one of the largest hydrocarbon finds so far in the South China Sea.

One estimate of the value of total oil reserves in the South China Sea is US$1,000 billion. Most of the claimant countries are badly short of oil, and China moved from oil surplus to oil deficit in 1993. In 1995 China received its first tankers of oil from the field off Malacca in which it has one-third of the equity. But everyone sees that the Chinese have a stronger navy than any of the others and it is naval power that is likely to resolve the question in the end. Li Duc Anh of Vietnam discussed the issue with Jiang Zemin in 1993 and agreed verbally to shelve the Spratlys issue, but China now seems to insist that its own sovereignty be recognised by the others before joint development can begin. Meanwhile various military manoeuvres have been staged by China to brandish the fist, including a large-scale amphibious landing exercise, and the construction of a military airfield on Woody Island which could be used as a base for China's SU-27s to cover the Spratlys and Paracels. In 1994 Vietnamese naval ships interfered with a Chinese vessel conducting a seismic survey of the bloc awarded by Beijing to Crestone of the USA. According to the Vietnamese, the Chinese navy has made similar interferences.

In the summer of 1995, China reportedly fired missiles in the course of naval manoeuvres in the Gulf of Tonkin, near an Atlantic Richfield natural gas drilling platform which was part of a joint project to pipeline gas to China Light and Power Co. of Hongkong – a project financed by China National Offshore Oil Corporation, Kuwait and Arco in collaboration. A discouraging case of left hand, right hand?[6]

It is far from certain that China's so-called 'historic claims' of territorial water, though inherited from the predecessor Guomingdang government, could be defended under modern international law. The area of sea claimed goes up to between 15 and 200 nautical miles from the coasts of the other states. China's domestic law on its territorial water claim 'goes beyond what is permissible under the Law of the Sea', according to Philip Bowring.

The stakes are high in the South China Sea. So are the risks. If a Japanese tanker or Korean freighter is accidentally damaged in the course of the infighting among the islands by these six governments, a full-scale international crisis could immediately flare up. If international oil companies are to engage in exploiting the offshore fields in the South China Sea, and if they are vulnerable to strafing or boarding by other armed forces, the damage to regional peace and stability would be enormous. A keen young Chinese army officer told a Western scholar recently that China would not press its claim in the Spratlys 'until we have the military capability to do it' – raising the age-old question, do civilian and military leaders in China have different agendas? All in all, the Spratlys issue must be considered the gravest threat to the security of east Asia.

It would not be so bad if China were to make its long-term intentions in southeast Asia much clearer. Understandably, it does not actually forswear helping the overseas Chinese out in the event of some kind of holocaust. But statements about the kind of southeast Asia China would like to see are very rare, and can be provocative. Consider the comment made by a Chinese scholar writing in a left-wing Hongkong magazine in 1991. Southeast Asia, he says, can become stable through a process of Finlandisation, after which it can become 'an integrated economic sub-belt within the West Pacific economic belt, with Singapore and Hongkong as the capital cities, linked up with the coastal region of South China ... China, together with Hongkong, Taiwan and Macao, after going through the stage of "taking off", can play the role of an authoritative elder that the others can depend on.'[7] The habit of seeing southeast Asia as a sort of junior playground, where immature schoolboys roam more or less at will under the kindly, watchful and experienced eyes of teachers from the north, dies hard.

South Asia is less flammable. Despite the small Himalayan war of 1962 with India, there is a reciprocity of intellectual respect between India and China which is now unusual in world affairs. It is almost as if the creative spirits on both sides are capable of rising above petty nationalism and believe themselves to be a part of an overarching civilisation rather than of a petty nation state in the European mould. Chinese historians concede that much of China's civilisation came across the Himalayas from India. They point to Bodhidharma, the sixth-century sage, who died as a Buddhist 'missionary' in China, and his predecessors. China's image of India in those days was as a Buddhist paradise, as one might have expected, but also as a source of scientific learning.

Since then scholars on both sides have identified parallelisms and mutual influence.[8] Jawaharlal Nehru wrote in 1937 that India and China had 'traded in ideas, in art, in culture and grown richer in our own inheritance by the other's offering'. He predicted that the two countries, 'sister nations from the dawn of history, with their long tradition of culture and peaceful development of ideas, had to play a leading part in this world drama, in which they themselves are so deeply involved.'[9] One of his colleagues, Srimati Sarojini Devi, later made this comment on Nehru's enthusiasm for China.

> It appears almost as if he has an ancestral memory of the country ... I think I understand his mystical passion for China to some extent. He belongs not to any *one* race nor any *one* country. He is heir to all the countries and to their cultures. And what country has produced such great culture, such serenity, wisdom and courage as China? It has not lost its integrity through ages and centuries.[10]

India and China found a common agenda with the Atlantic powers in the early 1940s to resist fascist aggression, and in 1940 Nehru proposed an Eastern Federation in Asia led by India and China as the senior partners.[11] The contemporary bond between Indian and Chinese intellectuals was the need to preserve an independent Asia free from both Western imperialism and Japanese fascism. Thirty years later another Indian politician, Subramaniam Swami of the Jan Sang, wrote that the ultimate aim of Indian policy should be to create an alliance between China and India to expel the white powers from Asia.[12]

Chiang Kai-shek was widely praised in India for the strong words which he addressed to the British – his allies against Japan! – on their duty to grant India independence. A few Indians responded by actually serving in the Chinese civil war, though on the Communist side. The Bengali Marxist, M.N. Roy, became the Comintern agent in China liaising between the Chinese Communist Party and the Kremlin, though his efforts were not greatly successful. A Maharashtrian, Dr D.S. Kotnis, displayed conspicuous bravery in the medical treatment of Communist Chinese guerrillas in the fight against Japan.[13]

Rabindranath Tagore began to visit China in the 1920s and made friends with many Chinese artists, writers and intellectuals. He later established a Cheena Bhavan, or China Hall, at his Santikinetan University near Calcutta and brought in a Chinese teacher to start a course of Chinese studies, the first of its kind in modern India.

When the Pacific War ended, India and China became fully absorbed in their domestic struggles, China in civil war, India fighting for independence. After that, the Chinese Communists were somewhat isolated in Asia, so Nehru tried at the Bandung

Afro-Asian Conference in 1955 to bring his counterpart, Zhou Enlai, into the Asian circle. The other Asian leaders were made to feel that Nehru was doing them a favour by introducing his very good friend, Mr Zhou, and the Chinese delegation felt that they were being patronised.

Then the border dispute began to take shape, in areas of the high Himalayas which had never been properly surveyed, and were virtually uninhabited. Nehru warned his parliament in 1959 that 'a strong China is normally an expansionist China.'[14] The voluminous cartographical evidence favours the Chinese more than the Indian side, however. Nehru was not well served by the emotional nationalism with which his own aides and the Indian media treated the issue. It ended in war, in 1962, on a very limited scale, and with Nehru disillusioned.

That left a stalemate, and some twenty years of diplomatic frost, during which China befriended Pakistan and other neighbours of India. When the thaw came in the 1980s, there was still no border resolution because China was no longer ready to compromise, as had been bruited in the 1960s. The southern slope of the eastern Himalayas is now found by Chinese scientists to be rich in minerals and hydro-electric potential, as well as being suitable for agriculture. The war almost broke out again in 1987, and remains a possible future threat because of the many strategically located canyons over which both sides try to assert military control from time to time. The frontline positions remain in some sectors only ten yards apart.[15] Yet some of the passes were opened in 1995.

There is tacit agreement that the Himalayas do not warrant another war as such, and both sides are likely to prevent large-scale fighting again. A settlement is now a matter of India accepting a modest loss of pride and China finding some compensatory sweetener. Meanwhile the status of the various small Himalayan states, some independent, some semi-autonomous, is linked with the India–China border problem. At about the time of the India border war, China proposed a confederation of Himalayan states, and this was later elaborated by George Patterson, the Tibetan specialist, to involve not merely Nepal and Bhutan, but also Tibet, Nagaland and Kashmir – all mountainous territories, all out of ethnic and cultural step with their metropolitan governments, and all theoretically interested in ganging up together to keep metropolitan interference to a minimum – but it is unrealistic.[16]

As could have been anticipated, China has conspicuously cultivated India's smaller neighbours, while India has done the same to China's. In 1985 a commander of China's eastern fleet brought a destroyer to call at Karachi and Colombo. Unlike its predecessor under the eunuch Admiral Zheng He five centuries earlier, this was a fleet 'with balls' in the form of guided missiles – a foretaste of future naval rivalry in the Indian Ocean. A few years later when India imposed an economic blockade on disobedient Nepal, the Chinese kept Katmandu's options open by flying crucial gasolene and kerosene into Katmandu to frustrate India's blackmail.

Both India and China have to transit the Malacca Straits when sending their ships between the Indian and Pacific Oceans, and those ships are monitorable by Singapore, Malaysia and Indonesia. Russian frigates ordered by India passed through the Malacca Straits, and so did Russian submarines purchased by China.

With Pakistan, China's hoped-for counterweight against India, there is co-production of the F-7P fighter aircraft at Pakistan's Kamra aeronautical complex. The Chinese have long supported Pakistan's nuclear effort, to help Pakistan remain outside India's orbit. Even American protest has not cut this Chinese lifeline. But from India's point of view, China is arming India's potential enemy. In 1990 India gave tit-for-tat help to the nuclear research of Vietnam, the main irritant on China's southern border – yet India buys Chinese uranium for its nuclear plant at Tarapur.[17]

The non-convergent dreams of Nehru and Zhou Enlai lie under the ground, but in 1988 a replay was begun, it seemed, when Nehru's grandson (Premier Rajiv Gandhi) went to Beijing to talk to Zhou Enlai's adopted son (Premier Li Peng). The lack of emotional warmth compared with earlier phases was made up for by better practical organisation. From 1992 modest programmes of mutual investment have begun in such areas as dry farming, soil conservation, specialised irrigation and agro-industries.[18] It stands to reason that there are areas of agriculture and industry where one of the two countries has specialised more than the other, or has been the first to reach a solution of a development problem common to both.

Han Suyin, the Chinese writer whose marriage to Vincent Ruthnaswamy, an Indian army engineer, is itself a microcosm of the re-emerging rapport between the two nations, helped to get some of these programmes started by discussing them in both capitals. Another area in which exchanges are taking place is space science, ironically encouraged by an American ban on technology transfer to the Indian space organisation.[19] Now in the Asia of the 1990s India and China find themselves broadly agreed on such issues as trade, military exchanges, the precedence of employment over human rights, the sovereignty of Tibet and the need to resist American pressures.

The younger generation on each side of the Himalayas recognises the importance of the other country, although India, as the more free society of the two, manifests the greater interest. Take one example: Vikram Seth, author of the best-selling novel, *A Suitable Boy*, did his conventional student stint at Oxford and Stanford, where he studied Chinese. He then surprised his friends by going on to Nanjing University, spending two years in China on economic research, and publishing a set of lively English translations of three eighth-century Chinese poets.[20] He may have set a new pattern for the intellectual relationship to revive.

China's interest in India is partly dictated by the strong traditional links which Tibet has enjoyed with India, culminating with the existence in Dharamsala of a 'court' of the nominal ruler of Tibet, the Dalai Lama. His entourage in India is sometimes referred to as a government in exile, or a cabinet. But the Indian government regards the Dalai Lama as a religious exile and not a head of government.

To the westward, there are broadly similar considerations for China to cultivate the Islamic countries of the Middle East, since these exert a continuing influence on the Muslim populations of China's western provinces, especially Xinjiang, as well as exporting oil. Beijing looks for a security buffer against outside interference in its western provinces, a means of pressure to stop the undesirable influence of Teheran, Ankara, Riyadh and Cairo over the Chinese Muslims, and an acceptance of China's status and pre-eminent position in central Asia. Currently these concerns appear to have crystallised into an informal alliance with the 'northeastern tier' of the Middle East, namely Iran and Pakistan (although the rapprochement with India may confuse this). China has also cultivated the Egyptian leaders, supplying spare parts in the 1970s for the Migs which Egypt had obtained from the Soviet Union.[21]

In earlier decades the Chinese dallied with Middle East extremists, but by 1990 the simmering Muslim insurgency in China's own western provinces led it to make common cause with Middle East moderates themselves threatened by Islamic fundamentalism. By 1993 China was running a trade exchange of $2.3 billion with the countries of the Middle East. In 1993 Yasser Arafat chose China as his first destination to visit outside the Arab world after signing his historic treaty with Israel.[22] Many expect China to take on the role of patron of the PLO now that it has an actual state to run.

China supplied Silkworm missiles to Iran which the Iranians then trained on American ships in the Persian Gulf in 1987. China is likely to become the most important external player in the Middle East after the USA. The Gulf War enabled China to recover some international standing after Tiananmen. The Chinese strongly condemned the Iraqi invasion of Kuwait, and supported UN motions against Iraq, with the exception of resolution 678 permitting the use of armed force to overcome Saddam Hussain (on which China abstained).[23]

But China's investment in the Middle East is not solely military. It signed a contract to build two 300 MW nuclear power stations in Iran, and is discussing other projects of that size in Egypt and Pakistan. Despite their relatively close ties to the Arab countries in the past and to the 'northeastern tier' Middle East countries in more recent years, the Chinese also deal with Israel. Formal diplomatic relations were not established until 1992, but there has been a long history of co-operation on defence projects, including work on China's next generation of fighter air-to-air missiles and tank programmes. According to the American CIA, defence contacts go back to the 1970s, and run into several billion dollars, although this is denied by the Israelis. A later American report that China and Israel had produced a prototype for the Lavi fighter plane, of which production would soon start in Chengdu in southwest China based on American design and technology, was also denied by both Chinese and Israeli officials.[24] China's interest in Israeli equipment is not quixotic: Israel had captured, studied and reproduced Soviet weapons in its wars with Arab neighbours from the 1960s onwards, when China was denied Soviet materiel.[25]

Beyond the Middle East lies Africa, where China once ran an extraordinary and expensive campaign to win the support of small weak states against Taiwan. Those were the days when China was a net donor of aid. The Chinese expressed solidarity with the Sudanese, for example, who had, after all, taken Charles Gordon, the British perpetrator of the sacking of the Summer Palace in Beijing in 1860, out of circulation. In those days Zhou Enlai could sound the clarion call on leaving Africa: 'revolutionary prospects are excellent throughout the African continent', and Chinese went so far as to open discussion with Africans whose support they needed at an international meeting with 'we blacks'...[26]

The Africans learnt something from China. The Ujamaa villages created by President Nyerere of Tanzania were partly inspired by the People's Communes of China. But otherwise little mark has been left: the Chinese interfered in palace revolutions, supplied arms to revolutionaries and extended useful economic aid for a short period. The Tanzam railway between Tanzania and Zambia was the showpiece, but it ran into considerable difficulties and its usefulness is now lessened by alternative transport developments.[27]

It is sad to record that the many African students who have been officially welcomed at Chinese universities have often experienced prejudice and violence. In 1988 Africans at Nanjing University arrived at a dance with Chinese girl partners who were asked for identification, and this led to a clash between thousands of Chinese and African students. On the following day the dormitory housing seventy of the African students was surrounded by 2,000 Chinese students, some shouting, 'Kill, kill.' The authorities had built a wall around this dormitory to control entry and exit, especially of Chinese girls, but the African students knocked it down.[28]

Part of the trouble was the special treatment given to African students by way of cigarettes and foodstuffs, allowing them more of these items than the Chinese students themselves. There are about 1,500 African students in China, and many of them come away disillusioned. Chinese society is sufficiently isolated to be rather open in racial prejudice. There are still Chinese who will approach a black visitor and rub his face 'to see if the colour comes off'.[29]

Beyond Africa in turn lies Latin America, where China also sought in the 1960s to win friends and influence votes in the United Nations. It is not clear that the Latin Americans always identify the Chinese correctly, since the Peruvians, for example, erroneously call their ethnic-Japanese president, Alberto Fujimori, 'El Chino'. In these parts, Chinese and Japanese look alike. Yet China has supplied Peru with more than US$100 million in soft loans for tractors, construction equipment and hydro-power. It is a big investor in Peru's loss-making public enterprises, helping the privatisation programme by buying out the Hierro Peru iron mine for US$120 million and promising another $150 million over the next three years. This was through the state-owned Shougang steel conglomerate.[30]

With Brazil, China co-operates in space technology, building research and communications satellites in a $200 million joint project. There is also a joint venture in iron mining, and Brazilian companies have bid for $700 million-worth of Chinese dam-construction contracts.[31]

But, as in Africa, these economic collaborations are piecemeal and do not add up to an overall strategy, let alone a political plan. China's role is ambiguous. In population the Chinese represent one-third of the so-called Third World, and its aid to these countries would be classified under UN terminology as 'South–South'. But the Third World is losing its unity, while China gradually takes up its destined role as the largest single state in the world, and therefore active in virtually every country.

A former Indian ambassador to China offers the comment that most Chinese have a superiority complex which makes them feel it is their lot to dominate the world – not militarily, which would be both impossible and suicidal, but politically, culturally and economically. Yet this very quality which instils such drive in them makes them less able to understand the nuances of other countries' values, ways and psychology. Their grasp of the cultural factors in international relations is weak. Although they may have in the end more power than others to dictate events, they may not necessarily be able to use that power to manipulate foreign countries as successfully as some of the old diplomatic hands like Britain and France. By the time China reaches that stage in the early twenty-first century, the necessary interdependence of nations will have grown to the point where no one state, not even the biggest, can realistically expect to push others about in the manner of the nineteenth-century Western imperialists.[32]

CHAPTER 21

CHINA AND THE WEST: PLAYING THE GAME

Chinese scholars have found evidence that Chinese sailors of the Qin dynasty crossed the Pacific Ocean in the year 218 BC, before English or German history had even begun, and landed in America. This put China's history and scientific achievements in a brilliantly better light from the point of view of modern American critics of China. The late Professor Joseph Needham of Cambridge University agreed that these Qin sailors might have influenced the development of the Mayan civilisation of Mexico and might partly account for its accurate calendar, architecture, metal-working, maize and cotton cultivation and pictographic script.[1] More recently, however, China has seemed to need to borrow almost everything from the West in order to modernise. The notion that Chinese seamen might have preceded Christopher Columbus by more than sixteen centuries in discovering America was a gratifying salve for Chinese bruised by their new dependence on the outside.

But today China is seriously tackling its economic development, and the former one-way street of cultural and technical imports from the West has become two-way. Trade is better balanced, and China takes a more assertive position in world affairs, though the West has not quite surrendered its mission to change China into its own image. When Margaret Thatcher lectures China on adhering to treaties, and when Bill Clinton excoriates the Chinese for running too large a trade surplus, they are reflecting past attitudes which are taking time to die away. Meanwhile the Chinese leaders show, by inference if not directly, that they accept many of the American roles in Asia – containing

Russia in the past, restraining Japanese militarism in the present, promoting Asia–Pacific dialogue at the highest level – as beneficial to the region and helpful to China.

One of the appeals of China to the Western mind was its image as the underdog. Westerners slightly guilty about their former imperialism in China, or vaguely nostalgic about the labours of their missionaries in the Celestial Kingdom, retain a patronising sympathy for China. Now the underdog is eating better and growing into a more substantial and well-fed hound. How long can Western sympathy stretch in those circumstances, and how long will China have the benefit of the doubt in international affairs?

A minimal readiness to work with the West on international problems and the avoidance of adventures should assure China of a soft landing on the big power game-board. Compared with other upwardly mobile countries earlier this century, China is already a 'satisfied' state, with few territorial claims of significance against neighbours, and enjoying the prestige of a permanent seat and veto on the UN Security Council – something of which the Chinese are proud, and use carefully. In the 1990s, for instance, China collaborated discreetly with Western powers in the UN over the Gulf War, Cambodia and Bosnia.

Deng Xiaoping once gave a marvellously studied definition of the ideal foreign policy for China. 'Observe the development soberly,' he advised, 'maintain our position, meet the challenge, hide our capacities, bide our time, remain free of ambitions, and never claim leadership.'[2] Confucius himself could hardly have spoken better, and in many respects the advice has been followed.

Sympathetic or not, Western leaders cannot yet buck the habit of making demands for China to change her policies. In 1995 there were five major areas of policy on which Western countries were urging the Chinese government very hard to make 'improvements'. The major one was human rights, but there was also pressure regarding democracy, the arms trade, protection of the environment and the drug trade.

The Tiananmen killings in 1989 led Western governments to reassess their dealings with the reformist China of Deng Xiaoping. They tried to do more to promote human rights and democracy there. Communism was in rapid retreat after

Gorbachev's failure in Moscow, so why should China not be nudged into some form of democracy?

It was not only China that seemed to lag behind in this respect. The lashes from a rattan cane received by a bloodied American teenage vandal in Singapore caused immense protest in the USA. But the Chinese government hit back, arguing that human rights were actually better in China than in America because of the high incidence of murder, robbery, rape, drug abuse and racial discrimination in the USA. 'The human rights situation in China,' it was officially stated, 'is not completely satisfactory, but it is better than that in the United States in many aspects.'[3]

George Bush had been the official envoy of the United States in China for some years, and was better informed about China than any of his predecessors. But after the Tiananmen killings he instigated a partial economic boycott of China designed to demonstrate to the Chinese that they could not flout the international ideals of the West so lightly. The hard-headed Henry Kissinger demurred. 'The American human rights approach to China,' he complained, 'elicits next to no support from most other governments. Not a single Asian nation supports it; not one of them would stand with America if a major crisis resulted.'[4] Kissinger, of course, was the man who had supposedly confessed in 1972 that, 'after a dinner of Peking duck, I'll sign anything.'

Dr America's punitive medicine for China in the years immediately following Tiananmen was one part suspension of high-level visits, and one part threatened trade sanctions. Without formally organising themselves, Western politicians tried to avoid going to Beijing or meeting Chinese leaders. But China soon offered bait to entice weaker Western heads of government: in 1991 Giulio Andreotti, then Prime Minister of Italy, tested the water in Beijing and secured the release of several Catholic priests. John Major and James Baker were subsequently rewarded with releases of students and trade unionists of particular interest to their governments.

Such horse-trading could not settle down to be a habit. The prisoners released were only a small proportion of China's high-profile political prison population, leaving thousands unhelped. In any case, to release an individual prisoner does not change

China's basic position on human rights, nor does it promote free speech. Not one dissident thus released was willing to talk to foreign pressmen on the record about his or her political beliefs.

The most numerous releases came a year after Tiananmen to deflect the American threat of withdrawing Most Favoured Nation treatment from China. Eight hundred were freed, and President Bush was able to veto the Congress resolution calling for MFN status to be withheld. He argued that 'constructive engagement' was better than always trying to punish China. Closing the door on Chinese trade and investment would hurt just those politically progressive elements in China who were engaged in Western trade and trying to push their government to become more liberal. It would play into the hands of Beijing's hardliners who were more inclined to isolationism. The realisation that there was now a Greater China economic circle, which would cause the withdrawal of MFN to hurt 'innocent' Chinese economies dependent on Chinese trade such as Hongkong and Taiwan, was perhaps the clinching factor.

President Clinton altered the system of annual review of the MFN for China, thus putting the issue on a back burner for his presidency. The upshot is that China has seen the potential strength of an American trade retaliation, without actually having to suffer from it so far, which seems a well-judged formula for ensuring China's 'good behaviour' – assuming that the repressed resentments do not burst out at a later stage.[5]

Within the broad category of human rights, there is one arena which arouses uncomprehending fury among Western liberals, and that is Tibet. Virtually all Western governments historically accepted China's legal sovereignty over Tibet, but Western politicians find it impossible to swallow the brutality with which that sovereignty is exercised by China. It has become a point of honour among Western statesmen to meet the Dalai Lama merely to show China their exasperation over its régime in Tibet.

Over the past ten years or so the Chinese have tried to defend their human rights position in the one way open to them, namely to say that attaining a minimum economic level in the society must have priority. Madame Peng Peiyun, the Minister of Family Planning, told the *New York Times* in 1993 that 'the most important human right is the people's right to survival.'[6] A Western lawyer would see no reason why survival and freedom should be mutually exclusive, but it would not be difficult for a Chinese to explain how political freedoms of the kind enjoyed in the West would blunt the actions of the Chinese government in support of economic development: you cannot keep a backward economy on a 10 per cent a year forced march while observing democracy. The impact of both these arguments seems to be having some quiet effect behind the scenes on the respective decision-makers. President Clinton's second term opened in 1997 with a bilateral will for better Sino-American relations, even exchange visits by Jiang and Clinton.[7]

The economic semi-miracle of the 1980s and early 1990s enables the Chinese government to justify to its own population the wisdom of the autocratic style, including the clamp-down on the students in 1989 which was robustly justified to foreign statesmen. In any case there has been a significant change in the past fifteen years in China: the Communists no longer interfere so deeply or systematically in family life, in return for citizens agreeing not to subvert their rulers politically – a new and improved 'social contract'.

China's stance on human rights was put by Premier Li Peng in measured words at the United Nations in 1992. 'A country's human rights situation,' he declared, 'should not be judged in total disregard of its history and national conditions . . . China values human rights and stands ready to engage in discussion and co-operation with other countries on an equal footing . . . seeking consensus while reserving differences.' This is a new China which is ready to talk constructively with the West about human rights instead of defensively shutting the door.

The same sort of thing is happening on the broader issue of democracy. The Western attack here is weaker, because its public is more upset by the fate of an individual beaten prisoner than by the inability of opposition parties to operate in China. In any case despotism is found in the capitalist world as well. When the West criticised Tiananmen, China called it a 'gross interference in China's internal affairs'. Then the Chinese realised that they were not the only ones in Asia to feel threatened by the democratic proselytising of the West. Lee Kuan Yew defended

China against some attacks of Western democrats, and Indonesia and Malaysia have similar views although they are still somewhat suspicious of China.

A third sector of Western pressure on China concerns the arms trade. This came to the fore during the two Gulf Wars when Western media publicised the weapons that China had sold to both Iran and Iraq. The Chinese have also sold arms to Pakistan, Syria and Saudi Arabia, though no one disputes America's pre-eminence as arms salesman. Over and above this, nuclear proliferation became an urgent issue when it was feared in Western quarters that China's nuclear co-operation with Algeria and Iran had acquired military implications. Because of this, the Americans refused to supply China with high technology which could have military uses.

American naval ships have already been hit (in the Gulf) by Chinese-made Silkworm missiles, and the Americans are putting a considerable effort into getting China to ban the export of missiles and to become a full member of the Missile Technology Control Régime. Here one sees China hesitantly crossing the line between the receiving end and the giving end of military high-tech, and sometimes getting stranded in between.

One of the most important concessions made by China to meet Western expectations was its agreement in 1991 to sign the Nuclear Non-Proliferation Treaty. Until then the Chinese had rejected that treaty as a hegemonist conspiracy designed permanently to disadvantage the Third World (a view shared by India). On disarmament, on the other hand, China's position has hardened. In the early 1980s China said it would join in multilateral nuclear disarmament as soon as the two superpowers made substantial cuts in their weapons, and in 1983 China put a figure of 50 per cent to that.

In the later 1980s when deep cuts in both American and Soviet nuclear arsenals made the attainment of this trigger level a real possibility, China shifted its ground to say that it would join in only when Washington and Moscow cut their arsenals to the same level as China's.[8] China thus required nuclear parity with Russia and the United States. Since then China has joined, subtly and privately, Western efforts to bring North Korea's nuclear programme into control. China would have the most to lose from a North Korean use of nuclear weapons.

A general point made by Chinese diplomats when the arms build-up is under fire is the recent availability of Russian weapons at bargain basement prices, which Moscow has to sell in a desperate chase for hard currency. The Chinese were enthusiastic buyers of these items, which fell neatly into their budget, but which were mostly one-off purchases not likely to be repeated. Ironically, these purchases from Russia were one of the factors leading to the American resumption in 1994 of regular military discussions with the Chinese, broken off since Tiananmen.[9]

The other targets of Western pressure are the same as in many Third World countries. One is environmental issues, since China's industrial development and the way it is carried out will affect not only the future environmental pollution among its own population but also among those of neighbouring states. There is not much point in altering all the Western refrigerators if the Chinese will not adapt theirs. Drugs is another well-known question of international concern, where the Chinese, because of their traditional drug-runs in Yunnan along the borders of Burma and Thailand, have a considerable responsibility which they are often unable to shoulder.

The Chinese too have an agenda, though they do not push it as vigorously as the West does. One question which will not be resolved for a very long time is the question of international cultural modes. China, like India and most other Third World countries, accepts the Anglo-Saxon system and values which are built into the major international institutions, such as the World Court, the World Bank, WTO, IMF and the UN itself. How long will China go on collaborating with this cultural monolith without seeking to introduce some 'cultural democracy', as it were, by way of Chinese modes?

These would differ from the Western model principally by favouring conciliation over judgement of right and wrong, and consensus over majority voting. If China did raise this lurking cultural issue it might well be supported by other Asian states, especially Japan. China might even become a leader in spearheading Asian values into the world system. By then China would have absorbed more of Western social culture, and might not see the present international practice as quite so alien.

China wants to join the world. Its disappointment at losing the 2000 Olympic Games was tangible, and widely felt. It was said with a lyrical flourish that one of the five rings on the Olympic flag is China, which was a vivid way of reminding the world that China has 22 per cent of the world's population and ought to be a major venue for such global events.[10] By 2000 the struggle for the succession to Deng Xiaoping and the retrocession of Hongkong and Macao will be over, a time perhaps for China to expect belated world recognition. There were complex reasons for Sydney's triumph, but every Chinese knew that it was yet another Western snub. Their confident hope is that China will host the 2004 Games.

China's foreign policy target had been set by the redoubtable Deng Xiaoping in 1984 in the words: 'China's policy of opening to the outside world will not be changed in this century and the first fifty years of the next century, and it can hardly be changed in the second fifty years.' A few months before that fine dictum Deng received a letter from Liang Heng, who had stood for election to the Hunan Provincial People's Congress as a non-Marxist candidate in 1980, seeking permission to marry the American Judith Shapiro.[11] Marrying a Westerner is slightly shocking to many Chinese and then still needed the approval of the highest person in the land. Another shock experienced by many a young intellectual is to see for the first time a Western map of the world in which the Atlantic Ocean, not China, sits in the middle. In these ways the Chinese are still sheltered from fully belonging to the world, and given the millions of relatively untutored stay-at-homes, China may actually be in the end the last country to join the world community. Some Chinese feel that China's conceited concept of itself as the world's pre-eminent kingdom prevents it from joining the world community.

So vulnerable does China feel to the blows of a more powerful, more experienced and more ruthless outside world that no holds are barred in the attempt to put the Chinese view of a situation on the map. When Han Suyin revealed that for years she had been 'lying through my teeth' defending China from Western critics, she was merely expressing what hundreds and thousands of diplomats and academics had done before her. It furnished a patriotic motive for the untruths she had uttered, as if that justified them.

But there are reasons to believe that a better and sounder view of the West is creeping through that open door. Fang Lizhi explains why most Chinese returning from study in the West bring something positive with them. 'If they are honest,' he says, 'all those who have been to foreign countries must admit that discipline, order, morality, culture and civilisation in those countries are superior to what they are in China ... in general terms, these countries are more civilised than we are.'[12] Fang exaggerates in the opposite direction from Han Suyin, but what he says here contains some truth.

Meanwhile reception of foreign broadcast news and features is spreading. John Simpson estimates that two million Chinese watch the BBC World Television Service every day. He goes on to attribute to this BBC exposure an enhanced capability of Chinese viewers to judge their 'discredited' régime.[13] That is to exaggerate the impact of foreign TV, which is widely watched and enjoyed, especially for its entertainment, but its political provocations are generally ignored – not out of timidity, or because of the government's control of the population, but because the Chinese tradition and the Chinese personality do not include the ambition to challenge the government of the day except in the most extreme cases.

For China, joining the world can be consummated either alone or as a member of a partnership or group. A suggested partnership with Japan has been discussed. Recently Chinese leaders met with their Iranian and Indian counterparts to discuss a possible alliance against American hegemonism in Asia. But China's size dictates a lonely role as a single actor, and its alliances are likely to be shallow and opportunistic.

The Chinese foreign policy specialists dealing with the West spend most of their time on US issues. Quite apart from the Most Favoured Nation problem that dominated the early 1990s, there are many other areas of contention in China–US trade ranging from intellectual property rights and patents, China's non-tariff barriers, the transparency of trade regulations and anti-dumping, to Chinese evasion of textile quotas under the Multi-Fibre Arrangement.[14] But these are run-of-the-mill disputes similar to those which the United States pursues with many other Asian countries. At least American salesmen and investors are refreshingly honest about their role. 'We are here to make a buck, not to save the world,' as a defence electronics salesman put it.

One problem in which politics and economics are richly mixed in the American mind is that of China's export of goods made by prison labour. There are hundreds of labour prison camps across China where a wide variety of commodities is produced, at virtual nil labour cost, by people condemned to punishment for offences. The mystery about these camps has been somewhat dispelled by the extraordinary feat of Harry Hongda Wu, who, after serving a sentence in them, managed to escape to America. He soon reappeared in China with a new name and nationality, an American girlfriend and a miniature pocket camcorder. On the strength of being an American he was allowed to visit many labour camps, and the resulting unauthorised footage made several good TV programmes in the West and the basis for a book as well.[15] Soon afterwards a Chinese official produced another book giving an extremely detailed and revealing official account of the camps.

The USA strictly forbids the import of prison labour goods, but the widening gap between prison-camp pay and wages in China's booming coastal factories creates a problem. How do you un-mix the prison-grown tea after it is blended with other Chinese teas for shipment abroad? China has responded to American complaints by prosecuting some trade corporations and labour reform camp managers, but it can also point out that it is the American importer's responsibility to abide by his own country's laws – and that the USA also exports prison labour goods, so that the moral case is by no means clear cut.

With Russia, which China used to see as the other superpower on her northern and western flanks, the problems are different. Military clashes over the disputed border on the Ussuri river brought the risk of war between the two nuclear powers very close. Now the two have patched up their quarrel, but the relationship is overshadowed by domestic unrest on both sides. The demonstrating Chinese students on the eve of Tiananmen in 1989 used Mikhail Gorbachev's visit to Beijing, which Deng had hoped would inaugurate a new constructive phase of this difficult relationship, in order to raise the stakes in their confrontation with Deng. Gorbachev was denied the full splendour of a state visit, and went home to find himself on his last legs: the Soviet empire finally crumbled in 1991, taking him and the Soviet Communist Party with it.

Now the focus seems to be on the Russian Far East, where there are still territorial disputes over the Ussuri river covering some 350 square kilometres. This has been settled between Moscow and Beijing, but the local government of Russia's Maritime Territory refused to go along with it, so there is an impasse.[16] The Russians are excessively frightened by the occasional statements from China that the tsars stole 3 million square kilometres from China at the end of the nineteenth century. The population figures tell why. China's three northeastern provinces hold more than 90 million people, whereas Russia's population east of Lake Baikal is less than seven million. A certain insecurity on the Russian side may be pardoned – though not its consequence, an unpleasant stepping-up of outright racism where, for instance, the Vladivostok government forbids Chinese citizens to own or rent property. The Chinese have almost completed their part of a new cross-border railway to take goods to Russia's Pacific coast, but the Russians are suspicious of growing Chinese influence in the region and are not very co-operative. The Chinese now profess to be scared of Russian chaos. In 1991, after the abortive coup in Moscow, China's Foreign Minister declared: 'Only China is stable. The whole world is in a mess.'[17]

Western Europe is somewhat detached from these Pacific issues. Europeans can collude with the modern representatives of another older civilisation as respectable as their own, and chuckle with them about who discovered those brash Americans first. It is more than 700 years, after all, since the first Chinese was received by an English king (it was a Chinese Xinjiang Christian, Rabban Sauma, and the Plantagenet King Edward I gave him money for the road).[18] The Chinese formed a special respect for Europeans: they used to say that whereas the Chinese have two eyes, the Europeans have only one – but then everyone else is blind. It is Europe as a whole which impresses, not so much the individual nation states. 'England,' wrote a nineteenth-century Chinese geographer dismissively, 'consists merely of three islands, simply a handful of stones in the Western Ocean.'[19]

France was the training ground of the first generation of Chinese Communists in the 1920s, but that has not saved it from clashes with China over arms sales. If you sell military aircraft or ships to Taiwan, China may retaliate, and vice versa. When the French sold sixty Mirage jets to Taiwan in 1992 China closed the French consulate in Guangzhou and kept French firms out of many large contract tenders thereafter.[20] But these tiffs do not usually last long. European governments know where their bread is buttered. When Chancellor Helmut Kohl went to China in 1993, he came back with nearly US$4 billion-worth of commercial contracts, and when Premier Li Peng returned the visit in the following year he concluded another $1 billion-worth, including the giant Siemens project to build a power station near Hangfeng.

The European Union is not, and will not become a Pacific power. The Europeans' interest in Chinese Christianity is muted, and their view of China's amenability to change through external trade threats is more measured and sceptical than the American.[21] In the case of Britain, the retrocession of Hongkong in 1997 causes bilateral difficulties because of Britain's quixotic late bid to introduce more democracy before handing over. But Sino–European relations as a whole are relatively unruffled, apart from such pinpricks as the British TV documentaries including new material (from a Chinese source) about Mao Zedong's sex life, about which the Chinese government protested.

One might think that the Chinese residents of Western countries would play some part in all this. There are 1.6 million in the USA, and 135,000 in Britain. But in practice they keep such a low profile that they do not become involved in state-to-state relations, and Chinese officials either look down on them or else find them of little use except in trade.

The Economist recently came out with the slightly extravagant recipe that we should treat China not with fear or with favour, but with delight.[22] It would be good for the West's peace of mind to acknowledge that China has emerged from its self-made trap of poverty and isolation, and has done so in a way which brings it into reasonably co-operative relationships with the outside world. But this does not mean that all the West's future dealings with China will be full of delight. Some of the problems mentioned here may well get worse, and other new ones appear, and there will always be hard work for Western diplomats.

China has become what Graham Hutchings of the *Sunday Telegraph* calls a 'semi-superpower'.[23] Some time early in the twenty-first century China will shed that 'semi' and hitherto repressed Chinese politicians may enjoy their first opportunity to throw their new weight around. But the Chinese appreciate the many acts of the West which were undertaken from a certain degree of conscience and right thinking over and above national interest: when Britain agreed voluntarily to give its colony in Hongkong back, for example, or when the Americans agreed, equally voluntarily, to maintain the Most Favoured Nation Treatment for China's trade which it was not legally obliged to do. Some Chinese decision-makers believe in the possibility of a right-dealing world to which they too could belong, and the West's interest is to enlarge their numbers.

Their experience before 1978 had not been sanguine, and it is perhaps an under-rated achievement of the West to have convinced China in the 1980s, despite all the petty disputes, that internationalism is worth while. The big future issues for China will mostly need to be solved with its Asian neighbours. The engagement with the West will concern frameworks for these issues rather than issues themselves – as befits two very large repositories of civilisation.

In the process China and the West will come to appreciate – and utilise – the new factor on China's side of the relationship, namely China's dependence on the outside world for her continuing domestic modernisation. China needs the West for its export markets, future grain imports, investments and technology. The West needs a powerful China to keep the rest of east Asia stable and thus facilitate Western economic activities there. In the very long term this could blossom informally into some kind of universal benevolent condominium.

PART SIX

THE FUTURE

CHAPTER 22

CONCLUSION: CHINA JOINS THE WORLD

The resurgence of China propels a new actor on to the modern world stage. The China which we see visibly growing in wealth and stature is not simply the China which went systematically downhill some two or three hundred years ago and is now coming up again smiling. The old Chinese empire was called by the historian Jonathan Spence 'the largest and most sophisticated of all the unified realms on earth', but it crumbled into too many unsalvageable pieces to be capable of reconstitution. The late Premier Zhou Enlai said when he left China as a student after the First World War that he hoped, when he returned, to see China 'flying aloft'.[1] His generation – and subsequent ones – yearned for the restoration of China's self-respect.

Lucian Pye, the MIT sinologist, used to describe China as a civilisation pretending to be a state. This double identity makes China difficult to analyse. The state continues under a new republican guise, while the civilisation undergoes sea changes with economic modernisation and the flooding in of outside influences. Changes within China and changes in the world outside make it impossible to revive the old China. What is emerging today is something we have never seen before: that is to say, China as a modern state, China with military and economic muscle.

This new China is a mixture of three distinct elements: the old China, aspects of which are still to be observed in people's behaviour; a new China which is naturally evolving out of the old under the influence of indigenous developments in the economy and politics; and finally another new China which is taking shape from the pressures outside the frontiers, especially those of the hitherto powerful Western world. The amalgam of these three, of which the second is the most potent, is what China will become as it reaches the peak of its modernisation in the early decades of the next century. This amalgamation of elements particularly affects the new China in three major sectors of its national development, namely the modernisation of society, of politics and of the economy.

China's social modernisation has sharpened people's materialism and individualism without there being an immediate means of curbing them. The gradual breakdown of the old family system, accelerated by the government's birth control programme limiting the number of children, has weakened the idea of collectivism which was so strong in the old China. Once individualism breaks out in this traditionally family- and clan-centred society it is not easily restrained. Many thoughtful Communist Party leaders now openly lament a spiritual gap in their system.[2]

Some surprising reports of change are beginning to come out of China. A sign of the new times is the *Youth* survey of the white-collar workers in Shanghai revealing that their family background and connections are now considered to be less important in their work than educational qualifications and personal effort. These sophisticated Shanghai people also hold liberal views about divorce, taking a lover or letting a family member go his own way.[3] But where is the self-restraint, the self-control?

The Chinese are now encountering the modern social problem of having more dependent old people and more spoiled single children in their midst. Yet the old ways have a knack of surviving. Jung Chang in *Wild Swans* was not the only one to notice that in the supposedly egalitarian people's communes of the 1960s and 1970s it was the ex-landlord and his family who usually turned out to be the best educated in the group, and, because their skills were needed by their former peasants, they and their sons were able eventually to regain some of the power and authority which the Maoists had stripped from them.[4] Here is a continuity factor to lay alongside the more visible destructive changes in society.

Political modernisation has not developed as energetically. There has been no systematic drive to create the institutions of freedom. The government and ruling party saw no reason to dilute their power, while the people saw no advantage in freedom because of their traditional acceptance of authority. In most of the demonstrations for democracy in China under the Communists, it has been seen as an ideal, and a distant one at that, rather than an actual political process to put in train. Traditional modes of authority therefore remain, and that is why Mao Zedong and Deng Xiaoping became so powerful.

Mao's was the worst case. His paranoia has been judged as having caused more deaths than Stalin and even his sanity in his final years has been questioned. The memoirs of Mao's personal physician, Dr Zhisui Li, portray an erratic, almost childish approach to government.[5] Yet his colleagues were too frightened to unseat Mao (the only try, by Marshal Peng Dehuai, was a fiasco). The kind of democracy capable of pulling down a leader like Mao will not exist in China for many years. There is not yet a substantial middle class in China as there is in most Western countries, and peasant apathy in political matters is notorious. The countryside was little moved by either the Cultural Revolution or the Tiananmen Square killings. Demonstrations are led and manned by students and urban workers only.

Yet there is a very gradual intrusion of Western ideas about politics, especially about open debate and open voting for candidates for councils and assemblies at the lower level. This kind of idea seeps in from Taiwan and Hongkong, where a sub-group of the Chinese people has already entered the world of the rule of law and contested elections. Chinese themselves visiting foreign countries and then returning to the People's Republic bring graphic accounts of democratic political institutions which excite interest, and the same goes for the overseas Chinese coming from those same countries.

But the process is extremely slow, even in such relatively large and sophisticated urban centres as Shanghai, Guangzhou or Beijing. The historic ground on which Anglo-Saxon democracy was constructed goes back to Magna Carta which the English barons negotiated with King John to limit his absolute power, and it took seven centuries after that to bring about the reforms of the nineteenth century which gave the vote to all adult males (women had to wait even longer). Chinese history has no such background. Even the student hunger-strikers in Tiananmen Square in 1989 warned in their final statement that 'democratic rule, to every Chinese person, is unfamiliar. Everyone in China must learn it from the very beginning.'[6]

We cannot therefore realistically expect effective democratic processes to be installed and working in China in the foreseeable future. Half of the Chinese students in the USA said in a survey that they did not expect democracy in China within twenty years.[7] If a democratic constitution were to be planted in the unprepared soil of Chinese society, it would be a frail and weedy plant, not vigorously nurtured by grass-roots involvement. The attitude of most Chinese would still be, 'let the rulers rule, and leave us alone – and we will leave them alone.' On particular controversial issues like the Sanxia dam and family planning policy, there can be strong surges of public opinion against government policy, but these are the exceptions which prove the rule.

Those mini-rebellions can happen today without a democratic structure, and would happen even more if there were a democratic constitution in force. But otherwise there would be much apathy, except perhaps at the very lowest levels, which is where the Communist Party reformers have encouraged some democratic procedures knowing that the habit could spread upwards to the higher levels. Political change is likely in fact to be selective and sluggish. Western countries would be wise to accept this, and to shed illusions about the realistic possibilities of rapid political development in China. Better encourage the things which have some chance of succeeding with outside encouragement rather than condemn what the Chinese people themselves acquiesce in at home. Taiwan is showing what kind of modern political system can be produced by Chinese, but the challenge for China's rural provinces is far greater and will take more time.

A good example of the development of grass-roots democracy is the People's Council of Gao village in Hebei. In under three years this elected council sacked more than fifty unqualified village Communist Party officers, vetoed more than seventy 'unreasonable' decisions made by those officers, and made over 700 decisions to boost the village economy. About RMB 3 million was saved that might otherwise have been wasted, and over eighty enterprises were established. Gao's experience has been copied by many other places, and the increase of village autonomy with a democratic foundation is becoming an important factor on the national political scene.[8] That is the base upon which Chinese democracy will be built, not the critical resolutions of Western parliaments or the United Nations, not the preaching of a Clinton or a Patten, not a series of condescending editorials in the Washington press or democracy propaganda broadcasts to China by Western radio and TV stations.

Economic modernisation is easier to monitor. The economic reforms of Deng Xiaoping have been largely successful, giving scope for indigenous forces to break out for the improvement of the local economic environment. These reforms can be maintained as long as there is a minimal consensus or unity at the centre. After Deng's decease this may come into question. But the best guess is that a modest momentum of reform – even in the most difficult area of state-owned industry – will be maintained.

Malaysia is a small country geographically close to China, and in territorial dispute with it over the Spratly Islands. Yet its Prime Minister, Mohammed Mahathir, recently predicted that 'a prosperous China will become the engine of growth, firstly for East Asia, including Southeast Asia, and then the world.'[9] He is in a position to form a better judgement than many Westerners. The Chinese themselves squirm at such remarks. They are all too aware of the long way they have to go to catch up with even Malaysian standards. The World Bank estimates China's Gross National Product per head of population at only a quarter of Malaysia's. The Chinese also fear that optimistic statements do them no good, because they encourage greater demands upon them by neighbours and by the international community. Deng told John Roderick, the veteran Associated Press reporter, 'We will always be a Third World country, never a superpower.'[10]

The other major feature of contemporary Chinese economics is the devolution of power to the provinces. If the provinces gain a certain measure of autonomy (and the coastal provinces are to some extent in that position already) then the centre will have less control and there will more inequality. Each province will go its own way more obviously than today. Chinese politicians are very concerned about the possibility of a fragmentation, but at least one can assert that authority would be exercised in such a scenario by provincial governors already committed to the modernisation process. They will not be like the old feudal-style warlords who so damaged China in the first half of this century, but more like 'peacelords' – or even GNP-lords. Meanwhile the economic sprint is unmistakeable – growth averaging about 9 per cent a year since 1978 (in Taiwan it has been 9 per cent on average since 1950, and in Hongkong even higher).

This is the pattern of China's likely progress over the next few years. How will people in other countries be affected, and how far will the new China accept foreign influences? The Chinese take comfort from the fact that the pain of change is softened by the intercession of their compatriots abroad – the denizens of 'Greater China' who are ethnic Chinese at a higher stage of economic and social development, in Taiwan, Hongkong and Singapore, and the overseas Chinese living in southeast Asia and America and, indeed, all over the world. The new role of the overseas Chinese was heralded by the return to Aw Boon Haw, the Malaysian magnate, of his assets in China after a quarter-century's sequestration. The Maoist constraint on Chinese abroad returning and investing in their motherland had always been disliked on both sides. The torrent of funds and technology from these offshore Chinese into China in the 1980s and 1990s – from tycoons like Y.K. Pao, Li Kashing, Dhanin Chearavanont and Liem Sioe Liong – became a major factor in the success of Deng Xiaoping's reforms.

China's double role as civilisation and state means a unique interaction of political and cultural factors in its development. The Chinese people in or out of the People's Republic are forging a new sense of cultural identity which must eventually extend into the political and economic spheres. The Chinese in China itself view their 'lost' relatives from Taiwan, Hongkong and southeast Asia as people whom they can immediately recognise culturally, though they may entertain strange and not always very Chinese ideas about politics and social relations – like the puritanically cost-conscious offshore Chinese who withdrew his vast donation to his family village on being served an inappropriately luxurious dinner feast by its leaders.

These offshore Chinese are of the greatest value as a perception buffer between China and the West. The Chinese in China are increasingly able to see how other Chinese people can adapt to modern ways, largely Western-originated, without losing all their sense of Chineseness. And we in the West can see the Chinese life of Taiwan or Singapore at a relatively high level of economic development, observe what kind of mix of Western and Chinese values is produced, and be reassured that the end product will not be entirely mysterious or threatening. The offshore Chinese introduce China to the world, and the world to China, and both sides must be immensely grateful to them.

The most valuable thing of all is that the Chinese in China, who have many historical, geographical and cultural reasons to be somewhat isolationist and minded to stick to their own basic values rather than cave in to Western pressures, may feel a little more relaxed about lowering their guard when they see how their kinsmen in Taiwan, Hongkong and southeast Asia have retained their core Chinese identity.

Efforts to pin down that identity, to find the precise mix between traditional Chinese and modern Western, have not so far been very fruitful, however. Martin King Whyte, the American sinologist, found that the reversion to household farming after 1978 helped keep families together, delaying their fragmentation and encouraging efforts to build up even larger households based on the clan.[11] This has all kinds of consequences. Parents win greater control over their children's choice of mate. The elders can be more assertive on such matters as ancestor worship and the elaborate celebration of weddings and funerals. The progress made by women in their struggle for equality is set back. Individualism is bridled once more. The commune of Mao was more egalitarian, even if it produced less food, whereas the materially better off household or family farming units of Deng are in some respects socially regressive.

On the other hand, rural dwellers are being brought closer to urban or Western patterns of life. The growth sector in the villages is not farming, but rural industry, and young people from the countryside are gaining a wider outlook and becoming more independent, especially if they migrate from home to find these jobs. Television, of course, promotes urban standards and consumerist ideas contrary to those of the older generation; and is not easily suppressed, as the government has found when seeking to restrict foreign broadcasts.

Michael Harris Bond, a psychologist at the Chinese University of Hongkong, comes to a similar conclusion.[12] The Chinese have moved away from their former passivity towards achievement, and therefore competition, with a modern intensity near to that of Western societies. Yet they retain their attachment to the solidarity of the group, the importance of harmony in personal relations, paternalism towards younger people or juniors, and the over-riding obligations within the close small family. Japan has been travelling this tortuous road from east Asian tradition to global modernity far longer than China, and some of the juxtaposition of values to be observed in contemporary Japan probably foretells what lies ahead for China, give or take a little. A Japanese today is increasingly attracted to democratic values and yet continues to hold on to the hierarchical idea of the traditional social structure, accepting the importance of authority and obedience.

The cultural question affects the rate of economic growth, and its success, and there is now a growing literature on the general dislike of the Chinese – whether in China, Taiwan, Hongkong or southeast Asia – for impersonal large-scale industrial management. They prefer the family-style personalism, where an organisation is hierarchically arranged and members are expected to defer to authority rather than argue, that has been the Chinese hallmark since before Confucius. Some Western economists wonder how far China will get in the modern world without a large number of successful giant conglomerates.

Even culture has international repercussions – both ways. Whether there will be a convergence of cultures between China and the West – and other countries – is much debated among sociologists and psychologists. The Chinese will certainly become more familiar with the West over the next half-century or so, and a little more like the West. At the same time more Westerners will penetrate Chinese culture, civilisation, history, language, ethics, etc. That suggests the possibility of a convergence in the very long run. Obviously the fewer obstacles that the West places on China's development and growth, and the more it can invest and trade there, the more politically and intellectually secure the prospects of cultural convergence will be.

The early post-war European governments and President Bill Clinton had the right instincts on diplomatic recognition and Most-Favoured-Nation issues. But the Japanese example suggests that a complete movement by China to a Western cultural style may be neither necessary nor desired. If China proves no more malleable than Japan, then the West will find itself dealing with a number of different countries in east Asia with a similar base but slightly different present-day features – an inner circle within the Chinese culture zone and an outer one of east Asia as a whole.

The most interesting question is whether those east Asian countries would band together, for all their differences, to secure a kind of cultural equality in world affairs, where international organisations like the United Nations would give as much scope for east Asian cultural values as they do for Anglo-Saxon ones. That would be a war, not of bombs, machine guns or aircraft carriers, but of computers, faxes, word processors and satellites, as Rupert Murdoch has foreseen.

If there is one thing which does puzzle a Westerner, it is the continuing Chinese rejection of the small nation-state as a unit of economic and political development. Europeans have a kind of proprietary pride in the nation state of perhaps 40 or 50 million people which has been so successful in their continent. China, by contrast, seems firmly set on being a large unified, or at best semi-federal state of 1,200 million people. But the Chinese are right in suspecting an ulterior motive in the West's advice.

If federalism proceeds in China, and provincial autonomy increases, the power of the centre may progressively be reduced to embrace in the end only foreign policy, military affairs and the higher level of international economic relations. Would that kind of China be as important as the unitary or semi-federal China? If the provinces broke free and followed the example of Europe, might not China – or thirty Chinas – be discounted by the rest of the world as a relatively ineffective player? That is one major reason why the Chinese leaders wish to avoid the federalist solution. In any case, by the time China goes federal, if it ever does, the world will have entered an age of high interdependence, making big countries more pacific and smaller ones safer.

One might perhaps have expected that the economic hardships inevitably caused by fast development, particularly unemployment and inflation, would lead to unrest in many parts of China. Yet that is not a detectably widespread trend. The Chinese government can follow a tight credit policy without causing major social disturbance. If there is retrenchment because of overheating and excessive inflation, the authorities are frequently able to make subsistence-wage payments to workers, and to control credit supply to the extent necessary. When two Jardine Fleming analysts visited northwest China in 1994 they found 'considerable tolerance of the economic hardships caused by unemployment and inflation'.[13] This is one reason why the central government can continue playing an economic role over a country whose size would make most Western administrators blench.

The West is most apprehensive about resurgent China's possible new versions of old Chinese vices. The most obvious one is that of territorial expansion and aggressiveness. Actually this fear has been overtaken by events. Today there is no discernible drive to territorial expansion in China: China is 'satisfied' without acquiring outlying territories beyond her present control. The question could be put the other way round, that some of the territories which China presently controls may not be legitimate in global eyes for China to possess permanently. There must be a question mark over China's long-term position in Tibet, and possibly in Xinjiang and Inner Mongolia as well. In these three interior regions, China faces a colonial-type situation with significant cultural–ethnic minorities, and could well go through the same variety of responses that Western imperialist powers did in the past – from consolidating the metropolitan power and suppressing minorities, to granting self-rule, genuine autonomy and conceivably even independence.

This is the only frontier on which China faces a real threat of invasion from neighbouring powers and forces, especially Islamic fundamentalism and possibly revived Russian nationalism as well, so this interior region will be the most tricky geographical area for China in the decades to come. Elsewhere the frontiers are broadly fixed, and the only major flashpoint is the Spratly Islands, over which other Asian countries have been surprised at the strong, not to say aggressive, attitude taken by China. This may be a poker game that China is playing, with oil and other economic resources at stake, or it may be a last fling of nationalism in an era where there will be few more chances of expressing and indulging it. It may also be a result of weak leaders at the centre feeling the need to play the nationalist card to gain military and civilian support in the transition period surrounding Deng's death. Western interests are not strictly involved in the Spratlys, only east Asian ones.

China did not, after all, use force to retake the lost territories of Hongkong and Taiwan, which many people in other countries might partly have excused.[14] What Chinese governments have done over the last twenty or thirty years indicates that China does not wish to extend the already formidable territory it has to control. On the contrary, China's political energies may increasingly have to be concentrated on holding the existing China together.

Indeed, some Western observers fear that China may lose itself in inward-looking self-contemplation, rather as it used to in earlier centuries. Western specialists on international affairs notice how little creative thinking there is currently in China about world affairs and how the world should be run. This consequence of dictatorship does not bode well for any hopes we may have of a China which would use its growing power and influence to help steer the world along constructive paths. In the United Nations China speaks on regional Asian affairs, and has been most collaborative on particular crises beyond its frontiers such as North Korea and Cambodia (concerting its tactics with the USA and Japan). When it comes to the wider issues that have to be debated, however, a distinctively thoughtful Chinese voice is not often heard. They are not ready for that, inhibited by their own inexperience and their domestic politics.

There are also fears about China's political future. Because the political machinery is not being put systematically in place for some kind of future democracy, people worry lest the Chinese government remain as unaccountable and dictatorial as it is today, or even more so. Here again there are contradictory forces at work, but it seems fair to assume that the inexorable growth of the economy, especially outside the state sector, will widen people's political horizons and lead them to seek more choice, more pluralism, more participation – and that the ruling élite will become more and more entwined with that process. That is not, strictly speaking, a legitimate Western concern. The Chinese will find their own political institutions, just as they have found their own economic development strategies.

On the other hand it is obvious that China must in the end become the new centre of an east Asian group or system of economies which is going to be dominant in world affairs, probably taking a lead in material terms over the West in the next two decades or so, though it would still lag behind in terms of length of experience in international affairs. Such a shift in the world power balance will have many consequences for the West, impinging even on its domestic affairs. William Rees-Mogg has noted in *The Times* the concern that the rise of the east Asian economies may eventually make it difficult for the Western countries to maintain their welfare state.[15] That is a question far bigger than the compass of this book, but it shows how issues could develop in the early part of the next century which would set China and the West on a course, not of collision in the military sense, but of bad feeling, mutual reproach and tension over environmental issues, trade balances, the World Trade Organisation and many other matters of global management.

Western perceptions of China today differ hugely. There are pessimists who point to the economic hazards that lie ahead for China – the incompleteness of the reforms, the growing shortage of natural resources by comparison with the size of population, and the continued growth and ageing of that population – to forecast a sorry China in twenty or thirty years losing its hold on economic growth and facing rising strife at home.[16] Other Western experts, equally well informed, say that even if China continues its growth at only a proportion of the current rate it will soar ahead of other countries, overtaking the rest of the world during the next two or three decades.[17]

The capacity of the people to endure, not only economic

hardship but political irresponsibility as well, suggests that China might hope to escape some of the upheavals which other countries have experienced on the road to modernisation. One cannot easily choose between the optimists and the pessimists, or between the extremes in either camp. A sensible stance would be one of cautious optimism based on the resilience of the Chinese people and their traditional social discipline. Many criticisms of inefficiency, mismanagement and corruption in China are exaggerated – not always malevolently – for cultural or ideological reasons. But we should be ready to stand back and wait patiently if there are periods of turmoil ahead.

The contradictions are great. China, for example, is probably going to have the biggest Gross National Product in the world, exceeding the United States, in about twenty years. Yet some localities in China away from the coast in inhospitable mountain and desert terrain encompass some of the worst poverty to be found in the world. China is so large that it can contain such extremes. Another contradiction is that China continues to behave in the world like a single power unit, with a foreign policy not overtly challenged by provincial leaders, and yet, internally, China often gives the appearance of containing a number of small kingdoms openly resisting central control. Again, the Chinese are fierce to fight, as they did in Korea and the Himalayas, and can be strident in their diplomacy, and yet within China foreigners are often allowed the most extraordinary latitude of the kind that such visitors as Paul Theroux and Mark Salzman – and the British TV crew which made *Beyond The Clouds* – have been able to exploit so fruitfully.[18] Chinese fierceness is often a disguise for insecurity.

The new China is thus a microcosm of the world, reduced to one-fifth. Everything can be found there, evidence for all arguments. But the basic story is that 1.2 billion people are shedding some of their former collectivism and testing the waters of individualism. They are moving rapidly from searing poverty to an economic life better than in most developing countries, with pockets around such big cities as Guangzhou and Shanghai approaching southern European standards. These changes are ongoing.

The Chinese are governed by an authoritarian Communist

Party that is not afraid to innovate, but which has no agreed procedure for leadership changes. Although it has conceded some democracy at the lowest level, the Party does not admit of any democracy at the top, and its deplorable handling of the Tiananmen Square demonstrators in 1989 showed that democratisation will be a very long-term matter. But China has never wielded such influence in the world as it does today, with the largest army in the world and a remarkable capacity for sabre-rattling.

That sometimes conveys an aggressive image, and looked at from the Western point of view, China's apparent hostility from time to time is conveyed in a different cultural language, and therefore appears doubly threatening. The answer is to puncture that threat by going halfway to meet China in the cultural game. If the West hopes to engage, tame or collaborate with China on the basis of the English language and values, it may have some little success, depending on the skill of its representatives. But if it pursues the game more seriously with a greater grasp of the Chinese language and some knowledge of Chinese civilisation, its chances of success would be doubled or trebled. For a country of China's size, importance and future wealth, it is worth doing.

While federalism may spread, outsiders would be wise not to count on it until it happens: even if independent, the provinces would still be culturally Chinese and some of them as well off as the Mediterranean states of southern Europe. China's economy will grow inexorably, having already passed the point of experimentation to adopt a consensually compulsive quick march. China will not be a threat unless we make it so by refusing to help repair Chinese self-respect. It will be an avuncular rather than a savage tiger, even if frustration and inexperience in global affairs make it scowl and roar. That is the bottom line of a rational verdict on a country about to surprise a world grown used to China's absence. China has much to teach us, and the twenty-first century will provide the first opportunity for enriching intercourse even more stimulating than Europe's eighteenth-century 'discovery' of India.

NOTES

Abbreviations used:
BBC/SWB/FE: British Broadcasting Corporation, Summary of World Broadcasts, Far East.
ICM: Inside China Mainland (Taipei).
While Chinese periodicals are cited in *pinyin*, most Taiwan and Hongkong pubications are cited in the Wade–Giles spelling.

Chapter 1 China's History: Strands From the Past

1. Some historians now criticise Marco Polo for plagiarism, but the jury is still out on that. (Few notes are supplied for the first two introductory historical chapters which cover reasonably well-known ground.)

2. The late Professor Joseph Needham of Cambridge exhaustively pioneered the history of China's scientific achievements in his many-volumed *Science and Civilization in China*, Cambridge, 1954 onwards.

3. See the evidence deployed in Frank Welsh, *A History of Hong Kong*, HarperCollins, London, 1993, pp.34–8.

Chapter 2 Mao: The Communist Whirlwind

1. Wu Ningkun, *A Single Tear*, Hodder & Stoughton, London, 1993.

2. Mao's doctor, Li Zhisui, did the same, burning forty of his personal diaries in the Cultural Revolution. After quitting China in 1988, he reconstructed his memoir into *The Private Life of Chairman Mao*, Chatto & Windus, London, 1994.

3. *Los Angeles Times*, 20 November 1994.

4. David Shambaugh (ed), *Deng Xiaoping, Portrait of a Chinese Statesman*, Clarendon Press, Oxford, 1995; Richard Evans, *Deng Xiaoping and the Making of Modern China*, Hamish Hamilton, London, 1993; David Bonavia, *Deng*, Longman, London, 1989; Deng Maomao, *Deng Xiaoping My Father*,

Basic Books, New York, 1995; and David Goodman, *Deng Xiaoping*, Cardinal, London, 1990.

Chapter 3 Politics: He Who Argues . . .

1. *Study and Exploration (Xuexi Yu Tansuo)*, no. 5, 1988, in ICM, February 1989.

2. See David Y.E. Ho, 'Chinese Patterns of Socialization', in Michael Harris Bond (ed.), *The Psychology of the Chinese People*, Oxford University Press, Hongkong, 1986, pp.35–6.

3. Frank Ching, *Ancestors; 900 Years in the Life of a Chinese Family*, Harrap, London, 1988, p.113.

4. Quoted in James H. Williams, 'Fang Lizhi's Expanding Universe', *The China Quarterly*, no. 123, September 1990, p.459. Lin Kang argues that Chinese culture fostered a servile mentality, robbing people of their individual character, *Issues and Studies*, February 1993, p. 137.

5. Truth, *The Nineties*, Hongkong, April 1994, in ICM, June 1995, Bridge, *Financial Times*, 12 October 1991.

6. Quoted by Lucian W. Pye, 'The State and the Individual; an Overview Interpretation', *The China Quarterly*, no. 127, September 1991, pp.443–66.

7. *Mingbao*, Hongkong, 4 November 1991, in ICM, January 1992.

8. Qing Guangyao in *Japan Times*, 29 April 1993. The singer is the blue-eyed Fei Xiang, whose father is American and of whom Culture Ministry officials have said approvingly, 'his attitude is earnest', *International Herald Tribune*, 26 October 1989.

9. *Liaowang Zhoukan (Outlook Weekly)*, 1 May 1989, in ICM, July 1980.

10. The heir, Yu Yan, played the stage role of a British M.P. hurling abuse at Selwyn Lloyd, then Foreign Secretary, over the Suez affair of 1956. See *Spectator*, 12 June 1993; *Sunday Telegraph*, 13 June 1993; and Tony Scotland, *The Empty Throne, the Quest for an Imperial Heir in the People's Republic of China*, Viking, 1993.

11. *Japan Times*, 7 April 1993.

12. Sun Longji (Lung-kee Sun), *The Deep Structure of Chinese Culture*, as quoted in *Far Eastern Economic Review*, 23 April 1987.

13. *Hong Kong Economic Journal*, 3 June 1993, in ICM, September 1993.

14. Bertrand Russell concluded after his visit to China in 1921 that 'the business of "saving face" . . . is only the carrying out of respect for personal dignity in the sphere of social manners. . . . Chinese life . . . is far more polite than anything to which we are accustomed,' Russell, *The Problem of China*,

Allen & Unwin, London, 1922, pp.204–5.

15. See the clarifying exposition of face by Michael Harris Bond and Kwang-Kuo Hwang in Bond (ed.), *The Psychology of the Chinese People*, Oxford, Hongkong, 1986, pp.243–9.

16. *China Youth*, Beijing, September 1993, in ICM, January 1994. See Lucian W. Pye, 'Factions and the Politics of Guanxi', *China Journal* (Canberra), July 1995 p. 35 at p. 43.

17. *International Herald Tribune*, 23 November 1993.

18. Speech of 29 November 1991, *Trend Magazine*, Hongkong, January–February 1992, in ICM, March 1992.

19. ICM, May 1988.

20. *Legal System Daily (Fazhi Ribao)*, 25 February 1988, in ICM, May 1988.

21. Lin Defu, *China Youth*, no. 2, 1993, *BBC/SWB*/FE/1668/B/2/1 of 21 April 1993.

22. *South China Morning Post*, 5 January 1990.

23. Wang, *International Herald Tribune*, 16 October and 21 November 1991; Professor Guo Luoji, *Japan Times*, 15 July 1992; Judicial official *BBC/SWB*/FE/2093/G/3 of 6 September 1994; and see William P. Alford, 'Double-Edged Swords Cut Both Ways: Law and Legality in the People's Republic of China', in *Daedalus*, American Academy of Arts and Sciences, Cambridge, Mass., spring 1993, p.45.

24. W.J.F. Jenner, *The Tyranny of History: The Roots of China's Crisis*, Allen Lane, London, 1992; Elegant, *International Herald Tribune*, 4 June 1992.

25. Gong Xiangrui, 'Political and Constitutional Change in China', Address to Durham University, 30 November 1987 (mimeo), p.4.

26. Brantly Womack (ed.), *Contemporary Chinese Politics in Historical Perspective*, Cambridge University Press, 1991, p.86. On China's gerontocracy, see Chiang Chen-ch'ang, 'The Influence of the "Old Guard" in Mainland Chinese Politics', *Issues and Studies*, July 1992, p.25. The Politburo asked the five active 'Immortals' to 'mediate' the tension between centre and provinces at the beginning of 1995, *BBC/SWB/FE* 2219/G17 of 4 February 1995.

27. *Far Eastern Economic Review*, 3 January 1991.

28. Yao, *The Times*, London, 27 December 1990.

29. Quoted by Orville Schell, *Discos and Democracy, China in the Throes of Reform*, Pantheon, New York, 1988, p.325.

30. See Daniel Southerland, *Washington Post* and *International Herald Tribune*, 18 July 1994.

31. Lin Zaifu and Liu Binyan quoted by Merle Goldman, *Sowing the Seeds of Democracy in China, Political Reform in the Deng Xiaoping Era*, Harvard University Press, Cambridge, Mass., 1994, p.184; Spender in

Stephen Spender and David Hackney, *China Diary*, Thames and Hudson, London, 1982, p. 166.

32. *Seeing China Through a Third Eye*, believed to be by He Xin, *Mingbao*, 12 August 1994, *BBC/SWB*/FE/2078/G/7 of 19 August 1994 at p.8.

33. *The Times*, London, 27 June 1989.

34. Deng met Bush when the latter visited Beijing in February 1989.

35. Wang Dan and Yang Ping, 'On the Urgency of Democratic Reforms in China', *Mingbao*, 5 September 1994, *BBC/SWB*/2108/G/11-13 of 23 September 1994.

36. *BBC/SWB*/FE/1808 of 25 January 1993.

37. John P. Burns, 'Political Reform in a Turbulent Environment', *The China Quarterly*, no. 119, September 1989, p.481; Lowell Dittmer and Yu-shan Wu, 'The Modernisation of Factionalism in Chinese Politics', *World Politics* 47, July 1995, p. 467; and the high-level debate on factions in *China Journal*, July 1995.

38. *Daily Telegraph*, 15 November 1993.

39. Comment on *River Elegy* by *Cheng Ming*, Hongkong, September 1988, in ICM, January 1989; for extreme examples of mimicking Western fashions, including performance artists of Beijing staging Gilbert and George shows with nudity and masturbation, see also *Mingbao*, 26 July 1994, *BBC/SWB*/FE/2062/G/13 of August 1994 and *Washington Post* 13 September 1994.

40. See Ho-jen Tseng, 'Peasant, State and Democracy: The Chinese Case', *Issues and Studies*, April 1993, p.34 at pp.49–50.

41. Wang, *Daily Telegraph*, 15 November 1993; letter *International Herald Tribune*, 17 May 1995.

Chapter 4 The Party: Staying in Power

1. Address of 1980, cited in *Baixing Semi-monthly*, Hongkong, December 1993, in ICM, February 1994.

2. *International Herald Tribune*, 9 November 1979.

3. *Dagongbao*, Hongkong, 4 February 1988; Steven Mufson, 'Signs of Dissent in a Chinese Vote', *Washington Post* and *International Herald Tribune*, 18 March 1995; Draft laws, *Mingbao*, Hongkong, 31 December 1994.

4. *Guardian*, 15 February 1988.

5. Arthur S. Ding, 'The Reform of the People's Congresses in Mainland China,' *Issues and Studies*, April 1994, p.14 at p.30.

6. *Dagongbao*, 31 March 1988, and *The Times*, London, 29 March 1988.

7. Taiwan delegates not actually from Taiwan but drawn from Taiwanese on the mainland.

8. *Dagongbao*, 7 April 1988.

9. Womack quoted in *International Herald Tribune*, 29 March 1995; Yan, *Daily Telegraph*, 5 August 1988.

10. Huang, *The Times*, London, 2 April 1992; *Daily Telegraph*, 3 April 1992; deputy, *Xinhua* 18 March 1995, *BBC/SWB*/FE 2265/G/5 of 30 March 1995.

11. *The Times*, London, 12 February 1993.

12. Lincoln Kaye, 'Flourishing Grassroots', *Far Eastern Economic Review*, 19 January 1995, p.23.

13. *Far Eastern Economic Review*, 4 November 1994.

14. *Renmin Ribao*, 22 August 1989 – i.e. after Tiananmen.

15. *Xinhua*, 15 September 1994, *BBC/SWB*/FE/2105/G/1 of 20 September 1994; and 'China's Parliament Delivers "Slap in Face for Leader"', *The Times*, 16 March 1995.

16. See John P. Burns, 'Civil Service Reform: the Thirteenth Party Congress Proposals', *The China Quarterly*, no. 120, December 1989, p.739; also L.S. Dong, 'The Recruitment of Cadres and Civil Servants in Mainland China', *Issues and Studies*, October 1993, p.63; and *Xinhua*, 30 July 1994.

17. Deng's speech to Politburo on 18 August 1980, cited in *Dagongbao*, 14 July 1986.

18. *Wenweibao*, Hongkong 1 December 1992, in ICM, March 1993.

19. *The Express News*, Hongkong, 8 June 1993, in ICM, August 1993.

20. Dick Wilson, 'The China Syndrome', *Management Today*, October 1990.

21. *Dagongbao*, 12 April 1988.

22. *Trend*, Hongkong, May 1994, in ICM, August 1994.

23. *Nineties Monthly*, Hongkong, June 1990, in ICM, August 1990.

24. *Financial Times*, 12 October 1991, and *Mingbao*, Hongkong, 4 June 1992, in ICM, August 1992.

25. See Barry Sautman, 'Neo-Authoritarianism in Recent Chinese Political Theory', *The China Quarterly*, no. 129, March 1992, pp.72–102.

26. *Far Eastern Economic Review*, 13 September 1990.

27. Cited by Sun Longji (Lung-kee Sun), 'To Be or Not to Be Eaten', see *Modern China*, vol. 12, no. 4, October 1986.

28. *Guardian*, 4 April 1988.

29. *Ibid.*

30. *Mingbao*, Hongkong, 23 September 1994, *BBC/SWB*/FE/2110/G/1 of 26 September 1994; and *Cheng Ming*, Hongkong, 1 May 1994, *BBC/SWB*/FE/1990/G/12 of 8 May 1994.

31. *Cheng Ming*, Hongkong, August 1994, in ICM, October 1994.

32. Quoted in Richard Evans, *Deng Xiaoping and the Making of Modern China*, Hamish Hamilton, London, 1993, p.259.

33. See Lucian W. Pye, 'An Introductionary Profile: Deng Xiaoping and China's Political Culture', *The China Quarterly*, no. 135, September 1993, p.412 at p.432.

34. *The Times*, London, 12 February 1993.

35. *Trend*, Hongkong, August 1994, in ICM, October 1994. Wang was Mao's chief bodyguard and figured frequently in Dr Zhisui Li's *The Private Life of Chairman Mao*, Chatto & Windus, London, 1994.

36. *Cheng Ming*, Hongkong, August 1994, in ICM, October 1994.

37. *Sunday Times*, 27 November 1988.

38. *The Nineties*, Hongkong, July 1994, in ICM, September 1994; and *Far Eastern Economic Review*, 27 October 1988.

39. *Washington Post* and *Guardian*, 7 May 1980.

40. *International Herald Tribune*, 19 May 1990; *Sunday Times*, 26 April 1992; and *New York Times* and *International Herald Tribune*, 7 September 1993.

41. *Far Eastern Economic Review*, 13 September 1990.

42. *Wenweibao*, Hongkong, 14 October 1993, in ICM, December 1993.

43. *Ibid.*

44. *Front Line Monthly*, Hongkong, October 1993, in ICM, December 1993.

45. *South China Morning Post*, 26 April 1990.

46. One journal noted that it was acceptable for Mark Thatcher to go into business because he was restrained by the law like everyone else; in China it was different. *Cheng Ming*, Hongkong, February 1986, in ICM, April 1986.

47. *Hong Kong Mirror*, quoted in *Observer*, 16 February 1992.

48. *South China Morning Post*, 20 July 1989. Children of Jiang Zemin and Qiao Shi were said to be examples.

49. *Mingbao*, Hongkong, 22 June 1992, in ICM, August 1992.

50. *South China Morning Post*, 20 July 1989.

51. *Asia-Pacific Economic Times*, Guangzhou, 15 December 1991, in ICM, February 1992.

52. *Hong Kong Economic Journal*, 8 May 1992, in ICM, July 1992.

53. *Family Ties in China*, published in Dalian. See *Trend*, Hongkong, April 1992, in ICM, July 1992.

54. *Ibid.*

55. *Xinhua Collected Internal References*, no. 17, Beijing, in ICM, August 1992.

56. *South China Morning Post*, 23 July 1989; *Financial Times*, 21 February 1994; and Nick Rufford, 'China Fires Warning At Its Tycoon Elite?' *Sunday Times*, 26 February 1995.

57. See *Far Eastern Economic Review*, 6 March 1986; and *Cheng Ming*, March 1986, in ICM, May 1986.

58. *South China Morning Post*, 7 November 1989.

59. *Cheng Ming*, February 1986, in ICM, April 1986.

60. *Lien Ho Po* (*United Daily*), Hongkong, 27 July 1993, *BBC/SWB/*FE/1753/B2/1 of 29 July 1993.

61. Austin Hsu in ICM, June 1992, p.79.

62. Shenyang, *Renmin Ribao*, and *Cheng Ming*, Hongkong, 1 April 1994, *BBC/SWB*/FE/1973/G/1-3 of 16 April 1994; workers, *Mingbao*, 19 September 1994, *BBC/SWB*/FE/2124/G/5-6 of 12 October 1994.

63. *Financial Times*, 23 January 1993; Robert Tyerman in *Sunday Telegraph*. 26 February 1995; and Louise Evans, 'Chinese Scandal Keeps Its Secret', *Sunday Times*, 5 March 1995; also *Mingbao*, 4 March 1995, *BBC/SWB*/FE/2247/G/4 of 9 March 1995.

64. *China Youth*, Beijing, September 1993, in ICM, January 1994.

65. *BBC/SWB*/FE/2066/G/6 of 5 August 1994.

66. *China Youth*, Beijing, September 1993, in ICM, January 1994.

67. *Dagongbao*, 23 December 1993, in ICM, February 1994.

68. *Trend*, Hongkong, August 1993, in ICM, October 1993.

69. *Ibid*.

70. *Baixing News Weekly*, no. 17 of 1993, in ICM, October 1993.

71. *Dagongbao*, 14 November 1993, in ICM, January 1994.

72. Chen, *International Herald Tribune*, 4 October 1995; Li, *BBC/SWB/*FE/1752 and 1756.

73. *Cheng Ming*, Hongkong, 1 February 1994, *BBC/SWB*/FE/1912/G/2 of 3 February 1994.

74. Li, *Xinhua Digest*, no. 12, 1992, in ICM, May 1993; Hongkong, *BBC/SWB*/FE/2248/G/1 of 10 March 1995.

75. *Study and Exploration (Xuexi yu Tansuo)*, no. 5, 1988, in ICM, February 1989.

76. Quoted in Orville Schell, *Discos and Democracy, China in the Throes of Reform*, Pantheon, New York, 1988, p.132.

77. From an as yet unpublished work on social psychology.

78. *International Herald Tribune*, 22 June 1978.

79. Lee, *Far Eastern Economic Review*, 19 May 1988; CASS report by Kong Fan, *Renmin Ribao*, 19 September 1994, *BBC/SWB*/FE/2117/G/10 of 4 October 1994.

80. Xia Nairu, 'A late 20th Century Examination of Confucianism', *Academic Journal of Shanghai Normal University*, no. 2, 1992, in ICM, December 1992. New Asia became a component of the later Chinese University of Hong Kong.

81. *International Herald Tribune*, 2 September 1987; and *Japan Times*, 9 September 1987.

82. Liu Huishi, 'The Value of Confucian Ethics in the Construction of

Modern Chinese Thought', *Academic Journal of Shanghai Normal University*, no. 2, 1992, in ICM, December 1992. For an instructive Singaporean view see Martin Lu, *Confucianism, Its Relevance to Modern Society*, Federal Publications, Singapore, 1983.

83. Chan Kim-Kwong and Alan Hunter, 'Religion and Society in Mainland China in the 1990s', *Issues and Studies*, August 1994, p.52.

84. Lin Min, 'Individual Salvation and Ultimate Concerns – Liu Hsiao-feng's Formulation of Transcendent Human Universality in Contemporary Chinese Intellectual Discourse', *Issues and Studies*, February 1994, p.91.

85. *Tangtai (Contemporary)*, Hongkong, 15 June 1994, in ICM, August 1994; *Cheng Ming*, Hongkong, August 1994, in ICM, October 1994.

86. *Far Eastern Economic Review*, 7 October 1993; *Spring Magazine*, February 1993, in ICM, December 1993.

87. *Ibid.*, and *South China Morning Post*, 16 September 1992.

88. *Cheng Ming*, quoted in *Daily Telegraph*, 6 September 1990.

89. *The Times*, 26 December 1988.

90. *Guardian*, 19 August 1988.

91. *Cheng Ming*, Hongkong, September 1993, in ICM, December 1993.

92. *Xinhua*, 25 November 1994, *BBC/SWB*/FE/2166/G/3 of 30 November.

93. Andrew Nathan, Introduction, Susan Whitfield (ed.), *After the Event, Human Rights and their Future in China*, Wellsweep, London, 1993, p.9 at p.10.

94. Liu in Lin Min *op.cit.*, p.103; Zhang cited by Lincoln Kaye, *Far Eastern Economic Review*, 14 April 1994.

95. See the informed discussion of leadership factions in *Trend*, Hongkong, May 1995 in ICM July 1995 p. 7; Joseph Fewsmith, 'Neo-Conservatism and the end of the Dengist Era', *Asian Survey*, July 1995, p. 635.

96. Shanghai 'mafia', *BBC/SWB*/FE/2211/G/5 of 26 January 1995.

97. 'The New Nationalism', *Far Eastern Economic Review*, 9 November 1995; also Geremie R. Barmé, 'To Screw Foreigners is Patriotic: China's Avant-Garde Nationalists', *China Journal*, July 1995, p. 239.

Chapter 5 Tiananmen: The Objectors

1. See *Visit to China by the Delegation led by Lord Howe of Aberavon*, HMSO, London, 1993; and also 'China and Human Rights', *Britain-China*, no. 53, 1993/3, p.10; Susan Whitfield (ed.), *June Fourth Briefing Papers on*

China, June 4th China Support, London, 1993; and Susan Whitfield (ed.), *After the Event, Human Rights and their Future in China*, Wellsweep, London, 1993.

2. *Xinhua*, 13 March 1995, *BBC/SWB*/FE/2252/G/1 of 15 March 1995; *Wenweibao*, 14 March 1995, *BBC/SWB*/FE/2254/G/1 of 17 March 1995.

3. Chih-yu Shih, 'Contending Theories of "Human Rights with Chinese Characteristics"', *Issues and Studies*, November 1993, p.42.

4. Charles Humana, *World Human Rights Guide*, London, Hutchinson, 1983; Philip Baker, 'China, Human Rights and the Law', *Pacific Review*, vol. 6, no. 3, 1993, p.239.

5. *The Times*, 30 June 1993.

6. *Wenweibao*, 19 August 1993, *BBC/SWB*/FE/1773.

7. *Guardian*, 24 July 1989.

8. *Japan Times*, 13 May 1993; *International Herald Tribune*, 2 June 1993.

9. Liang Guoqing report admitting torture, injury and death in custody, *Guardian*, 30 April 1990; Qiao Shi, *Evening Standard*, 5 June 1990.

10. *International Herald Tribune*, 4 September 1992.

11. Numbers, *Xinhua*, 17 May 1994, *BBC/SWB*/FE/2006/G/13 of 28 May 1994; Winery, *Financial Times*, 4 April 1990. For a rigorous defence of the *laogai*, see *Fazhi Ribao* of 26 December 1994, *BBC/SWB*/FE/2198/G/10 of 11 January 1995.

12. *Sunday Times*, 24 June 1990.

13. *Far Eastern Economic Review*, 9 June 1984.

14. *International Herald Tribune*, 28 June 1989.

15. *Viewing China Through a Third Eye*, by 'Dr Leininger', see *Mingbao*, Hongkong, 12 August 1994, *BBC/SWB*/FE/2078/G/7 of 19 August 1994.

16. *Far Eastern Economic Review*, 16 November 1989; and Fang Lizhi, *Semi Monthly News*, Hongkong, 1 November 1987, in ICM, January 1988.

17. *International Herald Tribune*, 18 April 1992; *The Times*, 16 August 1993. Han is a Christian, and he contracted tuberculosis while in prison.

18. *Daily Telegraph*, 15 September 1993; interview, *Far Eastern Economic Review*, 4 November 1993.

19. *Daily Telegraph*, 8 February 1991 and 11 June 1993; and *Financial Times*, 5 June 1993 (a perceptive article). British Ministers had no such luck.

20. *Daily Telegraph*, 22 September 1993; *The Times*, 18 February 1994; *Japan Times*, 3 April 1994; Harry Wu, *Bitter Winds: A Memoir of My Years in China's Gulag*, John Wiley, New York, 1994.

21. *The Nineties Monthly*, Hongkong, February 1994, in ICM, April 1994.

22. The best accounts in the vast and growing literature on Tiananmen are Tony Saich (ed.), *The Chinese People's Movement: Perspectives on Spring*

1989, M.E. Sharpe, Armonk and London, 1990, on the background; Suzanne Ogden, Kathleen Harford, Lawrence Sullivan and David Zweig (eds), *China's Search for Democracy, The Student and Mass Movement of 1989*, Armonk, M.E. Sharpe, 1992 considers contradictory views of the confrontation; John Gittings, *China Changes Face: The Road from Revolution 1949–89*, Oxford, 1989, paperback edition of 1990 has an epilogue account of Tiananmen; the *Independent*'s little paperback by Michael Fathers and Andrew Higgins, *Tiananmen: The Rape of Peking*, London, 1989, conveys the heat and excitement of its title; and an even shorter political account, even sooner after the event, is Dick Wilson, 'Amenability Snaps in Tiananmen Square', *London Review of Books*, 6 July 1989.

23. *The Times*, 18 April 1989.

24. *Semi Monthly News*, 1 May 1989, in ICM, July 1989; *International Herald Tribune*, 1 July 1989.

25. *Japan Times*, 2 June 1993, a convincing picture of the site of the confrontation.

26. *International Herald Tribune*, 25 April 1989.

27. *Ibid.*, 28 April 1989.

28. *South China Morning Post*, 24 April 1989.

29. *Ibid.*, 20 May 1989.

30. The readiness of some workers, citizens and all kinds of disaffected groups to follow the student lead indicates raw material for bigger demonstrations in case of future Party bungling: see Andrew G. Walder, *Popular Protest in the 1989 Democracy Movement, The Pattern of Grass-Roots Organization*, Hongkong Institute of Asian-Pacific Studies, 1992.

31. *International Herald Tribune*, 28 April 1989.

32. *Observer*, 21 May 1989.

33. *South China Morning Post*, 28 May 1989; Peng Zhen, *Ibid.*, 30 May 1989.

34. *Hongkong Standard*, 3 November 1989.

35. *South China Morning Post*, 23 May 1989.

36. *The Times*, 18 May 1989.

37. *Sunday Times*, 13 August 1989.

38. *International Herald Tribune* and *South China Morning Post*, 19 May 1989.

39. *Japan Times*, 28 May 1989.

40. *South China Morning Post*, 30 May 1989.

41. *The Times*, 20 May 1989; *South China Morning Post*, 28 May 1989. For the army role at Tiananmen, see Timothy Brook, *Quelling the People: The Military Suppression of the Beijing Democracy Movement*, Oxford University Press, 1992.

42. *South China Morning Post*, 23 May 1989; *International Herald Tribune*, 21 June 1989.

43. *Sunday Times*, 21 May 1989; and army history book cited in *Lien Ho Po*, Hongkong, 18 July 1994.

44. *South China Morning Post*, 20 May 1989.

45. *Sunday Times*, 21 and 28 May 1989; *The Times*, 30 May 1989.

46. *South China Morning Post*, 24 May 1989; *The Times*, 26 May 1989.

47. *South China Morning Post*, 27 May 1989. Hu Qili, Yan Mingfu and many of Zhao's aides and reformist think-tankers were also dismissed.

48. *Observer*, 28 May 1989.

49. *South China Morning Post*, 31 May 1989.

50. From Hou Dejian's eye-witness account in *South China Morning Post*, 24 August 1989.

51. *South China Morning Post*, 10 September 1989.

52. *Spectator*, 17 June 1989.

53. *Financial Times*, 5 June 1989.

54. *Daily Telegraph*, 6 June 1989; *Lien Ho Po*, Hongkong, 20 July 1994, *BBC/SWB*/FE/2053 of 21 July 1994.

55. *Daily Telegraph*, 5 June 1989.

56. A student's eye-witness account, *Guardian*, 4 June 1990. The army denied the killing of occupants.

57. *Guardian*, 4 June 1990.

58. *Spectator*, 1 July 1989. See John Gittings, 'Accuracy and Chaos: Reporting Tiananmen', in Robin Porter (ed.), *Reporting the News from China*, Royal Institute of International Affairs, London, 1992, p.73.

59. See e.g. letter to the Editor from D.W. Nicholson of Cambridge in *Observer*, 18 June 1989. He criticises the 'intransigent' student leaders for their naïveté and arrogance. The anti-Communist Taiwan politician Ju Gao-geng cursed the 4 June demonstrators for their political incompetence, *Far Eastern Economic Review*, 31 May 1990.

60. *Financial Times*, 3 July 1989.

61. Chinese Communist Party Central Committee and State Council, 'Notice to the People of the Entire Nation', 5 June 1989, in ICM, August 1989.

62. *International Herald Tribune*, 19 May 1989. Jiang added that much trouble would have been avoided if assembly on the square had been banned from the outset.

63. Michael Fathers and Andrew Higgins, *op.cit.*, p.64.

64. *Mingbao*, 10 July 1990, in ICM, August 1990.

65. Richard Evans, *Deng Xiaoping and the Making of Modern China*, Hamish Hamilton, London, 1993, pp.298–9.

66. *International Herald Tribune*, 18 August 1989.

67. The Chinese Communist Central Committee's Directive Concern-

ing the Handling of the Counter-revolutionary Riots of June Fourth, 7 June 1989, ICM, August 1989.

68. *Far Eastern Economic Review*, 15 September 1994.

69. *Lien Ho Po*, 27 February 1995, *BBC/SWB*/FE/2241/G/4 of 2 March 1995; also Patrick Tyler in *New York Times* and *International Herald Tribune*, 27 February 1995.

70. Wang Juntao's talk at School of Oriental and African Studies, London, 27 June 1995.

Chapter 6 The Army: Out of a Gun Barrel

1. See Pauline Loong, *China, The Party and the Gun*, Jardine Fleming Securities, Hongkong, 1994.

2. *Financial Times*, 15 October 1990.

3. See ICM, October 1994.

4. *Financial Times*, *op.cit.*; also Michael Swaine in *Far Eastern Economic Review*, 4 March 1993.

5. See *South China Morning Post*, 17 and 22 August, 20 October 1989. When Yang and Zhao were both in disgrace later they were reported to be on friendly terms.

6. Ren Huiwen in *Hongkong Economic Journal*, no. 6, 6 November 1992, in ICM, January 1993; *Frontline Monthly*, Hongkong, November 1992 in ICM, January 1993; and *China Review*, October 1989.

7. *Far Eastern Economic Review*, 29 October 1992.

8. See Arthur S. Ding, 'The Recent Reshuffle of PLA Leaders', *Issues and Studies*, December 1992, p.116; also *China Review*, October 1989; and *New York Times* and *International Herald Tribune*, 5 December 1994.

9. *Open Monthly*, Hongkong, June 1992, in ICM, August 1992.

10. Arthur S. Ding, 'The Streamlining of the PLA', *Issues and Studies*, November 1992, p.86.

11. Samuel C.Y. Ku and Peter Kine-hong Yu, 'The Incomes of PLA Officers and Soldiers', *Issues and Studies*, November 1992, p.99 at p.104.

12. See *BBC/SWB*/FE/2057.

13. Thomas J. Bickford, 'The Chinese Military and its Business Operations', *Asian Survey*, May 1995, p.460.

14. *Far Eastern Economic Review*, 14 October 1993.

15. Tai Ming Cheung in *Far Eastern Economic Review*, 14 October 1993.

16. See Shirley Kan, 'China Arms Sales: Overview and Outlook for the 1990s' in *China's Economic Dilemmas in the 1990s*, US Congress Joint Economic Committee, Washington, April 1991, p.696; also *The China Quarterly* special issue on China's Military in Transition, June 1996.

17. *Financial Times*, 9 July 1993.

18. Zhao Xianfang, *Wenweibao*, 29 March 1993, in ICM, June 1993.

19. See Joseph R. Morgan, *Porpoises Among the Whales: Small Navies in Asia and the Pacific*, East-West Centre, Honolulu, March 1994, pp.33–7.

20. *Moscow Broadcasting Station*, 18 April 1993, in ICM, June 1993.

21. ICM, June 1993.

22. *BBC/SWB*/FE/1976/G/7 of 20 April 1993.

23. *The Times*, 7 March 1995.

24. The constant leap-frogging between China and Taiwan over the acquisition of the latest Western military aircraft is an outstanding example of mutual East Asian waste fuelling US, Russian and European profit. See Sheldon Simon, 'East Asian Security', *Asian Survey*, December 1994, p.1047 at p.1053. Taiwan buys F-16s and Mirage-2000s while Beijing spends on SU-27s and possibly Sukhois and Mig-31s.

Chapter 7 Economic Reform Strategy: The Ivy on the Wall

1. Chen followed this by reading statements by Richard Nixon, George Schulz and Giscard d'Estaing. *Dagongbao*, 19 February 1989.

2. *Jingji Kexue* (Economic Science), no. 3, 1985.

3. Li Xiannian, interview with Gerald Long of Reuters, *Japan Times*, 25 August 1979.

4. Talk in Shenzhen, *International Herald Tribune*, 29 January 1992.

5. *South China Morning Post*, 23 August 1989.

6. *Renmin Ribao*, 5 March 1987.

7. *International Herald Tribune*, 28 January 1993.

8. See also the story of the Wenzhou entrepreneur Wang Yuejin, *New York Times*, 28 January 1993.

9. The *Far Eastern Economic Review* of 10 October 1985 conveys the flavour of these debates.

10. William H. Overholt, *China, The Next Economic Superpower*, Weidenfeld & Nicolson, 1993, p.10.

11. Speech of Dr Goh Keng Swee, Conference on Doing Business with China, *Straits Times* and *Japan Times*, 26 August 1993.

12. *Xinhua*, 29 December 1993; *BBC/SWB* FE/1884/G/5 of 1 January 1994.

13. Hua Sheng, 'The Prospect of Economic Reform in China', lecture at Oxford University, 24 February 1993.

14. Zhang Weiying and Gang Yi, *China's Gradual Reform: A Historical Perspective*, Nuffield College, Oxford, April 1994, p.14 fn.32.

15. Zhang Weiying, 'Decision Rights, Residual Claim and Performance: A Theory of How the Chinese Economy Works, (mimeograph, Nuffield College, Oxford, 1994).

16. *Cheng Ming*, Hongkong, June 1993 and *Xinhua*, 1 June 1993, in *BBC/SWB*/FE/1705/B/2/1 of 3 June 1993.

17. *Ibid.*

18. *Dagongbao*, 29 December 1988.

19. 20 October 1984 Central Committee decision, see *Far Eastern Economic Review*, 1 November 1984.

20. See *The Thirteenth Party Congress and China's Reforms*, Beijing Review, Beijing, 1987.

21. *Ibid.*, p.58.

22. Quoted by Robert Benjamin from Changsha, *Baltimore Sun*, in *Japan Times*, 21 July 1993.

23. Zhu Rongji's speech in Shanghai, 13 May 1993, Xinhua, in *BBC/SWB*/FE/1689/B/2/1 of 15 May 1993.

24. *Mirror Monthly*, April 1989, in ICM, June 1989.

25. *Ibid.*

26. Talks in Hongkong, 26 May and 2 June 1993 in *Dagongbao*, 27 May 1993, *Wenweibao*, 3 June 1993 and *BBC/SWB*/FE/1707/B/2/1 of 5 June 1993.

27. Zhu, *Mingbao*, Hongkong, 5 August 1994, *BBC/SWB*/FE/2071/G/1 of 11 August 1994; Li Yungqi, 'China's Inflation, Causes, Effects and Solutions', *Asian Survey*, July 1989.

28. Zhu Rongji in Shanghai, and reporting to Chinese People's Political Consultative Conference on 6 October 1993, see *BBC/SWB*/FE/1884/G/7 of 1 January 1994.

29. *International Herald Tribune*, 17 April 1990.

30. Shanghai official Wang Qingzhang, Director, Shanghai Tourism Company (HK), *China Review*, February 1989. Jiang, see Chen Te-sheng, 'Economic Trends in Mainland China after the CCP's 14th Congress', *Asian Survey*, November 1989, p.1030.

31. See Prybyla's 'Mainland China's Economic System: A Study in Contradictions', *Issues and Studies*, August 1994, p.1.

32. Marcia Yudkin, *Private Businessmen in Socialist China*, Foreign Languages Press, Beijing, 1986, pp.8–9.

33. From a Hongkong economic journal cited in *Japan Times*, 16 September 1993.

34. Li Ruihuan in discussion with Hebei leaders, *Xinhua*, 5 July 1993, *BBC/SWB*/FE/1736/B/2/6 of 9 July 1983.

35. *Dagongbao*, 23 August 1984.

36. *Dagongbao*, 21 August 1988.

37. *Xinhua*, 25 November 1994, *BBC/SWB*/FE/2166/G/3 of 30 November 1994.

Chapter 8 The Farmers: Back to the Family

1. *China, Reform and the Role of the Plan in the 1990s*, World Bank, Washington, 1992, p.35; and 'The Titan Stirs', *The Economist*, 28 November 1992.

2. Estimate of the Chinese economist Sun Yangfang, *International Herald Tribune*, 24 April 1981.

3. *Daily Telegraph*, 17 February 1978.

4. *Wenweibao*, Hongkong, 17 November 1991, in ICM, February 1992. On Xiangyang see also Vivien Shue, 'The Fate of the Commune', *Modern China*, July 1984, p. 259.

5. Jiang Xiaowei, *South China Morning Post*, 7 September 1989.

6. World Bank, *op.cit.*, p.115.

7. Ramon H. Myers, 'Scarcity and Ideology in Chinese Economic Development', *Problems of Communism*, March 1978.

8. *Far Eastern Economic Review*, 26 September 1992.

9. Nicholas Lardy, 'Chinese Foreign Trade', *The China Quarterly*, no. 131, 1992, p.691.

10. *Economic Daily*, Beijing, 31 July 1992, in ICM, November 1992.

11. *International Herald Tribune*, 17 June 1992.

12. Tony Walker, 'China Determined to Head Off Farmland "Crisis"', *Financial Times*, 1 March 1995; *The Times*, 23 December 1987; *BBC/SWB*/FE/2257.

13. *Dagongbao*, 22 April 1993. Shujie Yao, 'Problems and Prospects of Grain Production in China' (mimeographed, Portsmouth University, 1993) argues China could maintain a high degree of self-sufficiency. Rice imports, *Mingbao*, Hong Kong, 15 February 1995. *BBC/SWB*/FE/2237/G/14 of 25 February 1995; and *Daily Telegraph*, 14 March 1995. One foreign study expects imports of 369 million tonnes of grain by 2030, on present trends, while the Japanese Overseas Economic Cooperation Fund predicts a 136 million tonne shortfall (one-fifth of domestic Chinese demand) by 2000; see OECD, *The Chinese Grain and Oilseed Sectors*, Paris 1995, also *China in the 21st Century*, Paris 1996.

14. Hua Sheng, Seminar on 'The Prospect of Economic Reform in China' at Oxford University, 24 February 1993.

15. *International Herald Tribune*, 4 April 1984.

16. *International Herald Tribune*, 11 January 1992; *Far Eastern Economic Review*, 23 April 1993; *Financial Times*, 28 August 1993. A similar story is

treated in the recent film *The Accused*, where a successful village chief is dismissed for arbitrary justice.

17. *Japan Times*, 21 May 1992.

18. See e.g. Elizabeth Croll, *From Heaven to Earth: Images and Experience of Development in China*, Routledge, 1994; and Thomas P. Lyons, *China's War on Poverty, A Case Study of Fujian Province 1985–1990*, Chinese University of Hongkong, 1992.

19. *Economic Daily*, Beijing, 16 December 1992, in ICM, March 1993; Wang Yi, *Semi-Monthly Talks*, Beijing, 10 November 1992, in ICM, March 1993; Cheng Jian, *Mingbao Daily News*, Hongkong, 1 January 1993 in ICM, March 1993; Lu Zixiu (Vice-Chairman of Anhui People's Congress), *Outlook Weekly*, Beijing, 12 April 1993 in ICM, August 1993; and Philip Bowring, *International Herald Tribune*, 20 July 1993.

20. *The Times*, 22 June 1993; *Japan Times*, 27 July 1993.

21. *Central People's Broadcasting Station*, Beijing, 29 May 1993, in ICM, August 1993.

22. *Xinbao*, Hongkong, 10 June 1993, in *BBC/SWB*/FE/1713/B/2/19 of 12 June 1993.

23. *Tangtai (Contemporary)*, Hongkong, 15 May 1994, *BBC/SWB*/FE/2011/G/4 of June 1994.

24. *Wenweibao*, 13 April 1992, in ICM, June 1993.

25. Lu Zixiu, *op.cit.*

26. *Guardian*, 22 June 1993. Xu Haiqing of Sheffield University argues that more rural rich migrate to cities than rural poor (paper to Chinese Economic Association in UK Annual Conference, London, December 1993).

27. Robert F. Ash, 'The Agricultural Sector in China: Performance and Policy Dilemmas During the 1980s', *The China Quarterly*, no. 131, 1992, pp.548 and 562. Frederick W. Crook, 'Primary Issues in China's Grain Economy in the 1990s Decade', *China's Economic Dilemmas in the 1990's*, US Congress Joint Economic Committee, Washington, April 1991, forecasts 2000 grain output at between 459 to 466 million tons, or some 35–40 million short of target; Ramon H. Myers, a seasoned observer of the rural Chinese scene, predicted at the outset of the reform that China would be lucky to achieve 2 per cent or 3 per cent annual agricultural growth, *The Chinese Economy, Past and Present*, Stanford University, 1980, p.239.

28. See 'Grain Price Fluctuation Foreshadows an Agricultural Crisis in Mainland China', *Issues and Studies*, February 1994, p.107.

29. Minquan Liu, 'Commune Responsibility System and China's Agriculture', in Qimiao Fan and Peter Nolan (eds), *China's Economic Reforms, The Costs and Benefits of Incrementalism*, St Martin's Press and Macmillan, 1994, p.104.

30. *Far Eastern Economic Review*, 17 November 1994.

31. William Hinton, *Shenfan*, New York, Random House, 1983. See also his earlier volume covering the land reform of the late 1940s, *Fanshen: A Documentary of Revolution in a Chinese Village*, New York, Monthly Review Press, 1966, and his later reflective essays in *The Privatization of China, The Great Reversal*, Earthscan, London, 1990. On co-operatives, see Andrew Watson, 'The Management of the Rural Economy: The Institutional Parameters', in Watson (ed), *Economic Reform and Social Change in China*, Routledge, London, 1992.

32. *Outlook Weekly*, Beijing, 23 January 1995, in ICM, May 1995, p.49. There is a useful discussion of this by Andrew Watson in Watson (ed), *Economic Reform and Social Change in China*, Routledge, London 1992, at pp. 188–95.

Chapter 9 Population: The Missing Girls

1. Frank Ching, *Ancestors: 900 Years in the Life of a Chinese Family*, London, Harrap, 1988; 'fake' boy, *Sunday Times*, 23 April 1989.

2. *Daily Telegraph*, 14 April 1989.

3. Steven Mufson, *Washington Post* and *International Herald Tribune*, 15 February 1995.

4. Mao once said: 'It is a very good thing that China has a big population. Even if China's population multiplies many times, she is fully capable of finding a solution; the solution is production ... Of all things in the world, people are most precious. Under the leadership of the Communist Party, as long as there are people, every kind of miracle can be performed', *Selected Works of Mao Zedong*, Beijing, 1961, vol. 4, pp.453–4. Chen Yun's dictum was about 1979, quoted in Chen Muhua, 'Developing Population Science and Making it the Goal of Controlling Population Growth', *Renkou Yanjiu* (Population Research), no. 3, 1981, p.1. The Beijing University President was Ma Yinchu.

5. Nicholas D. Kristof, *New York Times* and *International Herald Tribune*, 28 April 1993. For Beijing's denial see Jonathan Mirsky, *The Times*, 19 June 1993.

6. See generally Steven W. Mosher, *A Mother's Ordeal: One Woman's Fight Against China's One Child Policy, the story of Chi An*, Little, Brown, London, 1994.

7. *Japan Times*, 14 April 1992.

8. *Japan Times*, 18 May 1992.

9. *South China Morning Post*, 18 May 1990.

10. See e.g. Robin Porter (ed.), *Reporting the News from China*, Royal

Institute of International Affairs, London, 1992, p.85.

11. Dr Xiao Lubai closed her VD clinic in 1962 but reopened it in 1988, *Sunday Times*, 27 November 1998; see also, Lincoln Kaye, *Far Eastern Economic Review*, 14 April 1994, p.51; *Mingbao*, Hongkong, 26 July 1994, *BBC/SWB*/FE/2062/G/13 of 1 August 1994: and *Cheng Ming*, Hongkong, 1 April 1994, *BBC/SWB*/FE/1981/G/10 of 26 April 1994.

12. *The Times*, 9 September 1989; *Sunday Times*, 7 January 1990.

13. *Sunday Times*, 4 February 1990; see also Frank Dikötter, *Sex, Culture and Modernity in China*, Hurst, London 1995.

14. *Daily Telegraph*, 6 April 1988.

15. *Japan Times*, 15 December 1989 and 4 July 1991; see also Frank Dikötter, *op. cit.*

16. *Observer*, 7 August 1988.

17. *International Herald Tribune*, 17 February 1993.

18. See ICM, June 1993, p.70.

19. Chen Kai in *Japan Times*, 18 July 1991; Adam and Eve, *Daily Telegraph*, 2 March 1995.

20. *Japan Times*, 5 March 1987.

21. *Japan Times*, 29 April 1992.

22. *Daily Telegraph*, 24 April 1980.

23. From *Shaanxi Ribao*, Xian, 8 October 1993, *BBC/SWB*/FE/1854/G/11 of, 24 November 1993.

24. *Japan Times*, 2 July 1988.

25. *Observer*, 26 January 1992. An early report of this was the drowning of fifty baby girls in the space of two months in Hefei, Anhui province, in 1981 shortly after the population policy was implemented, Wong Siu-lun, 'Consequences of China's New Population Policy, *The China Quarterly*, no. 98, June 1984, p.220 at p.227.

26. See *International Herald Tribune*, and *Guardian*, 22 July 1993; also John S. Aird, *Slaughter of the Innocents: Coercive Birth Control in China*, American Enterprise Institute, Washington, 1990; scanners, *Xinhua*, 25 October 1995; *BBC/SWB*/FE/2137/G/7 of 27 October 1994.

27. *Observer*, 26 January 1992; *Wenweibao*, Shanghai, 1 August 1994; *Japan Times*, 2 August 1994; *Guardian*, 17 August 1995.

28. See *Far Eastern Economic Review*, 13 January 1994.

29. Wong Siu-lun, *op.cit.*, p.228.

30. *Xinhua*, 16 August 1994; *BBC/SWB*/FE/2089/G/8 of 1 September 1994.

31. *Japan Times*, 16 January 1992.

32. *China Youth Magazine*, Beijing, no. 3, 1993, in ICM, August 1993.

33. Dr Elizabeth Croll, School of Oriental and African Studies, London, talk to the Great Britain–China Centre, March 1994, in *Britain–China*, no.

55, 1994, 2, p.1 at p.4. See also Tyrene White, 'Birth Planning Between Plan and Market: The Impact of Reform on China's One-child Policy', *China's Economic Dilemmas in the 1990's*, US Congress Joint Economic Committee, vol. 1, Washington, April 1991, p.252.

34. *Xinhua*, 2 March 1995; *BBC/SWB*/FE/2247; see also FE/2203 and FE/2262.

Chapter 10 Industry and Finance: Factories Change Colour

1. Richard Conroy, *Technological Change in China*, OECD, Paris, 1992. The fan story was recalled by Gao Shanquan of the State Commission for Restructuring Economic Systems, at a Chinese Economic Association in UK conference in December 1992.

2. *BBC/SWB*/FE/1981/G/3 of 26 April 1994.

3. Zhang Weiying and Gang Yi, *China's Gradual Reform: A Historical Perspective*, Oxford University, April 1994, p.19.

4. Lu Mu, *Renmin Ribao*, 22 June 1994, *BBC/SWB*/FE/2030/B/6 of 24 June 1994. Some Western economists do not recommend privatisation in China, e.g. Patrick Bolton, London School of Economics, 'Privatization and Separation of Ownership and Control', paper for Chinese Economic Association in UK Conference, London, December 1993, p.8. Peter Harrold, *China's Reform Experience to Date*, World Bank, Washington, 1992, p.35 refers to a process of 'privatisation from below', using marketisation and the non-state sector to bring about state enterprise efficiency short of privatising ownership. Two UNCTAD discussion papers play down the role of privatisation, Dwight A. Perkins, 'China's "Gradual" Approach to Market Reforms', December 1992; and Ajit Singh, 'The Market and Evolutionary Market Reform in China', December 1993.

5. Yia-Ling Liu, 'The Private Economy and Local Politics in the Rural Industrialization of Wenzhou', *The China Quarterly*, no. 130, June 1992, p.293; and British Consulate-General, Shanghai, '"Island of Capitalism" on the East China Coast', *China-Britain Trade Review*, December 1991, pp.8–9. For a similar development, see Lin Dahui, 'Foshan: A Successful Case of Chinese Gradual Reform and Rapid Growth', Chinese Economic Association paper, London, December 1993.

6. *Financial Times*, 11 November 1992; *Window*, Hongkong, 6 November 1992.

7. *International Herald Tribune*, 5 August 1992; *Financial Times*, 27 January 1994.

8. *Far Eastern Economic Review* cover story, 21 January 1993.

9. *BBC/SWB*/FE/2062/G/5 of 1 August 1994; and *BBC/SWB*/FE/2007/G/9 of 27 May 1994.

10. *Financial Times*, 26 April 1994.

11. *Chinese News Agency*, Beijing, 19 November 1993, in *BBC/SWB*/FE/1855/G/3 of 25 November 1993.

12. Li Peng, address of 20 March 1992, cited in World Bank, *China: Reform and the Role of the Plan in the 1990s*, Washington, 1992, p.106.

13. *Sunday Times*, 2 August 1992.

14. *Far Eastern Economic Review*, 13 February 1992.

15. See the State Planning Commission policy statement on car and motorcycle production, *Renmin Ribao*, 4 July 1994; *BBC/SWB*/FE/2050/G/4 of 18 July 1994.

16. *Semi-Monthly Talk*, no. 291, Beijing, 10 June 1992, in ICM, October 1992.

17. *Ibid.*

18. Authoritatively reviewed in *China Briefing*, Hongkong Bank, October 1994.

19. Dong He, 'The Stock Market and Industrial Performance: Lessons from the West for Stock Market Development in China', in Qimiao Fan and Peter Nolan (eds), *China's Economic Reforms*, St Martin's Press and Macmillan, 1994, p.191.

20. *Financial Times*, 22 May 1993.

21. See e.g. Dong He, *op.cit.*

22. *International Herald Tribune*, 6 April 1994.

23. World Bank, *op.cit.*

24. *Cheng Ming Monthly*, Hongkong, June 1993, in ICM, August 1993; and *Hongkong Economic Journal*, 17 June 1993, in ICM, August 1993.

25. *South China Morning Post*, 17 August 1989.

26. *South China Morning Post*, 27 September 1989.

27. *International Herald Tribune*, 7 April 1989.

28. From a most lively and down-to-earth article in *Legal Daily*, Beijing, 20 October 1991.

29. Another revealing article in *Xinhua*, 18 May 1993, in ICM, July 1993.

30. ICM, November 1988.

31. *Dagongbao*, 2 July 1987.

32. Mayor Chen Xitong (now disgraced) unrolled this saga of toilet paper shortage to National People's delegates in March 1987, *Dagongbao*, 2 July 1987.

33. See Qiao Gang, State Council researcher, 'China's Price Reform', London School of Economics paper, November 1988.

34. Thomas T. Wong, 'The Salary Structure, Allowance and Benefits of

a Shanghai Electronics Factory', *The China Quarterly*, no. 117, March 1989, p.135.

35. *Financial Times*, 13 June 1980.

36. *Economic Daily*, Beijing, 16 September 1991, in ICM, January 1992.

37. *Dagongbao*, 27 October 1988.

38. *Dagongbao*, 25 February 1988.

39. *Financial Times*, 1 May 1992; *International Herald Tribune*, 4 July 1992.

40. *Renmin Ribao*, 24 November 1992, from *Legal Daily*, 17 November 1992, in ICM, February 1993.

41. *Nineties Monthly*, Hongkong, August 1990.

42. *Japan Times*, 10 April 1994.

43. Zhang Dinghua, *Xinhua*, 24 October 1993; *BBC/SWB*/FE/1830/G/3 of 27 October 1993.

44. *BBC/SWB*/FE/1935/G/5 of 2 March 1994; and FE/1966/G/4 of 8 August 1994.

45. *Wenweibao*, 29 June 1994, in *BBC/SWB*/FE/2044/G/3 of 11 July 1994.

46. *Cheng Ming*, Hongkong, and *Renmin Ribao*, 1 April 1994 in *BBC/SWB*/FE/1973/G/1-3 of 16 April 1994.

47. *Tangtai*, Hongkong, 14 May 1994, in *BBC/SWB*/FE/2011/G/4 of 1 June 1994.

48. *Guardian*, 28 June 1988.

49. *Guardian*, 9 June 1988. Zhang once bagged a wolf on a hunt.

50. Rong Yiren, see *Financial Times*, 31 May 1979; *Daily Telegraph*, 5 October 1979; *International Herald Tribune*, 21 December 1985; 'The Marxist Millionaires', *Sunday Times Magazine*, 27 November 1988; and *Dagongbao*, 8 June 1994, in *BBC/SWB*/FE/2020/G/5 of 13 November 1994. Canary Wharf, *Sunday Express*, 5 June 1992; LME, *Financial Times*, 6 March 1995.

51. *Sunday Times Magazine*, 27 November 1988.

52. Interview with Wang in Hongkong. He told me in 1989, 'I am not a member of the Communist Party, and that is the truth... I was imprisoned three times, by the Japanese Military Police, by the Guomindang and by the Gang of Four in the Cultural Revolution...' See also *Sunday Times Magazine*, 27 November 1988.

53. *Financial Times*, 20 July 1989; *South China Morning Post*, 3 July 1989; and *Hongkong Business*, March 1990.

54. *Dagongbao*, 30 June 1983; and on vice-president Chen Wuzing, see *Financial Times*, 29 October 1985.

55. Shanghai Club, *The Economist*, 9 February 1985; Guangzhou Club, *Dagongbao*, 21 August 1986.

56. *International Herald Tribune*, 12 December 1992; *The Times*, 21 October 1992.

57. *Japan Times*, 29 November 1991.

58. *Far Eastern Economic Review*, 22 May 1986; *Dagongbao*, 20 October 1988.

59. *Hongkong Business*, December 1988.

60. *Financial Times*, 2 June 1993; *Far Eastern Economic Review*, 11 September 1981. See David Bonavia on the early problems of Baoshan, *Far Eastern Economic Review*, 8 June 1979; also *Financial Times*, 29 September 1980 and 3 November 1980; and *China Newsletter*, May 1981.

61. *Liberation Daily*, Shanghai, 2 December 1991, in ICM, February 1992.

62. *Liberation Daily*, Shanghai, 12 January 1995; *BBC/SWB/*FE/2214/52/7 of 30 January 1995.

63. Barry Naughton, 'The Third Front: Defence Industrialization in the Chinese Interior', *The China Quarterly*, no. 115, September 1988, p.351.

64. See Denis Fred Simon, 'China's Drive to Close the Technological Gap: S & T Reform and the Imperative to Catch Up', *The China Quarterly*, no. 119, September 1989, p.598; Richard Conroy, *op.cit.*; and papers by Eric Baark, Richard Suttmeier, Denis Simon, Marcia Smith and Mary B. Bullock in the science and technology section of *China's Economic Dilemmas in the 1990s*, US Congress Joint Economic Committee, Washington, 1991, vol. 2, pp.531–628.

65. B. Fert, 'China Imports French and British Technology for a Twin Unit PWR Station', *Nuclear Engineering International*, London, September 1987; Geoffrey Cuthbert, 'Chinese Power', *Achievement*, December 1988; Zan Yun Long, 'Presentation of the Project Status of the Guangdong Daya Bay Nuclear Power Station', February 1989, mimeo: *Far Eastern Economic Review*, 19 February 1993.

66. *BBC/SWB*/FE/1950/B/1 of 10 March 1994.

67. See Tatsu Kambara, 'The Energy Situation in China', *The China Quarterly*, no. 131, September 1992, p.609; and Vaclav Smil, *Energy in China's Modernization*, Armonk, New York, N.E. Sharpe, 1988, but see also comments of Elspeth Thomson in *The China Quarterly*, no. 115, September 1988, pp.467–72.

68. See the exhaustive article by Richard Louis Edmonds, 'The Sanxia (Three Gorges) Project: The Environmental Argument Surrounding China's Super Dam', *Global Ecology and Biogeography Letters*, July 1992, p.105. See also Dai Qing, *Yangtze! Yangtze!* Earthscan, 1994; Christopher Reynolds, *Los Angeles Times*, 22 June 1994; and *Environmental Impact Statement for the Yangtze Three Gorges Dam*, Science Press, Beijing, 1995.

69. Mayor Li Ziliu, *Far Eastern Economic Review*, 20 August 1992. See also *The Economist*, 15 August 1992; and *International Herald Tribune*, 30 September 1991.

70. *The Economist*, 30 April 1988.

71. *Hongkong Business*, February 1993.

72. World Bank, *op.cit.*, p.126. A Chinese economist at Cambridge University has argued strongly that whereas the stock market was important to Europe as an engine for risk-sharing, China's greatest problem is shortage of capital, for which there are other sources available; better not push the stock exchange artificially, therefore, but allow it to develop later when needs become more sophisticated: Dong He, 'The Stock Market and Industrial Performance: Lessons from the West for Stock Market Development in China', Qimiao Fan and Peter Nolan (eds), *China's Economic Reforms*, St Martin's Press and Macmillan, 1994, p.191.

73. *Japan Times*, 5 May 1992.

74. Nicholas Kristof, *New York Times* and *International Herald Tribune*, 31 May 1993.

75. *Far Eastern Economic Review*, 16 July 1992.

76. Liu Jinbao, 13 March 1994, *BBC/SWB*/FE/1952/S1/2-3 of 22 March 1994; and Tony Walker, *Financial Times*, 2 April 1994.

77. *Far Eastern Economic Review*, 23 June 1994.

78. *BBC/SWB*/FE/1910/G/9 of 1 February 1994.

79. *South China Morning Post*, 23 November 1989.

80. On Kit Tam, 'A Private Bank in China: Hui Tong Urban Co-operative Bank', *The China Quarterly*, no. 131, September 1992, p.766; *International Herald Tribune*, 8 August 1988; *China Daily*, 3 January 1989. The British visitor was John Elster.

81. *Far Eastern Economic Review*, 14 January 1993.

82. *Japan Times*, 8 July 1993 and 11 July 1993.

83. *International Herald Tribune*, 7 July 1993. See Li Yingqi (a People's Bank of China economist), 'China's Inflation', *Asian Survey*, July 1988, p.655 and the same author's 'Changes in China's Monetary Policy', *Asian Survey*, May 1991, p.422.

84. *Financial Times*, 2 December 1993; Tsang Shu-ki and Cheng Yuk-shing, 'China's Tax Reforms of 1994', *Asian Survey*, September 1994, p.769; and Steven Mufson. *Washington Post* and *International Herald Tribune*, 7 March 1994.

85. *New York Times* and *International Herald Tribune*, 3 December 1993.

86. Dr Goh's speech of 19 August 1993, *Straits Times* and *Japan Times*, 26 August 1993.

87. Seth Faison, *New York Times* and *International Herald Tribune*, 7 March 1995.

88. William H. Overholt, *China, The Next Economic Superpower*, Weidenfeld & Nicolson, 1993, p.116.

Chapter 11 Trade and Investment: Through the Open Door

1. *Vanity Fair*, October 1993, p.42.

2. *Peking Review*, 19 April 1974; Maoist economists, *Fundamentals of Political Economy*, Shanghai, 1974; see *Asian Wall Street Journal Weekly*, 7 April 1988.

3. *Dagongbao*, 10 April 1986.

4. A merchant bank adviser, David Lowes of Robert Fleming, comments: 'China is not a homogenous territory. For a start it is virtually impossible to shift goods from one end to the other. It is therefore not a market opportunity of over one billion people. It has to be looked at as segments. Businesses which want to cover the whole of China may need to set up five or six different joint ventures with different partners in different parts of the country' (*Acquisitions Monthly*, London, supplement, June 1994, on corporate investment in China, p.28). See also Wang Gungwu, *The China Quarterly*, no. 136, p.931.

5. The pitfalls for foreign managers are examined in Tang Jie and Zhang Cheng, *A Report on Poll Conducted on Cross Culture Management in Foreign Invested Ventures in China*, Sasakawa Peace Foundation, Tokyo, 1995.

6. *Los Angeles Times* story carried in *Japan Times*, 28 October 1983; *Daily Telegraph*, 14 June 1983.

7. *The Times*, 19 January 1993; and *Sunday Times*, 19 November 1986.

8. *Financial Times*, 2 October 1992; *Japan Times*, 16 May 1992.

9. Oranges, *South China Morning Post*, 20 November 1989; winery, *South China Morning Post*, 12 November 1989.

10. *Far Eastern Economic Review*, 15 October 1992.

11. *China Review*, October 1988.

12. *China Review*, October 1989.

13. *Asian Wall Street Journal*, 5 March 1991.

14. *Dagongbao*, 22 December 1988; *Financial Times*, 14 December 1988.

15. *Daily Telegraph*, 21 June 1993.

16. *Hongkong Business*, September 1988.

17. *Hongkong Business*, December 1992.

18. Zhu Rongji interview by Dow Jones in *Far Eastern Economic Review*, 23 December 1993; Lincoln Kaye, 'Role Reversal', *Far Eastern Economic Review*, 27 May 1993, p.10; and World Trade Organisation *1995 Inter-*

national Trade Trends and Statistics, Geneva, 1995, p. 75.

19. *Xinhua*, 10 April 1994 in *BBC/SWB*/FE/1969/G/10/ of 12 April 1994; and *BBC/SWB*/FE/2275.

20. *Far Eastern Economic Review*, 24 June and 2 September 1993.

21. Peter Harrold, *China's Reform Experience to Date*, World Bank, Washington, 1992, p.26.

22. Wendy Freeman, 'China's Defence Industries', *Pacific Review*, vol. 6, no. 1, 1993, p.57.

23. *Financial Times*, 29 October 1992; *Dagongbao*, 6 October 1988.

24. *China-Britain Trade Review*, no. 327, December 1991, pp.4–7.

25. Freeman, *op.cit.*; *International Herald Tribune*, 5 March 1993.

26. *Hongkong Standard*, 8 November 1992.

27. *China Business Report*, London, 1979, no. 2.

28. *Dagongbao*, 25 June 1987; *International Herald Tribune*, 8 July 1987.

29. *Japan Times*, 8 May 1988.

30. Junhao Hong, 'The Resurrection of Advertising in China', *Asian Survey*, April 1994, p.326.

31. David Wall, *Special Economic Zones and Industrialization in China*, University of Sussex, Brighton, March 1991.

32. World Bank, *China, Foreign Trade Reform*, Washington, 1994, 'China's SEZ Policy – An Evaluation', pp.221–45, and 'Economic Zones in China: A Taxonomy', pp.246–51.

33. *BBC/SWB*/FE/2248/51/1 of 10 March 1995.

34. See Fuh-Wen Tzeng, 'The Political Economy of China's Coastal Development Strategy', *Asian Survey*, March 1991, p.270.

35. See Martin Lockett, 'China's Special Economic Zones: The Cultural and Managerial Challenges', paper for *The Economist* Conference on Chinese Culture and Management, Paris, January 1986.

36. David Wall, *op. cit.*

37. *Financial Times*, 17 August 1993; *Financial Times* interview with Zhu Rongji 13 November 1995; and Philip Bowring, *International Herald Tribune*, 9 November 1995.

38. Words of a foreign lawyer, *International Herald Tribune*, 30 June 1992.

39. Cited by Fuh-Wen Tzeng, *op.cit.* p.274.

40. *Cheng Ming*, Hongkong, 1 March 1994 in *BBC/SWB*/FE/2007/G/20 of 27 May 1994.

41. Nicholas R. Lardy, *China in the World Economy*, Institute for International Economics, Washington, 1994, p.110.

42. Long Yongtu, '"Return to GATT" – New Challenges and Opportunities', *China Economic Review*, September 1992, p.16 at p.22.

43. See Hsu Kuang-tai, 'Peking's White Paper on the Protection of

Intellectual Property Rights', *Issues and Studies*, July 1994, p.105. The last Emperor's widow recently won a lawsuit about the copyright of his autobiography, *International Herald Tribune*, 1 February 1995.

44. Zou Jiahua, 'China's Economic Restructuring and Opening to the Outside World', address to Royal Institute of International Affairs, London, 1992, p.11.

45. Much of the next few paragraphs draws upon Paul M. Cadario, Kazuko Ogawa and Yin-Kam Wen, *A Chinese Province as a Reform Experiment: The Case of Hainan*, World Bank, Washington, 1992. See also *Asian Finance*, 15 August 1988; and *China Mainland*, April 1988.

46. *International Herald Tribune*, 14 November 1995.

47. Other Special Economic Zones focusing on links with neighbouring economies are discussed in chapter 18 below.

48. See 'New Policy Regulates Foreign Involvement in China's Motor Vehicle Industry', *China Briefing*, Hongkong Bank, October 1994, p.4.

49. See Pi Shenghao and Ling Xiaodong, *China's Trade Pattern and Trade Policy*, Sasakawa Peace Foundation, Tokyo, 1995; also Lardy, *op.cit.*, chapter 2.

50. *South London Press*, 8 November 1996.

Chapter 12 Economic Outlook: Cat on the Loose

1. See World Bank, *China, Reform and the Role of the Plan in the 1990s*, Washington, 1992, pp.49–52.

2. Ross Garnaut and Guonan Ma, 'How Rich is China?', *Australian Journal of Chinese Affairs*, no. 30, 1993. See also Sang Bingyan, 'On Methodology for International Comparison of GNP and GDP: is China the "World's Third Largest Economy?"', *China Economic Review*, September 1992, p.16. Nicholas R. Lardy, *China in the World Economy*, Institute for International Economics, Washington, 1994, also rejects the high estimate of the IMF (over $2000) in favour of something nearer $1000. The *World Bank Atlas 1995* gives $490 on conventional basis, $2,120 on the new Purchasing Power Parity basis.

3. *Human Development Report 1993*, Oxford, 1993.

4. *Far Eastern Economic Review*, 23 June 1994.

5. William H. Overholt, *China, The Next Economic Superpower*, Weidenfeld & Nicolson, London, 1993, p.18.

6. *Mingbao*, 13 January 1994; *BBC/SWB*/2211/S1/2 of 26 January 1995.

7. *BBC/SWB*/FE/0376.

8. World Bank, *op.cit.*, p.88.

9. Tru-Gin Liu, 'Income Inequality in the Rural Areas of Taiwan

During 1976–87', St Anthony's College Oxford thesis, see *Chinese Economic Association in the UK Newsletter*, December 1992, p.7.

10. *The Economist*, 19 June 1993.

11. *BBC/SWB*/FE/1826/G/5 of 22 October 1993.

12. *Financial Times*, 6 July 1993.

13. *Financial Times*, 18 November 1993.

14. Figure compiled by William H. Overholt, *op.cit.*, p.8.

15. See Baruch Boxer, 'China's Environmental Prospects', *Asian Survey*, July 1989, p.669; and also his 'China's Environment: Issues and Economic Implications', in *China's Economic Dilemmas in the 1990s*, US Congress Joint Economic Committee, Washington, 1991, p.290.

16. *Xinhua*, 23 March 1994, *BBC/SWB*/FE/1984/G/13 of 29 April 1994.

17. *International Herald Tribune*, 5 January 1994; *Japan Times*, 28 August 1993.

18. For the vicissitudes of CITIC see *Financial Times*, 16 March 1995.

19. World Bank, *op.cit.*, pp.155–6. On RMB convertibility see Sophie Roell in *Financial Times*, 29 November 1996.

20. Shuhe Li, 'The Potential and Sources of China's Growth in the Next 30 Years', *City Economist*, vol. 4, November 1994, City University of Hongkong.

Chapter 13 Restless Provinces: The Drift to Federalism

1. Cheng, see *Pacific Review*, vol. 7, no. 3, 1994, p.319; polarities from Hu Angang, see *BBC/SWB*/FE/2230/G/6 of 17 February 1995.

2. G. William Skinner, 'China's Regional Systems: An Analysis of Contemporary Spatial Inequalities', lecture at School of Oriental and African Studies, London, 13 May 1994; Dru C. Gladney, *International Herald Tribune*, 22 February 1995.

3. *Far Eastern Economic Review*, 2 April 1992; *The Economist*, 26 June 1993.

4. Andrew Watson, Christopher Findley and Du Yintang, 'Who won the "Wool War"?: A Case Study of Rural Product Marketing in China', *The China Quarterly*, no. 118, June 1989, p.213.

5. *Dagongbao*, Hongkong, 9 May 1990.

6. *Dagongbao*, 9 May 1990; *Wenweibao*, 9 July 1990; *International Herald Tribune*, 24 November 1990.

7. *The Economist*, 19 August 1989.

8. *The Economist*, 'A Great Leap Forward', 5 October 1991.

9. *The Economist*, 26 June 1993.

10. *South China Morning Post*, 5 March 1990.

11. *Japan Times*, 28 December 1991; *Chinese News Service*, Hongkong, 17 February 1992, in ICM, April 1992.

12. *Mingbao Daily News*, Hongkong, 15 February 1992, in ICM, April 1992.

13. William Overholt, *China, the Next Economic Superpower*, Weidenfeld & Nicolson, London, 1993, p.64. See also Terry Cannon, 'National Minorities and the Internal Frontier', in David S.G. Goodman (ed.), *China's Regional Development*, Routledge, London, 1989, p.164 at p.168; and Terry Cannon, 'Regional Spatial Inequality and Regional Policy', in Terry Cannon and Alan Jenkins (eds), *The Geography of Contemporary China, The Impact of Deng Xiaoping's Decade*, Routledge, London, 1990, p.28.

14. Rone Tempest, *Los Angeles Times*, 16 November 1994, in *China News Digest*, 27 November 1994.

15. *BBC/SWB*/FE/1894/G/9-10 of 13 January 1994.

16. *Xinhua*, 28 June 1993, in *BBC/SWB*/FE/W0292/A/6–7 of 28 July 1993.

17. *BBC/SWB*/FE/W/0292/A/6-7 of 28 July 1993 and W/0297/A/5 of 1 September 1993.

18. See *Far Eastern Economic Review*, 18 October 1990.

19. John P. Burns, 'China's Governance: Political Reform in a Turbulent Environment', *The China Quarterly*, no. 119, September 1989, p.481 at p.487.

20. Wang and Hu: *South China Morning Post* and *International Herald Tribune*, 21 September 1993; see also Yong-Nian Zheng, 'Perforated Sovereignty: Provincial Dynamism and China's Foreign Trade', *Pacific Review*, vol. 7, no. 3, 1994, p.309 at p.320. Yan: see Arthur Waldron, '"Warlordism Versus Federalism", the Revival of a Debate', *The China Quarterly*, no. 90, p.116; Yan's article on federalism in *China Now*, no. 143, winter 1992–93; Yan's book published by Mingbao Press, Hongkong, 1992.

21. See *Far Eastern Economic Review*, 25 May 1995. See also *Towards A Democratic China: The Intellectual Autobiography of Yan Jiaqi*, University of Hawaii Press, Honolulu, 1992.

22. Paul Theroux, *Riding the Iron Rooster*, Hamish Hamilton, London, 1989, p.101; and *Japan Times*, 31 August 1991.

23. Weiying Zhang and Gang Yi, 'China's Gradual Reform: A Historical Perspective', paper presented at London School of Economics, April 1994, pp.16–18.

24. *China, Reform and the Role of the Plan in the 1990s, A World Bank Country Study*, 1992, pp.21–2.

25. Martin Wolf, 'Problem of Revenue Decline', *Financial Times*, 7 September 1994. See also *Financial Times*, 17 February 1995, for central ban

on overseas bond issues, and generally *Financial Times*, 16 March 1995.

26. *Far Eastern Economic Review*, 4 April 1991.

27. Kenneth Lieberthal, in *China's Economic Dilemma in the 1990s*, Joint Economic Committee of US Congress, April 1991, p.17; Harry Harding, 'The Concept of "Greater China": Themes, Variations and Reservations', *The China Quarterly*, no. 136, December 1993, p.660 at p.682.

28. *Mingbao*, Hongkong, 24 May 1994, in *BBC/SWB*/FE/2006/G/10 of 26 May 1994.

29. *China's Economic Dilemmas in the 1990s*, vol. 1, p.17.

30. David S.G. Goodman, 'The PLA and Regionalism in Guangdong', *Pacific Review*, vol. 7, no. 1, 1994, p.29 at p.37.

31. Pretends, Interview with a former Indian ambassador to China; transfers, *Lien Ho Po*, Hongkong, *BBC/SWB*/FE/2254/G/2 of 17 March 1995.

32. *Tokyo Shimbun*, 17 May 1994, *BBC/SWB*/FE/2000/G/3 of 18 May 1994.

33. Gerald Segal, *China Changes Shape: Regionalism and Foreign Policy*, Brassey's, London, 1994, pp.63 and 64.

34. James D. Seymour, 'Toward an East Asian Confederation of Independent States?', *Bulletin of Concerned Asian Scholars*, vol. 25, no. 3, 1992, p.44 at p.48; see also Yamei Zhang, 'China, Democratization or Recentralization', *Pacific Review*, no. 2, 1995, p.249.

35. Jae Ho Chung, 'Studies of Central-Provincial Relations in the People's Republic of China: A Mid-Term Appraisal', *The China Quarterly*, no. 142, June 1995, p.487 at pp.501–2.

Chapter 14 Minorities: Tibet and Others

1. James D. Seymour, 'Toward an East Asian Confederation of Independent States?', *Bulletin of Concerned Asian Scholars*, vol. 25, no. 3, 1993.

2. *Daily Telegraph*, 4 April 1989.

3. *Ibid.*

4. For a discussion of Tibet's international status between 1912 and 1950 see Karl Rahder, 'The Tibetan Claim to Statehood', *Issues and Studies*, June 1993, p.97.

5. See Francis Watson, *The Frontiers of China*, Chatto & Windus, London, 1966, p.175; and Edgar Snow, *Red Star Over China*, Gollancz, 1968, p. 110.

6. Hu Yaobang, *South China Morning Post*, 13 April 1990; atheism, *Xizang Ribao* (Tibet Daily), Lhasa, 2 November 1994, *BBC/SWB*/FE/2254/5/3/2 of 17 March 1995.

7. *Observer*, 7 November 1993, *Xinhua*, 15 March 1995, *BBC/SWB/* FE/2254/5/3/2 of 17 March 1995.

8. *Sunday Times*, 12 March 1989.

9. *International Herald Tribune*, 31 May 1990.

10. *The Times*, Letter to the Editor, 11 April 1989.

11. *Guardian*, 24 April 1990 (many details on Markham).

12. *South China Morning Post*, 9 April 1990.

13. *International Herald Tribune*, 10 March 1989.

14. *Daily Telegraph*, 25 March 1989.

15. *Renmin Ribao*, 6 October 1989.

16. *Independent*, 3 March 1989.

17. Graham Hutchings, 'The Holy Men of Tibet clash with Peking', *Sunday Telegraph*, 5 November 1995.

18. *Financial Times*, 7 August 1993; *Daily Telegraph*, 7 March 1989.

19. 'The Dalai Lama: No Room at the Potala?', *Issues and Studies*, September 1994, p.121.

20. On Tibetan economic zone see *BBC/SWB*/FE/2011/G/2 of 1 June 1995. On joint ventures for processing Tibetan raw materials, foreign trade and modernisation of Gonga Airport see *BBC/SWB*/FE/1939/G/3-10 of 7 March 1994.

21. *BBC/SWB*/FE/1935/G/4 of 2 March 1994.

22. Hollis S. Liao, 'Tibet's Economic Reform Since Teng Tsiao-p'ing's South China Tour', *Issues and Studies*, March 1994, p.15.

23. Investment: *BBC/SWB*/FE/2093/G/5-9 of 6 September 1994. The newly modernising Tibet was described in Han Suyin, *Lhasa, the Open City*, Jonathan Cape, 1977.

24. *International Herald Tribune*, 25 May 1993.

25. See *Far Eastern Economic Review*, 16 June 1993.

26. For a general account of the Chinese Communists' efforts to consolidate their control over Xinjiang province see June Teufel Dreyer, 'The PLA and Regionalism in Xinjiang', *Pacific Review*, vol. 7, no. 3, 1994, pp.41–55.

27. Han pioneer settlements in Xinjiang set up by the Production and Conservation Corps were military-agricultural colonies similar in function to the *tuntian* settlements first established by settlers in the Han dynasty. See June Teufel Dreyer *op.cit.*, pp.42–3.

28. See Jasper Becker, *Guardian*, 24 December 1985.

29. See *Far Eastern Economic Review*, 3 August 1989.

30. *Far Eastern Economic Review*, 3 May 1990.

31. See Colina MacDougall, *Financial Times*, 28 December 1991.

32. Peter Ferdinand (ed.), *The New Central Asia and its Neighbours*, Royal Institute of International Affairs, London, 1994.

33. See *Far Eastern Economic Review*, 12 May 1994.

34. *Japan Times*, 5 June 1993 and 22 September 1993.

35. See Lilian Craig Harris, *China Considers the Middle East*, I.B. Tauris, London & New York, 1993.

36. *International Herald Tribune*, 26 October 1993.

37. Jencks, 'The PRC's Military and Security Policy', *Issues and Studies*, November 1994.

38. Nicholas Danziger, *Far Eastern Economic Review*, 29 August 1985.

39. Curiously, President Lee Teng-hui of Taiwan, welcoming the Mongolian Prime Minister to Taipei in 1993 and extending economic aid to Mongolia, said: 'Mongolians are just like a part of the big Chinese family', *Central News Agency*, Taipei, 10 December 1993.

40. *Daily Telegraph*, 1 November 1982.

41. *The Times*, 29 August 1986.

42. See Tomochelor Hao, 'Nationalist Challenge to Multi-ethnic State: Inner Mongolia and China', London School of Economics thesis, 1995.

43. See e.g. Terry Cannon, 'National Minorities and the Internal Frontier', in David S.G. Goodman (ed.), *China's Regional Development*, Routledge, London, 1989, p.164 and pp.176–7.

44. Dru C. Gladney, *China's Ethnic Awakening*, East-West Center, Honolulu, January 1995.

Chapter 15 Hongkong: The Front Door

1. Editorial, *Wenweibao*, Hongkong, 12 December 1993.

2. Richard Evans, *Deng Xiaoping and the Making of Modern China*, Hamish Hamilton, London, 1993, pp.46 and 57. See also Dick Wilson, *Hong Kong! Hong Kong!*, Unwin Hyman, London, 1990, chapter 3.

3. *The Times*, London, 24 July 1991.

4. Li, *BBC/SWB*/FE/F/2 of 16 March 1995; Yang, *Xinbao*, Hongkong, 5 September 1994, *BBC/SWB*/FE/2101/G/4 of September 1994.

5. See the volume *Hongkong in Transition 1992*, One Country Two Systems Economic Research Institute, Hongkong Institute of Asia-Pacific Studies of Chinese University of Hongkong and Centre for East-West Studies of Hongkong Baptist College, p.67.

6. *Cheng Ming*, Hongkong, 1 March 1994, in *BBC/SWB*/FE/1953/F/1 of 23 March 1993; also *Cheng Ming*, 1 April 1994 in *BBC/SWB*/FE/1978/F/1 of 22 April 1994; *Dagongbao*, 7 May 1994. For the Chinese army's likely role in Hongkong after 1997 see *BBC/SWB*/FE/1889/F/3 of 7 January 1994.

7. *Cheng Ming*, 1 June 1994, in *BBC/SWB*/FE/2018/F/1 of 9 June 1994.

8. *Financial Times*, 28 November 1996.

9. *Financial Times*, 30 November 1993.

10. *Report of the Working Party on Local Administration in Hongkong*, Hongkong government, 1966; the thesis is challenged by some, but without taking Chinese values into account, e.g. Steven Hoadley, *Far Eastern Economic Review*, 2 November 1967.

11. *International Herald Tribune*, 24 January 1994.

12. Speech by Anson Chang, Hongkong Government Chief Secretary, to the Hongkong Association in London, 25 November 1994.

13. Louise Lucas in *Financial Times*, 28 October 1994.

14. *International Herald Tribune*, 8 April 1994; *Financial Times*, 7 April 1994; and *BBC/SWB*/FE/1995/G/1 of 7 April 1994.

15. Qian, *Wenweibao*, Hongkong, 7 November 1993, in *BBC/SWB*/FE/1941/F/1 of 9 November 1993; Ting Wai, 'Hongkong's Changing Political Order and its Relations with Taiwan', *Issues and Studies*, August 1992, p.46 at p.53.

16. *Spectator*, 2 April 1994; see also Percy Cradock, *Experiences of China*, John Murray, London, 1994.

17. Chris Patten in *The Times*, 10 December 1993.

18. *Guardian*, 25 February 1994.

19. *Guardian*, 21 January 1994.

20. *Financial Times*, 2 July 1994.

21. *Wenweibao*, October 1993, in *BBC/SWB*/FE/1828/F/3 of 25 October 1993.

22. *Guardian*, 18 January 1994.

23. *Wenweibao*, editorial, 25 February 1994 in *BBC/SWB*/FE/1932/F/3 of 26 February 1994.

24. *Xinbao*, 8 December 1993, in *BBC/SWB*/FE/F/3 of 15 December 1993.

25. *Financial Times*, 14 January 1994.

26. Simon Holberton, Interview with Li Kashing, *Financial Times*, 23 March 1995.

27. See Kuan Hsin-chi and Lau Siu-kai, 'The Partial Vision of Democracy in Hongkong', *China Journal*, July 1995, p. 239.

28. *Financial Times*, 24 March 1995.

29. Lau Siu-kai and Kuan Shin-chi, *The Ethos of the Hongkong Chinese*, Chinese University of Hongkong, 1988.

30. *Far Eastern Economic Review*, 14 July 1988.

31. See Le Shiu-hing, 'The Politics of the Court of Final Appeal Debate in Hongkong', *Issues and Studies*, February 1993, p.105; also Louise de Rosario, 'Justice Under Siege', *Far Eastern Economic Review*, 26 January 1995, p.18.

32. *Cheng Ming*, Hongkong, 1 July 1994 in FE/2043/F/1 of 9 July 1994.

33. *Far Eastern Economic Review*, 16 December 1993, and see the issue of 9 November 1995 for a detailed survey of Hongkong vs Shanghai debate.

34. Australian and Canadian figures are unreliable because of the vigorous traffic of Hongkongers acquiring those nationalities to and from Hongkong.

35. Michael Richardson, 'Jardine Shifts Weight Southward', *International Herald Tribune*, 19 October 1994.

36. Richard Hughes thus sub-titled his book on Hongkong in 1968, but he borrowed the phrase from Han Suyin.

37. Nick Rufford, 'Sons of Mao's Revolution Turn into Hongkong Tycoons', *Sunday Times*, 22 May 1994; and *The Economist*, 7 May 1994.

38. *BBC/SWB* FE/2216.

39. *Cheng Ming*, Hongkong, 26 July 1994, in *BBC/SWB*/FE/2059/F/2 of 28 July 1994.

40. *Cheng Ming*, Hongkong, 1 June 1994, in *BBC/SWB*/FE/2018/F/1 of 9 June 1994.

41. *Guardian*, 14 April 1987.

42. Richard Louise Edmonds, 'Macau and Greater China', *The China Quarterly*, no. 136, December 1993, p.878; also J.I. Kamm, 'Macau's Economic Role in the West River Delta' in R.D. Cremer (ed.), *Macau, City of Commerce and Culture*, University of East Asia Press, Hongkong, 1987, p.165; and Herbert S. Yee and Le Shiu-hing, 'Macau in Transition: The Politics of Decolonization' in Donald H. McMillen and Michael E. DeGolyer (eds), *One Culture, Many Systems, Politics in the Reunification of China*, Chinese University Press, Hongkong, 1993. Marconi has ambitious telecommunciations plans for Macao, Louise de Rosario, *Far Eastern Economic Review*, 12 October 1995, p. 110.

43. Lu Ping, *Dagongbao*, Hongkong, 14 June 1994, in *BBC/SWB/*FE/2024/F/2 of 18 June 1994.

Chapter 16 Taiwan: The Other China

1. See Michael Rand Hoare, 'Taiwan Confronts the Past', *History Today*, May 1993. The classic account of the incident is in George H. Kerr's *Formosa Betrayed* (Eyre & Spottiswood, 1966). See also Lai Tse-han, Ramon H. Myers and Wei Won, *A Tragic Beginning: The Taiwan Uprising of February 28, 1947*, Stanford University Press, 1991.

2. Yu-shan Wu, 'Marketization of Politics, The Taiwan Experience', *Asian Survey*, 4 April 1989, p.385.

3. Dennis Van Vranken Hickey, 'Taiwan and Tiananmen: An Analysis of Taiwan's Policy Towards the Democracy Movement', *Journal of Northeast Asian Studies*, Fall 1990, p.3; Brian Murray, 'Tiananmen, the View from Taipei', *Asian Survey*, April 1990, p.348.

4. Yu-shan Wu, *op.cit.*, p.387. Information also from Kao-Chao Lee, Director of Economic Research Department, Council for Economic Planning and Development, Taipei.

5. James C. Hsiung and others (ed.), *Contemporary Republic of China, the Taiwan Experience 1950–1980*, American Association for Chinese Studies, New York, 1981; Samuel C.Shieh (then Governor of the Central Bank) 'Financial Liberalization and Internationalization: the Development of Taipei as a Regional Financial Centre in Asia', address to Royal Institute of International Affairs, London, 15 April 1992; and Laura Tyson, 'Market Hampers Taiwan Financial Ambitions', *Financial Times*, 17 October 1994.

6. See Andrew J. Nathan, 'The Legislative Yuan Elections in Taiwan, Consequences of the Electoral System', *Asian Survey*, April 1993; also Linda Chao and Ramon H. Myers, 'The First Chinese Democracy', *Asian Survey*, March 1994, p.213.

7. John F. Copper, 'Taiwan's 1991 Second National Assembly Election', *Journal of Northeast Asian Studies*, spring 1992, p.47.

8. 'Taiwan's Mayoral and Gubernatorial Elections', *Issues and Studies*, December 1994, p.113. DDP: interviews with Tsai Shih-yuan and Hank Ou in Taipei, March 1994.

9. *Red Star Over China*, p. 107 in the original 1937 edition, p. 110 in the expanded edition of 1968.

10. 'If they persist in advocating Taiwan independence . . .', Deng said, 'we must resolutely make a decision to achieve reunification of the motherland by military means,' *Cheng Ming*, Hongkong, 1 August 1994, *BBC/SWB*/FE/2066/G/4 of 5 August 1994; also *Daily Telegraph*, 2 February 1995. Dr Jason Hu has assembled a useful compendium on this, under the title *A Study of a Possible Communist Attack on Taiwan*, Government Information Office, Taipei, April 1992.

11. Ye, *Xinhua*, Hongkong, 14 March 1994, *BBC/SWB*/FE/1948/S/1/3; Jiang, *Xinhua*, 30 January 1994, *BBC/SWB*/FE/2214/G/1 of 31 January 1995.

12. Deng Xiaoping, 'Speech at the Third Plenary Session of the Chinese Communist Party Advisory Commission', 22 October 1984, as quoted by An-chia Wu in *Issues and Studies*, July 1994, p.11.

13. Qingguo Jia, 'Changing Relations Across the Taiwan Strait, Beijing's Perceptions', *Asian Survey*, March 1992, p.281; Liu Jinbao, *BBC/SWB*/FE/2254/S/3/2 of 17 March 1995.

14. *South China Morning Post*, Hongkong, 5 May 1990.

15. Hsu Kuang-tai, 'On Peking's Granting of Legislative Power to the Amoy Special Economic Zone', *Issues and Studies*, September 1994, p.50.

16. Cheng-Tian Kuo, 'The PRC and Taiwan, Fujian's Faltering United Front', *Asian Survey*, August 1992, pp.686–7.

17. *China Daily Business Weekly*, Beijing, 6 November 1994; *International Herald Tribune*, 18 February 1995.

18. In his ending of the state of war in late 1991.

19. *The Foreign Policy Stance of the Democratic Progressive Party* (First Draft Typescript of 20 June 1993) has some interesting and innovative ideas on the UN question and China, pp.14–15.

20. Dr Jason C. Hu, 'The Case for Taipei's UN Representation, "The Virtuous Will Not be Alone"', address to Atlantic Council of US, Washington, 17 September 1993.

21. Dr Bernard Joei, 'An Open Letter to President Clinton', *China News*, 29 July 1993. 'Recognition of the Republic of China,' Professor Joei explains, 'has sometimes butted on its name, as it contains "China" – which some see as a sort of proprietary trademark of the People's Republic of China ... We should not be stopped by so little. "Chung Hwa Ming Kuo" (literally "Middle Kingdom People's State") is as meaningful a name and bears the advantage of authenticity. And where the Republic of China found closed doors, we hope Chung Hwa Ming Kuo will find them open.' Dr Joei used to be Taiwan's ambassador to the UN, and remains active in lobbying UN members. Burma, Cambodia, Ceylon and Persia all switched to names which their inhabitants can recognise, though for reasons differing from Taiwan's possible case. (Interview with Dr Joei in Taipei, March 1994.)

22. *International Herald Tribune*, 2 March 1995.

23. Targets, Liu Huaqing, *Cheng Ming*, Hongkong, 1 September 1994, *BBC/SWB*/FE/2133/G/13 of 22 October 1994.

24. 'Yang Shangkun on China's Reunification', *Beijing Review*, 26 November 1990, p.11. quoted in Qingguo Jia, *op.cit.*, p.287.

Chapter 17 The Overseas Chinese: Offshore Assets

1. See George Hicks and J.A.C. Mackie, 'Overseas Chinese, A Question of Identity', *Far Eastern Economic Review*, 14 July 1994, p.46 at p.48.

2. Peter Chen, 'Chinese Dominate Asia's Economies', *China Post*, 29 March 1994.

3. 'China's Diaspora Turns Homeward', *The Economist*, 27 November 1993, p.79.

4. *Far Eastern Economic Review*, 26 August 1993.

5. *Asian Finance*, Hongkong, 15 August 1991, p.12.

6. Jennifer W. Cushman, *Family and State: The Formation of a Sino-Thai Tin-mining Dynasty, 1797–1932*, Oxford University Press, Singapore, 1993.

7. Elliott Kulick and Dick Wilson, *Thailand's Turn, Profile of a New Dragon*, St Martin's Press, 1992, pp.137–41.

8. Lynn Pan, *Sons of the Yellow Emperor, The Story of the Overseas Chinese*, Secker & Warburg, 1990, pp.230–35.

9. *The Economist*, 27 November 1993.

10. *Overseas Chinese Business Networks in Asia*, East Asia Analytical Unit, Department of Foreign Affairs, Canberra, 1995; see also *China Post*, 29 March 1994.

11. Victor Mallet, 'Indonesian Workers Turn on Chinese Businessmen', *Financial Times*, 24 April 1994.

12. Kulick and Wilson, *op.cit.*, chapter 5, 'Those Chinese Genes', p.83.

13. Botan, *Letters from Thailand*, DK Book House, Bangkok, 1977, p.389.

14. Lee Kuan Yew's speech at second World Chinese Entrepreneurs' Convention in Hongkong, November 1993, *International Herald Tribune*, 23 November 1993.

15. *BBC/SWB*/FE/1763/A/2/1 of 10 August 1993.

16. *Far Eastern Economic Review*, 14 July 1994.

17. *Ibid*, and Xiangming Chen, Taiwan Investments in China and Southeast Asia, *Asian Survey*, May 1996.

18. See *International Herald Tribune*, 28 January 1993.

19. 'A Profitable Homecoming', *Financial Times*, 15 December 1992.

20. See Hicks and Mackie, *op.cit.*, p.46.

21. Michael Vatikiotis, *Far Eastern Economic Review*, 14 July 1994.

22. Interview in Bangkok, 1991.

23. Aw: *Dagongbao*, Hongkong, 2 June 1983; Kitty: *Financial Times*, 15 December 1992.

24. *Xinhua*, 4 April 1995, *BBC/SWB*/FE/2272/G/1 of 7 April 1995.

25. Yet international scholars increasingly question the 'Singapore model': See David Martin Jones and David Brown (political science lecturers at the National University of Singapore), 'Singapore and the Myth of the Liberalizing Middle Class', *Pacific Review*, vol. 7, no. 1, 1994, p.79. Singapore's role between China and southeast Asia is also not easily defined: see Kanishka Jayasuriya, 'Singapore: The Politics of Regional Definition', *Pacific Review*, vol. 7, no. 4, 1994, p.411. Sie Hok Tjwan calls Singapore the fifth overseas Chinese state after short-lived predecessors in southeast Asia in earlier centuries, and predicts a sixth one covering underpopulated areas like Sarawak (*The 6th Overseas Chinese State*, Centre for Southeast Asian Studies, James Cook University of North Queensland, 1990).

26. Chen Jie, 'The "Taiwan Problem" in Peking's ASEAN Policy', *Issues*

and Studies, April 1993, p.95 at pp.116–22.

27. See 'Keeping it all in the Family', *South China Morning Post*, 26 June 1994. A German sociologist finds that small Chinese traders in Singapore are nepotistic in favour of their very close family – sons, brothers, wives and sisters – but will not employ more distant kinsmen or clansmen unless they match outside candidates in qualifications or diligence (Thomas Menkhoff, *Towards an Understanding of Chinese Entrepreneurship in Southeast Asia: Small Trading Firms in Singapore*, Sociology of Development Research Centre, University of Bielefeld, 1990).

28. *Window*, Hongkong, 8 January 1993, p.35 (Kevin Sinclair reporting from Johannesburg).

29. Maurice Freedman, *The Chinese in Southeast Asia: A Longer View*, China Society, London, 1965, p.5.

30. See e.g. Peter S. Li, *The Chinese in Canada*, Oxford University Press, Toronto, 1988; and Lee Tai To (ed.), *Early Chinese Immigrant Societies: Studies of North America and British Southeast Asia*, Heinemann Asia, Singapore, 1988.

Chapter 18 Greater China: Only Reconnect

1. See *Far Eastern Economic Review*, 20 July 1979; and Harry Harding, 'The Concept of "Greater China": Themes, Variations and Reservations', *The China Quarterly*, no. 136, December 1993, p.660 at p.663.

2. *South China Morning Post*, 15 and 17 April 1989.

3. *South China Morning Post*, 25 May 1989.

4. *International Herald Tribune*, 23 January 1992; *Japan Times*, 25 April 1992; and Chen Te-sheng, 'Conditions Not Yet Ripe for the Establishment of a Greater China Economic Sphere', *Issues and Studies*, February 1992, p.131 at p.132.

5. *Japan Times*, 11 March 1992.

6. See Peter C.Y. Chow, 'The Co-ordination of Chinese Economic Systems: Problems and Prospects', *Issues and Studies*, January 1983, p.99. Three important formulations were 'Greater China Economic Community' by Chen Kunyao and Chen Yiqong of Hongkong University and the Chinese Academy of Social Sciences respectively; 'Greater China Common Market' by Cha-yuan Cheng; and 'Asian Chinese Common Market' by Charles Kao both of the USA. See Charng Kao, 'A "Greater China Economic Sphere": Reality and Prospects', *Issues and Studies*, November 1992, p.49 at p.50.

7. *BBC/SWB*/FE/1848 of 17 November 1993.

8. Yong-Nian Zheng, 'Perforated Sovereignty: Provincial Dynamism

and China's Foreign Trade', *Pacific Review*, vol. 7, no. 3, 1994, p.309.

9. See references in note 20 to chapter 13 above.

10. Thomas B. Gold, 'Go With Your Feelings, Hongkong and Taiwan Popular Culture in Greater China', *The China Quarterly*, no. 136, December 1993, p.907.

11. *Wenweibao*, Hongkong, 22 May 1992.

12. Yong-Nian Zheng, *op.cit.*, pp.313–14. This catalogue of the economic circles of Greater China principally follows Huang Chih-lien's scheme, but also corresponds broadly with Robert A. Scalapino's Natural Economic Territories. ('China in the Late Leninist Era', *The China Quarterly*, no. 136, December 1993, p.949 at p.958).

13. See Yong-Nian Zheng, *op.cit.*, p.315. Won Bae Kim, 'Yellow Sea Economic Zone: Vision or Reality?', *Journal of Northeast Asian Studies*, spring 1991, p.35; Sueo Sekiguchi, 'Direct Foreign Investment and the Yellow Sea Rim', *ibid.*, p.56; Choon-ho Park, Dalchoong Kim and Seo-Hang Lee (eds), *The Regime of the Yellow Sea*, Yonsei University, Korea.

14. Lincoln Kaye, *Far Eastern Economic Review*, 14 May 1992; Tony Walker, *Financial Times*, 17 January 1994; *Regional Economic Cooperation in Northeast Asia, Proceedings of the Vladivostok Conference*, 25–27 August 1992; Won Bae Kim *et al.* (eds), Sasakawa Peace Foundation, chapters 9 and 18; and Sumio Kuribayashi (ed.), *Rethinking Development Strategy in Northeast Asia*, Sasakawa Peace Foundation, 1993. On the Tumen River Area Programme see UNDP Draft Action Plan, January 1992; UNDP 'Initiative on the Development of the Tumen River Basin' (typescript), n.d.; *UNDP Tumen River Area Development Mission Report*, Pyongyang, October 1991; and Lincoln Kaye, 'Hinterland of Hope' and 'Casualty of History' and Mark Clifford, Louise de Rosario and Lincoln Kaye, 'Trade and Trade-offs', *Far Eastern Economic Review*, 16 January 1992.

15. See Keun Lee and Chung H. Lee, 'Trade Between Bohai of China and Korea: An International Perspective', and Won Bae Kim, 'The Future of Coastal Development in the Yellow Sea Rimlands', in *Journal of Northeast Asian Studies*, Winter 1990, pp.15 and 53.

16. Harry Harding, *op.cit.*

17. Maria Hsia Chang, 'The Future of Taiwan Mainland Relations', *Issues and Studies*, February 1993, p.56 at p.75.

18. Tu Weiming, *The China Quarterly*, no. 136, December 1993, p.674.

19. See interview with Wang Gungwu, 'Lessons from the Past', *Eastern Express Extra*, Hongkong, 23 October 1995.

20. *Tide Monthly*, Hongkong, 16 November 1991, in ICM, February 1992.

21. *Ibid.* See also Denny Roy's interesting explanations for Sino-Singapore collaboration in 'Singapore, China and the "Soft Authoritarian-

ism" Challenge', *Asian Survey*, March 1994, p.231.

22. *Liberation Army Daily*, 5 September 1992, in ICM, November 1992.

23. Other analyses place Greater China firmly in its geographical place, i.e. among the following dynamic East Asian regional groupings: (1) Greater Korea, including North China and the Russian Far East, (2) Greater China, including Guangdong, Fujian, Hongkong, and Taiwan; (3) the Indochina peninsula including Southwest China, Thailand, Vietnam and Cambodia; and (4) the Singapore region, including Johor and parts of Indonesia. See Anchia Wu, 'The Political Implications of the "Co-ordination of Chinese Economic Systems"', *Issues and Studies*, April 1992, p.1 at p.3–4.

Chapter 19 China and Japan: Back to Back

1. Chae-Jin Lee, *Zhou Enlai, The Early Years*, Stanford University Press, 1944, p.100. The Chinese are more adept at finger language, using it where their own dialects or sub-languages differ. Some use it with foreigners, not realising that the written language is different.

2. But the result of the personal rapport was abrasive of Sino–Japanese relations, see Hidenori Ijiri, 'Sino–Japanese Controversy Since the 1972 Diplomatic Normalization', *The China Quarterly*, 1990, p.639 at p.655.

3. Through the island of Deshima, controlled by the Dutch.

4. Frank Welsh, *A History of Hongkong*, HarperCollins, 1993, p.315.

5. Interview with a Japanese diplomatic specialist on Chinese affairs.

6. Interview with Shuichi Kato.

7. Nagatomi, *Sunday Times*, 18 October 1992; Mo, Minerva Press, 1993.

8. Interview with Ikuhiko Hata.

9. 'A Sense of Place', *Look Japan*, August 1992, p.7.

10. E.g. Minoru Tada, *Japan Times*, 25 September 1992.

11. *Japan Times*, 24 October 1992; also *Observer*, 25 October 1992. An excellent overview of the Japanese anguish over the Imperial visit may be found in *Japan Echo*, vol. XIX, no. 4, winter 1992, pp.6–26, articles and discussion by Tanino Sakutaro, Eto Shinkichi, Kobori Keiichiro and Nakajima Mineo.

12. Interview with another Japanese diplomatic specialist on Chinese affairs.

13. *International Herald Tribune*, 15 July 1992.

14. *Issues and Studies*, October 1994, p.135.

15. K.V. Kesavan, 'Japan and the Tiananmen Square Incident', *Asian Survey*, July 1990, p.669.

16. *International Herald Tribune*, 15 August 1991.

17. *Honolulu Star-Bulletin*, 21 March 1994.

18. Interview with Hiroshi Hashimoto, former ambassador of Japan in China.

19. 'Professor Fujino' was the title of the story.

20. *Japan Times*, 3 July 1992.

21. See Pi Shenghao and Ling Xiaodong, 'China's Trade Pattern and Trade Policy', and Tan Hashida, 'Japanese Direct Investment in China and its Implications in North East Asia', papers for Northeast Asia Conference on Economic Co-operation, Seoul, 28–30 November 1994. A Sichuan county magistrate had no false pride when he urged a visiting Japanese businessman, 'In order to expand opening up and enliven the country's economy, by all means treat my country as a colony. All foreign business interests are welcome to exploit this place.' *Nineties Monthly*, Hongkong, January 1995, in ICM, May 1995, p.69.

22. Tokyo brokerage analyst, quoted in *Far Eastern Economic Review*, 9 September 1993.

23. *Modern Enterprise Herald*, Beijing, 1987, no. 4, p.43, as quoted in Glen Lewis and Sun Wanning, 'Discourses about "Learning from Japan" in Post-1979 Mainland Chinese Magazines', *Issues and Studies*, May 1994, p.69. See also Tang Jie and Zhang Cheng, 'A Report on Poll Conducted on Cross Culture Management in Foreign Investment Ventures in China', paper for Economic Co-operation in Northeast Asia Conference in Seoul, February 1995.

24. Robert Taylor, *The Sino-Japanese Axis, A New Force in Asia*, Athlone Press, London, 1985, p.116.

25. *Straits Times*, 14 May 1971. When China resumed nuclear testing in May 1995, Japan restricted its grants of economic aid, see Yoichi Kato of *Asahi Shimbun* in *Insight Japan* (London), November 1995, p. 28.

26. Interviews with Mineo Nakajima and Tatsumi Okabe, academic sinologists, and with Ministry of Foreign Affairs officials, in Tokyo, February 1994.

27. Yoh Kurosawa, 'Expect China to Stay United and Pro-Growth', *International Herald Tribune*, 2 March 1995.

28. The options are fully discussed by Qingxin Ken Wang, 'Toward Political Partnership: Japan's China Policy', *Pacific Review*, vol. 7, no. 2, 1994, p.171.

29. Frank Ching, 'China Cools to North Korea', *Far Eastern Economic Review*, 28 July 1994.

30. *Financial Times*, 1 November 1994.

31. *Pacific Review*, vol. 7, no. 1, 1994, pp.95–6.

32. Toru Kono, 'China Nudges Pyongyang', *Japan Times*, 16 July 1994.

33. See Jia Hao and Zhuang Qubing, 'China's Policy towards the Korean Peninsula', *Asian Survey*, December 1992, p.1137.

Chapter 20 The Third World: Shifting Platforms

1. Ji Guoxing and Hadi Soestrato (eds), *Sino-Indonesian Relations in the Post-Cold War Era*, Centre for Strategic and International Studies, Jakarta, 1992.

2. Pao-min Chang, *The Sino-Vietnamese Territorial Dispute*, Praeger, New York, 1986.

3. Mya Maung, 'On The Road to Mandalay', *Asian Survey*, 5 May 1994, p.447 gives a depressing view of Sino–Burmese events; see also Philip Bowring, *International Herald Tribune*, 3 February 1995; Philip Sherwell, *Daily Telegraph*, 27 December 1994; *Japan Times*, 27 December 1994 and 19 September 1992; and James Pringle, *The Times*, 27 December 1994.

4. Ji Guoxing, 'Sino-Indonesian Political Prospects for the 1990s', in Ji Guoxing and Hadi Soesastro (eds), *Sino-Indonesian Relations in the Post-Cold War Era*, Centre for Strategic and International Studies, Jakarta, 1992, p.120 at p.125. For other solutions, see Pieter Kien-hong Yu, 'A Critique of the Three Proposals for "Solving" the Spratlys Dispute: A Chinese View from Taiwan', *Issues and Studies*, January 1994, p.63.

5. Philip Bowring, *International Herald Tribune*, 18 October 1994; and *The Times*, 10 February 1995.

6. *Far Eastern Economic Review*, 5 Octboer 1995. See generally Michael Richardson, *International Herald Tribune*, 6 June 1994 and Nayan Chanda, *Far Eastern Economic Review*, 11 August 1994.

7. Xu Zehong, *The Mirror*, Hongkong, July 1991, cited in Ting Wai, 'The Regional and International Implications of the South China Economic Zone', *Issues and Studies*, December 1992, pp.53–4.

8. Benoy Kumar Sarkar in his stimulating work *Chinese Religion through Hindu Eyes*, Commercial Press, Shanghai, 1916, wrote of the 'Indianization of Confucianism' and the 'thorough-going Indianization of China' (p.252) during the seventh to the thirteenth centuries. Liang Jizhao told Tagore in the 1920s: 'India and China are like twin brothers. Before most of the civilised races became active, we two brothers had already begun to study the great problems which concern the whole of mankind ... India was ahead of us and we, the little brother, followed behind', Rabindranath Tagore, *Talks in China*, Arunoday Art Press, Calcutta, n.d., pp.2–3.

9. *Visva-Bharati Bulletin*, no. 24, Santiniketan, April 1938, pp.1–2.

10. Speech to Sino-Indian Cultural Society, 25 December 1946, in *Sino-Indian Journal*, vol. 1, Part 1, July 1947, pp.159–60.

11. Nehru, 'The Eastern Federation', *National Herald*, 28 October 1940,

cited in Sarvepalli Gopal, *Jawaharlal Nehru, A Biography*, vol. 1: *1889–1947*, Jonathan Cape, London, 1975, p.249.

12. *The Times*, 30 October 1970. See generally J. Mohan Malik, 'China-India Relations in the Post-Soviet Era: The Continuing Rivalry'; *The China Quarterly*, no. 142, June 1995, p.317.

13. Kotnis was later hyped by the Chinese into a folk-hero for Indian consumption: see Sheng Xiangong, *An Indian Freedom Fighter in China – A Tribute to Dr. D.S. Kotnis*, Foreign Languages Press, Beijing, 1983. See also *Dagongbao*, 3 February 1983.

14. Jawaharlal Nehru, 'India-China Relations', speech in Lok Sabha, 27 November 1969, Ministry of Information, Delhi, n.d., p.12.

15. See John W. Garver, 'China and South Asia', *Annals of the American Academy*, vol. 519, January 1992, p.67.

16. *Far Eastern Economic Review*, 6 May 1965. See also Sarjit Mansingh, 'India-China Relations in the Post-Cold War Era', *Asian Survey*, March 1994, p.285.

17. Garver, *op.cit.*; *BBC/SWB*/FE/2208.

18. Interview with J.N. Dixit, former Foreign Secretary of India.

19. Zheng Ruixiang, 'Shifting Obstacles in Sino-Indian Relations', *Pacific Review*, vol. 6, no. 1, 1993, p.63. India bought enriched uranium from China in 1995.

20. Vikram Seth, *Three Chinese Poets*, Viking, London, 1992.

21. Lillian Craig Harris, *China Considers the Middle East*, I.B. Tauris, London & New York, 1993.

22. *Far Eastern Economic Review*, 30 September 1993.

23. Yitzhak Shichor, 'China and the Role of the United Nations in the Middle East', *Asian Survey*, March 1991; John Calabrese, 'From Flyswatters to Silkworms: The Evolution of China's Role in West Asia', *Asian Survey*, September 1990; Deng-ker Lee, 'Peking's Middle East Policy in the Post-Cold War Era', *Issues and Studies*, August 1994, p.69.

24. *Financial Times*, 14 October 1993; *International Herald Tribune*, 30 December 1994.

25. P.R. Kumaraswamy, 'The Star and the Dragon: An Overview of Israeli–PRC Military Relations', *Issues and Studies*, April 1994, p.36.

26. *Daily Nation*, Nairobi, 13 March 1962.

27. Alan Hutchison, *China's African Revolution*, Hutchinson, London, 1975.

28. *The Times*, 27 December 1988. See also Philip Snow, *The Star Raft, China's Encounter with Africa*, Weidenfeld & Nicolson, London, 1988.

29. *Daily Telegraph*, 28 December 1988. See also George T. Yu, 'Africa in Chinese Foreign Policy', *Asian Survey*, August 1988; and Alec Russell, 'Trouble Building up for China in Africa', *Daily Telegraph*, 13 March 1995.

Racial prejudice in China is skilfully analysed by Frank Dikötter in *The Discourse of Race in China*, Hurst, London, 1992.

30. *Far Eastern Economic Review*, 23 June 1994, *Financial Times*, 14 January 1993.

31. *Japan Times*, 25 November 1993.

32. See for a good discussion of this Tony Walker, 'The Waters Beyond Mischief Reef', *Financial Times*, 16 March 1995.

Chapter 21 China and the West: Playing the Game

1. *Financial Times*, 13 February 1993. The Chinese may also have invented golf, on one interpretation of a fourteenth-century manual on 'ball-beating' with different clubs (*Daily Telegraph*, 6 May 1993). Is nothing sacred?

2. Quoted in Michael Yahuda, 'Deng Xiaoping: the Statesman', *The China Quarterly*, no. 135, September 1993, p.564.

3. *Daily Telegraph*, 28 February 1994.

4. *International Herald Tribune*, 28 May 1994.

5. Robert W. Barnett, 'America and China: The Goal is Human Welfare', *International Herald Tribune*, 10 May 1994; Andrew Nathan in *The Economist*, 30 April 1994.

6. *New York Times* and *International Herald Tribune*, 21 May 1993.

7. President Clinton softened his attitude to China after his re-election in 1996.

8. Simon Long, 'The Tree That Wants to be Still: The Chinese Response to Foreign Pressure Since June 1989', *Pacific Review*, vol. 5, no. 2, 1992.

9. *International Herald Tribune*, 20 October 1994.

10. *Far Eastern Economic Review*, 18 March 1993.

11. *The Times*, 10 September 1983.

12. Fang Lizhi quoted in Orville Schell, *Discos and Democracy, China in the Throes of Reform*, Pantheon, New York, 1988, p.132.

13. *The Spectator*, 15 May 1993.

14. See Xiaoxiong Yi, 'China's US Policy Conundrum in the 1990s, Balancing Autonomy and Interdependence', *Asian Survey*, August 1994, p.675, for an overview of US–China issues.

15. Harry Hongda Wu, *Laogai – The Chinese Gulag*, Westview Press, Boulder, Colorado, 1992.

16. Pi Ying-hsien, 'China's Boundary Issues with the Former Soviet Union', *Issues and Studies*, July 1992, p.63; *BBC/SWB*/FE/2230 of 17 February 1995.

17. *Daily Telegraph*, 2 October 1991.

18. Jeannette Mirsky (ed.), *The Great Chinese Travellers*, Unwin, London,

1965, pp.192–3. The first Han Chinese in England may have been Shen Fu-tsung who worked on Chinese books in the Bodleian Library at Oxford in 1685.

19. Xu Jiyu, *A Brief Description of the Ocean Circuit*, 1848.

20. Patricia Wellons, 'Sino-French Relations: Historical Alliance Versus Economic Reality', *Pacific Review*, vol. 7, no. 3, 1994.

21. David Shambaugh declares those differences as disadvantageous to the US: 'Peking's Foreign Policy Conundrum since Tiananmen, Peaceful Co-existence vs. Peaceful Evolution', *Issues and Studies*, November 1992, p.65 at p.85.

22. *The Economist*, 28 May 1993.

23. *Sunday Telegraph*, 22 August 1993.

Chapter 22 Conclusion: China Joins the World

1. Zhou: Chae-jin Lee, *Zhou Enlai, The Early Years*, Stanford, 1994, p.78.

2. But see Martin King Whyte, 'The Social Roots of China's Economic Development', *The China Quarterly*, no. 144, December 1995, p. 999.

3. *Daily Telegraph*, 25 January 1991.

4. Jung Chang, *op.cit.*, p.561.

5. Zhisui Li, Mao's physician, documents Mao's physical deterioration in *The Private Life of Chairman Mao*, Chatto & Windus, London, 1994. Sanity, Daniel Southerland, *Washington Post* and *International Herald Tribune*, 18 July 1994.

6. Statement of 2 June 1989.

7. Gu Weiqun, 'Political Attitudes of US-based Mainland Chinese Students and Scholars', *Issues and Studies*, January 1992, p.53 at p.62.

8. An-Chia Wu, 'Mainland China's Political Reforms and Chinese Family Problems', *The China Quarterly*, no. 130, June 1992, p.317.

9. *International Herald Tribune*, 30 May 1994.

10. John Roderick, *Covering China: The Story of an American Reporter from Revolutionary Days to the Deng Era*, Imprint, Chicago, 1994.

11. Martin King Whyte, 'Rural Economic Reforms and Chinese Family Problems', The *China Quarterly*, no. 130, June 1992, p.317.

12. Michael Harris Bond, *Beyond the Chinese Face*, Oxford University Press, Hongkong, 1991.

13. See Pauline Loong and Daryl Ho, *The Northeast: Coming of Age*, Jardine Fleming Securities Ltd., October 1994, pp.8 and 12.

14. E.g. India in Goa, Indonesia in Timor – and Vietnam tried in Cambodia.

15. *The Times*, 4 July 1994. For Western resentment at having to come to terms with perceived Chinese and other east Asian superiority, see Simon Jenkins' defensive commentary, 'Tony Joins the Tiger Party', *The Times*, 6 January 1996.

16. See Denis Dwyer (ed.), *China: The Next Decades*, Longman, Harlow, 1993. Vaclav Smil is a doubter on environmental grounds, *China's Environmental Challenge*, 1993; Gerald Segal on fragmentation grounds, *China Changes Shape: Regionalism and Foreign Policy*, Brassey's, London, 1994. Lucian W. Pye, after a masterly review of recent books on China's political future after Deng, concluded that neo-fascism is more likely than democracy, 'Chinese Politics in the Late Deng Era', *The China Quarterly*, no. 142, June 1995, p.572 at p.583.

17. See Jim Rowher's survey of China in *The Economist*, 1992; and William H. Overholt, *China, the Next Economic Superpower*, Weidenfeld & Nicolson, London, 1993.

18. Paul Theroux, *Riding the Iron Rooster*, Hamish Hamilton, London 1988; Mark Salzman, *Iron and Silk*, Random House, New York, 1986. Salzman's is the best book to give to anyone in need of persuading that the Chinese are human. On the making of *Beyond The Clouds*, see *Daily Telegraph*, 7 January 1995.

INDEX